Natal and Zululand
from earliest times to 1910

Natal and Zululand

FROM EARLIEST TIMES
TO 1910

A new history

Edited by

ANDREW DUMINY
and
BILL GUEST

University of Natal Press

Shuter & Shooter

COVER DESIGN:

'Cultural patterns' by David Moon; taken from diagrams depicting settlements in Natal in early times and in the nineteenth century.

Co-published by

University of Natal Press
P.O. Box 375
Pietermaritzburg 3200

and

Shuter & Shooter (Pty) Ltd.
Gray's Inn, 230 Church Street
Pietermaritzburg 3201

First edition 1989

ISBN 0 86980 695 5

Set in 11 on 13 pt Times Roman
Printed by Kohler Carton and Print
Box 955, Pinetown, 3600 South Africa

Contents

List of maps

Foreword

In 1965 a colleague of mine was asked by an official in the archives service: 'What more is there to write about the history of Natal?' That slightly plaintive rhetorical question reflected a not uncommon view about the inherent limitations of the historian's craft.

The fact that the question was put in the year in which Edgar Brookes and I produced our *History of Natal* is not wholly beside the point. That single-volume synthesis was made possible by the advances that had been chalked up in Natal historical studies during the preceding four decades, and it was exactly those achievements which, while pleasing, were also troubling to the mind of an archives man. All the major official collections had been worked on, and virtually all the researchable topics had apparently been covered. Dissertations had been written on white settlement in Natal, on the Boer republics, on Natal's constitutional development, on missionary endeavour, on the Colony's relations with its neighbours, on educational policy and practice, on the Indian 'question', on most of the more important aspects of Natal's economic development in the pre-Union period, on many of the territory's leading public figures, and on all the major episodes in Boer-British and black-white conflicts east of the Drakensberg. What more was there to do, therefore, beyond a bit of filling in here and there, and a bit of up-dating from time to time in respect of events in the post-Union period?

It says much for the vitality of Natal's historians that that view of a virtually satiated field of studies proved to be dramatically wrong. The exploration of Natal's past has continued vigorously, and new dimensions have been recognized which yield co-ordinates as exciting in their potential, if not in their range, as those yielded in respect of the physical world by a shift from the two-dimensional to three-dimensional representations of space. In these developments, the Africanist and the historical-materialist paradigms have both been profoundly influential; so, too, have those rare but remarkable individuals who, regardless of paradigm, have the perspicacity and the imaginative flair to turn from the present to the past in order to ask illuminating new questons. It is their sensitivity to the complexity and subtlety of human affairs that sets at nought the 'fixed sum' view of history.

To varying degrees these diverse influences are all discernible in the contributions to this, the first of two projected volumes in which experts in various fields combine to rewrite Natal's history. The authors have all been active in research in the years since 1965, and the editors are to be congratulated on bringing the work of these scholars together within the covers of a single volume. If there is cause for impatience it is in respect of a companion volume on the post-Union period. The need for such a volume is acute, and it is to be hoped that it will not be long in appearing.

But, it is not simply to that second volume that one looks forward with anticipation. In addition, one hopes that (in keeping with the Hegelian dialectic which, directly of indirectly, underlies so much of the revisionist history of recent years), 'Duminy and Guest' juxtaposed against 'Brookes and Webb' will generate the creative tension from which there will come – perhaps in time to greet the twenty-first century – a brave new synthesis of the history of Natal.

C. de B. Webb
Vice-Principal
University of Natal
Pietermaritzburg

Acknowledgements

The production of a book of this kind poses many problems. Above all, it requires a high degree of co-operation on the part of the contributors. After deadlines have been met, changes frequently have to be made to eliminate overlaps with other chapters, to remedy omissions, or to maintain a measure of stylistic uniformity.

The editors wish gratefully to acknowledge the co-operation of the authors of the various chapters, who all shared in the enthusiasm of a joint endeavour and made light of the difficulties entailed. Thanks are also due to Margot Pretorius, who transferred the material on to a word-processor before final editing, and to Helena Margeot and Jenny McDowell, cartographers of the University of Natal in Pietermaritzburg and Durban, respectively, for the maps. The search for suitable photographic material was generously financed by the University of Natal Research Fund and Peter Newman, of the Faculty of Architecture's photographic studio, processed many of the illustrations. Helpful assistance was received from the librarians and staff of the Don Africana Library, the Killie Campbell Africana Library and the Local History Museum in Durban, and of the Natal Archives Depot, the Natal Society Library and the Natal Witness in Pietermaritzburg. The Reverend Canon A. C. A. Parry and Dr W. H. Bizley provided invaluable information about the Natal Railways.

We would also like to record our indebtedness to our colleagues, especially John Benyon, Paul Maylam and John Wright, who made very useful comments on the sections of the book written by ourselves, and to Connie Munro, the Secretary of the Department of History in Durban, who assisted in ways too numerous to mention.

Note on orthography

In writing about the history of Natal and Zululand, the difficulty arises of spelling Zulu names and placenames. Some of these were corrupted in colonial writings or on maps compiled by cartographers with no knowledge of Zulu. Modern Zulu lexicography has also led to the abandonment of many archaic spellings. The policy followed in this book has been that of using, wherever possible, the correct modern spellings, even when these differ from those that are in common usage. The Tugela, Umfolosi, Umgeni and Umkomaas rivers thus become the Thukela, Mfolozi, Mngeni, and Mkhomazi. Where the editors were in doubt, they followed the spellings used by Colin Webb and John Wright in their editing of *The James Stuart Archive of Recorded Oral Evidence Relating to the History of the Zulu and Neighbouring Peoples* (University of Natal Press, 1976–86).

Abbreviations

The following abbreviations have been used in the Notes at the end of each chapter in this book.

ABC Archives of the American Board of Commissioners for Foreign Missions, Houghton Library, Harvard University

AYB *Archives Year Book for South African History*, Cape Town, Government Printer

BPP *British Parliamentary Papers*

CAB Cabinet Papers (British)

CHBE The Cambridge History of the British Empire, Cambridge, Cambridge University Press

CO Colonial Office (British)

CSO Colonial Secretary's Office (Natal)

GH Government House Records (in NA)

JSP James Stuart Papers

KCAL The Killie Campbell Africana Library, Durban

LG Lieutenant-Governor's Papers (Natal)

MMS Archives of the Wesleyan Methodist Missionary Society, London

NA The Natal Archives, Pietermaritzburg

NGG *Natal Government Gazette*

NPP *Natal Parliamentary Papers*

PRO Public Record Office

SNA Secretary for Native Affairs (Natal)

TA Transvaal Archives, Pretoria

USPG Archives of the United Society for the Propagation of the Gospel, London

Contributors

Charles Ballard
Senior Lecturer in History, University of Natal, Durban

Joy Brain
Professor of History, University of Durban-Westville

Peter Colenbrander
Formerly Lecturer in History, University of South Africa, Pretoria

Andrew Duminy
Professor of History, University of Natal, Durban

Norman Etherington
Professor of History, University of Western Australia

Bill Guest
Associate Professor of History, University of Natal, Pietermaritzburg

Carolyn Hamilton
Doctoral student at Johns Hopkins University, USA and co-ordinator of the Swaziland Oral History Project

John Laband
Senior Lecturer in History, University of Natal, Pietermaritzburg

John Lambert
Senior Lecturer in History, University of South Africa, Pretoria

Tim Maggs
Senior Curator-in-Charge, Department of Archaeology, Natal Museum, Pietermaritzburg

Aron Mazel
Curator, Department of Archaeology, Natal Museum,
Pietermaritzburg

Ritchie Ovendale
Reader, Department of International Politics, University College of
Wales, Aberystwyth

Paul Thompson
Senior Lecturer in History, University of Natal, Pietermaritzburg

John Wright
Senior Lecturer in History, University of Natal, Pietermartizburg

Chantelle Wyley
History Subject-Librarian, University of Natal, Durban

Introduction

ANDREW DUMINY and
BILL GUEST

In 1965 two important books on the history of south-east Africa were published. The first was *A History of Natal* by E. H. Brookes, Professor of History and Political Science at the University of Natal, and C. de B. Webb, at that time Senior Lecturer in History at the same university. The other was *The Washing of the Spears*, by Donald R. Morris, published in America.[1]

Both these publications were milestones in the history of this region. 'Brookes and Webb', as the *History of Natal* soon came to be known colloquially, was more than a first attempt to write the history of a region hitherto dismissed as an unimportant sideshow in the history of southern Africa. It was an ambitious attempt to explore a field which had been greatly neglected.

Although there were several widely-read histories of the region written by amateurs,[2] a glance at the bibliography of 'Brookes and Webb' will show just how small was the store of academic research upon which they could draw. Professor Alan Hattersley, Brookes's predecessor, had written several studies of Natal settler society and C. J. Uys, who had studied under Brookes in the 1930s when the latter was a lecturer at the Transvaal University College, had published a study of Theophilus Shepstone,[3] but the output from the universities was extremely paltry. There was a handful of MA theses, including that of T. R. H. Davenport on responsible government, but only three doctoral theses, two written by scholars who were to leave Natal and develop research interests in other fields at other universities.[4] Among the few published works was a study of Indian immigration by L. M. Thompson, Professor of History at the University of Cape Town, a study of Sir Benjamin Pine's 'native' policy by L. M. Young, and a collection of the letters of J. W. Colenso edited by

Wyn Rees (Young and Rees were both Senior Lecturers at the University of Natal).[5] In the field of archaeology very few excavations had been carried out, and what had been done was largely the work of persons who were untrained in modern techniques.

At the time when *A History of Natal* was being written, the English-language South African universities were feeling the effect of the Republican referendum and the Sharpeville unrest. Many leading scholars had left for overseas. Arthur Keppel Jones, who succeeded Hattersley as Professor of History at Natal University, had taken up a post at Queen's University, Kingston, Ontario, while L. M. Thompson had left the University of Cape Town for the United States, where after heading the African Studies Centre at the University of California in Los Angeles, he led a Southern African studies programme at Yale University. Generously funded, these *émigré* scholars were able to command the field. The *Oxford History of South Africa* was the most important result of their activity. The first volume was published in 1969, edited by L. M. Thompson and Monica Wilson, who had been a colleague of Thompson at the University of Cape Town.[6] An important contribution to Southern African historiography was also made by the established South Africanist Gwendolin Carter of Smith College, Northampton USA. She visited South Africa in the 1950s to research her monumental study of South African politics after 1948 and returned in the early 1960s on an ambitious search for primary political material.[7]

The History of Natal was a brave attempt by the Department of History at the University of Natal to compete with this output. It was originally hoped that funding from the Human Sciences Research Council would permit a six-volume publication, each researched and written by a different member of staff. It soon became clear, however, that the project would have to be trimmed, not least because a necessary preliminary was the compilation of a bibliography, together with a survey of Natal government publications. In the event, Webb's *Guide to the Official Records of the Colony of Natal* was published separately,[8] while the extensive bibliography – the first attempt to itemise the many published works relating to the history of south-east Africa – became a valuable appendix to the book itself. As each chapter was written, it was circulated to members of the history departments in Pietermaritzburg and Durban for their comments.

'Brookes and Webb' was soon overtaken by the changes that took place within the field of South African historical writing. The first of these was a movement in the 1960s to counteract the Eurocentric versions of African history that had been produced during the imperial phase. Among the leaders of this movement were British scholars who taught at the universities that had sprung up in Africa after the colonies had gained independence.[9] There were few South African academics who were at first interested in taking up this challenge. An exception was David Welsh at the University of Cape Town, who produced a substantial study of the operation of the 'Shepstone system' in Natal.[10] In addition, several social anthropologists, finding that their practice of studying 'tribal' societies was also being subjected to criticism, began to look at African societies in historical perspective.[11]

The first work to be written on the history of Natal and Zululand from an African perspective was *The Zulu Aftermath* (1966)[12] by John Omer-Cooper, a graduate of Rhodes University who had, after studying at Cambridge, lectured at Ibadan, Nigeria. A similar enterprise was Donald Denoon's *Southern Africa Since 1800* (1972).[13] After obtaining an honours degree in History at the University of Natal, Pietermaritzburg, he too studied at Cambridge before taking up a teaching post in Africa – at Makerere, Uganda. An even more influential work, as far as Natal history is concerned, was a study of the 1906 Bambatha disturbances entitled *Reluctant Rebellion* (1970) by Shula Marks,[14] a graduate of the University of Cape Town who had been directed towards African history at London University by Professor Roland Oliver, the East African specialist. Marks, who is now Director of the Institute of Commonwealth Studies at the University of London, has pioneered many new avenues of research in Natal and Zulu history and, as tutor and professor at the School of Oriental and African Studies, has attracted a large number of postgraduate students from the English-language South African universities.

In 1967 Marks published a vigorous criticism of 'Brookes and Webb',[15] contending that it illustrated the increasing isolation of South Africans from the outside world. 'From this *History of Natal*', she commented, 'it seems that even the English-speaking historians, for so long the upholders of fine academic standards in South Africa, are being cut off from the new thinking in their field'. The main thrust of her criticism was that there was 'little analysis of those historical processes in the nineteenth century which were solely African – little awareness of the response African peoples can and did make to colonial rule, whether in Natal or in Zululand'. Conspicuously lacking was 'an analysis of the role of missionaries and the growth of an educated élite' or of 'the relationship of Christian Africans and pagans; even a detailed analysis of how Natal Africans responded to

Shepstone's "indirect rule"'. Ironically, Donald Morris's work on the rise
and destruction of the Zulu kingdom – the work of an amateur – was thus
more favourably regarded. Morris had painstakingly sifted through the
published sources and had tried to view Zulu history through Zulu eyes.

The criticism that Brookes and Webb were out of touch with recent
trends was unkind, as least as far as Webb was concerned. He was one of
the few South Africans invited by L. M. Thompson to attend the Lusaka
conference in 1968, at which papers were presented by established experts
in the field of African history and at which the need for a major
reassessment of South African history was emphasized. Furthermore,
while working on the *History of Natal*, Webb had come across in the Killie
Campbell Africana Library in Durban a large collection of recorded
interviews conducted by James Stuart with some 200 informants, most of
them Africans, at the turn of the century. Stuart was a senior government
administrator who became Assistant Secretary for Native Affairs. Realizing that these records were an invaluable source of information on Zulu
history, Webb obtained funding from the University and secured the
appointment in 1971 of John Wright, one of his former students, as
co-editor and translator. The first volume of *The Stuart Papers*, edited by
Webb and Wright, was published five years later, after which additional
funding was obtained from the Human Sciences Research Council.
Volume 4 was published in 1986, while another three volumes are still
projected.[16] It would be difficult to overemphasize the impact which this
project has made on the study of Zulu history. It was seized upon by several
scholars who, employing new techniques in the interpretation of oral
evidence, have been able to piece together a history of preliterate south-east
Africa that overturns much of what appeared in the earlier histories, with
their heavy reliance on the work of A. T. Bryant during the 1920s and
1930s (see Chapter 3).

What Marks's criticism of South African historical writing also
overlooked was that in 1967 there were still vast areas of colonial history
that needed to be explored. Most existing studies had concentrated on
'imperial policy' or on 'Native policy', with no attention being paid to
white colonial society and the mechanisms of colonial politics. As far as the
settlers were concerned, there was a great deal of groundwork to be done,
for there was no biographical register and no systematic attempt had been
made to catalogue the available records. Furthermore, while much had
been written on the Anglo-Zulu War, little attention had been paid to the
mass of official and manuscript source material. In the History Depart-

ments on both the Pietermaritzburg and Durban campuses there was at that time an overwhelming emphasis upon the study of British, European and American history.

One of the effects of the exodus of university teachers that occurred at the time of Sharpeville was their replacement by young scholars who viewed it as their responsibility to engage in research in the sadly-neglected field of local history. Like their overseas counterparts, they were highly critical of much of what had been written in South African history. Furthermore, a small but significant number of overseas graduates began to return, some taking up posts in departments of African Studies and Sociology. One of the first steps towards the study of local settler history was a project initiated by Professor K. H. C. McIntyre and Shelagh Spencer to compile a biographical register of early Natal settlers.[17] Webb left in 1976 to become Professor of History at the University of Cape Town, but there was a continued interest in the nineteenth century and especially in the history of the Nguni-speaking population of the region and the Anglo-Zulu War. Twentieth-century Natal politics had also begun to engage attention. Initially, it was the behaviour of the English-speaking white population, outnumbered by the Afrikaners after Union in 1910, which attracted interest but, as the study of urbanization developed, the emphasis has been upon the interaction of the population groups of the region in the setting of industrial capitalism.

At the University of Durban-Westville significant developments were also taking place. The University had begun to fight against the controls that had been imposed upon it as one of the 'ethnic' universities established in 1961 by the South African government in opposition to the 'open' universities. In the early 1970s Surendra Bhana, who had obtained his doctorate at the University of Kansas USA, was appointed to the staff and immediately began to work on the neglected field of the Natal Indian community. He was joined by Joy Brain, with her special interest in Indian Christians. The result was that the study of the Natal Indians began at last to gather momentum, supplementing the work of *émigré* scholars like Bridglal Pachai, and that of imperial historians who were attracted to Natal history because of parallels with other parts of the Empire or through lasting fascination with the career of M. K. Gandhi.[18] Meanwhile, the University of Zululand, established like the University of Durban-Westville as an 'ethnic college', was beginning to produce students with an interest in joining the growing number of scholars who were engaged in reinterpreting the Zulu past.

While this was taking place in the universities, the Natal Museum in Pietermaritzburg began in 1972 to expand its archaeological activities, with the appointment of specialist archaeologists, including Tim Maggs, Martin Hall, and subsequently Aron Mazel, to undertake Stone Age research. Employing modern research techniques and applying theories that had been developed in other parts of the world, the scientific research of important Stone and Iron Age sites took place. Soon, a picture emerged which completely overturned many established beliefs, not least the commonly-held view that the settlement of Iron Age black people in south-east Africa occurred at about the same time as the south-west was being colonized by European settlers. Similarly, the scientific study of the rock art of the region was intensified. It is now recognized as one of the most extensive galleries of rock art in the world.

The result of this activity in the universities and at the Natal Museum was an explosion of knowledge during the 1970s. In 1978 the Department of History in Durban launched the *Journal of Natal and Zulu History* to cater for the upsurge in academic activity that was taking place, complementing *Natalia*, the journal which had been published in Pietermaritzburg by the Natal Society since 1971. It has appeared annually ever since, attracting contributions from scholars throughout the English-speaking world. Similarly, the results of much of the archaeological research has appeared in a new series of the *Annals of the Natal Museum*, published bi-annually since 1980.

During the 1970s South African historiography was shaken by the so-called 'Radical-Liberal debate'. A group of young historians, describing themselves as 'Radicals', had emerged in Britain. Many of them were political refugees from South Africa. Their criticism, added to that of the 'Africanists', was that South African historians had written from a 'liberal' standpoint which assumed that the origin of white racism lay in the frontier experience, especially that of the Afrikaner. Its real origin, they insisted, lay in class conflict. 'Liberal' historians were therefore wrong in blaming South Africa's misfortunes upon the 'racism' of Afrikaners. They were also wrong in believing that the answer to the South African race problem lay in further economic development. Because 'apartheid' was the product of the industrial capitalist system, they argued that it was complementary to it and could not be eradicated while the system itself survived.[19]

Had the position of the Radicals been simply that of stressing the greater need for emphasis upon social and economic forces, in which respect their influence has been most significant, they might not have attracted so much attention. Nor would they have done so had their main concern been that of criticizing the rather simplistic assumptions which during the 1950s had dominated South African political analysis, and not only South African historical writing. Both of these had in fact already come under scrutiny and attack in the South African universities themselves. The contest was however deep-rooted, for it involved disagreement between Marxist analysis and the open-ended tradition that had operated among empirical historians. This was pointed out in 1977 by the American historian Harrison Wright in a hard-hitting little book.[20] Amongst other things, he accused the Radicals of being inferior historians on the grounds that their a priori assumptions precluded them from making a fair appraisal of evidence.

The 'Radical-Liberal' debate did not divide the Natal academic community to the same extent as elsewhere, although some Natal university historians contributed to it, notably Wright, who argued that there was a conflict between two theoretical paradigms.[21] One reason for this was that its members were well-known to each other. Another was that the leading revisionist of Zulu history, Jeff Guy,[22] was a former student of Webb. This meant that there was a basis of personal acquaintance which facilitated continued contact amongst those who were then active in the field. Guy, furthermore, while adopting an essentially Marxist framework in reinterpreting the destruction of the Zulu kingdom, never abandoned his commitment to empirical inquiry.

In 1979, on the occasion of the centenary of the Anglo-Zulu War, a conference was convened by the Department of History at the University of Natal in Durban. It was one of the largest gatherings of its kind to be held in southern Africa. Papers were presented by scholars from other South African universities as well as by overseas academics, including Norman Etherington (the American scholar whose study of the Natal African Christian, or *kholwa*, community had led to a continuing interest in nineteenth-century Natal history), Frank Emery (author of *The Red Soldier*) from Oxford, and Adrian Preston (the editor of Wolseley's *Diaries*) from Canada. Six years later, when the University of Natal celebrated the 75th anniversary of its foundation, another conference was held, the theme on this occasion being the history of Natal and Zululand generally. Again the response was overwhelming, with nearly forty papers being presented, several by overseas academics, including Marks, Etherington, Emery and Bill Swanson, whose American doctoral thesis on the history of Durban had pioneered the study of urban history in this region.[23]

Apart from revealing the depth of research activity on the history of Natal and Zululand and the widespread public interest therein, these conferences were characterized by a free exchange of ideas between historians of all ideological positions. At the first, Webb delivered a paper on the origins of the Anglo-Zulu War in which he set out the differences which separated Marxist structuralists from other historians. He pointed out the extent to which the two schools of thought could be reconciled.[24] This was also the theme of the inaugural lectures of both the present incumbents of the History Chairs at the University of Natal.[25]

This volume is the first of a projected two which attempt to make available to the public the results of the spectacular developments that have taken place in the field of Natal history during the past twenty years. Each chapter is written by an expert. The varied approaches of the contributors again illustrates the degree of co-operation that exists between historians who are bound together by their common interest in the history of Natal and Zululand. Despite differences of emphasis, there is agreement on the main themes of the history of this region during the nineteenth century.

The overriding feature of the history of south-east Africa before the Colony of Natal entered the Union of South Africa in 1910 was the penetration of the European economy. This occurred during the age of British industrial and commercial supremacy and the growth of British imperial power throughout the world. Britain's initial interest in southern Africa arose from its strategic importance in relation to the slave trade and in relation to British commercial interests in India and the Far East. These considerations prompted the permanent acquisition of the Cape Colony at the conclusion of the Napoleonic wars.

Once the annexation of the Cape had taken place, a new set of dynamics came into play and these constantly forced the extension of British rule. The most important of these at first was the problem of stabilizing the Cape Colony's frontiers. This not only resulted in the steady eastward and northward expansion of the Colony's frontiers at the expense of KhoiKhoi (Hottentot), San (Bushmen) and Xhosa, but also forced the initial annexation of Natal during the early 1840s (see Chapter 5).

By then, Britain was also responding to two other major concerns. The first was with the Dutch-speaking, or Afrikaner, population as a system of colonial self-government began to be applied. Representative government was introduced to the Cape Colony in 1853, even though the British settler population was outnumbered by the Afrikaners. In this delicate situation, the existence of the independent Orange Free State and South African

Republics seemed to affect the loyalties of the Afrikaner population in the Cape Colony, and this caused the British imperial government to adopt a more belligerent policy towards them.[26]

The second concern was with the black population. The consequence of the extension of the Cape's eastern frontier in the 1840s and the imposition of direct government over Mfengu and Xhosa was that independent African polities, such as those of the Sotho and the Zulu (see Chapter 3), appeared to encourage the disaffection of the African peoples who were under direct imperial rule, in the same way as the existence of the independent Boer republics seemed to affect the attitudes of the Cape's Afrikaner population. Furthermore, these new African kingdoms were soon identified in the imperial perspective as threatening stability throughout the subcontinent. Modern research has revealed the extent to which, in these circumstances, British imperialism was encouraged by men on the spot, adopting a colonial view. At certain very crucial times, as before the outbreak of the Anglo-Zulu War in 1879, British imperial action was precipated by such individuals.[27]

The geographic area dealt with in this volume is bounded by the Indian Ocean to the east and the Drakensberg mountain range to the west. To the south it today borders on the Transkei. To the north the Phongolo River divides it from Mozambique, Swaziland and the province of the Transvaal. It today comprises the composite of regions controlled by the Natal Provincial Administration, with its headquarters in Pietermaritzburg, and the government of KwaZulu, with its headquarters at Ulundi, the site of the royal homesteads of both Mpande and Cetshwayo. In the early nineteenth century the region acquired a political identity under Shaka. Today, the idea of regional identity persists in the attempts that are being made to combine these two local authorities.

For the various population groups that inhabited this region in the nineteenth century the consequences of the growth of the capitalist market economy and of the 'imperial factor' were profound. For the Zulu it spelt rapid change as new systems of authority were engineered and as natural resources were plundered. In 1879 the kingdom was destroyed. What remained of the territory after sections had already been excised for occupancy by Boer and British farmers, was then callously partitioned by the British imperial authority with the intention of preventing the regrowth of Zulu power (see Chapter 8).

For the growing British settler population the consequences were also profound, for they provided proof of cultural and material superiority at a time when Natal, like other British colonies, was moving towards self-government. Economic development, furthermore, enabled the Colony to raise revenue and so devise new methods of social control, supported by military and para-military forces, equipped with sophisticated modern weaponry. By the late 1890s Natal's settlers were legislating to eliminate the competition of Indian traders and were envisaging the future consolidation of white privilege (Chapters 10 and 15).

What the British settler population did not realize was that British power in southern Africa would wane rapidly after the Anglo-Boer War of 1899–1902. There was understandable confusion when political initiatives passed into Afrikaner hands and only gradually did this harsh truth become obvious in the years that followed.

No apology is offered for the fact that, in surveying these events, great emphasis is placed on the economic forces that were at work. Such forces are seldom detected by the societies in which they operate. In Britain the transformation from a rural agricultural economy to an urban industrial economy is commonly referred to as the 'Industrial Revolution'. One of its features was the virtual elimination of a rural population which had been able to subsist independently and the emergence of a new class of wage labourers. In Britain, this development was accelerated towards the end of the eighteenth century by the growth of primary industry, by the purchase of land by wealthy capitalist farmers, often aided by an Enclosure Act which could force independent landowners to sell, and by poor harvests which made it impossible for the small independent producer to survive. In Natal, as elsewhere in southern Africa, similar developments were taking place in the late nineteenth century.[28] They were given an impetus in the first decade of the twentieth century by a fall in the price of agricultural commodities and by the effects of drought, animal and plant diseases and locust plagues. As in Britain, this caused major population displacement. To some extent, the wages of migrant workers could subsidise the rural economy but, in the longer term, for the under-capitalized and uneducated African and Indian rural population, there was little prospect other than that of being sucked into the growing urban labour force. Displaced whites could move into the expanding colonial public sector, to the new centres of industrial growth, especially the Witwatersrand, or to new areas of 'opportunity' such as the Rhodesias (now Zambia and Zimbabwe), where generous offers were being made to attract white settlers.

While considerable emphasis is placed upon these major themes, it is hoped that this will not appear to reduce individuals to a level of insignificance. History is about human endeavour and, while it is the task of historians to discern patterns in order to explain what happened, they must also engage in the challenge of understanding and appraising the actions of individuals. The history of Natal and Zululand provides a rich store of human experience which will continue to fascinate each new generation. As in any society, there are examples of the avarice of moneymakers and of the victims of their greed; of the arrogance of administrators, of the intrigues of ambitious politicians; and of the enterprise and courage of individuals who tried to alter the world in which they lived, not always from motives of self-interest. In some cases, ambitions were achieved, in others there was the tragedy of defeat. Some prospered, others became society's victims. Some were lucky. Some were clever. Others were unlucky or had no chance at all.

The ingredients that made up the various societies that inhabited Natal and Zululand were no different from those of other societies. It is their history that is unique.

Notes

1   E. H. Brookes and C. de B. Webb, *A History of Natal* (Pietermaritzburg, University of Natal Press, 1965); D. R. Morris, *The Washing of the Spears: a History of the Rise and Fall of the Zulu Nation* (British edition: London, Jonathan Cape, 1966).

2   As, for example, G. Mackeurtan, *The Cradle Days of Natal, 1497–1845* (London, Longmans, 1931); H. C. Lugg, *Historic Natal and Zululand* (Pietermaritzburg, Shuter & Shooter, 1948); C. T. Binns, *The Last Zulu King: the Life and Death of Cetshwayo* (London, Longmans, 1963).

3   C. J. Uys, *In the Era of Shepstone* (Lovedale, Lovedale Press, 1933); A. F. Hattersley, *Portrait of a Colony* (Cambridge, Cambridge University Press, 1940), and *The British Settlement of Natal: a Study in Imperial Migration* (Cambridge, Cambridge University Press, 1950).

4   T. R. H. Davenport, 'The Responsible Government Issue in Natal, 1880–82' (unpublished MA thesis, Rhodes University College, 1949); B. A. le Cordeur, 'Relations Between Natal and the Cape, 1846–79' (Ph.D. thesis, University of Natal, 1962. Published in *AYB*, 1965, 1); B. Pachai, 'The Emergence of the Question of the South African Indians as an International Issue, 1860–1961' (Ph.D. thesis, University of Natal, 1963. Published as *The International Aspects of the South African Indian Question*, Cape Town, Struik, 1971).

5   L. M. Thompson, 'Indian Immigration into Natal', *AYB*, 1952, 2; L. M. Young, *The Native Policy of Benjamin Pine in Natal, 1850–55*, *AYB*, 1951, 2; W. Rees (ed.), *Colenso Letters from Natal* (Pietermaritzburg, Shuter & Shooter, 1958).

6   M. Wilson and L. M. Thompson (eds.), *The Oxford History of South Africa*, 2 vols. (Oxford, 1969, 1971).

7   G. M. Carter, *The Politics of Inequality: South Africa since 1948* (London, Thames and Hudson, 1958); T. Karis and G. M. Carter, *From Protest to Challenge*, 4 vols. (Stanford, 1972, 1973, 1977).

8   C. de B. Webb, *A Guide to the Official Records of the Colony of Natal* (Pietermaritzburg, University of Natal Press, 1968). Expanded and revised edition published as *Webb's Guide to the Official Records of the Colony of Natal* (Pietermaritzburg, University of Natal Press, 1984).

9   See, for example, R. Oliver and J. D. Fage, *A Short History of Africa* (Harmondsworth, Penguin, 1962), T. O. Ranger, *Revolt in Southern Rhodesia, 1896–7* (London, Heinemann, 1967), G. Shepperson, *Independent African: John Chilombwe and the Origins, Setting and Significance of the Nyasaland Native Rising of 1915* (Edinburgh, Edinburgh University Press, 1958).

10 D. Welsh, *The Roots of Segregation: Native Policy in Natal, 1845–1910* (Cape Town, Oxford University Press, 1971).

11 See, for example, W. J. Argyle and E. M. Preston-Whyte (eds.), *Social System and Tradition in South Africa* (Cape Town, Oxford University Press, 1978).

12 J. D. Omer-Cooper, *The Zulu Aftermath* (London, Longman, 1966).

13 D. Denoon with B. Nyeko, *Southern Africa since 1800* (London, Longman, 1972).

14 S. Marks, *Reluctant Rebellion* (Oxford, 1970).

15 S. Marks, 'The Nguni, the Natalians, and their History', *Journal of African History*, 8, 3 (1970).

16 C. de B. Webb and J. B. Wright (eds.), *The James Stuart Archive of Recorded Oral Evidence relating to the History of the Zulu and Neighbouring Peoples*, 4 vols. to date (Pietermaritzburg, University of Natal Press, 1976–86).

17 S. O'Byrne Spencer, *British Settlers in Natal, 1824–57: a Biographical Register*, 4 vols. to date (Pietermaritzburg, University of Natal Press, 1981–7).

18 See, for example, R. Huttenback, *Gandhi in South Africa: British Imperialism and the Indian Question* (New York, Cornell University Press, 1976) and *Racism and Empire: White Settlers and Colored Immigrants in the British Self-Governing Colonies, 1830–1910* (New York, Cornell University Press, 1976); M. Swan, *Gandhi: the South African Experience* (Johannesburg, Ravan, 1985).

19 For a discussion of the Radical-Liberal debate see C. Saunders, *The Making of the South African Past: Major Historians on Race and Class* (Cape Town, David Philip, 1988); K. Smith, *The Changing Past: Trends in South African Historical Writing* (Johannesburg, Southern, 1988).

20 H. M. Wright, *The Burden of the Present: the Radical-Liberal Controversy over South African History* (Cape Town, David Philip, 1977).

21 See J. Wright, 'Clash of Paradigms', *Reality*, 9 (1977).

22 Guy, *The Destruction of the Zulu Kingdom* (London, Longman, 1979). Guy had researched this topic under Shula Marks at the London School of Oriental and African Studies.

23 N. Etherington, *Preachers, Peasants and Politics in South East Africa, 1835–80* (London, Royal Historical Society, 1978); F. Emery, *The Red Soldier: Letters from the Zulu War, 1879* (London, Hodder and Stoughton, 1977); A. Preston (ed.), *The South African Diaries of Sir Garnet Wolseley (Natal) 1875* (Cape Town, Balkema, 1971); M. W. Swanson, 'The Rise of Multiracial Durban: Urban History and Race Policy in South Africa, 1830–1930' (Unpublished Ph.D. thesis, Harvard, 1965). Several of the papers delivered at the 1979 conference were published in A. H. Duminy and C. C. Ballard (eds.), *The Anglo-Zulu War: New Perspectives* (Pietermaritzburg, University of Natal Press, 1981).

24 C. de B. Webb, 'The Origins of the War: Problems of Interpretation', in Duminy and Ballard, *The Anglo-Zulu War: New Perspectives*, pp. 1–12.

25 J. A. Benyon, *Mr Hoggenheimer's Weight Problem* (Pietermaritzburg, University of Natal Press, 1977; A. H. Duminy, *Truth and Illusion in History* (Pietermaritzburg, University of Natal Press, 1984).

26 See R. Robinson and J. Gallagher, *Africa and the Victorians: the Official Mind of Imperialism* (London, Macmillan, 1961).

27 See, for example, J. A. Benyon, *Proconsul and Paramountcy in South Africa, 1806–1910* (Pietermaritzburg, University of Natal Press, 1980).

28 W. R. Guest and J. M. Sellers (eds.), *Enterprise and Exploitation in a Victorian Colony: Aspects of the Economic and Social History of Colonial Natal* (Pietermaritzburg, University of Natal Press, 1985).

Chapter 1

The Stone Age peoples of Natal

ARON MAZEL

Some of the earliest discoveries of stone implements in South Africa were made in Natal during the last quarter of the nineteenth century.[1] Thereafter, very little was reported from this region until the late 1920s. In 1929 A. J. H. Goodwin and C. Van Riet Lowe published their highly influential volume *The Stone Age Cultures of South Africa*, the first comprehensive treatment of the South African Stone Age.[2] This publication stimulated a great deal of interest in archaeology, resulting in a considerable amount of field-work, with Goodwin[3] and Van Riet Lowe[4] themselves being active in Natal. After the Second World War had temporarily halted this activity, it was renewed in the late 1940s, with a prominent part being played by Dr Oliver Davies. A lecturer in Classics at the Natal University College, he had a strong interest in archaeology and, besides pursuing his own research, encouraged many others to do the same and was instrumental in the formation of a Natal branch of the South African Archaeological Society in 1949. Between the 1950s and early 1970s there was a constant flow of publications on the Stone Ages of Natal. These studies were generally descriptive, concentrating on the classification of individual sites and stone collections according to the Goodwin and Van Riet Lowe cultural-historical scheme, even though in the early 1930s it had already become recognized that the scheme was imperfect.[5]

In the 1960s South African Stone Age archaeology, influenced by developments elsewhere, underwent numerous substantial changes. There was a move away from the descriptive cultural-historical approach to one which was ecologically orientated, with emphasis being placed on the description and understanding of past environments and human subsistence strategies and settlement patterns.[6] This research focused primarily on the Later Stone Age. There was also an interest in regions rather than in individual sites. This method was first employed in Natal by

Patrick Carter[7] who, on the basis of the likely availability of food resources, hypothesized a seasonal movement of Later Stone Age people in southern Natal between the Drakensberg and the lower-lying regions. In the late 1970s and 1980s the excavation of Later Stone Age sites was undertaken in Natal on a regional basis, one of the aims being to test Carter's seasonality hypothesis. One of the projects concentrated on southern Natal and the other on the Thukela Basin.

EPOCHS	MAJOR STONE AGE DIVISIONS	TIME OF COMMENCEMENT	CHARACTERISTIC ARTEFACTS
HOLOCENE 10 000 years ago	LATER STONE AGE	*c.* 30 000 years ago	Adze Scraper Backed pieces
PLEISTOCENE	MIDDLE STONE AGE	*c.* 200 000 years ago	Blade Flake Segment Point
2 million years	EARLY STONE AGE	*c.* 1,6 million years ago	Chopper (Oldowan) Handaxe Cleaver (Acheulean)

Table 1. Schematic representation of the Stone Ages of Natal.

The reason why Early and Middle Stone Age sites have been neglected, and why their study has remained primarily sequence-orientated, is that few archaeological remains, other than stone artefacts, have been preserved on sites dating back to these periods. Later Stone Age sites contain a much greater variety of material. Besides stone and bone, the material recovered includes plant remains, shell (marine and freshwater), ostrich eggshell, charcoal, modified bone and wood, beads (manufactured from ostrich eggshell, landsnail, bone and glass), pottery, shell pendants and ochre. Using this material, it is possible to infer much about the economic and social systems of the societies that produced them. Until recently, Later Stone Age archaeologists paid little attention to the study of social organization. This was largely because the ecologically orientated approaches that have predominated during the last twenty years have provided an inadequate base for the study of such issues. However, as archaeologists focus more on social themes, they are today making greater use of social theory.

In this chapter, the major Stone Age periods are dealt with separately. Table 1 provides an outline of the periods, showing their dating and the tools which typify each of them. While clear cultural differences separate these periods, it should be remembered that in all of them people were hunter-gatherers, subsisting primarily by means of hunting animals and gathering plant foods.

The Early Stone Age

The earliest known stone artefacts were found in Ethiopia at Kada Gona and are about 2,5 million years old.[8] Thereafter, stone artefacts between 2,1 and 1,6 million years old have been recovered from a variety of geological contexts in East Africa. In South Africa, the earliest dated stone artefacts are the pebble tools recovered from Sterkfontein in the Transvaal, dated at 1,6 million years ago.[9] They are comparable to those described as the Oldowan and Developed Oldowan found in East Africa (Figure 1). Succeeding the Oldowan period is the Acheulian period and this comprises the rest of the Early Stone Age. The Acheulian period is characterized by handaxes and cleavers that were fashioned from the cores of stones (Figure 1). Even though no well-defined typological differences are discernible, the archaeologist Tom Volman has argued, on the grounds that there was a chronological break at about 1 million years ago, that the Acheulian period should be divided into Upper and Lower Acheulian and that assemblages referred to as Fauresmith, Late and Final Acheulian should be included in the Upper Acheulian.[10]

Known Early Stone Age sites in Natal are shown on Map 1. Davies, the only person to have researched this period in Natal intensively, has recognized both Acheulian and 'pre-Acheulian' (presumably Oldowan) artefacts.[11] 'Pre-Acheulian' artefacts have been recovered from raised beach gravels and ancient coastal dunes, while artefacts from nearly twenty raised beach localities have been described as pebble tools, mainly choppers (Map 1). Acheulian sites are more common than 'pre-Acheulian' sites, and are found in a greater variety of contexts, such as raised beach and river gravels, eroded areas and coastal dunes.

Davies has also identified Early (Lower) and Later (Upper) Acheulian occurrences, the Lower Acheulian artefacts being generally found in marine terrace gravels, and the Upper Acheulian occurrences mostly restricted to the interior.[12] No information is available on the foods eaten by

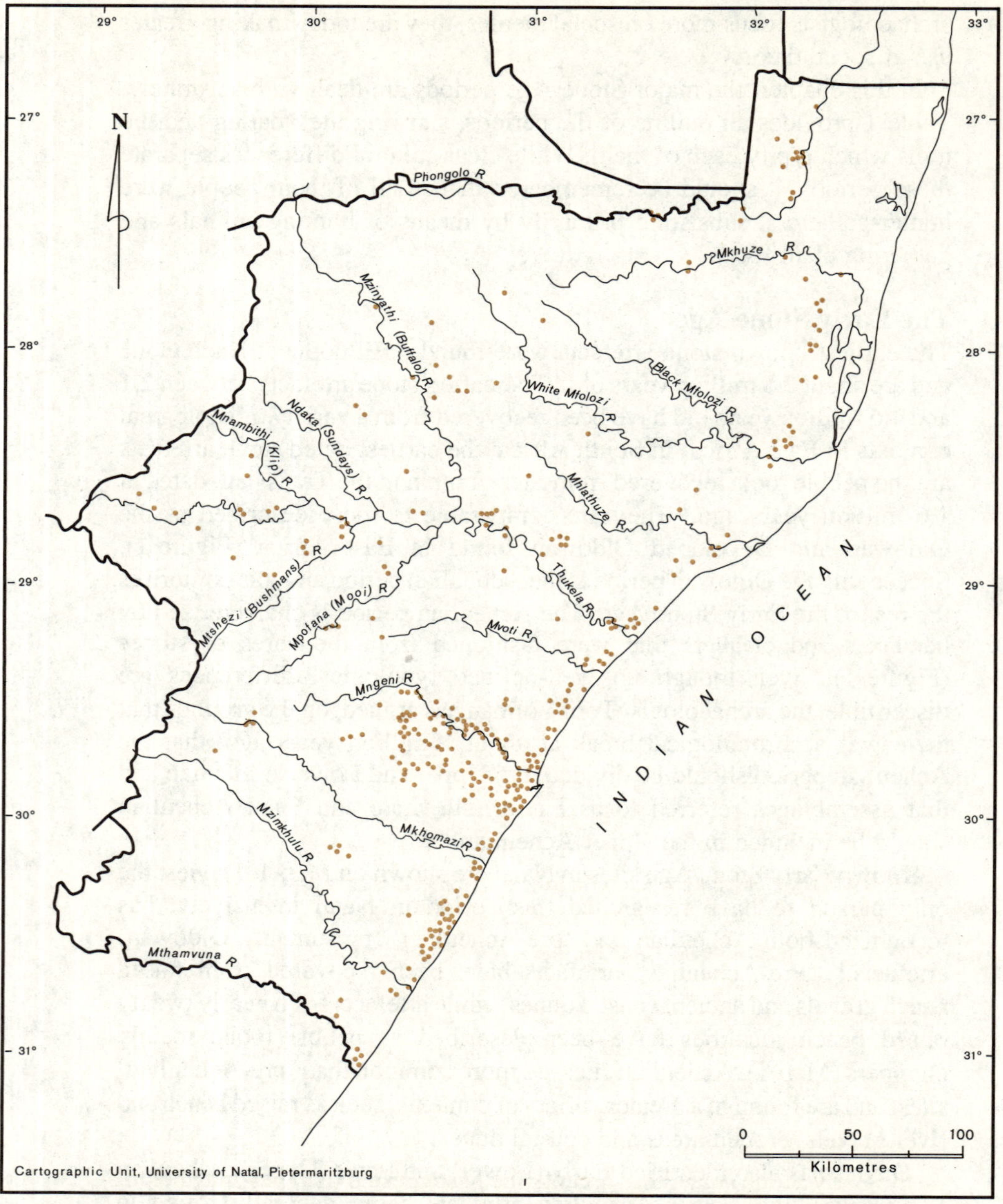

Map 1   Distribution of Early Stone Age sites in Natal

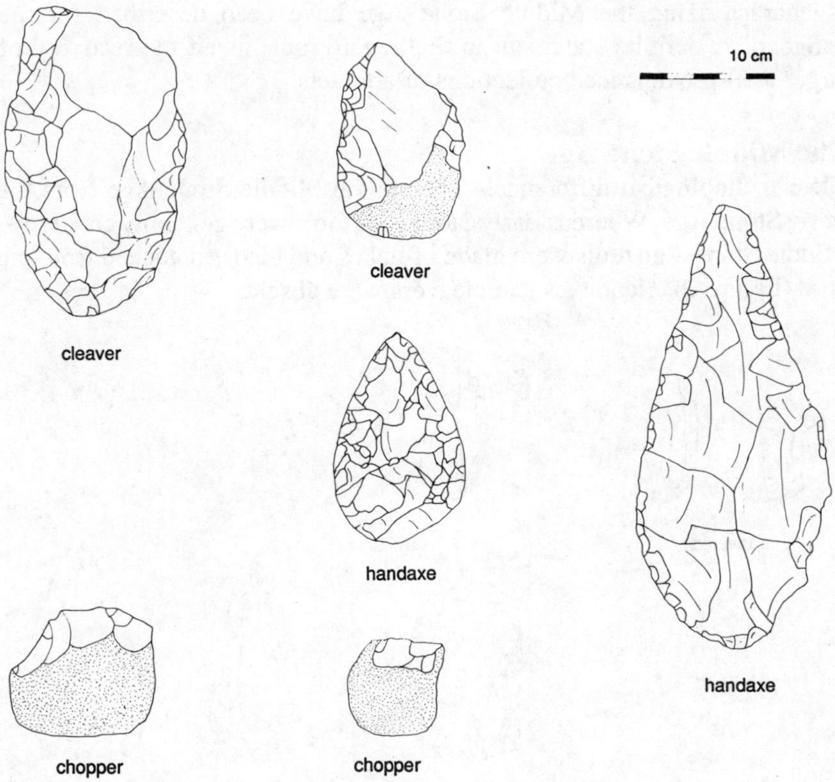

cleaver

cleaver

10 cm

handaxe

handaxe

chopper

chopper

Fig. 1   Early Stone Age artefacts

the Early Stone Age people in Natal, but it can be assumed on the basis of evidence on Early Stone Age people elsewhere that their diet consisted primarily of animals and plant foods. It was also during this period that people learnt to control fire.[13] All indications at present are that Acheulian artefacts were not produced in South Africa after 200 000 years ago.

Davies also identified what he called 'Sangoan' sites, primarily in the coastal region and occasionally between the coast and the first escarpment.[14] They are characterized by scrapers and picks; handaxes and cleavers being rare. Although these sites are generally viewed as belonging to the Early Stone Age, it has recently been suggested that they may belong to an early phase of the Middle Stone Age, dating to between about 200 000 and about 130 000 years ago.[15] This suggestion is not without problems because none of the technological attributes generally accepted as characterizing the Middle Stone Age have been described for the Sangoan. A definite statement in this regard must await the recovery of large, well-provenanced collections of artefacts.

The Middle Stone Age

Clear technological differences separate the Middle Stone Age from the Early Stone Age. Whereas Early Stone Age tools were generally core tools, Middle Stone Age tools were made of flakes and blades detached from the core (Figure 2). Handaxes and cleavers were absent.

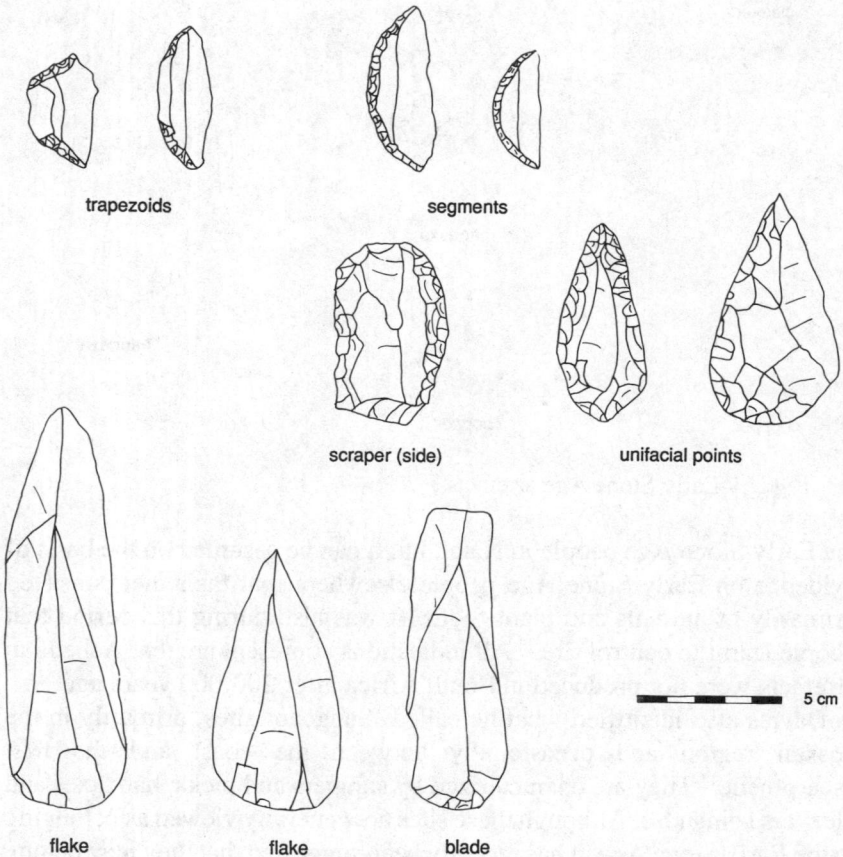

trapezoids   segments

scraper (side)   unifacial points

5 cm

flake   flake   blade

Fig. 2   Middle Stone Age artefacts

Apart from being located in similar contexts to those of the Early Stone Age, Middle Stone Age sites are also found in rock shelters. They are distributed over much of the region (Map 2), the major gaps appearing on the map probably reflecting gaps in our knowledge rather than an actual dearth of sites. There has been some debate as to whether Middle Stone Age occupation occurred in the Drakensberg above 1 200 metres (about 4 000 feet). One argument is that the area was overgrown with impenetrable *Podocarpus* (yellowwood) forest, making occupation impossible.[16] This has been countered by the argument, based on palaeoenvironmental data obtained from the excavation of large caves with long sequences in eastern Lesotho, that the major factor influencing site distribution would have been the amount and duration of snow.[17] Recent discoveries have in fact indicated that there probably was an ephemeral Middle Stone Age occupation of this area.[18]

Middle Stone Age deposits have been recovered from five excavated rock shelters in Natal, but only Border Cave has been comprehensively described.[19] The other sites are Sibhudu Shelter,[20] Holley Shelter,[21] Umbeli Belli Shelter,[22] and Umhlathuzana Shelter.[23] Using technological criteria, the Middle Stone Age has been divided into four stages: Middle Stone Age 1, Middle Stone Age 2, Howieson's Poort and Middle Stone Age 3.[24] The earliest reliably dated Middle Stone Age assemblage at Border Cave (Middle Stone Age 2) is between 130 000 and 100 000 years old,[25] being characterized by large narrow flakes and blades which decrease in average length through time. Overlying Middle Stone Age 2 are Howieson's Poort deposits, which date from about 100 000 to between 85 000 and 75 000 years ago. They are easily distinguished from the overlying and underlying deposits by characteristic backed artefacts, particularly segments and trapezoids (Figure 2), which are either rare or absent in the other stages.[26] The final stage of the Middle Stone Age at Border Cave has, on technological grounds, been subdivided into a stage dating between 75 000 and 64 000 years ago and a later stage dating from 64 000 to 50 000 years ago.[27] It has been argued by Volman, who initiated the division of the Middle Stone Age into these four stages, that Middle Stone Age 3 assemblages are not readily distinguished as a group from Middle Stone Age 2 assemblages.[28]

As yet, there is no unequivocal final dating of the Middle Stone Age. Excavations at Border Cave suggest that it was replaced by an Early Late Stone Age, perhaps as early as 45 000 years ago.[29] However, at excavated sites in Lesotho, Namibia and the southern Cape, as well as in Natal, the

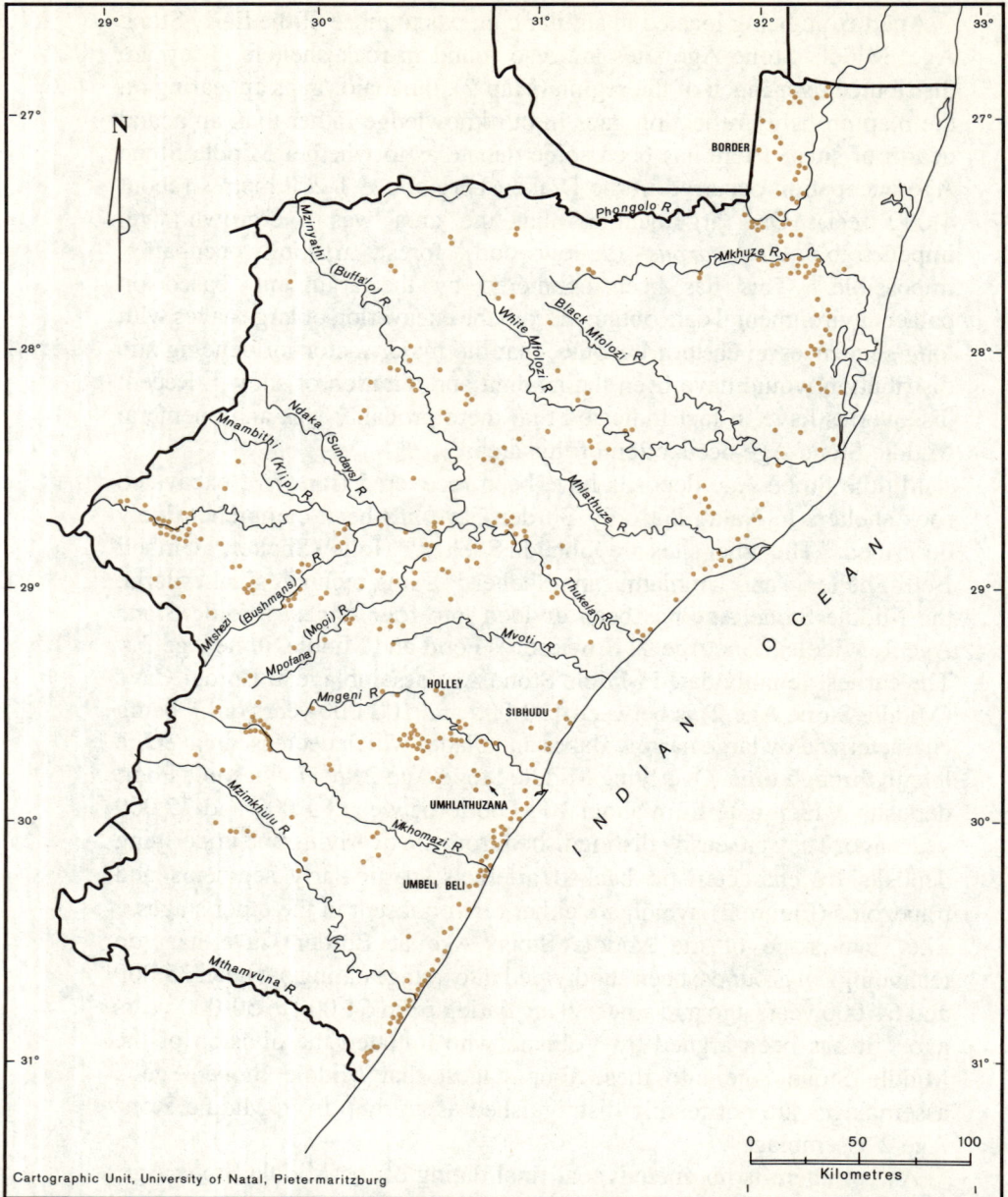

Map 2   Distribution of Middle Stone Age sites in Natal

Middle Stone Age perseveres until between 30 000 and 20 000 years ago. It is unlikely that people using Middle Stone Age and Later Stone Age artefacts would have lived in such close proximity for such a long period, so this problem remains to be solved by archaeologists.

Relatively little is known about the particular types of foods that the Middle Stone Age hunter-gatherers ate. Border Cave is the only site from which information is at present available.[30] In due course, it will be supplemented by the results of excavations at the Umhlathuzana and Sibhudu Shelters. Small quantities of a wide variety of animals were found in the Border Cave excavations. These included honey badger, dassie, Burchell's zebra, bushpig, warthog, hippopotamus, steenbok, oribi, mountain reedbuck, waterbuck, roan/sable, impala, blesbok, hartebeest/tsessebe, blue wildebeest, springbok, greater kudu, nyala, bushbuck, eland, Cape buffalo and possibly an extinct giant Cape horse *(Equus capensis)*. A handful of seeds was also found at Border Cave, while grindstones, which may have been used in the processing of plant foods, have been recovered from the Middle Stone Age levels at Umhlathuzana Shelter.[31] No local evidence exists to indicate that seafood was consumed, but shell middens dating to about 100 000 years ago have been recorded in the Cape.[32] It is thus not improbable that marine resources were exploited in Natal at roughly the same time.

Evidence of the manufacture of cultural articles from materials other than stone first appears during the Middle Stone Age. So also does evidence concerning religious practices, the final Middle Stone Age stage at Border Cave producing the earliest known burial in South Africa, and the only burial so far attributed to the Middle Stone Age.[33] A perforated *Conus* shell was found in association with this skeleton, and ochre may have been strewn over the body at the time of burial. This shell must have come from the Natal coast, roughly 80 kilometres to the east, and it therefore provides evidence of the movement of items over long distances during the terminal Middle Stone Age. Other significant cultural items recovered from the upper Middle Stone Age levels at Border Cave include 'daggers' of pig tusk, bone fragments with distinct small notches and utilized *Acacia* thorns.[34]

The Later Stone Age

A lot more is known about the Later Stone Age than about the earlier periods. This is because organic remains are generally better preserved in Later Stone Age rock shelter deposits, which are within the range of

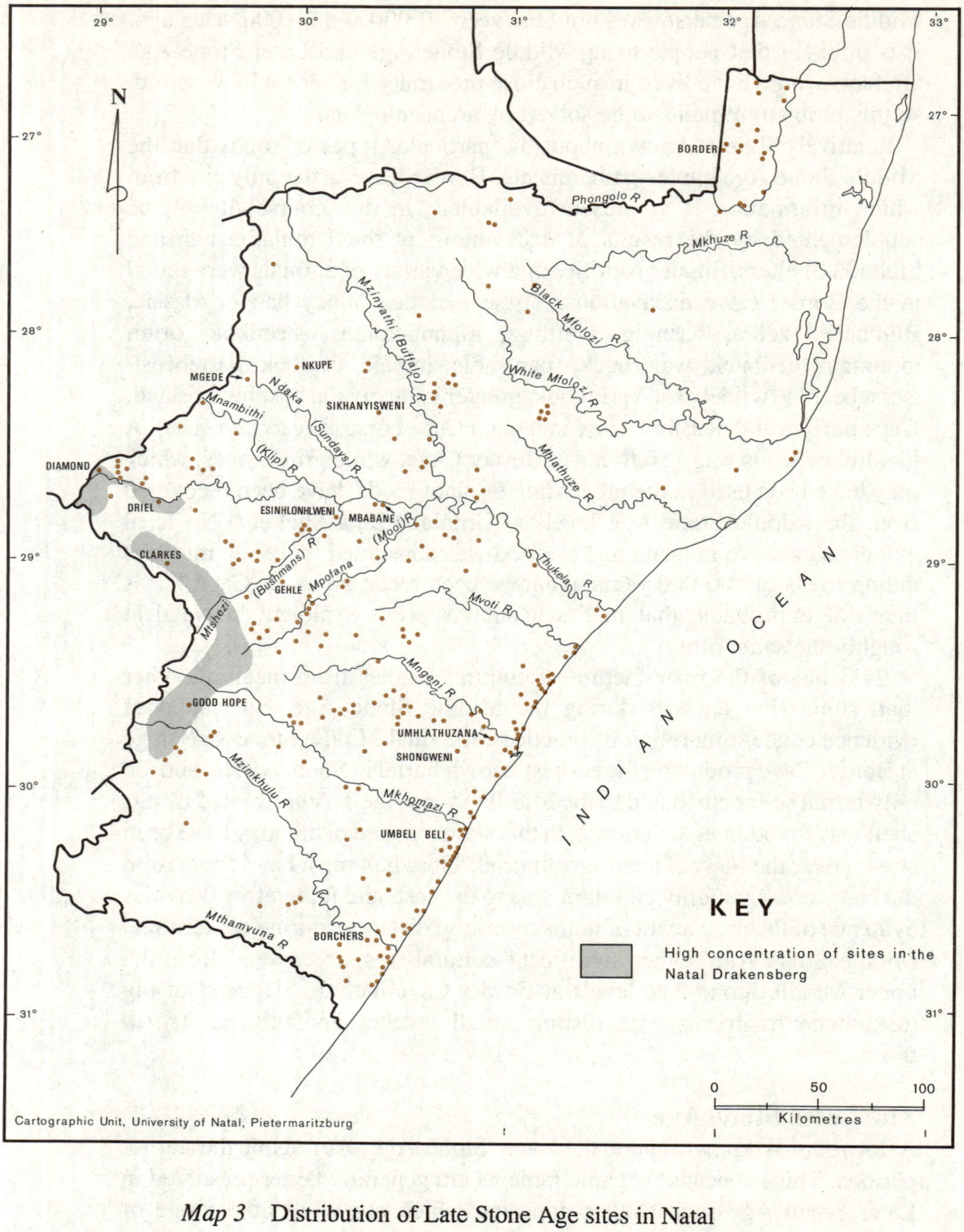

Map 3   Distribution of Late Stone Age sites in Natal

KEY

High concentration of sites in the Natal Drakensberg

Cartographic Unit, University of Natal, Pietermaritzburg

0   50   100

Kilometres

N

29°   30°   31°   32°   33°

27°

BORDER

Phongolo R

Mkhuze R

28°

Mzinyathi (Buffalo) R

Black Mfolozi R

White Mfolozi R

MGEDE   NKUPE

Mnambithi   Ndaka   SIKHANYISWENI

(Sundays) R

Mhlathuze R

DIAMOND

(Klip) R

DRIEL   ESINHLONHLWENI   MBABANE

CLARKES   GEHLE   (Mooi) R

(Bushmans) R   Mpofana   R

Mtshezi   Thukela R

INDIAN OCEAN

GOOD HOPE   Mvoti R

Mngeni R

UMHLATHUZANA

SHONGWENI

Mzimkhulu R

Mkhomazi R

UMBELI BELI

Mthamvuna R   BORCHERS

radio-carbon dating. Furthermore, archaeologists are more confident about using ethnographic analogies, especially during the Holocene (the period which followed the end of the Ice Age about 10 000 years ago), than when they are dealing with the earlier periods.

Later Stone Age sites abound in Natal (Map 3). In the Drakensberg alone, the only area which has been comprehensively surveyed, roughly 250 sites have been recorded, while another 250 or more, although containing only rock paintings, belong in all likelihood to the Later Stone Age. As with the Middle Stone Age, the large gaps on the map probably do not reflect an actual dearth of sites, for there may be many as yet undiscovered. It has, however, been argued that in the southern Natal Midlands the paucity of sites is due to the fact that the area was occupied only by small bands, living in transitory open-sites while moving between the Drakensberg and the coastal belt.[35]

Stone artefacts are overwhelmingly the most common cultural item recovered from the excavations that have been carried out, followed by pottery (belonging to the last 2 000 years), ground, polished and shaved bone, beads and ostrich eggshell. In studying these, archaeologists classify each of them according to the material from which they are made, their morphology, their size, their function and the nature of their modification. For example, stone artefacts are first classified according to raw material type, then according to whether they are waste material, utilized pieces or formally fashioned tools. In each category, there are further subdivisions and some of the artefacts are measured. Such methods of classification make it possible to compare cultural assemblages with those belonging to different periods or those found in different localities. Scrapers, adzes and backed pieces together generally comprise more than 90 per cent of the formal stone tools recovered from any one assemblage and they have been the tools most studied (Figure 3). The scrapers were probably used for removing the fat from animal skins before these were pegged out to dry. Adzes were probably used for shaving wood and, to a lesser extent, bone; while backed pieces, of which there are different types, were probably employed in hunting and in cutting up carcasses.

A great deal of information about the foods Later Stone Age hunter-gatherers ate has been obtained from animal, plant and marine and freshwater shell remains. In some cases, it has been possible to identify the remains of individual species. As small animals in particular are sensitive to environmental fluctuations, these remains can also tell us much about past environments. Botanical remains are also very useful, for seeds can

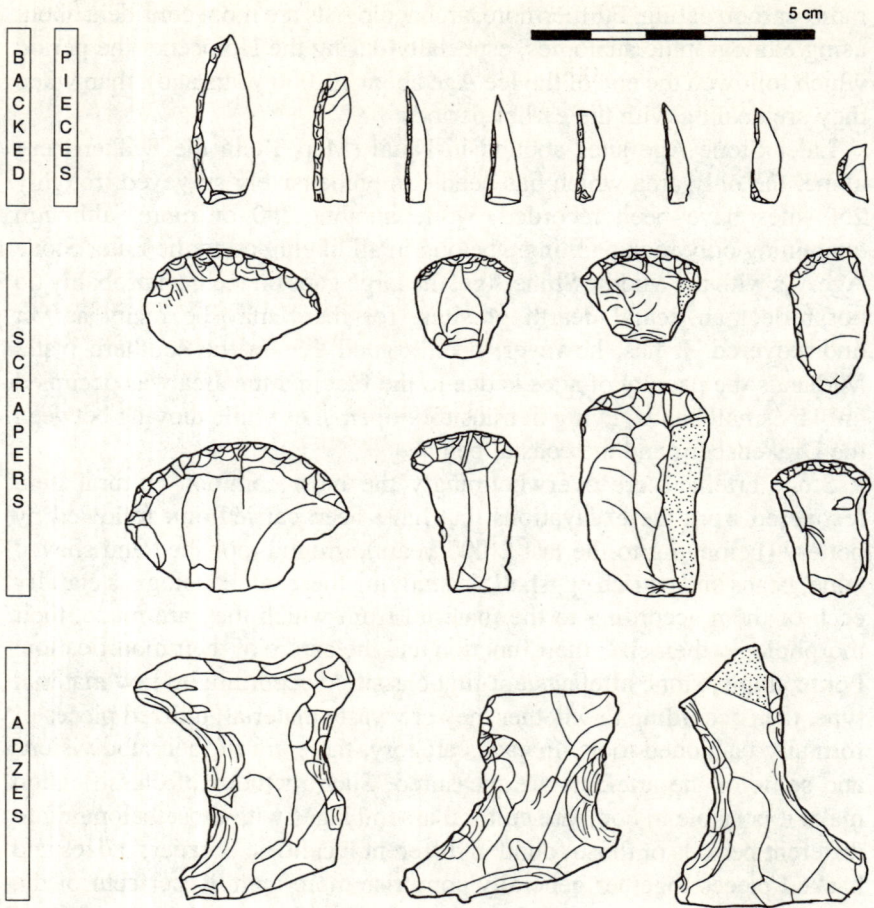

Fig. 3   Later Stone Age artefacts

indicate which fruits and berries Later Stone Age people ate. And, because fruits and berries are seasonal, they can also provide information about the months during the year when sites were occupied.

Only two Natal sites (Shongweni South Cave and Umhlathuzana Shelter, Map 3), which are less than 10 kilometres apart, have so far been dated at between 30 000 and 10 000 years ago.[36] The Shongweni South Cave excavation produced little diagnostic material, whilst the Umhlathuzana Shelter collections, which are considerably larger, are still being researched.

Of the Holocene Later Stone Age sites that have been excavated in the Thukela Basin and southern Natal, only two have so far been dated at between 10 000 and 7 000 years ago. At Sikhanyisweni Shelter, a small portion of these deposits was sampled and it has not been possible to classify the stone tool collection, whereas at Good Hope a slightly larger, and more diagnostic, stone sample was recovered. The Good Hope stone artefacts have affinity with the Albany Industry (known from excavations in the southern Cape and elsewhere in South Africa),[37] which generally dates to between 12 000 and 8 000 years ago, being characterized by large scrapers with few other tools. The Albany Industry is somewhat enigmatic as it is bracketed in time between industries dominated by small stone tools. Although it has been argued that it represents an adaptation to rapidly changing environments and subsistence potentials, no really satisfactory explanation has been produced for its occurrence.[38]

The Thukela Basin hunter-gatherer society
5000 BC – 50 BC

As most of the Later Stone Age research in Natal has focused on the Thukela Basin, this section concentrates upon this region. The many dated sites in the Thukela Basin show that it was intensively settled by Later Stone Age hunter-gatherers after about 7 000 years ago. Before then, it was virtually unoccupied. Around 2 000 – 1 500 years ago, Iron Age people entered the region (see Chapter 2). Unlike the Later Stone Age hunter-gatherers, who lived in rock shelters, and probably in temporary encampments out in the open, they lived in fairly large open-air villages, cultivated crops and kept domestic stock. Following the arrival of the Iron Age people, it is no longer possible to consider the Later Stone Age hunter-gatherers in isolation, for the archaeological record shows that there was interaction between these two communities.

Later Stone Age hunter-gatherer economic practices changed considerably between 7 000 and 2 000 years ago. Not only was the exploitation of certain foods increased, but a greater variety of foodstuff was consumed. This is indicated by the recovery from archaeological sites of both food remains and stone artefacts connected to food gathering and processing. At Nkupe Shelter and Mgede Shelter, whose deposits date from 4500 BC to 500 BC and 4500 BC to 2500 BC respectively, large quantities of plant remains were found. Remains of underground plant foods were absent in the lowermost levels at these sites, but were present in small quantities in the levels dated to before 4 000 years ago, and at Nkupe Shelter continued to increase in the overlying levels. Seeds from fruits and berries were recovered from all the levels at both sites, but increase in quantity and variety. A marked increase occurs in the remains of all plant-foods at Nkupe Shelter between 4 000 and 2 500 years ago. *Podocarpus falcatus* (yellowwood) seeds, whose fruits are edible,[39] were the most common seeds recovered at both sites.

Although the remains of underground plant foods have been recovered from only two sites, the increase in the number of adzes found at all the sites suggests that the Later Stone Age hunter-gatherers consistently increased their exploitation of them. As adzes were woodworking tools, they would have been used primarily to fashion and maintain wooden digging-sticks, which would have been used to dig up underground plant foods. These digging sticks were sometimes weighted with bored stones, particularly when it was necessary to break hard ground such as is found in the Drakensberg, the grasslands and the thornveld. An increase in adzes would therefore reflect an increase in the use of digging-sticks and this, in turn, would suggest a greater exploitation of underground plant foods.[40] Many paintings of digging-sticks, either separately or, at times, carried by women (sometimes with bored stones), have been found in the Drakensberg.[41]

Further evidence of the intensified exploitation of underground plant foods by Later Stone Age hunter-gatherers is provided by the discovery of an increasing number of grindstones, which were probably employed in the processing of these foods. While the 5000 BC – 2050 BC and 2050 BC – 50 BC deposits that have been excavated in the Thukela Basin are more or less similar in volume, a maximum number of six grindstones was recovered from the sites dating back to the earlier period and at least twenty from the sites dating to the later period.

Along with the increase in the consumption of plant foods, there occurred a general increase in the exploitation of dassies and hares at all the sites, and of small mammals such as mice, rats and shrews at Nkupe Shelter. No such increase in the consumption of small animals occurs at the other sites. Hunter-gatherers north of the Thukela River also began exploiting fish about 4 000 years ago, as evidenced by the recovery of fish vertebrae from Mgede Shelter, and of fish hooks from this site and Nkupe Shelter. Thereafter, fish remains were recovered from Sikhanyisweni Shelter and Nkupe Shelter.

All the sites produced antelope remains. The smaller and medium-sized antelope such as oribi, klipspringer, grysbok, steenbok, vaalribbok and mountain reed-buck are predominant in all the sites except Diamond 1, where the larger antelope such as blesbok, hartebeest and wildebeest are more common.

A highly significant addition to the archaeological record is pottery. The earliest pottery recovered from Stone Age hunter-gatherer sites comes from the Drakensberg and adjacent area and has been dated to about 2 000 years ago.[42] This pottery is unlike that of the contemporary Iron Age communities. There are three possible explanations for its origin amongst Later Stone Age hunter-gatherers. One is that it developed locally. The second is that there was contact with farming communities, with modifications being introduced by the hunter-gatherers. The third is it was introduced from elsewhere. Further research should shed light on which of these explanations is the most plausible. It is, however, pertinent that pottery, quite unlike Natal Early Iron Age pottery and dated at around 50 BC, is also known in the northern and southern Cape. Even though the origin of the Natal Later Stone Age pottery cannot be identified, its introduction must have had great impact on the food processing of the hunter-gatherers and increased the range of plants they could exploit, not least because for the first time they had a container in which water and food could be boiled.

The economic changes that can be identified between 7 000 and 2 000 years ago were associated with changes in the structure of Thukela Basin hunter-gatherer society. Recent research on contemporary farmers and hunter-gatherers has assisted archaeologists by showing that cultural artefacts can be signifiers of relations between people,[43] and this has enabled us to draw new inferences about past hunter-gatherer societies.

The Nkupe Shelter and Gehle Shelter (Map 3) cultural artefacts, which are dated at between 7 000 and 5 500 years ago, show similarities that are not found thereafter in sites north and south of the Thukela River. There are, for example, a large number of segments,[44] ground stones and a particular type of scraper at both sites. The inference drawn from this is that the hunter-gatherer communities which occupied these sites, about 110 kilometres apart, were part of the same extended social network that existed in the upper and upper/central Thukela Basin. At some time between 5 500 and 4 000 years ago, this network disintegrated and it appears that two, and perhaps three, distinct social networks emerged in its place. Once established, these social networks appear to have remained intact until the arrival of the Iron Age people between 2 000 and 1 500 years ago. The sites to the south of the Thukela River become distinguishable from those to the north by the absence of ostrich eggshell (pieces and beads), ground ochre and ground stones, as well as by the very low frequency of segments and modified bone. To the north of the Thukela River, similar local differences emerge. In the Sikhanyisweni Shelter there is a greater frequency of ostrich eggshell than in the Nkupe Shelter, while there are also differences in the types and numbers of modified bone and in the types of backed pieces. Sikhanyisweni Shelter is also the only site in the Thukela Basin which reveals evidence of ostrich eggshell bead manufacture.

Simulation studies have shown that for a group of people to be able successfully to reproduce itself, it must contain a minimum of 175 people of all ages.[45] The social networks that developed in the Thukela Basin may therefore represent areas of viable mating pools. This suggests that, although at the initial stages of their occupation of the region the Later Stone Age hunter-gatherers may have maintained geographically extensive social contacts to ensure the reproduction of their community, with time the range of these contacts decreased, resulting in the emergence of three mating networks shortly before 4 000 years ago.

The social and economic changes experienced by Thukela Basin hunter-gatherer society are consistent with what one would expect from a growing population. Population growth is also suggested by the increasing number of known sites occupied by the Later Stone Age hunter-gatherers during this time. It would, however, be wrong simply to ascribe the economic and social changes to population growth,[46] as research among modern hunter-gatherers has shown that they are able to regulate population growth.[47] It is also unlikely that these changes were precipitated by changing environmental conditions, another line of argument favoured by Later Stone Age archaeologists.[48] Available evidence indicates that the environment remained stable from the beginning of intensive hunter-gatherer occupation of the Thukela Basin 7 000 years ago until around 3 000 years ago. Moreover, the environment acts as a constraining force on human actions, so that changing environmental conditions merely alter the options available to people. The explanation for the changes must lie in the complex social and economic mechanisms operating within society, which either stimulated, or allowed, population growth. It would be premature to speculate on these mechanisms, as research on them has only recently begun.

Seasonal mobility

One of the main themes of Later Stone Age research in South Africa, including Natal, has been that of seasonality. It has been hypothesized, on the basis of an analysis of the seasonal movements of large antelope, that the food resources of southern Natal would have been exploited on a seasonal basis by hunter-gatherers.[49] According to this hypothesis, they would have occupied the Drakensberg in summer and the thornveld and coastal areas during winter, traversing the Midlands along ridges rather than in the valleys. Recent field-work based on this hypothesis has suggested that in southern Natal during the last 3 500 years, hunter-gatherers would have occupied the Drakensberg in spring and summer (October to March), the coastal zone in winter (April/May to August), and the Midlands in autumn and late winter (March/April and September). This seasonal hypothesis, which has still to be tested in the Thukela Basin, has given rise to the speculation that while they were in the Drakensberg, the hunter-gatherers would have lived in large groups and would have operated from large home-base sites. One of the results of the formation of these larger social units could have been an increase in ritual activity. Social organization in the Midlands, however, would have been characterized by the small mobile groups that traversed the zone, while in the coastal zones larger groups, but not as large as those in the Drakensberg, would have been found.[50]

Rock paintings

Any examination of the Later Stone Age in Natal would be incomplete without mention of rock paintings. The first recordings of rock paintings in the Drakensberg were made over 100 years ago. Since then, they have been the focus of extensive research and of numerous publications.[51] On completion of a three-year survey of painting sites in the Drakensberg in 1981, 516 sites, containing a total of 29 874 paintings, were known.[52] Rock art occurs, but less frequently, in other areas of Natal but it has never been adequately surveyed and researched.

A great problem lies in establishing the age of the art, but some advances have been made. The earliest dated paintings in southern Africa are from the Apollo 11 Cave in southern Namibia.[53] Dated to about 26 000 years ago, these paintings are about as old as the earliest palaeolithic art in western Europe. The Apollo 11 dates are based on the age of the deposits in which slabs of painted rocks were recovered. The next oldest known art in southern Africa are pieces of engraved stones from Wonderwerk Cave in

Aron Mazel

Trance buck from Clarke's
Shelter (scale in cm)

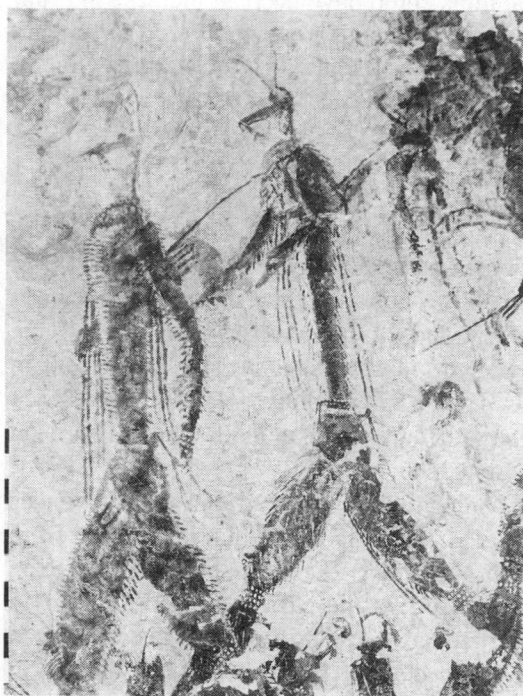

Aron Mazel

Therianthropes from
Procession Shelter
(scale in cm)

the northern Cape, dated to around 11 000 years ago.[54] An increasing number of painted and engraved stones date to within the last 10 000 years, especially the last 4 000 years, but none are from Natal. In the Natal Drakensberg, besides the paintings of cattle and sheep which, in all likelihood, postdate the arrival of the Iron Age farming communities 1 500 to 2 000 years ago and those of horses, wagons and whites which postdate AD 1800, we are unable to put dates to the paintings. However, as the area is high in rainfall and experiences great temperature variations, both of which cause weathering in rocks, it is unlikely that the earliest paintings still visible on the rocks are more than a few thousand years old. New and improved radio-carbon dating techniques, which have been used with success in the western Cape,[55] offer some hope of our being able to establish the age of the wall paintings in the not too distant future.

Interpretation of the paintings is a source of continuing controversy. There are three main theories. The first is that they were executed merely to illustrate what was seen, in other words, 'art for art's sake'. The second is that they represent a form of sympathetic magic, reflecting a belief that the painting of appropriate scenes before a hunt, or after a successful hunt, would enhance the prowess of the hunters. The third is that they are symbolic, related to hunter-gatherer religious practices, primarily trance performance, and perform important social functions.

Hunter-gatherer historical records as well as ethnography both favour what has been loosely phrased the 'trance hypothesis',[56] for many features of trance performance and trance vision are identifiable in the paintings. During trance dances, shamans enter trance and perform certain tasks such as the maintenance of social relations, the promotion of economic activity by, for example, guiding antelope into ambushes and controlling rain, and the maintenance of sound links between bands by means of 'out of body travel', in which they 'visit' associated bands. It has also been speculated that the art may have been a way of preparing novices for religious experience and an instruction for those who had not, or would not, experience trance. Thus, the shaman's art was not 'a luxury indulged in leisure time to provide pleasure and relaxation', but a 'remarkable aesthetic achievement' which lay at 'the very heart of the functioning of San society'.[57]

The 'trance hypothesis' appears to provide an explanation for many enigmatic paintings found in the Drakensberg, such as those found at Clarkes's Shelter and Procession Shelter (see photographs). These include the trance buck from Clarke's Shelter and therianthropes from Procession

Trance buck; line projection from nape of neck; arms back; bleeding nose or epistaxis

Therianthrope; bleeding nose or epistaxis; lines from top of head

Therianthrope; arms back; 'erect' hairs

Therianthrope: This represents a conflation of animal and human forms, and depicts the fusion of the shamans (in trance) with the source of their potency, which is derived from their 'possesion' of animals, in particular eland, which are considered 'strong' things.

Trance buck: A form of therianthrope.

Arms back: The position adopted by shamans when asking God to put potency into their bodies.

'Erect' hair: Hair has two known trance associations: in the form of lion's hair appearing on the shaman's back, representing evil or dangerous potency; or as a metaphor for the symbolic death of the shaman in trance and conceptually related to the death of the eland. The eland's hair stands erect while it is dying.

Bleeding nose or epistaxis: Shamans in trance sometimes experience nasal haemorrhaging, which is also a feature of the death of antelope. The shaman's nasal blood is rubbed on patients in the belief that its smell will ward off evil and sickness.

Line projection from the nape of the neck: The shamans expel the sickness they remove from their patients from the nape of the neck.

Lines from the top of the head: These lines most likely represent out of body travel.

Table 2. Some of the trance metaphors represented at Clarke's Shelter and Procession Shelter, based on paintings from these sites.

(Information for this table comes from: J. D. Lewis-Williams, 'Cognitive and Optical Illusions in San Rock Paintings', *Current Anthropology* 27 (1986); J. D. Lewis-Williams and J. H. N. Loubser, 'Deceptive Appearances: a Critique of Southern African Rock Art Studies', *Advances in World Archaeology* 5 (1986) and J. D. Lewis-Williams, 'The San Artistic Achievement', *African Arts* 18 (1985).)

Shelter, the arms back posture and line projection from the nape of the neck of the Clarke's Shelter trance buck, the 'erect' hair and lines from the head of the Procesion Shelter therianthropes, and the bleeding from the nose of the figures from both sites. The significance and meaning of these images are presented in Table 2.

The last two thousand years

The last two thousand years of the Later Stone Age in Natal has been intensively studied in the Thukela Basin through the excavation of many hunter-gatherer rock shelter and Iron Age village sites. It would appear that up to AD 1000 these Stone and Iron Age communities experienced close and equitable relations and may even have interbred. The distribution of sites, although not conclusive, suggests that the central Thukela Basin was occupied by the hunter-gatherers only after the arrival of Iron Age people in this area. There does not appear to have been competition for food resources between these two groups, while a study of their social systems and the nature of symbolic expression suggest more reasons for amicable co-existence between them than antagonism.[58] This is also the conclusion that may be reached from the study of manufactured items, which as noted earlier can reveal a great deal about social relationships. Items associated with the Later Stone Age, such as particular types of modified bone, ostrich eggshell pieces and beads are found on Early Iron Age sites, while Iron Age decorated pottery and iron ore have been recovered from the Mbabane Shelter hunter-gatherer site.[59] Talc schist and soapstone, which outcrop only in the Early Iron Age area, have also been found on hunter-gatherer sites, while the recovery of almost identical stone spatulae from the Driel Shelter hunter-gatherer and Msuluzi Confluence farming community sites also suggest that there was social and economic interaction between the two groups. It is also likely that the later hunter-gatherers used iron. Athough no iron has as yet been found at these sites, the use of a metal knife is suggested by the occurrence of faceted bone which seems to have been shaved by a sharp implement.

The study of manufactured articles of hunter-gatherer origin also indicates that the three social networks that had evolved before about 2000 BC (see above) disintegrated, to be replaced by one that was geographically more extensive. Marine shells, for example, are absent from the 2050 to 50 BC deposits, but are thereafter found in rock shelters from the Natal thornveld to as far inland as the mountains of Lesotho. The widespread distribution after 50 BC of ostrich eggshell and modified bone, as well as the presence of soapstone at Sikhanyisweni Shelter and talc schist at Driel Shelter, provides further evidence that there was widespread contact between the hunter-gatherers in the Thukela Basin. It is possible that, while the hunter-gatherers and Iron Age farmers established close reciprocal bonds, these new circumstances may have aroused a sense of insecurity among the hunter-gatherers and caused them to strengthen and widen their social networks.

There is less information available about the relations between the Later Stone Age and the Iron Age peoples after AD 1000. Indications are that they remained in contact, but not as closely as before.[60] At this stage, the Iron Age communities underwent changes in social organization which saw the emergence of social inequalities (see Chapter 2),[61] and this might have affected attitudes towards Later Stone Age hunter-gatherers, whose society remained egalitarian. A possibility, at present under investigation, is that the Later Stone Age hunter-gatherers became clients of the farmers, exchanging meat and ivory for domestic plant foods, as was indeed to happen during the colonial period in other regions of Southern Africa. What is certain is that the Later Stone Age hunter-gatherers survived in Natal to confront white settlers in the early nineteenth century, when they were referred to as 'Bushmen'.

One of the most tragic episodes in Natal's history is the decimation of the San (as the 'Bushmen' are now known) between the late 1830s and the 1880s, following the establishment of white settlements.[62] Both the Trekkers and the British settlers looked upon the San hunter-gatherers, who took to raiding their live-stock, largely as pests to be shot on sight as if they were animals. Three main periods of hunger-gatherer stock raidings have been identified, although raiding was by no means confined to these periods. The first was from 1845 to about 1852, the second from 1856 to the early 1860s and the third from 1868 to about 1876. A total of sixty-four raids was recorded during this time, with seven being the most in any one year. The evidence suggests that raids were not merely undertaken for food but were part of a response by the hunter-gatherers to the increasing encroachment by whites on their territory. Initially, their resistance met with some success, for large tracts of land remained unoccupied by the whites. However, as settler military resources increased and as the tactics of the settlers became more refined – as for example, the creation of a series of buffer zones of Africans along the Drakensberg foothills – the tide was finally turned, so that by the 1880s the occupation of Natal by its oldest known inhabitants had come to an end.[63]

Notes

1   For example, C. L. Griesbach, 'On the Geology of Natal in South Africa', *Quarterly Journal of the Geological Society of London*, 27 (1871), pp. 52–72; R. Andree, 'Die Steinzeit Afrika', *Globus*, 41 (1882), pp. 185–90; W. D. Gooch, 'The Stone Age of South Africa', *Journal of the Royal Anthropological Institute*, 11 (1882), pp. 124–82.

2   A. J. H. Goodwin and C. Van Riet Lowe, 'The Stone Age Cultures of South Africa', *Annals of the South African Museum*, 27 (1929), pp. 1–279.

3   A. J. H. Goodwin, 'A New Variation of the Smithfield Culture from Natal', *Transactions of the Royal Society of South Africa*, 19 (1930), pp. 7–14; A. J. H. Goodwin, 'The Rhodesian Origin of Certain Smithfield "N" Elements', *Proceedings of the Rhodesian Scientific Association*, 34 (1934), pp. 28–34.

4   C. Van Riet Lowe, 'The Smithfield "N" Culture', *Transactions of the Royal Society of South Africa*, 23 (1936), pp. 367–72.

5   H. C. Stein, 'Stone Implements from the Cathkin Peak Area', *Bantu Studies*, 7 (1933), pp. 159–81.

6   This new research paradigm, which became dominant throughout the western world, is commonly known as American 'new archaeology'.

7   P. L. Carter, 'Late Stone Age Exploitation Patterns in Southern Natal', *South African Archaeological Bulletin*, 25 (1971), pp. 55–8.

8   R. Lewin, 'Ethiopian Stone Tools are the World's Oldest', *Science*, 211 (1981), pp. 806–7; R. C. Walter and J. L. Aronson, 'Revisions of K/Ar Ages for the Hadar Hominid Site, Ethiopia', *Nature* (London), 296 (1982), pp. 122–7.

9   T. P. Volman, 'Early Prehistory of Southern Africa', *Southern African Prehistory and Palaeoenvironments*, ed. R. G. Klein (Rotterdam, Balkema, 1984), pp. 169–220.

10   Ibid., p. 180.

11   O. Davies, 'Pleistocene Beaches of Natal', *Annals of the Natal Museum*, 20 (1970), pp. 403–42; O. Davies, 'The Older Coastal Dunes in Natal and Zululand and their Relation to Former Shorelines', *Annals of the South African Museum*, 71 (1976), pp. 19–32.

12   O. Davies, 'The Palaeolithic Sequence of Umgababa Ilmenite Diggings', *Annals of the Natal Museum*, 25 (1982), pp. 41–59.

13   R. Mason, *Prehistory of the Transvaal* (Johannesburg, Witwatersrand University Press, 1962).

14   O. Davies, 'The "Sangoan" Industries', *Annals of the Natal Museum*, 22 (1976), pp. 885–911.

15   Davies, 'Palaeolithic Sequence', p. 58.

16   A. R. Willcox, 'Reasons for the Non-Occurrence of Middle Stone Age Material in the Natal Drakensberg', *South African Journal of Science*, 70 (1974), pp. 273–5.

17   P. L. Carter, 'The Effect of Climatic Change on Settlement in Eastern Lesotho during the Middle and Later Stone Age', *World Archaeology*, 8 (1976), pp. 198–206; P. L. Carter, 'The Prehistory of Eastern Lesotho' (unpublished Ph.D. thesis, University of Cambridge, 1978).

18   A. D. Mazel, 'Evidence for Pre-Later Stone Age Occupation of the Natal Drakensberg', *Annals of the Natal Museum*, 25 (1982), pp. 61–5.

19   P. B. Beaumont, 'Border Cave' (unpublished MA thesis, University of Cape Town, 1978); P. B. Beaumont, 'The Stone Age Culture Stratigraphy of Border Cave' (unpublished paper presented at a workshop on 'Towards a Better Understanding of the Upper Pleistocene in Sub-Saharan Africa', organized by the Southern African Association of Archaeologists, Stellenbosch, June 1979).

20   A. D. Mazel, 'The Ecology of the Holocene Later Stone Age Communities of the Northern Natal Drakensberg and Tugela River Catchment', (1983/84 HSRC Progress Report, 1984); A. D. Mazel, 'The Holocene Later Stone Age Prehistory of the Tugela Basin', (1984/85 HSRC Progress Report, 1985).

21   J. G. Cramb, 'A Middle Stone Age Industry from a Natal Rock Shelter', *South African Journal of Science*, 48 (1952), pp. 181–6; J. G. Cramb, 'A Second Report on Work at the Holley Shelter', *South African Journal of Science*, 57 (1961), pp. 45–8.

22   J. H. C. Cable, 'Economy and Technology in the Late Stone Age of Southern Natal' (Oxford, British Archaeological Reports, 1984, BAR International Series 201), pp. 1–267; information obtained personally from J. H. C. Cable.

23   Information obtained personally from J. M. Kaplan.

24   Volman, 'Early Prehistory', pp. 195–211.

25   Beaumont, 'Culture Stratigraphy', p. 19.

26   Backed artefacts display an abrupt retouch (usually at a 90° angle) along one or more edges. This retouch is used for either reshaping the piece or blunting an edge to expedite hafting a handle.

27   Beaumont, 'Culture Stratigraphy', pp. 17–18.

28   Volman, 'Early Prehistory', p. 207.

29   Beaumont, 'Border Cave'; Beaumont, 'Culture Stratigraphy'.

30 Beaumont, 'Border Cave; R. G. Klein, 'The Mammalian Fauna from the Middle and Later Stone Age (Later Pleistocene) Levels of Border Cave, Natal Province, South Africa', *South African Archaeological Bulletin*, 32 (1977), pp. 14–27.

31 Information obtained personally from J. M. Kaplan.

32 Volman, 'Early Prehistory', p. 212.

33 Ibid., pp. 216–17.

34 Beaumont, 'Border Cave', p. 60.

35 Cable, 'Economy and Technology', p. 205. He advised that his hypothesis has yet to be substantiated by means of field-work.

36 O. Davies, 'Excavations at Shongweni South Cave: the Oldest Evidence to Date for Cultigens in Southern Africa', *Annals of the Natal Museum*, 22 (1975), pp. 627–62; information about Umhlathuzana Shelter obtained personally from J. M. Kaplan.

37 J. H. C. Cable, K. Scott and P. L. Carter, 'Excavations at Good Hope Shelter, Underberg District, Natal', *Annals of the Natal Museum*, 24 (1980), pp. 1–34.

38 J. E. Parkington, 'Time and Place: some Observations on Spatial and Temporal Patterning in the Later Stone Age Sequence in Southern Africa', *South African Archaeological Bulletin*, 35 (1980), pp. 73–83. See also replies to this article which follow it.

39 F. W. Fox and M. E. Norwood Young, *Food from the Veld: Edible Wild Plants of Southern Africa Botanically Identified and Described* (Johannesburg, Delta Books, 1982).

40 A. D. Mazel and J. Parkington, 'Stone Tools and Resources: a Case Study from Southern Africa', *World Archaeology*, 13 (1981), pp. 16–30.

41 H. Pager, *Ndedema: a Documentation of the Rock Paintings of the Ndedema Gorge* (Graz, Akademische Druck, 1971), pp. 116, 225, 324, 325; P. Vinnicombe, *People of the Eland: Rock Paintings of the Drakensberg Bushmen as a Reflection of their Life and Thought* (Pietermaritzburg, University of Natal Press, 1976), pp. 276–85.

42 A. D. Mazel, 'Diamond 1 and Clarke's Shelter: Report on Excavations in the Northern Drakensberg, Natal, South Africa', *Annals of the Natal Museum*, 26 (1984), pp. 25–70.

43 I. Hodder, *Symbols in Action: Ethnoarchaeological Studies of Material Culture* (Cambridge, Cambridge University Press, 1982); J. R. Sackett, 'Style and Ethnicity in the Kalahari: a Reply to Wiessner', *American Antiquity*, 50 (1985), pp. 154–9; P. Wiessner, 'Style or Isochrestic Variation? A Reply to Sackett', *American Antiquity*, 50 (1985), pp. 160–6.

44   A crescent-shaped backed piece (see Note 26 above).

45   M. W. Wobst, 'Boundary Conditions for Paleolithic Social Systems: a Simulation Approach', *American Antiquity*, 39 (1974), pp. 147–78.

46   Parkington, 'Time and Place', pp. 73–83.

47   F. A. Hassan, *Demographic Archaeology* (New York, Academic Press, 1981), pp. 143–56.

48   A. D. Mazel, 'The Archaeological Past from the Changing Present: towards a Critical Assessment of South African Later Stone Age Studies from the Early 1960s to the Early 1980s', *Papers on the Prehistory of the Western Cape, South Africa*, eds. J. Parkington and M. Hall (Oxford, British Archaeological Reports, 1987, BAR International Series 332), pp. 504–29.

49   Carter, 'Later Stone Age'.

50   Cable, 'Economy and Technology', pp. 4, 219.

51   M. A. Cherry, 'Bibliography of Rock Art in Natal and Lesotho: 1974–1981', *Annals of the Natal Museum*, 25, 7 (1982), pp. 173–220; A. R. Willcox, *Rock Paintings of the Drakensberg, Natal and Griqualand East* (London, Parrish, 1956); H. Pager, *Ndedema*; P. Vinnicombe, *People of the Eland*; J. D. Lewis-Williams, 'Believing and Seeing: an Interpretation of Symbolic Meanings in Southern San Rock Paintings' (unpublished Ph.D. thesis, University of Natal, Durban, 1977); A. D. Mazel, 'Up and Down the Little Berg: Archaeological Resource Management in the Natal Drakensberg' (unpublished MA thesis, University of Cape Town, 1981). The most important of these studies are those of Willcox, Pager, Vinnicombe, Lewis-Williams and Mazel. My project was of a different nature to the others as it covered the entire Natal Drakensberg and not a specific region within this area.

52   Mazel, 'Up and Down'. If the number of paintings recorded by Vinnicombe and Lewis-Williams for which we have no exact figures were added, the total would far exceed 30 000.

53   A. I. Thackeray, 'Dating the Rock Art of Southern Africa', *New Approaches to Southern African Rock Art*, ed. J. D. Lewis-Williams (Cape Town, South African Archaeological Society, 1983, Goodwin Series, 4), pp. 21–6; W. E. Wendt, 'Art Mobilier from the Apollo Cave, South West Africa: Africa's Oldest Dated Works of Art', *South African Archaeological Bulletin*, 31 (1976), pp. 5–11.

54   A. I. Thackeray, 'Dating the Rock Art'; A. I. Thackeray, J. F. Thackeray, P. B. Beaumont and J. C. Vogel, 'Dated Rock Engravings from Wonderwerk Cave, South Africa', *Science*, 214 (1981), pp. 64–7.

55   N. J. van der Merwe, J. Sealy and R. Yates, 'First Accelerator Carbon-14 Date for Pigment from a Rock Painting', *South African Journal of Science*, 83 (1987), pp. 56–7.

56 R. Yates, J. Golson and M. Hall, 'Trance Performance: the Rock Art of Boontjieskloof and Sevilla', *South African Archaeological Bulletin*, 40 (1985), pp. 70–80.

57 J. D. Lewis-Williams, 'The San Artistic Achievement', *African Arts*, 18 (1985), p. 59. See also Lewis-Williams, 'The Social and Economic Context of Southern San Rock Art', *Current Anthropology*, 23 (1982), pp. 429–49.

58 A. D. Mazel, 'Mbabane Shelter and eSinhlonhlweni Shelter: the Last Two Thousand Years of Hunter-Gatherer Settlement in the Central Thukela Basin, Natal, South Africa', *Annals of the Natal Museum*, 27 (1986), pp. 389–453.

59 Ibid.

60 Ibid.

61 M. Hall, 'The Role of Cattle in Southern African Agropastural Societies: more than Bones Alone can Tell', *Prehistoric Pastoralism in Southern Africa*, eds. M. Hall and A. B. Smith (Cape Town, South African Archaeological Society, 1986, Goodwin Series, 5), pp. 83–7; M. Hall, 'Archaeology and Modes of Production in Precolonial Southern Africa', *Journal of Southern African Studies*, 14, 1, (1987), pp. 1–17.

62 J. B. Wright, *Bushman Raiders of the Drakensberg, 1840–1870* (Pietermaritzburg, University of Natal Press, 1971).

63 Ibid., pp. 35, 185.

Chapter 2

The Iron Age farming communities

TIM MAGGS

Controversy still surrounds some aspects of the question of Iron Age origins in sub-Equatorial Africa, including South Africa. However, one thing has become clear as a result of research undertaken since 1960. This is that surviving oral traditions do not have sufficient time depth to be of relevance, since radio-carbon dating has shown that Iron Age settlement is of far greater antiquity. This point is particularly important in any discussion of the origins of Natal's black population, because most previous academic debate on the topic has centred on the interpretation of oral traditions by writers such as A. T. Bryant (see Chapter 3). It is now accepted that local oral traditions do not go back earlier than the beginning of the Late Iron Age (*c.* AD 1000) and that they are of doubtful value when they deal with events that occurred earlier than about the mid-eighteenth century. It is therefore necessary to turn to archaeological methods as the main source of information on the pre-literate periods of Natal's history.

The different types of source material and methods required by archaeology and history make it difficult to dovetail the results of these two fields of research. For example, we cannot always equate communities defined on the basis of material culture with political or other groups known from written historical sources. The attempt, however, must be made to integrate the archaeological evidence of the last few centuries with the earliest written and oral sources so as to provide an adequate perspective of the region's history.

The Early Iron Age

The advent of the Iron Age saw not only the introduction of metallurgy. Of even greater significance was the introduction of agriculture, necessitating a settled, village way of life instead of the nomadic patterns of the Stone Age. It also provided for an appreciable increase in population density, as well as a more complex life-style. Richly decorated pottery is a hallmark of these early settlements. Domestic animals including cattle, sheep, goats and dogs were also a feature of the Iron Age, although current information indicates that they had already reached parts of South Africa, but apparently not Natal, during the Late Stone Age, through the agency of Khoisan herders.[1]

To the historian, one of the most pertinent questions is: who were these people? The evidence from excavated burial-sites in Natal is still very tentative, so that reliance must be placed on that from the Transvaal sites, which indicates that they were of Negro physical type, not distinguishable from today's black population. There is no possibility of ever finding direct evidence as to the language they spoke. However, since the basis of the Iron Age way of life is that of the historical Bantu-speaking peoples, and since the distribution of the Iron Age south of the Equator essentially coincides with the historical distribution of Bantu languages, most researchers equate the spread of the Iron Age with that of the Bantu-speaking peoples. The Early Iron Age people were therefore certainly black and very probably Bantu-speaking. Culturally, however, they were sufficiently different from any historical black group as to rule out any 'ethnic' label. For example, they were certainly not 'Nguni' or 'Sotho', in whatever way one might try to define these terms, although they were surely the ancestors of both.

There is by no means general agreement amongst archaeologists as to how the Iron Age reached this area. On the evidence of pottery styles, it has been argued that there were two or even three migrations from Equatorial Africa. It is, however, possible that in Natal later stylistic differences may have developed within the earliest stream and did not therefore arise from a second migration. On one point archaeologists seem agreed. This is that the earliest Iron Age sites in South Africa, including Natal, relate to an eastern coastal and lowland cultural tradition with links as far north as the Kwale sites of eastern Kenya. This tradition has been named 'Matola', after a site in southern Mozambique which provided close typological links between the Natal and eastern Transvaal sites.[2]

The inference to be drawn from the distribution of Matola and related pottery is that the first Iron Age people reached Natal as part of a migration down the eastern side of the continent which had reached southern Africa by the third century AD. The Natal evidence itself strongly reinforces this interpretation, for all of the thirty or so known sites are within a few kilometres of the coast (Map 4). This migration does not appear to have penetrated much further south than modern Scottburgh, for archaeological

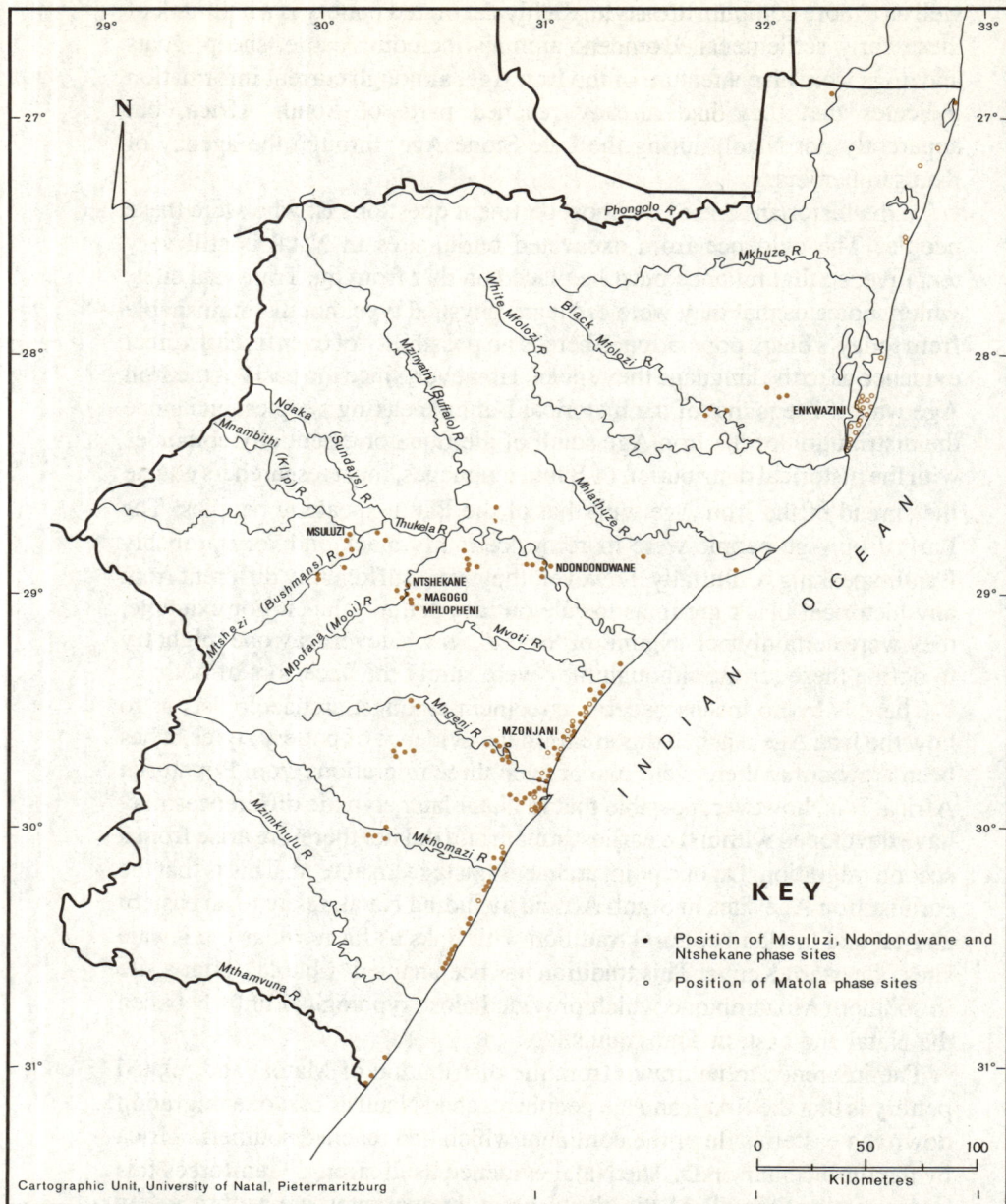

Map 4   Known Early Iron Age sites in Natal
Note: the distribution is restricted to coastal lowlands and river valleys further inland.

research on the South Coast and in the Transkei, though by no means complete, has so far failed to identify Matola material south of the Mzimayi River. As yet, only two Matola sites in Natal have been excavated, both of which are dated to around AD 300.[3] The preservation of organic material in both was poor, so that there is very little direct evidence concerning the economic activities of these people. The presence of slag at some sites proves that iron smelting took place on a small scale, while shells, especially of brown mussel, show that marine resources were exploited.

The specific environments of the sites give us further clues as to their ecology. Almost all of them are on the belt of ancient dunes which would have been covered by coastal forest at the time. In the St. Lucia area especially, sites are concentrated at the inland foot of the dunes, where these meet seasonally-flooded grassland. It has been argued that these sites were the first choice of immigrant farmers because they afforded some open, but not flooded, space. The sandy soils are poor and leached but the accumulated forest humus would have ensured good crops for the first year or two after they had been cleared. Apart from being attracted by this agricultural potential, the Matola people exploited the wild plant and animal resources of the forest and adjacent sea-shore. Although no direct evidence of agriculture has as yet been obtained from Natal sites, seeds of bulrush millet (a tropical African cultigen), have been recovered from a Matola site in the Transvaal.[4] Bulrush millet is still a favoured crop on the dunes around Kosi Bay. Evidence of domestic animals has yet to be found on any Matola site and it seems likely that they were rare, if present at all. The forest environment would certainly have been unsuitable as pasture for domestic animals. Marine mussels may therefore have played an important part as a protein source in place of meat or milk.

Matola sites indicate the existence of relatively small villages, of perhaps two to three hectares in extent, each occupied for only a few years. As yet, virtually nothing is known of their layout or architecture. The communities seem to have been small groups of perhaps a few dozen slash-and-burn cultivators, moving into a landscape sparsely inhabited by Khoisan hunter-gatherers.

Most Early Iron Age sites in Natal are later than the Matola period and are classified according to ceramic styles known as 'Msuluzi' (AD 500 – 700), 'Ndondondwane' (AD 700 – 800) and Ntshekane (AD 800 – 900). By this time villages, often about eight hectares in size and probably containing a hundred or more people, had become common in the lower-lying and savannah areas, below an altitude of 1 000 metres. They were most common along the major rivers and in the coastal belt (Map 4), where there was good deep soil, sweet year-round grazing, and timber for building and fuel.

Although relatively little is known about architecture and village layout, recent excavations are providing some clues. Stock-pens seem to have been built towards the edge of the site. At Ndondondwane (Map 4), a stockaded enclosure in a fairly central position apparently served as a working area for ivory-carving and iron smelting.[5] It may also have served a religious function because fragments of ceramic sculpture were found there. Huts were evidently made of poles and thatch, their walls being plastered with clay. In contemporary Transvaal sites, hut floors raised above ground level have been found, but none of these have thus far been uncovered in Natal. A typical Early Iron Age feature, found from central Africa southwards, is a refuse-pit often containing among the refuse a pot, the bottom of which had been knocked out.

Diet was based on agriculture and pastoralism with a little supplementary hunting, fishing and gathering of wild plants and shellfish. Crops identified from seeds include several grains (bulrush millet, finger millet and probably sorghum), and probably the African melon.[6] Cattle, sheep, goats and dogs have been identified among the animal remains, cattle and sheep evidently providing most of the meat.[7]

Most villages had one or more iron smelting areas and therefore produced their own requirements. In some cases, such as at the Mamba-Thukela confluence, a greater quantity of iron was produced than would have been necessary for local needs, indicating that it was used for trade. Other trade items of this period were decorative seashells, soapstone and ivory.

Economic interaction evidently continued to take place with Late Stone Age hunter-gatherer communities. This is indicated by the presence of Late Stone Age cultural items, including stone implements, bone arrowheads and ostrich eggshell beads. The last are of particular interest because ostriches would not have occurred in the wooded environment of the sites, the nearest ostrich habitats probably being the open grassland of the Natal hinterland. This indicates that hunter-gatherers were evidently making and trading eggshell beads with the lowland Iron Age settlements. The stone and bone artefacts frequently found in these village sites indicate that the hunter-gatherers were also probably engaged in hunting activities for the Iron Age villagers.

Ndondondwane represents a pottery style clearly developed from

Msuluzi (Figure 1), there being no break in time between the two styles. It is dated to the middle of the eighth century. Several of these sites saw an earlier Msuluzi occupation, or perhaps continuous occupation from this time onwards. In addition to choice of site, other aspects of cultural and economic life seem to have remained essentially as before. There is sufficient skeletal material from the Transvaal to confirm that the Iron Age people of this period were of Negro physical type. The Natal evidence suggests the same, and we expect that confirmation will come from recently-excavated material awaiting analysis.[8]

The final stylistic phase of the Early Iron Age is known as 'Ntshekane' (Map 4 and Figure 1), dating from about AD 800 to 900. Little is known about it as only one site has been excavated.[9] Its distinguishing feature is a ceramic style which almost certainly developed from Msuluzi and Ndondondwane. Other aspects of the culture remained unchanged – the same kind of village settlement occurring in the same environmental setting – while there seems to have been a preference to rebuild on Msuluzi sites.

The rarity of Ntshekane sites as compared with earlier ones must still be confirmed by further sampling. If this confirmation is obtained, it might indicate that environmental degradation had taken place. The savannah areas have a fragile ecology and this may have been appreciably degraded during the relatively dense occupation of the Msuluzi period. The areas would then have been unable to support as large a population as they had done one or two centuries earlier. It is also perhaps of significance that the Ntshekane excavation yielded a larger proportion and variety of wild animal bones, again suggesting a degraded environment that was unable to support large numbers of domestic animals.

The Late Iron Age

Following the lead of Zambian and Zimbabwean archaeologists, South African archaeologists introduced the concepts of an *Early* and a *Late* Iron Age to the local sequences a decade ago. As in the Stone Age, these terms are primarily based on artefact styles (in this case pottery), although they also have a chronological and stratigraphic significance.

The Early Iron Age, with its relatively similar pottery styles over long distances, is more homogeneous than is the Late Iron Age, which has much greater regional diversity. As in many other areas of sub-Equatorial Africa, there is a distinct break in the Natal ceramic sequence, marking the beginning of the Late Iron Age. Attempts to explain this have been for the

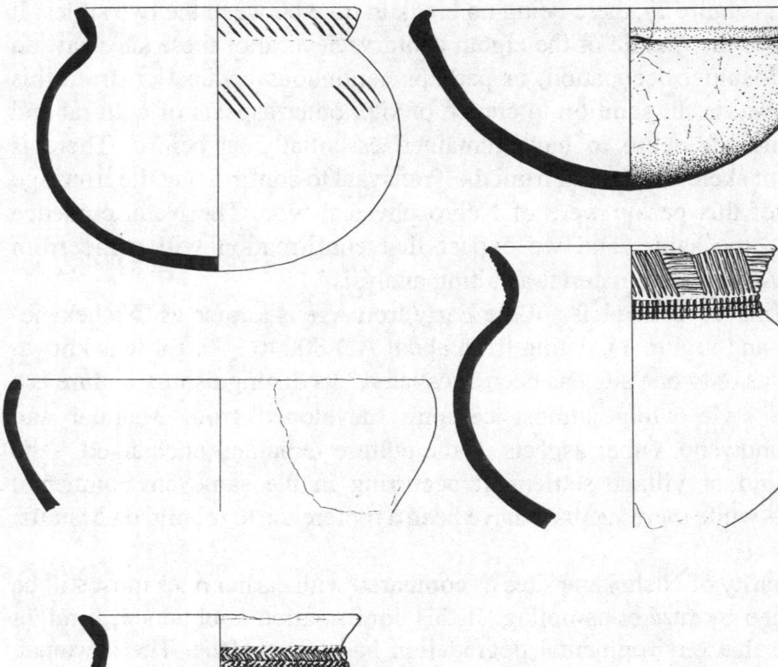

Fig. 1   Development of pottery styles during the Early Iron Age
Top row: Mzonjani *c.* AD 300; *second row:* Msuluzi *c.* AD 600; *third row:*
Ndondondwane *c.* AD 750; *bottom row:* Ntshekane *c.* AD 850.

most part rather simplistic, invoking population explosions and large-scale migrations.[10] The archaeological evidence from Natal itself has thrown little light on the reasons for this change. However, recent work in the Limpopo Basin has shown that larger-scale and more complex societies were emerging during the period AD 800 – 1200.[11] It seems likely that the changes that occurred in the Natal region were the result of similar socio-political factors, rather than of purely demographic ones.

The first half of the present millenium is the least understood part of the Iron Age sequence in Natal. Sites of this period are relatively inconspicuous and there has not been much excavation. However, enough is known to draw a number of contrasts between it and the Early Iron Age, which indicate many significant changes in addition to that of pottery style. Settlements were different in both layout and location. They were no longer sited in valleys beside rivers but were placed on higher ground. With the exception of the Moor Park group, described below, settlements seem to have been much smaller, with only a few huts. The implication would seem to be that society underwent a change away from the large Early Iron Age villages and towards the individual family homesteads of the historic Nguni-speaking peoples.

While the basic elements of the Iron Age economy – the crops, the domestic animals and the metallurgy – remained, there was some technological change, as reflected in different types of grindstones and iron-smelting equipment. Change in the organization of economic activities also took place. For example, evidence of iron-smelting is no longer found in virtually every settlement, indicating that many of them must have depended on trade for their metal requirements. There are also indications of ideological change. The well-developed ceramic sculpture of the Early Iron Age[12] was no longer produced and the buried pots from which the bottoms had been broken out are no longer found. It has been suggested that the social and religious importance which was attached to cattle by the more southerly of the black farming peoples in historical times may have originated during this period. The evidence for this is slim as cattle were already common in the earlier period. However, there was a slight increase in the number of cattle relative to small stock at some sites.[13]

The two sites of Blackburn[14] and Mphambanyoni[15] (Map 5), dated around AD 1000, provide some idea of life at this time in the coastal strip of Natal. Each occupied the top of a small hill, with middens of discarded shell around the edge of a small cluster of huts in the centre. The local

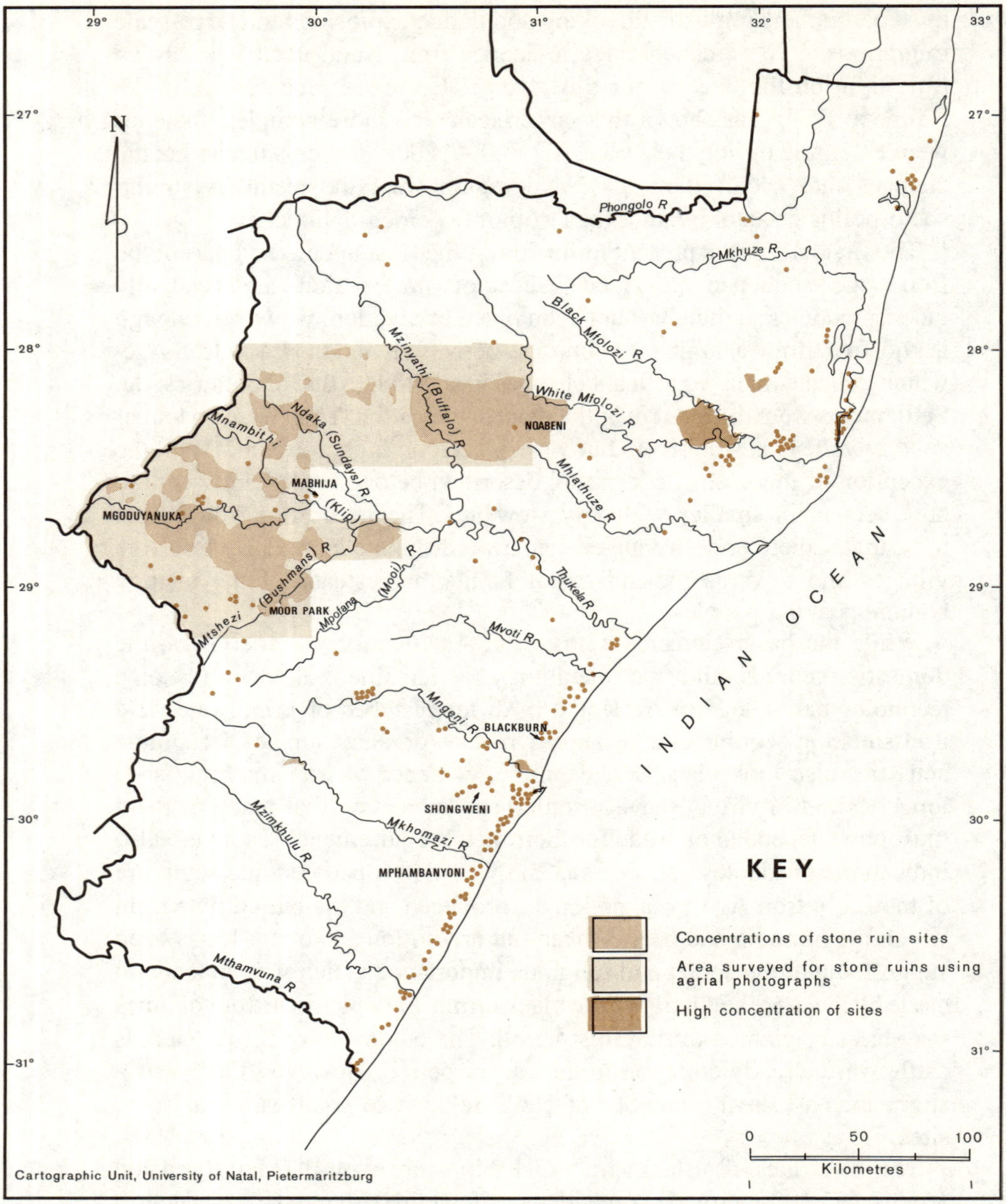

Map 5   Recorded Late Iron Age sites in Natal
Note: the concentrations indicate areas of intensive research rather than intensive settlement.

environment – coastal forest with the sea-shore only a few kilometres distant – seems to have greatly influenced diet, which included quantities of marine and forest animals. There were few, if any, domestic animals, while slash-and-burn agriculture appears to have been important. The dry rock-shelter at Shongweni (Map 5), 25 kilometres inland from the coast at Isipingo, contains well-preserved bulrush millet dated around AD 1000, and sorghum around AD 1200. Other crop plants found at this site, although not necessarily from exactly this time, include finger millet, African melon and bottle gourd.[16]

Inland from the coastal forest, domestic stock was probably a staple part of the diet, as was the case around AD 1300 at Moor Park, [17] near Estcourt (Map 5). This large site is one of a series built on spurs or isolated hilltops, with stone walling supplementing the natural defences (Figure 2). Most are in grassland areas and their distribution reaches almost to the foothills of the Drakensberg. They represent a distinct departure from the Early Iron Age sites in terms of construction, choice of situation and environment. Significantly, they are the earliest evidence of Iron Age penetration into pure grassland areas and may well reflect the advance into areas hitherto occupied by Late Stone Age hunter-gatherers (see Chapter 1). The poor winter grazing and exposed positions of some of the sites suggest that they may have been summer grazing camps, but this possibility has still to be tested by means of further field-work.

As things are at present, little else can be said of this period except that several unexcavated sites with related styles of pottery tend to confirm that the settlements were generally small and located in elevated positions. Sites are relatively inconspicuous unless they incorporate shell-middens, as is the case with coastal sites, or stone-walling, as is found in the Moor Park group. This low archaeological visibility, characteristic also of later sites, suggests that they were not occupied as intensively, or for such long periods, as those of the Early Iron Age.

After about AD 1500 the evidence clearly indicates that the Iron Age people of the Natal region were directly ancestral, culturally, linguistically, and physically, to today's black population. There is nothing to suggest that the cultural traits that distinguish Nguni-speaking groups from others within the Late Iron Age originated or developed outside the historic Nguni-speaking regions. The archaeological evidence alone would disprove the diffusionist argument, as advanced by Bryant and others (see Chapter 3), for there is nothing remotely 'Nguni' in style from the Iron Age of, for example, Malawi, Zambia or Zimbabwe in this or earlier periods.

Fig. 2

~	Contours	⬭ ⌒	Cleared terraces for huts
Cliff			Stone walling

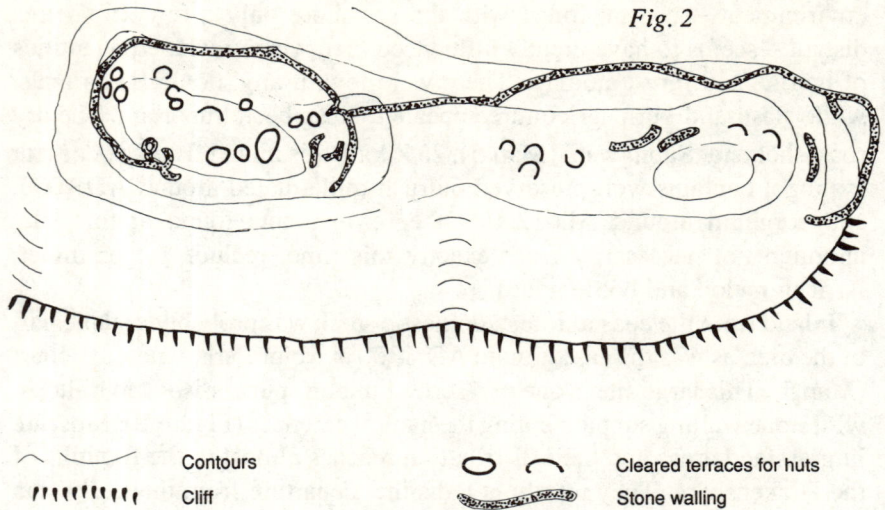

Above: *Moor Park stone-walled settlement c. AD 1300, demonstrating choice of naturally defended, hill-top situations. Maximum length 330 metres.*

downhill

Left: *Mgoduyanuka c. AD 1700 — a typical homestead, with stone cattle-pen, from the interior grasslands.*   Right: *Typical Zulu homestead of the 19th Century.*

Indeed, there are hints during the earlier period, between AD 1000 and 1500, of the development in the Natal region of cultural patterns asociated with the Nguni-speaking peoples, as for example the smaller settlements.

In researching this and other problems relating to this later period, the archaeological evidence can be supplemented by information obtained from shipwrecked Portuguese and other European mariners, who traversed lowland and coastal Natal on their way northwards to Mozambique, or who spent some time in the area prior to being rescued. These accounts are deficient in many respects, including precise information as to where the shipwrecks occurred, as well as the routes that were followed by the survivors. Previously, many authors tended to rely on G. M. Theal for the geographic location of the shipwrecks and description of the routes followed by the survivors. His accounts were, however, based upon little more than speculation, since the wrecks themselves were unknown. Recent research has established the sites of several of the wrecks, many of them at a considerable distance from where they were previously thought to have occurred. The wreck of the *Sao Bento*, for example, which was confidently asserted to have taken place 'somewhere between the Kasuka and the Mtata' has now been located at Msikaba, 100 kilometres north-east of the Mtata River.[18]

The evidence of written sources shows that, by the 1550s, while the coastal sourveld of Pondoland was thinly inhabited, coastal Natal from the Mtamvuna northwards was already well populated. A settlement of twenty hemispherical huts built of poles and thatch is described as being typical of the coast at the time.[19] A later report confirms that such 'small villages' were the homes of kinship groups, each under the authority of a senior man.[20] There can have been little difference between these homesteads and those of the nineteenth century in Natal and Zululand.

The agro-pastoral economy of the Iron Age prevailed throughout the coastal regions, with cultivation typically a combination of grains, legumes and vegetables of the pumpkin-melon family. There were three types of grains, one being sorghum and another a smaller-seeded millet, specific identification being difficult to establish from the old Portuguese documents. Vegetables included beans, African groundnuts (both legumes), gourds, watermelons and pumpkins, while sorghum was cultivated for its sweet pith as well as for its seeds. The presence of cultivated figs and sesame, as recorded in the written sources, requires more research before it can be accepted. There is, however, evidence to show that tobacco was being cultivated and smoked by 1686.[21] Cattle, sheep and goats were seen in quantities, as were chickens from southern Natal northwards.[22]

That the inhabitants were Nguni-speaking can be shown by the fact that documents dating from 1593 record the use in southern Natal and as far north as St. Lucia of words like *inkosi* for king or chief, *isinkwa* (bread) for millet loaves and *halala* (hurray!) as a greeting.[23] In 1635 the words *umlungu* (white person) and *umkhulu* (great) were recorded on the Transkei coast.[24] It is, however, clear that there have also been linguistic changes. The word *pombe* for beer and the greeting *nanhata*, used south of the Mzimkhulu and in Maputaland, seem to have fallen away without trace, although the former survives in Swahili.

Many of the customary practices described in surviving documents of the sixteenth and seventeenth century remained essentially unchanged down to the nineteenth century. These included grain storage in pits, young men's initiation, including circumcision, lobola (bridal exchange for cattle or metal goods), and the sacrifice of cattle for the 'continuance of their health'.[25] However, the custom of polling cattle horns seems to have fallen away in later times.[26]

In the nineteenth century, a significant linguistic and cultural boundary can be discerned separating Nguni and Tembe Thonga. Those parties of shipwreck survivors that walked northwards to Mozambique must have crossed this 'boundary' somewhere between the Thukela and the Thonga kingdom of Inhaca on the southern shores of Delagoa Bay. There are hints that this was the case. For example, the AD 1554 survivors[27] gave the name *Pescaria* (fisheries) to an estuarine lake, which is almost certainly the Mhlathuze Lagoon, where they bought quantities of fish for the first time on their journey northwards. As organized fishing is associated with Tembe Thonga and not with Nguni, this suggests that the former extended as far south as the Mhlathuze in the sixteenth century. The 1593 account recorded a change in architectural style on the coastal plain from the St. Lucia area northwards, where the hemispherical huts of the Nguni gave way to what appears to have been a cone-on-cylinder style associated with the Tembe Thonga.[28]

The evidence shows that political organization was on a small scale, at least in the coastal regions of Natal. In this discussion, the Nguni word *inkosi* (plural *izinkhosi*) is used for the political leaders because the English words, king or chief, have some inappropriate connotations. The most detailed information comes from a Portuguese report in the year 1593 that, on the rich coastal plain from about the Mkhomazi to the Thukela, the Portuguese passed through the territories of no less than nine *izinkhosi*. This would give an average width of about 15 to 20 kilometres per territory. While this may seem particularly small, even by the standards of pre-colonial southern Africa, it is comparable with the approximately 15 to 20 kilometres width of territories in central Zululand prior to the larger state-formation processes of the late eighteenth and early nineteenth centuries.[29]

The precise powers exercised by an *inkosi* are not defined by the early writers. It is, however, evident that there were at least two tiers within the category *inkosi*. In 1686 it was reported that, when a court case was considered to be of great importance, the 'king' would refer 'the parties to an older king in his neighbourhood'.[30] A contemporary record relating to the Xhosa makes a similar reference to an *inkosi*, Sotopa by name, whose authority was limited by the fact that 'Togu was then the paramount ruler of the tribe'.[31] To the south of the Mkhomazi River, larger political units existed. This is indicated by the listing as early as 1686 of several major subdivisions of the southern Nguni: the Mpondomise, Mpondo, Thembu and Xhosa.[32] However, it is doubtful whether these units were always effectively united under a single *inkosi*.

Oral tradition suggests the existence in the Natal interior of larger groups comparable to those in the south. The relatively well documented case of the Hlubi in the late eighteenth and early nineteenth centuries provides an example.[33] *Inkosi* Bhungane, at the height of his power, ruled a substantial area of some 5 000 square kilometres in what is now northern Natal. In the process of extending his rule, a number of lesser *izinkhosi* would have been subjugated, although they may have retained some of their authority, as was the case with the *izinkhosi* under Dingiswayo a few years later (see Chapter 3). This form of expansion tended to bring with it the seeds of its own destruction for the larger political units were threatened by fission, either from the lineages that had been subjugated or from rivalry within the ruling lineage. In the case of the Hlubi, for example, rivalry between Bhungane's sons after his death seriously weakened the unity of the realm.

There were a number of other large groups in the Natal hinterland during this period – for example the Bhele, the Zizi and the Dlamini – but it appears from the oral traditions that they possessed even less political cohesion than did the Hlubi.[34]

Trade, particularly in small ornamental items, had developed over long distances during the first millenium AD. The earliest evidence of overseas trade to southern Africa in the form of imported glass beads on Limpopo valley sites dates around the ninth century. The east coast Islamic trading system penetrated as far south as Vilanculas by this time, or a little later; it may even have reached Delagoa Bay, but there is as yet no definite archaeological evidence of such trade from our area. The first marine trade we know of is from the sixteenth century, through the natural harbour of Delagoa Bay, first with the Portuguese and subsequently with other

European traders. Among the kingdoms around the bay, there was competition for the control of this trade leading to the expansion of some at the expense of others. In the 1550s, the Inhaca lineage controlled little more than the peninsular and islands on the southeast side of the bay, while in 1593 they apparently had a subordinate *inkosi* just east of the Lubombo mountains in the Mkhuze area.[35] By about 1750, however, the succeeding Maputo ruling lineage had extended its power southwards to St. Lucia and inland to the Phongolo River.[36]

There is evidence to show that, by 1593, mercantile trade, presumed to have come from Delagoa Bay, had penetrated as far south as the Transkei and as far inland as the Nongoma area.[37] Ivory was the main export, while beads and copper were the main imports. Already by this time, imported cloth was in demand north of the Thukela, while copper was worth less there than further south, where it was still rare.

Attempts to control this trade may account for the fact that the shipwreck parties often encountered resistance when crossing rivers on their way through the Zululand coastal area. As rivers were often political boundaries, the explanation might be that each *inkosi* was anxious to control any trade to, or passing through, his territory. The coastal area between the Thukela and St. Lucia continued to be one of strife until the nineteenth century and to some extent this was the result of trade rivalry. Trade through Delagoa Bay came to be supplemented by trade through the 'river of Natal' (Durban), which by the late seventeenth century was frequently visited by small trading vessels.[38]

While the importation of relatively high-value and high-status items, like beads, brass rings and cloth, evidently had considerable effect on political developments north of the Thukela, the daily life of the people remained essentially that of the Iron Age. An exception was the introduction of maize, which became a staple in some of the higher-rainfall areas during the eighteenth century, if not earlier.[39] In the Natal region, as in other parts of South Africa, this may have produced important social changes. Compared with the African grains, maize has a far higher carbohydrate yield per unit of labour and land. It would therefore have allowed for substantial population increases in parts of the region favourable to its growth.

The archaeological record may indeed contain evidence of such population expansion, for one of the most conspicuous features of this later period is the very large number of stone and stone-faced earthwork structures, each of which was the livestock pen at the centre of a homestead

(Figure 2). They occur in extensive areas of the Natal interior grasslands (Map 5), where the relatively cool and moist climates are less suited to African cereals, but more so to maize, than are the savannah areas. Moreover, two excavated grassland sites[40] have produced evidence of maize as a staple, while the stone-built settlements in general are commonly associated with particularly large lower grindstones, which are thought to reflect the preparation of maize rather than the smaller African grains.[41]

Chronologically the focus of these stone-built settlements is in the period just before the warfare, population upheavals and political amalgamation of the 1820s, known as the Mfecane (See Chapter 3). From historical sources we can broadly link the settlements with the Nguni-speaking peoples living in the grasslands at this time.[42] The fact that they occur in such numbers in areas which previously saw relatively little Iron Age occupation, together with their association with maize cultivation, strongly suggests that the introduction of this exotic grain allowed for considerable population increase in these areas during the centuries before the Mfecane.

The use of stone in construction has made for the preservation of much detail, so that it is possible to make comparisons between these grassland sites and the settlement pattern that is characteristic of the Zulu in the nineteenth century (Figure 2). A significant difference is that a wide variety of design exists in the grassland homesteads, in contrast to the uniformity that is found in nineteenth-century Zulu settlements. This may reflect a greater flexibility of social structure than is suggested by ethnographic sources on the Zulu people. There are, however, clear links with cultural patterns of the Nguni-speaking peoples at several levels. In particular, many of the stone settlements reveal a pattern in which several homesteads form a cluster, separated from similar neighbouring clusters.[43] Anthropologists have observed the same pattern within contemporary Nguni-speaking communities, which is the result of several male agnates – descendants of a common male ancestor – building their homesteads in close proximity to one another.[44] This agnatic clustering has evidently been a characteristic of Nguni-speaking communities for several centuries.

In addition to social change during this period, the evidence reveals an increase in specialization, particularly in metal production. In the Natal region, where there is a virtual absence of non-ferrous ores, this was limited to iron and steel. The shipwreck evidence, confirmed by archaeology, indicates that iron was in relatively short supply south of the Thukela

Group of fourteen furnaces on the Mabhija Iron Smelting Site near Colenso. Slag heap at top right. Foreground scale is 0,5 metres.

Basin, but northwards was quite readily available. The oral traditions tell us that particular groups of people became specialist smiths, who traded with their neighbours. Environmental factors played a part in this because of the restricted distribution of suitable ore and wood for charcoal. Nevertheless, it is clear that the social organization of this industry was very different from that of Early Iron Age times, when virtually every village had one or more smiths. In later centuries, there were thus large areas of settlement, for example those in the grasslands, which were entirely reliant on trade for their metal requirements. Conversely, large concentrations of smelting sites, such as around Mabhija (Map 5) on the Thukela,[45] must have been partly dependent on metal production and trade. There is evidence of trade from the Thukela as far afield as what is now the Orange Free State, where goods were exchanged with Sotho groups.[46]

The production of iron and steel by specialists and the trade in these commodities would thus have enhanced the effect that mercantile trade and maize production had upon society. Like them, it enhanced the differential distribution of resources regionally and therefore the economic interdependence of the many small, autonomous political units. To an extent, economic factors influenced the process of state formation discussed in the following chapter. The degree of economic interdependence certainly exacerbated the hardships which were to occur later with the dislocations caused by the Mfecane.

Notes

1   R. G. Klein, 'The Prehistory of Stone Age Herders in the Cape Province of South Africa', *Prehistoric Pastoralism in Southern Africa*, eds. M. Hall and A. B. Smith (Cape Town, South African Archaeological Society, 1986, Goodwin Series, 5).

2   T. Maggs, 'Mzonjani and the Beginning of the Iron Age in Natal', *Annals of the Natal Museum*, 24, 1 (1980), pp. 71–96.

3   Ibid; M. Hall, 'Enkwazini: an Iron Age Site on the Zululand Coast', *Annals of the Natal Museum*, 24, 1 (1980), pp. 97–110.

4   M. Klapwijk, 'An Early Iron Age Site near Tzaneen, North Eastern Transvaal', *South African Journal of Science*, 10 (1973), pp. 137–61.

5   T. Maggs, 'Ndondondwane: a Preliminary Report on an Early Iron Age Site on the Lower Tugela River', *Annals of the Natal Museum*, 26, 1 (1984), pp. 71–93; J. H. N. Loubser, 'Excavations at Ndondondwane on the Tugela River' (unpublished report for KwaZulu Monuments Council, 1984).

6   T. Maggs, 'The Iron Age South of the Zambezi', *Southern African Prehistory and Palaeoenvironments*, ed. R. G. Klein (Rotterdam, Balkema, 1984), pp. 329–60.

7   E. A. Voigt, 'The Faunal Remains from Magogo and Mhlopeni: Small Stock Herding in the Early Iron Age in Natal', *Annals of the Natal Museum*, 26, 1 (1984), pp. 141–63; Voigt and A. Von den Driesch, 'Preliminary Report on the Faunal Assemblage from Ndondondwane, Natal', *Annals of the Natal Museum*, 26, 1 (1984), pp. 95–104.

8   Information provided personally by L. O. van Schalkwyk.

9   T. Maggs and M. A. Michael, 'Ntshekane: an Early Iron Age Site in the Tugela Basin, Natal', *Annals of the Natal Museum*, 22, 3 (1976), pp. 705–40.

10   T. N. Huffman, 'The Origins of Leopard's Kopje: an 11th Century Difaqane', *Arnoldia*, 8, 23 (1978), pp. 1–23; D. W. Phillipson, *The Later Prehistory of Eastern and Southern Africa* (London, Heinemann, 1977).

11   Maggs, 'The Iron Age South of the Zambezi'.

12   T. Maggs and P. Davison, 'The Lydenburg Heads', *African Arts*, 14, 2 (1981), pp. 28–33.

13   Voigt, 'The Faunal Remains from Magogo and Mhlopeni'.

14   O. Davies, 'Excavation at Blackburn', *South African Archaeological Bulletin*, 26 (1971), pp. 165–78.

15   T. Robey, 'Mpambanyoni: a Late Iron Age Site on the Natal South Coast', *Annals of the Natal Museum*, 24, 1 (1980), pp. 147–64.

16   Davies, 'Excavations at Shongweni South Cave'; O. Davies and K. Gordon-Grey, 'Tropical African Cultigens from Shongweni Excavations, Natal', *Journal of Archaeological Science*, 4 (1977), pp. 153–62; M. Hall and J. C. Vogel, 'Some Recent Radiocarbon Dates from Southern Africa', *Journal of African History*, 21, 4 (1980), pp. 431–55.

17   O. Davies, 'Excavations at the Walled Early Iron Age Site in Moor Park near Estcourt, Natal', *Annals of the Natal Museum*, 22, 1 (1974), pp. 289–323.

18   G. M. Theal, *History and Ethnography of South Africa before 1795*, 2 (London, Swan Sounenshein, 1909); G. Allen and D. Allen, *The Guns of Sacramento* (London, Garton, 1978); C. Auret and T. Maggs, 'The Great Ship *Sao Bento*: Remains from a Mid-Sixteenth Century Portuguese Wreck on the Pondoland Coast', *Annals of the Natal Museum*, 25, 1 (1982), pp. 1–39; G. Bell-Cross, 'Problems Associated with the Location and Identification of Early Shipwrecks', *South African Museum Bulletin*, 14, 8 (1981), pp. 326–40; T. Maggs, 'The Great Galleon *Sao Joao*: Remains from a Mid-Sixteenth Century Wreck on the Natal South Coast', *Annals of the Natal Museum*, 26, 1 (1984), pp. 173–86.

19   G. M. Theal, *Records of South-Eastern Africa*, 8 (Cape Town, 1898–1903; facsimile reprint, Cape Town, Struik, 1964).

20   J. Bird, *The Annals of Natal, 1495 to 1845*, 1 (Pietermaritzburg, P. Davis and Son, 1888; facsimile reprint, Cape Town, Struik, 1965).

21   D. Moodie, *The Record: or a Series of Official Papers Relative to the Condition and Treatment of the Native Tribes of South Africa* (Cape Town, A. S. Robertson, 1838–41; facsimile reprint, Amsterdam, Balkema, 1960).

22   Theal, *Records of South-Eastern Africa*.

23   C. R. Boxer, *The Tragic History of the Sea* (Cambridge, Hakluyt, 1959).

24   Theal, *Records of South-Eastern Africa*; I am grateful to Prof. A. S. Davey for his assistance.

25   Moodie, *The Record*.

26   Boxer, *The Tragic History of the Sea*.

27   Theal, *Records of South-Eastern Africa*.

28   H. A. Junod, 'The Condition of the Natives of South-East Africa in the Sixteenth Century, according to the Early Portuguese Documents' (South African Association for the Advancement of Science, 11th Annual meeting, Lourenço Marques, 1913); *South African Journal of Science*, 10 (1914), pp. 137–161; Boxer, *The Tragic History of the Sea*.

29   A. T. Bryant, *Olden Times in Zululand and Natal* (London, Longmans Green, 1929); M. Hall and K. Mack, 'The Outline of an Eighteenth Century Economic System in South-East Africa', *Annals of the South African Museum*, 91, 2 (1983), pp. 163–94.

30   Bird, *Annals of Natal*, 1.

31   Theal, *History and Ethnography of South Africa Before 1795*, 2.

32   Moodie, *The Record*; M. Wilson, 'The Early History of the Transkei and Ciskei', *African Studies*, 18, 4 (1959), pp. 167–79.

33   J. B. Wright and A. Manson, *The Hlubi Chiefdom in Zululand-Natal: a History* (Ladysmith Historical Society, 1983).

34   Bryant, *Olden Times in Zululand and Natal*.

35   Boxer, *The Tragic History of the Sea*.

36   D. W. Hedges, 'Trade and Politics in Southern Mozambique and Zululand in the Eighteenth and Nineteenth Centuries' (unpublished Ph.D. thesis, London School of Oriental and African Studies, 1978).

37   Boxer, *The Tragic History of the Sea*.

38   Moodie, *The Record*.

39   M. Hall and T. Maggs, 'Nqabeni: a Later Iron Age Site in Zululand', *Iron Age Studies in Southern Africa*, eds. N. J. van der Merwe and T. N. Hoffman (Cape Town, South African Archaeological Society, 1979, Goodwin Series, 3); T. Maggs, 'Mgoduyanuka: Terminal Iron Age Settlement in the Natal Drakensberg', *Annals of the Natal Museum*, 25, 1 (1982), pp. 83–113; D. W. Hedges, 'Trade and Politics in Southern Mozambique and Zululand'.

40   Hall and Maggs, 'Nqabeni: a Late Iron Age Site in Zululand'; T. Maggs, 'Mgoduyanuka: Terminal Iron Age Settlement in the Natal Drakensberg', *Annals of the Natal Museum*, 25, 1 (1982), pp. 83–113.

41   Maggs, 'Mgoduyanuka'.

42   Bryant, *Olden Times*; A. F. Gardiner, *Narrative of a Journey to the Zoolu Country in South Africa* (London, Crofts, 1836); J. Sanderson, 'Memoranda of a Trading Trip into the Orange River Sovereignty and the Country of the Transvaal Boers', *Journal of the Royal Geographic Society*, 30 (1851–2), pp. 233–55.

43   T. Maggs, D. Oswald, M. Hall and H. Ruther, 'Spatial Parameters of Late Iron Age Settlements in the Upper Thukela Valley', *Annals of the Natal Museum*, 27, 1 (1986) pp. 455–79.

44   W. D. Hammond-Tooke, 'In Search of the Lineage: the Cape Nguni Case', *Man*, 19, 1 (1984), pp. 77–93.

45   T. Maggs, 'Mabhija: Precolonial Industrial Development in the Tugela Basin', *Annals of the Natal Museum*, 25, 1 (1982) pp. 123–41.

46   D. F. Ellenberger, *The History of the Basuto: Ancient and Modern* (London, Caxton, 1912).

Chapter 3

Traditions and transformations
The Phongolo-Mzimkhulu region in the late eighteenth and early nineteenth centuries

JOHN WRIGHT and
CAROLYN HAMILTON

To reconstruct the history of the Phongolo-Mzimkhulu region before the arrival of literate observers in the 1820s, the historian must use evidence drawn from archaeological research and from recorded African oral tradition.[1] By far the most important collections of tradition available are those made in the late nineteenth and early twentieth centuries by Alfred Bryant and James Stuart. Stuart's original notes have been preserved, but are relatively inaccessible, and the traditions which he recorded are only now being published.[2] Bryant's notes have apparently not survived, but the syntheses of oral tradition which he published are widely regarded as the most authoritative sources available on the pre-colonial history of the region.[3] The most influential of these works has been his *Olden Times in Zululand and Natal*, which first appeared in 1929. Even though recent research has shown that it contains many flaws,[4] some scholars continue uncritically to accept many of its interpretations. In this way, *Olden Times* continues to shape the way in which historians use evidence drawn from the traditions recorded by Stuart and others. The first part of this chapter sketches out a critique of the central notions which underlie Bryant's interpretations of oral tradition. The second puts forward a revised conceptualization of the history of the Phongolo-Mzimkhulu region in the late eighteenth and early nineteenth centuries.

A. T. Bryant (1865–1953). After attending Birbeck College in London, he emigrated to Natal in 1883 and became associated with the recently established Mariannhill Mission Station. In 1887 he was ordained as a priest in the Order of St. John of Lateran, becoming known as Father David. He then returned to mission work in the Transkei and Zululand, where he established a mission station at the Ngoye ridge. In 1920 he was appointed Lecturer in Bantu Studies at the University of the Witwatersrand and subsequently retired to England.

Killie Campbell Africana Library

Part 1: *Olden Times* and beyond

The history of south-east Africa as recounted in *Olden Times* falls into three phases. The first, dating from about AD 1500 to 1700, was the period when the peoples whom Bryant calls the 'Nguni' migrated into the region from the north and north-west, and dispersed in their separate 'clans' (Bryant's term) to the localities where many of them were still to be found at the beginning of the nineteenth century.[5] The second, which constitutes what Bryant calls the 'Golden Age' of East Nguni history, was a period when the people lived in peace and stability in numerous small-scale clans under benevolent patriarchal rule. The third phase, the 'era of autocracy', began with the accession of Shaka to the chiefship of the Zulu 'clan' in about 1816. This event, according to Bryant, inaugurated a period of 'drastic political change' in which 'the primordial system of numberless clans and independent chieftains [was] . . . gradually demolished, and upon and out of its ruins [was] built up a grandiose nation ruled by an imperious despot'.[6]

Bryant's interpretation is founded on two linked assumptions. The first is that the oral traditions from which he derives his evidence can be taken more or less at face value. The second is that the 'clans' referred to in the traditions were historically real entities whose internal organization remained essentially unchanging even when they altered in size. From these notions follow the major misconceptions of his historical account. Bryant's view of oral traditions as a source of historical information is clearly stated in his published works. In his opinion, the amount of information that can be gleaned from the traditions is strictly limited, since they focus mainly on warfare and raiding.[7] Where traditions do survive, he argues, they may, with qualifications, be taken as containing a core of historical fact.

> As a general rule, we may say that every early Native historical tradition is based upon and born of fact; and secondly, that that basic fact is the only reliable element in the tradition . . . The various minor circumstances in the progress of an event do not appeal strongly to the Native mind; to it the only matter of real importance is the main issue, the fundamental fact. Each separate Native witness will report the same occurrence in a slightly different manner; will fix upon such details only as made an impression upon his own mind, and repeat statements in his own wording; and all alike will embellish their narrative according to their own peculiar gifts of verbosity or imagination.[8]

Variations of a tradition, in this view, are simply the products of individual 'Native minds'. The business of the historian who uses this kind of evidence is, in Bryant's words:

> . . . to put the crooked straight and to fill in the gaps, linking together disconnected facts by probabilities based on other knowledge, moulding discrepant statements so that they harmonize with their surroundings, drawing conclusions following naturally from well-founded premises.[9]

Where different versions of traditions existed, he writes, 'we . . . have selected that for presentation here which bore the weightier evidence, or, at any rate, an equal measure of probability . . .'.[10] His express concern, then, is to produce an internally consistent and coherent account by ironing out contradictions and inconsistencies, and filling in gaps by means of informed conjecture.

The view that oral traditions can be taken at face value as sources of historical information was common enough in Bryant's time,[11] but it has

James Stuart (1868–1942). Born in Pietermaritzburg, by the age of twenty he was fluent in the Zulu language and served as an interpreter before holding various posts in the Natal, Swaziland and Zululand administrations. He was magistrate in several divisions before being appointed Assistant Secretary for Native Affairs in Natal in 1909. From an early stage in his career he systematically collected information about the history, social customs and language of the Zulu and neighbouring peoples.

Natal Archives, C80

long since been displaced by more critical perspectives. In the 1960s and 1970s oral traditions came to be seen less as factual than as 'political' statements which reflected the imposition on society of images of the past that served primarily the interests of ruling groups. In this view, traditions operate as part of an ideology which serves to legitimize the right of ruling groups to control the resources of the territories which they dominate, and to exercise authority over subject groups in those territories.[12]

More recently, it has been recognized that the ideological content of oral traditions is not simply a reflection of rulers' interests, but is the product of political struggles that take place between rulers and ruled. In the course of these struggles, traditions come to express the world-views not only of the rulers but also to some extent of the ruled, the better to neutralize the potential antagonism of ruled to rulers. The disjunction between the essentially opposed world-views which they are trying to reconcile will often be revealed in the form of patterns of internal contradictions and inconsistencies. These can often be 'unpacked' by the historian to reveal something of the conflicts which produced them, and hence to throw light on past political struggles, as well as on the roots of social and political inequalities which the 'official' voice in the traditions seeks to obscure.[13]

The second of Bryant's misleading assumptions is that the group histories which are contained in many of the traditions are to be read as the histories of discrete polities. As he sees it, the basic political unit throughout the pre-colonial period was the 'clan', which he describes as:

> . . . the magnified family, in which all alike were descended from the same original ancestor, all were now ruled by that ancestor's direct living representative, and all . . . dwelt and moved together in one great block . . .[14]

The clan was thus at once a political unit, a descent group, and a residential group, with a high degree of internal cohesion.

Given Bryant's literal reading of the traditions, it is easy to understand how he arrived at this view, for the historical narratives which the traditions contain are often cast in the form of histories of bounded 'clans', with an objective existence of their own. Moreover, at the time when Bryant was writing, the notion of the bounded 'tribe' as the characteristic social and political unit of Africa had been central to British anthropological thought for several decades.[15] Conventionally, the tribe was seen – as it still is in certain kinds of South African history-writing[16] – as a group of people occupying a specific territory under the political authority of a hereditary chief. It was economically more or less self-sufficient, politically more or less autonomous, and to a large degree united by ties of kinship, culture and language.[17]

In recent years, the notion of the 'tribe' has been abandoned by many academics. Not only is it disliked by many African scholars and political leaders as a pejorative term, but it is also seen as a term which confuses political units, descent groups and ethnic groups, and fails to distinguish between political units of different types.[18] Use of the term effectively prevents analysis of change in basic social relationships. The fact that African oral traditions often speak of social units which approximate to the European notion of 'tribe' cannot be used to argue in favour of retaining the term. In its place need to be set ideas of polities whose composition, internal organization, culture, traditions, ethnic affiliations and boundaries were fluid and subject to various forms of internally and externally induced change.

Two major misconceptions in Bryant's historical account follow from his assumptions that oral traditions can be taken at face value, and that they reflect the histories of discrete and unchanging 'clans'. The first is his elaborate schema of the migrations and dispersal of what he sees as the ethnically united 'Nguni' group of clans. The second is to be found in his notion that the processes of state formation which culminated in the emergence of the Zulu kingdom can be seen as the amalgamation of numbers of small political units into a single, enlarged unit of essentially the same type.

The name 'Nguni', Bryant asserts in *Olden Times*, is one by which, in times gone by, the peoples of Zululand, Natal and the eastern Cape 'generically distinguished themselves from the other two types around them', that is, from what he calls the 'Sutu' and 'Tonga' peoples. He gives no evidence in support of this statement, and in fact there is very little in the traditions which he records to substantiate it. He admits as much when, at another point in *Olden Times*, he writes that the peoples themselves 'nowadays are almost wholly ignorant of what was probably their own original generic name, viz. *abaNguni* . . .'.[19]

It is significant that Bryant's usage of generic terminology changed markedly over the years. In his 'Sketch of the Origin and Early History of the Zulu People', published in 1905, the word 'Nguni' did not appear at all: at this stage he was still using the then common terms 'Zulus' and 'Kaffirs'. In the series of historical articles which he published in 1910–13, he was beginning to use 'Nguni' in compound forms like 'Zulu-Nguni' and 'Tonga-Nguni', but it was not until the publication of *Olden Times* in 1929 that the word became fully established in his work as a generic term for the black peoples who historically had inhabited the region from Swaziland to the eastern Cape. This was the meaning of 'Nguni' that was rapidly adopted by academics in the 1930s, and which has remained entrenched in the literature ever since.[20]

In the precolonial societies of south-east Africa, the word (in the forms *umNguni*, *abaNguni*, *abeNguni*, and their cognates) had a different meaning. In the words of a recent commentator, it seems rather to have connoted 'great antiquity and extensive political authority'.[21] As late as 1923 one of its meanings was recorded as 'an ancient; a person belonging to an ancient stock'.[22] As such, 'Nguni' was a designation that lent itself to appropriation by politically dominant groups concerned with underpinning their authority by claiming rights to genealogical seniority and historical primacy, and by newly-formed communities seeking to establish a corporate identity for themselves. There is evidence in tradition and in documents that the term was used in these ways over a long period, resulting in the proliferation of claims to being 'Nguni' which confronted

Bryant and other researchers in the early years of the twentieth century.[23] They not surprisingly mistook what were essentially historically contingent claims as claims to primordial ethnic affiliation, and concluded that the 'clans' of Zululand-Natal were all descended from a single clan that had once called itself 'Nguni'.

Bryant goes on to interpret the traditions of origin of the individual 'Nguni' clans in a way which allows him to classify them into three distinct ethnically related 'families', which he calls the Ntungwa, the Mbo, and the Lala.[24] In his view, the clans which made up each of these shared a common origin and culture, and had migrated together into the Phongolo-Mzimkhulu region. But close investigation of the traditions of origin which both he and Stuart record does not bear out this conclusion. Far from being groupings of genealogically related clans, the Ntungwa, Mbo and Lala in fact turn out to consist of clans which are demonstrably unrelated. By the same token, clans and sometimes even sections of clans, which are demonstrably related, are placed by Bryant in different groupings. Contradictions of this sort indicate that claims to Ntungwa, Mbo and Lala affiliation must be seen, not as reflections of primordial ethnic relationships as Bryant contends, but of political struggles which occurred at some point before he recorded the traditions current in the early twentieth century.[25] As is argued later in this chapter, the making of these identities was in all probability a product of the conflicts associated with the emergence and consolidation of the Zulu kingdom in the 1820s and after. The view of the Ntungwa, Mbo and Lala as having a corporate existence that extends back into the remote past is based on a combination of conjecture and misinterpretation of the evidence.

If Bryant's notion that the peoples of the Phongolo-Mzimkhulu region historically constituted a homogeneous ethnic group must now be rejected, so too must his charting of their historical migrations. As is revealed in the previous chapter, archaeological evidence that has emerged since the early 1970s provides a completely different picture of the nature and timing of the process in which the region was settled by farming peoples.[26] Analysis of the traditions of migration which Bryant records reveals that there is actually nothing in them to support his account of long-distance population movements.[27] In fact, they may not even reflect real migrations at all, since, as is now well recognized, traditions of origin and migration among pre-colonial societies often constitute 'founding charters' which have little, if any, basis in fact.[28] It is noteworthy that in his earliest historical work, the 'Sketch' of 1905, Bryant deliberately avoided conjecture about the early 'wanderings' of the peoples who eventually came to inhabit Zululand-Natal, but, by the time he came to write the articles of 1910–13, he was wholeheartedly embracing the theory of migrations.[29] From a historiographical perspective, it is not difficult to understand why he did so, for the theory of 'Bantu migrations' was then becoming dominant among scholars as an explanation of the origin of the historical peoples of sub-equatorial Africa.[30]

It is evident that no 'Nguni' ancestral clan ever existed, and the word was never used as a generic term by the peoples to whom Bryant and other contemporary scholars came to apply it. The *amantungwa*, *amalala* and *abambo* were not groupings of clans that could demonstrate a common descent, but of clans whose traditions of common descent developed in a process of political struggle during the course of the nineteenth century. Strictly speaking, 'Nguni' should be used only as a linguistic term, as in 'Nguni languages', and 'Nguni-speaking peoples'. Continued use of this term as an ethnic designation helps to conceal the conclusion to which recent archaeological research (see Chapter 2), as well as research on recorded oral traditions of Zululand-Natal points – that the historically known African societies of the region did not 'migrate' into it in fixed ethnic units, but emerged locally from long-established ancestral communities of diverse origins and heterogeneous cultures and languages.

The second of Bryant's historical misconceptions concerns the nature of the changes which were entailed in the emergence of centralized states north of the Thukela. The central theme of *Olden Times* is the rise of the Zulu kingdom, which according to him entailed changes of political scale and methods of government without changes of social structure. In his words, 'The Zulu daily life of a hundred, perhaps a thousand, years ago was precisely that which it is today', and 'What the Zulus were like one hundred years ago . . . that they continued to be right up to the time of the Zulu War in 1879 . . .'.[31] In spite of 'drastic political change', he states, 'the social habits of the people would mostly continue undisturbed'.[32]

The origins of this notion may be traced back to the earliest writings on Zulu history in the 1830s,[33] but if Bryant was not its originator he was certainly its chief codifier. For half a century after the publication of *Olden Times* it went virtually unchallenged. Although by 1940 the social anthropologist Max Gluckman was in some ways edging towards a theory of structural change in his treatment of the origins of the Zulu state, in effect he arrived at a position similar to that of Bryant, as did the historian

J. D. Omer-Cooper a generation later.[34] In the works of both these authors, as in that of other contemporary writers on Zulu history, the focus remained narrowly on military and political organization within 'tribal' society.

It was not until the second half of the 1970s that some historians began to argue that in south-east Africa during the late eighteenth and early nineteenth centuries a deep-seated transformation from one kind of society to another had taken place[35]. Where Bryant focused primarily on the details of military conquest, and on the role of individual leaders, these later authors trace the emergence of social and political institutions of a kind which enabled political leaders to wield far more authority over their own adherents than before, and to hold conquered peoples much more firmly in a position of subordination. The emergence of states entailed not simply an increase in the size and in the degree of militarization of political units, but also comprehensive changes in the nature of political, social, ideological, and to some extent, economic relations between rulers and ruled. Bryant's failure to discern this led him to explain historical change in terms of the 'genius' of great leaders, such as Dingiswayo of the Mthethwa and Shaka of the Zulu.[36] As will be indicated in the second part of this chapter, simplistic 'great man' theories of this sort have now given way, at least in the academic literature, to explanations which place greater emphasis on structural change.[37] All of which is not to say that *Olden Times* and Bryant's other historical works should now be left to gather dust as relics of a past generation of history-writing. Far from it: they remain indispensable works for the historian, but now less as histories than as source-books for the rewriting of history.

Part 2: Towards a reconceptualized history

Our knowledge of the Phongolo-Mzimkhulu region in the late eighteenth and early nineteenth centuries derives primarily from a corpus of oral traditions recorded a century or more after the events which they purport to describe.[38] Although comparatively little evidence on the nature of socio-political organization before the emergence of the Zulu kingdom in the late 1810s and early 1820s can be extracted either from the traditions or from the shreds of documentary evidence which exist, there is enough to suggest that in the mid-eighteenth century the inhabitants of the Phongolo-Mzimkhulu region lived in numerous, small-scale political units which varied in size, in population and in political structure. In size they ranged from a few hundred to several thousand square kilometres, and in population from a thousand or fewer individuals to several thousand or more. In structure, they varied from chiefdoms in which the ruling chief exercised a lightly-felt 'managerial' and ritual authority over the people who recognized his rule and paid him tribute, to aggregations of chiefdoms, or 'paramountcies' as they may be called, in which the dominant chief's power was to a greater extent based on the organization and deployment of physical force.[39]

Chiefdoms were made up of a fluctuating number of local communities which were themselves composed of shifting clusters of homesteads. Ties of neighbourhood, of kinship (real or fictive), of clientship, and of marriage operated to bond communities, while at the level of the chiefdom a measure of political cohesion was provided through acts of allegiance made by people to chief, and through the partial redistribution of accumulated tribute from chief to favoured or politically important adherents. Non-political ties tended to cut across political boundaries, and communities and chiefdoms alike were generally fluid and unstable entities, enlarging, splitting, forming and reforming, sometimes peacefully, sometimes violently, as members quarrelled over access to material resources and to the sources of power. This fluidity and instability was an indication of the degree to which power in these polities was uncentralized. This was because there were no institutions through which the chief could exercise more than a temporarily effective command over the armed men of the chiefdom as a whole. Men mobilized on a local basis under their own community leaders, with the result that the chief was not usually able to command enough armed manpower to enable him easily to confront and subdue dissident factions, or to prevent them from abandoning their allegiance to him and hiving off from the chiefdom.

By the same token, these chiefdoms of the mid-eighteenth century and earlier were not divided on what could be called class lines, for there was no means by which a ruling group could capture for itself exclusive control of a chiefdom's basic resources. Even if the political authorities were responsible for allocation of land, the fact that it was notionally held in common prevented the emergence of marked imbalances in its distribution. Possessing as they did a degree of control over armed followings, community leaders were usually able to resist attempts on the part of the chief to extract more tribute in kind or in labour-service than they found acceptable. If resistance failed, moving away to give allegiance to another chief was another possible course of action. This is not to say that these polities were free of other forms of social division, for there were clear inequalities of status between local communities, between men and women, and between older and younger people. These inequalities did not however add up to the existence of permanently opposed groups of 'haves' and 'have-nots'.

Paramountcies formed when one chief was able to subordinate others, through conquest, through manipulating rights to local resources, or through extending control over strategic points on trading routes. Subordination was expressed through declarations of formal allegiance and through payments of tribute. It entailed recognition of the paramount's superior status, but not necessarily of his right to make laws for the subordinate chiefdoms. By virtue of his usually greater wealth, the paramount was often able to attract more adherents than were his subordinate chiefs, and could thus deploy more coercive power, but this was not generally on a scale which enabled him to subjugate chiefdoms to the point of being able to incorporate them under his direct rule. The subordinate chiefs therefore remained to varying degrees autonomous within their own chiefdoms; essentially they were 'tributaries' rather than 'subjects' of the paramount. Polities of this sort were somewhat more complex in their make-up than were individual chiefdoms, and exhibited more pronounced social and political inequalities. But, as they had no permanent and centrally controlled apparatus of repression and exploitation, and tended to be unstable and liable to fragment into their constituent chiefdoms, they cannot be described as fully fledged 'states'.

Evidence from oral traditions suggests that in perhaps the third quarter of the eighteenth century a decisive shift from the patterns of social and political relationships described above began to take place. In several localities between Delagoa Bay and the Thukela River, there began a process of political centralization and more or less simultaneous geographical expansion (see Map 6). East of the Maputo River, in what is now southern Mozambique, the Mabhudu chiefdom began to establish its dominance at this time. To the south-west, in what is now northern Zululand, the region round Magudu saw the emergence of an aggressively expanding Ndwandwe chiefdom, while still further south, between the lower Mfolozi and the Mhlathuze Rivers, the Mthethwa chiefdom was rising to prominence. Other chiefdoms in the region may also have been expanding at this time, but these three seem initially to have been the most important.[40]

The causes of this process of expansion have in recent years been the subject of debate among historians. In place of Bryant's 'great man' theory, several alternative hypotheses have emerged. One is the idea that political

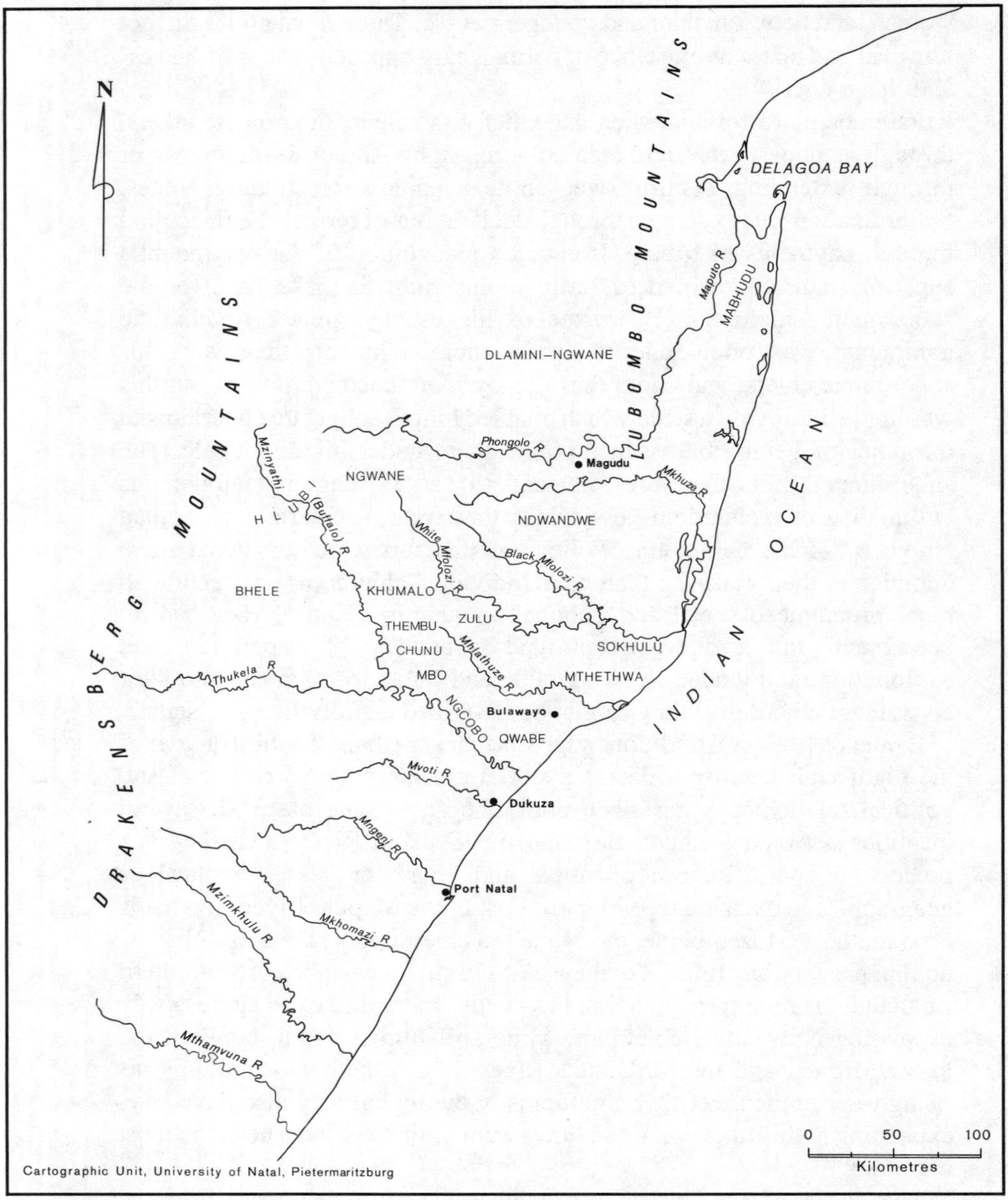

Map 6   The Phongolo-Thukela region before the formation of the Zulu
kingdom

change in late eighteenth-century south-east Africa was a product of intensified conflict over resources consequent on the growth of the region's human population. This idea was first articulated by Gluckman, and uncritically adopted and popularized by Omer-Cooper in his well-known book, *The Zulu Aftermath*.[41] Even if the region's population was growing (see Chapter 2), there is no evidence that it had reached critical density. As other commentators have pointed out, there is actually very little evidence on which demographic explanations of this nature can be based.[42]

A variation of this explanation sees the causes of intensified conflict over resources as lying not so much in an increase of population as in a decline in the productivity of grazing and agricultural land resulting from centuries of unscientific farming practices.[43] In opposition to this line of argument, some archaeological research suggests that there is no evidence that the natural environment in Zululand-Natal would have been subject to ecological strains of this kind.[44] In any case, like the 'demographic' argument, the 'environmental' argument is speculative, not based on firm evidence, and cannot by itself explain why conflict over resources should have begun when and where it did, nor why it should have produced the particular political effects that it did.[45]

The most persuasive arguments so far put forward are based on the hypothesis that the initial dynamic, at least, was provided by the effects of international trade. That the impact of this trade could in particular circumstances precipitate political conflict which led to the formation of states where previously there had been none is well attested in evidence from other parts of Africa.[46] Recent studies of the effects of external trade on the societies of the Delagoa Bay-Thukela region show that the beginnings of the process of expansion and centralization coincide closely with the revival of the European ivory trade at Delagoa Bay from the mid-eighteenth century onwards.[47] A spasmodic trade in ivory had been conducted at Delagoa Bay, as at other parts of the south-east African coast, by visiting European merchants, mainly Portuguese, from the mid-sixteenth to the early eighteenth century, but it was too intermittent and on too small a scale to have had any lasting political effects on the chiefdoms beyond the vicinity of the bay. From the mid-eighteenth century, however, the ivory trade expanded over a period of perhaps thirty years to attain an unprecedented volume. English merchants, in particular, were active in exchanging cloth, beads and metal for ivory, most of which apparently came from the regions to the south of the bay.

Prior to the beginnings of this trade, ivory had simply been a by-product of hunting elephants for food, with little, if any, social importance attached to it. With the growth of demand for ivory as a trading commodity, its social value grew rapidly, and control of ivory resources and of trade routes began to become matters of increasing importance to chiefdoms in or near ivory-producing regions. Within many of these chiefdoms, there was increasing conflict between the ruling house and subordinate groups over the rights to produce and exchange this commodity. In some cases, subordinate groups were able to assert their own rights against those of the dominant one, and in the process often weakened or even destroyed the chiefdom's political cohesion. In other cases, the ruling group was eventually able to establish its own control over the production and trading of ivory, and, as a consequence, to extend the scope of its authority over subordinate groups. When this happened, its increased degree of command over the chiefdom's manpower enabled it permanently to subordinate neighbouring chiefdoms as well in a way that had not previously been possible.

Documentary evidence strongly suggests that the expansion of the Mabhudu state was linked to its control of trade routes from Delagoa Bay southwards.[48] Though no direct evidence survives to indicate that the emerging states further to the south like the Ndwandwe and the Mthethwa were linked to the Delagoa Bay trade, there is no other hypothesis that can adequately explain why political centralization and external expansion should have begun in this region in the later eighteenth century. Why these processes should have begun in these particular chiefdoms and not in others is more difficult to explain. Geographical and environmental factors such as the accessibility or otherwise of the bay, and the availability of sufficient numbers of elephant were of course important; so too were the political forces at work in each individual chiefdom prior to the beginnings of the ivory trade. Particular combinations of these factors shaped the specific ways in which individual chiefdoms responded to the penetration of international commerce, but on the precise processes involved the evidence unfortunately has virtually nothing to say.

Whatever the exact nature of the forces that made for centralization and expansion, in all three of the chiefdoms mentioned, these processes entailed deep-seated social and political changes that centred on the transformation of the functions performed by the bodies of young men known as *amabutho* (singular *ibutho*).[49] The *amabutho* seem originally to have constituted circumcision schools which were periodically formed when the ruling chief banded together a number of young men, all of roughly the same age and drawn from groups which recognized his authority, for the purpose of conducting them through the rites which marked the transition from youth to manhood. In effect, such bands, which had their own names, insignia, and corporate loyalties, constituted bodies of young men which, temporarily but periodically, were under the ritual authority of the ruling chief, and could be turned to his own services.

Given the growth in demand for ivory in the outside world, the incentive was for the chief to turn these *amabutho* towards hunting elephant on his behalf. The ivory thus produced was turned into wealth in the form of prestige imported goods. This wealth was used to enlarge the chief's circle of dependants and clients, thus increasing the coercive power at his disposal. More coercive power ultimately meant more wealth, both in the form of imported prestige goods acquired through the ivory trade, and also in the form of increased tribute, especially in cattle, extracted from subject groups. More wealth, in turn, meant the enhancement of the ruling chief's capacity to distribute largess to politically important subordinates and to the *amabutho*, and hence the further strengthening of the *amabutho* system. The penetration of external trade, once begun, can thus be seen as having set in motion a self-reinforcing process of political centralization and social stratification.

As their command over their *amabutho* was extended, ruling chiefs began turning them to use in conflicts with one another. *Amabutho* were also employed as standing forces to maintain the political subordination of subjected communities and to extract an increased quantity of tribute from them. The expansion of the internal scope of the authority of the chiefs was thus paralleled by the expansion of its geographical span, with the increasingly militarized *amabutho* now serving more and more often in the capacity of army and police force.

The evidence for the developments outlined above varies in quality. That the Mabhudu, the Ndwandwe and the Mthethwa chiefdoms were all expanding geographically in the later eighteenth century is well attested;[50] in addition, traditions indicate that in the Mabhudu and Mthethwa chiefdoms, at least, *amabutho* with the functions described above were emerging at the same time.[51] The evidence for internal political transformation is less easy to find, but nevertheless a careful reading of the traditions points to the emergence at this time of a fundamentally new way of structuring political relationships between ruling houses and subordinate groups.

The evidence is clearest in the case of the Mthethwa chiefdom. In the earliest phase of Mthethwa expansion, associated with the reign of Khayi in roughly the third quarter of the eighteenth century, communities newly subjected to the overlordship of the Mthethwa ruling house were incorporated into the Mthethwa chiefdom through manipulation of their traditions of origin in a way that enabled them to be able to claim to be kinsfolk of the ruling house. In the reigns of Khayi's successors, Jobe and Dingiswayo, which spanned the turn of the century, political incorporation began to take place on a different basis. Chiefdoms subjected to Mthethwa rule were now no longer incorporated into the core group which claimed kinship links with the ruling house; instead, they were deliberately prevented from making such claims, and so came to form a stratum within the Mthethwa polity that was politically and socially quite distinct from, and subordinate in status to, the core of groups linked to the ruling house. The emphasis on common origins that had earlier served to unite subjected groups with the Mthethwa ruling house now gave way to an emphasis on the distinctions that existed between the core of the older groups and the newly subjected ones, with the latter being excluded from certain rights and privileges enjoyed by the core, and subjected to demands for tribute in cattle and labour.[52] The emergence of this distinction can be seen as marking the beginnings of the formation of embryonic social classes within an embryonic state. In this polity, the power exercised by the emergent aristocracy over the class of commoners was increasingly based not only on the ruling chief's ritual and managerial authority but also on the growing coercive power at his disposal. A similar two-phase pattern of political incorporation may be discerned in the traditions of the emergence of the Ndwandwe state, although in this case the evidence is much less clear.[53]

A rather different pattern of political incorporation seems to have characterized a number of other states that were emerging a little after the Mthethwa and Ndwandwe. Among the states in this second category were the Qwabe in the coastal region south of the Mhlathuze, the Mbo and Ngcobo in the Thukela valley, the Hlubi on the upper Mzinyathi (Buffalo) River, and the Dlamini-Ngwane in the south of what is now Swaziland (see Map 6). In all these polities, at least partially militarized *amabutho* were being formed by the early years of the nineteenth century, while processes of geographical expansion were also under way. But, unlike the rulers of the Mthethwa and, even less, of the Ndwandwe, the rulers of this second category of states were by and large unable to establish close control over subjected groups, or to establish a firm social and political distinction between the dominant group and a subordinate class of subject groups.

Their polities were at once less centralized and less stratified than those of the Mthethwa and Ndwandwe.[54]

It is noteworthy that the states of this second category were located in an arc which stretched from the lower Thukela up the valley of the Mzinyathi and round into the valley of the Phongolo. This region was geographically distinct from that where the Mthethwa and Ndwandwe states were emerging. This distinction, together with the slightly later emergence of the states of the second category, and the difference of their political organization, suggests that the forces underlying their emergence were rather different from those which had produced the Mthethwa and Ndwandwe. Their origin seems to have owed less to trade than to a defensive reaction on the part of chiefdoms on the peripheries of the aggressively expanding Mthethwa and Ndwandwe trading states.

Once they had come into existence, states of this second category may well have tried to break into existing trading networks and, as they became caught up in conflicts with the Mthethwa and Ndwandwe and with one another, distinctions between the two categories tended to blur. Their common characteristic was the growing dependence of ruling houses on the *amabutho* system, both for maintaining their power over their subjects and for extending the span of that power outwards. As this dependence grew, so did the necessity for rulers to acquire extra resources of cattle for redistribution as largess and reward to the *amabutho*. There was no way in which these needs could be met from the ruling houses' own cattle holdings, or from the cattle which it was politically safe to extract from their subordinates in the form of tribute. To meet their immediate demands, cattle could be acquired only by raiding them from other chiefdoms. The rise of *amabutho*-based states therefore saw the development of raiding as a structural necessity. Raids had no doubt been frequent enough among these chiefdoms before the emergence of states, but from the late eighteenth century they increased in frequency and scale. And, as the political importance of cattle as a means of supporting the *amabutho* system increased, so raids began to turn into wars of territorial conquest aimed at bringing regions of good grazing land under the permanent control of expanding chiefdoms.

Conflict over cattle and grazing lands was further intensified in the last years of the eighteenth century by the decline of the Delagoa Bay ivory trade and the rise of a trade in cattle. At this time, British and American whalers first began to use the bay as a base of operations, creating a new local demand for provisions, including cattle.[55] As the region around the bay was not good cattle country, local chiefs were soon importing cattle from the ecologically more favoured regions further to the south for sale to the whalers. Whereas ivory had been a 'luxury' item, whose production and exchange had directly involved few commoners, cattle played a pivotal role in the life of every household. For chiefdoms involved in the trade, exports of cattle were a potentially serious drain of crucial resources. The development of the export trade would therefore have provided yet further incentives for these chiefdoms to seek to replace exported cattle by raiding other chiefdoms.

In the early years of the nineteenth century, conflict over cattle and land was sharpened still further by the effects of a major drought, still remembered a hundred years later as the *Madlathule* ('let him eat and remain silent').[56] With livestock dying in large numbers, competition for surviving herds would have been fiercer than ever. By this time the political scene in south-east Africa was dominated by the rivalry between half a dozen newly emerged states: the Mabhudu, Dlamini-Ngwane, Hlubi, Ndwandwe, Mthethwa and Qwabe. By the 1810s the rivalry between the Ndwandwe and Mthethwa was gradually coming to overshadow other conflicts,[57] with the Ndwandwe expanding southward across the Mkhuze towards the Black Mfolozi, and the Mthethwa pushing inland up the valley of the White Mfolozi.[58] Of the two, the Ndwandwe was the more centralized and militarized state, with its ruling house, under Zwide kaLanga, enlarging the territory under its control by means of ferocious conquest.[59] The Mthethwa state under Dingiswayo kaJobe was less tightly knit, with subordinate chiefs retaining a considerable measure of autonomy, including control of a proportion of their armed men. For as long as they acknowledged his overall authority, Dingiswayo allowed, or was constrained to allow, the ruling houses which were subjected in the course of Mthethwa expansion to remain dominant over their own chiefdoms. In the face of a growing threat from the Ndwandwe, he went so far as to encourage some of his strategically-placed subordinate chiefdoms, in particular the Sokhulu in the east near the mouth of the Mfolozi and the Zulu in the west on the middle White Mfolozi, to expand their autonomous military capacity.[60]

By about 1816, the Mthethwa and Ndwandwe were facing each other across a frontier that stretched from near the mouth of the Mfolozi to the present-day Vryheid area. The following year, the confrontation between them came to a head when the Ndwandwe launched an attack on the Mthethwa, defeated their main army, and captured and killed their king

Dingiswayo.[61] The Ndwandwe were now poised to dominate the whole region from the Phongolo to the Thukela, but in the south there remained one final obstacle to be overcome. This was the budding Zulu state, whose chief, Shaka kaSenzangakhona, had come to power with Mthethwa assistance and, as a tributary of Dingiswayo, had been encouraged by the Mthethwa chief to create a firm regional basis of resistance to the Ndwandwe. Possibly as part of a deliberate ploy to escape the overlordship of the Mthethwa, Shaka had held back his army on the occasion of the Ndwandwe attack: consequently, when, in about 1818, the Ndwandwe made their expected attack on the Zulu, his force was intact, and strong enough to beat the invaders off.[62] After the withdrawal of the Ndwandwe, the Zulu leadership rapidly set about increasing the size of the army at its disposal and bringing it under centralized control. More of the surrounding chiefdoms were bullied into accepting Zulu overlordship or cajoled into a Zulu-dominated political and military alliance. The manpower thus brought under Zulu authority was drafted into newly-created Zulu *amabutho*, whose focus of allegiance was the person of the Zulu chief. Large numbers of cattle were extracted as tribute from newly subordinated chiefs and added to the Zulu herds. Only the relatively powerful Qwabe and Khumalo polities offered strong resistance to Zulu expansion. The capacity of the Zulu ruling house to offer smaller chiefdoms a form of organized protection against the Ndwandwe drew them, however grudgingly, to yield up much of their manpower and many of their cattle to the rulers of the aggressively expanding new state into which they now found themselves incorporated.[63]

A second attack by the Ndwandwe on the Zulu was successfully parried, and when, in about 1819, Zwide launched a third expedition, the Zulu leadership felt secure enough to meet it head-on. In a pitched battle on the banks of the Mhlathuze River, the result of which could easily have gone the other way, the Ndwandwe were defeated. The Zulu at once counter-attacked, overran the Ndwandwe territory, and drove Zwide and the remnants of his forces north-westwards over the Phongolo.[64] Overnight, the Zulu had become the predominant power in the Phongolo-Thukela region. Hitherto preoccupied with defence, the Zulu leadership under Shaka now found itself confronted with the necessity of controlling a region much larger in area, and containing a larger population, than had ever before been subjected to the authority of any chief in south-east Africa.

The literature, both academic and popular, on the emergence and early history of the Zulu kingdom has focused overwhelmingly on the figure of Shaka the warrior-king, the founder of empire, the heroic leader, the tyrant. In the century and a half since his death in 1828, one account after another, whether denigratory or adulatory, has repetitively highlighted the force of his personality, his prowess as a military and political leader, the dominance which he exercised over a wide area of south-east Africa. He is seen in the great bulk of the literature as the main driving force behind the rise of the Zulu power. Very little attempt has been made to situate him in the social and political context of his times. Until very recently, there has been a dearth of source material on his reign,[65] with the result that no critical study of his career has yet been written. Nor has any assessment yet been made of the way in which, over the years, writers have cast and recast his literary image in essentially the same form. Where the three Zulu kings who succeeded him all emerge as distinct historical personalities, Shaka remains a stereotyped, often mythologized figure.[66]

While it is clear from the existing evidence that Shaka was a man of extraordinary energy, skill and ruthlessness, both as a military leader and as a politician, he was also very much a product of his own times. The social and political upheavals that were taking place in south-east Africa in the early years of the nineteenth century were pushing to the fore a new kind of leader: men who owed their positions as much to their aggressiveness, powers of initiative, and ability to make quick decisions as they did to their diplomatic and organizational talents. Among them were chiefs like Zwide of the Ndwandwe, Matiwane of the Ngwane, Ngoza of the Thembu, and Mzilikazi of the Khumalo, together with many less well-known figures who were able to seize the opportunities that came their way to enhance their personal power and status. That it was Shaka, rather than any other leader, who was able to establish his supremacy in the Phongolo-Mzimkhulu region was the product of the meshing of circumstance, accident, and personal ability in a process of historical change that historians of the period still have to untangle.

A factor that is likely to delay the successful pursuit of this enterprise is that in recent years the history of south-east Africa in the first half of the nineteenth century has been written very largely round the notion of the so-called *mfecane* (or *difaqane*). The term has been used in a number of different and sometimes contradictory ways, but common to all of them is the idea that the dramatic changes in the political map of south-east Africa which took place in the 1820s and 1830s were caused initially by the destabilizing effects of the rise of the Zulu kingdom. Recent research has not only queried this idea, but has challenged the usefulness of the whole notion of the *mfecane* as an organizing concept.[67] It is clear that the Phongolo-Thukela region was only one of several quite separate epicentres of political instability that were emerging in south-east Africa at this time, and that to ignore the others, as *mfecane* theory invariably does, is to give a greatly distorted view of the forces that were shaping the region's history. Until a new and integrated conceptual framework for analysis of the period has been developed, assessments of the careers of individual leaders run the risk of serving merely to entrench existing historical stereotypes.

If it is difficult to establish the precise historical role of individuals like Shaka, it is clear that the most important political changes of the time were those associated with the expansion of Zulu power. The dominance which the Zulu ruling house proceeded to establish after its victory over the Ndwandwe depended directly on its ability to maintain the highly centralized control and the tight discipline which it had succeeded in imposing on the *amabutho* formed during the emergency which it had faced in 1818–19. The tightening of the *amabutho* system had been designed as much to underpin the tenuous hold on political power of the Zulu rulers as to increase the efficacy of the force at their command: it was both an instrument of internal social control and a means of external defence. After the defeat of the Ndwandwe, the system was extended to the large number of newly-subordinated and potentially rebellious chiefdoms that had suddenly been subjected to Zulu rule. Their young men were compulsorily drawn into the Zulu *amabutho*, segregated into specially-built royal homesteads or *amakhanda*, and forbidden to marry without the permission of the Zulu king. The *amabutho* system thus gave the Zulu state the means to divert the labour-power of young men from their fathers' homesteads and turn it to state purposes, and to socialize young men into identifying the Zulu king as their ritual leader and the source of their welfare. At the same time, the king assumed the authority to decide when young men could set up households of their own. Over time, as differences of social status began to emerge between the various *amabutho*, the system also served to locate individuals ever more firmly within an increasingly rigid social hierarchy.[68]

Forms of state control over young women were as necessary as those over young men for the continued dominance of the Zulu ruling line. As in agricultural societies everywhere, women in the agricultural societies of south-east Africa had always played a crucial role in productive as well as reproductive or 'domestic' labour, and control of these functions had always been a matter of profound social concern – and struggle. Given the expansion of the demands for tribute in the form of labour-power that were imposed on their subjects by the rising states of the late eighteenth and early nineteenth centuries, the productive and reproductive functions of women took on an added political importance and, in a process of conflict about which oral traditions are mostly silent, women became subjected to certain forms of state regulation.[69]

This was achieved mainly through two institutions, both of which may have been emerging in some of the more centralized chiefdoms of the early nineteenth century, but which reached their full development under the Zulu state.[70] One of these was constituted by the female *amabutho*, into one or other of which most of the women of the kingdom were placed, according to age. They functioned primarily as units through which the state could control both the destination of women as marriage partners and the timing of their marriages. Members of each female *ibutho* were permitted to marry only men from male *amabutho* specified by the king, and only after permission to marry had been given by him.

The other institution of control was that represented by the *izigodlo* (singular *isigodlo*), or the king's establishments of women. These consisted of young women who had been presented as tribute to the king by his more important subjects, and who were kept physically secluded in the royal quarters at his *amakhanda*.[71] They have often been portrayed in popular literature as 'harems', but in fact their functions extended far beyond that of concubinage. As the 'sisters' and 'daughters' of the king, they were his to dispose of in marriage to wealthy or powerful men, and it was he who received the bridewealth handed over in return. Essentially, then, the women of the *izigodlo* constituted a source of royal patronage.

The extension of state control over the lives of young men and women was accompanied by important changes in gender relations and in homestead structure. Though some women of the Zulu aristocracy were able to attain very high status and accumulate considerable political power as heads of *amakhanda*, in general the emergence of a highly centralized and stratified social order was accompanied by a decline in the already inferior social status of women. This was evidenced in a considerable increase in the degree of their subordination not only to the political authorities but also to the heads of their homesteads, whether fathers or husbands. Accompanying this was an increase in the burden placed on women in the sphere of productive labour, as they took over some of the tasks of the young men who were withdrawn from homestead labour to serve the state in the new kind of production unit represented by the *amabutho*. The social superiority of men in general was enhanced by the growth in the political importance of cattle, and hence of the productive labour of men, the herders. The militarization of society and the development of an ethos which placed greater and greater emphasis on male military prowess also served to diminish the status of women.[72] At the same time, controls over marriage imposed by the state meant that the rate of formation of new homesteads slowed down, established homestead heads were able to take more wives and thus extend the size of their establishments, and young men and women remained within their fathers' homesteads longer than previously.[73]

Though the *amabutho* system gave the emerging Zulu aristocracy a powerful instrument both for maintaining and legitimizing its domination over the heterogeneous society which it was struggling to bring under its control, maintenance of the system faced the Zulu leadership with major problems. Chief among these, as previously mentioned, was the system's generation of an unending need for cattle for redistribution to politically important office-holders and to notable warriors. This created the need for constant expansion into new territories. After the defeat of the Ndwandwe in about 1819, the Zulu leaders moved rapidly to extend their rule northward of the Black Mfolozi over the chiefdoms formerly tributary to Zwide. Subsequently, forms of Zulu hegemony were extended still further to the north-east over the Mabhudu and other Ronga chiefdoms, partly to extract tribute from them, and partly to keep control of the trade routes to Delagoa Bay.[74] For fear of the still-powerful Ndwandwe, who were reconsolidating under Zwide in what is now the eastern Transvaal, the Zulu leaders did not seek actively to expand their power beyond the Phongolo to the north-west.[75]

South of the Thukela, organized communal life had largely been destroyed by groups like the Bhele, the Thembu, the Chunu and others which had moved southwards to distance themselves from Zulu power in the first phase of its expansion.[76] Only in the lower Thukela valley and in the coastal regions were coherent chiefdoms still to be found, and in the early 1820s these became clients of the Zulu state.[77] By the mid-1820s, Zulu armies were raiding as far south as the Mpondo country in their search for cattle. In 1826 Shaka moved his capital from Bulawayo, near present-day Eshowe, to Dukuza, near what is now Stanger, and proceeded to colonize the coastal region between the Thukela and Mkhomazi by quartering a number of *amabutho* and establishing a string of royal cattle posts in it. This extension of Zulu authority placed rich resources of agricultural and grazing land at the monarchy's disposal, and brought it closer to the British traders who had established themselves at Port Natal in 1824 (see Chapter 5).[78]

The society that emerged in this process of expansion was composed of three tiers.[79] At the apex were the king and the aristocracy, which consisted of members of the Zulu ruling house and the closely associated groups which had been incorporated into the Zulu chiefdom in the first stage of its expansion. Linked to them by a common interest in preserving the existing social hierarchy were the more important chiefs and notables of the chiefdoms subjugated in the ensuing stage, who were encouraged to align themselves politically with the Zulu aristocracy, and allowed to sit in the king's councils. The rest of the members of these chiefdoms comprised the second tier of Zulu-dominated society: from their ranks were drawn the young men whose labour-power, exploited through the *amabutho* system, underpinned the very existence of the state. Members of these chiefdoms may be seen as having been full 'subjects' of the Zulu king, with certain rights as well as obligations. To foster the growth of a sense of corporate identity among them, they were encouraged by their Zulu rulers to regard themselves as all being of *amantungwa* descent.[80] In time, they did in fact come to think of themselves as sharing a common origin and culture. *Ntungwa*-ness thus constituted an ethnic identity which, like all ethnic identities, developed in specific political circumstances.[81]

The third and lowest tier comprised the majority of the people of the peripheries of the Zulu kingdom. They were variously known by members of the other two tiers by derogative names such as *amalala* (menials), *amanhlwenga* (destitutes), *iziyendane* (those with a strange hairstyle), and the like. The subjugation of these peoples was carried out only in the final phases of Zulu expansion, and they were ruled less as 'subjects' of the king than as despised 'outsiders', who were seen as being ethnically inferior to the peoples of the *amantungwa* chiefdoms. Their chiefly houses were required to maintain identities clearly separate from that of the Zulu ruling house, and their leaders, although accorded a number of privileges which distinguished them from the bulk of their subjects, were excluded from certain of the central decision-making processes. Their young men, far from being recruited into the ranks of the king's *amabutho*, were put to work at menial tasks like herding cattle at outlying royal cattle posts. Altogether, members of these chiefdoms seem to have had fewer rights and heavier obligations than members of the *amantungwa* chiefdoms of the kingdom's heartland.[82]

The deep-seated divisions and inequalities which came to exist within Zulu-dominated society were not maintained simply by force. They were also maintained through an ideology of state which sought, firstly, to legitimize Zulu domination by portraying the royal line as ruling by right of genealogical seniority rather than by right of conquest and, secondly, to obscure the nature and extent of social inequalities by emphasizing ethnic divisions – *ntungwa*, *lala*, *nhlwenga* and others – rather than class divisions. To broaden the basis of its power, the new aristocracy also sought to extend state control in the sphere of ritual by reserving for the king alone the right to initiate the performance of politically important ceremonies such as those connected with rainmaking, the opening of the planting and harvesting seasons, and the doctoring of the army.

All this is not to say that the Zulu ruling house did not face strong resistance from subordinate groups as it sought to establish its hegemony. A dramatic manifestation was the well-known attempt, probably by Qwabe dissidents, to assassinate Shaka in 1824.[83] The history of internal opposition to the Zulu state in its early years has only recently begun to be investigated, but it is clear that the tyrannical nature of Shaka's rule needs to be explained more in terms of the shaky nature of Zulu dominance for much of the 1820s than, as is so often the case in the literature, in terms of the quirks of the king's personality.[84]

The sensitivity of the Zulu leadership to internal opposition was heightened by the external threat to its domination posed by the reconstituted Ndwandwe state. The reality of this threat was made clear when, in 1826, the Ndwandwe attempted to invade the Zulu kingdom. In the ensuing battle, fought at Ndololwane north of the upper Phongolo River, the Ndwandwe were routed.[85] It was only at this stage that Shaka felt secure enough to move his capital, as already described, to Dukuza in the south-eastern marches of his kingdom. But political tensions within the kingdom remained high. This was vividly illustrated by the massacre which followed the death of Queen Nandi, Shaka's mother, in 1827. This episode has often been portrayed as a symptom of Shaka's 'bloodthirstiness': it was in fact to a large extent a move on the part of the king to rid himself of political opponents.[86]

The tensions that existed between the ruling house and its subject groups intersected with tensions within the ruling house itself. For reasons that have not yet been fully investigated, a conspiracy to get rid of the king was building up in his court in the later 1820s.[87] As is well known, it culminated in his assassination at the hands of two of his half-brothers in September 1828. In the event, Zulu hegemony proved to be strongly enough established for the ruling house to be able to ride out the ensuing crisis of succession, and the kingship passed relatively smoothly to Dingane, Shaka's half-brother and one of his assassins (see Chapter 4).

The consolidation of the Zulu state by the late 1820s marked the culmination of the processes of political centralization which had been taking place north of the Thukela since the mid-eighteenth century. In place of a large number of small, relatively uncentralized and unstratified chiefdoms, there had emerged a polity that was not only much larger and militarily more powerful than any of its predecessors, but also, in crucial respects, differently structured. Before the mid-eighteenth century, political institutions had been characterized by the virtual absence of state structures. The role of force in the maintenance of social cohesion and the ability of powerholders to extract tribute from those subordinate to them had both been limited, and the emergence of permanent class divisions thus inhibited. By the 1820s, an emergent Zulu aristocracy was using a well-established state apparatus to maintain by force its position at the apex of an increasingly rigid hierarchy of embryonic social classes, and to extract tribute in various forms and amounts from the different categories of its subordinates. In the space of a little over half a century the nature of society in the Phongolo-Mzimkhulu region had been radically transformed.

Notes

1   We wish to thank Philip Bonner for reading and commenting on preliminary drafts of this chapter.

2   Stuart's notes of his interviews are to be found in the James Stuart Collection of the Killie Campbell Africana Library at the University of Natal, Durban. These notes are currently being published by the University of Natal Press in a multi-volume series entitled *The James Stuart Archive of Recorded Oral Evidence Relating to the History of the Zulu and Neighbouring Peoples.* Four volumes, edited by C. de B. Webb and J. B. Wright, have been published since 1976, a fifth is in preparation, and two more will follow.

3 Bryant's first major historical work was the essay entitled 'A Sketch of the Origin and Early History of the Zulu People', which was published as a preface to his *Zulu-English Dictionary* (Mariannhill, 1905), pp. 12*–66*. This was followed by a series of articles published in the newspaper *Izindaba Zabantu* in 1910–13; these were reprinted in A. T. Bryant, *A History of the Zulu and Neighbouring Tribes* (Cape Town, Struik, 1964). His main history, *Olden Times in Zululand and Natal*, was published in London in 1929. His major ethnographic study, *The Zulu People as They Were Before the White Man Came* (Pietermaritzburg, Shuter & Shooter, 1949), begins with two historical chapters.

4 Two pioneering revisionist reviews of Bryant's work were made in the late 1960s by Shula Marks and Anthony Atmore, but neither claimed to be anything more than a preliminary re-assessment. See S. Marks, 'The Traditions of the Natal "Nguni": a Second Look at the Work of A. T. Bryant', in *African Societies in Southern Africa*, ed. L. Thompson (London, Heinemann, 1969), ch. 6; S. Marks and A. Atmore, 'The Problem of the Nguni: an Examination of the Ethnic and Linguistic Situation in South Africa before the Mfecane', *Language and History in Africa*, ed. D. Dalby (London, Frank Cass, 1970), pp. 120–32.

5 Bryant, *Olden Times*, ch. 1, 2, and pp. 232–5, 313–17.

6 Ibid., ch. 9. The quotations appear on p. 71.

7 Bryant, *History of the Zulu*, p. 139.

8 Bryant, *Olden Times*, pp. 18–19.

9 Ibid., p. viii.

10 Ibid., p. x.

11 For an outline of early studies of oral traditions as historical source material see J. Vansina, *Oral Tradition: a Study in Historical Methodology* (Harmondsworth, Penguin, 1973), pp. 2–18.

12 See Vansina, *Oral Tradition*, especially ch. 4; D. P. Henige, *The Chronology of Oral Tradition: Quest for a Chimera* (Oxford, Clarendon Press, 1974), especially ch. 1; J. C. Miller, 'Introduction: Listening for the African Past', *The African Past Speaks*, ed. J. C. Miller (Folkestone, 1980), ch. 1.

13 New methodological perspectives on the existence of patterned contradictions in oral traditions are discussed in C. Hamilton, 'Ideology, Oral Traditions and the Struggle for Power in the Early Zulu Kingdom' (unpublished MA thesis, University of the Witwatersrand, 1985), ch. 1.

14 Bryant, *Olden Times*, p. 15.

15 R. Cohen and J. Middleton, 'Introduction', *From Tribe to Nation in Africa: Studies in Incorporation Processes*, eds. R. Cohen and J. Middleton (Scranton, Pennsylvania, Chandler, 1970), pp. 1–2; J. Iliffe, *A Modern*

History of Tanganyika (Cambridge, Cambridge University Press, 1979), pp. 323–4; R. Thornton, 'Evolution, Salvation and History in the Rise of the Ethnographic Monograph in Southern Africa 1860–1920', *Social Dynamics*, 6 (1980), pp. 14–23.

16   See for example J. S. Bergh and A. P. Bergh, *Tribes and Kingdoms* (Cape Town, D. Nelson, 1984).

17   See A. W. Southall, 'The Illusion of Tribe', *The Passing of Tribal Man in Africa*, ed. P. C. W. Gutkind (Leiden, Brill, 1970), pp. 28–9.

18   See for example Southall, 'The Illusion of Tribe', pp. 28–48; M. H. Fried, *The Notion of Tribe* (Menlo Park, California, Cummings, 1975), *passim*; P. King, 'Tribe: Conflicts in Meaning and Usage', *West African Journal of Sociology and Political Science*, 1 (1976), pp. 186–94; M. Godelier, *Perspectives in Marxist Anthropology* (Cambridge, Cambridge University Press, 1977), ch. 3; T. O. Ranger, 'Race and Tribe in Southern Africa: European Ideas and African Acceptance', *Racism and Colonialism: Essays on Ideology and Social Structure*, ed. R. Ross (The Hague, Martinus Nijhoff Publishers for the Leiden University Press, 1982), ch. 8; A. W. Southall, 'The Ethnic Heart of Anthropology', *Cahiers d'Etudes Africaines*, 100 (1985), pp. 567–72.

19   Bryant, *Olden Times*, pp. 4, 288.

20   The historical usages of the term 'Nguni' are discussed in J. Wright, 'Politics, Ideology and the Invention of the "Nguni"', *Resistance and Ideology in Settler Societies*, ed. T. Lodge (Johannesburg, Ravan, 1986), pp. 96–118.

21   Hedges, 'Trade and Politics in Southern Mozambique and Zululand', p. 255.

22   R. C. A. Samuelson, *The King Cetywayo Zulu Dictionary* (Durban, Commercial Printing Co., 1923), p. 316.

23   Wright, 'Politics, Ideology and the Invention of the "Nguni"', pp. 107–11.

24   For Bryant's discussion of these terms see *Olden Times*, pp. 31–5, 232–3, 313–15. In *Olden Times* Bryant sees the Lala as a sub-group of a 'family' which he calls the Thonga-Nguni. In his later work, *The Zulu People*, he substitutes Lala for Thonga-Nguni, and as Lala has generally come to be used in the literature it is retained in the present discussion.

25   Our argument is drawn from Hamilton, 'Ideology, Oral Traditions and the Struggle for Power', ch. 5, 8; and C. Hamilton and J. Wright, 'The Making of the Lala: Ethnicity, Ideology and Class-Formation in a Precolonial Context', unpublished paper presented to the Third History Workshop conference, University of the Witwatersrand, 1984, pp. 8–18.

26 See also T. Maggs, 'The Iron Age Sequence South of the Vaal and Pongola Rivers: some Historical Implications', *Journal of African History*, 21 (1980), pp. 1–15; 'Iron Age Settlement and Subsistence Patterns in the Tugela River Basin, Natal', *Frontiers: Southern African Archaeology Today*, eds. M. Hall *et al.* (Oxford, British Archaeological Reports, 1984, BAR International Series 207), ch. 17; 'The Iron Age South of the Zambezi', ch. 8.

27 This point was first made by Shula Marks in 'The Traditions of the Natal "Nguni"', pp. 130–1.

28 Miller 'Listening for the African Past', pp. 31–4; Hamilton 'Ideology, Oral Traditions and the Struggle for Power', pp. 166ff.

29 Bryant, *Dictionary*, p. 30*; Bryant, *History of the Zulu*, ch. 7.

30 Two particularly influential works in this field were G. W. Stow, *The Native Races of South Africa* (London, Swan Sonnenschein, 1905), ch. 21, 22, 24–6; Theal, *History and Ethnography of Africa South of the Zambesi*, 1, ch. 3.

31 Bryant, *Olden Times*, p. 74; Bryant, *Zulu People*, p. 72.

32 Bryant, *Olden Times*, pp. 70–1.

33 See Hamilton and Wright, 'The Making of the Lala', pp. 3–5.

34 M. Gluckman, 'The Kingdom of the Zulu of South Africa', *African Political Systems*, eds. M. Fortes and E. E. Evans-Pritchard (London, Oxford University Press, 1940), pp. 25–46; 'Analysis of a Social Situation in Modern Zululand', part B, *Bantu Studies*, 14 (1940), pp. 147–54; 'The Rise of a Zulu Empire', *Scientific American*, 202 (April 1960), pp. 157–68; 'The Individual in a Social Framework: the Rise of King Shaka of Zululand', *Journal of African Studies*, 1 (1974), pp. 113–44; Omer-Cooper, *The Zulu Aftermath*, pp. 24–37.

35 See H. Slater, 'Transitions in the Political Economy of South-East Africa before 1840' (unpublished Ph.D. thesis, University of Sussex, 1976), ch. 9–10; Hedges, 'Trade and Politics', ch. 6, 7; P. L. Bonner, 'The Dynamics of Late Eighteenth Century, Early Nineteenth Century Northern Nguni Society: some Hypotheses', *Before and after Shaka: Papers in Nguni History*, ed. J. B. Peires (Grahamstown, Institute of Social and Economic Research, Rhodes University, 1981), ch. 2; P. L. Bonner, 'Classes, the Mode of Production and the State in Pre-Colonial Swaziland', *Economy and Society in Pre-Industrial South Africa*, eds. S. Marks and A. Atmore (London, Longman, 1980), ch. 3; P. Bonner, *Kings, Commoners and Concessionaires: the Evolution and Dissolution of the Nineteenth-Century Swazi State* (Johannesburg, Ravan Press, 1983), ch. 2.

36 Bryant, *Olden Times*, especially ch. 10–15, 18, 19, 21–6.

37   See the comments of P. R. Maylam, *A History of the African Peoples of South Africa: from the Early Iron Age to the 1970s* (Cape Town, David Philip, 1986), pp. 29–32.

38   Bryant, *Olden Times*, ch. 9; *The Zulu People*, ch. 3, 11; M. M. Fuze, *The Black People and Whence they Came*, trans. H. C. Lugg, ed. A. T. Cope (Pietermaritzburg, University of Natal Press, 1979), ch. 9–11. Some of the traditions recorded by Stuart that bear on the period have been examined in Hamilton, 'Ideology, Oral Traditions and the Struggle for Power', ch. 2, 3.

39   The formulations which we put forward in the paragraphs that follow are based on our reading of the recorded traditions, and on conceptions of the differences between 'stateless' societies and states, derived from the literature on political anthropology and on modes of production. Our thanks go to Peter Delius for his criticisms of an early draft of the model which we present here; the responsibility for it remains our own.

40   On the Mabhudu see Hedges, 'Trade and Politics', pp. 133–42; on the Ndwandwe see Bonner, *Kings, Commoners and Concessionaires*, pp. 10–12; on the Mthethwa see Hamilton, 'Ideology, Oral Traditions and the Struggle for Power', pp. 110–15.

41   See Gluckman, 'The Kingdom of the Zulu', p. 25; 'Analysis of a Social Situation', pp. 148–51; 'The Rise of a Zulu Empire', p. 161; 'The Individual in a Social Framework', pp. 137–8; Omer-Cooper, *Zulu Aftermath*, pp. 25, 27.

42   L. M. Thompson, 'Co-operation and Conflict: the Zulu kingdom and Natal'. *The Oxford History of South Africa*, 1, eds. M. Wilson and L. M. Thompson (Oxford, Clarendon Press, 1969), p. 341; J. J. Guy, 'Ecological Factors in the Rise of Shaka and the Zulu Kingdom', *Economy and Society*, eds. Marks and Atmore, pp. 112–13; D. S. Chanaiwa, 'The Zulu Revolution: State Formation in a Pastoralist Society', *African Studies Review*, 23, 3 (1980), p. 5.

43   This hypothesis has been argued in its most sophisticated form by Jeff Guy: see his 'Ecological Factors', pp. 102–18.

44   M. Hall, *Settlement Patterns in the Iron Age of Zululand: an Ecological Interpretation* (Oxford, British Archaeological Reports, 1981, BAR International Series 119), ch. 5–9, and especially pp. 177–8.

45   In an original interpretation, Chanaiwa has attempted to explain what he calls 'the Zulu revolution' in terms of an intensification of conflict between wealthy ruling élites and the mass of poor commoners led by displaced and deprived royal princes. But he too fails to specify why this process would have begun when it did. See Chanaiwa, 'The Zulu Revolution', pp. 1–20.

46   See C. Coquery-Vidrovitch, 'Research on an African Mode of Production', *Perspectives on the African Past*, eds. M. Klein and G. W. Johnson (Boston, Little, Brown, 1972), pp. 33–51; and 'The Political

Economy of the African Peasantry and Modes of Production', *The Political Economy of Contemporary Africa*, eds. P. C. W. Gutkind and I. Wallerstein (Beverly Hills, Sage Publications, c.1976), ch. 3; *Pre-Colonial African Trade: Essays on Trade in Central and Eastern Africa before 1900*, eds. R. Gray and D. Birmingham (London, Oxford University Press, 1970), especially pp. 15–22; E. Terray, 'Long-Distance Exchange and the Formation of the State: the Case of the Abron Kingdom of Gyaman', *Economy and Society*, 3 (1974), pp. 315–45; M. Mason, 'Production, Penetration and Political Formation: the Bida State, 1857–1901', *Modes of Production in Africa: the Precolonial Era*, eds. D. Crummey and C. C. Stewart (Beverly Hills, Sage Publications, 1981), ch. 8.

47   A. Smith, 'The Trade of Delagoa Bay as a Factor in Nguni Politics, 1750–1835', *African Societies*, ed. L.M. Thompson, ch. 8; 'Delagoa Bay and the Trade of South-East Africa', *Pre-Colonial African Trade*, eds. Gray and Birmingham, ch. 13; 'The Struggle for Control of Southern Mocambique, 1720–1835' (unpublished Ph.D. thesis, University of California, Los Angeles, 1970), ch. 5, 6; Slater, 'Transitions in the Political Economy of South-East Africa', ch. 7, 9; Hedges, 'Trade and Politics', ch. 3, 6.

48   Hedges, 'Trade and Politics', pp. 141–3.

49   On the centrality of the *amabutho* in the political transformations that were taking place in the later eighteenth century see Slater, 'Transitions in the Political Economy of South-East Africa', pp. 277–81; Hedges, 'Trade and Politics', pp. 195–9; J. B. Wright, 'Pre-Shakan Age-Group Formation among the Northern Nguni', *Natalia*, 8 (1978), pp. 22–30; Hamilton, 'Ideology, Oral Traditions and the Struggle for Power', pp. 116–19, 330–3.

50   On the Mabhudu see Hedges, 'Trade and Politics', pp. 137–41; on the Ndwandwe see Bonner, *Kings, Commoners and Concessionaires*, p. 12, and Bryant, *Olden Times*, pp. 158–61; on the Mthethwa see Hamilton, 'Ideology, Oral Traditions and the Struggle for Power', pp. 110–15.

51   Hedges, 'Trade and Politics', pp. 153–4; Hamilton, 'Ideology, Oral Traditions and the Struggle for Power', pp. 116–19.

52   Hamilton, 'Ideology, Oral Traditions and the Struggle for Power', pp. 112–18, 122–30.

53   Bryant, *Olden Times*, pp. 160, 162, 276–7, 686, 690, 691; Bryant, *History of the Zulu*, pp. 12–13; Hedges, 'Trade and Politics', pp. 156–64.

54   On the Qwabe see Hamilton, 'Ideology, Oral Traditions and the Struggle for Power', pp. 156–60; on the Mbo and Ngcobo see Bryant, *Olden Times*, pp. 404–5 and ch. 46, and Hedges, 'Trade and Politics', p. 176; on the Hlubi see Wright and Manson, *The Hlubi Chiefdom*, pp. 9–11; on the Dlamini-Ngwane see Bonner, *Kings, Commoners and Concessionaires*, ch. 2.

55   Hedges, 'Trade and Politics', pp. 145–52. On local whaling see also A. R. H. Booth, *The United States Experience in South Africa 1784–1870* (Rotterdam, Balkema, 1976), pp. 32–40; P. Duignan and L. H. Gann, *The United States and Africa: a History* (Cambridge, Cambridge University Press, 1984), pp. 66–72.

56   Bryant, *Olden Times*, pp. 63, 88; Guy, 'Ecological Factors', pp. 111–12; Bonner, *Kings, Commoners and Concessionaires*, pp. 20–3.

57   Bryant, *Olden Times*, ch. 18.

58   Wright and Manson, *The Hlubi Chiefdom*, pp. 12–13; Hamilton, 'Ideology, Oral Traditions and the Struggle for Power', pp. 123–9.

59   Bonner, *Kings, Commoners and Concessionaires*, pp. 23–4, 27–8.

60   Hamilton, 'Ideology, Oral Traditions and the Struggle for Power', pp. 117–20, 124–35.

61   Bryant, *Olden Times*, pp. 162–6; Hamilton, 'Ideology, Oral Traditions and the Struggle for Power', pp. 136–8.

62   Bryant, *Olden Times*, ch. 19; Hamilton, 'Ideology, Oral Traditions and the Struggle for Power', pp. 135–6, 246–7.

63   Hamilton, 'Ideology, Oral Traditions and the Struggle for Power', pp. 172–90, 246–64.

64   Bryant, *Olden Times*, ch. 22, 25.

65   A considerable amount of information on the subject is now becoming available in the successive volumes of the *James Stuart Archive* (see Note 2 above).

66   For contrasting examples of how Shaka has beeen presented in recent literature, see E. V. Walter, *Terror and Resistance: a Study of Political Violence* (London, Oxford University Press, 1969), ch. 7; J. K. Ngubane, 'Shaka's Social, Political and Military Ideas', *Shaka, King of the Zulus in African Literature*, D. Burness (Washington, Three Continents Press, 1976), pp. 127–64.

67   The pioneering rethinking has been done by Julian Cobbing. See his unpublished paper, 'The Case against the Mfecane' (presented at the Centre for African Studies, University of Cape Town, 1983) and a revised version with the same title (presented at the African Studies Institute, University of the Witwatersrand, 1984).

68   On the role of the *amabutho* in the emerging Zulu kingdom see Slater, 'Transitions in the Political Economy of South-East Africa'; pp. 300–2, 307–8; Hedges, 'Trade and Politics', pp. 208–14; Guy, 'Ecological Factors', pp. 115–17; Hamilton, 'Ideology, Oral Traditions and the Struggle for Power', ch. 6.

69   Guy, 'Ecological factors', pp. 116–17; Slater, 'Transitions in the Political Economy of South-East Africa', pp. 266, 281.

70   The place of women in the emerging Zulu kingdom is discussed in Hamilton, 'Ideology, Oral Traditions and the Struggle for Power', ch. 7.

71   Ibid., pp. 446–51.

72   Ibid., ch. 7. More generally on changes in gender relations in precolonial south-east Africa see E. A. Alpers, 'State, Merchant Capital, and Gender Relations in Southern Mozambique to the end of the Nineteenth Century: some Tentative Hypotheses', *African Economic History*, 13 (1984), pp. 39–43.

73   On changes in the rate of homestead formation in the early Zulu kingdom, see Guy, 'Ecological Factors', pp. 115–17. On changes in homestead structure see Slater, 'Transitions in the Political Economy of South-East Africa', pp. 319–21.

74   Bryant, *Olden Times*, ch. 26; Hedges, 'Trade and Politics', pp. 214–16.

75   Bonner, *Kings, Commoners and Concessionaires*, p. 37.

76   Bryant, *Olden Times*, ch. 30–2, 39.

77   Hamilton, 'Ideology, Oral Traditions and the Struggle for Power', ch. 8.

78   Slater, 'Transitions in the Political Economy of South-East Africa', pp. 326–40; Hamilton, 'Ideology, Oral Traditions and the Struggle for Power', pp. 353–63.

79   The arguments in this paragraph are detailed in Hamilton, 'Ideology, Oral Tradition and the Struggle for Power', ch. 5.

80   The term *intungwa* (plural *amantungwa*) may have been derived from an ecological characteristic of the region which the Zulu were incorporating at an early stage of their expansion. Such ecological referents are common in African generic naming practices.

81   On the nature of ethnic boundaries and naming practices in precolonial south-east Africa, see the discussion in Hedges, 'Trade and Politics', pp. 25–8.

82   Hamilton and Wright, 'The Making of the Lala', pp. 11–17; Hamilton, 'Ideology, Oral Traditions and the Struggle for Power', ch. 8.

83   An eye-witness account of this incident is given in H. F. Fynn, *The Diary of Henry Francis Fynn*, eds. J. Stuart and D. McK. Malcolm (Pietermaritzburg, Shuter & Shooter, 1950), pp. 83–5. See also the discussion in Hamilton, 'Ideology, Oral Traditions and the Struggle for Power', pp. 185–6.

84   See the discussions in Slater, 'Transitions in the Political Economy of South-East Africa', pp. 341–2; and Hamilton, 'Ideology, Oral Traditions and the Struggle for Power', pp. 174–5, 184–6, 354–5, 362–3, 506–8.

85   For an account of the Zulu campaign, see Fynn, *Diary*, pp. 122–8. See also the discussion in Hedges, 'Trade and Politics', pp. 201–2.

86   An eye-witness account of the massacre is given in Fynn, *Diary*, pp. 132–7. See also the discussion in Slater, 'Traditions in the Political Economy of South-East Africa', pp. 318–19.

87   See the discussion in Slater, 'Traditions in the Political Economy of South-East Africa', p. 348.

Chapter 4

The Zulu kingdom, 1828–79

PETER COLENBRANDER

Late in September 1828 Shaka, the founding father of the most powerful polity in south-east Africa, was murdered at his Dukuza homestead, the site of present-day Stanger.[1] His assassins were Dingane and Mhlangana, two of his half-brothers, and Mbopha kaSitayi, his senior *inceku* (personal assistant). Although not party to the deed itself, the moving force behind the plot was Mnkabayi, a full sister of Senzangakhona and thus Shaka's paternal aunt, and an influential figure in the affairs of the kingdom. She had been a close associate of Nandi, Shaka's mother, and her reputed motive for plotting against him was a deep sense of aggrievement at Nandi's death in 1827, for which she held Shaka directly accountable.[2]

The opportunity to assassinate Shaka had been provided by the absence of virtually all of the *amabutho* on campaign against Soshangane, who lived to the north in the vicinity of the Olifants River. Indeed, Dingane and Mhlangana may themselves have set out on this expedition, but took the opportunity to return to Dukuza shortly after its initial departure.[3]

Dingane and his fellow-conspirators were not simply exploiting the absence of a protective force; they were also aware that political circumstances favoured their purpose. Discontent had, by all accounts, increased as Shaka had grown more despotic and autocratic in the latter part of his reign, and especially in the wake of his mother's death. These developments are usually attributed to Shaka's allegedly disturbed and increasingly unbalanced state of mind. Recently, however, it has been argued that Shaka was asserting himself more emphatically for rational and readily explicable reasons; namely, to counter a series of growing political crises that confronted him.[4]

The new rulers now set about securing their power. Of Shaka's councillors, only Sothobe kaMpangalala, who had led the recent ill-starred embassy to the Cape, was present at the time of his assassination. Initially inclined to take physical revenge on the murderers, he was soon won over to their cause after being reminded of his own opposition to Shaka's recent excesses. Clearly, however, the conspirators needed more than powers of personal persuasion if they were to survive any challenge to their position. In the absence of the bulk of the army, the only soldiers available to them were the young bearer-boys recently detached by Shaka from the Soshangane expedition and constituted as the *iziNyosi* regiment. To supplement this inexperienced unit, the two co-rulers turned to the *iziYendane*, or tributary peoples, resident in the western marches of the kingdom. Hitherto only employed as menials and auxiliary cattle guards, they were now banded together in a new regiment, which was given the title *Hlomendlini* ('Home Guards'). It was divided into two separate sections and placed under the overall command of Sipingo kaHengqwa. Its first task was to collect Shaka's cattle depastured in Natal, to forestall their seizure by the Mpondo and Bhaca peoples.[5] Meanwhile the *iziNyosi* were employed in attacking and killing Ngwadi, Shaka's maternal half-brother. A great favourite of the late king, he had been allowed considerable political latitude and had amassed substantial herds and a not insignificant following, for which reasons Dingane and Mhlangana had plausible grounds for fearing that he might rally wider opposition to them.[6]

It was not long before the two royal conspirators began to plot against each other. The ostensible cause of conflict was the allocation of Shaka's cattle, but Dingane allegedly had the superior genealogical credentials and apparently had long regarded himself as the rightful claimant to the kingship. Supported by Mnkabayi, Dingane was able by means of a ruse to eliminate his rival. At the same time, Mbopha, a commoner who had no entitlement to the throne, was rewarded politically and materially. However, as a regicide, he was understandably suspect and he too was subsequently removed from the scene.[7]

Dingane had still to win the allegiance of the main body of *amabutho*, which returned from Soshangane's country soon after Mhlangana's death. This does not appear to have been difficult. Apart from the general discontent arising from Shaka's recent policies, the regiments had their own particular grievances. In 1828 they had first been dispatched against the Mpondo, and then, before they could fully recover, were ordered out against Soshangane. To compound these hardships, they had been deprived of their bearer-boys by Shaka, with the result that they had suffered the indignity and inconvenience of having to carry their own provisions and equipment.[8] Furthermore, the campaign itself had been a fiasco.

VII.—VIEW OF THE KRAAL, OR CAPITAL, OF THE KAFIR CHIEF DINGAAN.

The detail shown on this early woodcut, included in W. C. Holden's History of the
Colony of Natal *(1855), suggests that it accurately portrays the layout
of Dingane's royal kraal at Mgungundlovu.*

Forewarned by a Zulu traitor of the approach of the force, Soshangane had
been able to frustrate its purpose. As if that were not enough, the expedition
was ravaged by illness and hunger. It was thus a dispirited, weakened and
disorganized army that returned to Zululand, and one which was neither
willing nor able to oppose the new king. Indeed, the soldiers may have
welcomed Dingane's accession, since they were thus spared the
punishment that Shaka would have visited upon them for failing in their
task.

But the relative smoothness of the transition to Dingane's reign goes
deeper than this. Whatever the tensions evident in the Zulu state, and
whatever the latent fissiparous tendencies, the kingship had nonetheless
acquired widespread legitimacy at the political, economic and ideological
levels.[9] This is a truly remarkable achievement, given the brevity of the
prior existence of the kingdom. In essence, therefore, the dramatic political
events of 1828 amounted to a dynastic rebellion, not a revolution.

Generally speaking, Dingane's kingship has received a bad press.
Largely as a result of the lurid portrayals by the early Port Natal settlers and
of his subsequent conduct towards the Voortrekkers, he has emerged as a
capricious, untrustworthy and cowardly despot, who shared none of
Shaka's redeeming features. In fact, it is worth stressing that he began his

reign on a distinctly conciliatory note. Mindful of the disaffection that Shaka's excesses had elicited, he inaugurated his reign by permitting several of his *amabutho* to marry, by relaxing military discipline, by promising a more peaceful era and by subjecting his subordinate chiefs to less exacting supervision.[10] It is true that some of Shaka's councillors were replaced by men more favourably disposed to himself, but by no means all of Shaka's lieutenants met violent deaths at his hands, and some indeed were placated and wooed with generous gifts of cattle.[11]

This lenient approach, however, proved short-lived. In about 1829 the Qwabe people under Nqetho rose in revolt and fled south-westwards. The Qwabe had been left relatively undisturbed by Shaka. Perhaps Nqetho had concluded that Shaka's comparatively benign disposition towards him and his people would now count against him. However, there are other references to Shaka's having displayed particular vindictiveness towards the Qwabe in the aftermath of his mother's death (see Chapter 3), engendering perhaps general disaffection with Zulu rule among the Qwabe.[12] Whatever the reasons, the Qwabe decided to exploit the more relaxed conditions to cast off their allegiance. This must have given Dingane cause for concern, more especially as the pursuing Zulu forces were unable to defeat them decisively, or to seize all their livestock.

Henceforward, any threat, real or imagined, to the cohesion and security of the state or to its territorial integrity, was dealt with ruthlessly. At various times during Dingane's reign, generally successful punitive measures were taken against, among others, the returned fugitive Matiwane, chief of the Ngwane; Zihlandlo and his Mkhize people on the middle reaches of the Thukela; the Cele in the coastal lands to the south of that river; Bheje's Khumalo at Ngome mountain; Mlotsha's Khumalo on the upper stretches of the Mkhuze River; the Qadi people; and the Hlubi in the strategic Mzinyathi frontier zone.[13] In the process, several chiefs were violently replaced, livestock was expropriated, and community life was often severely disrupted. Similar steps were taken against male members of the Zulu ruling dynasty, for fear that they might serve as rallying-points for opposition. Of Dingane's close male kin, only Mpande and Gqugqu were to survive these purges. In addition to these coercive measures, Dingane attempted to cement domestic political alliances by giving several of his female relatives in marriage to important subordinates.[14]

In his foreign policy, Dingane is not usually remembered as having been militarily active and assertive, except in respect of the incoming Boers during the latter part of his reign (see Chapter 5). He lacked his predecessor's powers of generalship and seldom, if ever, accompanied his forces on campaign. But, notwithstanding his initially pacific declarations, he proved by no means averse to mounting expeditions beyond the borders of his realm. The Bhaca, the Mpondo, the Swazi, the 'Nkentshane' Sotho near modern Middelburg on the highveld, and Mzilikazi's Ndebele were all visited by Zulu armies during his reign, some on more than one occasion.[15] He also intervened militarily against the European enclaves at Delagoa Bay and Port Natal. Discounting these latter episodes for the moment, the need to counter a military threat was rarely a major consideration in initiating the campaigns. More persuasive was the necessity of keeping the *amabutho* gainfully employed so as to retain their loyalty and efficiency. Although their functions were not exclusively military, the rituals that they practised and the ideology they enshrined was distinctly martial in tone and placed great stress on prowess in battle.[16] That apart, raiding was indispensible for acquiring additional cattle with which to feed, clothe, equip and reward the large number of enlisted men. In short, the logic and workings of the *amabutho* necessitated frequent campaigning.[17]

However, Dingane's forces enjoyed less than consistent success in the field. On occasion, long distances, harsh terrain and inclement weather frustrated their endeavours.[18] More disturbingly, their adversaries began to adopt successful counter-tactics. The Swazi, for example, proved adroit at taking refuge in mountain caves, thus neutralizing the Zulu advantage of mobility and numbers. Consequently, Dingane was constrained to summon the assistance of Port Natal gunmen[19] (Shaka had also adopted this solution when faced with a similar predicament). Furthermore, Dingane made increasingly insistent demands on the European traders, and later the missionaries, to supply him with firearms and train his men in their use. Perhaps, too, firearms were desired because military discipline was never restored to Shakan levels. Certainly, as late as 1831, one of Dingane's military lieutenants was voicing grave misgivings on this score.[20]

By far the most pressing and far-reaching, not to mention fateful, dilemma that Dingane had to face stemmed from the growing white presence in the outer reaches of his kingdom. Three distinct communities were involved; the Portuguese at Delagoa Bay, the English trading settlement at Port Natal, loosely associated after 1836 with the missionaries, and, subsequent to 1837, the Voortrekker settlers to the south-west of the Thukela and Mzinyathi rivers. The various communities posed Dingane with three sets of often inter-related challenges; commercial, political and territorial.

Dingane was apparently in a position to conduct trade with Delagoa Bay and Port Natal very much on his own terms for the greater part of his reign. By exploiting the commercial rivalry between the two entrepôts, he was generally able to obtain the commodities he desired at favourable rates of exchange, or to acquire from the one what was denied him by the other. Thus, even after the English traders stopped supplying firearms in the mid-1830s, he continued to obtain them from Delagoa Bay, though he never received them in sufficient volume to satisfy his full requirements.[21] And, if all else failed, he could resort to force. In 1831, for instance, he sent a detachment of soldiers to punish John Cane, a Port Natal settler, for allegedly mischievous and deceitful conduct.[22] Cane had failed to report to the king after leading an unsuccessful mission to the Cape Colony on his behalf. Much more spectacular was his intervention two years later at Delagoa Bay, when the Portuguese fort was attacked, the Governor being killed and replaced with a more compliant substitute. This episode perhaps represents the high water mark of Zulu influence in the affairs of southern Mozambique, large areas of which now came under their sway.[23]

These latter actions were not unrelated to Dingane's dealings with Port Natal, which were much more complex. While the regulation of the affairs of the white settlement there was his ultimate concern, he was generally inclined to act with great circumspection. Not only did he value the commercial connection, but he wished to avoid giving offence to the British at the Cape, with whom the Port Natal settlers were closely linked.[24] In consequence, areas of mutual discord tended to remain unresolved and grow more acute, so that by the mid-1830s Zulu relations with Port Natal had sunk to a low ebb.

Dingane's perceptions of white political activities and ambitions were to a significant extent influenced by Jacob Msimbiti, a Xhosa-speaking African, who had been imprisoned on Robben Island before coming to Zululand to act as interpreter for the earliest British settlers during Shaka's reign. Jacob had told Dingane of the white expansion that had occurred on the Cape Colony's eastern frontier, and had also raised fears about their territorial interests in Natal. While these latter reports may have been premature, and while he had fallen from Dingane's favour by the early 1830s,[25] there is good reason to believe that he had nurtured in Dingane and his counsellors a nagging, and ultimately well-founded, distrust of white motives.

Moreover, Dingane was clearly annoyed by the recent discontinuance by the settlers of the sale of firearms, while the settlers resented his consistent ability to manipulate the general terms of trade to his advantage.[26] He was also disturbed by settler attempts to trade directly with his people. This he could not countenance, for the royal monopoly over exchange relations was vital to the maintenance of political control over his subjects and, more especially, his tributaries. It was not, however, always possible for him to stem this undermining process, particularly in the case of the African peoples residing closer to Port Natal.[27]

Even more irksome and threatening from Dingane's point of view, was the flight of refugees to the white settlement. Zulu subjects living south of the Thukela had been seeking refuge at Port Natal from a very early stage in its history. Shaka had tolerated this because he saw it as a means of stabilizing the southernmost reaches of his realm with the minimum of effort.[28] However, under Dingane, not only did the numbers of refugees swell (there were about 2 500 of them at Port Natal by the middle of the decade), but a growing proportion of them came from Zululand itself. Indeed, in 1834 an entire Zulu regiment is said to have defected.[29] Consequently, Port Natal now harboured a significant concentration of political malcontents, and the threat which they posed could no longer be dismissed lightly, especially as there was a growing disinclination among the settlers, who could now deploy some two to three hundred muskets, to conform to their earlier role as loyal subordinate chiefs.[30]

By as early as 1832 countermeasures had been instituted. Sothobe, assisted by Lukwazi, was appointed to superintend the peoples living on the Natal side of the middle stretches of the Thukela. On the coastal lands, the inhabitants were ordered to withdraw across first the Thongati River and, shortly afterwards, the Thukela itself. The *Hlomendlini* units were now stationed in south-western Zululand to guard the strategic territories facing Port Natal.[31] Still the flight of refugees persisted. By 1835 Dingane had decided that the continued right of the trading settlement to operate was conditional upon the repatriation of all future refugees. But this arrangement, concluded with Captain Allen Gardiner, a newly-arrived missionary, very soon came to nothing. In the face of the traders' failure to honour the terms of the agreement, Dingane slapped a ban on all commerce and prohibited all whites except Gardiner from entering Zululand. The annexationist sentiments which the traders and their allies in the Cape had been harbouring over the last few years grew shriller (see Chapter 5).[32]

Serious as the problem of Port Natal had become, the gravest threat to the cohesion and integrity of the Zulu kingdom arose from another source, the Voortrekkers. Late in 1837 the Trekker leader, Piet Retief, arrived at

This document, in which king Dingane cedes 'the place called Port Natal, together with all the land annexed, that is to say from Tugela to the Umzimvubu River westward, and from the sea to the north', was allegedly found in Retief's hunting bag when his body was recovered in December 1838. Its authenticity is still disputed.

Dingane's capital Mgungundlovu, to negotiate the cession of all the territory south of the Thukela. Dingane tentatively agreed, provided that Retief retrieved several hundred cattle which had been raided recently from the north-western region of the kingdom by Sekonyela, the Tlokwa chief. That mission having been accomplished, Retief returned in February 1838 to claim his part of the bargain. It was then that he and his party were put to death. Immediately after Retief's death, Zulu forces proceeded to attack Boer laagers in Natal in an apparent effort to annihilate the Trekkers in one fell swoop. In the event, Dingane did not succeed in dislodging or destroying all the Trekkers – though his forces did seize some 35 000 of their cattle – and he and his people were later to pay dearly for this failure. In the short term, however, further military setbacks befell both the Trekkers and the Port Natal settlers, the latter hoping to exploit the prevailing uncertainty to free themselves from Dingane's overlordship. But towards the end of 1838, the demoralized Trekkers rallied around a new leader, Andries Pretorius, under whose command they inflicted a crushing defeat on Dingane's forces at the Ncome (Blood) River, during the course of which engagement some 3 000 Zulu sacrificed their lives. In terms of the ensuing peace treaty, Dingane undertook to restore the Boer livestock he had earlier seized, to refrain from further aggression, and to cede the territory south of the Thukela as well as a strip of territory to the east of the river.[33] Following his defeat at the Ncome River in December 1838, Dingane unsuccessfully attempted the conquest of southern Swaziland, so that he could vacate the territory ceded to the Boers, distance himself from them and allow himself time to recoup his strength for the further apparently inevitable conflicts with them.

In all this train of events, only Dingane's motives for acting as he did against Retief need elaboration. It is this episode which, pre-eminently, has shaped the almost universally hostile historical depictions of Dingane. Moreover, it has come to serve as a potent symbol in Afrikaner folk-consciousness, and is a subject which still evokes strong emotions. Dingane's conduct was not beyond reproach, but cannot simply be written off to incomprehensible, mindless savagery. His behaviour can and should be rationally explained.

The general import of Jacob's prognostications about white expansion has already been noted. Perhaps, in the light of the difficulties with Port Natal which had developed in the intervening years, his warnings had acquired greater, if belated, credibility. In any event, Dingane had no trusted European confidant to whom he could turn for up-to-date

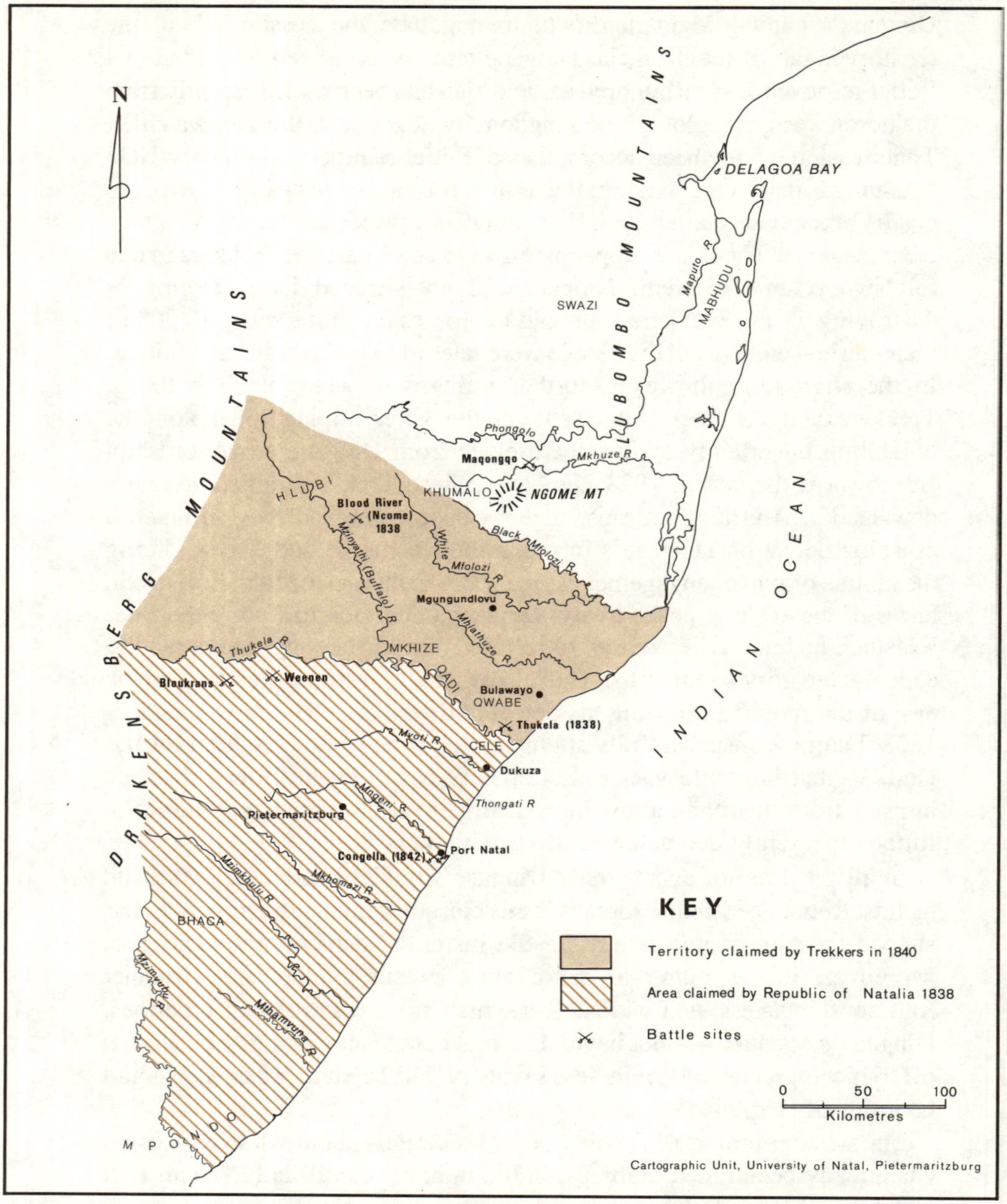

Map 7 The Zulu kingdom and the Republic of Natalia

information about these strangers who had descended so unexpectedly in quest of land.[34]

The subsequent activities of Retief and the Trekkers probably exacerbated Dingane's anxiety. Even before Retief had carried out his side of the bargain, the main Trekker parties, comprising several thousand people, came down the Drakensberg into northern Natal. This was alarming enough in itself, but was made more so when the Trekkers set up laagers – in effect a kind of mobile fort – in the area and started seizing grain from neighbouring homesteads.[35] Moreover, Dingane had probably learned of the prowess of these mounted gunmen against such formidable foes as Mzilikazi's Ndebele. His growing fears for the physical safety of his kingdom were heightened by a threatening letter he received from Retief shortly after their initial meeting, in which he was warned of the dire fate awaiting kings who broke their word. Thereafter, by the simple trick of handcuffing the unsuspecting Sekonyela, Retief had been able to extract the stolen Zulu cattle, as well as a handful of horses and guns. Successful as this ploy was, it can only have unsettled Dingane even further.[36] To cap it all, at their second fateful meeting, Retief refused to surrender Sekonyela's firearms – the very technology that Dingane so feared and coveted – and devised a show of force by way of a mock cavalry charge by the sixty-odd riflemen who had accompanied him. It was shortly after this display that Dingane gave the order for the Trekker party to be massacred. It has been argued that the refusal to surrender the Tlokwa firearms was the decisive issue in the whole bloody episode.[37] It remains possible, however, that Dingane had already decided upon, or at least seriously contemplated, his course of action prior to this development, not least because of the growing pressure on him from his councillors and soldiers to take a stand.[38] Moreover, it seems inherently unlikely that Dingane would have adopted so hazardous a policy for the sake of fewer than a dozen firearms.

Dingane's troubles were not, however, over by 1839. Neither party viewed the peace agreement with any great confidence, and it was not long before hostilities were resumed. This time, Trekker ambitions triggered and interlocked with dynastic opposition in the Zulu royal house. During the latter part of 1839 Mpande, the half-brother of the king, fled across the Thukela and entered into a political and military alliance with Pretorius. In January 1840, two military columns, the one Boer, and the other comprising Mpande's adherents, advanced into Zululand and by early the following month Dingane's forces had been decisively defeated at the bloody battle of Maqongqo, near the present village of Magudu. Shortly afterwards, Dingane, now a fugitive, was put to death by the Nyawo people, apparently with Swazi assistance and support.[39] The Boers, having earlier recognized Mpande as the 'Prince of the Emigrant Zulus', now proclaimed him king, even though the military contribution which their commando had made to Dingane's overthrow was negligible. Within a matter of months, Mpande had been raised from a position of relative obscurity to the apex of the political structure.

For several reasons, the year 1840 was an important milestone in Zulu political history. Not only had a new king acceded, but white intervention in his succession presaged the increasingly altered circumstances under which both he and his successor Cetshwayo were to rule. While the Zulu were to retain their independence, their influence in south-east Africa therefore became less decisive. Moreover, many of the problems they had to face at home and in the region as a whole arose from or were complicated by white settlement in the Transvaal and Natal, and the subsequent consolidation of European domination over most of the subcontinent. Initially, the weakness of the Trekker and British communities, and the rivalry between them, provided room for manoeuvre but, as European penetration of the subcontinent increased, the policy options available tended to diminish and assumed a more reactive character.

Mpande is often portrayed as an unworthy successor to Shaka and Dingane – ineffectual, indolent, obese, peaceable and even cowardly.[40] These characteristics, it is implied, help to explain why he was the only Zulu king to die a natural death, and this after a reign of thirty-two years, by far the longest in the history of the kingdom. This stereotype, while containing some germ of truth, is largely the result of the relatively limited attention his reign has received from historians.[41] It ignores or under-estimates the considerable difficulties that beset him during his reign and the degree of his success in steering the Zulu kingdom through a period of accelerated political change.

Mpande began his reign on a very precarious footing. He was born in about 1798 and, like Shaka and Dingane, was the son of Senzangakhona, who then ruled the insignificant Zulu chiefdom. Although animosity and suspicion were the hallmarks of relations between male members of ruling dynasties in Nguni-speaking societies, Mpande attained a position of some trust under Shaka. He claimed to have served as 'captain' on several of Shaka's campaigns and was given the responsibility of fathering a son for the king, Shaka hoping to minimize the risk of usurpation at the hands of an ambitious heir by not fathering his own children.[42] Dingane's attitude to

Mpande was more complex than that of Shaka. As a usurper, he had, as we have seen, systematically eliminated almost all of his father's other sons, leaving Mpande to exercise a limited degree of authority over the south-eastern reaches of the Zulu kingdom, where his homesteads were situated. A further indication of the confidence Dingane had in him was that he was again entrusted with the task of fathering an heir, Dingane's motives presumably being the same as Shaka's. In return, Mpande appears loyally to have attended to the king's interests, such as when he warned Dingane that the Cele chief Magaye seemed intent on defecting southwards.[43]

The reasons for Dingane's trust in – or tolerance of – Mpande are not clear. According to one source, it had a lot to do with Ndhlela kaSomphisi, the Ntuli chief, a man of considerable wealth and influence, who served as Dingane's leading councillor and who is believed to have persuaded Dingane not to put Mpande to death along with the king's other sons. Ndhlela's support of Mpande may have stemmed from some kind of political affiliation, for the Ntuli domain lay close to Mpande's homesteads. He seems to have promoted Mpande's interests by the unlikely means of referring pejoratively to his alleged cowardice, inferior geneological status and physical and mental deficiencies. It has been suggested that he did so because he saw that Mpande alone could guarantee the continuity of the Zulu kingdom as only he had produced heirs.[44] If this is true, his reasoning points to the unforeseen hazards of both Shaka's and Dingane's avoidance of procreation.

After the failure of Dingane's 1838 expedition against the Swazi, he called on Mpande to furnish reinforcements and prepare to move northwards with all the people of the south. Mpande's temporizing response confirmed Dingane's long-held suspicions. Ndhlela, however, sent messengers to warn Mpande that Dingane had decided to kill him, whereupon Mpande undertook his flight to the Boers, an event described in Zulu oral tradition as 'the breaking of the rope that held the nation together'.[45]

The fugitives who accompanied Mpande comprised most of the inhabitants of the area to the south of the Mhlathuze River. Some estimates place his following at almost half the Zulu nation, but about 17 000 is probably nearer the mark.[46] Not all of those who fled did so because they were his loyal followers. Many were simply the victims of Dingane's recent policy of evacuating the coastal areas of Natal and seized the opportunity presented by Mpande's defection to re-establish their independence on their ancestral lands. As they were *amalala*, that is, were members of an ethnically-defined class of super-exploited tributaries, their incentive for flight was the greater.[47] Even among the more privileged fugitives, personal fidelity to Mpande was by no means always the motive for joining the flight. Zulu kaNogandaya, for example, perhaps the greatest of Shaka's warriors, who had been admitted to the ranks of the military *izinduna* in recognition of his courage, despised Mpande as a coward. Moreover, he doubted his own prospects of survival under Mpande's leadership, particularly as he had earlier succeeded in wooing a girl whom Mpande also desired. He and his party therefore seized the first opportunity after crossing the Thukela to seek refuge with the English settlers at Port Natal and he was never to return to his native land.[48] Others joined the southward flight to avoid further conflict with the Boers, or because they shared the widespread disenchantment with Dingane's policies, particularly his proposals for northward resettlement. In any event, it must have been clear to many that, by association, they had become implicated in Mpande's recent disloyalty to Dingane, so that flight offered the best chance of survival. Indeed, Mpande himself may have had no other purpose in mind, for it has been suggested that he had at the time no ambitions for a political and military alliance with the Boers but was driven to this by the pressures that were exerted on him after his flight.[49]

An incident which occurred during Mpande's brief sojourn in Natal illustrates the low esteem in which he was held by many of his party. At the same time as Mpande was designated 'Prince of the Emigrant Zulus', by the Boers, Mpangazitha kaMncumbatha, formerly an important functionary under Dingane, was appointed by them as one of his *izinduna*. Shortly afterwards, Mpangazitha was mauled to death by the crowds in attendance. Historical interpretations of this event differ, but Zulu oral testimony portrays Mpangazitha's death as the expression of popular feeling against a man notorious for his overbearing ways, explicitly denying Mpande's complicity. The incident therefore suggests that Mpande's attraction as king to many of his influential followers lay in the belief that he was a weak man whose wishes could easily be flouted.[50]

If the allegiance of many of Mpande's southern supporters was dubious and if his followers were fewer than some estimates suggest, his influence in the north, where he was an unknown quantity, was even more tenuous. Mpande assured the Boers that he could count on the loyalty of three northern chiefs[51] but he failed to identify them. He may have been referring, among others, to Klwana kaNgqengelele, of the Buthelezi people, and

Maphitha kaSojiyisa of the Mandlakazi branch of the Zulu royal house, who had tendered their submission to the Boer commando shortly after Dingane's final defeat.[52] Mpande's appeal to these men may be attributed to common prudence, but they may also have been influenced by his reputation for weakness. Maphitha, for example, was a powerful person in his own right, whose responsibilities included superintendence of the tributary chiefdoms in the vicinity of the Lubombo mountains. He was in fact quick to exploit the unsettled conditions that followed Mpande's accession, appropriating to himself many of Dingane's cattle and *isigodlo* girls before forwarding the remainder to the new king.[53]

Mpande's problems were further compounded by the terms that the Boers imposed on him. Even before then, the Trekkers had insisted that Dingane demobilize his young regiments and allow their members to marry. Dingane had complied, ostensibly in deference to their demands, but in reality to facilitate his proposed settlement of southern Swaziland, realizing that this would require accelerated homestead formation.[54] Ingenious as this was from Dingane's viewpoint, the move greatly weakened the military power base of his successor. In 1840 the Trekkers went further. Apart from seizing a vast herd of 36 000 cattle, they designated the Black Mfolozi as the new boundary, thereby depriving Mpande of half the former kingdom (see Map 7). They also required that Mpande recognize their overlordship, specifically requiring him not to carry out executions for witchcraft or to wage war against other African chiefdoms without their consent. In the event, neither the territorial provisions, nor Boer suzerainty, were translated into effective action,[55] but this was not something Mpande could have known at the time.

However, like Dingane before him, one of Mpande's main assets was that the institution of kingship had acquired widespread acceptance. Thus, like his predecessors, he continued to enrol *amabutho*, to control marriages, to maintain *izigodlo*, to officiate at national ceremonies and to exercise the other rights and duties of kingship. With these assets, his position was relatively secure, provided he could control the members of the ruling lineage who might otherwise serve as the rallying point for rebellion on the part of his subjects and chiefs.[56]

By contrast, it has sometimes been argued that during the 1840s and early 1850s the outflow of refugees to Natal from the Zulu kingdom reached enormous proportions, indicating that the very idea of kingship and the state was being negated.[57] Although this argument is based upon contemporary statistics, Theophilus Shepstone (see Chapter 7) himself

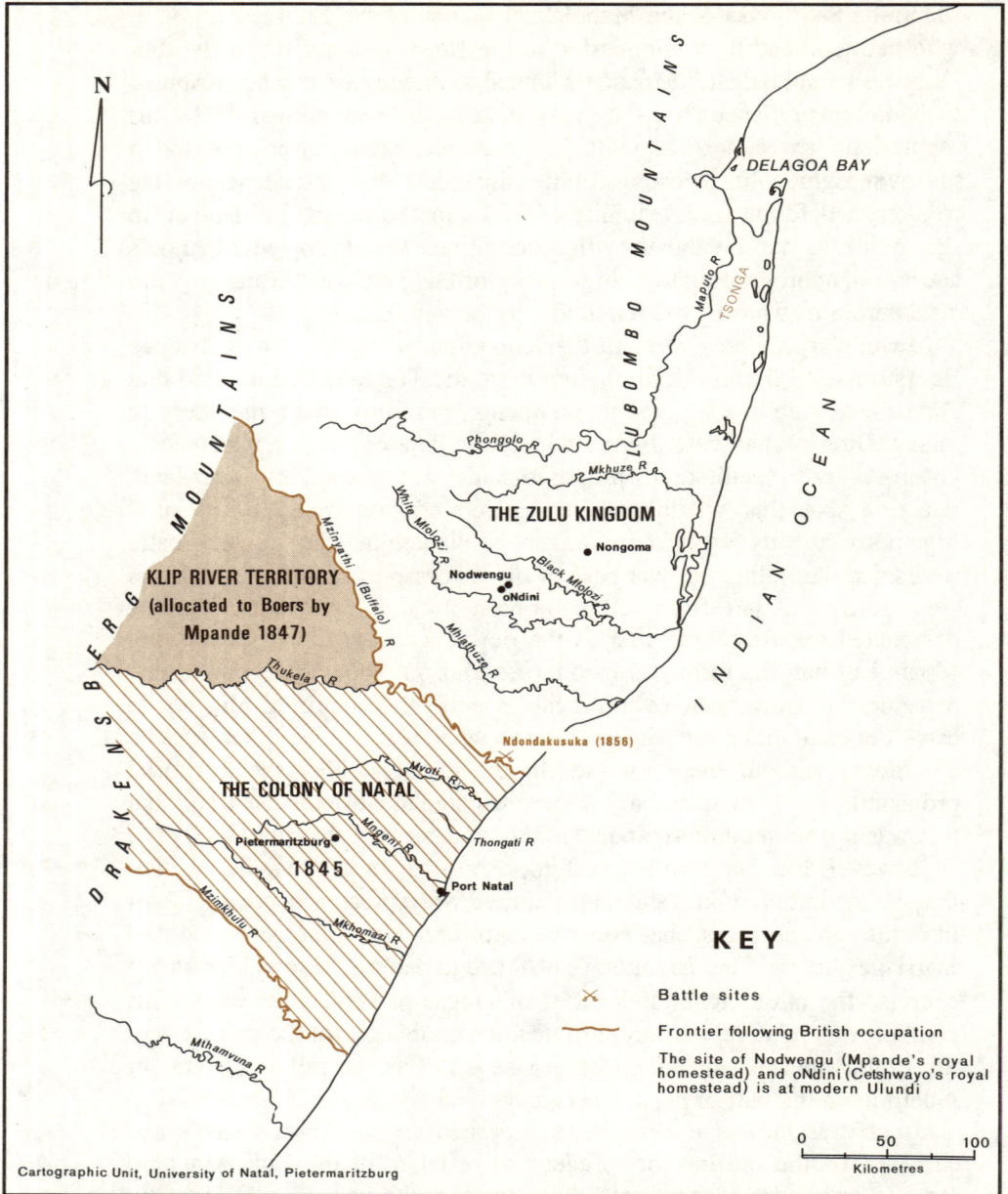

Map 8   The Zulu kingdom and the Colony of Natal, 1840–79

believed that these estimates were greatly exaggerated.[58] Moreover, the largest influx appears to have occurred in the early 1840s, when by far the majority of refugees were people who had never been fully assimilated into Zulu society. It is true that the general problem was serious enough for Mpande to take steps to staunch the outflow. It is also true that at various times during the 1840s and 1850s, he depopulated a strip of territory along his southern frontier, establishing military posts there. For their part, the authorities in the Colony repatriated refugees' cattle to Zululand, introduced new regulations in 1854 to provide for the apprenticeship of fugitives to white employers for a period of three years, and even contemplated the appointment of a resident in southern Zululand. Even so, it is unlikely that the refugee question was ever much more than an irritant.[59]

Very little is known about the first years of Mpande's reign. The prospect of renewed Boer intervention no doubt caused him to act with circumspection. By the same token, it probably encouraged widespread Zulu acceptance of his leadership. At a very early stage, he seems to have realized that the way to counter the Boer threat to his kingdom was to seek the support of the British settler community. As early as 1841, he began cautiously to cultivate the goodwill of the British garrison at Port Natal and by 1842/3 he had given a pledge of Zulu military support against the Trekkers, though this was never taken up.[60]

Within weeks of the British victory over the Boers at Port Natal in mid-1842 (see Chapter 5), Mpande acted to secure his internal position, attacking those of his subjects who had taken up residence near the mission station of the Reverend Aldin Grout at Empangeni, so forcing the missionary to leave Zululand. Like his predecessors, Mpande viewed religious affinity as being indistinguishable from political allegiance.[61] At much the same time, he attacked those who had remained loyal to Dingane in 1839, seizing their cattle. The survivors fled to Natal, where they were pejoratively dubbed 'Ndhlela's rectum'.[62] In about 1843, he then turned on Gqugqu, the only other surviving son of Senzangakhona, whose genealogical claims to the kingship may have been stronger than his own. Gqugqu appears to have been building up local support in the vicinity of the Ntontela barracks in south-eastern Zululand and, following his death, some two to three thousand people led by Mawa, the sister of Senzangakhona and the *inkosikazi* of Ntontela, fled to Natal, taking numerous cattle with them.[63]

Not all of Mpande's domestic initiatives can be dated with such precision, but his reign is remembered in oral tradition for the frequency with which he expropriated the herds of his most affluent subjects.[64] His more regular resort to this time-honoured practice whereby the Zulu kings eliminated their over-mighty subjects may have arisen from the depletion of the national herd by the Boers as well as by the flight of refugees. But, like his predecessor, Mpande did not rely on coercion alone. He raised up several of his favourites as local administrators and entered into marriage alliances with men of wealth and influence. This strategy was facilitated by the large size of his *izigodlo* and was made more attractive by the inflated bride-price he could demand. He was also known for the liberality with which he *sisa'd* (loaned) cattle, thus building up an extensive network of dependents.[65]

Military expeditions abroad did not occur during Mpande's reign on the same scale as they had under his predecessors, though he was by no means inactive. From the outset of his reign, his main objective was Swaziland, which he saw as a rich source of cattle and a potential territorial haven. Initially, too, he must have been disturbed at the growing friendship that developed between the Trekkers of Natal and the Swazi, dating from the time of Dingane's defeat. Restrained for the time being from actively prosecuting his plans by the likelihood of Boer, and later British, disapprobation, he concentrated on launching a number of raids against several minor tributary chiefdoms to the north-west of his kingdom, including those of Langalibalele, Magonondo and Phutini. In Langalibalele's case, he was probably motivated by anxiety at that chief's growing independence on a particularly sensitive frontier. A dynastic dispute in Swaziland in 1846 provided him with his long-awaited opportunity and, having first pre-empted British censure by making it appear that the Swazi were the aggressors, he launched an attack late in 1846 which netted many cattle, following this up with a full-scale invasion early in the ensuing year. Large tracts of southern Swaziland were at first brought under Zulu control but, after the Swazi had sought refuge in caves and had entered into an alliance with the party of Trekkers which had recently settled in the eastern Transvaal, the Zulu were forced to withdraw.[66]

It was during this period that the most serious rupture occurred between the Zulu kingdom and the Colony of Natal. The dispute arose after Mpande allowed a group of Boers to establish an independent republic under his overlordship in the Klip River district during the first half of 1847, thereby violating the Anglo-Zulu treaty of 1843 which had established the Thukela and Mzinyathi rivers as the border. One reason why he embarked on this risky course may have been that he had never been fully reconciled to the loss of the Klip River district, which historically had been an important area for tribute extraction and which contained rich grazing lands. In addition, the region was strategically important because it straddled the escape route of refugees across the Mzinyathi. Mpande may also have reasoned that, if the district were controlled by Boer vassals, the British would be less able to intervene against him in his operations against the Swazi. Perhaps too, there was an element of pique and desperation: having failed late in 1846 to obtain British military assistance against the Swazi and their eastern Transvaal allies, he hoped to match the latter's firepower by recruiting his own Boer gunmen. A further possibility is that he hoped to nullify the Swazi-Boer alliance, realizing that the Transvalers were unlikely to fire on their kinsmen when hostilities against the Swazi recommenced. Whatever the reason, Mpande repudiated the alliance in late 1847, after strong objections had been raised by the British Government. As it happened, by then he no longer had any need of Boer assistance against the Swazi.[67]

During 1848, Mpande recommenced his offensives upon Langalibalele and Phutini, who thereupon fled to Natal. His objective was to secure a bridgehead preparatory to a further attack on south-western Swaziland, which he then proceeded to launch. Temporarily without their Transvaal allies, the Swazi were obliged to submit and may even have become his tributaries. Mpande may have had to stop short of outright conquest because a series of minor crises blew up at this time with the British at his rear over a number of infringements of the Natal boundary. Moreover, Sir Harry Smith's victory over the Boers at Boomplaats in August 1848 may finally have convinced him of the extent of British power.[68] Henceforward, Mpande went out of his way to avoid provoking Natal.

The final onslaught on the Swazi occurred in 1852, after they had attempted under Mswati to free themselves from Zulu overlordship. A very large Zulu force succeeded in capturing numerous cattle, but Mpande was again obliged to back off, not only because of British disapproval but because many of his leading chiefs had opposed the expedition from the outset.[69]

While the Zulu were engaged in these operations in Swaziland and its south-western environs, Mpande reasserted Zulu overlordship over the Tsonga people to the north-east, who had long been suppliers of valuable tribute to the kingdom. The opportunity to intervene decisively occurred when a dynastic dispute developed in the Mabhudu chiefdom, enabling

This illustration from a nineteenth-century publication showing Mpande seated in the foreground with an elephant being dismembered and its foot about to be roasted was, like other early pictorial representations, processed in England, but it seems to retain much of its authenticity.

Courtesy of S. Bourquin

Mpande to elevate his own candidate, Noziyingeli, to the chieftainship. The Zulu army was also active in 1851 in an attack upon the Pedi in the north-eastern Transvaal, the outcome of this operation being unclear.[70]

By the early 1850s, Mpande was at the height of his power. So confident was he that in 1849 he risked allowing the return of missionaries to Zululand, in the person of Hans Schreuder, whose most immediate appeal was his skill in alleviating his ailments.[71] The next few years were, however, to witness a dramatic reversal of his fortunes, for a succession dispute erupted into full-scale civil conflict early in December 1856. The main protagonists were two of Mpande's sons, Cetshwayo and Mbuyazi, whose supporters were known respectively as the *Usuthu* and *Isigqoza*. Behind the rivalry of these two claimants lay a host of political and economic frustrations and aspirations.[72]

In Zulu society, there existed an elaborate set of rules governing succession and inheritance. Expressed in their simplest form, they stipulated that the heir to a chief or king was the first-born son of the great wife, who was specifically wedded for this purpose. Whereas a commoner's heir was the eldest son by the first wife, a chief would choose his great wife only when he was advanced in years, so as to minimize the risk of usurpation. In practice, it was seldom possible to order matters so neatly and the rules of succession, far from being an immutable prescription, could be manipulated, especially by means of genealogical gerrymandering. This meant that they did not preclude competition, although they did succeed in defining the field of competitors, providing a legitimating basis for their respective claims.[73]

In Mpande's case, as well as those of his immediate predecessors, these rules had apparently been set aside, for he had forcibly dethroned Dingane, Dingane had assassinated Shaka and Shaka had supplanted Sigujana, for a brief period Senzangakhona's successor as Zulu chief. Indeed, Mpande was to proclaim, as he surveyed the growing animosity between his two sons:

> I won my kingship by force of arms; so must others do likewise . . . Our house did not gain the kingship by being appointed to sit on a mat . . . Our house gained the kingship by stabbing with the assegai.[74]

In this instance, however, events were to show that flouting the settled principle of succession was by no means the preferred option among the Zulu, nor a guarantee of success.

Mpande himself had not always displayed such contempt for the conventions. Contrary to the assertion that he had never clearly designated an heir,[75] he had in fact nominated Cetshwayo, at the time of his sojourn in Natal.[76] He had however changed his mind by the early 1850s and, when he began to foster Mbuyazi's cause, he claimed the right to repudiate his earlier action on the grounds that he himself had not been king at the time. He further argued that, as he had fathered Mbuyazi for Shaka, Mbuyazi was therefore, in terms of Zulu levirate custom, the true heir to the great founding father.[77] It would seem that it was only when this manipulation of the ideology of succession had clearly failed to undermine support for Cetshwayo's candidature, that Mpande began to advocate a more violent solution, in the hope thereby of securing Mbuyazi's right of succession. Perhaps he was only trying to intimidate his opponents to acquiesce. In the event, he merely strengthened their resolve.

Cetshwayo was born in the late 1820s or early 1830s. He was the son of Ngqumbazi, the daughter of Mbonde, the Zungu chief.[78] At some stage during the 1840s, Mpande set up Ngqumbazi in her own royal homestead, along with a number of other wives associated with her house. This homestead, Gqikazi, was situated in the northern marches of the kingdom, not far from the present Nongoma. Such practices were common for they enabled the king to spread his control and to prevent quarrels between co-wives and rival sons, while taking better advantage of available natural resources.[79] In the case of Gqikazi, the need to extend royal influence was an especially important factor, for it was in this area that Masiphula, his leading councillor, and Maphitha, who were already immensely influential in the affairs of state, had their regional power bases. When Gqikazi was estabished, Mpande refused to allow his sons to accompany their mothers, for he realized that the dispersal of royal homesteads facilitated the formation of potentially dangerous dynastic and regional alliances, and would provide the princes with the opportunity to cultivate personal followings. In Cetshwayo's case, his prohibition proved only temporarily effective. Possibly because Mpande was prevented by his infirmities from visiting the region in person, Cetshwayo was soon able to build up a core of support centred on the Gqikazi and associated Bazeni homesteads.[80]

The structure of Zulu military institutions lent itself to Cetshwayo's purpose. It is often assumed that, until such time as the soldiers were demobilized after many years of service, the Zulu age regiments were permanently stationed at the various centrally-located royal headquarters to which they had been allocated. In reality, the period of active service was not continuous. Normally, sections of each regiment, sufficient only to cater for the immediate requirements of the royal household, took turns in serving at the royal barracks. This arrangement may have been a recent innovation necessitated by the curtailment of raiding opportunities, but it may equally have been devised by Shaka himself.[81] Mpande thus did not have an absolute monopoly of coercive power, though the forces at his disposal outnumbered those available to any of his subordinates, provided that there were no alternative focuses of loyalty such as the one Cetshwayo was beginning to establish. Cetshwayo was also able to take advantage of the practice whereby young recruits foregathered for a fairly protracted period at particular royal homesteads, before proceeding to the king to be enrolled in a regiment. Special bonds developed between these prospective soldiers and the princes attached to the homestead where they had initially assembled. These ties tended to be consolidated over time, since soldiers were permitted to undertake their periodic service at the royal barracks nearest their own homes, rather than at their generally more distant regimental headquarters. This meant that the hard core of Cetshwayo's Usuthu party was drawn from all the king's regiments.[82]

By 1856, Cetshwayo could count on the support not only of his immediate adherents, but also on that of the leading chiefs. Two significant supporters were Masiphula and Maphitha, who had numerous followers of their own, and could use their powerful positions in the national political and military structure to ensure that others followed suit.[83] Their support of Cetshwayo may have arisen from their belief that they would be able to manipulate him once they had installed him as king. Another possibility is that Mpande's frequent expropriation of livestock belonging to his richer subjects caused them to look for a possible successor. It is also possible that their opposition was provoked by Mpande's policy towards the Swazi, as well as Natal and the Pedi.[84]

The opposition to Mpande which was now emerging around the person of Cetshwayo was able to capitalize on widespread popular grievances in Zulu society. These centred mainly on the military system and, more particularly, on the decline in raiding which had occurred as the result of settler expansion. Notwithstanding Mpande's various campaigns, his policy of domestic confiscation and his generosity in loaning cattle, he was failing to provide sufficient booty to satisfy his followers and meat to feed his troops. As he met the shortage by plundering his wealthy chiefs, they in turn made further demands upon their subordinates.[85] The resultant discontent was further heightened by famine in 1852–3 and by Mpande's

This photograph, one of the earliest taken in Natal, shows Joshua Walmesley with the frontiersman John Dunn (left) prior to the Battle of Ndondakusuka in 1856.

Local History Museum, Durban

deferment of the age of demobilization. This policy was dictated by Dingane's premature demobilization of so many of his soldiers in the late 1830s, thereby creating a shortfall in active manpower reserves.[86] Many disaffected soldiers now backed Cetshwayo because they saw in a civil upheaval the prospect of a large-scale redistribution of cattle.

It can thus be seen that, when in the early 1850s Mpande began to favour Mbuyazi, Cetshwayo had already built up a basis of support which ruled out both assassination as well as successful intrigue on Mbuyazi's behalf.[87] By the latter part of 1856, when the crisis was rapidly coming to a head, Mpande saw the need for external support. He instructed the *Isigqoza* to occupy the south-eastern corner of his kingdom, his former sphere of influence, and to solicit the assistance of Natal. Mbuyazi visited Joshua Walmesley, the Natal border agent, but emerged only with the backing of John Dunn, the white frontiersman whose extraordinary involvement in Zulu affairs now began, and a handful of African gunmen. The mercenary force was not sufficient to deter Cetshwayo and, within days, the *Isigqoza* were overwhelmed at Ndondakusuka, near the mouth of the Thukela. The pursuing Usuthu force, numbering 15 000 men, was more than twice as strong.[88] Mbuyazi and five other of Mpande's sons died, as did several thousand of his followers. Some were killed in the battle itself; others died in flight, attempting to cross the swollen river.

Cetshwayo's military ascendancy was thus assured. For the best part of the ensuing decade, Mpande survived only by employing considerable guile and ingenuity. He unsuccessfully sought support from Natal, and even briefly flirted once more with the Boers. For a time, he successfully created the impression in his kingdom that such help would be forthcoming, largely by means of pointing to the assistance which Dunn had given to Mbuyazi at Ndondakusuka. Early in 1857, two of Mbuyazi's brothers, Mkhungo and Sikhotha, fled to Natal, where they enjoyed the patronage of both Theophilus Shepstone and Bishop Colenso and this he could again produce as evidence of white support. During the latter part of the 1850s, Mpande also allowed a greatly increased amount of missionary activity, both because he wished to create a favourable impression in Natal, and because he sought the services of the missionaries as political advisers and as interlocuters with the Colony.[89]

These subterfuges did not prevent Cetshwayo from continuing to consolidate his political position, so that by late 1857 Mpande was obliged to accept an arrangement whereby they shared power, with himself as the lesser partner. Undeterred, he began to groom yet another of his sons, Mthonga, as his successor. Tension, occasionally erupting in factional violence, continued and was not dispelled even after Shepstone had visited Zululand early in 1861 and, from motives of his own, proclaimed Cetshwayo heir (see Chapter 7). Even so, Mpande had not become a mere figurehead. Despite his ill health, he continued to perform rituals, while his sanction was still required in important matters of policy such as the enrolment of regiments and the granting of permission to marry. He could still, moreover, count on British and Boer support to restrain his son. By 1865, he and Cetshwayo were finally reconciled, for they both recognized the need to present a united front in the face of growing Boer encroachment in north-western Zululand. After this, he began to withdraw more and more from national affairs, and two years later he allowed Cetshwayo to don the headring and so to acquire the formal status of manhood.[90]

Perhaps the most serious legacy of the protracted dynastic struggle was that it gave rise to territorial disputes with the Transvaal Boers. Both protagonists in the civil war had at various stages in the early 1860s attempted to buy the support of Boer mercenaries by means of allowing them to occupy land.[91] When the Boers claimed that the land had been ceded to them, the Zulus could only plead in vain for British arbitration.

Mpande, who died in 1872, has remained an underrated figure in Zulu history. Whatever his failures, he must surely be given credit for the fact that his kingdom, although bruised, was intact when he died.

Cetshwayo, whose reign formally began on his father's death, had to cope with a number of problems both at home and abroad, of which the lingering Transvaal land dispute was the most urgent. He was also to be confronted by the effects of the discovery of diamonds in Griqualand West in the late 1860s. This led to intensified capitalist development that was to affect all parts of the subcontinent, enormously enhancing the strength of the European presence in South Africa.[92] In the new era of economic growth, furthermore, the wish of imperial policymakers to tie up British interests in the subcontinent was to produce the idea of a confederation later in the 1870s. For the Zulu kingdom, this meant that its parochial territorial squabbles with the Transvaal, which was annexed by Britain in 1877, became of far wider geopolitical significance. After being regarded as a useful check on Boer expansion, the Zulu kingdom came to be regarded as a dangerous hindrance to the achievement of confederation, so that its destruction became an unavoidable necessity (see Chapter 7).

All this lay in the future, however. Meanwhile, Cetshwayo recognized that the protracted dispute with his father had left the kingdom in no condition to meet the challenges of an increasingly hostile world. By the late 1860s, he had already begun to reassert Zulu interests in the territories to the north and north-east of the kingdom. He had also initiated a large-scale firearms procurement programme,[93] with the object of securing the Zulu state against external threat and, with Mpande's death clearly imminent, of defeating any possible princely challenge. His first act as king was to invite Shepstone to preside over his formal installation, hoping thereby to ensure Natal's support in the boundary dispute with the Boers, as well as to put paid to the dynastic pretensions of Mkhungo, and more especially Mthonga, who were both still at large. As it happened, this was a serious mistake, for it lent credibility to Shepstone's privately-held dreams of expansion (see Chapter 7).[94] Moreover, in the late 1870s, Shepstone and High Commissioner Frere were to cite Cetshwayo's non-compliance with guidelines put forward for the amelioration of Zulu governance at the 'coronation', as additional justifications for war.[95]

Cetshwayo attempted to consolidate his position at home by raising up a number of new chiefs to counterbalance the influence of those who had exploited the earlier dynastic rivalry for their own aggrandisement.[96] Where regimental discipline and morale had declined, he enforced the marriage regulations with fresh vigour[97] and prepared for a new round of campaigning against the Swazi. The Swazi kingdom was by then enticing not only as a traditional raiding ground, but also because, freed from Zulu attack since the mid-1850s, it had emerged as the dominant power in south-central Mozambique and was thus in a position to threaten valuable tribute resources, as well as the supply of firearms through Delagoa Bay. Moreover, like his predecessors, Cetshwayo thought of Swaziland as the territory to which he could retreat and establish a new state in the event of his expulsion from Zululand, a prospect which seemed increasingly real as the 1870s progressed. The lure of conquest and of booty was at this time made even more attractive because Zululand was experiencing a resource crisis, caused by unfavourable climatic conditions, pasture degeneration, lungsickness epidemics, the export of cattle, the maldistribution of wealth, and possibly population growth.

Cetshwayo's plans regarding the Swazi were thwarted by the opposition of the Natal Government, whose goodwill he still regarded as vital to the resolution of the boundary dispute with the Boers, and by the opposition of certain of his leading chiefs. He therefore had to be satisfied with the seizure of a number of mountain fastnesses in the Lubombo range, which might serve as a useful launching pad for later expansion into southern Swaziland, and was obliged to embark upon a far less ambitious programme of cautious expansion across the Phongolo. He is known to have sent several missions to the Pedi, with a view to forming an alliance against their common enemies, the Swazi and the Transvaal Boers, but nothing seems to have resulted.[98]

Cetshwayo's political initiatives, like those of Mpande, did not extend to major institutional reform. This meant that the structural basis of Zulu society remained recognizably the same as it had been in the days of Shaka.[99] Not even the missionaries, many of whom blamed their failure upon the obstruction of the Zulu authorities, had made any real impression (see Chapter 11). By the late 1870s, their relations with Cetshwayo had reached crisis point, largely as a result of the publication by one of them of very damaging reports in the Durban Press about political conditions in Zululand. With good reason, he also suspected that they were party to moves to persuade the British Government to undertake a war to destroy his kingdom. By the beginning of 1878 all of them had left.[100]

Greater than the impact of the missionaries was that of the hunters and traders, who for decades had been attracted by the kingdom's resources of cattle and game. A recent study has argued that the self-sufficiency of the Zulu economy was not irretrievably undermined, and that trade with Natal was assimilated into existing economic patterns, so that 'traditional' processes and the relations of production were not greatly affected.[101] This possibly underestimates some of the consequences of trade. The importation of large numbers of hoes, a standard barter commodity, for example, helped undermine the indigenous iron-working industry, while the firepower available to the hunters from Natal resulted in a drastic decline in game resources. As regards Zulu cattle holdings, the impact of the traders should also not be underrated, especially as they introduced and transmitted cattle diseases, of which lungsickness was the most lethal. By the late 1870s, Cetshwayo was obliged to fund the purchase of firearms by allowing the recruitment of labourers drawn from petty Tsonga tributary chiefdoms, obtaining in return a rake-off in capitation fees as well as a healthy proportion of the labourers' earnings.[102]

These developments again illustrate the extent to which, at the outbreak of the Anglo-Zulu War in 1879, the Zulu economy was becoming more enmeshed in the capitalist system. Not the least important consequence was that it encouraged the ambitions of Cetshwayo's subordinates, most notably Zibhebhu kaMaphitha.

Notes

1   I wish to thank Professor Colin Webb and John Wright for their comments on an early draft of this chapter. For any remaining deficiencies I alone am responsible.

2   Bryant, *Olden Times*, p. 659.

3   Thompson, 'Co-Operation and Conflict', p. 351. But see also Fuze, *The Black People*, p. 71.

4   C. A. Hamilton, 'Shaka: One Kind of Folklore or the Other', *Weekly Mail*, 6 November 1986, p. 22.

5   Bryant, *Olden Times*, pp. 666–8; Wright and Manson, *The Hlubi Chiefdom*, pp. 21–3.

6   Bryant, *Olden Times*, pp. 668–9.

7   Ibid., pp. 122–3, 668–70.

8   Ibid., p. 626.

9   C. A. Hamilton, 'The AmaLala in Natal, 1750–1826' (unpublished seminar paper, Department of History, University of the Witwatersrand, 1982), p. 5.

10   Bryant, *Olden Times*, p. 674; F. N. C. Okoye, 'Dingane: a Reappraisal', *Journal of African History*, 10, 2 (1969), p. 221; Slater, 'Transitions in the Political Economy of South-East Africa', pp. 307–8, 348.

11   Bryant, *Olden Times*, p. 671; Hedges, 'Trade and Politics', pp. 211, 221; 'Cetywayo's Story of the Zulu Nation and the War', *A Zulu King Speaks*, eds. C. de B. Webb and J. B. Wright (Pietermaritzburg and Durban, University of Natal Press and Killie Campbell Africana Library, 1979), p. 10.

12   Bryant, *Olden Times*, pp. 391, 614–15.

13   Ibid., pp. 389, 413, 493–4, 601–3; Bryant, *A History of the Zulu People*, pp. 51–3, 84ff; Fuze, *The Black People*, pp. 73, 83–4; Wright and Manson, *The Hlubi Chiefdom*, pp. 24–8.

14   Bryant, *Olden Times*, pp. 46–7, 49.

15   Ibid., p. 324; Bonner, *Kings, Commoners and Concessionaires*, pp. 40–2; R. Rasmussen, *Migrant Kingdom: Mzilikazi's Ndebele in South Africa* (London and Cape Town, Rex Collings and David Philip, 1978), p. 87.

16   Killie Campbell Africana Library, JSP, File 58, Notebook 15: Evidence of Mtshapi kaNoradu, 11 May 1918, pp. 23–31.

17   Slater, 'Transitions in the Political Economy of South-East Africa', pp. 312–14; Hedges, 'Trade and Politics', pp. 211, 214, 223.

18   Bryant, *Olden Times*, p. 398; Rasmussen, *Migrant Kingdom*, pp. 128–9.

19   Bryant, *Olden Times*, p. 322.

20   Okoye, 'Dingane', p. 233.

21   Hedges, 'Trade and Politics', pp. 248–9; Smith, 'The Trade of Delagoa Bay as a Factor in Nguni Politics', pp. 188–9.

22   Okoye, 'Dingane', p. 224.

23   G. Liesegang, 'Dingane's Attack on Lourenço Marques in 1833', *Journal of African History*, 10, 4 (1969), pp. 56–79; Hedges, 'Trade and Politics', p. 242–4.

24   Okoye, 'Dingane' pp. 223–4; Hedges, 'Trade and Politics', pp. 244, 246.

25   Okoye, 'Dingane', pp. 225–7.

26   Hedges, 'Trade and Politics', p. 245; Okoye, 'Dingane', p. 225.

27   Hedges, 'Trade and Politics', p. 231–2, 241, 245; Slater, 'Transitions', pp. 310, 386–7.

28   Hamilton, 'The AmaLala in Natal', p. 30.

29   Wilson and Thompson, *Oxford History of South Africa*, 1, p. 352; Maylam, *History of the African Peoples*, p. 83.

30   Hedges, 'Trade and Politics', p. 246.

31   Bryant, *Olden Times*, pp. 388, 399, 546, 560.

32   Slater, 'Transitions', pp. 372–400.

33   Omer-Cooper, *Zulu Aftermath*, p. 46.

34   Wilson and Thompson, *Oxford History of South Africa*, p. 359.

35   Slater, 'Transitions', pp. 408–9.

36   Omer-Cooper, *Zulu Aftermath*, p. 44.

37   Okoye, 'Dingane', pp. 234–5.

38   Wilson and Thompson, *Oxford History of South Africa*, 1, pp. 359–60.

39   Bonner, *Kings, Commoners and Concessionaires*, p. 44.

40   For a recent restatement of this view see D. Denoon and B. Nyeko, *Southern Africa since 1800* (London, Longman, 1984 edition), p. 78.

41   Bonner, *Kings, Commoners and Concessionaires*; P. A. Kennedy, 'The Fatal Diplomacy: Sir Theophilus Shepstone and the Zulu Kings, 1839–1879' (unpublished Ph.D. thesis, UCLA, 1976); R. Mael, 'The Problems of Political Integration in the Zulu Empire' (unpublished Ph.D. thesis, UCLA, 1974). These studies cover aspects of Mpande's foreign policy, his relationship with Natal and the succession dispute with his son Cetshwayo, but his kingship as such awaits systematic investigation.

42   Minutes of the Volksraad, 15 October 1839, Bird, *Annals of Natal*, 1, p. 537; Webb and Wright, *James Stuart Archive*, 2, p. 162.

43   J. B. Wright and D. R. Edgecombe, 'Mpande kaSenzangakhona, *c.* 1798–1872', *Black Leaders in Southern African History*, ed. C. Saunders (London, Heinemann, 1979), p. 47; Webb and Wright, *James Stuart Archive*, 3, p. 82.

44   Ibid., 1, pp. 19, 127, 198; 2, pp. 88–9, 200–1.

45   Bonner, *Kings, Commoners and Concessionaires*, pp. 42–2; Wright and Edgecombe, 'Mpande', p. 49.

46   Mael, 'Political Integration in the Zulu Empire', pp. 89–90.

47   *BPP* Despatch with Enclosures from Lt. Governor Scott to His Grace the Duke of Newcastle, No. 34, 1864, Native Affairs (published separately, 26 February 1864), *passim*; Hamilton and Wright, 'The Making of the Lala', pp. 1–22.

48   Webb and Wright, *James Stuart Archive*, 2, pp. 181–2.

49   Minutes of the Volksraad, 15 October 1839, cited in Bird, *Annals of Natal*, 1, p. 538.

50   Mael, 'Political Integration in the Zulu Empire', pp. 96–7; Webb and Wright, *James Stuart Archive*, 2, p. 237; 3, p. 128.

51   Minutes of the Volksraad, 15 October 1839, cited in Bird, *Annals of Natal*, 1, p. 539.

52   A. Delegorgue, *Travels in Southern Africa*, cited in Bird, *Annals of Natal*, 1, p. 573.

53   Bryant, *History of the Zulu*, p. 19; JSP, File 70, Evidence of Socwatsha kaPapu, 1 January 1902 and 24 January 1904, pp. 12 and 104.

54   Bonner, *Kings, Commoners and Concessionaires*, pp. 42–3.

55   Kennedy, 'The Fatal Diplomacy', pp. 52–3.

56   This issue is discussed at length in M. Gluckmann, *Order and Rebellion in Tribal Africa* (London, Cohen and West, 1963); and M. Gluckmann, *Custom and Conflict in Africa* (Oxford, Oxford University Press, 1973 edition). See also Bonner, *Kings, Commoners and Concessionaires*, pp. 211–13, for the analogy in Swaziland.

57   P. A. Kennedy, 'Mpande and the Zulu Kingship', *Journal of Natal and Zulu History*, 4 (1981), p. 34.

58   *Natal Colony; Proceedings of the Commission Appointed to Inquire into the Past and Present State of the Kafirs in the District of Natal*, 6 (Pietermaritzburg, Archbell, 1852), p. 97.

59   Kennedy, 'The Fatal Diplomacy', pp. 98–9.

60   Kennedy, 'Mpande and the Zulu Kingship', p. 31.

61   Mael, 'Political Integration in the Zulu Empire', pp. 117–22.

62   JSP, File 58, Item 18: Evidence of Singfocela, 3 April 1910, pp. 4–5.

63   Mael, 'Political Integration in the Zulu Empire', p. 124; Webb and Wright, *James Stuart Archive*, 2, p. 216.

64   Ibid., 3, pp. 180–1.

65   Ibid., pp. 151–2; Kennedy, 'Mpande and the Zulu Kingship', p. 32; JSP, File 73: Evidence of Ndukwana kaMbengana, 12 September 1900, pp. 131–2.

66   Bonner, *Kings, Commoners and Concessionaires*, pp. 49–56; Wright and Manson, *The Hlubi Chiefdom*, pp. 23, 30–3.

67   M. M. Behn, 'The Klip River Insurrection, 1847' (unpublished MA thesis, Natal University College, 1932), *passim*; Kennedy, 'The Fatal Diplomacy', pp. 59–67.

68   Ibid., pp. 68–71, 81–9; Wright and Manson, *The Hlubi Chiefdom*, pp. 32–8; Wright and Edgecombe, 'Mpande', p. 52; Bonner, *Kings, Commoners and Concessionaires*, p. 60–1, 93.

69   Ibid., pp. 61–3.

70   Mael, 'Political Integration in the Zulu Empire', pp. 151–2; P. Delius, *The Land Belongs to Us: the Pedi Polity, the Boers and the British in the Nineteenth Century* (Johannesburg, Ravan Press, 1983), p. 30; Webb and Wright, *James Stuart Archive*, 1, pp. 63–5; 2, p. 142.

71   JSP, File 65, Item 4: Evidence of Revd Stavem, 2 June 1907, p. 1; Wright and Edgecombe, 'Mpande', p. 53.

72   N. A. Etherington, 'Anglo-Zulu Relations, 1856–78', *The Anglo-Zulu War: New Perspectives*, eds. A. H. Duminy and C. C. Ballard (Pietermaritzburg, University of Natal Press, 1981), p. 15. In this essay, he argues that the civil war 'emphasized anew the most fundamental defect in the constitution of the kingdom; the lack of a settled principle of succession'.

73   J. L. Comaroff, 'Rules and Rulers: Political Processes in a Tswana Chiefdom', *Man*, 13 (1978), pp. 1, 4 and 13.

74   Webb and Wright, *James Stuart Archive*, 2, p. 165.

75   Wright and Edgecombe, 'Mpande', p. 55.

76   Webb and Wright, *James Stuart Archive*, 2, pp. 215–16.

77   Ibid., p. 162; JSP, File 70: Evidence of Ndhlovu kaTimuni, 7 November 1902, p. 33.

78   Mael, 'Political Integration in the Zulu Empire', p. 168.

79   Webb and Wright, *James Stuart Archive*, 3, pp. 203, 267; J. J. Guy, 'Segmentation and Nguni History' (unpublished seminar paper, n.p., n.d.), pp. 1–3.

80   Mael, 'Political Integration in the Zulu Empire', pp. 170–1; Webb and Wright, *James Stuart Archive*, 3, p. 302; 1, p. 36.

81   Bryant, *The Zulu People*, p. 497; J. J. Guy, *The Destruction of the Zulu Kingdom* (London, Longman, 1979), pp. 55–6; J. Cobbing, 'The Evolution of the Ndebele Amabutho', *Journal of African History*, 15, 4 (1974), p. 607; Wright and Edgecombe, 'Mpande', p. 54.

82   Gluckman, 'The Kingdom of the Zulu', pp. 31–2; Mael, 'Political Integration in the Zulu Empire', p. 171; Webb and Wright, *James Stuart Archive*, 2, p. 244.

83   Ibid., p. 190, 227; JSP, File 70: Evidence of Ndhlovu kaTimuni, 7 November 1902, p. 34; File 57, Notebook 5: Evidence of Ndabazezwe ka Mfuleni, 24 June 1921, p. 6.

84   Mael, 'Political Integration in the Zulu Empire', pp. 176–7; Webb and Wright, *James Stuart Archive*, 3, p. 179.

85   Webb and Wright, *James Stuart Archive*, 1, p. 30; 2, p. 259; 3, pp. 180–1; JSP, File 60, Notebook 25: Evidence of Tununu ka Nonjiya, 1 June 1903,

p. 11; File 58, Notebook 15: Evidence of Mtshapi kaNoradu, 11 May 1918, pp. 38–40.

86   JSP, File 58, Notebook 5: Evidence of Socwatsha kaPapu, 27 August, 1921, p. 24; File 73: Evidence of Ndabazezwe kaMfuleni, 16 September, 1900, p. 139.

87   Webb and Wright, *James Stuart Archive*, 2, pp. 227, 241–3; 3, pp. 291–4; JSP, File 58, Notebook 17: Evidence of Mtshapi kaNoradu, 1 April 1918, pp. 3–8.

88   Kennedy, 'The Fatal Diplomacy', pp. 126–9; Webb and Wright, *James Stuart Archive*, 2, pp. 223–4; 3, pp. 291–4; JSP, File 58, Notebook 17: Evidence of Mtshapi kaNoradu, 1 April 1918, pp. 3–7.

89   Etherington, 'Anglo-Zulu Relations', pp. 16, 29.

90   Wright and Edgecombe, 'Mpande', p. 57–8.

91   Bonner, *Kings, Commoners and Concessionaires*, p. 113.

92   J. J. Guy, 'Cetshwayo kaMpande, *c*.1832–1884', *Black Leaders*, ed. C. Saunders, pp. 79–82.

93   J. J. Guy, 'A Note on Firearms in the Zulu Kingdom, with Special Reference to the Anglo-Zulu War, 1879', *Journal of African History*, 12, 4 (1971), pp. 557–70.

94   Etherington, 'Anglo-Zulu Relations', pp. 26–8, 34–7.

95   Brookes and Webb, *A History of Natal*, pp. 98, 134.

96   Mael, 'Political Integration in the Zulu Empire', footnote 15, p. 55.

97   Guy, *Destruction of the Zulu Kingdom*, pp. 38–9.

98   Bonner, *Kings, Commoners and Concessionaires*, pp. 129–50; Delius, *The Land Belongs to Us*, pp. 193, 232–8; P. Colenbrander, 'The Zulu Political Economy on the Eve of the War', *Anglo-Zulu War*, eds. Duminy and Ballard, pp. 82–92.

99   Guy, *Destruction of the Zulu Kingdom*, pp. 14–5, 18.

100 N. A. Etherington, 'The Rise of the Kholwa in South-Eastern Africa: African Christian Communities in Natal, Pondoland and Zululand, 1835–1880' (unpublished Ph.D. thesis, Yale University, 1971), pp. 181–200.

101 Ibid., pp. 17, 78, 83–7, 239–46.

102 Colenbrander, 'Zulu Political Economy', pp. 86–8; P. J. Colenbrander, 'External Exchange and the Zulu Kingdom: Towards a Reassessment', *Enterprise and Exploitation in a Victorian Colony: Aspects of the Economic and Social History of Colonial Natal*, eds. B. Guest and J. M. Sellers (Pietermaritzburg, University of Natal Press, 1985), pp. 99–121.

Chapter 5

Traders, Trekkers and colonists

CHARLES BALLARD

Lasting changes were brought about in those regions of the world that were part of the British Empire. From the humid 'oil rivers' of West Africa to the frigid reaches of Hudson's Bay in Canada, the impact of Britain's political economy was felt everywhere, as the colonies, protectorates and self-governing dominions produced raw materials for the industrial order and in turn provided markets for Britain's manufactures.

Just as the Industrial Revolution had transformed the economy and society of Britain, so too an indelible feature of British imperialism was the introduction of European material culture, Christianity and a capitalist ethos into non-European societies. This transmission was achieved through a multitude of agents as British traders, officials, missionaries and settlers made contact with the aboriginal inhabitants. British rule in south-eastern Africa thus inaugurated an era of major transformations for the region and its inhabitants.

The first permanent white settlement in south-east Africa was that established at Port Natal in 1824 (see Map 9) under the leadership of Francis Farewell and Henry Francis Fynn. Accompanied by four other adventurers from the Cape Colony, they acted as agents for Cape merchants who sought a large and ready market among the Zulu, from whom they could obtain ivory (including hippopotamus tusks), hides and maize.[1] They especially hoped to develop a flourishing trade with the northern Nguni and so capture some of the trade that was then flowing through Delagoa Bay.[2]

Fynn and Farewell fully recognized that they were beyond the protection of British law, which effectively terminated at the boundaries of the Cape Colony. Farewell wrote to Lord Charles Somerset, the Governor of the Cape Colony, urging the annexation of the Port Natal region, but Somerset,

Map 9   The Port Natal settlement
(Based on a map in A. E. Cubbin, 'Origins of the British Settlement at
Port Natal', Ph.D., UOFS, 1983)

*This drawing by H. F. Fynn of the settlement at Port Natal shows the homesteads of the
first white hunter-traders.*

in line with Colonial Office policy, refused to sanction any efforts by Farewell to lay claim to the area and implied that the traders were dependent upon their own resources in dealing with the indigenous peoples.[3] Pending a reply to this request, in August 1824 Fynn and Farewell opened communications with Shaka, and obtained permission to occupy and exercise authority over the land surrounding Port Natal. By obtaining permission to occupy land and to trade, they had, in effect, recognized the overlordship of the Zulu king. For his part, Shaka regarded the white traders as 'client-chiefs' and expected them to render 'service' to the Zulu state, like other tributary chiefs within the Zulu political orbit.[4]

The adoption of local African laws and customs was a significant feature of the settlement. Within six months of its establishment, northern Nguni refugees from the north began to congregate around it. Shaka's wars had depopulated the vicinity and a severe dislocation of chiefdoms had resulted. Once these uprooted Africans learned that the white traders had been given permission to settle, they began to cluster around them, seeking protection and a better livelihood.[5] These refugees were organized by the traders along African political lines, separated into villages acknowledging individual traders as their chiefs. The traders were too few in number and lacked the resources to impose a European-style, metropolitan system of government on them. Henry Fynn became chief of three homesteads, scattered from the Bluff southwards to the Mzimkhulu River. John Cane and Henry Ogle also governed three homesteads each, in the vicinity of the port.[6]

After 1832 other traders from British settlements in the eastern Cape joined the settlement, so that by 1838 the white population had increased to approximately forty.[7] These men also gathered refugees and fugitives from the Zulu kingdom as clients. James Collis, Robert Dunn, D. C. Toohey and Richard (Dick) King, assumed positions as chiefs over various homesteads.[8] Collis, Dunn, Alexander Biggar and his two sons brought numerous Khoikhoi (Hottentot) retainers with them when they arrived from the eastern Cape.[9] The Khoikhoi were employed in the same capacity as their counterparts in the Cape and Orange River regions – as hunters, interpreters and transport-riders.[10]

Another social characteristic of the settlement was the scarcity, if not total absence, of white women. The early settlers frequently took wives and concubines from the indigenous population.[11] In consummating these relationships, they frequently adhered to local African marriage customs, situating the wives' huts around their residences, as was the custom among

In 1835 Allen Gardiner, who had served as captain in the Royal Navy during the Napoleonic wars, established the Berea Mission Station on the hill above Port Natal. This illustration appeared in his book Narrative of a Journey to the Zooloo Country in South Africa in 1835 and 1836, *published after his return to England. He did not return to Natal but worked among the Indians in Bolivia, where he died of starvation in 1851.*

the Zulu.[12] Serious efforts were also made by several white chiefs to legitimize their marriages by means of lobola, the payment of the bride price in cattle.

While Port Natal's white population adapted to the culture of the Nguni-speaking people, their European values, in turn, made an impression on African society. The African refugees who had arrived at Port Natal were destitute, having been deprived of their most tangible source of wealth and status, cattle. They were forced to turn even more to hunting, fishing and agriculture to survive.[13] The traders at the port found this advantageous, for a regular supply of locally-produced foodstuffs meant they could devote more time and energy to their trading activities. African agriculturalists also freed them from the need to import expensive supplies from Algoa Bay or Cape Town. The Zulu kingdom, however, was influenced by the white traders to a much lesser extent than were the African refugees, for Shaka and his sucessor Dingane would not allow them to trade direct with their subjects.[14]

On 23 September 1828 king Shaka was assassinated. Dingane's subsequent efforts to legitimize his rule resulted in an increased flight of refugees to Port Natal. When this happened, the settlement was viewed more and more as a threat to the Zulu state.[15] The first rift in relations

developed in 1831, after the failure of Dingane's diplomatic mission to the
Cape Colony (see Chapter 4). Acting on the advice of his interpreter, Jacob
Msimbiti, who had spread unsubstantiated rumours of Cane's support of a
British plan for the invasion of Zululand, Dingane confiscated Cane's
cattle. This gave rise to the rumour that all the whites were to be liquidated.
Henry Fynn fled southward to the Illovu River, while the remaining whites
hid in the surrounding bush. It was not until several months later that the
traders returned, having received Dingane's assurances that they would not
be interfered with.[16]

In 1833 a second and more serious incident occurred when a Zulu
expedition was returning via Port Natal from an unsuccessful raid to
recover stolen cattle. Believing that the Zulu impi had killed several
traders, John Cane's clients reacted by attacking and killing 200 unresisting
members of the Zulu army.[17] Convinced that Dingane would seek revenge,
the British traders fled to Mpondoland. They eventually returned after
receiving another assurance from Dingane that no harm would come to
them.[18]

Dingane was clearly in a dilemma as to how he should deal with the
traders and their black wards. Like Shaka, he coveted the trade goods,
especially firearms, that the traders brought into Zululand, but the presence
of the Zulu exiles at the port, while not a direct challenge to his exercise of
power, nevertheless threatened to undermine his position at court. As early
as 1833, he was under pressure from his chiefs to send an impi to deal with
the refugees.[19]

In 1835 Dingane insisted that the British traders themselves halt the flow
of Zulu deserters, threatening to put a stop to their trading operations if this
was not done (see Chapter 4). The arrival of Allen Gardiner in February
1835 provided the means whereby a temporary solution to this impasse was
reached.[20] Gardiner was the first missionary to arrive in this frontier zone,
which previously had been exclusively a traders' preserve. Initially, the
traders gave him a cordial reception. They responded favourably to his
efforts to lay out the township of Durban, named after the Governor of the
Cape Colony, and to draw up a set of by-laws to control the population of
the settlement, while they also applauded his efforts to introduce
Christianity to the region.[21] He seemed the obvious person to intercede with
Dingane, and this he was persuaded to do. However, he succeeded in doing
no more than obtaining the king's agreement to respect the lives and
property of the inhabitants of the port, provided that in future all Zulu
escapees would be returned to Zululand.[22]

For three months there was an uneasy peace. Anxious to ingratiate himself with Dingane in order to begin mission work in the Zulu kingdom, Gardiner was instrumental in returning fugitives with the aid of the traders, notably James Collis. At the end of June 1835, however, two white traders violated the agreement by encouraging Zulus (especially young women) to renounce their allegiance and move to the port. Dingane retaliated by prohibiting all trade with the port, refusing to allow any European, with the exception of Gardiner, to cross the Thukela River. That the Zulu king did not launch an attack upon the settlement is attributable to the fact that all the traders and many of their African clients possessed firearms.[23]

In 1837 the balance of power between the Zulu kingdom and the growing settlement at Port Natal was affected by the arrival of Trekkers from the Cape Colony, under the leadership of Piet Retief and Gerrit Maritz. Their arrival encouraged the traders to hope that they would soon be released from the economic and political control of Dingane. On learning of the impending Trekker migration to Natal, the possibility had been raised of forming an alliance with them, not only to shake off Zulu overlordship but to establish 'a government of our own', which would be 'free from the false measures and wavering policy of the neighbouring [Cape] Colony'.[24]

The Trekkers constituted a much more serious threat to Zulu hegemony in south-east Africa than had the Port Natal trading settlement. The thirty-or-so traders and their African clients could be fairly easily contained in the vicinity of the port, whereas the more numerous Trekker pastoralists demanded large tracts of land in territory regarded by the Zulus as their sphere of influence. With their experience of over thirty years of almost continuous warfare on the Cape Colony's eastern and north-eastern frontiers, the Trekkers were also geared to military action. Before their arrival in Natal, they had shown in their military enagagements on the Highveld their capacity for offensive action, as well as their ability to establish defensive positions utilizing the laager. Dingane's reaction to Retief's request for a considerable amount of land was to kill the Boer leader and the other members of his party, and to launch a swift attack on the Boer encampments. Over 600, including women and children, were killed (see Chapter 4).

Dingane's actions cemented a Trekker-trader alliance to challenge Zulu military power. The first offensive against the Zulu state came from Port Natal, when an expedition of 2 100 Africans under Cane successfully raided Zulu villages. It returned in early April 1838 with 4 000 cattle and over 500 Zulu women and children, who were to be integrated into the Port

Natal community as wives and labourers.[25] In the same month, Alexander Biggar and Cane led a second expedition, which was almost completely annihilated at the Battle of Thukela by a Zulu army under the king's brother, Mpande. In late April the remaining Europeans evacuated the settlement before it was sacked and burnt by the advancing Zulu army.[26] By the middle of 1838, Zulu impis had inflicted severe defeats on both the Boer and British settlers, but their success was shortlived as Trekker reinforcements, under the command of Andries Pretorius, arrived in November of the same year.[27]

On 16 December 1838, the Zulu army was decisively defeated by the Boers at Blood River.[28] The Zulu dominance of south-east Africa was broken and Dingane's credibility within the Zulu kingdom was weakened to the extent that rival princes and factions could openly challenge his authority. These divisive tendencies surfaced in September 1839 when Mpande revolted and fled with his followers to seek an alliance with the Boers. Taking advantage of this political rupture in the Zulu royal house, the Trekkers concluded an alliance with Mpande's faction and Dingane's forces were routed at the Battle of the Maqongqo Hills. After Dingane's flight, Mpande was recognized as king of Zululand (see Chapter 4).

The warfare between the Trekkers and the Zulu alarmed the British authorities in the Cape, and in December 1838 a detachment of 100 soldiers occupied Port Natal to restore peace. After the defeat of Dingane, this small garrison withdrew in December 1839. In the same year the victorious Trekkers concluded a treaty with Mpande, in terms of which he handed over to them all the territory Retief had requested, with the Thukela River as the boundary in the north and the Mzimvubu River in the south. The Trekkers called their new state the Republic of Natalia and established Pietermaritzburg as their centre of government. There was no written constitution, but it was agreed to elect representatives from the various Trekker parties to a Volksraad of twenty-four members, performing all legislative, executive and judicial functions.[29]

The Republic of Natalia was shortlived. The Trekker presence seemed to pose a threat to Britain's strategic interests, while there was a danger that a foreign power might exploit the situation and occupy the harbour at Port Natal, thus threatening Britain's sea-route to India. Moreover, the Zulu-Boer conflict precipitated instability to the north of the Thukela, leading to a massive flood of Nguni-speaking peoples southwards, as those who had been subjected to Zulu overlordship now returned to their former homes. The movement of nearly 60 000 refugees into the territory that now

A sketch by an unknown artist of Durban Bay with the British military encampment on Dunn's Hill (Seaview) in the foreground. The drawing is dated 5 May 1842.

constituted the Republic of Natalia between 1839 and 1842 meant increased competition for the grazing and agricultural lands that had already been apportioned to the Trekkers. Complaints of 'squatting' and cattle theft were common and Boer attempts to deal with this by means of commando action led, as it had on the Cape Colony's frontiers, to indiscriminate raiding and harsh retaliation. Boer commando raids on the African chiefdoms to the south of the Mzimkhulu, accused of cattle theft, threatened stability on the eastern frontier of the Cape Colony, as did the Volksraad's plan to relocate the 'surplus' African population on lands on or near those settled by eastern Cape chiefdoms.[30]

The British Governor of the Cape Colony, Sir George Napier, despatched a force of 237 troops to occupy Natal, and on 4 May 1842 the Union Jack was hoisted over Durban. The Trekkers retaliated by repulsing the British at the Battle of Congella and beseiging the garrison. It was then that the early Port Natal settler, Dick King, made his legendary ride of 600 miles to Grahamstown to summon aid. Thereupon, on 25 June, the frigate *Southampton* relieved the beleaguered garrison, forcing the Boers to withdraw from Durban.[31]

On 31 May 1844 Natal was annexed as an autonomous district of the

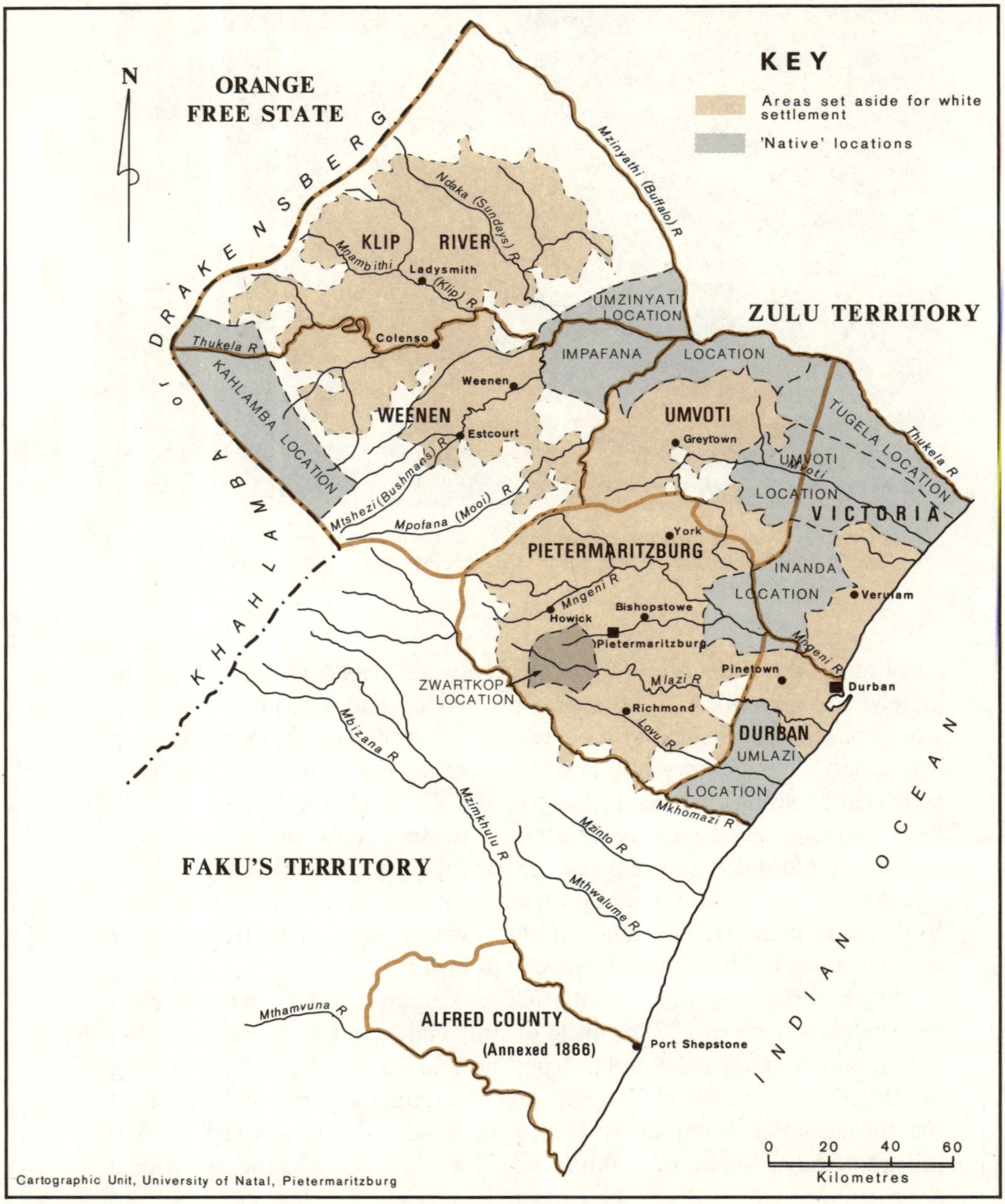

KEY

Areas set aside for white settlement

'Native' locations

ORANGE FREE STATE

ZULU TERRITORY

N

DRAKENSBERG

KLIP RIVER

Ndaka (Sundays) R

Mzinyathi (Buffalo) R

Mzambithi

Ladysmith

(Klip) R

Colenso

UMZINYATI LOCATION

Thukela R

IMPAFANA   LOCATION

KAHLAMBA LOCATION

Weenen

UMVOTI

TUGELA LOCATION

Thukela R

WEENEN

Estcourt

Greytown

UMVOTI

Mtshezi (Bushman's) R

LOCATION

VICTORIA

KHAHLAMBA

Mpofana (Mool) R

York

PIETERMARITZBURG

INANDA

LOCATION

Verulam

Mngeni R

Howick

Bishopstowe

Mngeni R

Pietermaritzburg

Durban

ZWARTKOP LOCATION

Mlazi R

Pinetown

Mzizana R

Richmond

Levu R

DURBAN

Mzimkhulu R

UMLAZI

FAKU'S TERRITORY

Mzinto R

LOCATION

Mkhomazi R

INDIAN OCEAN

Mthwalume R

Mthamvuna R

ALFRED COUNTY

(Annexed 1866)

Port Shepstone

0   20   40   60
Kilometres

Cartographic Unit, University of Natal, Pietermaritzburg

Map 10   The Colony of Natal, 1845

Cape Colony. The annexation was reluctantly ratified by the Imperial Government, which was swayed by the argument that continued instability in the region would destabilize the Cape Colony's eastern frontier, while it was imperative for strategic reasons to contain the Trekker population in the interior of the subcontinent. Apart from these strategic considerations, the new Colony was of little economic value.[32] While the presence of coal was known, there were no other mineral deposits of any value to boost the territory's development. Ivory, hides and skins provided the only immediate source of export income. The Boers, numbering several thousand, far outnumbered the few hundred British settlers, who were clustered around the immediate vicinity of Durban. The African population was unsettled, returning in increasing numbers to reoccupy the land from which it had fled during the Shakan period.

These were the major problems and conditions that confronted the new British colonial administration that took office in the new Colony in December 1845. It was headed by a Lieutenant-Governor, assisted by a Colonial Secretary, a Crown Prosecutor and a Diplomatic Agent to the Native Tribes. The posts of Colonial Treasurer, Postmaster and Registrar of Deeds were assumed by the Surveyor-General, reflecting the caution and extreme economy exercised by the British Parliament over Colonial Office finances. The Lieutenant-Governor was subordinate to the Cape Governor, while the Natal Executive Council, composed of the Lieutenant-Governor and his top-ranking officials, was not empowered to pass any legislation: this could only be done by the British Parliament or the Cape Legislative Council.[33]

With limited finances and a skeleton staff, the new administration nevertheless implemented major reforms which dramatically affected the subsequent history of the region. The appointment in 1846 of Theophilus Shepstone as Diplomatic Agent to the Native Tribes was an event of especial importance. The son of a Cape missionary, he had grown up on the Cape's eastern frontier and was a fluent southern Nguni linguist. Before his appointment in Natal, he had been a Diplomatic Agent representing the interests of the Cape Government across that Colony's eastern frontier. For nearly thirty years he was to dominate the administration of African affairs in Natal, from the formulation of policy down to its implementation and enforcement (see Chapter 7). Practically unaided, and with little money, he supervised the movement of nearly 80 000 Natal Africans during 1846 and 1847 into locations he had demarcated for their occupation, the rest of the area being cut up into farms for white ownership.[34] These were governed according to 'native customary law', and not the Roman-Dutch law that applied to the Colony's white inhabitants. These measures soon aroused the criticism of the white settlers, both British and Boer, on the grounds that the reserve areas were too large. As the development of farming began to generate a need for labour, the cry was also soon raised that the 'abundance' of land available to Africans made them economically independent and unwilling to enter the employ of white settlers.[35]

Many of the Trekkers had left the Cape Colony to escape what they regarded as the unacceptable controls of the Cape administration. The annexation of the Colony of Natal, once their armed resistance had been overcome, was met with considerable resentment, even before the new administration began to implement reformist humanitarian policies in accord with those being followed in the Cape Colony. Despite the efforts of Sir Harry Smith, the flamboyant Cape Governor, who visited Natal in 1848 and attempted to win their co-operation by means of generous land grants, most soon resolved to trek once more into the interior.[36] As they did so, British immigrants began to pour into the Colony.

The event that was to usher in profound changes in the fledgeling Colony of Natal was the immigration of white settlers, most of them from the British Isles, between 1849 and the mid-1850s. Like Australia, Canada and New Zealand, Natal thus became a colony of white settlement, although the number of settlers was nowhere near as large as that attracted to Australasia and North America at this time. The severe depression then gripping the industrial economies of Britain and Europe, combined with the bad weather, poor harvests and the devastations of the potato blight which brought further misery to the poor and unemployed, spurred a renewed interest in emigration. A number of colonization schemes, supported by the British Government, by speculators, by philanthropists or by religious bodies, offered assisted passages and allotments of land in the colonies to 'suitable settlers', a description which included labourers, traders, artisans, farmers and individuals with modest capital.[37]

Between 16 May 1849 and 6 February 1852 nearly 5 000 immigrants arrived in Natal, most of them under schemes of this sort. The most important of these enterprises was Joseph Byrne's Emigration and Colonization Company, with which was associated a number of Wesleyan societies, like the Christian Emigration and Colonization Society which settled 400 colonists at Verulam on the north coast. Most of the Byrne Settlers were located near Richmond in the Byrne Valley.[38] A sprinkling of immigrants arrived from western Europe. They were in most cases

*An artist's impression of settlers leaving England for Natal in 1850.
('The Embarkation', from the* Illustrated London News, *6 July 1850.)*

*This undated photograph shows an early white settlement in the Umkomaas valley. As
soon as they began to prosper, the settlers built more substantial houses.*

Natal Archives, C402

Transport-riding provided a better living than farming for some of Natal's white settlers, and also for black entrepreneurs. This undated photograph records a typical scene before the construction of railways.

associated with Lutheran missions (see Chapter 11), many of the missionaries electing to remain in the Colony with their families. In this way, Germans established thriving settlements at Hermannsburg, Wartburg, New Hanover and New Germany.[39] A handful of settlers arrived from the British Colony of Mauritius and, with their experience in sugar farming, were instrumental in establishing Natal's sugar industry (see below).

Although the hopes of those who had been taken in by the glossy promises of the settlement companies were seldom if ever realized, many of these colonists soon flourished. Abandoning the attempt to make ends meet on the land they had been allocated, they turned to trade. A wagon-load of goods could usually be obtained on credit from some established supplier in Pietermaritzburg or Durban and these could be exchanged at highly profitable rates for frontier commodities. Having acquired sufficient capital, successful traders could establish trading stores in the remote areas, open businesses in the growing urban centres, or return to farming, where they could now experiment in more capital-intensive operations. The whole of the Natal-Zululand region thus rapidly became covered by a commercial network. By 1855, the establishment of the towns of Richmond, York and Greytown in the Midlands bore witness to this growing economic activity. Pietermaritzburg, the capital of the former Republic of Natalia and of the Natal Colony, became the new commercial centre and at that time had a white population of nearly 2 000, while Durban, the only seaport, was about the same size.

In all these centres, the building of churches and the establishment of libraries, sporting clubs, agricultural shows, horticultural societies and botanical gardens reflected the intent of the British settlers to create a society like that which they had left in Britain. They soon built substantial houses, manufacturing their own bricks but importing corrugated iron and fashionable furniture, stained glass windows and cast-iron ornaments. Their intent to recreate British society was reflected also in the establishment of schools, modelled closely on those in Britain. Those children of the Colony's élite who were not sent to schools in Britain or the Cape were provided for by privately-funded schools. Hilton College, founded in 1872, and Michaelhouse, founded in 1896, catered for boys. Girls attended St. Anne's Diocesan College, which was established at Richmond in 1869 before being transferred to Pietermaritzburg in 1881 and then moved to its present premises at Hilton in 1905, while the Girls' Collegiate School in Pietermaritzburg was established in 1876, St. John's Diocesan School in Pietermaritzburg founded in 1897, and the Durban Young Ladies' Evangelical Collegiate Institute (now Durban Girls' College) established in 1877. Most settler families, however, sent their children to government-supported schools. In 1863 the Pietermaritzburg High School, or Maritzburg College as it was later known, was founded, followed three years later by Durban High School. Although most of these schools admitted black children, provided that they conformed to 'European habits and customs', the education of the Colony's African children was almost exclusively in the hands of mission schools, the most important of which was Adams College, founded in 1853 by the American Board of Missions (see Chapter 11).[40]

Another feature of colonial life was newspapers, which soon appeared in each centre. The *Natal Witness* was first published in Pietermaritzburg in 1846 and the *Natal Mercury* first appeared in Durban in 1852. Apart from keeping their readers informed about political and social events in Europe, with reports frequently being simply reprinted from British newspapers, these newspapers soon began to champion the local interests of the communities they served, so that lively debates frequently took place between them. The altercations between frequently outspoken editors often

This view of the inner-anchorage in Durban Bay was painted by Charles Maclean, upon whose early life the story of John Ross is based. The painting forms part of a larger chart of Durban Bay.

The outer-anchorage in 1879. The breakwaters had been constructed in an attempt to eliminate the sand-bar, which prevented all but the smallest of vessels from safely entering the harbour.

split the small colonial populace into violently antagonistic political groups.

Some of these disagreements were about the expenditure of government funds on roads (and later railways), a matter that was of great importance to farmers, traders, contractors, and property speculators, who hoped for rising property values in isolated towns or villages. Others centred around the unending problem of the Colony's finances, as the government attempted to raise the revenue necessary to meet the costs of its small but growing administration. It had also to undertake capital works. Apart from the construction of the roads, it was necessary to improve the Durban harbour by means of expensive attempts to reduce the height of the notorious sand bar, which made the harbour inaccessible to most ocean-going vessels. Surprisingly, in view of the great importance to the local community of improving the harbour, the Board of Commissioners responsible for harbour administration was inefficient. In 1877 a Harbour Board was constituted, but it too proved to be ineffectual until it was reconstituted in 1881, following a government Commission of Inquiry.[41]

Christianity was part of the cultural baggage that was brought to Natal by the colonists. A variety of denominations was represented. While Congregationists from America were the pioneers in founding mission stations among the Africans, German and Norwegian Lutherans also ministered mainly to the African population (see Chapter 11). The Dutch Reformed Church was dominant among those Boers who remained in the Colony after its annexation by Britain in 1845, most of them occupying northern Natal. In the 1860s it established mission stations for the Africans around Ladysmith and Greytown. In 1852 Jean-Baptiste Sabon and Bishop Allard established the Roman Catholic Church in the Colony and began to work among both the colonial and African populations.

The largest denomination among the early British colonists was Methodism, so that settlements such as Howick and Verulam were almost exclusively Methodist. The first substantial church building in Durban was that built by W. C. Holden in 1850, replacing the wattle-and-daub structure that had been erected in 1845 by his predecessor, J. Archbell. The most outstanding Methodist missionary was James Allison, who after leading his following of African Christians from Swaziland, founded two large mission stations, one at Intaleni in 1847 and another at Edendale, near Pietermaritzburg, in 1851.[42]

Anglicans, members of the Established Church of England, were about as numerous as Methodists and, in the early years of the Colony, were probably representative of the more well-to-do settlers who had arrived in the Colony with capital to invest. Their community was rent by the controversy surrounding John William Colenso, who was consecrated the first Bishop of Natal in 1853. In 1855 he established his residence and headquarters at Bishopstowe, near Pietermaritzburg, where a year later he opened a school, *Ekukanyeni*, for the education of African children. A man of formidable intellect, he translated much of the Bible into Zulu, compiled the first Zulu-English dictionary and produced Zulu readers for use in schools. Confronted by the problems of explaining Christianity to Africans, he questioned the literal interpretation of the Bible and in 1862 published *The Pentateuch and the Book of Joshua Critically Examined*. After he had refused to recant or modify his position, he was found guilty of heresy and excommunicated, a rival bishop being appointed in his place. At that time, controversy centred around such issues as the Church's attitude towards polygyny, which Colenso believed should be condoned (see Chapter 11).[43] Other points of disagreement have developed between the two factions of the South African Anglican community so that it remains divided today.

A prominent feature of the white settler society was its racialism. Britain, perhaps more than any other European nation, was in the nineteenth century imbued with the belief that its political and cultural institutions were superior to those of other nations and ethnic groups. British settlers carried these ideals and prejudices with them. Blacks were thought to be in an infant stage of cultural development, so that it was only 'natural' that the settlers should maintain their superiority in all spheres of human endeavour in order to guide, goad and, if necessary, coerce their 'childlike' wards along the path to 'civilization'.[44] The editor of the *Natal Witness* provided a typical expression of this attitude when he wrote in January 1847:

> The other class of our colonial population consists of men in a state of infancy as regards civilization. They are far more numerous than the Europeans, and their numbers are likely to be increased by additions from the adjacent tribes. Scattered over large tracts of country, and unimpelled by want, they have worn their lives away up to the present time in slothful indolence, to the full development of the depravity of human nature.[45]

During the first two decades after British annexation, white settler

Natal Archives, C2783

The Ashby Sugar Mill near Umhloti, established in 1876.

farmers gradually came to grips with the region's environment and agricultural possibilities, although many experiments failed disastrously. Among these failures were cotton-growing schemes in the coastal regions during the 1840s and early 1850s, which failed because of erratic yields and improper cultivation.[46] Thereafter, coffee tree plantations were established at the coast and these flourished until the early 1870s, when they were destroyed by a blight.[47]

The coastal lowlands (see Map 11) were found to be suitable for the cultivation of sugar-cane, tea, coffee and arrowroot after cultivars had been imported from similar bioclimatic regions, especially the British Colony of Mauritius.[48] Sugar farming was soon to become Natal's premier agricultural industry. E. F. Rathbone, Adolphe de Terrason and Henry Milner, all of whom came from Mauritius, imported cane cultivars into the Colony as early as 1848 and grew experimental patches of 'Bourbon' and 'Green Natal' cane near Durban.[49] Edward Morewood was the first settler to erect a mill for the processing of cane sugar on his estate Compensation, north of Verulam. In 1854 Milner and J. B. Miller auctioned the first batch of sugar in Durban's market square, and by 1860 over 3 000 acres of cane

Newcastle

Utrecht

Vryheid

Dundee

Ulundi

Ladysmith

Z U L U L A N D

Weenen

Empangeni

Eshowe

Estcourt

Greytown

N A T A L

Stanger

Pietermaritzburg

Verulam

INDIAN OCEAN

Richmond

Durban

N

Ixopo

Relief

metres
above 1800
1800

1400

900

400

0

Bioclimatic Zones

Highlands

Midlands

Coastal lowlands

0   50
kilometres

Port Shepstone

MAPWORK BY B.MARTIN Cartographic Unit, University of Natal, Pietermaritzburg

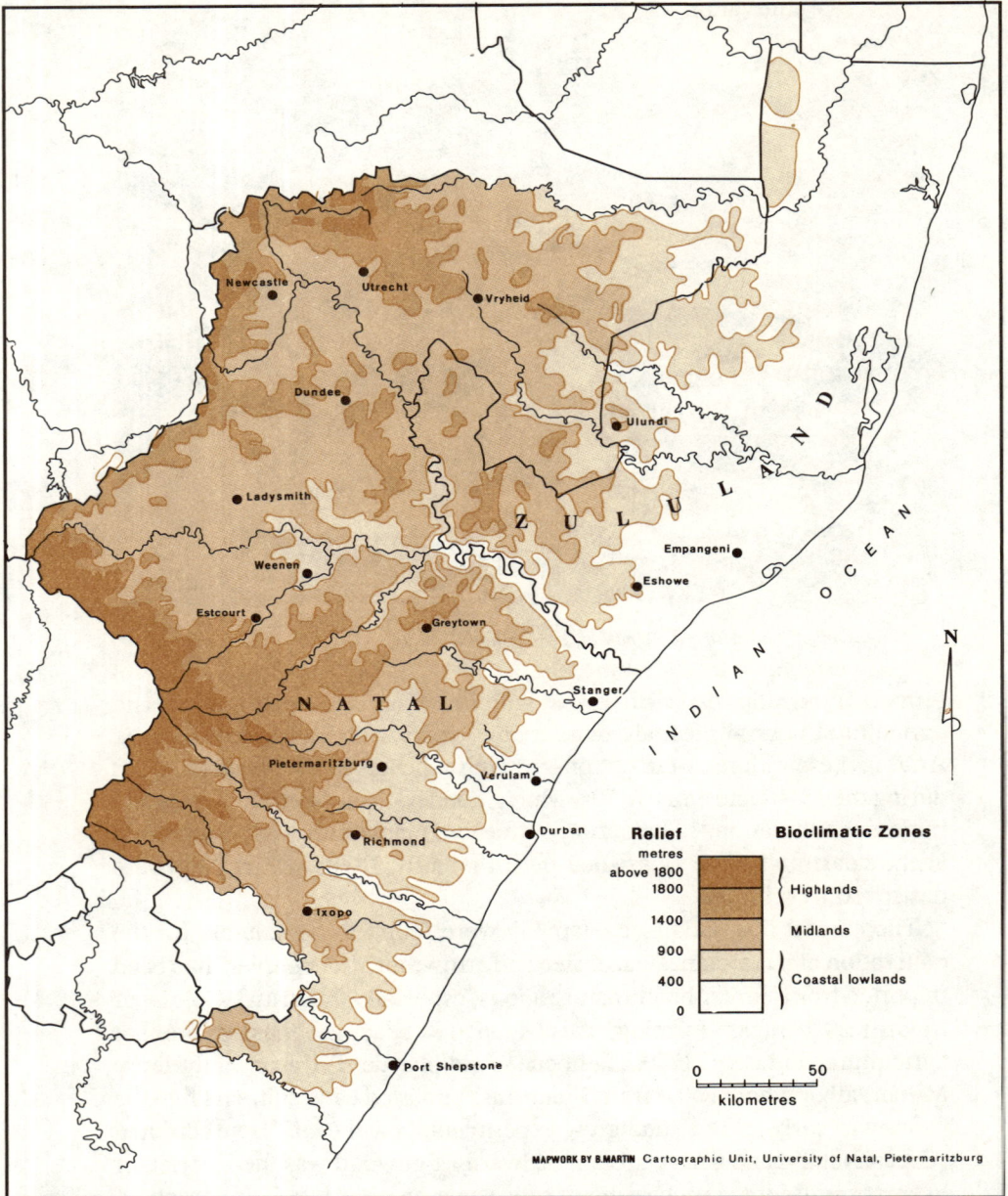

Map 11   Bioclimatic zones, Natal and Zululand

were under cultivation in Victoria and Durban counties and several large mills were in operation, notably at Springfield and Isipingo. The development of the industry was from the first impeded by a shortage of capital and labour, while new varieties of cane had to be found to suit local conditions[50] and it was with difficulty that these basic problems were overcome (see Chapter 12).

In the interior, the Midlands mist belt (see Map 11) was suitable for maize cultivation, dairy farming and the extensive grazing of cattle and sheep on the hilly and broken terrain. By the middle of the nineteenth century, wool farming was well-established in the Cape Colony and it was from there that merino sheep were introduced to Natal in the 1850s, a prominent part being played by immigrants from Australia, among them J. S. Dobie. After a promising beginning, the industry was to be affected by the economic depression of the late 1860s, while farmers also had to contend with the noxious burr weed and sheep diseases such as scab, which was not brought under control until the introduction of compulsory dipping (see Chapter 12). In the decade of the 1870s the sheep population numbered about 350 000, producing a woolclip that averaged 1 000 000 pounds (453 592 kilograms).[51]

In the early 1880s, wattle plantations were planted successfully, with the aim of producing bark for tannin.[52] At an even higher altitude, the highland sourveld (see Map 11) soon became the principal sheep-farming region of the Colony. Maize, root and fodder crops were also established there, along with cattle ranching. Higher still, on the foothills and slopes of the Drakensberg, where there were severe frosts and occasional droughts, the indigenous fauna was shot off and extensive grazing farms for cattle and sheep were established. Some maize, and later wattle, was also grown with moderate success.[53]

Throughout most of the nineteenth century, climatic and environmental conditions were generally favourable for sustained increases in crop and livestock production. The region was not, of course, immune from drought or stock disease, but these were relatively shortlived or were fairly easily combatted. Between 1860 and 1895 a general drought occurred throughout the region on average every six years[54], with 1878 and 1881 being particularly bad. During these years, sugar and maize crops were cut by as much as half[55], so that maize was imported from the United States of America to feed Africans on the verge of starvation in several locations.[56] In the mid-1850s, peripatetic white traders introduced bovine pleuro-pneumonia, or lungsickness, and this killed thousands of cattle, especially in Zululand. A renewed outbreak occurred in 1872 and it is estimated that this wiped out approximately half the cattle in the Zulu kingdom alone.[57] Horsesickness was an almost perennial scourge and bluetongue took a heavy toll of sheep in the 1860s and 1870s.[58] No disastrous insect infestations occurred before 1895, except for a small swarm of locusts near Durban in 1851.[59]

The diversified nature of settler agriculture, combined with the financial interests of speculators and merchant capitalists, produced noticeable divisions within the settler farming community. There were the wealthier but numerically smaller 'planters' who grew cash crops along the humid subtropical coastal belt. These farmers required large gangs of labourers to produce mostly sugar, tea and, to a lesser extent, coffee and arrowroot, and were distinguishable from the so-called 'up-country' or Midland farmers who made a living from mixed farming and pastoral products.[60] A complicating factor as far as agriculture was concerned was the existence of the land companies, of which the most important was the Natal Land and Colonisation Society, formed in London in 1860. They did not actively engage in farming but held vast areas of fertile farming land, especially in the Midlands, on speculation, often finding it profitable to rent them to African tenants while awaiting the increase in land values that was expected to follow upon the further white immigration which some of them tried to promote. Much of the Colony's maize, sorghum and livestock was produced by such rent-paying peasants (see Chapters 11 and 15).[61]

The emergence of an economically independent African farming class, together with the viability of the homestead economy, caused many Africans to shun working for the less attractive remuneration offered by the settlers. Most colonists blamed the shortage of labour upon Shepstone's location system (see Chapter 7) and upon the practice of the large land companies of allowing African 'squatters' on their land. As the British Government refused to allow higher taxes to force Africans to earn cash wages or legislation that would reduce African economic independence through restricting their access to land,[62] the Natal Government administered and partly financed several schemes to recruit labour abroad. In the late 1850s an agreement was reached with the Indian Government to allow the recruitment of indentured Indian labour (see Chapter 10), a development that was crucial for the sugar industry[63] (see Chapter 12). A second scheme was introduced when, between 1865 and 1874, Indian labour recruitment was halted by the Indian Government due mainly to complaints that had been received regarding maltreatment, poor food and harsh punishments on some sugar plantations (see Chapter 10). During this period, the labour crisis was alleviated by means of an agreement with king Cetshwayo of Zululand, whereby thousands of Tsonga labourers, recruited in southern Mozambique, were allowed to travel through Zululand to work in Natal. The Natal Government appointed a salaried Protector of Emigrants for Zululand and several agents to supervise these operations.[64]

After completing their indentures, many 'Free Indians' remained in the Colony and quickly established themselves as productive market-gardeners along the entire coastal belt of Natal in the 1870s and 1880s.[65] In the vicinity of Durban, they soon became the chief suppliers of vegetables and maize to the white urban community (see Chapter 10).

In these years, the main stimulus to the economy was provided by the expansion of trade with neighbouring territories. Although the original trading settlement at Port Natal had been established by Cape merchants, the Colony soon found itself at a disadvantage in regard to the Cape trade. Until well into the 1860s, Natal was dependent on the Cape for the forwarding of goods and Cape merchants skimmed off a percentage of the profits in the form of interest on credit, handling and shipping charges. Moreover, Cape merchants unloaded inferior goods on Natal's inhabitants and they were subject to double duties as they passed through customs houses in both Cape Town and Durban.[66] The Natal Colony's erratic trade in primary raw products such as ivory and hides meant that the Cape exported much more to Natal than it received in return, particularly as Cape merchants preferred to import sub-tropical goods from Mauritius, following trading patterns that had been established earlier in the century.

The figures for imports and exports indicate the extent to which the Colony was a supplier of raw materials, mostly to Britain but also to other British colonies. Unfinished commodities such as ivory, hides and wool or non-animal agricultural products such as sugar and wattle comprised approximately 80 per cent of the total value of goods produced for export.[67] Conversely, imports from Britain and the western world in general were composed of finished and manufactured goods. Import items that ranked consistently high in value were clothing and textiles of every description, machinery and metal tools and utensils, saddlery, arms and ammunition, liquor and even food products such as coffee, flour, meal and tinned and preserved meats and fish.[68] The Colony was thus dependent on Britain and the industrialized world for almost every conceivable manufactured tool or device.

Trade was crucial to the Colony's finances because customs and excise duties, together with the hut tax, were the principal sources of revenue. In 1849 customs duties realized £11 200, or 54 per cent of total revenue, and in 1875 customs garnered £114 777 or 41 per cent of government revenue. Because the financial foundations of the Colony rested so heavily on this base, fluctuations in the customs revenue were near infallible indicators of the state of trade and the general condition of the Colony's economy at any given time.[69]

The dependence of the Colony on trade with Britain meant that it was highly sensitive to fluctuations that occurred in the international economy. Between 1860 and 1864 Natal thus experienced a brief period of prosperity and expansion when the price of wool rose as a consequence of a shortage of cotton during the American Civil War. This not only affected wool farmers in the Colony; it also greatly stimulated the Overberg trade with the Orange Free State, where farmers also benefitted from the boom. Between 1860 and 1864 the value of imports that passed through Durban thus rose from £355 000 to £592 000, while the value of exports jumped from £410 000 to £620 000. The buoyant conditions in Britain and the Cape at this time also contributed to the expansion of the sugar industry in the form of greater demand, firmer prices and the injection of much-needed capital.[70]

This boom came to a halt in 1865 when cotton exports from America were resumed. This triggered an economic down-turn in Natal and in southern Africa generally as wool and sugar prices dropped sharply.[71] The fall-off in trade produced widespread bankruptcy and this led to a sudden drop in revenue from customs, so that the government's budget deficits rose from £12 000 in 1865 to £27 000 in 1867.[72] The Colonial Government attempted to balance its budget by means of imposing additional taxes in the form of increases in the duties on popular consumer goods such as tea, tobacco, wine, spirits and imported processed foods.[73] In 1869 a graduated tax on marriages was introduced as a device to extract additional revenue from the Colony's large African population. The measure yielded an average of £4 500 per annum until it was abolished in 1875.[74]

By the end of the 1860s the Colony had begun to feel the effects of the opening of the diamond-fields at Kimberley. Thereafter, a further unexpected boost to the economy was provided by the outbreak of the Anglo-Zulu War, during which there was a demand for heavy equipment and provisions for the British military. This prosperity was, however, short-lived for in the mid-1880s the British economy again entered a

By the 1870s, Durban had become a busy commercial centre. This photograph shows the Market Square in 1875. Today the City Hall stands on this site.

depression. When this happened, lower prices and lower demand for Natal's primary exports and a corresponding drop in the Overberg trade with the Orange Free State and the Transvaal triggered a sharp depression which affected not only merchants, traders and transport-riders, but farmers, labourers and artisans as well.[75]

To the Natal commercial interests, whose voice could not be ignored in the Legislative Council, it seemed that the Colony could only be lifted out of its financial difficulties by means of securing a greater share of the transit trade. The Cape had already constructed a railway line to Kimberley. The difficulty was that, with the Colony's treasury empty, the construction of the line linking Durban with the interior could not be undertaken without the Imperial Government's support. This provided the British Government with a useful tool with which to persuade the Colony to co-operate in the scheme which it was pursuing at this time to confederate the states of southern Africa (see Chapter 6). Following the founding of the Natal Government Railways at the beginning of 1876, the construction of the main line to the interior began and by the end of 1880 the railhead had reached Pietermaritzburg. By 1886 it had reached Ladysmith and two coastal lines linked Durban with Verulam to the north and Isipingo to the south.[76]

After the late 1870s railway construction gathered momentum. The numerous rivers and difficult terrain posed many engineering challenges. This photograph depicts the opening of the bridge over the Mbilo River, near Durban.

These lines provided local farmers with access to the major urban centres and to the port. Railway receipts, however, did not at first come up to expectations, even before the trade depression of the mid-1880s led to a 54 per cent fall in revenue. Whereas the Colony had previously been able to balance its budgets by means of customs duties and the hut tax, the construction of railways had burdened the Colony with an enormous debt and had increased its dependence upon the Overberg transit trade. The development of the Witwatersrand gold-fields after 1886 rescued it from this bleak financial condition.

Notes

1   M. R. Barbour, 'Natal: 1824–1856: a Review of some Economic Aspects of the Colony from its Foundation to the Granting of Representative Government' (unpublished Honours research essay, University of Natal, 1972), p. 1; A. E. Cubbin, 'Origins of the British Settlement at Port Natal, May 1824–July 1842' (unpublished Ph.D. thesis, University of the Orange Free State, 1983), pp. 6–56. Much of the text on Natal's frontier phase is based on C. C. Ballard, 'Natal 1824–44: the Frontier Interregnum', *Journal of Natal and Zulu History*, 5 (1982), pp. 49–64.

2   Fynn, *Diary*, p. 56.

3   Bird, *Annals of Natal*, p. 71.

4   Wilson and Thompson, *Oxford History of South Africa*, 1, ch. V and VI.

5   Fynn, *Diary*, pp. 22–3.

6   Webb and Wright, *Stuart Archive*, 1, pp. 99, 109–11.

7   A. F. Hattersley, *The British Settlement in Natal: a Study in Imperial Migration* (Cambridge, Cambridge University Press, 1950), pp. 14–1 5.

8   G. MacKeurtan, *The Cradle Days of Natal* (facsimile edition, Durban, T. W. Griggs, 1972), p. 31.

9   Minutes of the Natal Executive Council, 7 January to 17 September 1846.

10   Webb and Wright, *Stuart Archive*, 1, p. 99.

11   Wilson and Thompson, *Oxford History of South Africa*, 1, pp. 238–41.

12   Brookes and Webb, *History of Natal*, p. 20. Until the arrival of James Collis from Algoa Bay in 1832, only Francis Farewell had brought his wife to the port, see E. J. Krige, *The Social System of the Zulus* (London, Longmans, 1936), pp. 34–40.

13   Fynn, *Diary*, p. 24.

14   Ibid., p. 143.

15   Okoye, 'Dingane', p. 222.

16   Ibid., p. 224. Jacob is a prime example of a 'non-white' frontiersman who entered the Natal frontier zone and attached himself to the legitimate authority of the Zulu king as a means of acquiring privileges and power denied him by the British traders. Jacob's influence was considerable during this period,until the traders prevailed on Dingane to have him executed for his rumour-mongering.

17   Gardiner, *Journey to the Zoolu Country*, pp. 289–90. Gardiner gave evidence to the Aborigines Committee of the House of Commons condemning the traders' lifestyle.

18   Okoye, 'Dingane', pp. 231–2.

19   Ibid., p. 230; Cubbin, 'Origins of the British Settlement', pp. 102–9.

20   Ibid., pp. 231–2.

21   MacKeurtan, *Cradle Days*, pp. 202, 239.

22   Gardiner, *Journey to the Zoolu Country*, pp. 129–33.

23   Fynn, *Diary*, pp. 242–50.

24   Mackeurtan, *Cradle Days*, pp. 202–39; Cubbin, 'Origins of the British Settlement', pp. 135–49.

25   J. S. Galbraith, *Reluctant Empire: British Policy on the South African Frontier, 1834–1854* (Berkeley, University of California Press), p. 185; Cubbin, 'Origins of the British Settlement', pp. 150–61.

26   Brookes and Webb, *History of Natal*, p. 34.

27   Galbraith, *Reluctant Empire*, p. 186.

28   Brookes and Webb, *History of Natal*, pp. 31–2.

29   Brookes and Webb, *History of Natal*, p. 35; Cubbin, 'Origins of the British Settlement', pp. 165–73.

30   Galbraith, *Reluctant Empire*, pp. 193–6.

31   Brookes and Webb, *History of Natal*, p. 39; Cubbin, 'Origins of the British Settlement', pp. 240–75.

32   Bird, *Annals of Natal*, 2, p. 86.

33   Brookes and Webb, *History of Natal*, p. 54.

34   E. H. Brookes and N. Hurwitz, *The Native Reserves in Natal*, Natal Regional Survey, Vol. 7, ch. 1 (Cape Town, Oxford University Press for the University of Natal, 1957).

35   Brookes and Webb, *History of Natal*, p. 56.

36   A. L. Harington, *Sir Harry Smith: Bungling Hero* (Cape Town, Tafelberg, 1980).

37   The most detailed study of British immigration to Natal during the 1840s and 1850s is Hattersley, *The British Settlement of Natal*.

38   Spencer, *British Settlers in Natal*, 1, pp. xvii–xx.

39   G. G. Bruss, 'The Impact of the First World War on the German Community in Natal' (unpublished MA thesis, University of Natal, Durban, 1981); Killie Campbell Africana Library, B. E. Camp, *A History of the District of Alfred* (unpublished manuscript); S. A. Feather, 'A Cultural-Social Study of the Norwegian Settlement at Marburg' (unpublished MA thesis, Natal, Pietermaritzburg, 1980); S. Kjonstad, 'The Development of the Marburg Settlement, Natal', *Journal of the Natal Geographical Association*, 5 (1987).

40   At Verulam, a separate black Wesleyan school was established as early as 1859 (see M. G. Park, 'The Early History of Verulam', *AYB*, 1953, 2, p. 272). For the history of education in Natal see Brookes and Webb, *History of Natal*, pp. 78, 164–5; A. M. Barrett, 'A History of Michaelhouse, 1896–1952' (M.Ed. thesis, University of Natal, 1968); A. F. Hattersley, *Hilton Portrait: South African Public School, 1872–1945* (Pietermaritzburg, Shuter & Shooter, 1945); S. Vietzen, *A History of Education for European Girls in Natal, 1837–1902* (Pietermaritzburg, University of Natal Press, 1973); M. P. Kiernan, 'The Work for Education in Natal of Robert James Mann, 1857–65' (unpublished M.Ed. thesis, Manchester, 1982).

41   L. Heydenrich, 'Port Natal Harbour', *Enterprise and Exploitation*, eds. Guest and Sellers, pp. 17–46.

42   Brookes and Webb, *History of Natal*, pp. 26–7, 72.

43   For details of Colenso's life, see J. J. Guy, *The Heretic: a Study of the Life of John William Colenso, 1814–1883* (Johannesburg and Pietermaritzburg, Ravan Press and University of Natal Press, 1983).

44   C. Bolt, *Victorian Attitudes to Race* (London, Routledge and Kegan Paul, 1971).

45   *Natal Witness*, 15 January 1847.

46   Hattersley, *The British Settlement of Natal*, pp. 93–6.

47   Ibid, pp. 93–6; Brookes and Webb, *History of Natal*, p.80.

48   J. Phillips, *The Agriculture and Related Development of the Tugela Basin and its Influent Surroundings* (Pietermaritzburg, Natal Town and Regional Planning Commission, 1973), ch. 1.

49   Hattersley, *British Settlement of Natal*, pp. 235–6.

50   Brookes and Webb, *History of Natal*, p. 80.

51   Phillips, *Agriculture and Related Development*, ch. 1; J. M. Sellers, 'The Origin and Development of the Woolled Sheep Industry in the Natal Midlands in the 1850s and 1860s', *Enterprise and Exploitation*, eds. Guest and Sellers, pp. 151–80; C. C. Ballard and G. Lenta, 'The Complex Nature of Agriculture in Colonial Natal, 1860–1909', ibid., pp. 121–50.

52   Hattersley, *British Settlement of Natal*, pp. 260–71.

53   Phillips, *Agriculture and Related Development*, p. 66.

54   C. W. de Kiewiet, *A History of South Africa: Social and Economic* (London, Clarendon Press, 1950), p. 189.

55   *Natal Departmental Blue Books*, Resident Magistrates' reports, 1878, 1879 and 1881; *Natal Statistical Blue Books*, Returns for Agriculture, vols. 29 (1878), 30 (1879) and 32 (1881).

56   *Natal Blue Book*, Resident Magistrates' reports, 1881; S. C. Rolando, 'The Establishment of Veterinary Services in Natal: the Career of Samuel Wiltshire, 1874–96' (unpublished BA Honours essay, Natal, Durban, 1987).

57   C. C. Ballard, 'The Role of Trade and Hunter-Traders in the Political Economy of Natal and Zululand 1824–1880', *African Economic History*, 10 (1981), pp. 1–16.

58   Hattersley, *British Settlement of Natal*, pp. 270–2.

59   *Natal Mercury*, 3 May 1895.

60   Ballard and Lenta, 'The Complex Nature of Agriculture in Colonial Natal pp. 123–34.

61   N. Hurwitz, *Agriculture in Natal, 1860–1950* (Natal Regional Survey, 12, Pietermaritzburg, University of Natal Press, 1957), pp. 54–66.

62   For a detailed discussion of the labour situation see D. Welsh, *The Roots of Segregation: Native Policy in Natal, 1843–1910* (Cape Town, Oxford University Press, 1971).

63   Brookes and Webb, *History of Natal*, pp. 84–7.

64   C. C. Ballard, 'Migrant Labour in Natal, 1860–79, with Special Reference to Zululand and the Delagoa Hinterland', *Journal of Natal and Zulu History*, 1 (1978).

65   Slater, 'The Changing Pattern of Economic Relationships', pp. 257–83.

66   *Supplement to the Blue Book for the Colony of Natal (Departmental Reports)*, 1885. Annual report of the Resident Magistrate of Alexandra County.

67   Charles Barter, *The Dorp and the Veld, or Six Months in Natal* (London, William S. Orr, 1852), p. 16.

68   C. C. Ballard, 'A Survey of Selected Vital and Economic Statistics for the Colony of Natal, 1844–1909' (Department of History, University of Natal, Durban, 1981), pp. 27–105.

69   Ibid.

70   See particularly M. F. Bitensky, 'The Economic Development of Natal, 1843–1885' (unpublished MA thesis, London School of Economics, 1955), pp. 218–21.

71   Ibid., pp. 45–7.

72   *Natal Statistical Blue Books*, 1865–7.

73   Bitensky, 'The Economic Development of Natal', pp. 218–21.

74   *Statistical Year Book for the Colony of Natal*, 1 (1900): Statistical Summary of Public Finance.

75   D. van Zyl, 'Boom or Bust: the Economic Consequences of the Anglo-Zulu War', *Journal of Natal and Zulu History*, 9 (1986), pp. 26–55.

76   D. H. Heydenrych, 'The Construction of Public Works and the Constitutional Status of Natal, 1875–1893: the Railway Case' (unpublished paper delivered at the Conference on the History of Natal and Zululand, University of Natal, Durban 2–4 July 1985), pp. 1–2.

Chapter 6

Colonists, confederation and constitutional change

BILL GUEST

The spasmodic demands for constitutional change that were made by Natal's white colonists during the second half of the nineteenth century were in keeping with the process that was evolving in other parts of the Empire. In each of the colonies of white settlement in Canada and Australasia bicameral representative systems were introduced, in most cases evolving out of a nominated advisory council. The progress of each colony from Crown rule to autonomous control varied in pace in accordance with the particular relationship that existed between individual colonial governors and their respective councils, and the intensity of the agitation for self-government on the part of each settler community. At the same time, the Imperial Government was constantly torn between the political expediency of yielding to settler demands and the wish to defend the interests of aboriginal populations, as championed by missionaries and the well-organized Aborigines Protection Society lobby.[1]

Of particular relevance to Natal was the example of the Cape Colony where, despite British reservations about entrusting political power to a white minority, representative government was introduced in 1853 and responsible government in 1872. In the wake of the Reform Acts of 1832 and 1867, British settlers throughout the Empire tended to regard representative institutions as a birthright, and those in southern Africa gained further inspiration from the creation of politically-independent Boer republics in the interior. Moreover, the Natal colonists were always keen to assume more effective control over 'native' administration, a portfolio monopolized for nearly thirty years by the Colonial Office appointee, Theophilus Shepstone (see Chapter 7). They also became increasingly irritated by what they perceived as the Imperial Government's unduly protective attitude towards Natal's Indian population and its neglect of the

Colony's economic interests, particularly with regard to inland railway construction in competition with the Cape for the trade of the interior republics.[2] Yet, the fact that Natal was one of the last British colonies with a white population to acquire responsible government was not due only to the concern of imperial officials that the settler community constituted such a small minority of the population. It was due also to the reluctance of many colonists to assume, under such circumstances, responsibility for their own internal security and external defence.

The Colony was granted its first representative institutions in terms of the 1856 Charter of Natal,[3] which separated it from the Cape and endowed it with an independent administrative structure. This consisted of a Governor or Lieutenant-Governor, who was to be assisted by an Executive Council of Crown officials and advised by a Legislative Council of sixteen members. Twelve of these were to be elected from eight electoral divisions and the other four were to be nominated by the Crown. In practice, these four were the same persons who sat on the Executive Council, being the Colonial Secretary, the Colonial Treasurer, the Attorney-General and the Secretary for Native Affairs. The elective seats were to be held for four years, and the franchise was limited to males over twenty-one years of age who owned immovable property valued at £50, or who rented such property to the annual value of £10. Prior to the Franchise Amendment Law of 1883, these property qualifications effectively excluded a substantial number of white males who came to be known as 'lodgers' but, like the Cape constitution of 1853, the franchise clauses of Natal's Charter did not discriminate on grounds of race. Some Indians succeeded in acquiring the vote and, theoretically, Africans could do so as well, provided they were granted exemption from the authority of tribal law. Indeed, as in the Cape Colony, the low franchise qualification was envisaged by the Colonial Office as affording a measure of protection to persons of colour. In practice, however, in the hands of local officials, the property qualifications were usually sufficient to exclude such rare applicants from the franchise, while the effect of Law 11 of 1865 was virtually to eliminate any further possibility of Africans gaining the vote and to confine participation in elections almost entirely to white adult males. It stipulated that, in addition to the prevailing franchise qualifications, African applicants should have resided in Natal for five years and been exempted from tribal law for seven. Their loyalty to the Crown had also to be vouched for by voters who had known them for at least two years. It has been argued that this measure was agreed to by the British authorities because it secured the approval of the colonial legislature for the Native Land Trust and enabled the colonial executive to retain control of the £5 000 reserve fund which had been established by the Charter for African administration and welfare. The missionaries at this time displayed no interest in African voting rights. There appears to have been general agreement among them that African land ownership was more important than the franchise.[4]

The presence of a large unenfranchised indigenous and Indian population gave the Imperial Government good reason to delay as long as it did in granting Natal responsible government. Moreover, the relationship between the Colony's Legislative Council and its successive governors was seldom sufficiently stable to inspire confidence in the ability of the white settler community to assume the responsibilities involved. Experience acquired in other parts of the Empire, including the Cape, reinforced the notion that a long apprenticeship of non-responsible representative government was appropriate in Natal's case, particularly as 'responsible' colonies were expected to be financially self-supporting and capable of providing for their own defence.[5]

Nevertheless, when in 1865 the British Parliament passed the Colonial Laws Validity Act empowering colonial legislatures to amend their own constitutions, subject to royal veto, the elected members of the Natal Legislative Council launched their first attempt to gain a larger measure of governmental control.[6] They were led by G. H. Wathen, a representative of Pietermaritzburg County, and John Robinson, the proprietor of the Durban newspaper the *Natal Mercury* and member for Durban Borough, who was subsequently to become the leading proponent of responsible government for the Colony, and its first prime minister in 1893.[7] The select committee proposed by them to consider amending Natal's constitution duly reported in favour of fully-fledged responsible government but, realistically, it did not recommend its immediate introduction, on the grounds that the Colony still lacked sufficient men with the necessary political expertise.[8] Instead, acting on a suggestion by Robinson, it proposed as a step in that direction the addition of six elected members to the Legislative Council, as well as the nomination of two non-official members to the Executive Council, in order to give the colonists a voice in that chamber. These recommendations hardly served to enforce the principle of responsibility. They nevertheless failed to elicit the unanimous support of the Legislative Council, though Acting Lieutenant-Governor Bisset supported the first proposal, so long as the proportion of nominated members in the legislature (one in four) was retained.[9]

The new Secretary of State for the Colonies, Lord Carnarvon, was sympathetic to both recommendations, but these were shelved in view of the financial crisis to which the depression of the late 1860s gave rise in Natal (see Chapter 5). In addition to postponing any prospect of constitutional reform, the crisis led to a protracted political struggle when the executive members of the legislature insisted that the Colony's shortage of administrative funds should be met by increased taxation, while the elected members demanded public retrenchment. The latter group insisted upon the legislature's constitutional right to control expenditure and in 1869 and 1870, when the estimates failed to reflect the reductions demanded, they resolutely refused to pass the administration's supply bills. Lieutenant-Governor Keate's new Native Taxation Bill further aggravated the dispute by proposing additional powers for the executive, so that it could impose heavier taxation on the indigenous population and provide more adequately for the welfare of chiefs.[10] Taxation and expenditure 'for Native purposes' was already a sensitive issue, having led to a dissolution of the Legislative Council in 1858 and again in 1861, as well as a petition from that body demanding the removal from the Colony of Lieutenant-Governor Scott, who had stoutly defended Shepstone's location system (see Chapter 7) against the growing opposition of the settler community.[11]

The revival of a matter which had been the cause of such bitter disagreement ten years previously prompted another, more radical attempt to increase the elective element in government. In May 1869 Charles Barter, who was later to become well-known as a magistrate and editor of the *Times of Natal* and was then representing Pietermaritzburg County, introduced a bill proposing the creation of a Legislative Council of twenty elective and four official members coupled with an Executive Council of four non-official members, drawn from the legislature, and three official appointees. In the same session, Barter also proposed the amalgamation of the offices of Colonial Secretary and Secretary for Native Affairs. The intention in Keate's view was 'the transfer of the control of the Natives from the Crown to the Local Legislature', so that 'they should supply with certainty and at a cheap rate the manual labour required by the Colonists'.[12] Neither of Barter's bills were approved, but later that year an attempt was made to break the deadlock by extending the mixture of elective and official members from the lower to the upper house when the Lieutenant-Governor was empowered to appoint two elective members of the Legislative Council to the Executive.[13] Keate dutifully selected two of the most influential elective members, J. W. Akerman, the chemist and former farmer who represented Pietermaritzburg City, and J. R. Goodricke, the Durban advocate and businessman representing Durban Borough, but the measure failed to dilute the antagonism that prevailed between the Colony's executive and legislature. Keate was so discouraged that at the opening of a new Legislative Council the following year he made no appointments at all.[14]

The elective members were jubilant when in February 1871 a dispatch from Lord Kimberley, Secretary of State for the Colonies, censured Keate's financial policy and affirmed the Council's right to control expenditure. It prompted yet another proposal to amend the constitution, on this occasion led by R. E. Ridley, member for Pietermaritzburg County. It was strongly supported by the *Times of Natal*, of which Ridley was the editor, and by Robinson's *Natal Mercury*.[15] Robinson had previously opposed the notion of immediate responsible government, arguing that the Colony was not yet ready for it and unable to undertake its own defence. His change of heart at this juncture aroused considerable criticism, including that of Colenso who dismissed him as 'Mr Facing-both ways . . . a mere weathercock veering with the popular breeze'.[16] The bishop was among those who suspected the motives of the 'scheming politicians' who advocated constitutional change, observing that they longed 'to manage their natives as they please' and expected to be the 'foremost officials' under a new dispensation.[17]

Yet Robinson, for one, was strongly influenced by developments further afield, including the imminent establishment of responsible government at the Cape and the apparent desire of the imperial authorities to achieve a self-supporting federation of states in southern Africa that would justify a complete withdrawal of British military forces from the region. Furthermore, the idea of unification was very much in the air, for the unification of Germany and of Italy had just been completed, the United States had only recently endured a bitter civil war to forge more securely its bonds of union, the British North America Act of 1867 had brought into being the Dominion of Canada and, by the end of the century, the Australian colonies had also been federated. Robinson realized that, if southern Africa was similarly soon to be federated, it was first essential for Natal to secure responsible government, so that it could enter such an association on an equal footing with the Cape and the interior Boer republics.[18] However, while the British Government remained committed in principle to allowing responsible government in all the colonies of white

John Macfarlane. As resident magistrate at Estcourt since 1855, he earned a reputation for strictness and on several occasions prior to the crisis of 1873 clashed with Langalibalele and his Hlubi followers.

Natal Archives, C108/26

settlement, Natal with its small settler population of not more than 18 000 persons and an indigenous population of at least 250 000, remained an exception. As Kimberley explained to Lieutenant-Governor Pine:

> It would be in accordance with the general views of Her Majesty's Government that any further change should be in the direction of Responsible Government, but unless circumstances should present themselves favourable to the admission of Natal into a federation including a large population of European descent, it does not appear probable that the Colony will at an early date become capable of receiving a more advanced Constitution than it at present enjoys.[19]

If federation was to be a necessary pre-requisite for any further advance towards responsible government, Natal's Legislative Council did at least succeed in increasing its elective majority when, in 1873, it passed a law to add three more elective and one nominated member to its own strength.[20] In the following year, the Natal colonists made their first formal request for full responsible government when a proposal to that effect was passed at a public meeting in Pietermaritzburg, and by a majority of the elected members in the Legislative Council.

The Constitution Bill, introduced by Charles Barter on 21 September 1874, was prompted by the administration's inept handling of the Langalibalele episode during the preceding few months. The crisis developed in 1873 when the Resident Magistrate at Estcourt, John Macfarlane, instructed the powerful local chief Langalibalele to hand in all

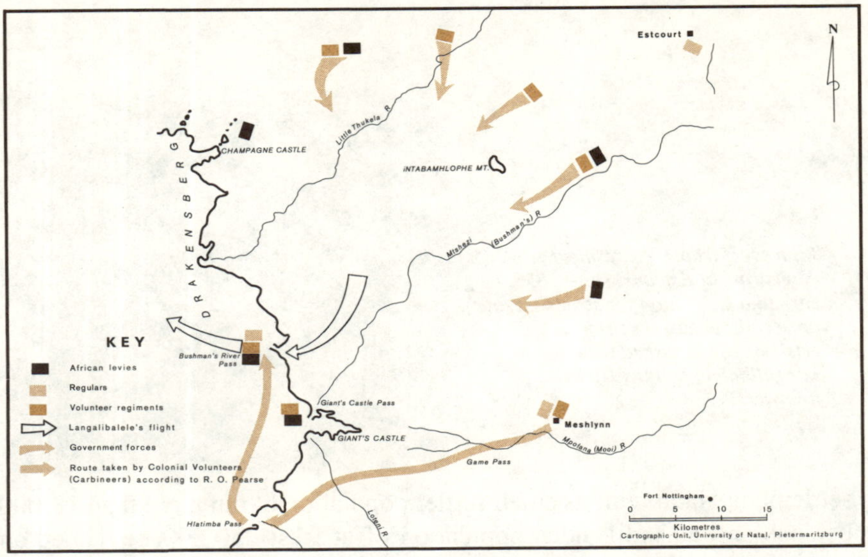

Map 12 Military operations against Langalibalele, 1873
(Based on a map in R. O. Pearse, *Barrier of Spears*, Howard Timmins, 1973, p. 231.)

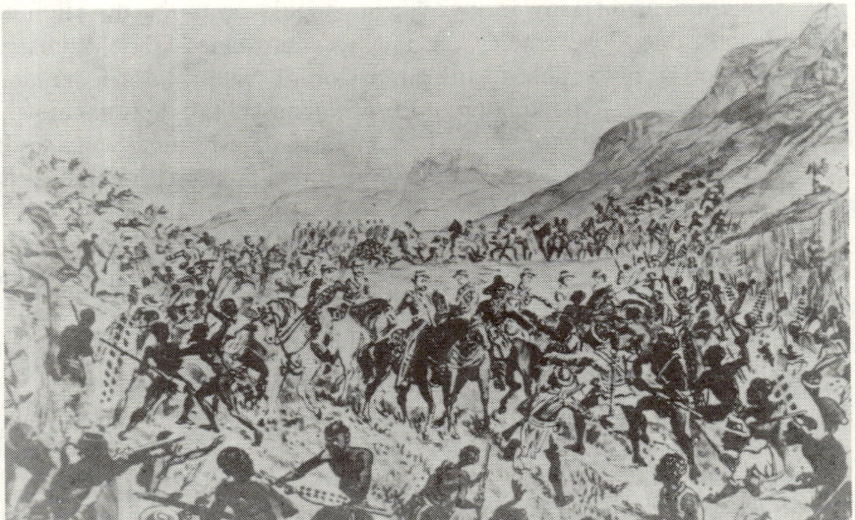

Killie Campbell Africana Library

A water-colour sketch by Thomas Baines (d. 1875) of the confrontation at the Bushman's River Pass. Based on a pen and ink etching provided by an eye-witness and described by the Natal Mercury *of 7.2.1874, it portrays Major Durnford (on horseback, centre) remonstrating with the Hlubi; Charles Barter is on his left and Elijah Kambule (the interpreter who was killed in the ensuing skirmish) on his right.*

Major (later Colonel) A.W. Durnford, who commanded the government forces in the Bushman's River Pass skirmish on 4 November 1873.

Natal Archives, C782

African auxiliaries were employed in the military operations against the Hlubi and Ngwe. (From the Mercury Pictorial, *21 January 1909.)*

Don Africana Library

the unregistered firearms which his Hlubi followers had acquired in exchange for their labour on the Griqualand West diamond-fields. Macfarlane may have intended to make an example of him as a warning to others after Langalibalele had on several occasions found excuses not to register the guns in compliance with Natal's Gun Law and had refused to obey an order to appear in person before Shepstone.[21]

Ever since being settled in 1849 on their location in the Drakensberg foothills between the Bushman's and Little Thukela rivers, the Hlubi and

Natal Archives, C790

Chief Langalibalele and seven of his sons, photographed in 1874 after their capture.
Malambule (rear, second from right) was exiled with his father for firing on the
government forces at the Bushman's River Pass.

related Ngwe people had performed valuable service to the Colony's white
stock-farmers by providing a protective screen against San raids. By the
early 1870s these incursions had ceased and the Hlubi had aroused the envy
of their white neighbours through their success in producing cash crops.
Moreover, Langalibalele was not a government-appointed or 'unborn'
chieftain, but had established himself as one of the most powerful
hereditary chiefs in Natal, while building up a reputation as a rainmaker.[22]
Possibly because he sensed that a plot was being hatched to deprive him of
his land, Langalibalele and a number of his people fled to Basutoland,
pursued by a large force of white volunteers and African militia. In a

skirmish at the top of the Bushman's River Pass (see Map 12), three of the colonial volunteers and two of Shepstone's indunas were killed.[23]

This tragedy sealed Langalibalele's fate. Those of his followers, mainly women and children, who had remained in Natal were flushed out of hiding-places and driven from their location (which was later sold off to white farmers), while their cattle was confiscated and used in part to reward those 'loyal' Africans who had assisted the colonists. The same treatment was meted out to the neighbouring Ngwe. Langalibalele, having been deposed from his chiefdom, was captured with the assistance of military forces from the Cape Colony and brought to Pietermaritzburg for trial. He was found guilty of 'treason' and 'rebellion' under a weird combination of Native and English Criminal Law and banished for life to the Cape Colony. This sentence not only far exceeded the powers that had been conferred upon the Lieutenant-Governor as 'Supreme Chief' but had no precedent in African 'usage, custom and law'. In subsequent trials, seven of Langalibalele's sons, two indunas and 200 of his followers were sentenced to varying terms of imprisonment. One son, Malambule, was banished for five years because he had fired upon the government forces in the engagement at the Bushman's River Pass.[24]

By September 1874, when Barter's bill requesting the introduction of responsible government came before the Legislative Council, these events had already attracted a great deal of unfavourable publicity in Britain, due largely to the efforts of Bishop Colenso, who brought them to the attention of the Aborigines Protection Society.[25] The majority of Natal's white settlers, who had previously been so critical of Shepstone, now rallied to his support, even though the crisis also highlighted the long-felt need for the colonists to gain more direct control of 'native' administration for themselves. In his capacity as a captain in the colonial volunteer forces, Barter had been personally involved in the military operations against Langalibalele's followers.[26] Despite the prevailing excitement in the Midlands and upper districts of Natal, his Constitution Bill was opposed by the less affected coastal representatives, who feared that the Colony would now be saddled with the cost of its own defence. Seeing that the debate was going against them, Barter's supporters questioned whether the official Council members were entitled to vote on a measure involving their own premature retirement and, when the Speaker ruled that their votes were indeed illegal, the coastal members withdrew in protest. Lieutenant-Governor Pine thereupon refused to give his assent to the bill on the grounds that the Speaker's ruling was itself illegal.[27]

Lord Carnarvon, who had returned to the Colonial Office as Secretary of State in February of that year, approved Pine's refusal to condone the bill but, in response to his advice that the existing constitution could not be retained for much longer in the face of growing dissatisfaction with it, he was emphatic that responsible government for Natal was at that time out of the question.[28] Indeed, the Langalibalele crisis justified serious misgivings as to the Colony's ability to assume responsibility for its own administration, including that of the substantial African majority. Moreover, it provided a convenient opportunity for constitutional changes of another sort to be effected in Natal, as a small step towards the realization of that broad confederal solution to the problems of southern Africa which Carnarvon had already been contemplating.

During the 1850s, in his capacity as Colonial Under-Secretary, Carnarvon had opposed Sir George Grey's advocacy of federation as the panacea for the ills of the subcontinent and as the means of honourably discharging the Imperial Government's moral responsibility for the whole region. He had questioned how 'colonies or states so unequal in size, population, development and natural resources' might be federated and, with reference to the financial difficulties of the other prospective confederal partners, had asked if 'these collective deficiencies' were 'to be made good by the Cape Colony? and if so by what inducement will this last be tempted to so losing a bargain?'[29]

However, by the 1870s Carnarvon had become convinced that the time was ripe for the application of such a solution. By then he had already been instrumental in carrying through the British North America Act of 1867, which created the Dominion of Canada, and it was therefore not unnatural that he should have sought the distinction of creating a second dominion within the Empire. That objective was also in keeping with his personal interest in a much broader strategy of overall imperial defence, in which connection he was involved in establishing the interdepartmental Committee on Colonial Defence in 1878. Carnarvon was convinced of the continued strategic importance of the southern African coastline. He believed that a confederated South Africa would also reduce Britain's expenditure and contribute substantially towards the consolidation of the British Empire, at a time when other European powers were taking an increasing interest in the acquisition of territories abroad, and in the African continent in particular. As Robinson's *Natal Mercury* pointed out at the time, by effecting a South African confederation 'the home government is relieved from its responsibilities; the colonists are allowed to participate in the privileges of selfgovernment, and the British Empire is strengthened by the consolidation of a new dominion'.[30] Recent studies emphasize that southern African confederation must be seen in terms of the need, following the discovery of diamonds, to create conditions which were conducive to capitalist intrusion and industrialization in the subcontinent. These included the provision of a larger and more reliable supply of labour and a greater measure of political stability.[31]

Whatever the underlying causes of the policy of confederation may have been, Carnarvon's intervention in Natal became imperative by late 1874, when the outcry against the treatment of Langalibalele and his followers reached a crescendo with Colenso's arrival in London to plead for the Hlubi chief in Whitehall.[32] Further, the infringement of Imperial Statute (32 Vict. Chap 10: The Colonial Prisoners' Removal Act) involved in the Cape Government's decision to accept Langalibalele as a prisoner on Robben Island simply could not be ignored, even at the risk of antagonizing a colony still conscious of its responsible government status and which, it was hoped, would assume the role of senior partner in the confederal association that Carnarvon had in mind.[33] After weighing all the evidence and interviewing both Colenso and Shepstone, he announced a mitigation of sentence for the convicted chief, compensation for his dispossessed followers, and substantial changes in Natal's constitutional composition.[34] Far from following the Cape Colony towards the attainment of responsible government, Natal was confronted with a return to virtual Crown Colony rule. This retrogression infuriated the settlers, who were already excited over the 'rebellion' and trial, but it did promise to give Carnarvon more effective control of at least one of the variables in the complex southern African equation for which he was seeking a solution. The situation demanded the services of a strong and experienced trouble-shooter to impose the necessary changes upon the Colony, and necessitated the removal of Lieutenant-Governor Pine, who was held responsible for mismanaging the Langalibalele crisis. Much to the annoyance of the colonists, he was recalled and retired on pension.[35]

Major General Sir Garnet Joseph Wolseley, GCMG, KCB, was not Carnarvon's first choice as Special Commissioner to Natal, but proved to be more than equal to the task. In the course of five military campaigns, he had already demonstrated his self-assurance and efficiency, while the most recent, in Ashanti, had earned him a reputation as a specialist in African crises.[36] Natal was to provide him with his first appointment of a quasi-political nature, together with the prospect of participating in an

Sir Garnet Wolseley (third from left) and his staff posing outside Government House in Pietermaritzburg.

Anglo-Zulu War that already seemed to be in the offing. Yet, privately, he had no enthusiasm for the assignment, though he was assured that it need not take longer than six months and that the only problem likely to confront him was 'the ill mannered behaviour of the low ruffians who constitute the representative assembly'.[37] In fact, the job was completed in a whirlwind five months, which one local journal described as 'the most momentous period that has marked our brief but chequered colonial history. . .'[38] Indeed, as Wolseley himself put it, the necessary reforms were achieved 'by a *coup de main* never giving the people here breathing time to think over what they were about until the deed was done . . .'[39]

Wolseley had been instructed by Carnarvon to effect constitutional changes in the direction of quasi-Crown Colony rule, so as to ensure Natal's support for confederation and to gain closer control of all aspects of 'native' administration. He lost no time in making his intentions clear at his very first Executive Council meeting on 2 April 1875 and, four days later, he published his instructions from Carnarvon in the Government Gazette.[40] Local resistance was softened up by an initial bombardment of flattery and dinner invitations emanating from the Royal Hotel in Durban, where Wolseley took up temporary residence, and from Government House in

Pietermaritzburg, where the campaign was focused more specifically on members of the Legislative Council.[41] His very capable staff, most of whom had served with him in Ashanti, were instructed to dance special attendance upon the most influential wives in the Colony, while Wolseley himself handled the local religious leaders, entertaining both the Bishop of Natal and his rival, the Bishop of Maritzburg, to dinner. Confronted by the difficulty that his attendance at the services of either might show partisanship, he attended communion with the garrison at Fort Napier.[42] After an unsuccessful attempt to acquire control of Robinson's *Natal Mercury*, by mid-April he had secured the bi-weekly *Times of Natal* at a cost of £50 a month, paid out of his own pocket, and had arranged for its editorials to be written under his direction by members of his own staff.[43] Another significant gain was the capture of two of the Colony's principal executive posts: Wolseley succeeded in persuading the Colonial Treasurer, John Ayliff, and the Immigration Officer, Colonel B. P. Lloyd, to take sick leave. Both vacancies were then promptly filled with his own appointees, Colonel Sir George Pomeroy Colley and Major William Butler, who could be relied upon to assist in pushing the necessary legislation through as speedily as possible.[44]

When, on 5 May 1875, Wolseley faced the Legislative Council, he emphasized the necessity for a greater degree of executive control in order to ensure the Colony's internal stability and to promote its interests through immigration, investment and improved public works, including the construction of a railway line to the interior.[45] His Natal Constitution Amendment Bill, which proposed to strengthen the executive by equalizing the number of elected and nominee members in the Legislative Council, provoked three motions of opposition within the House and two public petitions, presented to the legislature from Pietermaritzburg and Umvoti County, requesting that it be withdrawn. But it was R. E. Ridley (former editor of the *Times of Natal*) who, despite serious illness, emerged as the Bill's most implacable opponent, both in Council where he proposed amendments to it, and through the medium of his editorials in the *Natal Witness*.[46] The Bill finally passed its third reading on 31 May by a majority of ten to seven, but only after a compromise had been reached, whereby the number of nominee members was reduced from fifteen to thirteen in a House to be composed of twenty-eight members, including the Speaker.[47]

Wolseley was fortunate that the successful passage of his bill coincided both with the absence from the House of Ridley, who was too ill to attend, and with the absence from the Colony of Barter and A. Fass, a member for Pietermaritzburg Borough. As consistent opponents of greater executive control, they had expected to return in time to resist the measure but failed to anticipate the speed with which Wolseley conducted his campaign.[48] The threat of coercive imperial legislation or of a general election in which some current members might lose their seats, as well as the Colony's desire for a larger garrison and an imperial guarantee for railway and immigration loans, also played their parts in securing the Legislative Council's reluctant consent to one of the most extraordinary proposals to be placed before a colonial legislature.[49] The Natal Constitution Amendment Law was sanctioned by the Imperial Government on 5 August, and on 24 September 1875 came into effect for a period of five years. It was not entirely without precedent, for a similar 'voluntary' surrender of representative institutions had already taken place in 1870 in the colony of Honduras, and was to occur again in 1876 in Grenada and St. Vincent.[50] 'Jamaica reform' did not gain for the Crown unlimited power in Natal, but Wolseley was satisfied that he had done enough to 'enable Her Majesty's Ministers through the Governor here to direct the future policy of Natal and to prevent hasty and dangerous local legislation . . .'[51] The *Natal Witness*, an opponent to the end, even after Ridley had died in June, commented at the time of Wolseley's departure:

> Sir Garnet found Natal loyal, he leaves it servile. He found it full of political life, he leaves it a political corpse . . . Routs and parties, champagne and sherry, only tended to rivet the fetters prepared for us. The work was to be done thoroughly, and thoroughly has it been performed . . .[52]

The Colony did enjoy some compensation, in the form of two bills drawn up by Carnarvon to authorize railway construction and the raising of necessary funds. Furthermore, the sweeping changes in 'native' policy that had been envisaged by Carnarvon never materialized because reliance was placed upon the advice of Shepstone, who impressed Wolseley with his 'sound practical judgement'. The new Native Administration Bill which was eventually passed on 5 December 1875 did not therefore introduce any radical changes.[53] In theory, the judicial powers of the Secretary for Native Affairs were substantially reduced because the African population was placed under the jurisdiction of the ordinary criminal law of the Colony, while a Special Native High Court was established to try civil cases and to hear appeals against decisions of the local magistrates' courts. In practice, however, the new law did not significantly alter the powers previously exercised by the Secretary for Native Affairs or by the local chiefs.[54] Moreover, the codification of 'native' customary law which was envisaged in 1875 as a preliminary step towards its amendment and assimilation into the ordinary colonial law, was only completed in 1878. It proved to be contradictory and confusing, due to disagreements within the Board of Native Administration which was responsible for its compilation. A subsequent re-codification undertaken by a new Board was only completed in 1891 and had similar serious limitations. Far from promoting its eventual reconciliation with the system of Roman-Dutch law that applied to the Colony's white population, codification robbed customary law of its earlier flexibility, as Shepstone had predicted, and inhibited its subsequent evolution (see Chapter 15).[55]

In the years immediately following the constitutional amendment of 1875, there were occasional outbursts of recrimination in the Natal Press against Wolseley and the Imperial Government, though the colonists generally appear to have resigned themselves to the limitations placed upon their further progress towards responsible government.[56] Wolseley's successor, Lieutenant-Governor Sir Henry Bulwer, considered the new constitution decidedly cumbersome. After experiencing difficulty in filling the newly-created nominee posts in the Legislative Council, the original qualifications had to be modified. The nominated members subsequently proved to be an uncertain element, periodically asserting their independence and voting against the Government. The Colony nevertheless experienced a period of political stability, in contrast to the unrest of the early 1870s.[57]

Carnarvon had been convinced that 'Jamaica reform' would ultimately assist Natal along the path towards responsible government, through the medium of confederation. Despite the contention that responsible government should precede confederation, the idea of closer union with the other southern African states did not immediately fall into disfavour with Natalians. Not only did confederation promise economic prosperity, it also offered the prospect of greater security to a settler community which was decidedly jittery in the wake of the Langalibalele experience, and which became even more so in 1878–1879, just prior to the outbreak of the Anglo-Zulu War.[58]

However, Carnarvon's confederation proposals did not strike such a responsive chord in the Cape, where his celebrated dispatch of 4 May 1875, proposing a conference of South African delegates to discuss the matter, came hard on the heels of the Imperial Government's disallowance of Act No. 3 of 1874, whereby the Colony's newly-installed responsible government had provided for Langalibalele's incarceration. Castigated by its Opposition for subservience to the Imperial Government, and resentful of Carnarvon's nomination of the eastern Cape separatist leader John Paterson as a delegate to the proposed conference, J. C. Molteno's Cape Ministry was determined to assert itself.[59] Moreover, when viewed from Cape Town, confederation appeared to be an attempt by Britain to offload its responsibility for southern Africa, requiring the Colony to assume an even greater burden of defence and to share its customs revenues with her poorer neighbours. The Langalibalele crisis merely confirmed this lack of enthusiasm.[60] The replacement of Molteno by Gordon Sprigg in February 1878 raised hopes in Natal that confederation would proceed, but it soon became clear that the Cape Government would remain as reluctant as ever to assume the responsibilities involved in the scheme.[61]

Consequently, Natal's settler community was obliged to consider the alternative of political alliance with one or both of the interior Boer republics, wherein its economic interests increasingly lay, although it much preferred the greater security associated with union with the Cape. The idea of an eastern confederation, incorporating Natal and the Boer states to the exclusion of the Cape Colony, was however only seriously contemplated at times when considerations of basic security did not enjoy precedence over prospects for commercial advancement. It was particularly attractive just after Shepstone's annexation of the Transvaal in 1877 (see Chapter 7), but met with sullen hostility from the Boers.[62] The attitude of her prospective confederal partners, and the prospect of having to share her lucrative customs revenue with them, eventually contributed to Natal's own disenchantment with confederation, a process which was completed by the unnerving experience of the Anglo-Zulu War and the uncertain settlement of Zululand that followed it. Any surviving thoughts of an eastern confederation, incorporating Natal and her Overberg neighbours, dissolved in December 1880 when the Transvaal Boers took up arms to recover their independence from British rule.[63]

From a political point of view, the effect of the failure of the confederation movement upon Natal was particularly severe, for confederation had been the banner under which the Imperial Government had forestalled the demand for responsible government. This was a struggle which therefore remained to be resolved.

Notes

1   Sir J. Robinson, *A Life-Time in South Africa: Being the Recollections of the First Premier of Natal* (London, Smith, Elder, 1900), pp. 175–6; V. Harlow, 'The New Imperial System, 1783–1815' and J. R. M. Butler, 'Colonial Self-Government, 1838–1852', both in *CHBE*, 1940, 2, eds. J. Holland Rose, A. P. Newton and E. A. Benians, pp. 129–57 and 335–82; C. A. G. Bodelsen, *Studies in Mid-Victorian Imperialism* (Copenhagen, Gyldendal, 1960), pp. 19–20.

2   GH 1217, No. 93, pp. 24–35: Keate to Granville, 22 October 1869, and Granville to Keate, 15 and 16 March 1870; KCAL Colenso Papers, Folio X50: Mrs Colenso to C. Bunyon, 16 April 1874, and Folio 511: Colenso to Revd T. H. Steel, 31 July 1873; D. Welsh, *Roots of Segregation*, pp. 42–50, 202; J. L. McCracken, *The Cape Parliament, 1854–1910* (Oxford, Oxford University Press, 1967), pp. 7–17, 124–7.

3   See G. von W. Eybers, *Select Constitutional Documents Illustrating South African History, 1795–1910* (London, George Routledge, 1918), pp.188–94.

4   Eybers, *Select Documents*, pp. 194–7; T. R. H. Davenport, *South Africa: a Modern History* (Johannesburg, Macmillan, 1977), p. 78; E. H. Brookes, *The History of Native Policy in South Africa, 1830 to the Present Day* (Cape Town, Nasionale Pers, 1924), pp. 58–61; S. Trapido, 'Natal's Non-Racial Franchise, 1856', *African Studies*, 22 (1963), pp. 22–32.

5   M. Wight, *The Development of the Legislative Council, 1606–1945* (London, Faber & Faber, 1946), p. 102; J. R. M. Butler, 'Imperial Questions in British Politics, 1868–1880' in *CHBE*, 3, eds. E. A. Benians *et al.*, p. 20; A. F. Hattersley, *Portrait of a Colony: the Story of Natal* (Cambridge, Cambridge University Press, 1940), p. 98; B. O. Williams 'The Dispute between Lieutenant-Governor Keate and the Legislative Council, Natal, 1867–72' (unpublished MA thesis, Natal-South Africa, 1935.)

6   *Natal Legislative Council Votes and Proceedings*, 1 June 1865; Bodelson, *Mid-Victorian Imperialism*, p. 20; Wight, *Development of the Legislative Council*, p. 77.

7   For a more detailed account of the role played by Sir John Robinson in the political life of colonial Natal, see J. Lambert, 'Sir John Robinson and Responsible Government, 1863–1897' (unpublished MA thesis, Natal, 1975) and J. Lambert, 'Sir John Robinson, 1839–1903', *Journal of Natal and Zulu History*, 3 (1980), pp. 45–56. Earlier specialized studies focusing on the responsible government issue in Natal include J. G. Loudon, 'The Responsible Government Issue in Natal, 1880–1882: Parliamentary Elections in Coastal Constituencies' (unpublished MA thesis, Natal University

College, 1940); T. R. H. Davenport 'The Responsible Government Issue in Natal, 1880–1882' (unpublished MA thesis, Rhodes University College, 1949) and T. R. H. Davenport, 'The Responsible Government Issue in Natal, 1880–1882', *Butterworth's South African Law Review* (1957), pp. 84–133; D. J. N. Denoon, 'Sir John Robinson: his Career from 1884 until . . . 1893' (unpublished BA Honours essay, Natal, 1962); C. J. Talbot, 'Harry Escombe and the Politics of Responsible Government in Natal, 1879–1885: a Search for Power' (unpublished MA thesis, University of Natal, Pietermaritzburg, 1974).

8   NA Accession 349: *Some Papers on the Constitution of Natal, 1862–1890*, p. 105; Lambert, 'Robinson and Responsible Government', pp. 11–14.

9   *NPP*, Vol. 248, 14 June 1866; GH 1215, No. 82, pp. 346ff: Bisset to Cardwell, 6 August 1866.

10   GH 46, No. 4, pp. 28ff: Carnarvon to Bisset, 12 October 1866; B. J. T. Leverton, 'Government Finance and Political Development in Natal, 1843–1893' (D.Litt. et Phil. thesis, University of South Africa, 1968) in *AYB*, 1970,1), p. 148; Williams, 'Dispute between Keate and Legislative Council', p. 32.

11   A. B. Theunissen, 'Natal under Lieutenant-Governor Scott, 1856–1864' (unpublished MA thesis, Natal-South Africa, 1936), *passim*; A. F. Hattersley, *Pietermaritzburg Panorama: a Survey of One Hundred Years of an African City* (Pietermaritzburg, Shuter & Shooter, 1938), p. 12.

12   *Natal Legislative Council Votes and Proceedings*, 24 and 27 May 1869; GH 1216, No. 75, pp. 528ff: Keate to Granville, 20 September 1869 and 1217, No. 93, pp. 24–35: Keate to Granville, 22 October 1869.

13   GH 50, No. 67, pp. 223ff: Granville to Keate, 6 December 1869; Davenport, 'Responsible Government Issue' (unpublished MA thesis), pp. 11–12; Lambert, 'Robinson and Responsible Government', pp. 15–16.

14   GH 1217, No. 32, p. 209: Keate to Granville, 19 May 1870 and Vol. 1299, Confidential, pp. 331ff: Keate to Kimberley, February 1871.

15   GH 53, No. 60, pp. 194ff: Kimberley to Keate 18 February 1871; *Times of Natal*, 29 April 1871; *Natal Mercury*, 1 August 1871; Loudon, 'Responsible Government', pp. 1–2.

16   KCAL Colenso Papers, Folio 25Y: Colenso to Shaen, 14 December 1873; *Natal Mercury* 5 February, 10 March 1870, 4 and 25 May 1871, 5 and 10 August 1871.

17   KCAL Colenso Papers, Folio 25Y: Colenso to Shaen, 14 December 1873.

18   C. J. Uys, *In the Era of Shepstone* (Lovedale, Lovedale Press, 1933), pp. 76–8; A. W. Palmer, *A Dictionary of Modern History, 1789–1945* (Harmondsworth, Penguin, 1963), pp. 25–6, 37, 48, 59, 280; Lambert, 'Robinson and Responsible Government', pp. 16–25 and 'Sir John Robinson', pp. 46–7.

19   GH 50: Kimberley to Pine 3 June 1873; 1217, No. 93, pp. 24–35: Keate to Granville, 22 October 1869; E. A. Walker, *A History of South Africa* (London, Longmans, 1957), p. 345.

20   G. M. Theal, *History of South Africa from 1873 to 1884*, 1 (London, Allen and Unwin, 1919), p. 225.

21   *BPP* XLV of 1874 (C. 1025), pp. 43–76: Pine to Kimberley, 1 February 1874, enclosing minutes of Langalibalele's trial; LIII of 1875 (C. 1119 No. 10), pp. 8–44: Officer Administering the Government to Carnarvon, 9 May 1874, enclosing minutes of the trial of the tribe; W. R. Guest, *Langalibalele: the Crisis in Natal, 1873–75* (Durban, Department of History, University of Natal, 1976), pp. 31–6.

22   SNA 1/3/5 No. 33: J. MacFarlane to Secretary for Native Affairs, 19 February 1856; 1/3/8, pp. 306–9: MacFarlane to Secretary for Native Affairs, 31 January 1859 and 1/3/13 No. 23: MacFarlane to Secretary for Native Affairs, 1 December 1863; GH 1540: MacFarlane to Pine, 29 January 1874; Wright, *Bushman Raiders of the Drakensberg*, pp. 78, 82, 93–4; Guest, *Langalibalele*, pp. 24–30; N. A. Etherington, 'Why Langalibalele Ran Away', *Journal of Natal and Zulu History*, 1 (1978), pp. 4–10.

23   *BPP* XLV of 1874 (C. 1025), pp. 9–14: Pine to Kimberley, 13 November 1873; *Natal Mercury*, 11 November 1873; Guest, *Langalibalele*, pp. 36–44; Etherington, 'Why Langalibalele Ran Away', pp. 10–24.

24   *BPP* LIII of 1875 (C.1141): Colenso's Pamphlet 'Langalibalele and the Amahlubi Tribe'; Guest, *Langalibalele*, 45–60; Etherington, 'Why Langalibalele Ran Away', pp. 2–4.

25   KCAL Colenso Papers, Folio 511: Colenso to Revd J. Reynolds, 4 April 1874; Guest, *Langalibalele*, pp. 60, 63–4.

26   See Guest, *Langalibalele*, p. 41.

27   *Natal Legislative Council Votes and Proceedings*, 21 September 1874; *Natal Mercury*, 5 and 7 November 1874; GH 1380, p. 253: Message to the Legislative Council No. 65; Eybers, *Select Constitutional Documents*, pp. 199–200; Lambert, 'Robinson and Responsible Government' pp. 41–2.

28   GH 1300, pp. 64ff, Confidential: Pine to Carnarvon, 15 December 1874, and 281, pp. 897ff, Confidential: Carnarvon to Wolseley, 22 February 1875; Lambert, 'Robinson and Responsible Government', pp. 40–2.

29   *Select Documents on British Colonial Policy, 1830–1860*, eds. K. N. Bell and W. P. Morrell, pp. 191–4, quoting Carnarvon's minute of 7 January 1859 on Grey's despatch to Sir E. Bulwer-Lytton, 19 November 1858 (CO 48/390).

30   *Natal Mercury*, 19 November 1874. For an explanation of the confederation policy based upon Carnarvon's personal ambitions and strategic interests, see C. F. Goodfellow, *Great Britain and South African Confederation, 1870–1881* (Cape Town, Oxford University Press, 1966), pp. 49–59.

31   For more detailed socio-economic analyses of the policy of confederation, see A. Atmore and S. Marks, 'The Imperial Factor in South Africa in the Nineteenth Century: Towards a Reassessment', *Journal of Imperial and Commonwealth History*, 3 (1974), pp. 105–39 and R. L. Cope 'Strategic and Socio-Economic Explanations for Carnarvon's Confederation Policy: the Historiography and the Evidence', *History in Africa*, 13 (1986), pp. 13–34.

32   *Natal Mercury*, 30 January 1875; Guest, *Langalibalele*, pp. 56–64.

33   GH 597: Barkly to Pine, 8 July 1874; *BPP* LIII of 1875 (C.1121), pp. 64–6: pamphlet *re* Langalibalele's case with Counsel's opinion, left by Colenso with Carnarvon, 5 October 1874; *Carnarvon's Speeches on the Affairs of West Africa and South Africa*, ed. R. G. W. Herbert (London, John Murray, 1903), p. 167.

34   GH 62, No. 142: Carvarvon to Pine, 3 December 1874, and 63, No. 144: Carnarvon to Barkly, 4 December 1874 (copy); *BPP* LII of 1875 (C.1342–1), pp. 32–4: Barkly to Carnarvon, 4 June 1875; Uys, *Era of Shepstone*, pp. 92–96; Goodfellow, *South African Confederation*, p. 61.

35   *BPP* LIII of 1875 (C.1121), pp. 92–5: Carnarvon to Pine, 3 December 1874; *Times of Natal*, 6 January 1875; Guest, *Langalibalele*, pp. 64–8.

36   Goodfellow, *South African Confederation*, p. 61; *The South African Diaries of Sir Garnet Wolseley 1875*, ed. A. Preston (Cape Town, Balkema, 1971), pp. 1–4, 21–53, 75–95, 116–17.

37   NA Sir Evelyn Wood Papers, File VII: Wolseley to Wood, 19 February 1875; *BPP* LIII of 1875 (C. 1187), pp. 5–8: Carnarvon to Wolseley, 18 February 1875.

38   *Natal Mercury*, 2 September 1875. For more detailed accounts of Wolseley's Natal mission, see Wolseley, *Diaries*, pp. 114–40, and R. W. Wells, 'The Operation of the Jamaica Reforms in the Natal Constitution, 1875–1880' (unpublished MA thesis, Natal-South Africa, 1935).

39   Wolseley, *Diaries*, p. 233, entry for 9 August 1875.

40   Wolseley, *Diaries*, p. 158, entry for 2 April 1875; *NGG*, Vol. XXVII, No. 1523, 6 April 1875; F. B. Maurice and G. C. A. Arthur, *The Life of Lord Wolseley* (New York, Doubleday, 1924), p. 8.

41   *Natal Mercury*, 17 April 1875; Wolseley, *Diaries*, p. 157, entry for 1 April; p. 164, entry for 15 April; p. 165, entry for 17 April, and p. 166, entry for 19 April 1875.

42   Wolseley, *Diaries*, p. 160, entry for 4 April; p. 188, entry for 27 May 1875; H. Brackenbury, *Some Memories of my Spare Time* (London, William Blackwood, 1909), p. 239. For details of the religious controversy in Natal see P. Hinchliff, *John William Colenso, Bishop of Natal* (London, Nelson, 1964), ch. 5. Wolseley's staff in Natal consisted of Napier Broome as Colonial Secretary, Major H. Brackenbury as Private Secretary and Clerk to the Executive Council, Colonel George Pomeroy-Colley as Colonial Treasurer, Major W. F. Butler as Immigration Agent, and Captain Lord Gifford as aide-de-camp. All but Napier Broome, the only civilian, had served with him before. See Wells, 'Jamaica Reforms in Natal', p. 35.

43   Wolseley, *Diaries*, p. 158, entry for 2 April and p. 162, entry for 11 April 1875; NA Shepstone Papers, File 29: T. Shepstone to Henrique Shepstone, 21 September 1875; Brackenbury, *Memories*, p. 237.

44   Wolseley, *Diaries*, p. 160, entry for 6 April 1875.

45   *Natal Legislative Council Votes and Proceedings*, 31 May 1875; Wolseley, *Diaries*, p. 175, entry for 5 May 1875.

46   *Natal Legislative Council Votes and Proceedings*, 5 to 31 May 1875; *NPP*, 471: petitions 3 and 4 of 18 May 1875; Wolseley, *Diaries*, p. 175, entry for 5 May; p. 177, entry for 7 May; p. 180, entry for 12 May; p. 181, entry for 13 May; p. 183, entry for 18 May and p. 185, entry for 20 May 1875.

47   GH 1219, No. 119, pp. 91–94: Wolseley to Carnarvon, 1 June 1875; Wolseley, *Diaries*, p. 191, entry for 31 May 1875.

48   Wolseley, *Diaries*, pp. 144–5, entry for 20 March 1875.

49   Wolseley, *Diaries*, p. 168, entry for 24 April 1875; Maurice and Arthur, *Life of Wolseley*, pp. 79–82; Uys, *Era of Shepstone*, p. 111.

50   *BPP* LII of 1876 (C.1401–1), p. 86: Carnarvon to Bulwer, 29 October 1875; Maurice and Arthur, *Life of Wolseley*, pp. 79, 85; Eybers, *Select Constitutional Documents*, p. 199; Wells, 'Jamaica Reforms in Natal', pp. 3–7.

51   GH 1219, No. 119, pp. 91–4: Wolseley to Carnarvon, 1 June 1875. See also Wolseley, *Diaries*, pp. 139–149.

52   *Natal Witness*, 24 August 1875; Wolseley, *Diaries*, p. 196, entries for 15 and 16 June 1875.

53   NA Shepstone Papers, File 14: Carnarvon to Shepstone, 26 October 1874; GH 1219, No. 131, pp. 101–13: Wolseley to Carnarvon, 14 June 1875; *Natal Legislative Council Votes and Proceedings*, 5 December 1875; D. H. Heydenrych, 'The Construction of Public Works and the Constitutional Status of Natal, 1875–1893: the Railway Case' (unpublished paper, Conference on the History of Natal and Zululand, University of Natal, Durban, 1985), pp. 1–2.

54   *Ordinances, Laws and Proclamations of Natal*, Col. 2, 1870–78, p. 1140 (Law No. 26 of 1875); GH 1219, No. 18: Bulwer to Carnarvon, 14 February 1876 and 69, No. 195: Carnarvon to Bulwer, 6 March 1876, enclosing J. W. Akerman to Aborigines Protection Society, 18 December 1875.

55   *Natal Witness*, 4 July 1878; Eybers, *Select Constitutional Documents*, pp. 247–364; Welsh, *Roots of Segregation*, pp. 152–72, 176.

56   *Natal Colonist*, 3 September 1875; *Natal Witness*, 2 and 16 November 1875, 6 July 1877.

57   NA Shepstone Papers, File 13B: Bulwer to Shepstone 25 April, 18 July and 15 August 1877; GH 1636: Sir G. Wolseley Memoranda, 1875, containing letters from proposed nominee members; *Natal Legislative Council Votes and Proceedings*, 1875–1880.

58   *Natal Mercury*, 10 January 1874; GH 274, pp. 148ff, Secret; Carnarvon to Wolseley, 13 May 1875; *BPP* C–1399, No. 1: Carnarvon to Barkly, 4 May 1875; Goodfellow, *South African Confederation*, pp. 49–67. For an examination of white settler attitudes in Natal towards confederation proposals at this time, see B. Guest, 'Natal and the Confederation Issue in the 1870s' (unpublished MA thesis, Natal, 1967) and B. Guest, 'The War, Natal and Confederation' in *The Anglo-Zulu War: New Perspectives*, eds. Duminy and Ballard, pp. 53–77.

59   *BPP* LII of 1876 (C. 1399), pp. 1–3: Carnarvon to Barkly, 4 May 1875 and pp. 58–83: J. A. Froude to Carnarvon, 10 January 1876; LII of 1875 (C. 1342–1), pp. 32–4: Barkly to Carnarvon, 4 June 1875; Uys, *Era of Shepstone*, p. 96; P. A. Molteno, *The Life and Times of Sir J. C. M. Molteno*, 2 vols. (London, Smith, Elder, 1900), 1, pp. 336–43.

60   *BPP* LII of 1876 (C. 1399), pp. 29–35: Barkly to Carnarvon, 20 October 1875; *Cape Argus*, 10 and 12 June 1875; Molteno, *Life of J. C. M. Molteno*, 1, pp. 345–7; 2, pp. 21ff.

61   Guest, 'Natal and the Confederation Issue', pp. 38–40, 95–6, 112–14.

62   Ibid., 85–6, 94, 129–30.

63 GH 1501: Report of Sub-Committee of Natal Executive Council, 29 November 1878, and Memorandum by T. Polkinghorne (Treasurer), 8 May 1879; GH 1220, pp. 489–93: Colley to Kimberley, 26 December 1880; *Natal Mercantile Advertiser*, 12 and 28 February 1880, 10 February 1881; *Natal Witness*, 27 September 1879 and 8 April 1881; *Natal Mercury*, 25 September 1879 and 28 March 1881; B. Guest, 'The Meaning of Majuba for Natal', *Natalia*, 11 (December 1981), pp. 27–8.

Chapter 7

The 'Shepstone system' in the Colony of Natal and beyond the borders

NORMAN ETHERINGTON

In 1846, at the age of twenty-eight, Theophilus Shepstone was appointed Diplomatic Agent to the 'Native Tribes' of Natal. For the next three decades, his little office in Pietermaritzburg was primarily responsible for all of the following functions of government: keeping the peace and administering justice among the African population; collecting taxes, fines and fees imposed on Africans by the government; regulating the movement of Africans across the internal and external boundaries of the Colony; and maintaining diplomatic relations with independent African states throughout south-east Africa. Both his contemporaries and later historians marvelled that he did so much with such limited resources and so few apparent failures. Shepstone, who did not talk much about himself, did not contradict those who said he succeeded because he mysteriously 'knew the native mind'. He played the role of African chief with pomp and swagger. He believed that his Nguni name *Somtseu* inspired awe and respect everywhere. However, he was very well aware that his administration rested on more prosaic foundations.

The *mfecane* and the Voortrekker Republic of Natalia had upset but not destroyed the old framework of African life in Natal (see Chapters 3 and 4). The British annexation finally obliterated the police power of the Zulu kingdom south of the Thukela and drove away a great many of the Voortrekkers who had challenged it before them. The inhabitants could reclaim their land. People still knew and respected the traditional supports of law and order. So long as these were not fundamentally threatened, it did not require much effort to keep the peace.

At the outset, Shepstone doubted that he could succeed. His first policy

*Theophilus Shepstone (1817–93)
photographed at an early stage of his
long career.*

Natal Archives, C108/16

memorandum painted a gloomy picture of African life in his jurisdiction.[1] Fragments of broken chiefdoms with a history of bloodshed were caught up in never-ending disputes which 'no mere native authority' could 'quell or set at rest'. He predicted that anarchy could continue unless the government pushed the black population onto reservations under the watchful eye of white magistrates. Each magistrate would enforce 'good behaviour' and control the movement of people in and out of his reservation. He would resolve disputes and try criminals. He would encourage 'industrious habits' and the production of commodities for the market places of the world. Similar advice was given in 1846 by the Commission for Locating Natives, of which Shepstone was a member. According to the Commission's report, 100 000 Africans in Natal were living 'without any law whatsoever actively and efficiently operating among them'. They needed missionaries to teach them Christianity and to stamp out 'immoral' customs. They needed 'industrial schools' to teach them how to work and a force of black policemen under white officers to keep the peace.[2]

The Colonial Office rejected these ambitious schemes because they would cost too much. To Shepstone's surprise, Natal did not fall into chaos. Instead, the African people proved to be a mine of human and material resources which propped up the feeble Colony during the pioneering decades. Shepstone and his colleagues on the Location Commission realized that the Africans would not stay peaceful unless they were given enough land to support their families in accordance with accepted standards. Therefore, they marked out 'locations' in areas already inhabited by Africans but not claimed by white farmers.[3] These lands alone would not have been enough to support the whole African population. Fortunately, there was a further reservoir of unsurveyed Crown Land and unoccupied farms on which Africans were able to live undisturbed for many years. As long as this necessary foundation of family life existed, Shepstone was able to leave the government of the Natal Africans largely in the hands of the people.

He did this by putting a layer of British judicial and administrative machinery on top of pre-colonial African institutions. Shepstone conceived his system as a pyramid of authority:

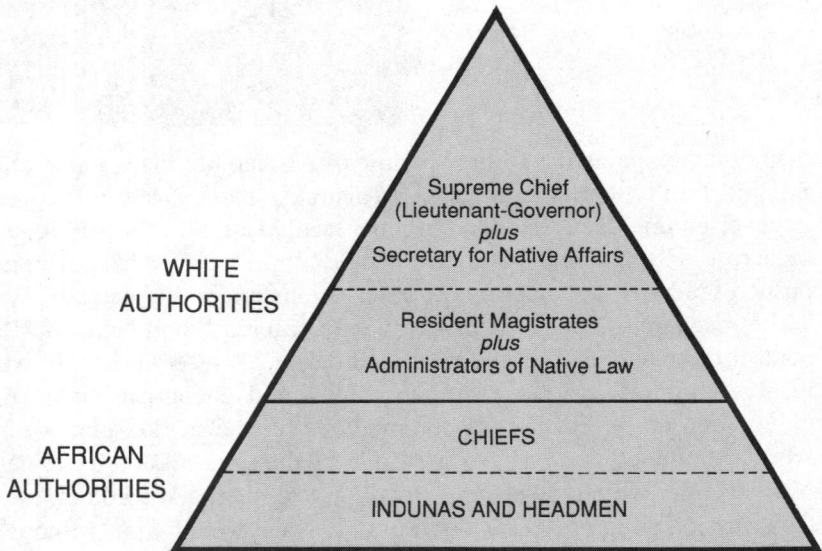

WHITE
AUTHORITIES

Supreme Chief
(Lieutenant-Governor)
plus
Secretary for Native Affairs

Resident Magistrates
plus
Administrators of Native Law

AFRICAN
AUTHORITIES

CHIEFS

INDUNAS AND HEADMEN

At each level of the hierarchy, officials were supposed to make decisions in accordance with 'Native Law'. The customary practices of Natal's indigenous population were assumed to be the basis of Native Law but no one systematically studied them or wrote them down. Consequently, Native Law was what its interpreters said it was. At the lowest levels of Shepstone's pyramid, indunas and 'headmen' decided such cases as Africans chose to bring to them. Occasionally, magistrates allowed them to settle disputes without a formal trial. At another level, hereditary and appointed chiefs declared the law, although the frequency with which they sat in judgment and the categories of cases they handled varied from district to district. One white magistrate remarked in 1859 that there had been a decline in cases decided by chiefs over a period of years. In other districts, influential chiefs such as Teteleku claimed to be deciding most disputes 'about cattle, in cases of *ukulobola*, or about ground, or goats' as late as the 1880s. Interpretations of Native Law in chiefly courts varied according to the prejudices of the chiefs. For example, Teteleku decided cases in the light of his understanding of traditional practice. Johannes Khumalo, on the other hand, who was a Christian headman, said that he passed judgement 'as near as I know to the white man's law'.[4]

At the next level, cases were heard by white, salaried Resident Magistrates and Administrators of Native Law.[5] Africans could appeal to their courts against decisions of chiefs or headmen. They could also bring cases directly to them, although the higher fees charged discouraged most people from doing so. The magistrates had great discretionary powers. Without written codes or old case records to guide them, they were supposed to arrive at just decisions by utilizing their 'knowledge of the customs of the natives', by 'comparing numerous precedents' and by applying 'rules of equity, whether these are to be found in English or Native precedents'.

At the summit of the pyramid, law was made by the decrees of Shepstone, the Lieutenant-Governor and the Legislative Council. Shepstone justified ruling by decree on the ground that Zulu monarchs had possessed absolute power. The Governor, he argued, now stood in the place of the monarch and, as 'Supreme Chief', could do as he liked. Since the introduction, interpretation and enforcement of these decrees was mostly in the hands of Shepstone and his assistants, there were numerous anomalies and inconsistencies.

Africans often expressed confusion and anger at their subjection to Shepstone's patchwork system of Native Law. At a meeting called in 1863 to protest against the system, one man summed up the bewilderment felt by many people:

> He said he did not know how many laws there were in Natal. English, Kafir, and Roman Dutch he had heard of. There was also a mixture of all; by all of which the natives got the worst of it. He said they wanted a written law – not one in which the brains was [sic] the only book to which reference was to be made.[6]

Another man complained that 'the way we see the laws promulgated now is by seeing someone going to prison for disobeying them'.[7]

These, however, were problems for Africans, not problems for Shepstone. For a relatively small cost, the makeshift arrangement kept the peace and settled disputes. By rewarding his indunas and chiefs with portions of the fines they collected and booty they acquired on punitive expeditions, Shepstone secured a loyal following. His apparatus of government also provided channels for the collection of revenue. Taxing Africans produced an unexpected bonanza which paid for almost the whole government of Natal. The foundation of the system was the hut tax imposed on every black head of household, according to the number of huts in his homestead. As the population grew, so did the number of huts. From time to time, the base rate was raised by the Legislative Council. Fines and fees charged for the registration of marriages were another source of funds which grew with the population. By a proclamation of 1869, a charge of £5 was imposed for the registration of every African marriage. Registration of a divorce cost £1.

Most lucrative of all were the customs duties charged on goods imported into Natal. At first glance this might appear to be a colour-blind tax. However, the Legislative Council tried to put as many charges as possible on goods used exclusively by Africans. For example, there were no customs duties on silk stockings, top hats, frock coats or any of the other apparel worn by the well-to-do. On the other hand, cotton and woollen blankets, used by Africans throughout the subcontinent, were heavily taxed. In 1873, ordinary hoes were charged only sixpence but so-called 'Kaffir' picks and hoes attracted a tax of a shilling each. The 'manufactured' tobacco smoked by Europeans could be imported for one shilling and sixpence per hundred weight. The coarser tobacco snuffed and burned by Africans was charged more than twice that amount. Beads used in trade to the interior were taxed heavily. So were alcohol and firearms. Although sales of both to Africans in Natal were severely limited by law, such was not the case in the independent black territories of east and central Africa. Despite the fears of white settlers that firearms sold beyond the borders might someday be turned against them, the gun lobby of Durban managed to block all attempts at control.[8] Sale of ammunition was a government monopoly which bolstered revenue. Thus, it was not just the blacks who lived in the Colony whose taxes supported the government; customs charges on goods used in the interior trade were passed on to distant African purchasers in the form of higher prices. Whenever more revenue was needed, new charges were levied on African consumer goods. So, when the decision was made to import Indian labour for sugar plantations, the new schedule of tariff charges was known as the 'Coolie tariff'. African workers thus contributed largely to the cost of the importation of their competitors on the labour market.

By the final years of Shepstone's administration, the balance sheets showed how spectacularly successful had been the strategy of making Africans pay for their own government. After the deduction of interest payment and technical charges, the total revenue in 1872 was £191 196.[9] Of that total, £81 915 came from customs charges largely passed on to black consumers, £27 656 came from hut taxes, £10 468 came from fines and fees charged for African marriages, and £10 086 came from sales of ammunition. Fines imposed by colonial courts, which mostly fell on African offenders, raised £3 620, and sales of land (which had of course belonged entirely to Africans before white settlement) raised £7 819. Taken together, the funds contributed by Africans amounted to about £142 000 (roughly 75 per cent of all revenue).

On the other side of the balance sheet, expenditure (after the deduction of technical accounting items) amounted to £150 675. Only £5 891 of the money was spent for 'Native Purposes'. The other £144 784 – a sum just slightly more than the total revenue raised from Africans – paid for: the salaries of all government officials, all the hospitals, all the gaols, all the grants to white schools, all the ammunition bought by the government, all the money spent on colonial defence, the postal services, roads, streets, bridges, and the Legislative Council which levied the taxes. In other words, while Africans suffered taxation without representation, white settlers enjoyed representation virtually without taxation.

This result could not have been achieved without the growth of African purchasing power. It was the money they earned through supplying food to colonial markets, working for white employers and trading that enabled them to pay taxes and buy the goods on which customs charges were levied.[10] It was this increasing prosperity, as much as the maintenance of African structures of authority, that enabled Shepstone to rule with so little open resistance from the people. Nevertheless, he had to engage in a constant struggle to prevent white politicians from killing the goose which laid the golden eggs. His most determined enemies were the so-called 'up-country' people from the farms and villages of inland Natal. These settlers believed that, if black labour could be made cheaper and more plentiful, they could achieve the prosperity that they had hoped for ever since their arrival. The poorer white farmers and workers also resented competition from black producers. The up-country party in the Legislative

Council argued that raising hut taxes and cutting down the size of the locations would force 'lazy' Africans to come out to work for them.[11]

Shepstone believed, and often said, that those policies would lead to instability and eventual rebellion. He was supported by important sections of white opinion. Coastal sugar planters backed him because they needed reliable labour more than they needed cheap labour. They accepted his argument that reliable labour was more likely to be obtained from stable families on the locations than from unruly, unhappy, impoverished people pushed off their ancestral lands. His old friend Bishop Colenso believed that it was 'the most influential planters on the Coast – those who have the most invested in the colony, and therefore most to lose from mismanagement' who were 'warm supporters of Mr Shepstone'.[12] Another important group of backers comprised landowners who made money by renting property to Africans. As the latter expanded their operations, they were happy to pay for the right to occupy better land than was available in the locations. Absentee landowners such as the Natal Land and Colonization Society supported Shepstone against the up-country people who wished to squeeze Africans off Crown Lands and private property alike.[13] British governors and other officials also backed Shepstone. They feared that a concerted attack on African security would invite rebellion and lay the Colony open to a Zulu invasion. Lieutenant-Governor Musgrave estimated in 1872 that African men in Natal were already supplying as much labour as could reasonably be expected.[14] If more was required, they would simply demand higher wages so that they could continue to support their families.

Shepstone and his supporters looked beyond the borders of the Colony of Natal for solutions to its economic problems. They believed that the Colony was ideally situated to be the gateway to the African interior. In the language of their time, they conceived their task to be 'the opening of Africa'. By this they meant, not simply exploring expeditions such as David Livingstone's, but what they called the 'exploitation' of natural and human resources. Exploitation did not in those days carry its present unsavoury connotations. It was a Victorian expression of optimism and the spirit of progress. Introducing mining and a cash economy to new territories was expected to enrich Europeans and to 'raise' Africans from 'savagery' to 'civilization'.

Like Shepstone's system of indirect rule, this expansive vision was part of the African inheritance for, during the preceding half-century, ribbons of migration had pushed into the far interior from the Natal region. Many of these black trekkers left relatives behind in Zululand and Natal. That meant that they also left claims and obligations concerning women, children and cattle which only time and distance could gradually extinguish. There was therefore continual movement between Natal and distant lands. As Secretary for Native Affairs, Shepstone could not avoid taking notice of these long-distance relationships. One of the tasks of his border agents was to record the movements and to check the credentials of all Africans who passed the frontier. Magistrates and Administrators of Native Law sat in judgment on very complicated lobola cases involving 'foreigners' which came to them on appeal from the courts of chiefs and headmen. Shepstone's own incorrigibly suspicious mind led him to interrogate messengers from faraway chiefs in order to uncover external or internal threats to security. He was not making an idle boast when he sent the following message to the Ndebele king Lobengula of Zimbabwe in 1871:

> The Lieutenant-Governor of Natal thanks Lobengula . . . for his friendly message . . . he also accepts the tusk of ivory . . . The Government of Natal is the largest Native power in South Eastern Africa, and its territory is the resort of refugees of all ranks from surrounding Tribes. The Lieutenant-Governor is looked upon as The Father of all, and hears what all have to say. He is therefore intimately acquainted with the domestic circumstances of surrounding populations, he does not seek for this information, it comes to him.[15]

Exploring parties seized gratefully upon Natal's established lines of communication to the interior. Shepstone willingly put his official resources at the disposal of promising expeditions. In 1870, for example, he sent his official messenger, Elijah Kambule, and one of his border agents, Frederick Elton, to help the London and Limpopo Mining Company in a bid to win a mining concession in Matabeleland.[16] The leader of another exploring party hailed Shepstone's name as 'a host itself among the Native tribes of Central Africa'.[17] In contrast to the up-country people who resented Shepstone for locking up labour on the locations, the visionaries who hoped to 'open up Africa' from Natal saw him as 'the one-day-to-be Governor-General of all the native tribes residing between the Cape and the Zambezi'.[18] Shepstone agreed. He believed that the general model of administration he had evolved in Natal could be applied elsewhere on the continent, so long as Africans could pay hut taxes and provide the basic services of local government.[19]

What he failed to realize was that the system was dynamic, not static. It contained built-in potential for trouble. Within Natal, there was a contradiction between growing black involvement in the economy and a system of segregation administered by a government of British officials and white settlers. Beyond the frontier, there was a contradiction between 'opening up Africa', and maintaining peaceful relations with independent states. During Shepstone's lifetime, these contradictions manifested themselves in a series of internal and external crises.

Another flaw in Shepstone's policy was that it was based upon the theory that Africans lived as identifiable chiefdoms on specified lands. Anyone who wished to move was supposed to get a signed pass from the local magistrate. In cases of serious crime, Shepstone would invoke the principle of 'tribal responsibility' which made each chief responsible for the conduct of every member of his 'tribe'. The reality of African life in Natal was at odds with this theory in many respects, for not only did as many people live outside the locations as in them, but many Africans had no recognized chief at all. Shepstone estimated that, at the time he assumed office as Diplomatic Agent, only 'one-third, or at most one-half' of the people were living under hereditary chiefs. Consequently, he had to make 'tribes' and chiefs. In some cases, he attached individuals and fragments of chiefdoms to existing chiefs. In other cases, he rewarded trusted African assistants by putting them in charge of entirely artificial chiefdoms.[20]

A difficulty in governing according to the principle of 'tribal responsibility' was that it was often incompatible with government based on geographical units. Natal's magistrates and Administrators of Native Law were responsible for particular areas. It frequently happened that chiefdoms overlapped the boundaries of magisterial authority, while the search for good land, better wages, and access to colonial markets increased the distance between Africans and the chiefs to whom they were theoretically responsible. Of course, it was open to any magistrate to punish chiefs in his district for offences committed far away. However, the object of upholding 'tribal responsibility' was not to punish chiefs but to maintain law and order. Shepstone, perennially short of staff, was inclined to ignore illegal activities carried on by isolated individuals in remote places. But, if members of a large chiefdom with an important head flouted the law, he brought the full weight of armed force to bear on the offenders.

In 1857 the chief Sidoi in southern Natal made an unauthorized attack on a neighbouring chiefdom and, when summoned to account for it by the local magistrate, went into hiding. Shepstone commanded that Sidoi's people surrender their chief or face extinction as a tribal unit. After Sidoi and some of his followers escaped from the Colony, Shepstone confiscated the property and destroyed the homes of those who remained.[21] A select committee of the Legislative Council which investigated the affair reported that Shepstone had acted precipitately and that innocent people had been brutally punished.[22] (Their condemnation was undoubtedly merited but their motives were less than pure. The up-country party hoped to use the incident to break up the locations, so that more labour could be forced on to the market.)

Within a few months of Sidoi's flight, a second chief was charged with rebellion. This time, it was Matshana of northern Natal who refused a magistrate's order to deliver for trial men who had killed a person believed to be a witch. Shepstone sent his younger brother, John, with a large force to bring Matshana in. After luring the chief to a meeting with a promise to come unarmed, John Shepstone and his men produced concealed weapons and attempted a capture. Although wounded, Matshana and part of his retinue escaped to Zululand.[23] The remainder of the chiefdom was broken up and scattered. A nearby missionary reported to his superiors that Matshana had been respected by white and black alike and expressed the belief that, if the truth were known in London, both Shepstones would lose their positions.[24] In fact, the two incidents strengthened Shepstone's authority. The fate of the two extinguished chiefdoms was held up as an example of what lay in store for others who did not obey orders. One magistrate later reported that their punishment had exercised a most salutory influence in his district. When another magistrate found chiefs reluctant to support his plan for an 'industrial village', he simply mentioned Sidoi's name and opposition melted.[25] Chief Langalibalele of the Hlubi, who had been in dispute with his magistrate in 1858, 'expressed great contrition' when he was reminded of Matshana's ruin.[26]

In villages and towns, Shepstone faced other problems which the system of locations and indirect rule could not solve. African workers in the towns came from widely scattered areas, some from far beyond the Colony's borders. They were not under the effective control of any chief. They mingled with, and sometimes cohabited with, the poorer white residents. They were frequently accused of crime. Shepstone's preferred method of dealing with such people was to subject them to strict control. The Refugee

Law of 1854 made all individual immigrants liable to three years' service for white employers at fixed wages. Labourers recruited in gangs had no legal rights if they left their assigned employers. Africans from within Natal needed passes signed by their magistrates before they could legally enter a town. Curfew laws forbade all except Europeans to be out after certain hours. No alcoholic drinks could be legally sold to Africans. In 1873 Shepstone further curbed what he called 'the attractive but unwholesome liberty' of Africans in the main towns of Pietermaritzburg and Durban by requiring every 'Native' who was not a householder, renter or servant in monthly employment to register as a *togt* (day) labourer or jobber.[27] After five days in town, every jobber had to accept any work offered at a fixed low wage or face imprisonment with hard labour for up to three months. This not only controlled African movements, but helped to increase Shepstone's popularity among white employers. By such measures, he assisted the development of shanty slums and labour barracks which had become established features of the urban landscape even before he left office in 1875. A missionary wrote in 1877 that the only shelter Africans could find in Pietermaritzburg was:

> . . . at the outskirts of the Town in the lowest localities, in tumble-down uninhabitable houses; or perhaps two diminutive rooms in a row of houses called the 'Barracks' where they are packed together in a most unwholesome manner for body as well as soul, with the most profligate characters in Town. And in these places very often the single room is converted into a Beer house for Kafir Beer, as the only means of livelihood for the hapless woman with her four or five children.[28]

During the Shepstone years, the combined effects of limited administrative resources, settler ascendancy and economic growth made a mockery of the initial promise that there should 'not be in the eye of the law any distinction of colour, origin, race or creed'. Shepstone believed that he needed Native Law to keep the peace in rural districts and that he needed Draconian rules to prevent urban areas from being overrun by Africans. Both he and the all-white Legislative Council knew that equal rights would threaten the unique taxation system of the Colony which forced unrepresented Africans to pay nearly the whole cost of government; while settler opinion revolted at the idea of accepting them as equals. In order to safeguard their respective interests, officials and settlers contrived to make it all but impossible for any African to escape the strictures of Native Law.

Natal Law 11 of 1864 laid down rigid procedures for exempting Africans from the system. For more than a decade after the proclamation of that law, no exemptions were granted and, when at length a few score of Africans did succeed in complying with the regulations, they found themselves exempt in name but not in substance. A similar enactment in 1865 ensured that few, if any, Africans would ever be permitted to vote. One of the men who drafted the law later declared that its complexities were deliberately formed to stop them from exercising the franchise.[29]

The economic growth which enabled the government of Natal to milk African taxpayers also drew streams of temporary workers to the Colony in search of wages. As early as 1855 Shepstone had noticed that 'many, if not the majority of our labourers, do not belong to the tribes of our immediate neighbourhood; they come from a distance, numbers from beyond the Drakensberg, and some from lattitudes far north of Delagoa Bay'.[30] The importance of these aliens to the economy of the Colony increased as alternative centres of employment opened up, for example the Cape Railways and the Kimberley diamond-fields. One answer to the problem of assuring a supply of labour was to import indentured workers from India, a practice that began in 1860.

In 1872, after the diamond rush had raised black wages and consequently diverted migrants from Natal, a Select Committee of the Legislative Council investigated the question. Evidence submitted showed that, in addition to sea-borne migration from Mozambique, there were three principal overland migration routes.[31] One ran through Zululand, another through the Transvaal Republic, and a third through territory claimed by both the Zulu kingdom and the Transvaal. Attempts to increase migration along these routes involved Shepstone and the government of Natal in thorny diplomatic problems which they were ill-equipped to handle. Nevertheless, they plunged boldly in.

Shepstone had perpetually meddled in the affairs of his neighbours. From the early 1850s he had promoted schemes for moving Natal's 'excess' African population – those who could not be accommodated on the locations – to some nearby territory where he would rule them as Supreme Chief through an administration paid for by hut taxes and tariffs.[32] At first he had looked south to Mpondoland, but by 1860 he had shifted his attention to Zululand. In that year he and Sir George Grey failed by just a whisker to annex the disputed territory between the Transvaal and Zululand.[33] During the next ten years, he was involved in schemes to annex Basutoland.[34]

In the 1870s Natal's labour difficulties caused Shepstone's attention to focus once more upon Zululand. Employers in the Colony reacted enthusiastically to the news that Britain intended to conclude a treaty suppressing the slave trade from Zanzibar because they expected that 'free' migrant labour would be diverted to South Africa. The editor of the *Natal Witness* expressed the hope in 1872 that workers from East Africa would be carried down the coast on the shipping packets being introduced by William Mackinnon. The editor thought British intervention in East Africa would:

> . . . open up the trade all along the coast, and place Natal in a better position for pressing on the Imperial Government the necessity of buying the Portuguese Government out of the country south of the Zambezi . . . Natal must consequently carry out a Monroe Doctrine of its own, and insist that the Anglo-Saxon race shall hold undisputed sway from Cape Town to the Zambezi. Besides, we wish to obtain a supply of labour for our coast planters from these localities, and this we will never be able to do satisfactorily until we have control of the various ports.[35]

Frederic Elton, a retired army captain who had been one of Shepstone's border agents, was sent to Zanzibar to look after Natal's interests and stayed on as British Consul to Mozambique. There he clandestinely worked to end Portuguese rule.

Shepstone shared the belief that only the expansion of British dominion could solve the long-term economic and security problems of Natal. Portugal and the Transvaal Republic hindered the movement of black labour and the expansion of trade. The Zulu kingdom and other martial states kept regiments of able-bodied young men tied down with military duties. Mineral discoveries, the expansion of commerce and the trade in firearms were constantly strengthening the power of Natal's white and black neighbours. If a general African onslaught on British Africa occurred,[36] discontented blacks in Natal might rise in sympathy. These fears, justified or not, dominated his domestic and foreign policies in the early 1870s, so that the curbing of the independence of the Zulu kingdom, and the extension of British rule northwards along the south-east coast of Africa assumed a new urgency.

The year 1873 was a jittery one in Natal. White public opinion had been edgy, not least because there had been a panic over the alleged threat of sexual assaults on white females by African men, even though few Africans had ever been convicted of such a crime. Rumour said that black workers on the Kimberley diamond-fields were buying guns and bringing them back to Natal without complying with the stringent registration laws.

When Langalibalele – perhaps remembering Matshana, whose fate had been brought to his attention by the local magistrate, John Macfarlane, fifteen years previously – did not comply with the instruction to bring in unregistered firearms, the case was referred to Shepstone.[37] Unfortunately, the Secretary for Native Affairs was far too preoccupied with Zulu affairs at the moment to deal with the matter. Shepstone's interest in the Zulu kingdom at this juncture had been brought about by the death of Mpande in 1872 and the succession of Cetshwayo. He seized eagerly on an invitation to attend the coronation, portraying it to his government as an invitation to install the new monarch (see Chapter 4). He hoped to use his meeting with Cetshwayo to revive his proposal to annex the disputed borderlands, to make firm arrangements for the passage of Tsonga labourers from the northeast, and to make certain of the new king's friendship. These goals would not be easy to accomplish because Cetshwayo had a long-standing distrust of Shepstone. After the Zulu civil war of 1856 Shepstone had harboured refugees from factions who had opposed Cetshwayo. In 1861 he had tried to undo the damage by conferring 'official' recognition upon Cetshwayo as heir-apparent, but was angrily rebuffed.[38]

During the coronation expedition of August-September 1873, Shepstone strove to overawe the Zulu nation. Although the Colonial Office had refused him not only the power to discuss annexations of territory but also the escort of regular troops he had requested, it approved the use of colonial volunteer militia. (By an accident of fate, the volunteers chose to hold their preparatory manoeuvres at Escourt, thereby frightening Langalibalele into thinking that he was about to be attacked.) When at length Shepstone entered Zululand with his pompous entourage, he had trouble finding the man he was proposing to crown. The great men of the country had already proclaimed Cetshwayo king the previous month. He was put off with one excuse after another for nearly three weeks before managing to hold his superfluous ceremony on 1 September.[39]

In the negotiations that accompanied the 'coronation' Shepstone promised to limit missionary activity in Zululand and never again to support rival claimants to the throne. Cetshwayo, for his part, conceded nothing more than an agreement regularizing the migration of labour

King Cetshwayo's 'coronation' by Shepstone on 1 September 1873 was a diplomatic device aimed at securing greater influence over the Zulu kingdom.

At the 'coronation' ceremony, Shepstone (seated, centre) adorned Cetshwayo (seated left) with a 'crown' decorated with tinsel. The 'crown' was looted by British troops, along with Cetshwayo's other possessions, following his defeat in 1879.

through his domain. A veteran Anglican missionary in Zululand judged the whole expedition to have been 'a farce'. So it might have been remembered, except that Shepstone used the occasion to deliver what he called a kind of 'ordination sermon or Bishop's charge'.[40] In this public speech, he recommended that fewer sentences of death be imposed on wrong-doers, that all trials be open and that there should be an unrestricted right of appeal to the king. Although no one claimed at the time that these injunctions had any legal force, five years later the British High Commissioner in South Africa would cite the alleged breaking of these 'laws' as one of his excuses for making war on Cetshwayo.

All Natal breathed a sigh of relief when Shepstone brought the expedition safely home, for he could now confront Langalibalele. In reviewing the events that followed (see Chapter 6), the Secretary of State for the Colonies, Lord Carnarvon, agreed with Colenso that the trial of Langalibalele had been a farce and the punishment of the Hlubi a gross miscarriage of justice, but he did not share the Bishop's conviction that Shepstone's system of African administration was to blame.[41] While in London to plead his side of the story, Shepstone could point to three decades of apparent peace and increasing revenue as proof that the system worked.[42] He could also argue that it would have worked even better if he had had more resources and less obstruction from ignorant settler politicians. He contended that the system could be applied to 'any class, country or nation' of Africans south of the Zambezi. Given sufficient land and intelligent, firm administrators, Africans anywhere could be made to pay for their own government. Furthermore, he told Under-Secretary Herbert that, if the territory in dispute between the Transvaal and Zululand were annexed and governed by his methods, a permanent avenue could be opened to the interior of Africa – an avenue for labour migration to Natal and for the export of 'surplus black families' from the Colony.[43]

Shepstone's advice and the objective of federating South Africa thus outweighed Colenso's moral pleadings. A significant offshoot of the Langalibalele crisis was that settlers, who had previously complained of Shepstone's excessive kindness to Africans, now found unsuspected virtues in his administration. Instead of denouncing Native Law as barbaric, they began to see it as a device to ensure that ordinary civil rights would never be extended to Africans. Shepstone himself was knighted in 1876 and sent by Carnarvon to the Transvaal to secure, by persuasion if possible or by proclamation if necessary, its entry into the proposed confederation. Shepstone chose to annex by proclamation on 12 April

Cetshwayo kaMpande, photographed in August 1882, during his visit to London following his deposition and exile.

1877. As administrator of the Transvaal government for the next four years, he was in a good position to advance the expansionist programmes he had long advocated in Natal.

The Zulu kingdom was the next casualty of Carnarvon's scheme. Natal's new Governor, Sir Garnet Wolseley, decided within a few weeks of his arrival in Natal that it must be brought under control before it posed too great a military threat.[44] He suggested justifying annexation on the grounds that Cetshwayo had 'broken the laws' proclaimed by Shepstone at the

Coronation of 1873.[45] While Carnarvon hoped that the annexation could be put off until more urgent matters had been attended to, he agreed that it 'must and ought to come eventually'.[46] So did Sir Bartle Frere, whom Carnarvon sent to South Africa as High Commissioner and who soon found himself fighting a war against the Xhosa on the Cape's eastern frontier. Once Shepstone had been installed at Pretoria, Cetshwayo faced a formidable array of enemies. Shepstone had earlier supported the Zulu in their land dispute with the Transvaal because he hoped to acquire that land for his own black kingdom and road to the north. Now he could secure these objectives by means of upholding the Transvaal claim to the territory, a change of front which he justified by saying that his inspection of archives in Pretoria had convinced him that the Zulu people were in the wrong. He thereafter fed Frere and Carnarvon a stream of correspondence emphasizing 'the menace' of Zulu militarism, linking this to the possibility of a general rising against whites in southern Africa. At the end of 1877 he wrote:

> We might as well surrender at once as do anything that would confirm all these populations in their suspicions that we fear the Zulus. Nor do I think it would be a very difficult thing to break up the Zulu power, and when that is done, you may calculate more certainly upon peace in South Africa. Cetshwayo is the secret hope of every . . . independent chief, hundreds of miles from him, who feels a desire that his colour should prevail, and it will not be until this power is destroyed that they will make up their minds to submit to the rule of civilization.[47]

Frere and Carnarvon got similar advice from Elton, who was now the British consul at Mozambique. His reports stressed the dangers presented by the virtually unrestricted gun trade through Portuguese territory, recommending that Britain do everything possible to buy Portugal out of east Africa.[48] Most of the information available to the High Commissioner and the British government therefore indicated that the Zulu kingdom was a hindrance to the development of British South Africa. The Colonial Office had for several years regarded annexation as inevitable; the War Office thought it necessary for security; Shepstone said it should come sooner rather than later. Sir Henry Bulwer, who succeeded Wolseley as Governor of Natal, dissented from this opinion. He thought there was nothing in the recent behaviour of either Cetshwayo or his subjects to suggest aggressive intentions.[49]

Bulwer's moderation delayed but did not prevent the war. In October 1877 Shepstone met Cetshwayo's chief minister Mnyamana ka Ngqengelele near Blood (Ncome) River and revealed his change of heart on the Transvaal-Zulu boundary dispute. The Zulus came away from that acrimonious meeting convinced that he had declared personal war on their kingdom, and they were not mistaken. In October he sent secret messages to Anglican and Norwegian missionaries, hinting strongly that a British invasion was imminent.[50] But in January 1878 Carnarvon intervened, warning his South African High Commissioner that because of difficulties elsewhere in the Empire, 'a native war is just now impossible'.[51] Although Carnarvon resigned from the Cabinet soon after sending this instruction, his successor at the Colonial office, Sir Michael Hicks Beach, took the same line. Without backing from London, Shepstone and Frere needed a good cause if they were to provoke the 'inevitable' war.

The most suitable pretext for war was undoubtedly the border dispute. Bulwer had appointed a commission to arbitrate, so that from the time it began its proceedings in March 1878, the fate of the Zulu kingdom hung in the balance. From the point of view of Shepstone and Frere, the results were however extremely disappointing. Although John Shepstone was one of the three commissioners, the eventual report supported Zulu claims. Overriding Bulwer, Frere thereupon took personal command of the

Britain's ultimatum was read to a Zulu delegation on the bank of the Thukela River. The fig tree pictured in this photograph still stands below the site of Fort Pearson.

situation. On 11 December 1878 he had the results of the Commission announced to a Zulu delegation, but coupled the good news with the announcement that the Boers who had settled in the region were to be allowed to stay, notwithstanding the recognition of Zulu sovereignty. He then went on to deliver an ultimatum amounting to a declaration of war, demanding that within twenty days a Zulu who had been accused of violating the Natal border be turned over to British authorities, together with the payment of a fine of 600 cattle. Beyond this he announced that, unless the Zulu army disbanded within thirty days, unless missionaries who fled after Shepstone's invasion scare of 1877, or who had been expelled by Cetshwayo, were readmitted, unless the 'coronation laws' of 1873 were implemented, and unless a British Resident were stationed at court, the redcoats would invade.[52] No reasonable person could imagine that Cetshwayo could accept terms that required the destruction of the social and political structure of the kingdom. War came on 12 January 1879.

Notes

1   *BPP* XXXVIII of 1850 (C. 1292): Shepstone to Lt. Governor West, 26 April 1845.

2   *BPP* XLII of 1847–48 (C. 980): Report of the Commission.

3   ABC 15.4.4: Daniel Lindley to B. Anderson, 16 November 1855.

4   SNA 1/3/9, Annual Report of Windham, RM, 1859; statements of Teteleku and J. Khumalo in *Evidence Taken Before the Natal Native Commission, 1881* (Pietermaritzburg, 1882), pp 183, 323.

5   Resident Magistrates could try cases involving anyone. Administrators of Native Law could not try any case involving whites.

6   *Natal Witness*, 27 March 1863.

7   *Evidence Taken Before the Natal Native Commission*, pp. 368–73.

8   N. A. Etherington, 'Labour Supply and the Genesis of South African Confederation in the 1870s', *Journal of African History*, 20 (1979), pp. 235–53.

9   This figure and those which follow are taken from *The Natal Almanac and Register*, 1874 (Pietermaritzburg, 1873) pp. 186–214.

10 For a general treatment of African peasant production see C. Bundy, *The Rise and Fall of the South African Peasantry* (London, Heinemann, 1979). For a description of black enterprise in Natal see Etherington, *Preachers, Peasants and Politics*, pp. 145–75.

11 An insight into the minds of Shepstone's settler enemies can be gleaned from the *Proceedings and Report of the Commission Appointed to Inquire into the Past and Present State of the District of Natal* (Pietermaritzburg, 1853).

12 KCAL Colenso Papers, Folio Y: Colenso to Shaen, 14 December, 1873.

13 Henry Slater, 'Land, Labour and Capital in Natal: the Natal Land and Colonisation Company 1860–1948', *Journal of African History*, 16 (1975), pp. 257–83.

14 CO 179/111: Musgrave to Kimberley, 6 January 1873.

15 CO 178/102: Keate to Kimberley, 6 June 1871, enclosure.

16 SNA 1/3/21: Lucas to Shepstone, 24 July 1871; CO 179/99: Keate to Kimberley, 23 September 1870; SNA 1/1/20: Levert to Shepstone, 30 May 1870; *Natal Witness*, 29 July 1870.

17 *Natal Witness*, 2 March 1869.

18 *Natal Witness*, 12 May 1868.

19 Etherington, 'Labour Supply', pp. 247–8; R. E. Gordon, *Shepstone: the Role of the Family in the History of South Africa, 1820–1900* (Cape Town, Balkema, 1968), pp. 182–3.

20 For a fuller discussion, see N. A. Etherington, 'The Rise of the Kholwa in Southeast Africa' (unpublished Ph.D. thesis, Yale University, 1971), pp. 48–53.

21 SNA 1/3/6: Hawkins to Shepstone, 21 September 1857, and Minute by Lt. Governor J. Scott on letter from Fynn dated 27 January 1858.

22 *NPP* No. 235 of 1858.

23 Etherington, 'Rise of the Kholwa', notes 106 and 107, p. 68.

24 Ibid., note 108, p. 68.

25 Ibid., notes 109 and 110, p. 68.

26 Ibid., notes 111, p. 68.

27 SNA 1/7/8: Memorandum by Shepstone, 26 May 1873.

28   USPG B.32: Quarterly report by Markham, June 1877.

29   See Welsh, *The Roots of Segregation*, pp. 243–6, 290.

30   CO 879/1: *Natal. Despatches, Reports, etc. Relative to the Management of the Natives*, p. 5.

31   *Natal Legislative Council Minutes.*

32   J. W. Colenso, *Church Missions among the Heathen in the Diocese of Natal* (London, R. Clay, n.d.), p. 8.

33   Kennedy, 'The Fatal Diplomacy', pp. 185–86.

34   Gordon, *Shepstone*, pp. 192–93.

35   *Natal Witness*, 11 October 1872.

36   Fear of the 'general combination' is a constant factor in official thinking from the 1850s onwards. See, for example, SNA 1/6/2: Shepstone's transcript of a message from Mswazi, 12 March 1862; PRO Carnarvon Papers, 30/6/23: Keate to Kimberley, 22 June 1871; CO 179/102: Sargeaunt to Carnarvon, 22 November 1877,

37   Etherington, 'Why Langalibalele Ran Away', pp. 1–25; Wright and Mason, *The Hlubi of Natal*, pp. 46–50; Guest, *Langalibalele*, pp. 25–30.

38   Etherington, 'Anglo-Zulu Relations', pp. 17–21.

39   Ibid., 26–33.

40   SNA 1/7/7: Report by Shepstone of the Expedition to Install Cetshwayo, August 1873, pp. 16–17.

41   The friendship between Colenso and Shepstone and its rupture are treated at length in Guy, *The Heretic*.

42   See Goodfellow, *Great Britain and South African Confederation*.

43   Gordon, *Shepstone*, pp. 192–93; CO 179/116: Shepstone to Herbert, 30 November 1874.

44   Wolseley's secret thoughts and sentiments are revealed in his *Diaries*.

45   PRO Carvarvon Papers 30/6/33: Wolseley to Carnarvon, 16 May and 8 July 1875.

46   CO 179/123: Minute on Bulwer to Carnarvon, 27 April 1877.

47   PRO Carnarvon Papers 30/6/23: Shepstone to Carnarvon, 11 December 1877.

48   N. A. Etherington, 'Frederic Elton and the South African Factor in the Making of Britain's East African Empire', *Journal of Imperial and Commonwealth History*, 9 (1981), pp. 260–1.

49   See Guy, *The Heretic*, pp. 254–67.

50   Etherington, 'Anglo-Zulu Relations', pp. 43–4.

51   C. W. De Kiewiet, *The Imperial Factor in South Africa: a Study in Politics and Economics* (Cambridge, Cambridge University Press, 1937) pp. 221–22.

52   For a clear yet relatively detailed account of the preliminaries of the war, see Brookes and Webb, *History of Natal*, pp. 124–135. Cetshwayo's comprehension of the same events is given in *A Zulu King Speaks*, pp. 25–9 and 53–6.

Chapter 8

The reduction of Zululand, 1878–1904

JOHN LABAND and
PAUL THOMPSON

The Anglo-Zulu War of 1879 was not greeted with great enthusiasm in
either Natal or Zululand. Although Sir Bartle Frere was able to raise some
colonial opinion, notably in the *Times of Natal* and the *Natal Mercury*, he
found no groundswell of enthusiasm for war.[1] Similarly, the Zulu king,
Cetshwayo kaMpande, found the men of his younger *amabutho* anxious to
'wash' their spears, but the leaders of the Zulu nation viewed a conflict with
Britain with great foreboding.[2]

Frere envisaged a short and successful war. The new Colonial Secretary,
Sir Michael Hicks Beach, made it quite clear that his government did not
want *any* war, because of a crisis looming with Russia over Afghanistan;
however, the telegraph from London went only as far as Madeira and
messages then went by ship to South Africa. Frere had used this delay in
communication of several weeks to present the British government with the
fait accompli arising from the ultimatum that had been delivered to the Zulu
kingdom on 11 December 1878.[3]

Frere's plan then entered the military stage. The conduct of British
operations was the responsibility of Lieutenant-General Sir Frederick
Thesiger, 2nd Baron Chelmsford, the commander of imperial forces in
South Africa. He brought some 17 000 troops to the frontier for the
invasion of Zululand. About two-fifths were British regulars, the rest
colonials of one kind or another, but the great majority, indeed half his total
force, consisted of the Natal Native Contingent, black auxiliaries whom the
Natal government had allowed to be drafted into the imperial service under
white officers.[4] The invading force was predominantly infantry; the 1 700

mounted troops were almost all colonial units of varying discipline and training, and the want of adequate reconnaissance would be keenly felt in the first advance.

Chelmsford's plan was to invade Zululand on five lines converging on oNdini (Ulundi), the seat of the Zulu king. The numerically greater Zulu army enjoyed pre-eminence in local reputation as warriors, but Chelmsford was confident that British troops, with their more sophisticated organization and weaponry, could defeat them. Indeed, his concern was that his own army might appear too formidable and thus discourage the Zulu from giving battle in their traditional manner, so that the British could demonstrate their superiority in open battle and thereby procure Zulu submission.[5]

His first concern was with logistics and this soon clouded the optimistic expectation of a speedy drive to victory. The commissariat department until recently had been the Cinderella of the British army, and it still lacked sufficient organization and trained personnel. The preparations for the Zulu campaign strained it almost to breaking point, for it was obvious that the difficult ground that would have to be traversed in an invasion of the Zulu kingdom, almost trackless and sodden by summer rains, could be covered only by ox-wagon. A struggle therefore ensued to obtain and maintain the thousands of wagons that were necessary, each requiring a span of oxen. It was just as well that the decision had been made to reduce the lines of advance to three.[6]

The Natal government was extremely chary of involvement. Sir Henry Bulwer, the Lieutenant-Governor, wished to involve Natalians minimally and envisaged a defensive posture for the Colony. During 1877 and 1878 the government had done little more than step up the building of a number of stone- or brick-walled enclosures, indiscriminately called 'laagers', at administrative centres, where the settlers could rally in self-protection. The Colony's Boers, who were stand-offish, were encouraged to build their own laagers with some government help. In this way, the government sought to secure the safety of the estimated 22 000 whites. It could do little about the estimated 290 000 blacks and worried that they might create disorders of their own in the event of a war. Chelmsford himself feared that Zulu forces might slip past his advancing columns to raid the Natal countryside and cut his lines of communication. In December 1878 the Colony was divided into seven Defensive Districts and two Subdistricts (Pietermaritzburg and Durban) under local commandants, with wide discretionary powers in case of an emergency. In addition, the three

Districts bordering Zululand and the Durban Subdistrict (the base of operations) were placed under British regular officers, who would co-ordinate imperial and colonial measures. In the same Districts, the chiefdoms which had not furnished men in large numbers for service in the Natal Native Contingent, were detailed to provide a Native Border Guard, also under white officers.[7]

After the ultimatum had expired on 11 January 1879, the invasion of Zululand commenced promptly. One column advanced from the lower Thukela, brushed aside a Zulu force in the brief but sharp action of Nyezane or Wombane on the 22 January, and took possession of the abandoned mission station at Eshowe. Another column advanced from the Transvaal to the White Mfolozi, with some heavy skirmishing. In between these two, the third column, which Lord Chelmsford himself accompanied as virtual commander, crossed the Buffalo (Mzinyathi) River at Rorke's Drift and, after struggling forward in the shadow of the Nquthu range, had after ten days penetrated about thirty kilometres into Zululand (see Map 13).[8]

Not comprehending Frere's purpose and wishing to placate the British, Cetshwayo remained on the defensive. He knew that his own field forces outnumbered those of the enemy and that he would continue to enjoy this numerical advantage, provided that reinforcements were not brought in from overseas. Hoping to minimize this possibility, he attempted to show that the Zulu would do no more than defend their own country, strictly enjoining his commanders not to take the offensive outside its borders. Through informers and spies he knew the placement of the British, but he could only guess at their intentions when he dispatched his army, which was already assembled when the war began, against the invading columns. A large reserve was stationed at oNdini, to be held in reserve in the unlikely event of a cavalry dash upon his headquarters or a sea-borne expedition from Delagoa or St. Lucia Bay.[9]

Chelmsford's column took local resistance to be the main Zulu force, while cavalry reconnaissance did not locate an impi drawing close in the hills off the left flank. Myopic staff discounted suggestions of Zulu troops where they were not expected. As the Zulu main force, some 20 000 men, hovered in proximity to his camp at Isandlwana on the morning of 22 January, Chelmsford divided his own force, taking half to support a small vanguard of colonials engaged in an awkward skirmish some fifteen kilometres away. Colonel H. B. Pulleine, 1/24th Regiment, was left in charge of the camp, which had not been laagered because the wagons would be needed shortly to haul supplies. He was superseded by Colonel

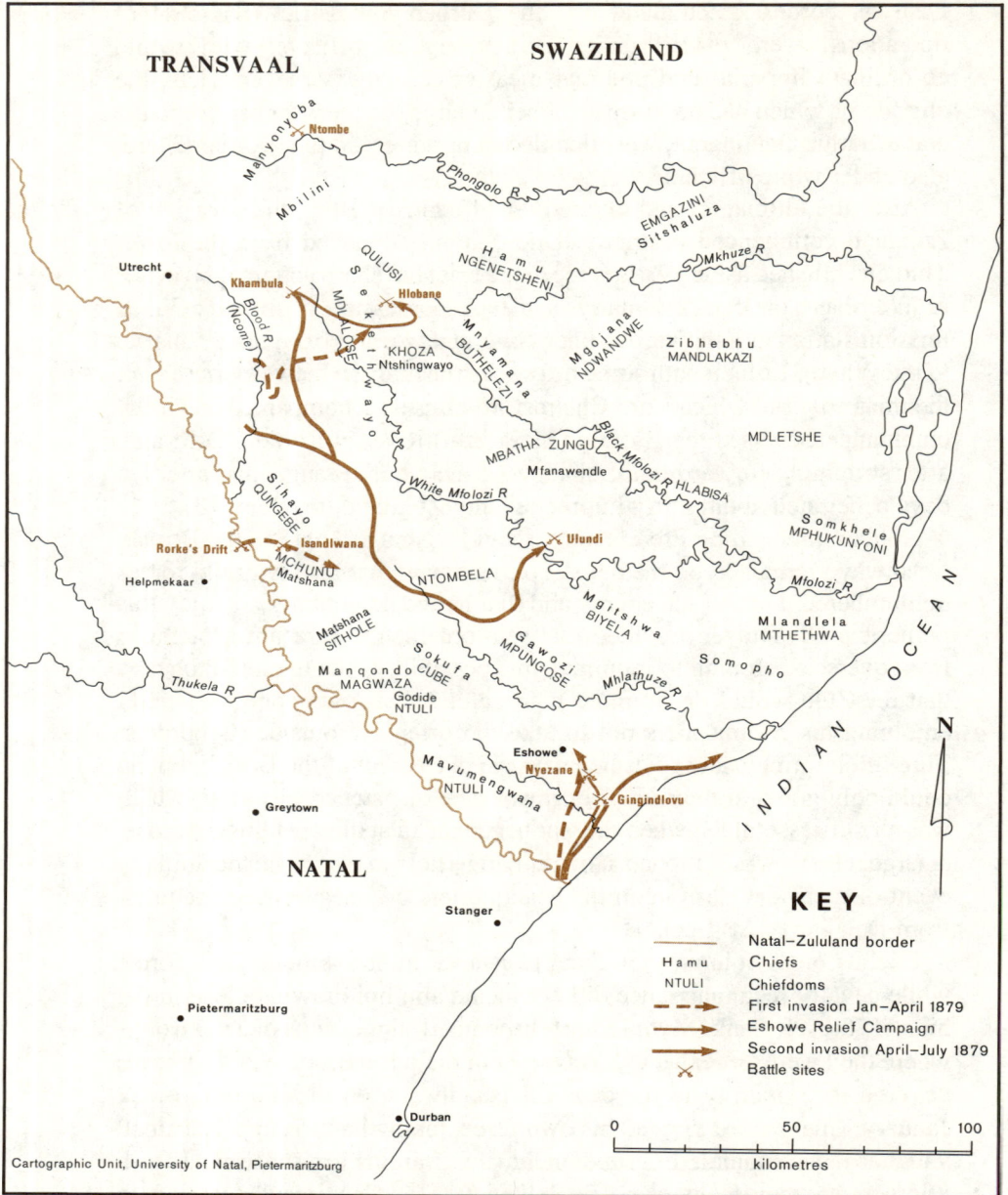

TRANSVAAL

SWAZILAND

Malnyonyoba
Ntombe

Mbilini

Phongolo R.

EMGAZINI
Sitshaluza

Utrecht

QULUSI

Hamu
NGENETSHENI

Mkhuze R.

Khambula

Hlobane

Blood R.
(Ncome)

MDLALOSE

Sekethwayo

Mnyamana
BUTHELEZI

KHOZA
Ntshingwayo

Mgojana
NDWANDWE

Zibhebhu
MANDLAKAZI

MBATHA ZUNGU

Black Mfolozi R. HLABISA

MDLETSHE

White Mfolozi R.

Mfanawendle

Sihayo
QUNGEBE

Rorke's Drift
Isandlwana
MCHUNU
Matshana

Helpmekaar

NTOMBELA

Ulundi

Somkhele
MPHUKUNYONI

Mfolozi R.

Matshana
SITHOLE

Sokufa
CUBE

Gawozi
MPUNGOSE

Mgitshwa
BIYELA

Somopho

Mlandlela
MTHETHWA

Thukela R.

Manqondo
MAGWAZA

Godide
NTULI

Mhlathuze R.

INDIAN OCEAN

N

Greytown

Mavumengwana
NTULI

Eshowe
Nyezane
Gingindlovu

NATAL

Stanger

KEY

Pietermaritzburg

	Natal–Zululand border
Hamu	Chiefs
NTULI	Chiefdoms
----→	First invasion Jan–April 1879
—→	Eshowe Relief Campaign
═→	Second invasion April–July 1879
×	Battle sites

Durban

0   50   100

Cartographic Unit, University of Natal, Pietermaritzburg

kilometres

Map 13   The Anglo-Zulu War, 1879

A. W. Durnford, commander of the 1st Regiment of the Natal Native Contingent, who arrived and then sped off with reinforcements to support Chelmsford. Before leaving, some of his mounted troops who had been ordered on to the ridge to the left, inadvertently discovered the Zulu impi that was lurking there. The chiefs Ntshingwayo kaMahole Khoza and Mavumengwana kaNdlela Ntuli, the Zulu commanders, had not intended to fight that day because of the new moon but, now that their force was known to the enemy, they had no choice. Instantly, the Zulu army assumed its traditional attack formation. Pulleine threw his infantry into line, but the Zulu 'chest' bore it back regardless of losses, while the 'horns' gathered in Durnford's force on Pulleine's right flank and swept around his left flank. Without a laager or other all-round defence, the British were doomed and in less than two hours the battle was over. A third of Chelmsford's column, including half of the regulars, were annihilated.

The triumphant Zulu plundered the camp and removed their casualties – perhaps as many as a thousand had fallen – while Chelmsford, belatedly aware that something had gone wrong, marched the rest of his column back to the camp. After spending the night on the battlefield, he retreated to his base in Natal the following morning.[10]

The ramifications of the Battle of Isandlwana were many. With the collapse of Chelmsford's invasion, Frere's plan had fallen apart, making it clear to the British government that the unwanted war would be longer and costlier than anticipated. Its reaction was to prosecute it to a successful conclusion and support its embarrassed agents, and it ordered reinforcements post-haste to reverse the defeat. The battle was a pyrrhic victory for the Zulu. It cost them dearly, yet it magnified their warlike image in British eyes.[11] Cetshwayo's defensive strategy was furthermore abandoned in the aftermath, when his half-brother, prince Dabulamanzi kaMpande, ignored the king's orders and led the reserve force that had missed the Isandlwana battle to attack Chelmsford's depot at Rorke's Drift on the other side of the Buffalo (Mzinyathi). For nearly twelve hours, the Zulu unsuccessfully attempted to overrun the company-strength garrison inside the hastily-fortified position. About 500 casualties were lost in an engagement which showed what a small force with superior firepower could do in a prepared position.[12] Moreover the battle of Rorke's Drift or KwaJimu was construed as the repulse of a Zulu invasion of Natal.

After the repulse at Isandlwana, the Centre Column remustered at Rorke's Drift and Helpmekaar, while the Left Column fell back to the Transvaal border. They now fortified their positions – never again would

Prince Dabulamanzi kaMpande (centre), the Zulu commander at the Battle of Rorke's Drift

The Battle of Khambula, 29 March 1879

they leave a camp exposed as at Isandlwana. The Right Column held on to Eshowe, but sent its mounted forces and vehicles back to the lower Thukela. Irritated at the lodgement in his territory, Cetshwayo thereupon gave the order that the place be invested.[13] In the border districts of Natal, the settlers poured into the laagers, while in the major towns, buildings were fortified and barricades prepared to shelter refugees and protect the burgesses against Zulu marauders. A general rising of the Colony's black population was a constant fear, but it remained passive, if uneasy. Although the Natal Native Contingent lost half its strength through desertion and disbanding, the Native Border Guard maintained its watch along the rivers and black levies were raised in the interior to augment it.[14]

The war languished until March, when large British reinforcements began to arrive from overseas. Just over 4 500 troops disembarked at Durban in March and 4 100 in April, including the King's Dragoon Guards and the 17th (Duke of Cambridge's Own) Lancers.[15] With these forces at his disposal, Chelmsford was able to move to relieve the Eshowe garrison. As the column advanced up the coast, the border forces demonstrated vigorously along the front. Cetshwayo, perhaps deceived by them as to British intentions, sent his main force under Chief Mnyamana kaNgqengelele Buthelezi against the left column commanded by Colonel Sir Evelyn Wood leaving Chief Somopho kaZikhala Mthembu with the force about Eshowe to resist the relief column, led by Chelmsford himself. Both Zulu commanders had been cautioned against attacking the British in prepared positions but could not restrain their subordinates.[16] Chelmsford's column laagered and repelled Somopho's attack with relative ease at Gingindlovu on 2 April, before advancing to the relief of the Eshowe garrison.[17] Meanwhile, Mnyamana's impi overtook Wood's mounted men on an over-ambitious sally at the Hlobane Mountain and routed them. On the following day, the 29th March, Wood saved his reputation and column at Khambula when the Zulu attacked his fort and laager. They fought with the same ferocity as at Isandlwana, and with even greater obstinacy, for the battle lasted four hours. The result was, however, never in doubt and a British riposte finally precipitated the exhausted warriors into a disorderly flight in which they suffered further heavy casualties.[18]

After Isandlwana the Zulu nation could not win the war and, after Gingindlovu and especially Khambula, it was apparent that they would lose it. The slaughter – over a thousand at Gingindlovu, perhaps two thousand at Khambula – sent a shudder through the land. The disheartened warriors dispersed to their homes, while Natal border agents told of the crying and mourning that was taking place in homesteads to which the warriors did not return.[19] Cetshwayo himself seems to have abandoned hope of a military solution, but all his overtures to negotiate in order to save his kingdom were rebuffed.[20]

After Khambula, there were two columns available for the final onslaught upon Ulundi: Major-General H. H. Crealock's First Division at the coast, and a combination of Major-General E. Newdigate's Second Division and Wood's 'Flying Column' from the Transvaal. Preceded by another demonstration along the border, the advance commenced at the end of May.[21] Although the winter had made the ground firmer for the wagons, logistical problems were now amplified by the size of the invading force. Chelmsford's column lumbered forward at an average rate of only two to three kilometres a day, laagering every camp and fortifying depots at strategic points, with the fresh imperial cavalry being employed in shepherding convoys and reconnoitring front and flank.[22] Along the coast Crealock, who had been told that his main task was to distract a part of the Zulu army, made even slower progress, his advance being held up by sickness, so that it was not able to move until mid-June.[23] Cetshwayo soon realized that Crealock's column would not get off the plain, and was therefore able to concentrate his force against Chelmsford's column.[24] Meanwhile, local Zulu forces raided across the border into the Umvoti district of Natal, as well as into the Utrecht district of the Transvaal; initiatives which did not deter the British advance, if indeed that was their intention.[25]

At the end of June, Chelmsford laagered his force on the Mthonjaneni heights, overlooking the Mahlabathini plain, where oNdini and twelve other military homesteads were concentrated. He then led a strong force down to the White Mfolozi on 4 July and, having crossed it, moved in a 'square' on oNdini. The assembled Zulu army attacked but could not break the formation, whereupon it was routed by British cavalry issuing from the square. British observers commented that the Zulu onset at the battle of Ulundi, or Nodwengu, which lasted less than an hour, lacked the sustained ferocity of earlier battles. Zulu casualties were nevertheless high and estimated at between 1 000 and 1 500, perhaps half being suffered in flight. Cetshwayo was not present, having probably anticipated the result of the battle. He had left the vicinity on the previous day and fled to find safety in one of Mnyamana's homesteads on the isiKhwebezi. The British burnt the royal residences on the plain and retired victorious to Mthonjaneni.[26]

The burning of oNdini after the battle, 4 July 1879. (From the Illustrated London News, *23 August 1879.)*

At this juncture Wolseley, the new High Commissioner for South Eastern Africa, arrived in Natal. With the war dragging on, with Frere unable to control events and with Bulwer and Chelmsford at loggerheads over the imperial use of colonial forces, the British government had sent the brilliant and ambitious young general back to Natal to improvise a quick end to the war.[27] He promptly dropped many of the conditions contained in the ultimatum, leaving Frere fuming in Cape Town. Chelmsford, having avenged Isandlwana at Ulundi, and with Zulu power ostensibly broken, withdrew his forces from Mthonjaneni and handed over his command to his new superior.[28]

Wolseley acted swiftly. He reduced the field army to two 'flying columns' and moved back to oNdini, where he sought to convince doubtful Zulu chiefs that they could have their land if they would give up their king. Many were inclined to accept his terms, for the flying columns had established British ascendancy in the heart of the Zulu kingdom, while tough mounted patrols were scouring the country for the fugitive

*The Zulu chiefs are here depicted accepting Wolseley's peace stipulations on
1 September 1879. (From the* Graphic, *25 October 1879.)*

Cetshwayo. Moreover, there was the possibility that Wolseley might at last
be able to activate the Swazi front, which Swazi diplomacy had succeeded
in keeping quiescent despite persistent British requests for military
assistance.[29] Although there were still some armed warriors ready to fight,
especially in the north-west, the Zulu nation as such had lost the capacity
for organized resistance. Its sufferings would only increase if the British
remained to interfere with the spring planting.[30] After Cetshwayo had been
captured in the Ngome forest on 28 August,[31] his leading chiefs and
advisors agreed at oNdini on 1 September to the suppression of the
monarchy and to the fragmentation of the kingdom into thirteen territories,
each under an appointed chief. Although these were formally independent,
they had to submit to the arbitration of a British Resident.[32] Cetshwayo was
exiled to Cape Town and during September the British forces withdrew
from Zululand.

    Almost immediately, critics began condemning Wolseley's settlement
and, ever since, historians have deplored it as a failure, responsible for

plunging Zululand into dreadful civil strife.[33] While it has been hailed for its 'Machiavellian quality',[34] it has been lambasted for having been inspired by nothing more than sheer 'political expediency, cultural arrogance and ignorance'.[35] In attempting to make a balanced judgement, it must be remembered that the British government had instructed Wolseley to end the war with honour and to devise a settlement that avoided the expense and responsibility of direct annexation. Exactly how this was to be achieved was left to Wolseley's discretion.[36] His approach to the problem was influenced by the British school of Indian defence, through which his Chief of Staff, Sir George Pomeroy Colley, had made his reputation.[37] His settlement thus closely resembled that which Lord Lytton had intended to impose on Afghanistan, whereby the North-West Frontier would be secured by breaking Afghanistan into a number of impotent principalities, ruled by chiefs amenable to British control in the form of Residents.[38] It was only when deciding on practical details, as into how many chiefdoms Zululand should be divided, and who should be set over them, that Wolseley turned to local advisers. From the proffered counsel of colonial officials and other local experts,[39] he accepted that of Sir Theophilus Shepstone, whose ideas largely coincided with his own because he was the leading proponent for the setting-up of a number of independent chiefdoms.[40] Shepstone argued that the preservation of the Zulu monarchy would prolong the life of the Zulu military system. Royal authority, he claimed, was very fragile because the various chiefs yearned for the independence their predecessors had enjoyed before the rise of king Shaka. The appointment of thirteen chiefs – a number he considered manageable – would ensure that royal influence would be stifled. Whether these chiefs were hereditary, with a tradition of independence, or whether they were new men owing their elevation solely to the British, they would collaborate in ensuring that the Zulu monarchy did not re-emerge.[41]

In actually choosing the chiefs, Wolseley felt he had found the perfect adviser in John Dunn,[42] Cetshwayo's white adviser, who had thrown in his lot with the British on the outbreak of hostilities. An important part was also played by John Shepstone, the acting Secretary for Native Affairs in Natal, who could reinforce his brother's advice. Dunn was rewarded for the confidence Wolseley placed in him by being made chief of the largest of the thirteen territories (see Map 14). Situated along the Thukela frontier with Natal, it was seen as a buffer between the Colony and the possibly less amenable chiefdoms to the north. As such, it was to serve the same function as Lord Lytton had envisaged for Kandahar, which was to have acted as a

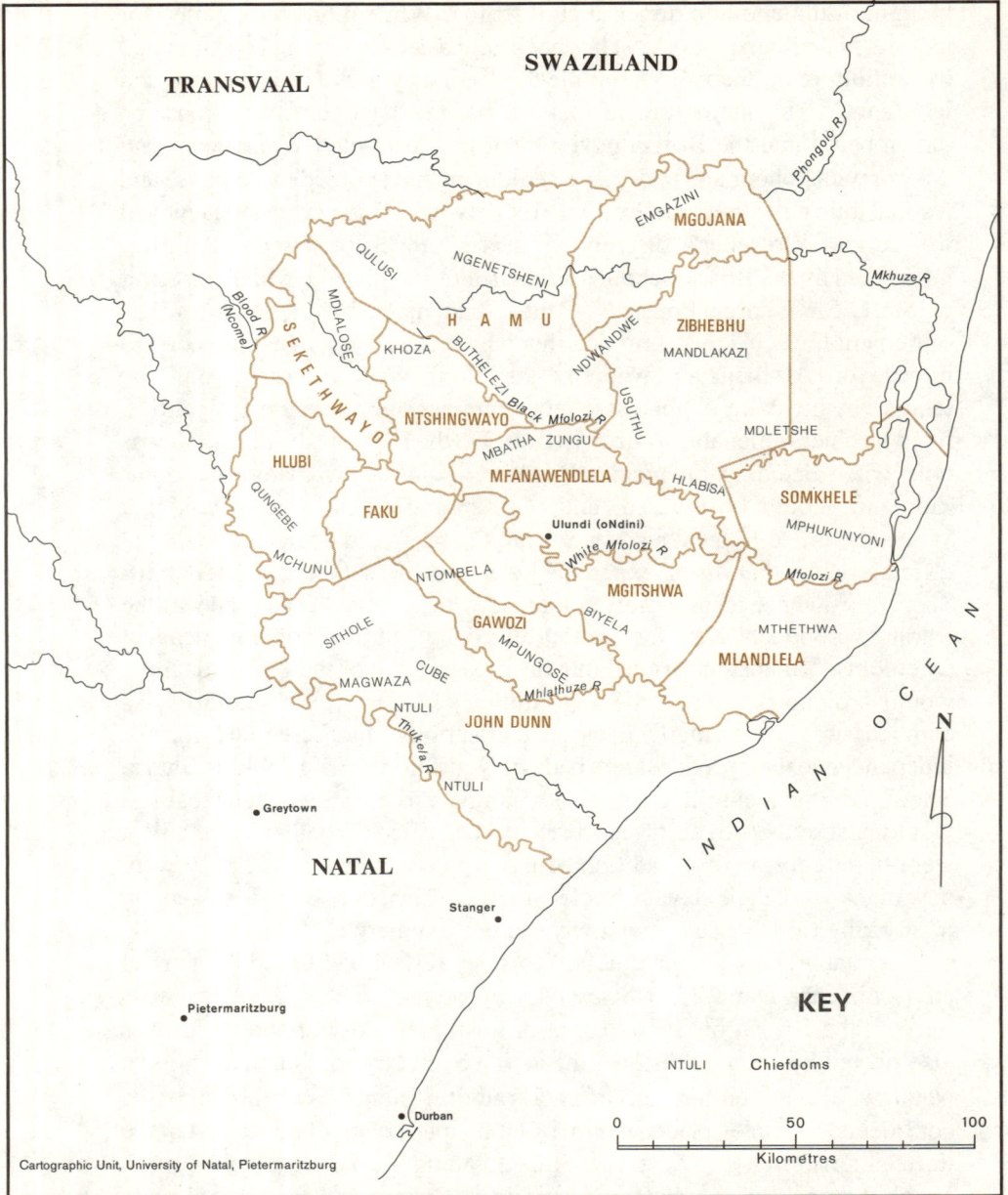

Map 14   The partition of the Zulu kingdom, 1879

*Zibhebhu kaMapitha, the
ambitious Mandlakazi chief*

Natal Archives, C740

bulwark against the more rebellious sections of Afghanistan.[43] The remaining stretch of territory bordering Natal, that along the Buffalo (Mzinyathi) River, was given to another alien, Hlubi of the Tlokoa, whose men had fought with the British during the war. The majority of the remaining chiefs also owed their appointment to the degree of trust Wolseley was able to place in them, either for their actual collaboration with the British, or for their sufficiently early abandonment of the royal cause. A number of them had no hereditary status at all and were to find it extremely difficult to assert their authority. Two, however, emerged as the dominant powers in northern Zululand and became the main instruments in the suppression of the aspiration of the royal house. One was Prince Hamu kaNzibe of the Ngenetsheni section of the Zulu. Despite his close family relationship with Cetshwayo (he was his half-brother), he had deserted to the British during the war and had long been suspected of designs on the throne. The other was Zibhebhu kaMaphitha, chief of the Mandlakazi

*Prince Ndabuko
kaMpande, the leader
of the royalist cause*

Natal Archives, C636

people, who had enjoyed a semi-independent position in the north-east of
the kingdom. Wolseley had quickly discerned their lust for greater power
and autonomy and had deliberately granted them their chiefdoms north of
the Black Mfolozi, not only because their own adherents were concentrated
there, but because this was an area where loyalty to the monarchy was
expected to remain particularly strong. Prince Hamu was set over the
fiercely royalist Qulusi people, and also over Chief Mnyamana and most of
the Buthelezi. Zibhebhu was to rule over a territory that included the
homesteads of prominent members of king Cetshwayo's family, such as his
eleven-year-old son Dinuzulu and his full brother, Ndabuko kaMpande,
who had after Cetshwayo emerged as leader of the royalist cause, as well as
those of many of the king's closest adherents, the uSuthu.[44]

Historians are probably justified in perceiving a recipe for civil war in Wolseley's settlement and especially in the arrangement north of the Black Mfolozi. Yet, at another level, the settlement must be appreciated for what it was: a pragmatic attempt to neutralize any future Zulu threat to Natal or the Transvaal, not through annexation but by dividing the kingdom against itself. In doing so, Wolseley exploited the long-standing conflicts that existed between the king at the centre and the more powerful chiefs, especially those on the periphery of the kingdom (of whom Zibhebhu is the most representative example), anticipating that they would continue to align themselves with the British in order to increase their political and economic power at the expense of the king and the uSuthu.[45]

Where the settlement fell down, even on its own terms, was in its failure to provide a mechanism for containing the conflict that was bound to erupt in Zululand and for ensuring that it did not spill over into Natal. The Natal colonists in general were quick to perceive this and, the more they reflected on the settlement, the more their opposition grew (as expressed through the newspapers and Legislative Council). This criticism cannot be ascribed solely to disappointment that Zululand would not be opened to white settlement, with the Zulu being brought onto the labour market. It was the widespread expression of a genuine belief that the security of the Colony depended upon the annexation of Zululand and the administration of the territory by white officials.[46]

The Natal official establishment's viewpoint was most articulately expressed by Sir Theophilus Shepstone, whose ideas on 'native affairs' it had by now wholeheartedly espoused.[47] Shepstone was able to propose an alternative to Wolseley's settlement, based on a system that had been operating in Natal for decades (see Chapter 7). Essentially, this was an expedient system of indirect rule. Shepstone was always conscious of the dangers inherent in a precipitate transition from an African to a colonial administration, and argued that hereditary chiefs should be left with the exercise of a modicum of their former powers under the supervision, as in Natal, of white officials. He claimed that under this arrangement (as had proved the case in Natal) the chiefs' authority would be gradually undermined and eventually negated once their adherents had come to realize that the effective source of power resided not with them, but with the white officials.[48] In concrete terms, Shepstone envisaged the annexation of Zululand to Natal, and the introduction of an administrative structure of white magistrates set over the chiefs.[49] In this way, Zululand would be turned into a giant location on the Natal model and, if the land were not

Melmoth Osborn, the first British Resident in Zululand and later Resident Commissioner of the Colony of Zululand. (From J. Y. Gibson, The Story of the Zulus, *Longmans, Green and Co., New York, 1911.)*

opened to white settlement, it could at least serve to resettle Natal's excess black population. The system would be paid for by the imposition of a hut tax, which would have the additional advantage of forcing the Zulu onto the labour market. For it was a feature of the Shepstone system in Natal that, by preserving a certain continuity with existing norms and practices of black society and by maintaining the homestead as the basis of the system of production, it was possible, without eliciting violent resistance, to divert a proportion of the surplus – as tax, rent or labour – from the chiefs to the colonial authorities. Wolseley's settlement, by guaranteeing the Zulu their land and cattle, had not disrupted their economic and social base, and Shepstone therefore presumed that his Natal system could be effectively introduced into Zululand.[50]

Yet a third viewpoint concerning Zululand's fate was that of Bishop Colenso and his family, notably his daughters, Frances and Harriette, who over the years consistently championed the royal cause in Zululand.[51] They warned that any settlement of Zululand which excluded the king and left Zululand in the control of rival contenders to the throne would certainly produce civil war.[52]

The first British Resident in Zululand was Melmoth Osborn, a former colleague of Sir Theophilus Shepstone, and a dedicated exponent of his policies.[53] Consequently, when the uSuthu and their associates, such as Mnyamana, complained of ill-treatment by Zibhebhu and Hamu and went to Pietermaritzburg in May 1880 to plead for the return of the king, Osborn threw his influence behind their oppressors. So outspoken was his support of them at a meeting at Nhlazatshe in May 1881, that Zibhebhu and Hamu were emboldened to turn on the uSuthu and drive their leaders, including Prince Ndabuko, from their homes. The uSuthu and others who had suffered because of Wolseley's settlement, naturally drew together to resist and, as Osborn had no armed force at his disposal with which to intervene, the country began to slip into anarchy.[54]

Meanwhile, the exiled king Cetshwayo in Cape Town, alarmed by events in Zululand and encouraged by Bishop Colenso, who saw in his restoration the last hope for his country, had been petitioning the British government for permission to visit England in order to plead his cause. By September 1881 it seemed obvious to the officials of the Colonial Office in London that the Wolseley settlement had broken down irredeemably and that the only possible alternative lay in an accommodation with the king, as they wished to avoid direct annexation.[55] Cetshwayo was therefore allowed to travel to England in August 1882, fortified in his negotiating power by the pleas in April 1882 of a second deputation of uSuthu leaders to Pietermaritzburg. Lord Kimberley, the Colonial Secretary, agreed to his restoration. But, as he was under pressure from the Natal officials, who saw behind the restoration the spectre of a reunited Zululand, and who feared that the king would take his revenge upon the chiefs who had collaborated with the settlement and had suppressed the uSuthu, the conditions of Cetshwayo's reinstatement were not settled until some months later when they satisfied Natal interests.[56]

Thus, when Cetshwayo returned to Zululand on 10 January 1883, he found that his powers had been drastically curbed. His authority was confined to the central portion of his former kingdom, under the supervision of a Resident, H. F. Fynn, the son of the Natal pioneer (see Map 15). He was hemmed in by his arch-enemy, Zibhebhu, who had been awarded an additional large tract of land north of the Black Mfolozi, which included not only the homesteads of many of the uSuthu leadership but also the royalist Emgazini people and sections of the Buthelezi. It was intended that Zibhebhu would consolidate his power in this strong royalist area as a deliberate check to the king's ambitions. To the south, a Reserve Territory was created out of Dunn's and Hlubi's chiefdoms to act as a military buffer for Natal. The Reserve would serve as a sanctuary for those who wished to evade the king's rule. Although technically an independent territory under British protection, it was to be administered by officials recruited from Natal, consisting of a Resident Commissioner (initially John Shepstone

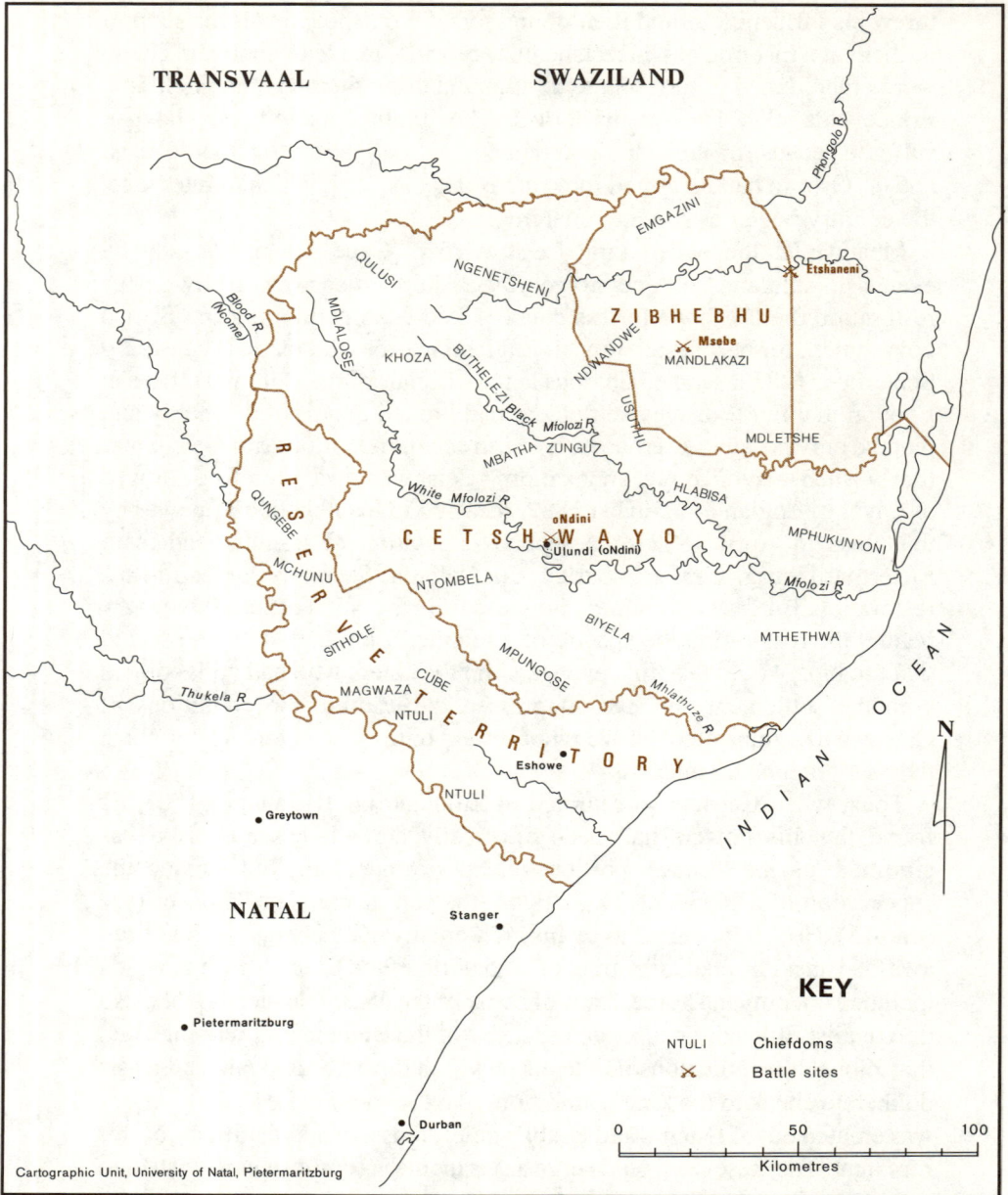

Map 15   The partition of Zululand, 1883

King Cetshwayo's restoration ceremonies in January 1883. He is portrayed seated in a chair receiving a deputation of his relatives. (From the Graphic, *10 March 1883.)*

and then Melmoth Osborn), assisted by sub-commissioners, ruling through the Zulu chiefs, the cost being met by a hut tax. This was nothing less than the extension of the Shepstone system and implied Natal control over the southern third of Zululand. The inhabitants of the Reserve were given the impossible choice of submitting to the system or, if they wished to remain loyal to King Cetshwayo, of abandoning their homes and moving into his district.[57]

In such circumstances, the king's return achieved nothing except to intensify the conflict in Zululand. In Cetshwayo's own territory, this was immediately made clear in the hostility of those chiefs whom the new settlement had deposed, while clashes soon erupted in the north-west between Hamu's Ngenetsheni and the royalist Qulusi and Mdlalose. In the Reserve, the divided loyalties of his adherents strained relations with the already antagonistic Natal officials. But his greatest threat lay in the north, where Zibhebhu precipitated full-scale war by insisting that his uSuthu subjects in his enlarged chiefdom acknowledge his authority or move into

Cetshwayo's district. Prince Ndabuko, Chief Mnyamana and others of the uSuthu leadership, whose homesteads were in the north of Zululand, organized an army to invade Zibhebhu's territory and eliminate him. Both sides enlisted the support of white mercenaries and on 30 March 1883 in the Msebe valley, Zibhebhu utterly routed the invaders, inflicting what were possibly the heaviest losses ever suffered by a Zulu army. He thereafter retaliated by taking the war to uSuthu territory and, aided by Hamu, systematically ravaged their districts in the north. Then, on 20 July 1883 he descended on oNdini, the homestead which Cetshwayo had built close to that which the British had razed to the ground in 1879. After the defenders had been scattered, at least fifty-nine of the most notable uSuthu leaders and men of influence in Zululand were massacred.[58]

This slaughter marked the real end of the old order in Zululand. The established leadership was destroyed and, after the king had fled to sanctuary among the Cube people in the Nkandla forest of the Reserve, the royal cause was left in total disarray. From the Reserve, Cetshwayo tried in vain to rally his supporters until, threatened by Zibhebhu's approach, on 17 October 1883 he put himself under Osborn's protection at Eshowe.[59] There he died suddenly on 8 February 1884. The uSuthu leadership, including his son Dinuzulu, were convinced that he had been poisoned on Zibhebhu's instructions.[60] With the king died Colenso's plan of restoring order to Zululand. Colenso's daughter Harriette faithfully supported the cause of his son Dinuzulu, but it was clearly no longer feasible to restore the kingdom in Zululand. The divisions now ran too deep. The vested interests of chiefs such as Zibhebhu were too strong, and officials such as Osborn were too powerful.

Despite the fact that parts of Zululand were in a state approaching anarchy, Gladstone's government resolutely declined to extend sovereignty or protection over Zululand beyond the Reserve.[61] Even in the Reserve, Osborn was encountering the greatest difficulty in collecting the hut tax, meeting with active resistance from uSuthu supporters who concentrated in the Nkandla forest. It was not until September 1884, after a confused period of skirmishes and cattle raids, that an uneasy peace emerged, brought about by the need of the uSuthu to plant their crops, and by Osborn's recognition that he had not the forces to quell them.[62]

The situation was at its worst in Cetshwayo's former territory. There, the uSuthu faced extinction as the result of Zibhebhu's and Hamu's deliberate policy of denying them access to their grain and cattle. The crisis enabled Prince Ndabuko and Chief Mnyamana to consolidate their leadership of the

Prince Dinuzulu kaCetshwayo (born 1868, died 1913)

Natal Archives, C6477

uSuthu as the guardians of Cetshwayo's fifteen-year-old heir, Dinuzulu. Allies had to be found and, in May 1884, they struck a bargain with Boers from the Transvaal, who for decades had been infiltrating western Zululand in search of grazing. In return for recognizing Dinuzulu as king of Zululand north of the Reserve and aiding him against his foes, they were to be allowed an unspecified number of farms in Zululand. On 5 June 1884 the uSuthu and their Boer allies duly defeated Zibhebhu at Etshaneni and forced him and the broken remnants of the Mandlakazi to flee to the Reserve, where a special location was set aside for them by the sympathetic officials. When the Boers claimed their part of the bargain, Dinuzulu was obliged to cede some 2 700 000 acres of western Zululand to them.[63] The price was exhorbitant because the area, renamed the New Republic, included much of the best grazing in Zululand. It incorporated the main homesteads of the uSuthu leadership, as well as those of their staunchest

TRANSVAAL   SWAZILAND

T Phongolo R.

EMGAZINI

QULUSI   NGENETSHENI

Mkhuze R.

MDLALOSE

Blood R.
(Ncome)

Vryheid

NEW REPUBLIC

KHOZA   BUTHELEZI

MANDLAKAZI

NDWANDWE   NDWANDWE

Ivuna
Ceza   ZIBHEBHU'S LOCATION 1888   ST. LUCIA

USUTHU

MBATHA   ZUNGU   MDLETSHE   BAY

Black Mfolozi R.

White Mfolozi R.

NQUTU   Nkonjeni

QUNGEBE

HLABISA

MCHUNU   Hlophekhulu   MPHUKUNYONI

NTOMBELA

Mthonjaneni   Mfolozi R.

ENTONJANENI

PROVISO B   BIYELA   LOWER UMFOLOZI

SITHOLE   MTHETHWA

NKANDHLA   MPUNGOSE

CUBE

MAGWAZA   St. Paul's

Thukela R.   NTULI

Mhlathuze R.

INDIAN OCEAN

NTULI

Eshowe

ESHOWE

Greytown

NATAL

Stanger

KEY

Pietermaritzburg

NTULI   Chiefdoms

Durban

British Magisterial division 1887
(boundaries incomplete at that
time)

X   Battle sites

0   50   100

Kilometres

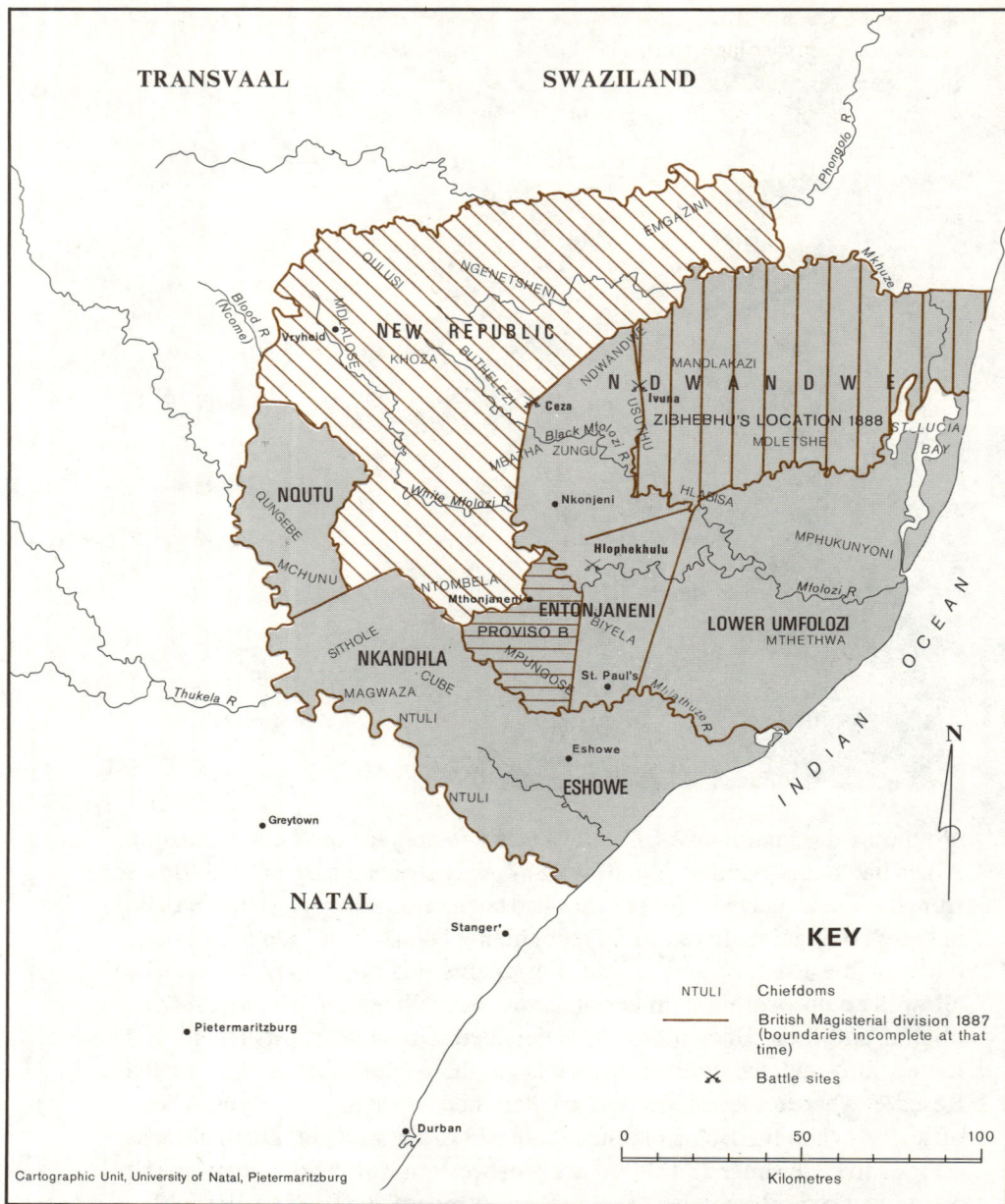

Map 16   The British Colony of Zululand, 1887–8

adherents, such as the Qulusi, Buthelezi, Mdlalose and Emgazini people. It was hardly any solace to them that their enemies, Hamu's Ngenetsheni, also fell under the sway of the Boers.[64] Moreover, the Boers soon proceeded to claim that those areas retained by Dinuzulu should also fall under their supervision. Appalled at the way in which the Boers were interpreting their agreement, the uSuthu prepared to resist.

It was at this point that Britain at last intervened, but its action was not a response to the desperate uSuthu appeals for help. Britain had been growing anxious at German interest in the area and feared a link-up with the Boers, who sought an outlet to the sea. The Liberal government thus reluctantly annexed St. Lucia Bay in December 1884.[65] It was not, however, until the fall of Gladstone's government in August 1886 and the advent of Lord Salisbury's Conservative administration, with its more fully-developed concern to safeguard imperial interests in south-eastern Africa as a whole, that Britain began at last to recognize that it could not shrug off all responsibility.[66] British intervention, when it came, was no boon to the Zulu, for the Boers were bought off in October 1886 by Britain's official recognition of the New Republic. In return, they dropped all claims to a protectorate over Dinuzulu and ceded control over a block of territory in central Zululand known as Proviso B, where they were nevertheless allowed to retain ownership of their farms. By January 1887 a boundary commission, set up under Melmoth Osborn, had completed the task of defining the boundaries (see Map 16).[67] This arrangement left the rump of Zululand independent but vulnerable. The uSuthu, who would have nothing to do with the setting of the New Republic's boundaries, had protested at Britain's official recognition of the alienation of so much Zulu territory, and at the loss of so many royal adherents to Boer jurisdiction. Within what remained of Zululand, they were threatened by Zibhebhu from the Reserve, constantly agitating for permission to return to his lands in the north.

Meanwhile, in Natal, the lobbying for the incorporation of the territory into the Colony's boundaries continued. While the British government contemplated this move, to which the only alternative now seemed to be to assume direct responsibility itself, the Governor, Sir Arthur Havelock, warned that the Colony did not have the resources to control the territory. Matters were brought to a head by Osborn who, alarmed at the deteriorating situation, on 5 February 1887 simply notified the uSuthu leadership that 'British protection' had been extended over them. To the uSuthu, protest seemed futile, while the British government, faced with a *fait accompli*, duly agreed to the annexation of central Zululand and the Reserve, which from 19 May 1887 became the British Colony of Zululand.[68] It can rightly be argued that Britain's anti-annexationist policy had spelled ruin for the Zulu people.[69] For, when in 1887 Britain finally shouldered the responsibility for its victory of 1879, it was over the devastated remnant of the former Zulu kingdom, still threatened by the bitter uSuthu-Mandlakazi rivalry that was the consequence of the intentionally divisive Wolseley settlement.

When Zululand became a British colony in 1887, it was understood that this would not be a burden on the British taxpayer. The administration of Zululand was thus financed by a hut tax, the official establishment being kept to a bare minimum. The Governor of Natal doubled as Governor of Zululand and administered the territory through a Resident Commissioner at Eshowe, who supervised the Resident Magistrates of the six administrative districts into which Zululand was divided (see Map 16). They were expected to enforce their authority through a small black police force although, as a last resort, they could call on a small detachment of imperial troops stationed in southern Zululand.[70]

At the time, the Colensos alleged that these officials were unfit for their task, a charge which has been repeated by some historians.[71] The truth is that, although most of them were selected for their expertise and ability,[72] they were all recruited from Natal. They were therefore all imbued with the Shepstone orthodoxy that the greatest threat to the peaceable establishment of British rule was the Zulu royal house.[73] The appointment of Melmoth Osborn as Resident Commissioner ensured that this perspective would be adhered to, while Shepstone himself had the ear of the Governor, Sir Arthur Havelock, and directly influenced the drafting of a Code of Laws and Regulations for Zululand, adapted from the Code of 1885 which had been introduced in British Bechuanaland.[74] The Zululand code thus emerged as a monument to Shepstone's concept of indirect rule, and effectively extended the Shepstone system of Natal to Zululand.

It could not have been expected that the uSuthu leadership, which had only accepted annexation for fear of worse, would easily acquiesce in their loss of power and status. The new code of laws, furthermore, soon made it clear to ordinary people that many traditional customs would be under pressure. The traditionalist resistance to British rule which erupted in 1888 was therefore a typical response, similar to those that occurred in similar circumstances in other parts of the Victorian empire.[75]

The epicentre of the revolt was the Ndwandwe District in the north of

R. H. Addison, Resident Magistrate of Ndwandwe (left), with Commander George Mansel and men of the Reserve Territory Carbineers, c. 1885

Zululand, where Dinuzulu, Ndabuko and the bulk of the uSuthu had their homesteads. The Zululand officials had been instructed to adopt a conciliatory approach during the difficult period of transition to British rule and R. H. Addison, the Resident Magistrate of Ndwandwe, and Melmoth Osborn, his immediate superior as Resident Commissioner, found themselves unable to deal with Dinuzulu's recalcitrance. The Governor thereupon summoned the uSuthu leaders to Eshowe, where, on 14 November 1887, he bluntly reminded them that power had passed to the British, underlining the lesson with a substantial cattle fine.[76]

It was at this stage that the officials resorted to a disastrous expedient. As early as February 1887, both Shepstone and Osborn had suggested using Zibhebhu, who was still in the Reserve, as a means of curbing the truculent uSuthu. It was not unusual in a colonial situation to employ collaborators as a cheap means of reducing rebellious elements and, in this case, Addison's police were inadequate and the Governor was reluctant to send regular troops against his new subjects. But, in the circumstance, the decision to use Zibhebhu was a grave miscalculation, for there were bitter animosities between the uSuthu and Mandlakazi. When, therefore, in late November 1887 Zibhebhu and his adherents returned under British auspices to their old territory (now in the Ndwandwe District), they were thirsting to avenge their defeat in the civil war and stridently demanded the expulsion of those uSuthu who had settled on their former lands. The uSuthu were naturally filled with alarm, and Addison added to their disquiet by openly taking Zibhebhu's side in every dispute, forfeiting all claim to impartiality in a blatantly unjust demarcation of Zibhebhu's new location, from which Zibhebhu thereupon proceeded, with Addison's connivance, to evict uSuthu (see Map 16). The uSuthu were thus driven into a position where they could envisage no redress except by force of arms. On 5 April 1888, Dinuzulu slipped across the border to raise armed support from the uSuthu living under the Boers and, on 26 April 1888 when the Zululand Police attempted to arrest some of the uSuthu leaders, they were prevented from doing so by a large party of armed uSuthu. In mid-May Dinuzulu and his adherents retired to Ceza mountain (a traditional fastness on the borders of the New Republic), where they supported themselves by raiding those whom they considered guilty of loyalty to the British, notably Chief Mnyamana's Buthelezi. On 2 June an attempt by police, this time supported by soldiers, to arrest the uSuthu leaders on Ceza was ignominiously repulsed in a running skirmish, after which there was an instant collapse of British authority in many other parts of Zululand.[77]

Most notably, Shingana kaMpande, one of the uSuthu leadership, collected a small force on Hlophekhulu hill in the Entonjaneni District in emulation of his nephew Dinuzulu. It was while the British were diverted by this new threat that Dinuzulu executed a most daring and doubtless satisfying stroke. Zibhebhu had been ordered up to help protect Ivuna, the seat of the Ndwandwe magistrate. There, on 23 June, the uSuthu descended on him after a night march from Ceza and, under the guns of the fort at Ivuna, put him to flight.[78] Zibhebhu and his shattered adherents were then evacuated to the south under British protection[79] and all the country north of the Black Mfolozi was abandoned by the British. In the Lower Umfolosi District Chief Somkhele kaMalanda of the Mphukonyoni, another prominent uSuthu, was encouraged by events to launch an attack on the magistrate's fort, which was beaten off.[80]

The uSuthu revolt was shortlived. Reinforcements were brought up from the Natal garrison and Shingana was dislodged from Hlophekhulu on 2 July. The military force then split into two columns and, during July and August, advanced through the disaffected areas, burning large numbers of huts as a punishment to rebels and a warning to others. Dinuzulu's position on Ceza became untenable and, on 7 August, he fled to the South African Republic. By 30 September, the troops had been withdrawn, and it was left to the civil authorities to reassert their authority and to resettle those uSuthu who surrendered. It was different for the uSuthu leadership. After Dinuzulu and his leading supporters had given themselves up to the British on 15 November 1888, they were put on trial at Eshowe. On 27 April 1889 Dinuzulu, Ndabuko and Shingana were found guilty of high treason, being sentenced respectively to ten, fifteen and twelve years imprisonment, to be served on St. Helena.[81]

The appalling consequences of employing Zibhebhu against the uSuthu, together with the expense of putting down the uprising, caused the British government once again to rethink its policy. Yet, it was not until 1893 that any move was made, by which time the British general election of 1892 had reinstated a Liberal government and Shepstone, who had exercised such a profound influence upon Natal's history for half a century, had died. In these circumstances, the retirement of Melmoth Osborn as Resident Commissioner of Zululand was seized upon as the opportunity to appoint Sir Marshall Clarke, the successful Administrator of Basutoland, with the expectation that he would implement an alternative to the Shepstone system, based on his experiences in Basutoland. Clarke attempted to reverse the tendency to play on factional differences, the essence of both the Wolseley settlement and the Shepstone system. In a sense echoing Bishop Colenso's original position concerning the restoration of Cetshwayo, he advocated the repatriation of Dinuzulu and the uSuthu exiles. Although Dinuzulu returned as a government induna, and not a paramount chief, it was hoped that he would use his influence to heal Zulu divisions and, by restoring Zulu confidence in the British, so help consolidate their administration.[82]

In January 1894 the British government agreed to Dinuzulu's pardon and return, but this was delayed by the intervention of the Natal government, whose objections now carried greater weight, responsible government having been introduced in the previous year (see Chapter 9). The Colony's interest in the matter derived not only from its security fears. There was also growing agitation from those who wanted closer control over Zululand's mineral resources. Farmers and developers eyed the coastal belt

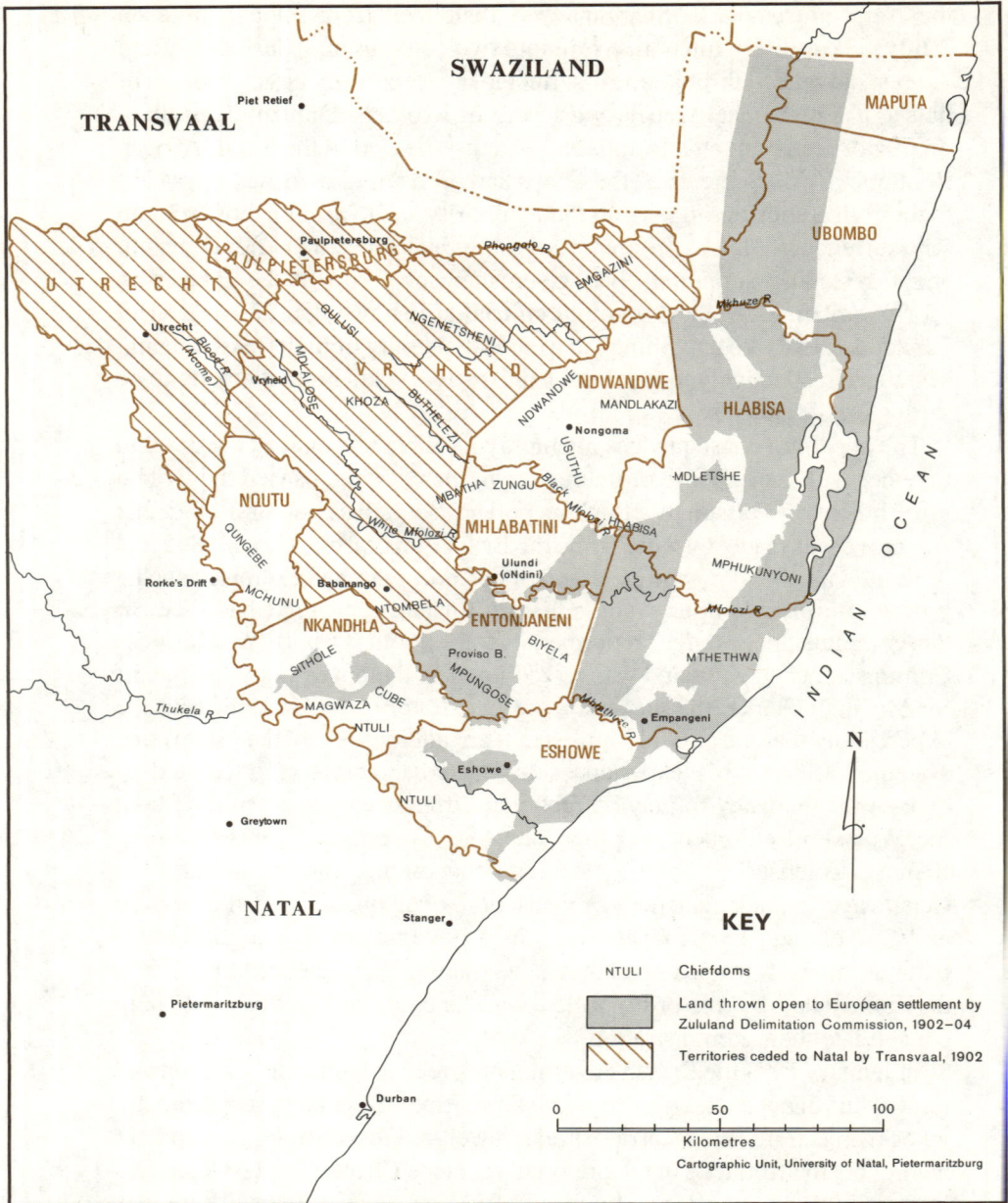

Map 17   Zululand, 1902–5

as suitable for sugar cultivation, fearing that Clarke's policy would close Zululand to white penetration.[83] While negotiations were in progress, the Liberal government fell in June 1895, after which the Natal government was able to negotiate an agreement with the new Colonial Secretary, Sir Joseph Chamberlain, whereby Dinuzulu's return was coupled with the annexation of Zululand by Natal. In the interests of his wider schemes for South African Federation, Chamberlain decided to conciliate Natal, with the result that, as in 1879, Zululand was again sacrificed to imperial expediency and settler interests. The territory that became incorporated on 29 December 1897 did not of course include the New Republic territory which had been lost to the Transvaal.[84] Included, however, was the Ingwavuma District which, although it had never formed part of the Zulu kingdom, had been annexed piecemeal by Britain in 1888, 1890 and 1895 in order to thwart the Transvaal's attempts to reach the sea, and had been incorporated into Zululand on 15 July 1895. Tongaland (or Amaputaland), fully annexed by Britain in 1897, had also been incorporated on 24 December 1897.[85]

Annexation by Natal spelt the end of Clarke's attempt to 'Basutolandize' Zululand. Having been incorporated into Natal's administrative system, Shepstonism was ultimately triumphant after nearly twenty years of conflict with competing solutions. It also meant the opening up of Zululand to white settlement, though five years were to elapse before the land was demarcated for it. A Commission duly set up in August 1902 submitted its final report on 18 October 1904. It set aside 3 887 000 acres as reserves for the Zulu, and excluded 2 613 000 acres for white occupation, most of which was soon turned into privately-owned sugar and wattle plantations (see Map 17).[86]

To outward appearances, the way of life of the Zulu people did not seem to have been radically transformed by the loss of political independence.[87] At the turn of the century, most Zulu continued to wear traditional dress and to live in scattered homesteads. Production proceeded as before, the kinship system and customary laws and practices persisted, and polygyny was practised. Cattle remained central to the economy, testifying as before to the wealth and power of men of rank, and were still used in lobola payments for wives, the effective agricultural producers in the homestead. Homestead heads, under the authority of chiefs, continued to regulate this pattern of life.

Even so, white observers at the time were in little doubt that, under colonial rule, the Zulu were steadily being made to conform to the requirements of an industrializing subcontinent.[88] A significant indication of this process was the way in which the young men of Zululand, who had once laboured in their age-grade regiments for their king, were becoming migrant labourers on farms and mines and in white towns. This fundamental re-allocation of labour was accelerated by the continued application of the Shepstone system to Zululand. It was equally a consequence of Shepstonism that the shift was muted, for it had always sought to manipulate or redirect the existing structures of traditional black society, so avoiding direct confrontation. Thus, when the colonial administrators of Zululand freed the young men from their obligation to serve the king and allowed them to labour outside the country for wages,[89] they not only served the interests of white farmers and industrialists, but also enabled the young men to earn enough money to marry and establish their own homesteads according to the traditional pattern. Young men were also induced to leave their homes in search of work by a hut tax of 14 shillings, first becoming payable in 1888,[90] and which became in Zululand, as it had been in Natal, the basic source of revenue. Cash was the preferred means of payment and, once the country had settled down following the suppression of the uSuthu 'rebellion', the young men were returning with sufficient money for it to be no longer necessary to tender cattle.

The introduction of money into the economy of Zululand had the effect of modifying certain aspects of Zulu society. Traditional homestead production continued to be vital, supporting the population between labour contracts, but ceased to be quite as predominant as before. White traders, attracted to the growing cash market of Zululand, opened more stores for the distribution of manufactured goods. Lobola changed from being a practice based on reciprocal obligation to one more often regarded as a form of sale. Colonial regulations promoted this process by insisting that the amount of lobola to be paid should depend on the status of a girl's father. This had the effect of augmenting the wealth of men of position, while widening the gap between them and the young men, who had to labour longer abroad to earn the cash for lobola, as well as for their contribution towards the hut tax, which it was the responsibility of the heads of homesteads to pay to the government. At the same time, the young men's long absences for work in the mines and towns of the Transvaal and Natal tended to weaken the hold of custom and the ties of kinship, breaking down their customary respect for elders and the traditions of the homestead, including those of homestead formation and marriage itself.[91]

The position of the chiefly class was also changing. While the chiefs retained their traditional status, they exercised their authority on a different basis. They were the deputies of the Governor who, as Supreme Chief, was regarded as having succeeded to what the whites considered to have been the absolute powers of the Zulu king. Consequently, they were subject to the Supreme Chief's pleasure, and received a cash pension in return for assuming responsiblity for the law-abiding behaviour of their people. In terms of the 1878 Natal Code of Native Law, extended to Zululand on its annexation in 1887, chiefs retained jurisdiction in minor civil cases and in less serious criminal ones, while benefiting from the fines and fees of their courts. Yet, such authority as they exercised fell under the supervision of the white magistrates set over them.[92] It is, therefore, not to be wondered at that, as paid officials dependent for their powers more on the approbation of the government than on that of their people, while upholding often unpopular or misunderstood colonial laws, they came to be held in less esteem.

The general dissolution of the traditional economy and of social relationships was hastened by a series of natural disasters which were part of a wider pattern of climatic deterioration and pestilence that began in 1895 and persisted for the next twenty years. In 1895–6 immense swarms of red locust swept bare the fields, and this recurred in 1898, 1903–4 and 1906. Between 1895 and 1907 there were six years of serious drought. In 1897 the most devastating blow of all struck the already weakened agricultural communities. Rinderpest, the contagious viral disease of ruminants, broke out among the cattle herds in mid-year and persisted until the end of October. Perhaps 85 per cent of the cattle, the chief form of storable wealth, succumbed. And, before the herds had had time to recover, they were infected in 1904–5 by the new and deadly tick-borne disease, east coast fever.

The combination of locusts, drought and livestock epidemics precipitated a major crisis for the people of Zululand. The destruction of large portions of the staple subsistence crops of maize and sorghum led immediately to widespread malnutrition and starvation. In the long run it led to the weakening of the whole tradional system of farming. The catastrophic loss of cattle undermined the very foundations of Zulu society, which had evolved around cattle-keeping, so that cattle were regarded as the basis of all social contracts and ceremonies.[93] Zulu society was the less able to resist these blows, or to recover from them because the colonial government gave no relief from the payment of the hut tax. Furthermore, traditional obligations of kinship had already been so eroded that they no longer could provide a safety-net against the consequences of economic disaster. The result was a further widening of the gap between wealthy men of status and the increasingly impoverished body of commoners, forced to depend ever more on the labour market outside Zululand. Some migrant workers, living so far from home, were tempted to cease sending their wages to their families and to abandon all obligation to their homesteads.[94]

The political subordination and fragmentation of Zululand had been accompanied by changes affecting labour patterns, traditional custom, kinship relationships and authority. They had also accentuated cleavages between rich and poor, and between those based on their homesteads in Zululand and those who now worked in the mining and industrial complexes of white South Africa. These developments were destined to become increasingly marked as Zululand moved further into the twentieth century.

Notes

1   The mixed feelings and different attitudes of Natalians towards the impending war are discussed by B. Guest in 'The War, Natal and Confederation', *The Anglo-Zulu War: New Perspectives*, eds. Duminy and Ballard, pp. 53–77.

2   The Zulu royal position on the war is given in 'Cetywayo's Story' and 'Ceshwayo's Letter', in *A Zulu King Speaks: Statement made by Cetshwayo kaMpande on the History and Customs of his People*, eds. C. de B. Webb and J. B. Wright (Pietermaritzburg, University of Natal Press, 1978), especially pp. 20–9 and 46–56.

3   Goodfellow, *South African Confederation*, pp. 160–9; C. de B. Webb, 'Lines of Power: the High Commissioner, the Telegraph and the War of 1879', *Natalia*, 8 (1978), pp. 31–7.

4 *Narrative of the Field Operations Connected with the Zulu War of 1879* (prepared by the Intelligence Branch of the Quartermaster-General's Department, Horse Guards, War Office; London, Her Majesty's Stationery Office, 1881), pp. 141–5. This official narrative of the war is still basic to an understanding of the British military campaign. (A useful supplement to it is *The South African Campaign, 1879*, comps. J. P. MacKinnon and S. Shadbolt (London, Hayward, 1882) with its lists and biographical details of officers and short histories of units in the imperial service.) Numerous books have appeared since the war, attempting to give a better account, but very few have surpassed the *Narrative*, even for the British side, and, of course, the Zulu side. Something of the Zulu perspective is given in J. P. C. Laband, *Fight us in the Open: the Anglo-Boer War through Zulu Eyes* (Pietermaritzburg and Ulundi, Shuter & Shooter and KwaZulu Monuments Council, 1985). The best recent comprehensive work, despite some distortion and errors in detail, is D. R. Morris *The Washing of the Spears: a History of the Rise of the Zulu Nation under Shaka and its Fall in the Zulu War of 1879* (New York, Simon and Schuster, 1965). For a survey of the literature on the war, see the section entitled 'References' in J. P. C. Laband and P. S. Thompson, *Field Guide to the War in Zululand and the Defence of Natal 1879* (Pietermaritzburg, University of Natal Press, 1983), pp. 118–20. Cetshwayo's version of events appears in *A Zulu King Speaks*. Lord Chelmsford's posthumous apologia is presented by Gerald French, *Lord Chelmsford and the Zulu War* (London, John Lane, 1939), to which the best and gentlest antidote is Sonia Clarke, *Zululand at War 1879: the Conduct of the Anglo-Zulu War* (Houghton, Brenthurst, 1984), containing the confidential correspondence of several imperial officers, especially prominent ones on the staffs of Lord Chelmsford and some of his column commanders.

5 Clarke, *Zululand at War*, pp. 65, 121. For the Zulu military system and tactics, see Laband and Thompson, *Field Guide*, pp. 3–7. The Zulu had firearms – 8 000 seems to be the lowest estimate for the war period – which could be called serviceable, but they were obsolescent (or obsolete) and had effected no significant change in tactics. The Zulu used rifles best as sharpshooters, as accounts of the battles of Rorke's Drift or KwaJimu and Khambula indicate. See J. J. Guy, 'A Note on Firearms in the Zulu Kingdom with Special Reference to the Anglo Zulu War, 1879', *Journal of African History*, 12, 4 (1971), pp. 557–570.

6 See J. Mathews, 'Lord Chelmsford and the Problems of Transport and Supply during the Anglo-Zulu War of 1879' (unpublished MA thesis, University of Natal, Pietermaritzburg, 1979); also Morris, *Washing of the Spears*, pp. 309–16. It must be added that the reduction in the number of lines of advance for logistical reasons is only inferred in this case.

7 The arrangements for the defence of Natal are treated in three works by J. P. C. Laband and P. S. Thompson: *Field Guide*, pp. 13–15; *War Comes*

to Umvoti: the Natal-Zululand Border, 1878–79 (Durban, University of Natal, Department of History research monograph, 1980), pp. 15–16, 28–35 *passim*, and, with Sheila Henderson, *The Buffalo Border 1879: the Anglo-Zulu War in Northern Natal* (Durban, University of Natal, Department of History research monograph, 1983), pp. 19–40.

8   *Narrative of the Field Operations*, pp. 22–7, 50–2.

9   *A Zulu King Speaks*, eds. Webb and Wright, pp. 29–31, 55–6, 59.

10   The great significance, drama and mystery of the Battle of Isandlwana has attracted considerable attention from military historians and other writers. The British official account is in the *Narrative of the Field Operations*, pp. 28–44. The classic monograph, although rather dated, is Sir Reginald Coupland, *Zulu Battle Piece: Isandhlwana* (London, Collins, 1948). A very concise account is given in Laband and Thompson, *Field Guide*, pp. 54–7, which seeks a balance between the British and Zulu aspects of the battle. The account in Morris, *Washing of the Spears*, pp. 352–88, has been cogently challenged in important details by F. W. D. Jackson, in 'Isandhlwana, 1879: the Sources Re-Examined', *Journal of the Society of Army Historical Research*, 43 (1965), pp. 30–43, 113–32. The differences evoked a correspondence between the two which almost achieved the level of controversy in *Soldiers of the Queen*, 29/30 (1982), pp. 3–22 and 33 (1983), pp. 9–20. For a recent and well researched account, which follows Jackson's line, but which is marred by its neglect of the Zulu side, see P. Gon, *The Road to Isandlwana* (Johannesburg, Ad Donker, 1979), pp. 212–48. A very useful compilation of contemporary records is N. Holme, *The Silver Wreath: Being the 24th Regiment at Isandhlwana and Rorke's Drift, 1879* (London, Samson Books, 1979). Critical reflections of British officers are to be found in Clarke, *Zululand at War*, pp. 73–108 and 119–37 *passim*, and of soldiers in Emery's *Red Soldier*, pp. 71–117. For a solid account with attention to the Zulu perspective, see J. Y. Gibson, *The Story of the Zulus* (London, Longmans Green, 1911). The most recent and comprehensive synthesis, emphasizing Chelmsford's responsibility for the British disaster, is in J. Mathews, 'Lord Chelmsford: British General in Southern Africa, 1878–1879' (unpublished D.Litt. et Phil. thesis, University of South Africa), pp. 114–220.

11   Goodfellow, *South African Confederation*, pp. 169–75; J. A. Benyon, 'Isandhlwana and the Passing of a Proconsul', *Natalia*, 8 (1978), pp. 38–45: Morris, *Washing of the Spears*, pp. 441–5. For more personal reactions, see Clarke, *Zululand at War*, pp. 109–18, and Emery, *Red Soldier*, pp. 107–10.

12   See the *Narrative of the Field Operations*, pp. 44–8; Morris, *Washing of the Spears*, pp. 389–420; and Emery, *Red Soldier* pp. 121–46: *BPP* LIII of 1878–9 (C. 2308), enclosure 6 in No. 14: statement of Ulankana, son of Undikile, 10 February 1879: 'The attack on Rorke's storehouse was directed

and led by Dabulamanzi, a prince, against the will and order of the king, who would have killed the leader if he had not been a prince.'

13   *Narrative of the Field Operations*, pp. 53–5. *A Zulu King Speaks*, eds. Webb and Wright, pp. 32, 33. For the British defences at Eshowe, see J. P. C. Laband, 'British Fieldworks of the Zulu Campaign of 1879, with Special Reference to Fort Eshowe', *Military History Journal*, 6, 1 (1983), pp. 1–5.

14   Laband and Thompson, *War comes to Umvoti*, pp. 35–44, and *The Buffalo Border*, pp. 43–59. See also P. S. Thompson, '"The Zulus are Coming!" The Defence of Pietermaritzburg, 1879', *Journal of Natal and Zulu History*, 6 (1983), pp. 28–47; and P. S. Thompson 'Captain Lucas and the Border Guard: the War on the Lower Tugela, 1879', *Journal of Natal and Zulu History*, 3 (1980), 30–44 *passim*.

15   *Narrative of the Field Operations*, pp. 60–3, 83–5, 154–5 *passim*.

16   Ibid., p. 63. For the demonstration see Laband and Thompson, *War comes to Umvoti*, pp. 45–51, and *The Buffalo Border*, pp. 62–5; Thompson, 'Captain Lucas and the Border Guard', pp. 39–40; J. P. C. Laband, 'Bulwer, Chelmsford and the Border Levies', *Theoria*, 57 (1981), pp. 6–8 *passim*. For the Zulu action see *A Zulu King Speaks*, eds. Webb and Wright, p. 33; Guy, *Destruction of the Zulu Kingdom*, pp. 56–7; J. P. C. Laband and J. Wright *King Cetshwayo kaMpande* (Pietermaritzburg, Shuter & Shooter and KwaZulu Monuments Council, 1983), pp. 17–18; and Bertram Mitford, *Through the Zulu Country* (London, Kegan Paul, Trench, 1883), pp. 277–9.

17   *Narrative of the Field Operations*, pp. 64–6, 82. Morris, *Washing of the Spears*, pp. 462–6. For an eye-witness account, see C. L. Norris-Newman, *In Zululand with the British* (London, W. H. Allen, 1880), pp. 133–54.

18   *Narrative of the Field Operations*, pp. 73–81; Morris, *Washing of the Spears*, pp. 475–97; Emery, *Red Soldier*, pp. 163–79 *passim*; *A Zulu King Speaks*, eds. Webb and Wright, pp. 33–4. A recent and detailed account is by J. P. C. Laband, 'The Battle of Khambula, 29 March 1879: a Re-Examination from the Zulu Perspective', in *There will be an Awful Row at Home about This*, ed. I. Knight (Shoreham-by-Sea, Zulu Study Group, Victorian Military Society, 1987), pp. 20–9.

19   Laband and Thompson, *War Comes to Umvoti*, p. 51; *The Fannin Papers: a Pioneer's Story of the Diamond Fields and the Zulu War*, comp. N. Fannin (Durban, Robinson, 1932), p. 44.

20   Cf. *A Zulu King Speaks*, p. 34, and French, *Lord Chelmsford and the Zulu War*, pp. 246–53. See also Morris, *Washing of the Spears*, p. 559; Frances E. Colenso, assisted by Lt.-Col. E. Durnford, *History of the Zulu War and its Origin* (London, Chapman and Hall, 1880), pp. 355–64; and Cornelius Vijn, *Cetshwayo's Dutchman*, ed. J. W. Colenso, (London, Longmans,

1880), pp. 129–50; J. P. C. Laband, 'Humbugging the General?: King Cetshwayo's Peace Overtures during the Anglo-Zulu War', *Theoria*, 67 (October 1986), pp. 1–20.

21   *Narrative of the Field Operations*, pp. 92–3, 101–2. For the demonstration see Laband and Thompson, *War Comes to Umvoti*, pp. 56–65, and *The Buffalo Border*, pp. 71–3; Thompson, 'Captain Lucas and the Border Guard', p. 41. In a British reconnaissance ahead of the Second Division on 1 June 1879, the Prince Imperial of France was killed.

22   *Narrative of the Field Operations*, pp. 96–8, 102–3, 109–10; Clarke, *Zululand at War*, pp. 203–12; Morris, *Washing of the Spears*, pp. 552–3. For the logistical difficulties, see Mathews, 'Lord Chelmsford and the Problems of Transport and Supply', and French, *Lord Chelmsford and the Zulu War*, pp. 216–34.

23   *Narrative of the Field Operations*, pp. 86–8; French, *Lord Chelmsford and the Zulu War*, pp. 279–80. Cf. Clarke, *Zululand at War*, p. 213.

24   *Narrative of the Field Operations*, pp. 104–8. Clarke, *Zululand at War*, pp. 213–27; *A Zulu King Speaks*, eds. Webb and Wright, p. 34; Morris, *Washing of the Spears*, pp. 553–4.

25   See Laband and Thompson, *War Comes to Umvoti*, pp. 67–73, and the *Natal Mercury*, 31 May, 3, 7, 17 and 28 June, and 1 July 1879.

26   *Narrative of the Field Operations*, pp. 110–17. Clarke, *Zululand at War*, pp. 229–44; Emery, *Red Soldier*, pp. 224–38; *A Zulu King Speaks*, eds. Webb and Wright, p. 34–5, 58–9; P. Dlamini, *Servant of Two Kings*, ed. S. Bourquin (Durban and Pietermaritzburg, Killie Campbell Africana Library and University of Natal Press,1986), pp. 70–2.

27   Laband, 'Bulwer, Chelmsford and the Border Levies', pp. 8–12.

28   *Narrative of the Field Operations*, pp. 117–18. Cf. Guy, *Destruction of the Zulu Kingdom*, p. 158.

29   British military and diplomatic activities are described in some detail in the *Narrative of the Field Operations*, pp. 119–31 *passim*, but with insufficient elucidation of strategies. *South African Journal of Sir Garnet Wolseley, 1879–80*, ed. A. Preston (Cape Town, Balkema, 1973), pp. 56, 60–1, 65, 74–7, 86–104. For the attempts to involve Swaziland in the war, see Bonner, *Kings, Commoners and Concessionaires*, pp. 150–4.

30   Guy, *Destruction of the Zulu Kingdom*, p. 59. Zulu war weariness is mentioned peripherally in Laband and Thompson, *War Comes to Umvoti*, pp. 78–89, and *The Buffalo Border*, pp. 77–80 *passim*. An incomparable narrative evincing the uncertainty and declining morale is reproduced in 'A Zulu Boy's Recollections of the Zulu War', ed. C. de B. Webb, *Natalia*, 8 (1978), pp. 6–21. Cf. E. Unterhalter, 'Confronting Imperialism: the People of Nquthu and the Invasion of Zululand', in *The Anglo-Zulu War: New Perspectives*, eds. Duminy and Ballard, pp. 98–119.

31   The pursuit and capture of the king is described from both sides in *A Zulu King Speaks*, eds. Webb and Wright, pp. 35–6 and 59 and *Narrative of the Field Operations*, pp. 132–6. See also Binns, *The Last Zulu King*, pp. 167–73; Vijn, *Cetshwayo's Dutchman*, pp. 53–77, 169–77; Guy, *Destruction of the Zulu Kingdom*, pp. 60–64.

32   Brookes and Webb, *History of Natal*, p. 146.

33   See, for example, ibid., p. 147.

34   L. M. Thompson, 'The Subjection of the African Chiefdoms, 1870–1898', in *The Oxford History of South Africa*, eds. Wilson and Thompson, 2, p. 265.

35   Guy, *Destruction of the Zulu Kingdom*, p. 76.

36   Benyon, *Proconsul and Paramountcy in South Africa*, p. 165.

37   Wolseley, *Journal*, pp. 2, 3; C. C. Ballard, 'Sir Garnet Wolseley and John Dunn: the Architects and Agents of the Ulundi Settlement', in *The Anglo-Zulu War: New Perspectives*, eds. Duminy and Ballard, pp. 130–1.

38   Wolseley, *Journal*, p. 318.

39   Notably that of Charles Brownlee, ex-Secretary for Native Affairs in the Cape, and Sir Henry Bulwer.

40   Guy, *Destruction of the Zulu Kingdom*, p. 71.

41   J. P. C. Laband, 'Dick Addison: the Role of a British Official during the Disturbances in the Ndwandwe District of Zululand, 1887–1889' (unpublished MA thesis, University of Natal, 1980), p. 10.

42   C. C. Ballard, *John Dunn: the White Chief of Zululand*, Johannesburg, Ad Donker, 1985), pp. 147–8.

43   Wolseley, *Journal*, p. 318.

44   J. P. C. Laband, 'The Cohesion of the Zulu Polity under the Impact of the Anglo-Zulu War: a Reassessment', *Journal of Natal and Zulu History*, 8 (1985), pp. 58–62; Guy, *Destruction of the Zulu Kingdom*, pp. 73–4.

45   Ibid., pp. 35–8, 74–5, 87.

46.   J. Pridmore, 'The Reaction of Colonial Natal to Sir Garnet Wolseley's Settlement of Zululand, June–December 1879' (unpublished BA Honours essay, University of Natal, 1983), ch. 2 *passim*, p. 8.

47   See, for example, F. E. Colenso, *The Ruin of Zululand* (London, Ridgway, 1884–5), 2 vols. and the pamphlet by Harriette Colenso, *The Present Position among the Zulus (1893), with some Suggestions for the Future* (London, Burt, 1893).

48   Guy, *The Heretic*, p. 285 and ch. 18 *passim*.

230 *Control and conquest*

49 J. P. C. Laband, 'The Establishment of the Zululand Administration in 1887: a Study of the Criteria behind the Selection of British Colonial Officials', *Journal of Natal and Zulu History*, 4 (1981), p. 64.

50 Ibid.

51 Laband, 'Dick Addison', pp. 5–9.

52 Pridmore, 'Reaction of Colonial Natal', p. 8.

53 J. J. Guy, 'The Role of Colonial Officials in the Destruction of the Zulu Kingdom', *The Anglo-Zulu War*, eds. Duminy and Ballard, pp. 153–5.

54 Guy, *Destruction of the Zulu Kingdom*, pp. 104–18

55 C. de B. Webb, 'Great Britain and the Zulu People, 1879–1887', *African Societies in Southern Africa* (London, Heinemann, 1969), ed. L. M. Thompson, pp. 313–14.

56 Guy, *Destruction of the Zulu Kingdom*, pp. 159–64.

57 Guy, 'Colonial Officials', p. 158.

58 Gibson, *Story of the Zulus*, pp. 242–58; Guy, *Destruction of the Zulu Kingdom*, pp. 166–79, 183–204. For a concise account, see Laband and Wright, *King Cetshwayo*, pp. 29–31.

59 Gibson, *Story of the Zulus*, pp. 259–63.

60 C. T. Binns, *The Last Zulu King: the Life and Death of Cetshwayo* (London, Longmans, 1963), pp. 225–6.

61 Brookes and Webb, *History of Natal*, p. 153; Webb, 'Great Britain and the Zulu People', pp. 316–7.

62 Intelligence Division of the War Office, *Precis of Information concerning Zululand* (London, Her Majesty's Stationery Office, 1895), pp. 94–6; Guy, 'Colonial Officials', p. 160.

63 Gibson, *Story of the Zulus*, pp. 270–2; C.T. Binns, *Dinuzulu: the Death of the House of Shaka* (London, Longmans, 1968), pp. 22–33; Guy, *Destruction of the Zulu Kingdom*, pp. 217–27; G. Dominy, 'The New Republicans: a Centennial Reappraisal of the "Nieuwe Republiek" (1884–1888)', *Natalia*, 14 (December 1984), pp. 87–97.

64 Guy, *Zulu Kingdom*, p. 235.

65 Webb, 'Great Britain and the Zulu People', p. 319.

66 Ibid., pp. 320–1; R. L. Cope, 'The British Annexation of Zululand, 1887' (unpublished BA Hons essay, University of Natal, 1959), p. 17, 20–1.

67 Binns, *Dinuzulu*, pp. 90–9.

68   Laband, 'Dick Addison', p. 10. For the hopelessness of Dinuzulu's position, caught between Boer and Britain, see the comments of A. J. van Wyk, 'Dinuzulu en die Usutu-Opstand van 1888' (unpublished MA thesis, University of the Orange Free State, 1972).

69   Webb, 'Great Britain and the Zulu People', p. 322.

70   Laband, 'Dick Addison', p. 222. For the distribution of troops, see War Office, *Precis*, p. 98.

71   See especially the two pamphlets by H. E. Colenso, *Mr Commissioner Osborn as one Cause of Confusion in Zulu Affairs* (London, Burt, 1892); and *The Zulu Impeachment of British Officials 1887–8, Confirmed by Official Records in 1892* (London, Burt, 1892). For Guy, see 'Colonial Officials', p. 162 and *Zulu Kingdom*, p. 237.

72   Laband, 'Zululand Administration', *passim*.

73   Ibid., pp. 64–5.

74   Laband, 'Dick Addison', pp. 2–9.

75   Ibid., pp. 217–20.

76   Ibid., pp. 57–62.

77   Ibid., pp. 18, 63–4, 91–4, 96, 101–12, 109–10, 114–5, 222–4, 238–41.

78   Ibid., pp. 118–19, 122–36; J. P. C. Laband, 'The Battle of Ivuna (or Ndunu Hill)', *Natalia*, 10 (December 1980), *passim*.

79   From 1889, after an abortive attempt to resettle in his location, Zibhebhu was obliged to reside in the Eshowe District. He was only allowed to go back to his redefined location in 1898, on the return of Dinuzulu from exile.

80   Laband, 'Dick Addison', pp. 151–2.

81   Ibid., pp. 156, 159–160; 162–3, 168–9, 175–80; War Office, *Precis*, pp. 100–3; Binns, *Dinuzulu*, pp. 134–9. For the detailed testimony of witnesses of the trial, see *The Court of the Special Commissioners for Zululand, 1888–9: Zulu Trials* (London, 1889).

82   R. Edgecombe, 'Sir Marshall Clarke and the Abortive Attempt to "Basutolandise" Zululand: 1893–7', *Journal of Natal and Zulu History*, 1 (1978), pp. 43–53.

83   Brookes and Webb, *History of Natal*, p. 186.

84   Edgecombe, 'Sir Marshall Clarke', pp. 51–2.

85   P. Harries, 'History, Ethnicity and the Ingwavuma Land Deal: the Zulu Northern Frontier in the Nineteenth Century', *Journal of Natal and Zulu History*, 6 (1983), pp. 17–21, 25–6; and *Webb's Guide to the Official Records of the Colony of Natal*, eds. J. Verbeek, M. Nathanson and E. Peel (Pietermaritzburg, University of Natal Press, 1984), p. xxi.

86   Brookes and Hurwitz, *The Native Reserves of Natal*, p. 12; Brookes and Webb, *History of Natal*, p. 186; *The Right to the Land*, eds. T. R. H. Davenport and K. S. Hunt (Cape Town, David Philip, 1974), pp. 28–9, and T. R. H. Davenport, 'The Fragmentation of Zululand, 1879–1918', *Reality*, 11,5 (September 1979), pp. 13–15.

87   The economic and social consequences of annexation still require considerable research, and current conclusions must be regarded as tentative. Nevertheless, some significant work has been done in the field, and the remainder of this chapter is largely drawn from two major contributions: Marks, *Reluctant Rebellion*, especially ch. 2 and 5; and J. J. Guy, 'The Destruction and Reconstruction of Zulu Society' in *Industrialization and Social Change in South Africa: African Class Formation, Culture and Consciousness 1870–1930*, eds. S. Marks and R. Rathbone, (London, Longman, 1982).

88   See R. Plant, *The Zulu in Three Tenses. Being a Forecast of the Zulu's Future in the Light of his Past and Present* (Pietermaritzburg, Davis & Sons, 1905), p. 62. Plant, a Senior Inspector of Native Schools, Natal, held the conviction that the 'Zulu in Natal', thanks to a longer period under 'European control', was much further advanced than the 'Zulu in Zululand'.

89   It is not altogether clear where the young men went to work. Guy, in 'Destruction and Reconstruction', pp. 176–7, suggests the Transvaal gold-fields and on the construction of Natal's railway line to the Transvaal. However, D. H. Heydenrych, in 'Indian Railway Labour in Natal, 1879–1895: the Biggest Indian Work Force in the Colony', a paper presented at a workshop on the development of Natal before Union held by the Department of Historical Studies, University of Natal, Pietermaritzburg, in October 1984, shows very convincingly that Indian employees on the railways in Natal outnumbered Africans by at least 2 to 1, and that the Africans never numbered more than about a thousand.

90   Payment, due on 1 June 1888, was delayed until October because of the uSuthu 'rebellion'. See Laband, 'Dick Addison', pp. 128–9, 193.

91   Guy, 'Destruction and Reconstruction', pp. 175–6, 181–2.

92   For a discussion on colonial regulations and the powers of chiefs in Zululand, see Laband, 'Dick Addison', pp. 3–9, 40–2.

93   C. C. Ballard, 'The Repercussions of Rinderpest: Cattle Plague and Peasant Decline in Colonial Natal', *International Journal of African Historical Studies*, 19, 3 (1986), pp. 428–30, 437–9, 444–50; Marks, *Reluctant Rebellion*, pp. 128–30.

94   Guy, 'Destruction and Reconstruction', p. 186.

Chapter 9

Towards responsible government, 1879–93

BILL GUEST

In November 1879, with confederation a dead letter and with Sir Garnet Wolseley's 'Jamaica reforms' due to expire automatically in September 1880 after five years (see Chapter 6), John Robinson optimistically revived the responsible government issue in Natal's Legislative Council with a motion insisting that no other form of government would now 'satisfy the requirements of the colony'. Five years previously, in common with the other coastal representatives, he had opposed Charles Barter's proposal for the introduction of responsible government as unlikely, under the circumstances, to be granted by the Imperial Government. Since then, he had become an outspoken advocate of that cause as a result of Wolseley's reforms which, in his view, had not only impeded the Colony's constitutional advance but its economic development as well. Disillusioned by the manner in which the imperial authorities had handled events in Zululand, without reference to the best interests of Natal, and embittered by the demand that the Colony should contribute to the expense of the war, he was now determined that the white settlers should gain control of their own affairs as rapidly as possible.[1]

A select committee of the Legislative Council, appointed on the same day that Robinsons's motion was introduced, reported in January 1880 with the recommendation that Natal should opt for a bicameral legislature and for five Ministers, chosen from and responsible to it, in a composite Cabinet which would include the Governor and the officer commanding

One of the features of Natal settler politics during the 1880s and early 1890s was the rivalry between the two Durban politicians Harry Escombe and John Robinson. This undated photograph of a scene outside the Durban Court House (now the Local History Museum) was taken during one of the election contests in which they competed.

the troops. The new Liberal Secretary of State for the Colonies, Lord Kimberley, agreed that the 'Jamaica reforms' of 1875 had served their purpose but rejected these proposals on the grounds that the white settler community was greatly outnumbered by the African population and unable to assume responsibility for its own defence. Instead, Natal was simply to revert to its pre-1875 constitutional status.[2]

During the campaign preceding the election of members to the Legislative Council in September 1880, which coincided with the expiry of Wolseley's Constitution Amendment Act, Robinson made it clear that he now regarded responsible government as a pre-requisite to any future confederation and as the essential means whereby long-neglected public works could be completed, a more effective 'native' policy initiated and local defences properly organized. The election campaign did not focus specifically on responsible government, though the matter was extensively discussed and for several candidates it was the key issue. Only one, Harry Escombe in Durban, expressed his vociferous opposition to responsible government proposals, as he had earlier done in the Council, unless the interests of the Colony's black majority were safeguarded by the creation of a separate Council of Chiefs or by the Crown's appointment of nominees to represent them. He and Robinson were both duly elected to represent Durban in the Legislative Council, for although then in disagreement on the constitutional issue, both enjoyed a considerable personal following.[3]

During the last two decades of the nineteenth century, Escombe and Robinson emerged as the pre-eminent and most capable personalities among an otherwise mediocre field of white Natal politicians in the colonial period. Often opposed to each other, sometimes in agreement and eventually fellow Cabinet ministers, they never became close friends. Yet both were highly respected for their sense of courtesy and personal integrity, and both demonstrated a much broader South African perception of politics than many of their more parochially-minded contemporaries, while continuing to advance what they regarded as Natal's best interests. It was appropriate that Robinson was to be asked to form the Colony's first responsible Ministry and that Escombe was to lead its second, though neither of them can be exonerated from the racial prejudices of the time and place in which they lived, in spite of Robinson's paternalistic belief in the obligation of whites to uplift blacks and Escombe's initial concern to provide Africans with political representation.[4]

In the years immediately following the 1880 election, it was Escombe who assumed the political initiative. In an open letter addressed to Durban electors in August 1881, he indicated that, while he was still opposed to the granting of full responsible government, a workable alternative would be attained if it was accepted that, in terms of the eighth clause of the 1856 Charter, the Governor was entitled to appoint elected members as heads of government departments. He proposed that these five appointees, at least a majority of whom should be electives, could then form a Ministry that would be required to resign if it lost the confidence of the legislature. These appointees, together with the Governor and the former (nominated) departmental heads, would constitute the Executive Council. He argued that, by 'giving greater political freedom to the colony without unduly lessening the power of the Crown', the latter would 'secure the strong support of many colonists who, like myself, admit we are not ready for responsible government but who claim that we are entitled to be freed from . . . the officialism of Downing Street'. Escombe thereafter insisted upon the appointment of another select committee. In December 1881 the Legislative Council accepted and forwarded to London its recommendation that the Charter of Natal be amended to permit the appointment of non-official members of the Legislative Council as heads of department, and that official (non-elected) members should eventually, though not immediately, be phased out as the Colony advanced to full responsible government.[5]

Escombe regarded it as a 'natural development of progressive institutions', but Kimberley saw no difference between this proposal and the earlier requests for responsible government. While reiterating his previous objections to this, he nevertheless conceded that, in view of the changes which had taken place in the subcontinent, including the recent recognition of Transvaal independence, in terms of the Convention of Pretoria, the British Government was prepared to grant responsible government if the colonists voted in favour of it in a general election. He emphasized that they would have to agree to the establishment of a nominated upper chamber, that adequate provision would have to be made to safeguard the interests of the Colony's black majority, and that Natal would have to assume responsibility for its own internal and frontier defence.[6] These conditions were by no means inviting and on receipt of Kimberley's dispatch, Bulwer dissolved the Legislative Council, forcing the proponents of responsible government to fight an election on very shaky ground.

The failure of the policy of confederation, finally dashed by the Anglo-Zulu conflict and the first Anglo-Boer War, had caused the British government to reappraise its strategy in southern Africa and to look with greater favour upon a devolution of responsibility to the white settlers in the interests of imperial retrenchment. Most Natal colonists had reacted with incredulity and disgust when the new Liberal government concluded a peace with the Boers without avenging the successive military defeats, culminating in the humiliation at Majuba. Prime Minister Gladstone was burnt in effigy in both Newcastle and Pietermaritzburg, where the Union Jack was hauled down in Market Square and, before being buried, was drawn on a wagon through the streets of the capital by a team of oxen, each of which was named after a prominent Boer leader.[7] Yet, with Isandlwana and Majuba both only recent memories, few Natalians could have believed that the Colony was indeed capable of defending itself. While Escombe rejected Kimberley's offer as constituting far more than the compromise which he had proposed, Robinson reluctantly advocated acceptance and was defeated at the poll, his fellow pro-responsibles winning only three of the fifteen seats in the Legislative Council. Opposition to responsible government was particularly strong in the Midlands and northern districts, where it was reported that 'the people do not want it, nor do they care for it and, what is perhaps worse, do not yet understand what it means'. Although Robinson was returned at a subsequent election in 1883, the mood of the electorate, coupled with the Colony's current economic difficulties, did not encourage a re-opening of the issue until as late as 1887.[8]

During the interim, while Natal, in common with the rest of the subcontinent, had to contend with a severe commercial and financial crisis,[9] the Colony's responsible government faction gradually regrouped and increased in numerical strength. The issue of defence was largely resolved in 1884 when the creation of the New Republic in north-western Zululand substantially diminished the possibility of Natal ever having to contend with a Zulu military invasion across her north-eastern frontier (see Chapter 8). The subsequent British annexation of Zululand in 1887 made that possibility even more remote. At the same time, the resurgence of Boer republicanism following the annexation of the Transvaal, as evidenced in the 1881–2 Anglo-Boer conflict, gave Natalians further cause to believe that their interests would best be served as a self-governing British colony.[10] Not least, Natal found itself at a decided disadvantage compared to its self-governing rival, as the longstanding competition with the Cape Colony for the Overberg trade increased in intensity during the 1880s. With both trying to overcome the prevailing recession, by 1884 the Cape's imposition of duties on goods imported from Natal had all but terminated the latter's trade with the diamond-fields. Moreover, Cape commercial influence was spreading rapidly northwards through the Transkeian territories, to the extent that customs houses were soon to be established on Natal's border with Griqualand East, while the Cape railhead had already reached the Orange River, whereas Natal's had penetrated no further inland than Howick.[11]

The spectre of economic isolation was rendered even more ominous by the failure of Natal's efforts to reach a commercial understanding with the Orange Free State, by the Boer penetration of Zululand, and by a trade agreement between the Portuguese and Transvaal governments, which allowed all goods to pass through Delagoa Bay to the Republic for a mere 3 per cent *ad valorem* transit duty. 'Railways and responsible government' had already become John Robinson's political rallying-cry, encapsulating the two key issues which, under the prevailing circumstances, were becoming increasingly interrelated. With Natal's financial lifeblood, the Overberg trade, in danger of drying up, the proclamation in 1886 of the Witwatersrand gold-fields made the need for rapid railway construction into the interior even more essential. The Colony required a loan of £500 000 to finance the venture, for which the approval of the Imperial Government was an essential prerequisite.[12]

The clashes which occurred in 1886 between the Natal Legislative Council and Governor Sir Arthur Havelock over the legislature's demand to be consulted on important issues, such as proposed tax increases, customs negotiations and the future of Zululand, simply confirmed the opinion of an increasing number of colonists that what they needed was a responsible Ministry to protect and extend their interests. The revelation that Havelock had been secretly corresponding with the government of the Orange Free State in connection with a customs convention proposed by the Volksraad, and that he had referred the matter to London without reference to the Natal Legislative Council, underlined the fact that, although his predecessors had done so, he was under no obligation to take that body into his confidence. In December 1886 Robinson successfully carried through the Council a vote of no confidence in the Governor, though this rare act of impeachment (especially in a colony that was still without responsible government) was ignored by the Colonial Office, which upheld Havelock's actions.[13]

After the events of 1886, Robinson was more determined than ever to achieve responsible government and when, in the following year, he visited London as Natal's representative at the colonial conference held to coincide with Queen Victoria's Golden Jubilee, he was able to confer with the Secretary of State, Sir Henry Holland. It transpired that the Imperial Government was not prepared to guarantee the £500 000 loan required for railway construction because it doubted the Colony's ability to repay it. Instead, Holland suggested three possible courses of action: the Legislative Council could drop its proposed railway extension, it could accept the tax increases that would be necessary to repay the loan, or it could accept responsible government and raise its own loan on the financial market. In the event of the third option being adopted, the issues of colonial defence, Natal's relations with neighbouring territories and, above all, the constitutional rights of her African population, would first have to be satisfactorily settled.[14]

Robinson returned to Natal convinced that the imperial authorities were now more than willing to grant responsible government, and at a public banquet held in his honour in July 1887 he strongly advocated its acceptance as an essential foundation for the Colony's future development.[15] He had by now become the undisputed leader of the pro-responsibles or 'Forward Party' and, in August 1888, with his eye on the election that was due to be held two years later, he persuaded the Legislative Council to appoint a select committee, chaired by himself, to investigate the Colony's political future. Not surprisingly, the committee reported in favour of responsible government. It pointed out that colonial defence was no longer an inhibiting factor, considering the Colony's ability to maintain internal law and order through its own police and volunteer forces and in view of the fact that the Cape, Transvaal and Imperial governments had assumed responsibility for the adjacent territories to the south and north. As far as Natal's relations with Zululand were concerned, it advocated unification as being in the best interests of both territories, subject to the retention of an imperial garrison in Zululand to symbolize the Crown's authority. On the thorny issue of African representation in Parliament, the committee advocated the creation of an upper chamber in which Crown nominees with considerable local experience would protect the interests of the 'natives'. It suggested that all measures concerning the taxation and control of Africans would have to be initiated in that chamber. As a further safeguard, it was suggested that a Permanent Under Secretary of Native Affairs should be appointed and a specific amount earmarked for expenditure on 'native' welfare and education.[16]

The Legislative Council accepted the select committee's report by a narrow thirteen to ten majority but, in forwarding it to Lord Knutsford (Holland's new title on being raised to the peerage), the Council indicated that it did not wish its action to be construed necessarily as approval of the contents, considering that the official members had not voted, probably because they had regarded it as a matter calling for an expression of popular opinion. As Knutsford pointed out in his reply, this reluctance to express a firm opinion made it difficult for him to deal with the issues raised. He did, however, indicate that although the Imperial Government was resolved to withdraw all British troops from Natal as soon as possible, if responsible government were instituted, it would be prepared to maintain a garrison there for up to five years while adequate colonial forces were being organized. The real stumbling-block to the achievement of responsible government remained, as before, the provision of adequate protection for 'native' interests, whose great champion, Bishop Colenso, had died in 1883. In Knutsford's opinion, the small increase that had taken place in the number of whites relative to that of the Colony's African population did not strengthen the case for responsible government or for the union of Natal and Zululand, while the proposals for African representation contained in the select committee report did not provide sufficient security for the voteless majority. In a subsequent dispatch, Knutsford suggested three possible safeguards: that all bills affecting the 'native' population should require the approval of the Crown; that a fixed annual sum should be appropriated out of the Consolidated Revenue Fund for expenditure on 'native' education and upliftment; and that a Native Protection Board (reminiscent of that created in Western Australia in terms of the Aborigines Protection Act of 1886) should be established, its members appointed by the Governor.[17]

The last of these suggestions was almost unanimously rejected by the Natal colonists. In June 1890 the Legislative Council approved, by twelve votes to ten, Robinson's motion that it was unable to accept any of them and that responsible government would have to include control of all sections of the population.[18] During the election campaign which got underway in the following month, the 'Forward Party' established a Reform Association with branches in both Durban and Pietermaritzburg. Its opponents formed the Natal Conservative Association under the leadership of Sir John Akerman, the long-serving member for Pietermaritzburg City, drawing support primarily from the farming community, which still feared the security implications of an imperial military withdrawal in the event of responsible government being implemented.[19]

To some extent, the contest developed into one between the Colony's two main urban centres, with Pietermaritzburg becoming the stronghold of the Conservative Association, while the pro-responsibles drew support from businessmen in Durban as well as from a working-class Labour League, whose members were most vociferous in demanding responsible government as a step towards curbing Indian competition. This necessitated a compromise, including a promise from Robinson that he would resist any further government-assisted Indian immigration. It alienated the Colony's handful of Asian voters,[20] but proved to be no disadvantage as far as the rest of the electorate was concerned. All three pro-responsible candidates (including Robinson and Escombe) were elected in Durban, while fourteen of the twenty-four members returned for the Colony as a whole were in favour of responsible government. These included all the coastal members, bar two in Victoria County, and all the representatives of the upper or northern regions, with the midland counties of Umvoti and Pietermaritzburg emerging in opposition. However, opinion within the white electorate still appeared to be fairly evenly divided, considering the number of seats that were uncontested, the percentage poll

By the 1880s ex-indentured and 'passenger' Indians had become the target for political agitation, especially from white working-class organizations. This undated photograph is of a meeting at the Point, Durban, addressed by the Durban lawyer and politician, Harry Escombe.

of barely fifty per cent, and the fact that the majority of voters in favour of responsible government was a slim 184 out of 4 121 votes cast.[21]

When the new Legislative Council met at the end of 1890, Robinson again secured the appointment of a select committee, chaired by himself, to draft a Constitution Amendment Bill that would endow Natal with responsible government while accommodating some of Knutsford's pre-conditions. The Bill eventually passed by the Council provided for the creation of a standing committee to report on any measures specifically affecting persons who were not of European descent and stipulated that proposals which discriminated against non-Europeans should require the Crown's assent. However, Knutsford still withheld his approval because the Bill made no provision for an upper chamber, it insisted that the Governor should act on the advice of his Cabinet in exercising his powers as Supreme Chief over the Colony's 'native' population, and it did not guarantee the provision of a fixed annual amount for 'native' education and welfare.[22] The first and last of these objections was met by a revised Bill which the Legislative Council passed in February 1892. It provided for a nominated upper house and fixed annual expenditure on 'native' upliftment, but the clauses in the earlier Bill providing for a standing committee and for the Crown's assent to all discriminatory measures were dropped, while that relating to the actions of the Governor as Supreme Chief remained virtually untouched.[23]

When, later that year, Robinson and G. M. Sutton, the progressive Midlands farmer and member for Weenen County, visited London to negotiate directly with the Colonial Office as representatives of the Colony, it transpired that this last clause had become the crucial issue. Knutsford was by then anxious to finalize Natal's constitutional future and, in a confidential Cabinet memorandum of October 1891, had already recommended that concessions be made to the settlers. He was evidently not particularly concerned about any guarantees for African rights that might be written into the constitution because the Governor would still have the right to reserve whatever bills he deemed necessary for royal assent. The exercise of the Governor's powers as Supreme Chief, however, was non-negotiable, though Knutsford assured Robinson and Sutton that, in practice, the Governor would always acquaint his ministers with any measures he proposed to adopt concerning 'native' policy. He persuaded them that this provision would in no way diminish Natal's responsible government status in comparison with other self-governing colonies. A compromise Bill, dropping the offending clause, was then dispatched to the Governor of Natal with instructions to call another election in order to test public opinion and, if approved, to place the Bill before the Legislative Council for consideration without alteration.[24]

Robinson plunged into the ensuing election campaign with vigour, addressing meetings all over the Colony during August and September 1892. The 'Forward Party' hoped that its cause would be strengthened by revelations that President Kruger now favoured the completion of the Natal line to the Witwatersrand and that the British Government still refused to approve the raising of any loan until the Colony accepted responsible government. It was suggested that the Transvaal Volksraad had only agreed to a survey of the proposed railway route on the understanding that Natal was soon to acquire responsible government and that the Colony would face a bleak economic future if it rejected this opportunity. However, only ten 'pro-responsibles' were returned, while fourteen successful candidates had opposed constitutional change.[25] The day was saved for the pro-responsibles when they successfully contested the results in the Newcastle and Weenen constituencies, each of which returned two members, on the grounds of irregularities concerning spoilt papers and rejected votes. The Supreme Court declared both results to be invalid and, in a subsequent by-election, the earlier outcome was reversed in Weenen, while two 'pro-responsibles' were returned unopposed in Newcastle.[26]

Although public opinion was obviously divided and a small majority of voters may still have been opposed to constitutional reform, the 'Forward Party's' slender majority in the Legislative Council was sufficient to carry Robinson's Responsible Government Bill, the passing of which coincided with the Colony's fiftieth anniversary celebrations in May 1893. Two months later, the Bill received royal assent and in September, when elections were held for the new Legislative Assembly following the introduction of the new constitution, Robinson topped the poll in Durban Borough, with Escombe second among the seven candidates. The new Governor, Sir Walter Hely-Hutchinson, then called upon Robinson to form the first responsible ministry.[27]

Natal Archives, C2196

The first Natal Ministry, following the introduction of responsible government in 1893, was like all others, a coalition in which many interests were represented. Standing (left to right): *H. Escombe (a Durban lawyer) and F. R. Moor (an Estcourt farmer).* Seated (left to right): *T. K. Murray (a Pietermaritzburg farmer and businessman), Prime Minister J. Robinson (editor of the* Natal Mercury*) and G. M. Sutton (a Howick farmer and businessman).*

During the 1890s the opening of a parliamentary session was always a glittering occasion. This photograph shows Church Street lined with troops and spectators for the arrival of the Governor at the Pietermaritzburg City Hall, which was used by the Legislative Council until it was destroyed by fire in 1898. The Council moved to the new Senate Building, alongside the Legislative Assembly building in Longmarket Street, in 1901.

Under the new constitution, the old Legislative Council was replaced by one consisting of eleven members, initially nominated by the Governor and thereafter to be chosen by the Governor-in-Council. Five of the first eleven members, identified by lot, were to retire after five years, but otherwise all members were to sit for ten years, thereby ensuring some continuity. The new Legislative Assembly comprised thirty-seven members elected on the existing franchise, which did not observe the 'one vote one value' principle and therefore gave a disproportionate value to votes cast in rural constituencies. All financial proposals had to originate in the Assembly and could be rejected but not amended by the Council. The Governor was empowered to designate up to six ministerial offices, all of which had to be occupied by members of one or the other House, with not more than two drawn from the Legislative Council. As in the Cape, ministers were entitled to speak but not vote in the chamber of which they were not members. The

Governor also enjoyed the constitutional right to reserve bills which, after two years, could then be disallowed by the Crown. He retained intact his powers as Supreme Chief, though he was instructed 'so far as may be possible' to consult with his ministers.[28]

Robinson had good reason to be satisfied with the outcome of his prolonged struggle for constitutional reform. With the raising of loans for public works no longer a major difficulty following the attainment of responsible government, his ministry gave prompt attention to the question of railway extension into the interior. The opening in December 1895 of the main line to Johannesburg was a feather in the cap of the new colonial government, for it seemed to secure Natal's economic prosperity for the foreseeable future, until that bright prospect was dimmed by the rapid deterioration in Anglo-Boer relations which characterized the last years of the nineteenth century (see Chapters 13 and 14).

Robinson could also derive satisfaction from the knowledge that the Colonial Office had considerably modified its position with regard to the protection of black interests in Natal and, in order to reduce its own financial commitments in the region, had ultimately approved a constitution which in practice ensured for the white colonists a minimum of imperial interference. The appointment of members to the Legislative Council was undertaken in close consultation with the ministry, even though the Governor was not constitutionally obliged to do this. Perhaps partly for that reason, the upper House subsequently played a very passive role in the political life of the Colony, never once rejecting a bill passed by the Legislative Assembly. At the outset, ministerial control was similarly established over appointments to the important post of Permanent Under Secretary for Native Affairs. Moreover, the Governor's powers as Supreme Chief were never exercised in practice,[29] much as Robinson had anticipated (see Chapter 6). The miscalculation of those, like Knutsford, who had believed that the constitution contained built-in guarantees sufficient to protect African rights was soon revealed when the Natal Parliament embarked upon legislation to stifle *kholwa* economic enterprise and induce Africans to seek employment on white-owned farms (see Chapters 11 and 15). This was paralleled by measures that were intended to abolish Indian enfranchisement, to curb the competition of Indian traders and to terminate Indian immigration, which dated back to 1860 (see Chapter 10).

Notes

1   Lambert, 'Robinson And Responsible Government', pp 36–9, 76, 83–4; Lambert, 'Sir John Robinson' (1980), pp 52–3.

2   *NGG*, Vol. XXXII No. 1830, 2 July 1880, p. 440; Davenport, 'The Responsible Government Issue', pp. 24–38, 55; Robinson, *A Life Time*, ch. 6.

3   *Natal Legislative Council Debates*, 2 December 1879; Lambert, 'Robinson and Responsible Government' pp. 95–9; Davenport, 'The Responsible Government Issue', pp. 43–7. For a more detailed account of the role played by Escombe in the political life of colonial Natal, see Talbot, 'Escombe and Responsible Government', *passim*.

4   See Lambert, 'Sir John Robinson', pp. 45–55; Denoon, 'Sir John Robinson, 1884–1893', ch. 1, pp. 1–14 and ch. 5, p 1; Talbot, 'Escombe and Responsible Government', pp. 13–18, 254–62.

5   NA Escombe Papers File 2/1/1: Escombe to Wood, 11 September 1881; *Natal Mercury*, 1 September 1881; *Natal Witness*, 3, 10 and 27 September 1881; *Natal Legislative Council Debates*, 18 October and 7 December 1881; GH 1222, No. 219 p. 136: Wood to Kimberley, 10 December 1881; Talbot, 'Escombe and Responsible Government' pp. 69–109.

6   NA Escombe Papers File 1/11: Memorandum by Escombe, 9 May 1882; File 2/1/4: Wood to Escombe, 29 June 1882; *BPP* XLVII of 1882 (C. 3174), pp. 13–15: Kimberley to Bulwer, 2 February 1882; *Natal Government Notice* No. 155 of 1882; Davenport, 'The Responsible Government Issue', pp. 93–102.

7   KCAL Colenso Papers, Folio 262: Colenso to Chesson, 10 April 1881; KCAL Memoirs of Robert James Mason (Typescript); B. J. Kline, 'The Establishment of Responsible Government in Natal, 1887–93', *Journal of Natal and Zulu History*, 9 (1986), pp. 55–70.

8   NA Robinson Papers, File 'Elections and Parliament': Sutton to Robinson, 7 April 1883; *Natal Mercury*, 11 March and 20 May 1882; Lambert 'Sir John Robinson', p. 54; Lambert, 'Robinson and Responsible Government', pp. 114–17, 121–2; Talbot, 'Escombe and Responsible Government', pp. 113–47.

9   Leverton, 'Government Finance and Political Development', pp. 234–53; S. P. M. O'Byrne, 'Natal during the Administration of Sir Arthur Havelock' (unpublished BA Honours essay, University of Natal, Pietermaritzburg, 1961). See also Chapter 5.

10 Lambert, 'Sir John Robinson', pp. 53–4; Dominy, 'The New Republicans', pp. 87–97.

11 Lambert, 'Robinson and Responsible Government', pp. 129–35; H. Heydenrych, 'Railway Development in Natal to 1895' in *Enterprise and Exploitation in a Victorian Colony*, eds. Guest and Sellers, p. 58.

12 Lambert, 'Robinson and Responsible Government', pp. 135, 144–6, 158–61.

13 O'Byrne, 'Administration of Sir Arthur Havelock', *passim*; Lambert, 'Robinson and Responsible Government' pp. 159–61.

14 Lambert, 'Robinson and Responsible Government', pp. 162–4.

15 *Natal Mercury*, 9 July 1887.

16 *Natal Legislative Council Debates*, 7 August 1888; *BPP* LVII of 1890–1 (C. 6487), pp. 1–21: Havelock to Knutsford, 28 October 1888; Lambert, 'Robinson and Responsible Government', pp. 165–72.

17 *Natal Legislative Council Debates*, 2 October 1888; GH 151, No. 29: Knutsford to Havelock, 5 March 1889 and 154, No. 108: Knutsford to Mitchell, 29 August 1889; Lambert, 'Robinson and Responsible Government', pp. 172–8; H. C. Lugg, *Historic Natal and Zululand*, pp. 39–40; See also Kline, 'Establishment of Responsible Government', pp. 57–60.

18 *Natal Legislative Council Debates*, 26 June 1890.

19 Lambert, 'Robinson and Responsible Government', pp. 178–80; Lambert, 'Sir John Robinson', pp. 54–5.

20 Lambert, 'Robinson and Responsible Government', pp. 184–5.

21 *BPP* LVII of 1890–1 (C. 6487), pp. 25–8: Mitchell to Knutsford, 16 October 1890; Lambert, 'Robinson and Responsible Government', p. 185–6.

22. *Natal Legislative Council Debates*, 3 December 1890; *BPP* LVII of 1890–1 (C. 6487), pp. 71–5: Knutsford to Mitchell, 28 May 1891; Lambert, 'Robinson and Responsible Government', pp. 186–92.

23 *Natal Legislative Council Debates*, 25 February 1892; *BPP* LX of 1893–4 (H.C. 216), pp. 24–37: Mitchell to Knutsford, 8 March 1892; Lambert, 'Robinson and Responsible Government' pp. 205–7.

24 *BPP* LX of 1893–4 (H.C. 216), p. 21: Knutsford to Mitchell, 29 February 1892; p. 39: Robinson and Sutton to Colonial Office, 17 June 1892; p. 40: Colonial Office to Robinson and Sutton, 25 June 1892; pp. 40–8: Knutsford to Mitchell, 28 June (telegram) and 5 July 1892; Lambert, 'Robinson and Responsible Government', pp. 208–210; Kline, 'Establishment of Responsible Government'.

25 Lambert, 'Robinson and Responsible Government', pp. 212–6.

26 *BPP* LX of 1893–4 (H.C. 216), pp. 50–5: Mitchell to Ripon, 10 October 1892; Lambert, 'Robinson And Responsible Government', pp. 216–17.

27   *Natal Legislative Council Debates*, 8 May 1893 and 10 May 1893; Lambert, 'Robinson and Responsible Government', pp. 217–18.

28   Eybers, *Select Constitutional Documents*, pp. 204–8.

29   Lambert, 'Robinson and Responsible Government', pp. 219–22, 231–2; Marks, *Reluctant Rebellion*, p. 9; Kline, 'Establishment of Responsible Government'.

Chapter 10

Natal's Indians, 1860–1910
From co-operation, through competition, to conflict

JOY BRAIN

Two broad categories of Indian immigrants arrived in Natal in the second half of the nineteenth century. The first was the indentured group, popularly known as 'girmitiyas' or 'grimitkaran',[1] who began to arrive in November 1860, following the decision taken the previous year by the government of India to include Natal in the indenture system which had been in operation in other parts of the British Empire since 1842. The second group consisted of free immigrants who arrived as traders and were usually called 'passenger' Indians because they paid their own passages. The first group were commonly referred to by the colonists as 'Coolies' from the term *Kuli* for a porter or labourer; the second group, because of their garments and because many were Muslims, were often called 'Arabs'.

Once the Indian community had become established in Natal, further groupings began to emerge. The largest consisted of 'free Indians', who had completed their contracts of indenture and had entered various trades and occupations. Yet another group was made up of the first and subsequent generations of colonial-born Indians, who were seeking new opportunities in the professional and commercial labour market. As a separate class, they were to challenge the political leadership of the 'Arab' traders. There were other smaller groups which maintained a separate identity, largely because they consisted of selected indentured immigrants, whose particular skills were required in the Colony. These included 'special servants', most of whom were employed in hotels and clubs, and Mauritian Indians who were brought out on contract for the Natal Railway Company between 1876 and 1878.

A total of 152 184 indentured Indian labourers were brought to Natal between 1860 and 1911. This group was photographed shortly after disembarkation. (From A. H. Tatlow, Natal Province: Descriptive Guide and Official Handbook, *South African Railways Printing Works, Durban, 1911.*)

Following an outbreak of cholera which claimed twenty-four lives in 1861, Indian indentured labourers were routinely confined on arrival in the lazaretto quarantine station on the Durban Bluff.

Local History Museum, Durban

The first phase of indentured Indian immigration lasted from 1860 to 1866, when the economic depression that affected the Colony brought it to a halt. Even when comparative prosperity returned, the complaints that the first returning labourers made to the Protector of Emigrants in Madras delayed the despatch of further shipments. A commission of inquiry, known as the 'Coolie Commission', was set up in 1872 to investigate the grievances of the indentured immigrants, and it was not until 1874 that India agreed to resume shipments.[2] The next phase, under new and improved conditions, lasted from June 1874 to July 1911, when immigration to Natal was terminated by the government of India. During the period of fifty-one years, a total of 152 184 men, women and children arrived to complete a five-year period of indenture, after which they could re-indenture for a further five years with the same or with another employer. Thereafter, they could claim a free passage to India, and thence to their village of origin, or they could stay and make a new life.[3] The original group which arrived between 1860 and 1866 had a third option of accepting a piece of crown land of equivalent value to the return passage. Of the number who chose this option, only fifty-two eventually took transfer of land; this was at Braemar on the south coast and took place after considerable delay.[4] The offer was then cancelled and was not included in the new conditions after 1874. In all, about 24 per cent had returned to India by 1911.[5]

Two-thirds of the indentured immigrants came from the Tamil- and Telugu-speaking districts of southern India, while one-third came from the Hindi-speaking districts of the north, particularly from the Ganges valley area (see Map 18). In many parts of nineteenth-century India, unfavourable environmental conditions, natural disasters and burdensome taxation had caused continuing economic distress, forcing many to contemplate the unpleasant prospect of indentured labour overseas. The shipping lists indicate that the immigrants belonged to a wide variety of castes, among them some brahmins.[6] The majority were from the lower castes, including not only agricultural labourers but also craftsmen such as weavers, leatherworkers and potters. The demand in Natal and elsewhere in the British Empire was largely for agricultural labour for work on sugar and other plantations, so that the predominantly agricultural background of most recruits suited both the recruiting agencies and the colonial employers.[7] As far as religion is concerned, about 86 per cent were Hindus, 12 per cent Muslim and 2 per cent Christians of whom the majority were Roman Catholic.[8]

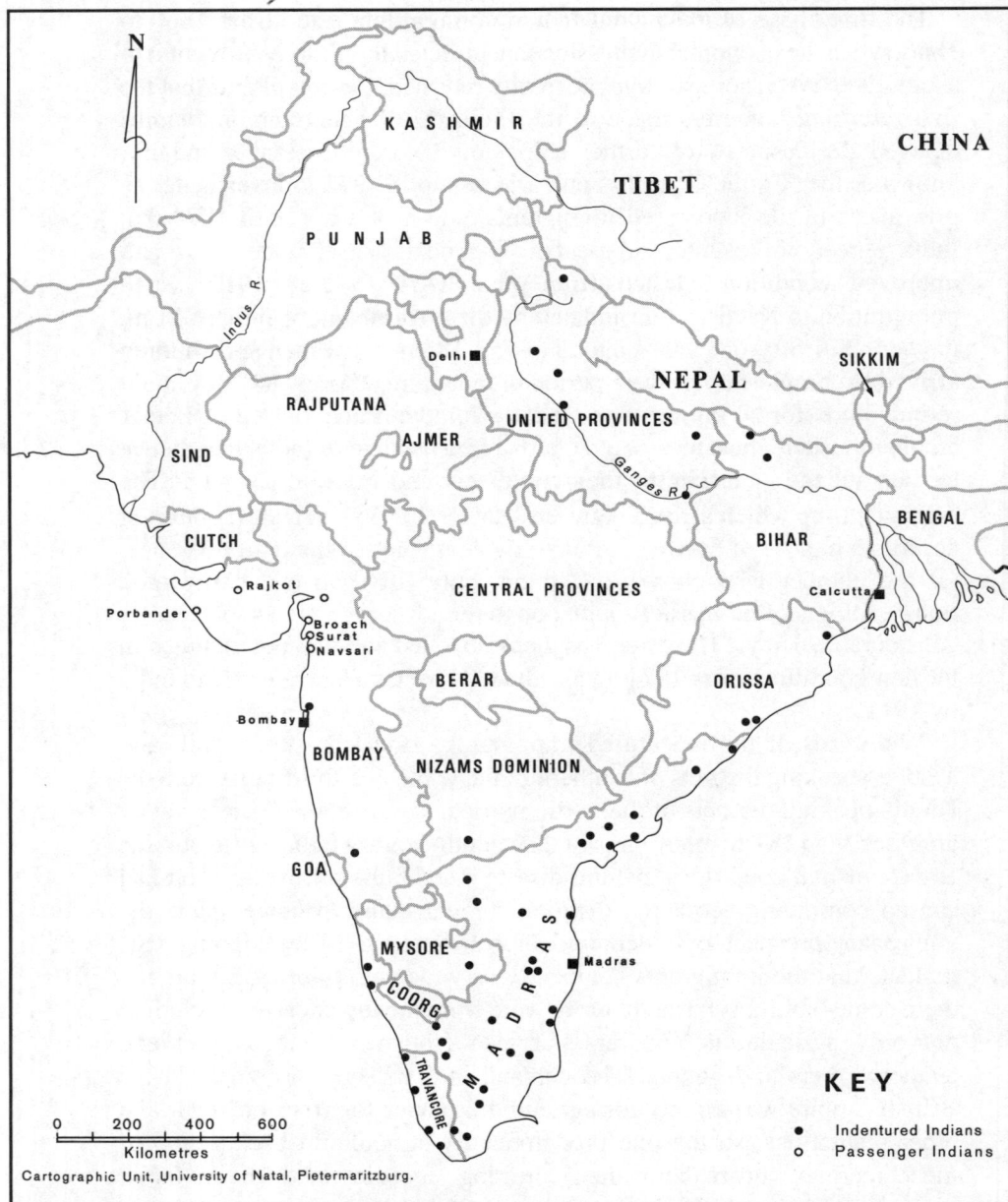

Map 18 India, showing the places of origin of Indians who emigrated to Natal

The employment of indentured Indian labour in Natal soon extended beyond the coastal estates, from Verulam in the north to Umzinto in the south, to which the first immigrants had been assigned. Later, they were allocated to employers in the Camperdown-Pietermaritzburg area and, after 1880, large numbers were used in the building of railways, both main and branch lines. By the late 1880s, they were in demand as coal-miners in northern Natal and in the wattle industry, while pastoralists in the Midlands and on the Colony's borders began to use them as shepherds and cattlemen.[9] By then, a handful of Indian employers also were using indentured labour. The labourers themselves had no say in the selection of their first employer, nor in the locality in which they were to work, although after 1904 it was agreed that they could not be sent to the coalfields for underground work without their consent. It was also found to be inadvisable to send newly-arrived men from south India, who were accustomed to a hot climate, to employers in northern Natal during the cold winter months.[10] While labourers had many justifiable grievances, employers also frequently complained that they had been allocated unsuitable, chronically sick or lazy workers. The allocation of indentured labour was made by the Coolie Agent and later by the Protector, who invited applications from employers each year. As ships arrived, labourers were distributed in order of requisition. The only stipulation was that families were always sent to the same employer and, where possible, people from the same village were kept together.

On paper, the contracts of the indentured Indians appeared reasonable enough at the time. Males were required to work nine hours daily for six days a week, receiving a basic wage of ten shillings (later twelve shillings) in the first year of service, with an increase of one shilling per month in each subsequent year. Women and minors were paid half this amount. In addition, the employer was required to supply food rations. An adult worker received two pounds of dhal, one pound of salt, two pounds of salt fish and one pound of ghee monthly, together with one and a half pounds of rice daily or two pounds of maize meal three times a week. The employer was also to supply a set of clothing on first employment, free medical attention and housing. Employers had also to contribute to the cost of hospitals for indentured workers at the rate of one shilling per worker per month, a considerable amount, at the time, for large employers to pay.[11]

In practice working conditions were far from satisfactory, for employers commonly spent as little as possible on the needs and welfare of their workers. On the labour-intensive sugar plantations, where between 60 and

Local History Museum, Durban

Large numbers of indentured Indians were employed as labourers in the sugar industry. This photograph was taken at the William Hartley Mill in Overport, Durban.

A small number of indentured Indians came to Natal as 'special servants', such as hotel waiters and chefs. This photograph is of the interior of the Commercial Hotel, Greytown, in about 1905. (From Twentieth Century Impressions of Natal: its People, Commerce, Industries and Resources, *Lloyds, London, 1906.)*

70 per cent of the Indians worked, a twelve- to fifteen-hour day was common practice during the busy seasons. Workers were often poorly housed and did not always receive their full rations, while there was a high incidence of intestinal diseases. Sanitation was usually non-existent and medical attention variable in quality. The death rate on some of the estates was particularly high and called for investigation by the Protector.[12] The disproportionate ratio of males to females – there were only three or four females to every ten males – resulted in social disturbances, quarrels between men over women, and prostitution. Even for those men who brought their wives with them or who married locally, a stable married life was difficult if not impossible.

Because non-plantation labour was generally better treated and better paid, many Indians preferred to work for the Natal Government Railways, the municipalities, or for a private concern like the Nelsrust Dairies at Baynesfield or the Clan Syndicate. Only after the end of the first period of indenture were they able to choose their employer. Even the coal-mines, despite their many hazards, were preferred by some workers to the large estates.

Despite the contractual nature of the system of indenture, which imposed conditions upon the employers and gave the indentured labourers recourse to the courts as well as a right of appeal to the Protector of Indian Immigrants, by the late 1880s informal as well as formal controls had whittled away their legal rights. The employers received sympathetic support from the local courts and the police, so that the powers of the Protector became progressively weaker. In the absence of formal channels for complaint, other forms of protest were employed. These included malingering, absenteeism, absconding, petty larceny and the destruction of property belonging to the employer. Organized protests were rare and, when they occurred, were small in scale and short-lived. One reason for this was that individual workers who showed organizing abilities and leadership potential could be quickly isolated.[13] Another explanation may be that it was common practice before 1906 for indentured workers to leave their original employer after the first contract expired; this resulted in a rapid turnover of the labour force and may have impeded the growth of worker consciousness.

Ex-indentured or free Indians who elected to remain in the country were able to sell their labour in most parts of South Africa, including the diamond and gold mining districts but excluding the Orange Free State, the Transkei and parts of northern Natal. The majority elected to remain in

On completing their indentures many Indians became market-gardeners and were soon supplying most of the fresh produce consumed in the towns. This is a photograph of the 'Indian Market' in Durban in the 1890s. (From Twentieth Century Impressions of Natal.*)*

Indian fruit-sellers at Verulam. Most of Natal's urban centres benefited from the presence of Indian market-gardeners and vendors. (From Tatlow, Natal Province: Descriptive Guide.*)*

Natal, where they entered the economy as farmers, smallholders, independent fishermen, tradesmen, hawkers or traders. For the first time, they found themselves in direct competition with colonists, Africans and coloured workers and thus began to create the same hostility as did the 'passengers'. In view of the employment history of most of the free Indians, it is not surprising that large numbers became successful market-gardeners and captured a dominant share of the market in the urban areas.[14] In the 1880s, the marketmasters at Durban and Pietermaritzburg were inundated with complaints from white farmers. This resulted in the imposition of certain restrictions upon Indians who wished to sell their goods in the market houses. There was competition also for arable lands, especially along the coastal strip, where Indians had been buying and leasing land from as early as 1866.[15] Indian artisans and tradesmen, whose skills had initially been welcomed in a colony where the white tradesman was in short supply, soon came into conflict with the white artisans, who complained bitterly about their loss of income due to the 'unfair' way in which Indians were cutting their costs. In 1886, for example, the Natal Working Men's Association petitioned the Governor, Sir Arthur Havelock, to stop all future importations of Indians on the grounds that 'artisans, small tradesmen would suffer from unfair competition at the hands of Indians, who have been brought here at the expense of the colony'.[16] Although the Protector denied the allegation in his reply, there seems no doubt that the white worker saw the Indian as a competitor. In 1896, the competition became overt when it was known that the Tongaat Sugar Company had arranged to bring in a group of skilled workmen from India at wages far below the market rate. White workers demanded legislation to prevent the importation of skilled men under the indenture system and the company, attacked on all sides for unjust practices, had to withdraw its application.[17]

As independent shopkeepers, the free Indian experienced competition with the 'passengers' from about 1880. From as early as 1863, small establishments owned and operated by free Indians had been set up in Durban. Baboo Naidoo, for example, had a shop in Field Street[18] and one Munsamy erected a store and dwelling on his land in Grey Street on which the mosque now stands.[19] By the 1880s, free Indians were running trading stores in Pietermaritzburg and in towns along the railway routes, where they catered for the needs of their compatriots, who were employed in large numbers by the Natal Government Railways. Pedlars and hawkers were also active in many districts, buying and selling items such as hides and

Cape Archives, C35/1

Anti-Indian excitement ran high among Natal's white settler population during the 1890s. This protest meeting was held at Durban Point in 1896.

skins or bartering for them with commodities known as 'Kaffir truck' or with items imported from India, such as cotton goods and spices.[20] Within a few years, however, most of the original shopkeepers had disappeared to be replaced by 'passengers'. In 1875, for instance, there were ten ex-indentured traders in Durban and one 'passenger'. Ten years later, only twenty-six free Indian traders, as compared with forty 'passengers', were trading in prime sites of the central business district.[21] In the next decade, the 'passenger' Indian established himself in trade, both wholesale and retail, while the free Indian tended to move into other sectors of the economy.

'Passenger' Indians, the second category, came mainly from western India, in what is today the state of Gujarat (see Map 18). They came from towns like Rajkot and Porbander and a host of villages in Kathiawar, as well as from Broach, Surat, Navsari and Bombay and the nearby villages. In addition to their varied places of origin, the 'passenger' Indians were characterized by differences of religion. There were Gujarati Muslims and Gujarati Hindus. Among the Muslims were groups like the Memons,

Bohras and Kokanis. Other groups included the Khojas, the followers of the Aga Khan, and the Parsis. A common origin or shared language or religion often created a strong bond among them and this frequently drew them to the same South African town. Hence Pietersburg, Potchefstroom and Bethal in the Transvaal attracted persons predominantly from Bhanvad, Ranavav and Eru respectively.[22] A few, like Aboobaker Amod, who set up a large and influential business in Durban as early as 1875, came via Mauritius, where there was a very large Indian population and good trading opportunities.[23]

Because the 'passengers' served the needs of the indentured and ex-indentured population, they settled largely in the coastal belt until about 1885. They then began to move into the hinterland, where they saw the opportunity to extend their activities to the African population, often underselling their white competitors. By 1900 the bulk of the African trade was in their hands. The extent of their penetration is shown by the fact that in 1908, despite the attempts of government and municipal authorities to

'Passenger' Indians were soon trading in all parts of Natal, underselling their white competitors. This photograph of the first Indian trading store to be erected in Old Main Road, Pinetown, was taken shortly before its demolition in the early 1920s.

Courtesy of Dr P. Brain

restrict Indian commercial activity, 1 008 licences were issued to Indians in all parts of Natal, with the exception of the township of Utrecht and the magisterial division of Paulpietersburg, where they were excluded by law. The total number of licences issued to non-Indians in that year was 2 034.[24]

The large-scale 'passenger', or 'Arab', traders and merchants had the advantage of being able to draw on the capital resources and expertise of family businesses. They were able to staff their shops with members of their extended families and, as the Protector remarked, employed few, if any outsiders of any race.[25] Hundreds of smaller Indian traders bought goods from them on credit for their retail outlets. Some idea of the scale of their operations is provided by the example of Abdulla Haji Adam, one of the three partners in the Durban-based firm of Dada Abdulla & Co. The company had branches in other parts of Natal as well as in the Transvaal and owned the steamships *Courland* and *Naderi*. The firm also had business connections in Bombay and Calcutta. Another example is that of M. C. Camroodeen, who had nearly 400 shopkeepers and hawkers on his books, owing him more than £25 500.[26] These and other large firms advertised their businesses in the *Natal Almanac and Register* as well as *Indian Opinion*. It is estimated that profits derived from Natal Indian trade in 1903–4 amounted to £502 000, while their property holdings in 1904 stood at £602 960.[27] It has been estimated that the annual combined turnover for both Indian traders and hawkers for South Africa as a whole was nearly £25 million in 1904, divided equally between the two.[28]

With the increase in the number of Indian and especially 'Arab' traders in the late 1880s, settler perceptions of them began to change. Whereas earlier, as the report of Superintendent of Police R. C. Alexander shows,[29] the 'passengers' had been praised for their law-abiding and courteous behaviour compared to the free Indians, as their businesses grew more numerous and more prosperous in the towns and as the rural African trade passed into their hands, they were seen as dangerous and unscrupulous rivals.[30] Nor were the 'Arabs' slow to voice their complaints, both by means of petitions and by statements in the Press. In 1878, a 9 p.m. curfew was introduced in Durban affecting Indians and in 1884 a petition, signed largely by members of the Indian commercial class, was submitted to the British government. The petitioners complained about the curfew laws, the closure of shops on Sundays, police brutality and the shortage of interpreters and other obstacles affecting Indians in the courts of law.[31] Economic depression in the Colony in the 1880s made the competition of the 'Arab' traders particularly unwelcome and, throughout the decade, tensions between white and Indian built up. Seeking to explain the increasing antagonism, the Wragg Commission reported in 1887:

> We are convinced that much of the irritation existing in the minds of European colonists against the whole Indian population of the colony has been excited by the undoubted ability of these Arab traders to compete with European merchants . . .[32]

The year 1893 was significant for both Natal colonists and for the Indian population. In that year, responsible government was granted (see Chapter 9) and the power to legislate against the Indians in various ways passed to the Natal Parliament, despite the advisory powers retained by the Secretary of State for the Colonies. For the Indians, and particularly the 'passengers', 1893 was an important year in that Mohandas K. Gandhi arrived in South Africa and was eventually to take up their cause.

In 1894 a bill was tabled which would have deprived Asians of the franchise. Royal assent was refused.[33] The following year the first part of a package of discriminatory legislation was introduced in the Natal Parliament. The Immigration Law Amendment Act No. 17 of 1895 imposed a £3 residential tax on all adult Indian males whose contracts had been drawn up in terms of this law. The first of these were due to complete their five-year period of indenture in 1901. After 1901, then, thousands of free Indians were left with three choices: to return to India, to re-indenture for a further period of five years, or to pay the £3 tax in addition to the £1 poll tax paid by males of all races. In view of their low earning capacity, the payment of the tax was, and was intended to be, beyond the ability of the majority. As Harry Escombe stated: 'Indians are appreciated as labourers only and are not welcome as settlers or competitors'.[34] In 1896 the Bill to deprive Indians of the franchise, which had been refused consent in 1894, was re-introduced and became law as Act No. 8 of 1896.

The following year, the Indian Restriction Act of 1897 and the Dealers' Licences Amendment Act were passed. Both were aimed directly at 'passengers' and traders. The first required that each immigrant be able to write and understand a European language and be in possession of at least £25. The second of these acts transferred the power to grant or refuse traders' licences to the local authorities and withheld the right of appeal to the courts. In this way, all hope of unprejudiced treatment of licence applications was removed, since the bitterest enemies of the Indian trader were to be found amongst his white competitors in the towns, where they were usually prominent members of the town boards or municipalities. This matter was taken up by the governments of Britain and India, and Natal was warned in 1899 that such unjust measures would bring to an end the Colony's participation in the indentured labour scheme.[35] The licence battle continued to be waged with increasing bitterness in the first decade of the twentieth century.

It is a sad reflection on the insularity and self-centredness of Natal's legislators that they chose to ignore the petitions and warning from the wider world, yet continued to depend on indentured labour for the growth of their economy. Harry Escombe was often a lone voice as he appealed to his colleagues and his constituents to adopt a more reasonable attitude towards Indians. He pointed out the contributions made by Indians of all classes to the prosperity of Natal and singled out the traders as serving a purpose in providing imported goods at low prices in inaccessible places.[36] Yet the politicians and legislators continued to ignore the protest until 1905. By then, public opinion in India had been aroused against the treatment of their compatriots in Natal. Joseph Baynes, who visited India in 1905, was alarmed at the strength of Indian feeling on the subject and recommended that a deputation from India be invited to visit the Colony.[37] Nothing came of the idea and, indeed, it was already too late since Natal's image was irretrievably damaged. It was left to Gandhi to marshall Indian protest within Natal.

With their large commercial interests, the traders considered themselves an élite group. The petty Indian traders, who were more numerous and whose interests were linked with those of the merchants, readily identified with them. This élitism made itself evident in the existence of exclusive cultural organizations, membership of which was narrowly defined by religion, language and caste. When their commercial and economic interests were threatened, they were able to organize politically and, in this way, the Durban Indian Committee launched a publicity campaign in Bombay and, through Bombay, to the British government, protesting against unfair treatment in Natal.[38] In the same way, the Natal Indian Congress, founded in May 1894 by leading merchants, reflected the interests of the trading class in its objectives.[39] Credit for the formation of the Natal Indian Congress is usually given to its first president, Abdulla Haji Adam.[40]

The part played by Gandhi in Indian politics in South Africa has been the subject of numerous studies, which until very recently were largely uncritical and mostly eulogistic. He arrived in South Africa in 1893, a London-trained barrister who had been briefed by a representative of the Porbander branch of the merchant Abdulla's firm, to assist in a lawsuit in Pretoria. The case arose out of a disagreement between Abdulla, who had extensive business interests, and the Pretoria firm of Tyeb Haji Khan Muhammed (usually known as Tyeb Sheth). Gandhi had intended to return to India at the conclusion of the case but, shocked by the prejudices against Indians in both Natal and the Transvaal and urged by the merchants, he decided to remain and did not return to India permanently until twenty-one years later.

Much of Gandhi's work in protesting against the treatment of Indians took place in the Transvaal in the post-war period and especially in 1907–8. In Natal he was involved in three important events. He was associated, in 1894, with the establishment of the Natal Indian Congress, which had as its objectives the 'establishing of a permanent institution that would cope with the legislative activity, of a retrograde character, of the first Responsible Government of the Colony with regard to the Indians, and protect Indian interests'.[41] The NIC was to play a significant role in the politics of both the Transvaal and Natal until 1914, but as the representative of the merchant class.[42] The second event was the establishment of the newspaper *Indian Opinion* in 1903. The first editor was M. H. Nazar, the joint secretary of the NIC, the printing and management being undertaken by Mandanjit Vijavaharik at his International Printing Press in Durban. Gandhi was associated with the project as adviser and contributor and most of the editorials published between 1903 and 1914 were probably written by him.[43] Printing of *Indian Opinion* was transferred to the Phoenix settlement in 1904. In the early years of the century, the NIC and *Indian Opinion* were in the vanguard of the fight against discriminatory laws in the Colony.

The third event of importance in Gandhi's sojourn in South Africa was the purchase of land outside Durban where he established his Phoenix settlement.[44] Gandhi was apparently influenced by the ideas of John Ruskin and Leo Tolstoy and his initial aim in acquiring the Phoenix property was to provide land on which workers could grow their own produce while drawing a small salary. An editorial in *Indian Opinion* in December 1904 elaborated on this idea, suggesting that 'the workers could live a more simple and natural life, and the ideas of Ruskin and Tolstoy be combined with strict business principles'. It has been pointed out that the American-educated Zulu editor of *Ilanga Lase Natal* , John L. Dube, had established a similar commune on a property close to Phoenix several years

M. K. Gandhi established a settlement at Phoenix, near Durban, modelled on the ideas of Ruskin and Tolstoy. The newspaper Indian Opinion *was produced there after 1903 in this building housing the International Printing Press.*

earlier.[45] It is not certain whether the two men were acquainted, but the idea of rural communes providing educational and other facilities seems to have been in vogue because Roman Catholic missionaries had established similar schemes in Pietermaritzburg and on the Bluff in the 1880s and 1890s.[46] In 1910 Gandhi established a settlement, similar to Phoenix, on land belonging to his friend Herman Kallenbach at Lawley near Johannesburg, which he called Tolstoy Farm. The settlement was to provide shelter and occupation for satyagrahis (followers of Gandhi) and their families and was planted with fruit trees and had ample water. Gandhi was dependent on financial help from local sources and from supporters in India, and had continuous financial problems which increased after 1910. Three years after its inception, he was obliged to close Tolstoy Farm and to return to Phoenix, where his family was settled, bringing some of his Tolstoy followers with him.[47]

It was in the early 1900s that Gandhi devised the political strategy of satyagraha, or passive resistance. This term has been translated as 'soul force', and for Gandhi it meant making one's own beliefs or resistance to injustice known by means of marches and other peaceful means of protest, without hatred, and refusing to resort to any form of violence, no matter what the provocation. Satyagrahis deliberately chose arrest and imprisonment rather than accede to the Transvaal government's enactment requiring them to register. This policy was followed also in Natal, but even at its height the kind of mass support that Gandhi had hoped for eluded him. The merchants in the Transvaal and Natal , who had initially supported him, had abandoned him by 1910 because of the apparent ineffectiveness of his tactics. He was thus increasingly forced to introduce new issues to revive a flagging campaign. One of these was to concentrate upon the threatened ban on interprovincial migration by Indians, which was contained in the Transvaal government's second Immigration Bill. In this way, he hoped to win the support of the educated élite in Natal. The groundswell of support which their involvement was expected to create did not, however, materialize, and it was only after 1910, when the campaign embraced issues affecting the masses, that mass support became a reality.

A third group among the Indians in colonial Natal was the 'new élite', a term coined in a recent study of Gandhi's role in South African Indian politics.[48] It comprised well educated and upwardly mobile Natal-born offspring of indentured or ex-indentured Indians, many of whom were Christians. Many of them had been educated in mission schools, where they had absorbed Western ideas and acquired proficiency in English. With high ambition they entered various professions, becoming lawyers, civil servants, accountants, teachers and interpreters. Prominent amongst them were individuals like the barristers James Godfrey, Joseph Royappen and S. R. Pather. P. S. Aiyar, the publisher and editor of the Pietermaritzburg weekly *Colonial Indian News*, and B. L. E. Sigamoney, the headmaster of Estcourt Indian High School, were to play a prominent part in the following decade. Other names well known in the period were L. M. Naidoo, S. P. Pillay and Suchitt Maharaj, all of whom were government interpreters, Vincent Lawrence, an attorney's clerk and Tamil language teacher, the photographers Brian and Lazarus Gabriel, and Charlie Nulliah Naidoo, a farmer and employer of indentured labour.[49]

These professional Indians formed their own organizations, such as the Hindu Young Men's Association, founded in 1905, the Catholic Young Men's Society and the Durban Indian Society. They also founded their own political organizations like the Natal Indian Patriotic Union, founded by P. S. Aiyar in 1908, and the Colonial-Born Indian Association, established in 1911. Like the trader-dominated Natal Indian Congress, these

St. Anthony's Young Men's Society in Durban, photographed c. 1908. This was one of several such organizations formed by young professional Indians at the beginning of the twentieth century.

organizations were, as the mouthpieces of Indians who were committed to upward social mobility, highly critical of discriminatory laws and practices which denied Indians access to equal opportunities. Although they intially supported the NIC, they became critical of its leadership, particularly after 1905, when they perceived it as doing nothing to further their economic interests. This can be seen clearly in the columns of the *African Chronicle*, edited by Aiyar. The free Indians who became market gardeners appear to have remained aloof from those organizations which they saw as being primarily for white-collar workers and representing urban interests. Suspicious of the merchants, they were removed from the mainstream of politics in the towns. When they combined, they did so in response to specific grievances, such as when they opposed moves by the urban authorities to protect white farmers, or when they resisted the establishment by Indian merchants of the Grey Street mosque market in Durban, seeing this as a move to monopolize the sale of their produce.[50]

Of the groups that formed the Indian community in Natal at the beginning of the twentieth century, the indentured Indians remain the least known outside the work situation. There is little evidence of how they spent their free time or how their social and religious needs were accommodated. Being largely illiterate, they left no personal records or diaries, while their employment on rural estates under the close supervision of compound officials made political organization difficult or impossible. For this reason, they have been described as a pre-industrial 'under-class'.[51] They did not make their needs and desires known and those who spoke on their behalf did so generally for whatever political advantage there was to be gained. In the 1900s, for example, merchants often advocated the termination of the indenture system as a lever for advancing their own interests, and not from any real concern for the plight of the indentured worker. A recent study suggests that the NIC repeatedly demanded the end of indentured labour in order to try and extract concessions from the Natal government for the free Indian community.[52]

The £3 tax was a burden on the free Indian from its inception but, during the depression after the Anglo-Boer War, it became insupportable. In 1903 the tax was extended to women, to girls over thirteen and to youths over sixteen years of age, and collection of the tax was more strictly applied.[53] The objectives were political in that it was hoped that more free Indians would return to India to escape the tax, and economic in that it was expected that the tax would force most of them back into indenture. The depression which followed the 1899–1902 war had resulted in a serious scarcity of jobs, so that unemployed whites were prepared to accept even menial occupations; free Indians, given the prejudices of the colonists, were soon in dire straits and with no hope of paying the tax.[54] A dramatic illustration of the hardships suffered by many free Indians is provided by the voluntary exodus of 2 000, who were in arrears with their tax, and who agreed to work for a private contractor who was building the Benguela Railway at Lobito Bay in Angola. The venture turned out disastrously, with as many as one quarter reported dead or missing.[55] Not surprisingly, the tax was a measure which rankled with the indentured community and was to be instrumental in radicalizing Indian politics in 1913, when Gandhi succeeded in organizing a passive resistance campaign on a large scale.[56]

It was not only discriminatory laws and taxation that gave the government of India a poor opinion of Natal. Indentured Indians complained bitterly of ill-treatment on their return to India, as well as lodging numerous complaints with the Protector in Natal concerning ill-treatment and poor conditions.[57] The suicide rate was unacceptably high, with the figure of 64 per 100 000 in 1904, higher than any other colony except Fiji.[58] Although many employers provided decent housing and health care, on some estates conditions were extremely poor and deaths from preventable intestinal diseases common. In 1904, for example, an official enquiry was held to investigate conditions on the Reynolds Brothers Estates, where there was a serious epidemic of dysentery. Perhaps the most damaging incident in a long series was the case of the vessel *Umfuli* which was engaged in 1906 to transport returning indentured labourers and their families to India. Among these were many 'invalids', a term used to describe anyone who was declared unfit to work. From the beginning of the indenture system, Natal had been in the habit of returning to India the sick, the old, the injured and anyone unable to work. The recruiting agents in Madras and in Calcutta had pointed out several times that it was difficult to persuade men and women to volunteer for Natal when each returning ship had on board groups of destitute and sick who were coming back to die and were certainly not a good advertisement for the Colony and its employers.[59] The *Umfuli* was found to be grossly over-crowded and with an unusually large number of 'invalids' aboard, estimated to exceed 30 per cent of the 642 passengers. On board also was a planter from Ceylon named Milo MacMahon and it was his statements, which appeared in the Press in Madras, that brought the whole matter to the notice of the Protector of Emigrants and the Government of India. The *Madras Mail*, for example, carried the headline:[60]

INDIAN EMIGRANTS FROM NATAL PACKED LIKE HERRINGS ON BOARD
A DISGRACE TO CIVILIZATION

Not even the fact that Indians working in Natal consistently sent or brought back more money than those from other colonies employing Indian labour,[61] could undo the harm that the *Umfuli* incident and the general casual treatment of the old and sick had done to Natal's reputation.

With the gradual improvement in the economy of South Africa as a whole and the optimism created by the Closer Union movement and the National Convention in 1908, employers of indentured labour began to take stock of their future labour needs. Whereas Natal was asking for steady recruitment of Indian labour, public opinion in India was strongly opposed to any plan to increase Natal's quota. Officially also there was little support in India for the continuance of the indenture system, which was eventually terminated in 1917, but in the case of Natal there was a determination to bring it to an end as soon as it was possible to do so. Meanwhile, the Natal government had appointed a commission to 'consider and advise on the question of Indian immigration to Natal'. In 1909 the Report of the Indian Immigration Commission (Clayton Commission) was published and showed that the Colony had learnt nothing from the criticisms so freely expressed in India. Indian labourers were still in demand by certain large-scale employers, but Indian settlers were not. The Commission recommended that indentured labourers should be returned to India immediately on expiration of their contracts, which should in future 'terminate not in Natal but in India or upon the high seas'.[62]

In February 1910, Professor Gopal Gokhale, a prominent member of the Indian National Congress and founder of the Servants of India Society, introduced a successful resolution in the Imperial Legislative Council recommending the prohibition of further indentured immigration to Natal. This was followed, in December of that year, by a similar resolution by the Indian National Congress, meeting in Allahabad. They called upon the government of India to prohibit the recruitment of Indian labour for South Africa, protesting against its policies as 'unwise, unrighteous and dangerous to the Empire'.[63] Eventually, it was decided by the Imperial Council that, unless Natal abolished the £3 tax, immigration to Natal would be prohibited. There was also severe criticism of the powers of the Protector who, it was asserted, 'was hardly ever a real protector'.[64] As a result, notice was served on the South African government in April 1911, prohibiting the recruitment of indentured labour from 1 July.[65] The last ship bringing Indian labourers, *Umlazi XLIII*, arrived on 21 July 1911 with 460 passengers on board, most of whom were indentured labourers.

In 1909, with the draft South Africa Act about to come before the British government for ratification, the Indian community decided to send a delegation to London to protest against certain articles in the Bill and to draw attention once again to the plight of the Indians in South Africa. Gandhi and Hajee Habib were selected to travel to London, while H. S. L. Polak led a delegation of four to India to whip up support there.[66] Gandhi agreed to go to London, not because it was part of his own strategy of satyagraha, but because an influential section of the Indian community felt that another tactic was called for. Members of this group were far from satisfied with the results of the previous passive resistance campaign. In London, Gandhi and Habib met the other South African delegations, including those of W. P. Schreiner, Dr A. Abdurahman, Revd W. B. Rubusana and J. T. Jabavu, who were protesting against the sections of the Bill which discriminated against all who were not of 'European stock'. For Gandhi, the special disabilities to which the South African Indians were subjected were of prime importance, nor was he prepared to accept legal restrictions on the immigration of Indians which were not also imposed on Europeans.[67]

Despite support and sympathy from many quarters, the demands of Gandhi and Habib were rejected. They returned to South Africa disappointed and Gandhi had to face financial difficulties and criticism from the members of the Natal Indian Congress, the Natal Indian Patriotic Union and later the Colonial-Born Indian Association over his failure to gain relief from the tax and redress for their other grievances. With the Union a *fait accompli*, new legislation was introduced to control the interprovincial migration of Asians, the recognition of marriages under rites that recognized polygyny and the immigration of Indian wives.

Natal entered the Union with its 'Indian problem' unsolved. Gandhi, who had long been the acknowledged leader of his compatriots, seemed to be losing the confidence of his supporters. The discriminatory laws were still in force and the number of committed satyagrahis shrinking. For the Indian community the future seemed dark indeed.

Notes

1   This term is derived from the English word agreement and means one who signed an agreement. The first form was used by the Hindi-speaking, the second by Tamils.

2   Thompson, 'Indian Immigration into Natal, pp. 55–66.

3   Law No. 12 of 1872.

4   NA 1785/1909, Indian Immigration Paper, II/1/168: A list of the original grantees and the owners in 1909 is provided in this document. A statement that Free Indians were not entitled to crown land in lieu of free passage is to be found in Legislative Council, *Votes and Proceedings*, Vol. 34, 1883. Questions relating to the transfer of the land at Braemar are referred to in GH 953, 1890, p 149.

5   NA II/1/179, 14/1911. The Protector quoted the figure, for persons returning to India, during the entire period from 1860 to December 1911, as 35 716 ex-indentured and 6 699 colonial-born children who accompanied them.

6   NA IIa/2/9, 460/1905 and 465/1905 refer to the presence of brahmins and the reluctance of the employers of labour to accept them.

7   See H. Tinker, *A New System of Slavery* (London, Oxford University Press, 1974).

8   The percentages for Hindus and Muslims are estimates; for Christians see J. B. Brain: *Christian Indians in Natal* (Cape Town, Oxford University Press, 1983).

9   Colony of Natal, *Report of the Protector of Indian Immigrants*, 1890.

10   *NGG*, Vol. XXXIII, 1897, 9 August 1881.

11   Law No. 19 of 1874.

12   The estates investigated by the Protector several times, because of high death rates, were Umhloti Valley Estates and Reynolds Brothers Estate. See, for example, NA II/1/139: 2709/1905 and NA IIa/2/14: 373/1907 for the former and NA II/1/156: 90/1906 and NA II/1/156: 3427/1907 for the latter.

13   M. Tayal, 'Indian Indentured Labour in Natal, 1890–1911', *Indian Economic and Social History Review*, 14, 4 (1977), pp. 519–547.

14   NA Pietermaritzburg Municipality, 7/4/1, 1856–82, p. 109; 7/4/2, 1882–93, p.127.

15   J. J. C. Greyling and R. J. Davies, *Land-Subdivision, Land-Ownership and Land Occupation* (Pietermaritzburg, Town and Regional Planning Commission, 1970), 1, pp. 23–4.

16   GH 1141, p. 90: Petition of the Natal Working Man's Asociation, 23 April 1886.

17   F. N. Ginwala, 'Class Consciousness and Control: Indian South Africans, 1860–1946' (unpublished Ph.D. thesis, Oxford, 1974), pp. 314–16

18   S. Bhana and J. B. Brain, 'Movements of Indians in Southern Africa, 1860–1911' (Preliminary Report presented to the Human Sciences Research Council, 1984), 2, p. 48. I wish to thank Professor Bhana for his many useful suggestions incorporated in this chapter.

19   J. B. Brain, 'Natal's Indians: Religion, Missionaries and Indentured Indians' (Paper read at the Conference to mark the 125th anniversary of the arrival of indentured Indians, University of Durban-Westville, October 1985), pp. 18–19.

20   *Report of the Protector 1886*, Deputy Protector's Report, p. A51.

21   *Report of the Indian Immigrants Commission* (Wragg) 1885–7, pp. 148–9: Evidence of R. C. Alexander; NA Durban Corporation Valuation Rolls, City Estate Office, 1880–1910.

22   Information on the origins of the 'passenger' Indians is based on an analysis of three volumes of the *South African Indian Who's Who* for 1938, 1940 and 1960. See also Bhana and Brain, 'Movements of Indians', 1.

23   S. Bhana, 'Indian Trade and Trader', *Enterprise and Exploitation*, eds. Guest and Sellers, p. 240.

24   GH 1599, 374/1908.

25   GH 1589, p. 210: R. C. Alexander on the progress of Arabs and Indians in Durban, 1886.

26   Swan, *Gandhi*, p. 9.

27   Konczacki, *Public Finance and Economic Development of Natal* (Durham, Duke University Press, 1967), p. 198.

28   A. J. Arkin, 'The Contributions of Indians in the Economic Development of South Africa, 1860–1970: an Historical-Income Approach' (unpublished Ph.D. thesis, University of Durban-Westville, 1981), p. 252.

29   R. C. Alexander, 'Our Indians', in Durban Corporation, *Mayor's Minute*, 1889, pp. 34–6.

30   See, for example, *NPP* 644: Petition No. 12 of 1885: Petition of the Pietermaritzburg Chamber of Commerce July 15, 1885 and CSO 1060, 95/86: Complaint of James Liddons of Curry's Post on the 'ever increasing number of Indian traders in the district', 6 January 1896.

31   B. Pachai, 'Aliens in the Political Hierarchy', *South African Indians: the Evolution of a Minority*, ed. B. Pachai (Washington, University Press of America, 1979), p. 10.

32   *Report of the Indian Immigrants Commission*, p. 74.

33   B. Pachai, *International Aspects of the South African Indian Question* (Cape Town, Struik, 1971), pp. 292–3.

34   *Speeches of Harry Escombe*, ed. J. T. Henderson, (Pietermaritzburg, P. Davis and Sons, 1903), pp. 292–3.

35   Pachai, *International Aspects*, p. 49. The same warning was given in 1904 (NA IIa/2/3: 317/04) and in 1910 (NA II/1/173: 2163/1910).

36   *Speeches of Harry Escombe*, ed. Henderson, p. 109.

37   Pachai, *International Aspects*, p. 23. The suggestion that an invitation be extended to the government of India is contained in NA IIa/2/8: 312/1905.

38 Swan, *Gandhi*, pp. 40–1. One such petition, from the merchants of Bombay, concerning the ill-treatment of Indians in Natal, was forwarded to Natal in 1891 and is to be found in GH 166, pp. 79–86.

39 GH 166, pp.49–52.

40 Ibid., p. 50.

41 Ibid., p. 49.

42 Ibid., pp. 50–1.

43 Ibid., pp. 57–8.

44 Pachai, 'Aliens in the Political Hierarchy', pp. 21–2.

45 Swan, *Gandhi*, pp. 59–60.

46 J. B. Brain, *Catholics in Natal*, 2, pp. 90–5.

47 Swan, *Gandhi*, p. 236.

48 See Swan, *Gandhi*, pp. 10–19 for short biographical accounts of the individuals mentioned.

49 Ibid., pp. 198–200.

50 Ibid., pp. 18–28.

51 Ibid., p. 61.

52 Pachai, *International Aspects*, p. 23.

53 J. B. Brain, 'Indentured and Free Indians in the Economy of Colonial Natal', *Enterprise and Exploitation*, eds. Guest and Sellers, p. 218.

54 Bhana and Brain, 'Movements of Indians', 2, pp. 61–2; GH 826, p. 178; GH 828, pp. 66, 80–172.

55 CO 179/253, 10 July 1909. See also E. Bradlow: 'Indentured Indians in Natal and the £3 tax', *South African Historical Journal*, 2 (1970), pp. 38–53; J. D. Beall and M. D. North-Coombes, 'The 1913 Disturbances in Natal: the Social and Economic Background to "Passive Resistance"', *Journal of Natal and Zulu History*, 6 (1983), pp. 48–81.

56 J. B. Brain and P. Brain, 'Nostalgia and Alligator Bite: Morbidity and Mortality among Indian Migrants to Natal, 1884–1911', *South African Medical Journal*, 65 (21 January 1984), pp. 98–102.

57 See, for example, NA IIa/1/11: 239/1906: Emigration Agent for the Colony of Natal, Madras, to Secretary of the Indian Immigration Trust Board, 5 July 1906.

58 *Madras Mail*, 17 October 1906. See also NA IIa/2/11: 340/1906 and NA IIa/2/13: 181/1907 for explanations and comment.

59 NA IIa/2/13: 181/1907, p. 1.

60   Report of the Indian Immigration Commission 1909, pp. 6, 11.

61   *Mahatma Gandhi: a Chronology*, comp. K. P. Goswami (New Delhi, Ministry of Information and Broadcasting, 1971), p. 39.

62   NA II/1/173: 2162/1910: 'Indians in South Africa: Debate in the Imperial Council'.

63   *Mahatma Gandhi*, comp. Goswami, p. 40.

64   Pachai, *International Aspects*, p. 59.

65   See, for example, NA II/1/162: 2023/1908 on the standard of rice issued to indentured men on the coalmines; NA II/1/160: 1159/1908 on the unacceptably high suicide rate among indentured workers; NA I/1/133: 164/905 and NA II/1/154: 2233/1908 on the assault of labourers by sirdars or employers; NA II/1/152: 1507/907 on general ill-treatment of indentured workers; NA. II/1/146: 3842/1906 on the standard of protection provided by the Protector and NA II/1/146: 3842/1906 on the conditions on the *Umfuli* and its invalided passengers. There are numerous other examples.

66   Pachai, *International Aspects*, p. 53.

67   E. A. Walker, *W. P. Schreiner* (London, Oxford University Press, 1937), pp. 326–7; J. D. Hunt, *Gandhi in London* (New Delhi, Promilla, 1978), pp. 108–9.

Chapter 11

Christianity and African society in nineteenth-century Natal

NORMAN ETHERINGTON

The rise of the Zulu monarchy provoked great interest among Christian missionary societies in Europe and America. At a time when obstacles of disease, communication and religious hostility made evangelization difficult or impossible throughout most of sub-Saharan Africa, the land of the Zulu seemed full of promise. Here was a great and highly-disciplined black state in a healthy environment, easily reached by sea. On the surface, it appeared to lack any form of organized religion which might prove resistant to preachers of the gospel. These advantages in an era of unprecedented Christian missionary activity eventually made Natal one of the most heavily-evangelized regions of the globe. Although the doctrines the missionaries preached challenged the fundamental ethical, metaphysical and social ideas of the Zulu, they generally acted as a counterpoise to white settlers and officials and came to know African life and problems better than did any other class of Europeans. They encouraged aspirations among their converts which had important political and economic consequences.

Missionaries came from many lands and many faiths: Anglicans, American Congregationalists, Scottish Presbyterians, English Methodists, French and German Catholics, Lutherans from Saxony, Prussia, and Scandinavia (see Map 19). Their strategies of conversion were almost as numerous as their denominations. American and Norwegian missionaries went out hoping that they could, by concentrating on the Zulu court, win the nation *en masse* to Christianity. The Hermannsburg Missionary Society planted villages of Germans in rural Natal, anticipating that the indigenous population would share their hope of recreating the communal piety of the Middle Ages. The first Catholic bishop attempted to frighten people by evoking the terrors of hell and damnation. The first Anglican bishop tried to

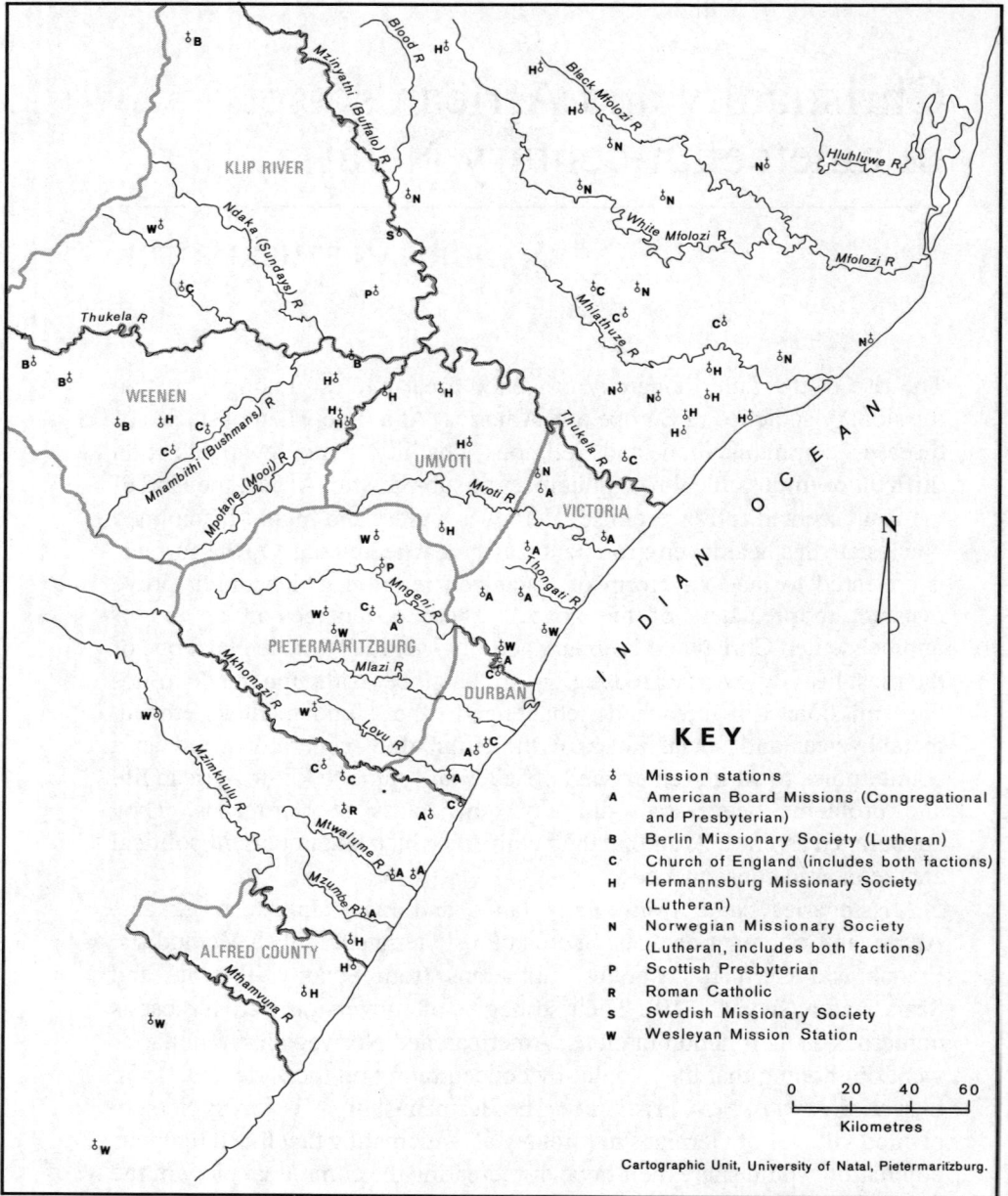

KEY

⌀	Mission stations
A	American Board Missions (Congregational and Presbyterian)
B	Berlin Missionary Society (Lutheran)
C	Church of England (includes both factions)
H	Hermannsburg Missionary Society (Lutheran)
N	Norwegian Missionary Society (Lutheran, includes both factions)
P	Scottish Presbyterian
R	Roman Catholic
S	Swedish Missionary Society
W	Wesleyan Mission Station

0   20   40   60
Kilometres

Cartographic Unit, University of Natal, Pietermaritzburg.

Map 19   Mission stations of Natal, Zululand and Mpondoland, 1835–80

cajole people by telling them that many of their cherished customs and beliefs already accorded with Christian truth. Some missionaries segregated their religious services; others resolutely opposed racial segregation.

Whatever the strategy adopted, success came very slowly. By the end of the century, African Christians did not comprise much more than 10 per cent of the black population. And when success came, it came most abundantly to those missionaries who adapted their approach to suit prevailing African realities.

Dreams of converting the Zulu nation *en masse* quickly faded.The retired British naval captain, Allen Gardiner, was in 1835 the first evangelist to test the receptivity of the court. As far as he could judge, the Zulu people had only vague notions of religion. They believed that the universe had begun with a single act of creation and that a divinity named Unkulunkulu had divided the first human beings into sexes and colours and had communicated to them the mournful knowledge that they must die. Spirits of the dead were believed to inhabit certain animals. Gardiner regarded the Zulu beliefs as a remnant of pre-Christian Judaism. They did not seem to be much of an obstacle to conversion, and he was favourably impressed by Dingane's intelligence and willingness to entertain new ideas.[1]

Dingane, in turn, respected Gardiner as a man who might help him bring order to the growing settlement of Port Natal, and gave permission for a missionary to be admitted. The captain then proved his good faith by returning to Zululand a group of people charged with crimes against the king and agreed to communicate to the Governor of the Cape, Sir Benjamin D'Urban, the king's views on diplomatic relations with Britain and the legal status of Port Natal.

Returning to London in 1836, Gardiner convinced the Church Missionary Society that they should send an ordained missionary to the Zulu kingdom. Their man, Francis Owen, arrived at Port Natal in 1837 to find three agents of the American Board of Commissioners for Foreign Missions already at work on the coast. The Americans had been encouraged by Dr John Philip, Superintendent of the London Missionary Society operations at the Cape, to believe that the Zulu monarchy offered possibilities for mass conversions, similar to those achieved in the Hawaiian kingdom during the 1820s. However, Gardiner's prior negotiations prevented them from finding the privileged position at court that was granted to Owen. For a few happy months, the English missionary served as schoolmaster to the greatest men in the land. But, before any lasting results could be achieved, his mission was embroiled in the tragic events that culminated in war between Dingane and the Voortrekkers (see Chapters 4 and 5). Owen fled after inadvertently being the only European eyewitness to survive the destruction of Retief's party, and the Church Missionary Society closed the mission.

The hostilities between the Zulus and the Trekkers nearly caused the Americans to give up as well, for they suspected that the advent of armed settlers would lead to the expulsion or extinction of the Zulu people, as had occurred with the Indians on their own western frontier. In 1840, however, Mpande 'anxiously, earnestly, and repeatedly requested' that at least one missionary reside near him, following his success in reconstituting the kingdom east of the Thukela River (see Chapter 4).

Aldin Grout answered the call, and proceeded to do irreparable damage to the cause of evangelization. Instead of working closely with Mpande, he allowed his mission station to become a political threat to the state. He boasted that some Zulus said openly 'that if Mpande does not treat them well, they will just walk off, or move their village upon my place, taking it for granted if they are upon the station, they are out of the way of Zulu authority'. In 1842 Mpande broke up the mission, complaining that the people called 'themselves the people of the missionary and refused to obey me . . . they cast off their allegiance to their king, and were of no use to me'.[2] In Zululand, where command over manpower was the principal support of the government, defections could not be allowed. Until 1850, Mpande thereafter absolutely prohibited missions in his country.

Norwegian Lutherans took up the crusade to convert the Zulu court after the Americans withdrew. Hans Schreuder, a giant of a man in mind as well as physique, planted a station on the Natal side of the border in 1848 and bided his time.[3] Opportunity knocked in 1850 when Mpande fell ill and sent to Schreuder for medicine. By making himself useful in this and other ways, Schreuder won the king's trust. He accepted, for the time being, Mpande's refusal to allow any Christian to perform the elementary act of swearing allegiance (*khonza*) which marked a person as a citizen of the realm. But he trusted that, in the long run, his respect for Zulu sovereignty would dim the memory of Grout's blunders. After tensions within the royal house erupted into civil war in 1856 (see Chapter 4), Mpande told Schreuder that more missionaries might come, a concession which the Norwegians interpreted as a wish for more white advisers to counterbalance the party of Cetshwayo.[4] Lacking Norwegian manpower to

*The Norwegian
missionary
H. P. S. Schreuder
founded the Mpumulo
Mission Station before
establishing others in
the Zulu kingdom. He
and his assistant
T. Udland (standing)
are here photographed
with their wives.*

Local History Museum, Durban

seize this unexpected chance, Schreuder turned to German Lutherans from
the Hermannsburg Missionary Society. They soon occupied as many
stations as the Scandinavians.

The Church of England gained a foothold in the country in 1860, when
Afrikaner encroachments on Zulu territory made Mpande think that
missionaries with official connections in Natal might strengthen his
position. Bishop Colenso, who at that time was known to be a close friend
of Shepstone, won permission to establish two stations in Zululand. The
first Anglican missionaries, Robert Robertson and S. M. Samuelson,
followed Schreuder's strategy. They attempted at every opportunity to
show they were loyal supporters of the royal house and to argue that
Christianity would strengthen rather than weaken the state.

During the next two decades, missionaries built houses and wagons for
Mpande. They wrote letters on behalf of the king and for Cetshwayo, the
heir apparent. They brought European medicines and trading goods into the
kingdom. But they did not succeed in breaking down the quarantine which
the state imposed on the Christian religion. By the middle of the 1870s,

there were no more than 450 black Christians in the country. Most of them had been imported from Natal to serve as examples but were more conspicuous for their activities in trade than in evangelism.[5] Growing numbers of missionaries doubted the efficacy of Schreuder's policy and prayed for the destruction of the royal authority which had so effectively thwarted their efforts.

Chiefly hostility was not the only obstacle to the spread of Christianity. Gardiner and the early American missionaries were mistaken in their initial perception that the Africans had few, if any, developed ideas about religion. They also grossly overestimated their own ability to change basic patterns of daily life by altering religious beliefs. In Natal, where the state erected no barriers to the spread of Christianity, missionaries encountered determined resistance at the grass roots of African society.

The American missionaries decided to stay in Natal even after Grout's folly had closed the door to Zululand, not least because Shepstone had offered them privileged sites for mission stations on large locations (see Chapter 7). There, hundreds of people came regularly to hear them deliver sermons in very imperfect Zulu, not only listening to what was said but repeating it with something approaching word-for-word accuracy. This convinced the missionaries that the people were not only highly intelligent but were hungry for instruction. Similar experiences greeted subsequent missionaries as they penetrated the far corners of the Colony, causing them to complain that they had been misled by the racial prejudices of intellectuals in Europe and America to expect simple-minded docility.

Instead, they found people who, as a French missionary bishop put it, were the equal of 'our European free thinkers' in debating ability. He gave as an example a young man who asked how a spiritual soul could be tormented by the material fires of hell. Questions of comparable difficulty were asked about theology. Why did an omnipotent God allow Satan to live? Why did God not send rain when it was needed? The most perplexing of all the theological problems confronting missionaries was that of explaining the Christian concept of sin. Africans readily agreed that actions could be designated right or wrong, but resisted the idea of a generalized quality of sinfulness built into every human being. Even less palatable was the idea that all their ancestors suffered death and torment because their sins had not been redeemed, a concept which struck at the root of the traditional belief that ancestral spirits directly affected the welfare of living people. Those rare individuals who contemplated or underwent conversion, were therefore interminably pestered to recant by their friends and neighbours. One man who left the church told a missionary that he would surely roast in hell for his apostasy but 'his friends had been to converse with him and they were very unwilling to have him become a believer'.[6]

Deeds as well as words were required of converts to Christianity. They had to clothe themselves according to missionary standards of decency. They had to rearrange the sexual division of labour and so take women out of agricultural labour and turn them into housewives. They had to try to live, as near as their income would permit, in European houses and clothes. But all these requirements were minor compared to the missionary assault on two basic institutions of family life: polygyny and lobola. Only one among the entire missionary clergy of Natal was prepared to baptize a polygynist, while no missionary allowed a convert to stay in the church if he took a second wife. These prohibitions were intended to do more than simply enforce the moral code of the New Testament, for Victorian missionaries believed they had a duty to 'raise the status of women'. Their theory was that the husband who cemented a marriage bond with a gift of cattle to his father-in-law was 'buying a woman'. The husband who married more than one wife was, in their opinion, purchasing slaves to satisfy his lust.

Missionaries were therefore amazed to discover that most Zulu women

A kholwa wedding ceremony in about 1880.

took a different view of status. It was generally accounted a privilege to be married to a man wealthy enough to support more than one wife. A relationship contracted without a gift of lobola carried a social stigma like that which marked illegitimacy in England or common-law marriage in America. As one African summed it up, 'any girl with a proper feeling would refuse to marry a man without being *lobola-ed*'.[7] Even though missionary societies tolerated the custom, they spoke out against it and solemnized marriages even when parents did not consent. They consequently acquired a reputation as enemies of family life and parental authority, for which reason most African women forbade their daughters to be educated at mission stations.

Chiefs in Natal were not as adamantly hostile to Christianity as were the monarchs of Zululand, but they also felt social pressures from their people to steer clear of preachers. In 1860 a Methodist missionary met 'a petty chief very friendly to Christianity who would himself believe but for his people and great men who tell him that by so doing he will forfeit his chieftainship and make himself a fool'. Another chief professed to be a 'lover of missionaries' but would not send his children to school because of the uproar it would create in his community.[8] Even so, many chiefs invited missionaries to reside near them because they valued their secular services such as letter-writing and intercession with British authorities.

As long as their basic fabric of family, community and religious life remained intact, the indigenous population resisted Christianization, no matter what intellectual or theological approach it took. None of them made much headway until the end of the century. Bishop Colenso, who denied the doctrine of eternal punishment, who permitted the baptism of polygynists and who supported hereditary chiefs, made fewer converts than did the American missionaries who preached hell-fire, temperance and monogamy. During the first five decades of evangelism in Natal, the work of hundreds of missionaries produced an African Christian population of less than 10 000, well under 10 per cent of the population.

The first converts, or *kholwa*, did not constitute a representative sample of the general population. About half the converts made before 1900 came from outside the region where their mission station was located,[9] this alien character being especially marked in Zululand because of the official ban on missionary activity. They were often accused of being morally peculiar as well. A magistrate grumbled in 1858 that missions were not 'particular about the character of the natives they admit to reside on their stations' and warned that 'the knowledge that some of the worst crimes are committed by those residing upon mission stations must have an injurious effect towards the spreading of the doctrines of Christianity among the surrounding population'. Some missionaries acknowledged there was truth in the charge that their missions were 'refuges for characters of the worst description'. According to the Anglican Henry Callaway, it was 'not the élite of . . . society which first gathers around a Missionary; it is not even an average specimen of the natives'.[10]

Callaway's own station at Springvale provides a good example of the social mix which characterized the early black Christian communities. The first residents were converts who followed him from Pietermaritzburg in 1853. Newcomers to the station over the next twenty years included six groups of refugees, seven families from the immediate vicinity, seven families from Methodist missions in the Transkei, ten families who came to join relatives, two former servants, a handful of brides acquired by male converts, and five hired teachers. There were representatives of the San and Griqua ethnic groups as well as of the Xhosa and Zulu.[11]

Missionaries liked to stress the purely religious motives of new converts, but their own reports reveal that many other forces were at work. Out of a group of 177 people whose reasons for going to live on missions are noted, 12 per cent were said to be attracted by religion, 26 per cent by prospects of employment, 15 per cent by relatives, and 14 per cent by their attachment to a missionary transferred from another posting. A further 33 per cent were refugees, including 3 per cent who had been accused of witchcraft and 10 per cent who wished to escape unpalatable marriages.[12]

Generalizing from these rough statistics, three significant factors can be singled out as formative influences on early black Christianity. The first is that mission stations attracted to Natal strangers who were lured by material opportunity or who had been pushed out of old homes by the turbulent events of the early nineteenth century. The second is that the people who needed land could get it from missionaries who possessed large tracts on private farms and 'mission reserves' granted by the government. The third is that people who found themselves uncomfortable, unwelcome or actively persecuted in their own societies could usually settle on mission stations with no questions being asked. Christian communities thus provided an escape hatch which had not previously been available to criminals, accused sorcerers, unwilling brides and psychologically disturbed individuals.

The Mariannhill Monastery, near Pinetown, was established in 1882 by a group of
Trappist monks led by Father F. Pfanner, seen here conducting a Sunday School
service.

Black Christians were not only held in disrespect by the heathen, there
was also a general contempt for missionary work among the white
community, even though it remained theoretically committed to the spread
and protection of the Christian religion. As far as the Trekkers were
concerned, they brought with them to Natal prejudices that had been
cemented on the Cape frontier. To the missionaries, they appeared as
irresponsible exploiters rather than as agents of European law and order.
One of Francis Owen's reasons for giving up his mission was the fear that
the Voortrekkers would 'never allow a station for missionaries' and that
Africans would run away to escape their tyrannical rule.[13] The Americans
who stayed hoped to be able to convert the Trekkers to 'true Christianity'
and thereby win permission to carry on their work among the blacks. At
first, the Volksraad refused to allow any mission to Mpande. When they at
last relented, it was over the strenuous objections of men who said that
missionaries set 'traps' for white settlers.[14] Grout reported that the
Trekkers:

> . . . granted Umlazi and Ifumi as places for mission stations, but they
> are now getting sick of it as they say the people on their places will

always be leaving them that they may stop on the station and there *be free* (I would not speak it aloud enough for them to hear, but that seems to show what they want and intend; they want slaves).[15]

Dr Newton Adams considered that the British annexation came just in time to prevent the breaking up of his mission.[16]

The English settler community was hardly less antagonistic to mission work. The Reverend Benjamin Markham encountered a colonist who agreed to contribute funds to missionary work if it was used for 'blowing Kafirs' brains out'.[17] Wilhelm Illing contrasted the respect shown to missionaries in his native Germany with the behaviour of Ladysmith whites, who would not permit their children to be baptized by a 'Kafir missionary'.[18] The American Silas McKinney was so disgusted by colonial prejudice that he refused for years to have any social contact with whites outside the missionary fraternity.[19]

At the top of the list of settler complaints about the missionaries was that they were indifferent to their need for land. The Native Commission of 1852, for example, said it had been a tragic mistake to appoint foreign missionaries to the commission which had laid out African Locations in the previous decade.[20] The land speculator and immigration promoter Joseph Byrne (see Chapter 5) encouraged public meetings in Pietermaritzburg and Durban to attack the American missionaries, whom he charged with preaching republican doctrines, undermining Britain's commercial strength and, most important, seeking land for Africans that ought to have been reserved for white colonists.[21] In 1862, a Select Committee of the Natal Legislative Council condemned Lieutenant-Governor Scott's plan for vesting control of African lands in appointed trustees, partly because it would tend 'as past experience proves, to give a control and preponderating influence to the clergy and missionaries'.[22]

The second big complaint against the missions was that they made Africans useless as labourers. While distributing tracts in Durban in 1861, a Methodist preacher was beset by a crowd of whites shouting that '"Missionary Kaffirs" were the worst in the country', and that missionaries 'hindered servants in their work'.[23] A Ladysmith woman told the local missionary that she could not afford the wages asked by black Christian women. What was worse, they 'always had a desire of going up to the Station to attend Divine services and Evening-School'. A plantation owner charged that 'by teaching the Kaffirs to read and write, and wishing them to dress' the missionaries 'made them proud and idle, and put them in possession of a power by which they became rogues and thieves'.[24] Benjamin Markham admitted that his converts demanded higher wages and said that, as a result, no more than half a dozen whites in the entire town of Pietermaritzburg sympathized with his work.[25] The opinion of the *Natal Witness*, expressed in 1871, was that:

> . . . the Colonist . . . would if pressed, give his vote in favour of the 'ignorance that is bliss' for the native, and prefer that his servants should enjoy their servitude, to their being educated into competitors. Hence, if there is not an open hostility to Missions, there is very slender sympathy in favour of their operations.[26]

The least supportable settler complaint was that missionaries failed to convert Africans. Or, to be more precise, that missionaries attempted to convert people who were not capable of becoming true Christians. According to a Methodist district superintendent, the major reason why settlers would not contribute to missions was 'scepticism as to the converting power of the gospel upon the native population'.[27] A candidate for the Legislative Council once told an election rally that 'a corps of police officers could do more to civilize the Kafirs, than all the missionaries in the Colony'.[28] Lieutenant-Governor Pine reinforced local prejudice by telling the Methodists that experience had taught him 'the extreme difficulty of really converting savage nations to a knowledge of our religion'.[29] For years it was popularly (but wrongly) rumoured that the veteran American missionary Daniel Lindley had said that he had yet to meet a truly Christianized African.[30] This sort of criticism puzzled the missionaries. It must, thought Henry Callaway, stem from 'an opposition to Christianity in any form, or in any country'.[31] Another speculated that, if this sort of unreasoning attack did not originate in secret atheism, it must come from 'the school of Dickens', which jeered at all dedicated Christian labours. He had:

> . . . heard it affirmed most confidently that there is not a converted kafir to be found. The most painful part of the case is, that those who say such things seem as if they wish them to be true – as if, in their judgment, it is a matter of congratulation that the heathen around us remain heathen still.[32]

It was as though the settlers unconsciously feared that Christian Africans would have a more powerful claim to equal rights than an uneducated population devoted to their ancient beliefs.

Isolation from both their white and their African neighbours spurred many of the *kholwa* towards material and educational progress. They sought security in an uncertain environment. Throughout South Africa, African agriculturalists were entering into colonial marketplaces as peasant producers (see Chapter 7). The *kholwa* were in the forefront of this movement in Natal, founding farms outside as well as within mission reserves. But, unlike most other African producers, they did not limit their entrepreneurial activities to farming. They became traders, carriers, artisans and landlords. In part, this broader range of economic enterprise was stimulated by missionaries, who applauded the acquisition of material wealth as proof of progress in 'Christian civilization'. In part, it reflected the exclusion of many African Christians from the lobola system of marriage which encouraged investment in cattle. In part, it was due to the superior educational opportunities available on mission stations which gave the *kholwa* a better knowledge of market forces and business methods.

While African Christians earned little by way of applause in Natal, they amazed European observers with the speed of their progress.[33] A committee of Anglican clergy investigating the affairs of Springvale mission, only sixteen years after its foundation, reported that 'there is not a village in England corresponding to Springvale where every man lives under his own vine and under his own fig tree'. The committee expressed surprise that the people were 'able to live without becoming servants', but noted that 'some American mission stations on the coast are far wealthier'. On one of these stations, Mvoti, there were by 1864 forty-eight houses constructed in the European manner, some of them quite as good as the missionary's own house. Mvoti people owned twenty-two ploughs, fourteen wagons worth £90 each, and twenty span of oxen worth at least £90 each. Two members of the community had personal net worth of more than £1 000.

Methodists could point to similar successes at Edendale and Driefontein. At the minor station of Verulam, a significant proportion of the *kholwa* had, by 1876, made the transition from wage earners to employers of non-Christian black labour. Berlin missions had a showplace of progress at New Germany. Even relatively impoverished communities such as the Anglican mission at Ladysmith boasted several residents with incomes exceeding £400 per annum by 1876.

Nearly all the Africans who won exemption from Native Law before the 1880s were Christians. Some of these men listed on their applications property holdings that would have been envied by most settlers in Natal. In 1881 the Methodist minister Daniel Msimang reported real estate consisting of two houses on 89 acres at Edendale, along with a large block of shares in the co-operatively owned farms of Driefontein and Kleinfontein. His moveable property included two ploughs, two wagons, thirty-six oxen, 260 goats and twenty cows. An even wealthier Christian, William Africa, owned 1 000 acres outright and shares in several farms.

The *kholwa* were pioneers in many branches of commercial agriculture, experimenting in the 1850s with cotton, coffee, arrowroot and sesame, and in the 1860s with sugar. The American mission at Mvoti led the way by establishing a plantation and crushing mill. The success of the venture encouraged similar enterprises to be started at Amanzimtoti and Ifumi.

Shortages of land on coastal mission reserves held the African planters back in these first ventures, as it did in most parts of the Colony. Freehold tenure, which was essential to commercial success, could not be had on government locations and was available only under special conditions on mission reserves. Plenty of land was available for rent from absentee landowners, but tenants hesitated to invest much money in farms which they did not own. Wherever they could, African farmers bought land, creating through their purchases areas which would one day come to be known as 'black spots'. These witnesses to thrift and enterprise began to appear in the 1850s. First at Edendale, then at Indaleni, the upper Mzimkhulu river valley and the hinterland of Ladysmith, Methodist men established farms by pooling resources. During the same period, a group of *kholwa* from the overcrowded Lutheran mission at New Germany bought a nearby farm and hired a white school teacher to continue the education of their children.

Land-buying continued in the 1870s with two more offshoots of Edendale appearing near Ladysmith, one on the Mlazi River and a fourth on the upper Mzimkhulu. Men from the Church of England mission at Ladysmith raised £2 010 towards the purchase of two farms. According to the Methodist missionary Joseph Allsopp, there were many counterparts to these ventures. He told the Natal Native Commission of 1881 that *kholwa* were 'forming companies and taking land' throughout the Colony; it being commonplace for them to be seen bidding 'publicly at sales of Crown Lands the same as white people'.[34]

In the bustling early years, *kholwa* often combined farming and trading.

Reports of their trading in Zululand date from as early as 1853. With increasing mobility acquired through the purchase of ox-wagons, *kholwa* traders spread a net of black commerce over half of southern Africa. Many community leaders, including the Congregational minister James Dube, derived most of their income from transport and trade. From Edendale, big wagon trains of thirteen and fourteen teams set off for the interior at regular intervals. Trading became so important to converts on American stations that in 1880 they demanded that mission newspapers give up-to-date reports on prices and markets.

Success in commerce owed much to educational facilities planted by the missions. For decades these were the only schools where Africans were taught. Government aid to education was channelled through the missions. Naturally, the *kholwa* were the best placed to take advantage of these schools and, by the 1880s, as many as 3 000 African pupils were being taught. Most of them studied only basic religion, arithmetic, reading and writing, but at some institutions impressively high standards were achieved, as is revealed by the government school returns for 1879, which include data on 2 440 elementary school pupils. Of these, 552 could 'read and understand English narrative containing words of two or more syllables' and 538 were 'able to write a fair small hand'. In arithmetic, 366 had advanced to subtraction, 225 to division, 117 to 'the compound rules' and 82 to 'the higher rules'.[35] At the Ladysmith Anglican school in the same year, forty-two students had attained an advanced level in English, German and Geography, six in English grammar, and two in music. St. Mark's school in Pietermaritzburg instructed black children in Latin and Greek. Four secondary schools provided advanced education, Adams College at Amanzimtoti, the Inanda Seminary, the Edendale Training Institution and the Pietermaritzburg Training School.

Nevertheless, *kholwa* demand for education perpetually exceeded what missionaries could supply.[36] African Christians caught up in the land-buying movement after 1870 could not wait for teachers to follow them and banded together to hire their own instructors. Parents frequently criticized mission schools for poor staff and failure to teach practical skills. Sometimes, they withdrew their children and started alternative schools. Wealthier people sent their children to the Cape to be educated. Converts from American stations began attending schools in Cape Town as early as 1864. By 1880, four years after American missionaries welcomed home Natal's first black university graduate (from Howard University in the United States), it had become commonplace for Methodist, Anglican,

At Mariannhill Monastery a variety of technical skills were taught. Here girls are shown learning to make western-style dresses.

Pupils at Mariannhill Monastery being taught how to taper a wagon wheel.

Presbyterian and Congregational families to pay for their children to be educated in racially-integrated Cape schools.

For everyone, educated or uneducated, white or black, the special circumstances which accompanied the creation of a new society in Natal stimulated an extraordinary ferment in ideas. The indigenous people barely had time to adjust to the new order of politics inaugurated by the Zulu monarchy before they faced the challenges of British colonialism and Christianity. Missionaries were as much challenged intellectually by African society as Africans were by the message of the evangelists. Settlers, who had distanced themselves from the moral, religious and political institutions of Europe, strove with evident difficulty to maintain their bearing. This period of mental ferment was stimulated and enriched by the presence of some remarkable minds which had been drawn to south-east Africa by the missionary movement.

Foremost among them was Bishop Colenso, whose face-to-face encounters with sceptical Africans inspired works of theological and biblical scholarship which sent shock waves through the Anglican communion in every part of the globe. Like the French bishop who had found Zulu intellectuals 'the equal of our European free thinkers', Colenso could not answer all the objections posed by people who had not been taught from infancy to regard the Bible as the literal word of God. As a follower of the English theologian F. D. Maurice, he believed that western Christianity did not possess a monopoly of religious truth.[37] His attempts to grapple with Zulu ideas led him to read the works of Germans and Britons, who were attempting to reconcile the gospel with scientific and historical scholarship. Colenso's published works brought him into conflict with the so-called 'High Church' or 'Anglo-Catholic' faction of his denomination in South Africa which was at that time seeking to remake Anglicanism in accordance with the ideas of the Oxford Movement in England.

After Colenso had been tried and found guilty of heresy by an ecclesiastical court convened by the Bishop of Cape Town in 1863, he retaliated by winning a judgment from the Judicial Committee of the Privy Council in London, confirming him as the legal Bishop of Natal. Thereupon, the opposing faction set up a rival 'Bishop of Maritzburg', thus splitting Anglicans in Natal into two bitterly divided camps. Many settlers were attracted by Colenso's doctrines and courage. They perceived in his challenge to the religious establishment a parallel to their challenge to the socio-political establishment of the mother country. Theological debate in colonial dining-rooms reached levels of sophistication equalled only by the

Ekukanyeni, the Christian community founded by J. W. Colenso at Bishopstowe, was destroyed by fire in 1884. A group of converts, including William Ngidi, are here photographed in front of the chapel.

levels of silliness achieved by the antics of the contending factions.

Africans were also stimulated to pursue unorthodox lines of thought through their encounters with missionaries. For example, the family of William Ngidi, 'the intelligent Zulu', helped inspire Colenso's biblical researches.[38] William, his brother Jonathan Ngidi, and their cousin Mbiyana Ngidi were all drawn to Christianity by American missionaries in the early 1850s. When the death of the pastor Samuel Marsh left Table Mountain station temporarily deserted, William and Jonathan moved to Colenso's newly-founded community of Ekukanyeni. William Ngidi embraced Christianity with a fervour that led the Bishop to nominate him as a candidate for the priesthood. However, in 1867 he suddenly left the church and led a movement for the reinstatement of old customs, including polygyny, lobola and the traditional sexual division of labour. His cousin Jonathan stayed on as one of Colenso's artisan assistants. In 1860, their cousin Mbiyana Ngidi joined with other converts on American stations to found an evangelistic movement known as the Native Home Missionary Society and in 1878 was ordained as a Congregational minister. However, when he was prevented from combining his evangelism with trading in Zululand (in partnership with cousin Jonathan) he broke away and in 1890 founded his own independent church. Thus, the Ngidi's experimented with a wide range of beliefs, combining in novel ways ideas drawn from different cultures and religious systems.

Another example of the fruitful interchange of ideas can be read in the annals of Springvale, the mission founded by Henry Callaway in 1858. Callaway had been a devout Quaker in his youth, believing that the profoundest religious truths could be communicated directly by God to individuals through 'immediate revelation'.[39] After medical studies in the early 1840s, he became a prosperous London physician. Gradually, he lost his Quaker faith and was drawn to the Church of England by the writings of F. D. Maurice, the same man who had awakened Colenso's missionary enthusiasm. In 1853, Callaway left his practice, took holy orders and joined Colenso in Natal. His medical training, his sympathy with theories of direct revelation and the missionary teaching of Maurice led him to make a very careful study of the beliefs of the people he proposed to convert. He was specially interested in the individuals known as 'doctors' (*inyanga*). His initial expectaton was that they would be his most formidable opponents, but he found that they showed far more interest in his medical and religious work than did ordinary people. Among the first residents of his station were families which included healers and diviners. Fascinated, Callaway began to make records of the customs, beliefs and healing practices of his parishioners and nearby Zulu doctors. Eventually, these records grew into two large books that influenced the development of late-Victorian anthropology.[40]

He discovered that there was not, as most people assumed, a single type of healer – the so-called witchdoctor. The Zulu word *inyanga* corresponded exactly to the English word 'doctor' inasmuch as it designated learning, combined with skill in any field. Some dealt only in pharmacology, others only in divination. Zulu specialists made referrals, just as London doctors did. While no *inyanga* could rival Callaway's skill in surgery because they lacked his knowledge of anatomy, they achieved cures in others ways, particularly with drugs, that he could not match. Callaway believed that some diviners possessed true powers of extra-sensory perception.

Some of Callaway's informants remained wedded to their old beliefs but others converted to Anglican Christianity. Still others mingled elements of old and new beliefs without committing themselves to either side. One member of his congregation was 'called' by dreams to the profession of diviner and left Springvale. Another resisted the call after a protracted struggle. That man's brother, Mpengula Mbande, became one of the first two Nguni priests of the Church of England. In Mbande's extended accounts of old beliefs which Callaway published as part of his ethnographic researches, we can read how one man came to disbelieve in the earthly powers of ancestral spirits. Similar mental journeys of exploration were being made all over Natal. Callaway predicted that they could eventually lead to new varieties of Christian and non-Christian religion. By the 1890s, his prediction was being borne out both by breakaways from established denominations, the Ethiopian churches, and by the rise of prophetic movements among people unconnected with the church in any formal way, the Zionist churches.[41]

Inevitably, the influence of many ideas that had been spawned in the religious arena spilled over into political life. From the moment that Captain Gardiner agreed to perform services for Dingane in exchange for a promise to admit missionaries, religion and politics were mixed up with each other. The Trekkers sought holy sanction for their war of revenge. Mpande closed Grout's mission in 1842 to stifle dissent in the kingdom and welcomed Lutheran missionaries in the 1850s to counter the threatening ambition of his son Cetshwayo. Bishop Colenso knew that his early friendship with Shepstone gave him a competitive advantage as an evangelist. Many Africans spurned Christianity because they perceived it as a disruptive force in the micro-politics of family and community life. The mixture of religion and politics was always volatile when issues of self-determination and equality were at stake.

Within mission communities, internal politics was often related to the question of who was to be in command. The aim of most missionary operations, even the Roman Catholic, was to raise up self-supporting, self-governing, self-propagating churches.[42] In the first instance, of course, a European missionary made converts and gathered them into a Christian congregation. During that early period, the missionary necessarily played a leading role. But, eventually, missionaries were expected by the societies that sent them to step aside and make way for African church leaders. However, who was to say when that time had arrived?

There are many examples of missionaries who attempted to rule their stations despotically. Their position was strengthened when they had control of land, either because their society owned it or because they occupied one of the mission reserves created by the government in the 1840s and 1850s. One American missionary went so far as to draft a set of rules and had them 'adopted and proclaimed as the laws of the stations' by the local magistrate.[43] Bishop Allard of the Catholic mission refused to allow people to cultivate land on his reserve unless they attended religious services.[44] Sometimes congregations rebelled against their missionaries, as for example at Edendale, when in 1860 Methodists expelled their missionary James Allison for allegedly cheating them of titles to their lands. At the American station of Mvoti, there was a general resistance to missionary authority, lasting from 1866 to 1875.[45]

Occasionally, the *kholwa* accused their missionaries of racial prejudice. Two decades before he broke with the church, Mbiyana Ngidi complained that 'while in the pulpit the missionaries said dear friends and brethren' but 'as soon as they came out of the pulpit they would not call them that because they were black'.[46] Towards the end of the nineteenth century, a number of missionaries did succumb to racial prejudice, some because of its newfound respectability in intellectual circles in Europe, some because they were discouraged by their slow progress in converting the African population.

There were many missionaries who, like Americans and Lutherans, changed from opposition to support of British intervention in Zululand. Anglican priest Robert Robertson, who at one time had hoped to convert the Zulu court by educating Cetshwayo's son Dinuzulu, became a British spy on the eve of the Anglo-Zulu War and is said to have shouldered a rifle in the campaign. Henry Callaway, the doctor who had showed such sensitive understanding of indigenous culture in his ethonographic studies of the 1860s, became Bishop of St. John's in the Transkei in 1873. Years of uphill exertion had exacted a toll. He decided it was wrong 'to keep out the struggling hardworking white man for such an unprogressive people as this' and for this reason recommended breaking up the old economy as a means of destroying resistance to Christianity. He supported the annexation of the Transkei and praised the British invaders of Zululand as a 'God-sent power'.[47]

There were, on the other hand, moments when the clergy stood up for the rights of non-Christian Africans. While sixty-nine ministers, representing every missionary society at work in the Colony, signed a memorial approving the 1873 punitive expedition against Langalibalele, Bishop Colenso threw away his longstanding popularity among the settlers by taking the side of the Hlubi.[48] Colenso also opposed the Anglo-Zulu War, compiling in the course of his agitation a massive *Digest on Zulu Affairs*, which remains our principal source of information about the Zulu side of the conflict and about the aspirations of Cetshwayo's uSuthu faction in the wars of the early 1880s.[49] Methodist missionaries in Mpondoland had neither Colenso's contacts in high places nor his polemical skills. But, in spite of instructions from their Society to stay out of politics, they did what they could to call attention to the injustice of the British annexation of Mpondo territory. Norwegian Bishop Hans Schreuder carried little or no weight with British public opinion, but he did stand by Cetshwayo when other missionaries deserted Zululand.[50]

The attractions of the Christian message increased as indigenous states lost their independence and as fundamental institutions of African life were buffetted by the forces of a new economic order. For some people, Christianity acquired prestige as the religion of the conqueror. For others, the gospel offered an explanation for what had gone wrong – God had punished the heathen – as well as a promise of relief in a life hereafter. Old Testament stories of the polygynous, pastoral Hebrews and their subjugation by foreign powers presented obvious analogies to the situation of the African. These were some of the messages propagated by a burgeoning army of black evangelists in the later part of the century. Conversions spread rapidly after 1890, so that by 1910 the conversion of the entire black population to some form of Christianity appeared to be only a matter of time.

The exponential growth of black Christian communities had important political ramifications. *Kholwa* farmers and businessmen had been arguing for years that, as civilized Christians, they should be exempted from the legal disabilities imposed on the rest of the African population. At a meeting near Pietermaritzburg in 1863 attended by *kholwa* from several denominations, Johannes Khumalo articulated their grievance.

> We have left the race of our forefathers; we have left the black race and have clung to the white. We imitate them in everything we can. We feel we are in the midst of a civilized people, and that when we became converts to their faith we belonged to them . . . We are under the wing of the Queen, let us ask for her law.[51]

As restrictions on land ownership and economic activity increased, the grievance was stridently reiterated. African nationalism was especially attractive to the *kholwa* because so many of them were descended from parents of different ethnic groups. In the mission station melting pots, they lost old identities and became simply African Christians. *Kholwa* from Natal were prominent in the founding of the South African Native

Congress, which carried on the campaign for equality in the twentieth century. Such notable leaders as John L. Dube, H. S. Msimang, A. W. G. Champion, Saul Mdsane and Albert Luthuli were all descended from the aspirant *kholwa*, who prospered in the mid-Victorian period but later found their advance blocked by restrictive legislation.

The brake applied by white authority to black economic activity, especially after the advent of responsible government, caused many talented individuals to seek an outlet for leadership ambitions within the Church. Before 1880, missionaries often complained that the most promising young men would not enter the ministry because they could earn far more money in business or agriculture. In later years, there were plenty of candidates but they were not men who were prepared to play a subservient role. Both the Methodist and the American Congregational missions faced crises in the closing decades of the century because white missionaries would not allow black ministers the same degree of freedom they themselves enjoyed as pastors.[52] The upshot was that disgruntled black preachers severed their connections with the missionaries and led many of the *kholwa* into independent churches.

White politicians were alarmed by the appearance of these breakaway movements, commonly known as Ethiopian churches. They feared that the drive for self-determination in religion would promote a similar drive in political life. The government of Natal acted to curb tendencies toward autonomy among the *kholwa* by attempting to gain control of education and the mission reserves. Most mission schools depended heavily on government grants. By specifying the conditions under which grants could be made, politicians could exert influence on the curriculum. A Special Committee Report to the Council of Education in 1902 criticized the missions for giving too much education.

> While we are in favour of the education of the natives . . . we still think that it would be unnecessary for them to attain to a high standard of education . . . The Native . . . if raised to a high standard, may find himself isolated because, while not being able to associate with Europeans, because of his colour, he is unable to associate with his own countrymen, because of his superior knowledge. It would be better to be contented with a rather lower standard of attainment. No grant should be made for proficiency beyond a certain standard except in the case of natives who are being trained to teach.[53]

In 1888 grants were given on condition that the top three grades be eliminated, except for student teachers, and that pupils be instructed in unskilled manual labour for at least six hours a day.

Mission reserves were criticized by a Lands Commission Report of 1902 for providing freehold property on which Africans could 'live in idleness'. The Mission Reserves Act of 1903 abolished all freehold tenure and instituted rents, half of which were to be paid to the missions, half to the government. To make sure that no African ministers controlled any mission reserves, another act of 1903 prohibited unlicensed clergy from officiating at marriages; while applications for licensing submitted by African ministers were refused.[54] When the Bambatha 'Rebellion' broke out in 1906, much of the Press and the legislature blamed Ethiopianism, even though there was little tangible evidence of *kholwa* complicity.[55] In 1907, the government forced a new constitution on the American mission which reinstituted total control by white missionaries. After these events, it would be difficult for anyone of any race in Natal to disentangle politics from religion.

Notes

1   Gardiner, *Narrative of a Journey to the Zoolu Country*, tells the story as Gardiner recalled it the following year (his diaries were lost). The sequel to Gardiner's mission can be read in *The Diary of the Rev. Francis Owen, MA, Missionary with Dingaan in 1837–8*, ed. G. E. Cory (Cape Town, Van Riebeeck Society, 1926).

2   Etherington, *Preachers, Peasants and Politics*, pp. 74–5.

3   The most extensive published account of Schreuder's mission is O. G. Myklebust, *H. P. S. Schreuder: Kirke og Misjon* (Oslo, Gyldendal, 1980).

4   Etherington, *Preachers, Peasants and Politics*, p. 76. The story of the early Norwegian missionaries is told in much greater detail in J. Sunensen, ed., *Norwegian Missions in African History, Vol. I: South Africa 1845–1906* (Oxford, Oxford University Press, 1985).

5   Ibid., p. 80–5.

6   Ibid., pp. 47–8, 55–7.

7   Statement of Maken, *Evidence Taken Before the Natal Native Commission, 1881* (Pietermaritzburg, 1882), p. 371.

8   Etherington, *Preachers, Peasants and Politics*, pp. 60–1.

9   Ibid., pp. 101–3.

10   SNA 1/3/9: Annual Report of Resident Magistrate Windham 1859; USPG folio D25: Callaway to Hawkins, 6 February 1863.

11   Etherington, *Preachers, Peasants and Politics*, p. 108.

12   Ibid., pp. 102–3.

13   KCAL Miscellaneous Missionary Papers: F. Owen, copy of an unaddressed letter, 26 April, 1838.

14   ABC 15.4.2: A. Grout to Anderson, 5 December 1840 and 17 January 1841,

15   ABC 15.4.2: A. Grout to Anderson, 2 September 1840.

16   Adams to Anderson, 15 February 1842.

17   ABC Folio E33: Markham, quarterly report, 5 February 1878.

18   USPG Folio E30: Illing, quarterly report, 29 June 1875.

19   ABC 15.4.7: Wilder to Anderson, 27 November 1862.

20   *Proceedings and Report of the Commission Appointed to Inquire into the Past and Present State of the Kafirs in the District of Natal, 1853* (Pietermaritzburg, 1854), p. 14.

21   ABC 15.4.4: A. Grout to Anderson, 31 January 1852; ABC 15.4.5: L. Grout to Anderson, 2 March 1852.

22   LG 283, 1862.

23   MMS J. Jackson, Jr. to the Secretaries, 1 July 1861.

24   USPG Folio E27: Illing to Secretaries, 3 March 1872.

25   USPG folio E32: quoted in T. Jenkinson, 'Church Missions in Natal', 1875.

26   *Natal Witness*, 27 October 1871.

27   MMS Cameron to Secretaries, 22 May 1875.

28   MMS Blencowe to Secretaries, 7 April 1850.

29   NA Methodist Papers, Folio 2/2: Pine to Pearse, 20 April 1850.

30   *Proceedings of the Natal Missionary Conference, 1878* (Durban, Natal Mercury, 1878), pp. 25–6.

31   Callaway, *Missionary Sermons* (London, 1875), p. 49.

32   F. Mason, 'Colonial Views Adverse to Mission Work and how to Meet Them', *Proceedings of the Natal Missionary Conference*, pp. 48–9.

33   Etherington, *Preachers, Peasants and Politics*, pp. 117–22.

34   *Evidence Taken Before the Natal Native Commission, 1881* (Pietermaritz-burg, 1882), p. 22.

35   *Natal Blue Book*, 1879.

36   Etherington, *Preachers, Peasants and Politics*, pp. 131–4.

37   Guy, *The Heretic*, pp. 69–92, 95–109.

38   Etherington, *Preachers, Peasants and Politics*, pp. 43, 50, 106, 133, 135, 137, 142, 144–5, 151, 150–62.

39   Callaway published a Quaker tract under that title in 1841.

40   *Nursery Tales, Traditions and Histories of the Zulus, in their own Words* (London, Trubner, 1866–8) and *The Religious System of the Amazulu* (London, Trubner, 1870). These works attracted the attention of Andrew Lang who used them to support his thesis that the meaning of classical myths could be elucidated by studying the folklore of living 'savage peoples'.

41   Etherington, *Preachers, Peasants and Politics*, 157–63; the two types were first delineated by Rengt Sundkler in *Bantu Prophets in South Africa* (2nd ed., Oxford, Oxford University Press, 1961).

42   For a discussion of the origins of these policies see W. R. Shenk, 'Rufus Anderson and Henry Venn: a Special Relationship', *International Bulletin of Missionary Research* 5 (1981), pp. 168–72.

43   ABC 15.4.8: G. Hance to Clark, 10 September, 1874.

44   SNA 1/3/9: Allard to Shepstone, 30 July 1860.

45   Etherington, *Preachers, Peasants and Politics*, pp. 141–3.

46   Ibid., p. 150

47   Ibid., pp. 44–5.

48   *Natal Witness*, 12 May 1874.

49   See Guy, *Destruction of the Zulu Kingdom, passim*.

50   O. G. Myklebust, 'Norsk Misjon og British Imperialisme in Syd Afrika', *Norsk Tidsskrift for Misjon* 31 (1977), pp. 65–72.

51   *Natal Witness*, 27 March 1863.

52 For an extensive account of the crisis in the American mission see L. E. Switzer, 'The Problems of an African Mission in a White Dominated Multi-Racial Society: the American Zulu Mission, 1885–1910' (unpublished Ph.D. thesis, University of Natal, Pietermaritzburg, 1971).

53 Quoted in Ibid., p. 252.

54 Ibid., pp. 433–6.

55 See Marks, *Reluctant Rebellion*.

Chapter 12

The new economy

BILL GUEST

During the last two decades of the nineteenth century, the economy of
Natal underwent some significant changes. These included substantial
infrastructural improvements, the development of large-scale agricultural
enterprises and an increase in the production of food crops, the
establishment of a much wider range of manufacturing industries and, not
least, the emergence of a local coal industry. The transformation of Natal's
economy beyond the level of 'a colony of samples' was a consequence of
the extraneous emergence of the gold-mining industry in the Transvaal.[1]
This not only created a market for many local producers, it also made
investment capital more readily available and promoted further
improvements in the local means of communications, thereby facilitating
the expansion of business and the transportation of bulky commodities.

Capital accumulation in colonial Natal is a theme which has only
recently begun to attract attention. The chronic shortage of local capital had
been only marginally alleviated by military chest expenditure, by the
modest sums of money imported by immigrants, and by the successful
speculative ventures of prominent land-owners like Jonas Bergtheil and
Adolph Coqui, who had tapped British metropolitan capital by floating the
Natal Land and Colonization Company in 1860, subsequently offloading
the shares with which the Company had bought their Natal landholdings on
the London stock market.[2] The formation of local capital was also assisted
by the establishment of banking institutions, the first of which were the
Natal Fire Assurance and Trust Company, founded in 1849, and the Natal
Bank, which opened in 1854. During the early 1860s three more local
banks, the Commercial and Agricultural Bank of Natal, the Colonial Bank
of Natal, and the Durban Bank were established, as well as branches of the
Standard Bank of British South Africa, and the London and South African

The Natal Bank in Aliwal Street, Durban (1854), was followed by others which promoted the accumulation of investment capital vital to the Colony's economic development.

Bank.[3] By the late 1870s there were only two banking institutions operating in the Colony, the Natal Bank and the Standard Bank, but the Bank of Africa joined them shortly thereafter and in 1882 the Natal Permanent Building Society was founded. In 1892 the African Banking Corporation began to operate in Natal, followed in 1895 by the National Bank of the South African Republic. Between 1895 and 1909 the deposits of the Colony's commercial banks increased from £2 481 020 to £3 823 157 and their local branches proliferated in number from eleven to thirty-five.[4]

The marked increase in banking activity in Natal during the 1890s and early 1900s was indicative both of the substantial increase in local merchant capital reserves, and of the growing interest of foreign investors in southern Africa, following the proclamation of the Witwatersrand gold-fields in September 1886. Consequently, established industries like sugar and new enterprises, notably whaling and coal mining, were able to draw upon financial resources both within the Colony and the metropolis.[5] The Natal government also found it easier to raise loans for urgently-needed infrastructural improvements, particularly after responsible government had been attained in 1893 (see Chapter 9).

The steady improvement in communications experienced in Natal during the latter part of the nineteenth century was similarly vital to the Colony's economic development. In 1873 the Natal government bought the privately-owned telegraph line which had been operating between Durban and Pietermaritzburg since 1864 and thereafter extended it in various directions. The overland link between Pietermaritzburg and Cape Town via Kokstad, Umtata and Kingwilliamstown was completed in April 1878. By the end of 1879 Natal was also linked by submarine cable from Durban through Delagoa Bay and Suez to Britain, and by telegraph through Newcastle to Pretoria.[6] A telephone system was developed during the early years of the twentieth century, while the postal service was much more frequent than it had been during its early days of dependence upon the military authorities and, from 1846, upon the 'Natal Witness Express'. This had provided weekly communication between Pietermaritzburg and Durban by means of 'native' runners who initially took two days to complete the journey.[7]

The improved postal service was largely a consequence of the gradual upgrading of Natal's road network. The military authorities readily assisted

Postal services in Natal and Zululand relied upon runners before the construction of roads made postcarts possible.

Local History Museum, Durban

In most parts of Natal, especially the Drakensberg region, the terrain made road construction extremely difficult.

in this undertaking, particularly in planning and constructing a more reliable route between Durban and the capital. The advent of the horse-drawn omnibus in 1860 provided a faster and more frequent postal service between the Colony's two main urban centres as well as conveying passengers, but the lighter 'postcart' proved even more efficient and extended mail deliveries further inland to Newcastle.[8] Apart from the link between the capital and the port, for most of the nineteenth century the Colony's other 'roads' were little more than wagon-tracks which were often impassable during the rainy summer months. Rivers had to be forded or, at best, crossed by pontoon, except for the 'iron tension' bridges which spanned the Mngeni and Msunduze from the late 1850s, though the second of these was destroyed in 1866.[9]

The discovery of the Kimberley diamond-fields in 1870 generated a heavier flow of through-traffic into the interior, which helped to establish a more recognizable 'road' between Pietermaritzburg and the Free State border. Enterprising black and white Natalians prospered by

Transvaal line to Delagoa Bay 1894

Pretoria

Delagoa Bay

Johannesburg 1895
Elsburg Junction

Heidelburg

SWAZILAND

Standerton

TRANSVAAL

ORANGE FREE STATE

Charlestown 1891

Kroonstad 1906

Utrecht 1910

Newcastle 1890

Vryheid 1903

Hlobane 1909

ZULULAND

N

Biggarsberg Junction
(Glencoe) 1889

Harrismith 1892

Dundee
(Talana) 1890

Somkele

Bethlehem 1905

Wesselsnek

1890

Mtubatuba 1903

Van Reenen 1891

Elandslaagte 1889

Ladysmith 1886

KwaMbonambi 1903
Empangeni 1903

Winterton 1907

Weenen 1907

Umhlatuze 1902

Estcourt 1885

Greytown 1906

N A T A L

Tugela 1898

New Hanover
1899

BASUTOLAND

Howick

Pietermaritzburg 1880

Tongaat 1897

Camperdown

Elandskop 1904

Botha's Hill

Verulam 1879

1880

1879

Donnybrook 1905

Richmond 1897

Pinetown
1878

Point Durban 1860
Bluff 1898

Creighton 1906

Isipingo 1880

Malenge 1909

Stuartstown

Umzinto 1900

Esperanza 1908

Park Rynie 1897

CAPE COLONY

N. Shepstone 1901

Port Shepstone 1907

Umzinto–Donnybrook 1908

0   50   100   150
Kilometres

Cartographic Unit , University of Natal, Pietermaritzburg

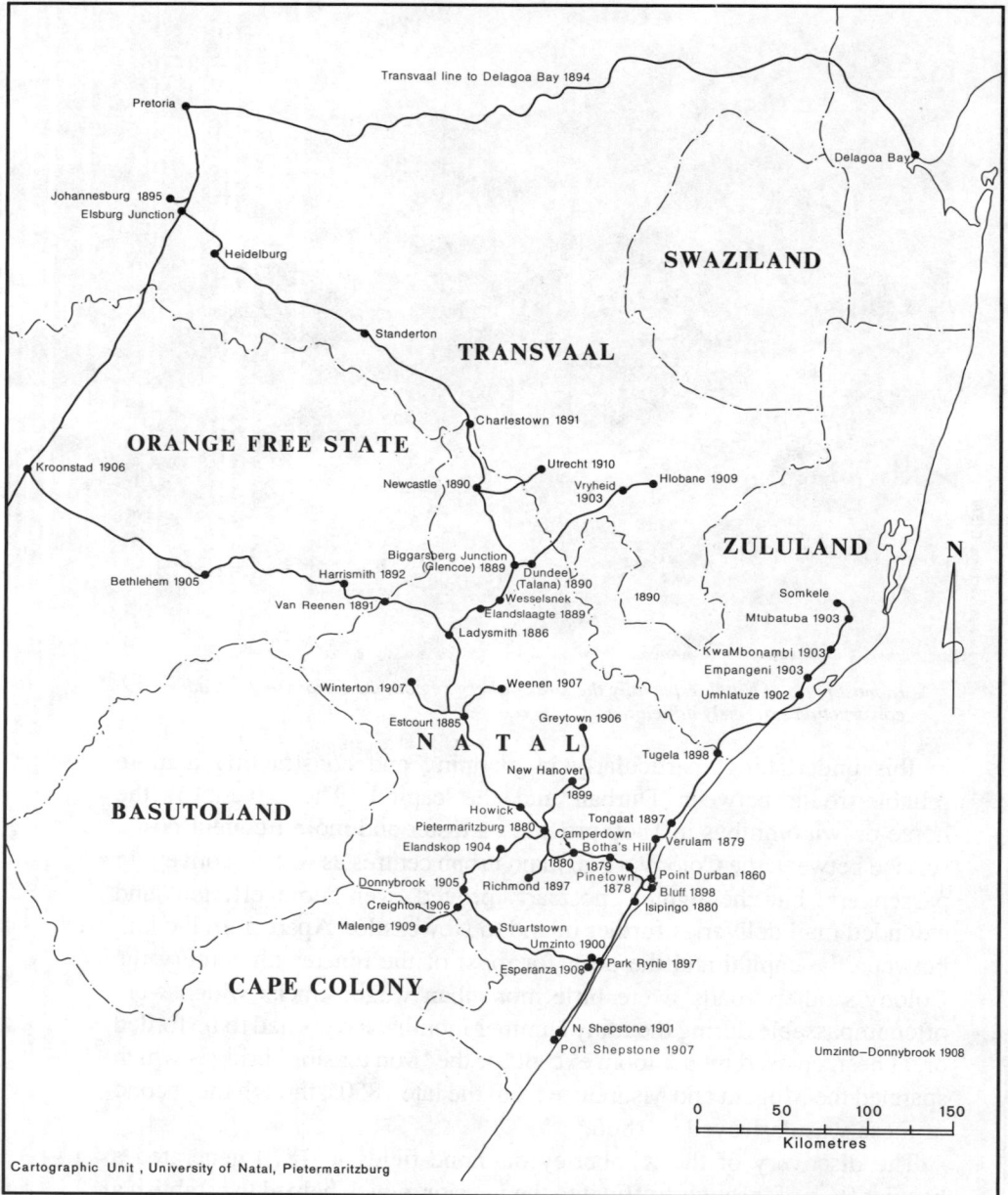

Map 20   Railway construction in Natal, 1878–1910

transport-riding on this route and from 1872 J. W. Welch, who had already monopolized the omnibus service between Durban and Pietermaritzburg, operated his weekly 'Royal Mail buses' through to Kimberley.[10] Similarly, the emergence of the Transvaal gold industry from the mid-1880s soon established a well-beaten path, through Ladysmith and Newcastle, upon which large British and American-type stage coaches, packed with fortune-seekers, became a familiar sight.[11]

The Overberg trade had always provided the primary incentive for railway construction into the interior, but it was the discovery of the main Witwatersrand gold reef which generated a new sense of urgency. Natal's Executive and Legislative Councils overlooked past differences of opinion to co-operate in authorizing extensions of the railhead from Ladysmith to Van Reenen's Pass, and from the Biggarsberg to Coldstream, on the Free State and Transvaal borders respectively. A convention was entered into with the Free State government to extend the line from Van Reenen's, which was reached in November 1891, to Harrismith, where the railhead arrived in July 1892[12] (see Map 20).

In addition to Indians and locally-recruited Africans, Tsonga labourers were imported via the Zulu kingdom for use in railway construction and other public works. This photograph was taken by James Lloyd, the pioneer Durban photographer. Much of his work was used by the Illustrated London News.

Courtesy of D. E. J. Watkins

The Transvaal was less easily penetrated, for although the line had been opened to Newcastle, with a branch to Dundee (Talana) in 1890, and as far as Charlestown near the republican border by April 1891, it was the Cape line that won the race to the Rand in September 1892, more than three years before the rail-link from Charlestown to Johannesburg had been completed.[13] This led to an immediate decline in the volume of goods imported through Durban, which was reflected in 1893 by a 22 per cent decrease in the Colony's railway receipts.[14] By contrast, in 1896 the Natal Government Railways earned £1 136 214 in revenues, representing a 116 per cent increase over 1895 and a net addition of £464 762 to the colonial exchequer after the payment of working costs and the interest on capital borrowed. Natal's investment in railway construction had been considerable, amounting to more than 76 per cent of the total colonial debt of over £8 million at the end of 1896 but, by that stage, the railways had already justified their construction by contributing no less than 51 per cent of the colonial government's income. By 1909 the Colony had £14 161 000 invested in its railways, while its net annual income from that source had reached £837 619.[15] As a revenue earner the railways were invaluable to Natal, and they also had an immediate impact on the local economy as an employer of black labour. By 1890 the Natal Government Railways was already the largest employer of Africans and Indians in the Colony, employing a record 3 137 and 2 606 respectively.[16]

Natal's ability to compete for the increasing interior trade depended not only upon railway construction but also upon the further development of Durban harbour. Harry Escombe, the Durban advocate who by the 1880s had emerged as a prominent figure in Natal politics, was chairman of the reconstituted Harbour Board from its inception in May 1881 until its dissolution in 1894. In that capacity, he perceived more clearly than most that the future prosperity of the Colony hinged upon the creation of 'a harbour accessible to ships of any draught, at all states of the tide, in any weather, by night as well as by day'.[17] The harmonious relationship which existed during the 1880s between him and the resident harbour engineer, Edward Innes, facilitated the efficient administration of the port and the implementation of yet another attempt to solve the perennial problem of the Bar. This involved the construction of a southern breakwater to protect the ebb-tide against northerly currents by overlapping the northern training wall and thereby reducing the height of the Bar through the elimination of sand travel from the south. Escombe supported the scheme, which initially appeared to be successful. While the depth of the water over the Bar

This early photograph of Durban's Point shows sailing vessels being offloaded near the railway station, constructed after the completion of South Africa's first railway line from there to Durban in 1860.

gradually increased, the facilities of the inner harbour were also improved. Following the arrival in 1886 of Durban's first pump-dredging equipment, more than twenty hectares of land was reclaimed at the Point, wharf space was enlarged, and pack-houses and storage provided.[18]

Cathcart Methven, the resident harbour engineer from 1888 (following the death of Innes in 1887) until his dismissal in 1894, was soon convinced that the extension of the southern pier beyond the northern breakwater had increased shoaling of the Bar by diverting and weakening the ebb-tide, and thereby reducing the tidal scouring effect which was so crucial to resolving the harbour's major problem. Whereas Escombe had come to the conclusion that the Bar could only be eliminated by total reliance on dredging, an expensive operation as yet little-tried in exposed sea conditions, Methven recommended a narrowing of the harbour entrance and increasing the scouring effect by extending the north pier further out to sea. In spite of the deteriorating relationship between the protagonists of these conflicting policies, the Harbour Board allowed Methven to begin implementing his proposals, and by 1892 the average depth of the entrance channel was 4,17 metres, an improvement of one metre over the previous year. In response to the increasing volume of shipping which was now able to enter the harbour, wharfage space was further increased, six hydraulic cranes and two steam-winches were brought into operation, and several steamer companies began loading local coal for bunkers on a regular basis.[19]

The controversy concerning the Bar and the relative merits of dredging and north pier construction nevertheless continued in the Harbour Board, at Legislative Assembly level, and among the general public, as indicated by frequent letters on the subject which were published by the local Press. The Escombe faction argued that the increase in the depth of the Bar was merely the result of temporary natural circumstances, a contention which seemed to be substantiated when, in April 1894, the depth of water at the harbour mouth decreased to a mere 2,6 metres.[20] However, Escombe's public support dwindled after he became Attorney-General, resigned as chairman of the Harbour Board, and then appeared to be largely responsible for its subsequent disbandment and the dismissal of Methven. Public meetings, pamphleteering, attacks through the Press, a parliamentary inquiry into Methven's dismissal and subsequent litigation against the colonial government failed to resolve the matter until, in October 1897, Escombe resigned his brief tenure as Prime Minister of Natal in favour of his arch-critic Henry Binns (see Chapter 13).[21]

In the meantime, the colonial government had earlier called upon Sir Charles Hartley and John Wolfe Barry for independent advice on future harbour development. Their proposals, which were accepted by the Natal Parliament in 1897, appeared to vindicate both sides of the controversy by recommending the adoption of a policy of tidal scour through north pier construction, coupled with large-scale dredging in order to reduce the Bar to a depth which would allow the passage of modern steamshipping. The importation of two new hopper suction-dredgers facilitated a more vigorous dredging programme, immediately improving the Bar depth to 6,14 metres in 1897, while north pier construction was completed to specification in 1900.[22]

The development of railway and harbour facilities during the latter part of the nineteenth century made Natal more dependent than ever before upon the Overberg trade. This proved to be a source of strength to the colonial economy in that Natal's fortunes were now more closely linked to the promising prospective development of the Witwatersrand. But it was also a source of weakness because heavy reliance upon income derived from railways and customs dues resulted in annual fluctuations in public revenues, while Natal's almost total dependence upon the inland traffic made it a suppliant for Transvaal favours (see Chapter 13). It was not until 1898, with the political storm clouds gathering rapidly over southern Africa, that the Colony was able to extricate itself by joining the South African Customs Union.[23]

Although the railway and harbour developments had been prompted primarily by a determination to maximize Natal's share of the transit and customs revenues to be derived from the increasing volume of traffic to and from the Witwatersrand, they also gave a boost to local producers. This was especially seen in the increased exportation of wattle bark, maize and other foodstuffs,[24] while the Natal Government Railways became an important consumer of local coal as well as providing access to the port at Durban, where the bunker and export trade could now be developed as improved harbour facilities attracted more shipping (see Chapter 14).

The numerous outcrops in northern Natal make it highly probable that coal was exploited as domestic fuel by the Iron-Age inhabitants of the region long before the arrival of white settlers, though it is unlikely that it

Before the installation of a mechanical loading plant in 1907, coal was carried on to ships at Durban's Point in this laborious fashion.

was used for smelting iron in uncoked form.[25] On their arrival in 1838, the Trekkers immediately detected and took advantage of the presence of coal, and by the early 1840s small quantities were already being transported for sale in Pietermaritzburg, in spite of the poor condition of the wagon roads. The existence of these large coal deposits in the interior played no part in influencing Britain's annexation of Natal to the Cape, even though an increasing volume of imperial steamshipping was anticipated off the coast of south-east Africa as the age of sail gave way to that of steam. In the absence of the necessary infrastructure to link the Colony's upper districts to the coastline, the exploitation of Natal's coal reserves could at that time be regarded as at best a very long-term proposition.[26]

Between the 1850s and 1880s, the white farming community of northern Natal discovered and made domestic use of numerous outcrops. In 1864 Peter Smith began to work a seam of good quality coal at his farm Dundee on the slope of Talana Hill and the same seam was subsequently worked by successive owners of the neighbouring property Coalfields. The activity on these two farms helped to ensure that the town of Dundee, which was laid out by Smith in 1882, had emerged as Natal's coal capital by the end of the century.[27] It was ideally situated for this purpose, being almost equidistant between the two extremities of the Klip River coalfield (Ladysmith in the

Natal's coal industry developed rapidly after the 1880s. Prior to that, there were many small-scale operations like this one in the Klip River district.

south and Newcastle in the north), in which most of the Colony's pre-Union coalmining activity took place. Initially, the demand for coal was limited and transport-riders equipped with ox-wagons could only undertake about thirty loads of 2,54 tons each per month during the dry season. The markets of Durban and Pietermaritzburg were still small and not easily accessible, while tests conducted on Natal coal in 1852 by HMS *Hydra* and the royal mail-steamer *Sir Robert Peel* were only moderately successful.[28]

The Anglo-Zulu and Anglo-Boer conflicts of 1879 and 1881–2 respectively gave temporary boosts to the local coal industry as the presence of large imperial forces in northern Natal provided a ready market and transport-riders, engaged in carrying commissariat stores up from the port, were only too willing to load their otherwise empty wagons with coal for delivery in Pietermaritzburg and Durban on the return journey.[29] In September 1881 the British geologist Frederic W. North, who had been appointed by Lieutenant-Governor Sir Henry Bulwer to investigate Natal's coal resources, reported that Klip River County incorporated a workable coalfield of no less than 1 350 square miles (3 496,5 square kilometres) in extent and contained 2 073 million tons of coal, even after a generous 50 per cent deduction to allow for intervening faults, dykes and barren ground. He also observed that, while the coal measures varied in quality, they mostly constituted, at the very least, good 'house coal' and that some would be suitable for use in steam locomotives.[30]

North's Report did not include any analysis of the extensive coal deposits of the Utrecht and Vryheid-Paulpietersburg districts, which were only annexed to Natal after the Second Anglo-Boer War, or of the coal and lignite reserves of Zululand, which was also not yet attached to the Colony. Nevertheless, his conclusions with regard to Klip River County were sufficient to arouse considerable interest in the region. In 1887, after the railhead had advanced the previous year as far inland as Ladysmith, the Natal government wisely anticipated an imminent increase in mining activity and organized a Mines Department, based in the capital, under Captain G. Nicholls, RE.[31] As North had anticipated, the extension of the main railway line into the interior from Ladysmith through Glencoe to Newcastle in 1889 at last facilitated the emergence of a large-scale coal-mining industry in northern Natal, first linking the Klip River coalfield to Durban and later, following the completion of the line to Johannesburg in 1895, to the expanding Witwatersrand market. The Natal Government Railways, in turn, benefited not only from the availability of a steady supply of cheap, locally-produced coal to substitute for the imported product that cost between 38s. and 50s. a ton, but also earned additional revenue by loading coal into goods trucks which would otherwise have returned empty to Durban after delivering their imported consignments inland.[32]

During the late 1880s and early 1890s, several colliery companies were formed to take immediate advantage of the new rail-link to the coastline. Frederic North returned to the Colony to purchase various properties in the vicinity of Newcastle on behalf of a powerful 'English Syndicate'. F. Reynolds, member for Alexandra County in the Legislative Assembly, and S. Mitchell Innes, a farmer of the Ladysmith district, floated the Elandslaagte Colliery at the southern end of the Klip River coalfield. A group of Durban mercantile and shipping entrepreneurs formed the Dundee (Natal) Coal Company Limited, under the chairmanship of the prominent businessman and civic leader Benjamin Greenacre, to mine the property Coalfields near Dundee and later also at Talana Hill and at Burnside in the Waschbank valley.[33] The Dundee Company was pre-eminent during the early years of the Natal industry, constructing its own railway line to meet the main line at Glencoe and contributing almost two-thirds of the Colony's total output in 1890. By 1899 it was still producing a third, but by 1909 it had slipped to fourth position in the output stakes, behind the Rand-financed Natal Navigation Collieries that had been established in 1898, Elandslaagte Colliery, and the new Durban Navigation Colliery, established in 1903.[34]

The Colony's infrastructural improvements, coupled with the presence of an expanding market in the Transvaal, also greatly enhanced the prospects for large-scale agricultural enterprises in Natal, although they did not immediately promote the production of large marketable surpluses. The new Witwatersrand market attracted the attention of the established food exporters of Australasia and of North and South America who, with the assistance of refrigerated shipping, were able to sell their produce more cheaply in southern Africa than could the local producers. Less favourable soil and climatic conditions, coupled with inadequate transportation facilities in some of the more fertile but remote agricultural regions of the Colony, made it difficult for Natal's farmers to compete with such sophisticated foreign competitors, who were already applying highly scientific methods to superior farmland.[35] Even so, by 1909 the total area of cultivated land in Natal had increased more than five-fold over that of the early 1870s, reflecting a much more extensive agricultural activity on the part of white Natalians in the production of export staples. Whereas African and Indian peasant agriculture continued to be directed specifically at the Colony's internal markets once subsistence needs had been met, as much as 75 per cent of the produce of white settler agriculture was intended for export. Domestic consumption therefore provided relatively little incentive for the increase in agricultural activity that characterized the last two decades of the colonial period.[36]

This was certainly the case with regard to sugar, which continued to be the primary export staple of the Colony's coastal lowlands, despite the extended crisis in the industry which began with the depression of the late 1860s. The reconstructed industry that emerged towards the end of the nineteenth century was similar to the older West Indian model in its financial structure and ownership, in contrast to what it had been in its own formative years. A concerted effort was made to improve efficiency and productivity in the face of increasing world competition, the decline in domestic and export prices, the scarcity of local credit facilities and the debilitating effects of natural disasters, soil exhaustion and crop disease. The frost-resistant and fibrous Uba cane was planted in place of the China cane and Green Natal varieties which had failed in the 1860s and 1880s respectively. In the attempt to enlarge milling capacity and reduce unit costs, technological innovations were introduced, the work force was more effectively manipulated, the consolidation of landholdings was accelerated and the number of operating mills reduced from seventy-five in 1877 to thirty-seven by 1898.[37]

The small plantation remained a feature of the Natal sugar industry to the end of the colonial period, but from the 1890s it was progressively overshadowed by a much larger and more highly capitalized unit of production which came to be known as the 'miller-cum-planter'. These concerns effectively combined central milling activities, including the crushing of cane for outside growers, with extended areas of production. They also assumed an increasingly corporate character, through which they were able to develop a monopolistic structure of ownership and control. The establishment of Reynolds Bros. Ltd in 1892 initiated the trend towards company ownership of the bigger estates and mills, sustained by an inflow of foreign and particularly British investment capital into the local sugar industry. In addition to Reynolds Bros. Ltd, Natal Estates Ltd and Tongaat Ltd were also originally incorporated in Britain, where a large proportion of the share capital was retained. After 1888 the fastest-growing of Natal's three sugar-broking companies was C. G. Smith and Co, which

The crossing of the Mngeni River was vital to the development of the Natal north coast. The railway bridge, constructed during the 1870s when the line to Verulam was built, was one of many that were washed away by floods.

by 1914 virtually controlled all sugar milling facilities south of Durban. The first refinery, established at South Coast Junction in 1898, was financed jointly by prominent shareholders in the Smith Group, Natal Estates Ltd and Tongaat Ltd.[38] By 1910 Huletts South African Refineries Ltd had emerged as a prominent producer on the north coast, with large estates at Tinley Manor, Darnall, Amatikulu and Umhlatuzi in Zululand.[39]

The emergence of these companies and the increasing influence of merchant capital upon the Natal sugar industry was facilitated by the fact that there was no attempt on the part of the colonial state to establish a central milling system. However, the Natal government was responsible for successfully negotiating the Colony's admission to the South African Customs Union from 1898. This gave local growers preference against Mauritian and other foreign sugars in the Cape market which, between 1852 and 1900, absorbed more than 50 per cent by value and weight of the Colony's sugar exports, and later also in the Transvaal market to which, from the late 1880s, an ever-increasing percentage of Natal's sugar output was directed.[40]

At this time, there was also an intensification of livestock production. This can be inferred not only from the increasing exportation of animal products but also from the fact that the Colony's sheep population more than trebled, from under 300 000 in 1870 to more than 900 000 in 1908, and there was an increase in head of cattle from 121 000 to nearly 230 000 during the same period.[41]

The history of animal husbandry in Natal as well as that of agriculture is bound up in the control and conquest of diseases, together with the identification and eradication of pests, many of which were imported into the region with contaminated stock. Bovine lungsickness made its appearance in mid-century, followed by rinderpest and east coast fever in the 1890s and after the Anglo-Boer War, while glanders, which attacked horses, was introduced at about the same time.[42] The northern coastal regions were to remain unsuitable for human occupation until malaria was brought under control following the identification of the anophales mosquito as a carrier and the use of quinine as a prophylactic. Even after this, outbreaks persisted, while nagana, or sleeping-sickness, also remained a scourge until the development of modern poisons made possible the effective control of mosquitoes and tsetse flies.[43]

The effect of these diseases was calamitous for many farmers and especially for Africans. Diseased animals as well as those that were apparently healthy were shot by government inspectors. As serious, whole crops could be destroyed by locusts or a blight. The casualties were likely to be the under-capitalized and often illiterate farmers (primarily black) who continued to follow outdated methods, who did not have the capital resources or access to credit facilities that would enable them to recoup their losses, and who could not afford the cost of diptanks and fencing as required by the legislation of a government that was largely controlled by successful white farmers.

The survivors were likely to be the large-scale capital-intensive farmers, practising 'scientific farming', as it was commonly described by its practitioners. They drew their expertise from the growing fund of scientific information that was being generated in the agricultural faculties of European universities and, following their establishment in South Africa in the early twentieth century, in the agricultural research stations such as Cedara, founded in 1902.[44] Joseph Baynes, for example, developed his farm Nelsrust, near Pietermaritzburg, into a model estate where, after experimenting with various crops, he concentrated on ranching and dairying. He was responsible for popularizing Friesland cattle in Natal and imported pedigree stock from several parts of the world in an effort to enhance the export quality of local beef and to develop a major dairy industry. His efforts were hampered by the prevalence of east coast fever

The government agricultural research station at Cedara was established in 1902 as part
of the post Anglo-Boer War strategy to develop agriculture in southern Africa through
the use of modern scientific farming methods. (From J. A. and A. Verbeek, Victorian
and Edwardian Natal, Shuter & Shooter, Pietermaritzburg, 1982.)

and of redwater, which he tried to overcome by supporting the research
being undertaken by the state vetinarian, Dr Herbert Watkins-Pitchford,
and by becoming one of the first farmers in the subcontinent to implement
systematic cattle-dipping. It was a practice he subsequently promoted
amongst other farmers and government officials, in the absence of any
programme of inoculation. Baynes established the first large-scale dairy in
Natal and successfully marketed its output through a chain of 'model
dairies' and tea-rooms in Durban, the first of which was opened in West
Street opposite Greenacre's store. In 1899 he established a butter factory at
Nelsrust, followed by another at Kroonstad in the Orange Free State. He
later also pioneered the local bacon industry with factories at Nelsrust and
Harrismith, where in 1910 he opened yet another dairy, the largest and best
equipped in South Africa, to cater more effectively for the growing market
in dairy products on the Witwatersrand.[45]

These developments in the local livestock industry, coupled with
population increases in the interior, promoted the production of food crops,
particularly maize. However, it was only at the turn of the century that
maize became a significant earner of foreign exchange for the Colony.
Some of the other industrial crops with which white farmers had earlier

hoped to make their fortunes, such as arrowroot and coffee, gave way to crops which were bioclimatically more suited to the region and for which there was a greater demand.[46] In 1903 the production of manufactured tea, in which J. L. Hulett had again played a pioneering role on his Kearsney estate, reached a record 2 681 000 pounds.[47]

Wattle, extensively planted during the early 1880s with the intention of producing tannin from the bark, also proved to be a more lucrative crop once it had been found that black wattle was superior to the silver variety as a tannin producer. The pioneering efforts of John Vanderplank, who in 1864 had planted the first wattle seed from Australia at Camperdown, were continued by other progressive farmers, including William Deane. Deane planted wattle quite extensively on his farm in the Mvoti district, where he practised scientific agricultural methods and founded the Natal Farmers' Co-operative Association in 1902.[48] George Sutton, the Midlands farmer who in 1903 became Natal's Prime Minister, actively promoted wattle planting through the medium of his agricultural column in the *Natal Witness*, written under the pen-name 'Agricola', and demonstrated on a sizeable scale that wattle bark could be used profitably as a tanning agent. Thereafter, increasing quantities of bark were exported and in 1910/11 exceeded £213 000 in value. Sutton, among others, was also responsible for the importation of eucalyptus varieties from Australia, producing timber for use as railway sleepers and mineprops. Tobacco was still produced on a small scale, though the product was considered unsuitable for cigarettes and was used instead as a low-grade pipe tobacco and in the manufacture of cigars and cheroots.[49]

Manufacturing industry was also stimulated by the new opportunities for expansion which emerged during the late nineteenth century, though it was still primarily focused upon processing the Colony's agricultural produce. Sugar, corn and flour mills were the most numerous form of industrial activity, but there were also mills for crushing wattle bark, tanneries, candle and soap factories, coffee processing and wool-washing plants, a bakery which produced ship biscuits and bread, saw mills, brick and tileyards, a wood-turning factory, a brewery, an aerated-water factory, coppersmiths and plumbers, iron foundries and several shipping and general engineering workshops, which in 1894 produced Durban's first locally built steam launch.[50] Wagon-makers had been in demand from the earliest days of white settlement in Natal and their numbers, together with those of builders and blacksmiths, increased as the colonial economy reached a wartime and postwar peak in 1902–3. The number of local manufacturers increased from 200 to more than 600 during the last three decades of the nineteenth century, though the size of these undertakings is unrecorded.

Even so, at the end of the 1890s approximately 85 per cent of Natal's inhabitants were still engaged in agricultural pursuits that contributed less than 20 per cent of its gross regional product, even allowing for the increasing exportation of maize, sugar and wattle bark. It seemed that the Colony was destined to export raw materials for use abroad in exchange for the wide range of manufactured articles that it was still unable to produce for itself.[51]

Notes

1   Konczacki, *Public Finance and Economic Development*, pp. 3, 9.

2   For an account of the Natal Land and Colonisation Company, see Slater, 'Land, Labour and Capital in Natal', pp. 257–283.

3   Konczacki, *Public Finance and Economic Development*, p. 24.

4   Ibid., pp. 24–5.

5   The development of the local sugar, whaling and coal-mining industries is discussed in more detail below in this chapter and in Chapter 14.

6   Theal, *History of South Africa from 1873 to 1884*, Vol. I, p. 225; Leverton, 'Government Finance and Political Development', pp. 169, 170, 192.

7   Hattersley, *Pietermaritzburg Panorama*, p. 57; A. F. Hattersley, *Portrait of a City* (Pietermaritzburg, Shuter & Shooter, 1951), p. 110 and *Portrait of a Colony*, pp. 170–2; Leverton, 'Government Finance and Political Development', p. 26.

8   Hattersley, *Pietermaritzburg Panorama*, pp. 55–7; Hattersley, *The British Settlement of Natal*, pp. 59, 272–7.

9 Hattersley, *The British Settlement*, pp. 59, 244, 272, 274–5; Leverton, 'Government Finance and Political Development', pp. 24–5, 42–3, 122–4, 192, 224–5.

10 Hattersley, *The British Settlement*, pp. 227–78; N. A. Etherington, 'African Economic Experiments in Colonial Natal, 1845–1880', *Enterprise and Exploitation*, eds. Guest and Sellers, pp. 274–5.

11 Hattersley, *The British Settlement*, p. 278; Leverton, 'Government Finance and Political Development', pp. 224–5, 248, 265–6; T. V. Bulpin, *To the Shores of Natal* (Cape Town, Timmins, 1953), p. 226.

12 For an account of railway development in Natal, see H. Heydenrych, 'Railway Development in Natal to 1895', *Enterprise and Exploitation*, eds. Guest and Sellers, pp. 47–69. See also Konczacki, *Public Finance and Economic Development*, pp. 22–3.

13 See Chapter 13.

14 J. Van der Poel, *Railway and Customs Policies in South Africa, 1885–1910* (London, Longmans Green, 1983), pp. 59–60, 69, 77.

15 Heydenrych, 'Railway Development in Natal', p. 63; Konczacki, *Public Finance and Economic Development*, p. 23.

16 Heydenrych, 'Railway Development in Natal', pp. 63–4.

17 J. Bond, *They were South Africans* (Cape Town, Oxford University Press, 1956), p. 98.

18 For an account of the development of Durban harbour, see L. Heydenrych, 'Port Natal Harbour', *Enterprise and Exploitation*, eds. Guest and Sellers, pp. 17–45. For the tenure of Edward Innes as resident harbour engineer, see pp. 33–5.

19 Heydenrych, 'Port Natal Harbour', pp. 35–7.

20 Ibid., pp. 37–8.

21 Ibid., pp. 38–9.

22 Ibid., p. 39.

23 Konczacki, *Public Finance and Economic Development*, pp. 18, 22, 65–7; Van der Poel, *Railway and Customs Policies*, pp. 76–9. See Chapter 13.

24 Konczacki, *Public Finance and Economic Development*, pp. 19–22, 68–70; Van der Poel, *Railway and Customs Policies*, pp. 94–101.

25 See T. Maggs, 'Mabhija: Precolonial Industrial Development in the Tugela Basin', *Annals of the Natal Museum*, 25, 1 (1982), pp. 123–41.

26 Commissioner of Mines Records (Dundee), File 550/1910: Commissioner of Mines, 'Natal Mining', n.d., p. 1; F. A. Steart, 'Coal in Natal', (Paper presented to the Third (Triennial) Empire Mining and Metallurgical Congress, South Africa, 1930) p. 1; Bird, *The Annals of Natal*, 2, p. 86: Napier to Stanley, 23 August 1842.

27   For an account of the Colony's coal industry, see R. Edgecombe and
     B. Guest, 'An Introduction to the Pre-Union Natal Coal Industry',
     Enterprise and Exploitation, eds. Guest and Sellers, pp. 309–51; for an
     account of the development of Dundee, see S. Henderson, 'Colonial
     Coalopolis: the Establishment and Growth of Dundee', *Natalia*, 12 (1982),
     pp. 14–26.

28   *NGG* Vol. 8, No. 389, 20 May 1856: Report of the Acting Surveyor-General
     (P. C. Sutherland) to Colonial Secretary, 10 May 1856; Edgecombe and
     Guest, 'The Natal Coal Industry', pp. 310–11.

29   *Blue Book for the Colony of Natal*, Vols. 29 and 32, 1878/1881: Magisterial
     Reports (Newcastle Division); Henderson, 'Colonial Coalopolis', p. 16.

30   Frederic W. North, *Report upon the Coal-Fields of Klip River, Weenen,
     Umvoti and Victoria Counties* (London, Harrison and Sons, 1881).

31   *Annual Report of the Commissioner of Mines*, 1909, p. 25.

32   North, *Report*, pp. 17, 6; *Supplements to the Blue Books for the Colony of
     Natal (Departmental Reports)*, 1887, 1889, 1890–91 and 1896: Reports of
     the General Manager Natal Government Railways, GN No. 1, 1899: Natal
     Government Coal Commission Report of 1898, p. 314.

33   *Supplements to the Blue Books for the Colony of Natal (Departmental
     Reports)*, 1889: Magisterial Report (Newcastle Division) and 1888: *Annual
     Report of the Commissioner of Mines*, p. H33; Henderson 'Colonial
     Coalopolis', p. 19; NA Dundee Coal Co. Ltd Minutes, Board of Directors:
     Add.1/1, General Account 31 December 1891, 1/1/3, 3 June 1909.

34   *Supplements to the Blue Books for the Colony of Natal (Departmental
     Reports)*, Annual Reports of the Commissioner of Mines: 1888, p. H33;
     1890/1, pp. H118, H160; 1899, p. H58; 1901, p. 42; 1909 p. 63.

35   See Ballard and Lenta, 'The Complex Nature of Agriculture in Colonial
     Natal', *Enterprise and Exploitation*, eds. Guest and Sellers, pp. 130–3.

36   Ballard and Lenta, 'Agriculture in Colonial Natal', pp. 126–8, 134–43.

37   See P. Richardson, 'The Natal Sugar Industry, 1849–1905: an Interpretative
     Essay', *Enterprise and Exploitation*, eds. Guest and Sellers, pp. 181–97,
     reprinted from *Journal of African History*, 23 (1982), pp. 515–27.

38   Richardson, 'The Natal Sugar Industry', pp. 192–3.

39   R. F. Osborn, *Valiant Harvest: the Founding of the South African Sugar
     Industry, 1848–1926* (Durban, South African Sugar Association, 1964),
     pp. 194–5. See also R. F. Osborn, *This Man of Purpose: Sir James Liege
     Hulett: Pioneer of Natal and Zululand: a Biography* (Umhlali, North Coast
     Sales Promotions, 1973).

40   Richardson, 'The Natal Sugar Industry', pp. 189, 191, 193–4.

41   Ballard and Lenta, 'Agriculture in Colonial Natal', p. 128, 130.

42   R. O. Pearse, *Joseph Baynes: Pioneer* (Pietermaritzburg, Shuter & Shooter, 1983), pp. 61–95; *Dictionary of South African Biography*, eds. W. J. de Kock and D. W. Kruger (Cape Town and Johannesburg, Government Printer, 1972), 2, p. 41.

43   M. Walker, 'The Provincial Council and Natal, 1924–32' (unpublished MA thesis, University of Natal, Durban, 1976), pp. 97–100.

44   L. C. A. Knowles and C. M. Knowles, *The Economic Development of the British Overseas Empire* (London, George Routledge, 1936), 3, p. 175.

45   Pearse, *Joseph Baynes*, pp. 61–95; *Dictionary of South African Biography*, eds. de Kock and Kruger, p. 41.

46   Ballard and Lenta, 'Agriculture in Colonial Natal', p. 128.

47   Natal Chamber of Industries, *Fifty Years of Progress*, p. 16.

48   Hattersley, *The British Settlement of Natal*, p. 279; W. E. Kaissier, 'An Economic Analysis of Wattle Farming in the Union of South Africa' (unpublished M.Sc. thesis, University of Natal, Pietermaritzburg, 1960); E. Rosenthal, *Southern African Dictionary of National Biography*, 4, pp. 108–9.

49   J. P. Doolan 'Country Notes by Agricola' (unpublished BA Honours essay, University of Natal, Pietermaritzburg, 1978); Hattersley, *British Settlement*, p. 279; Kaissier, 'Economic Analysis of Wattle Farming', p. 7; Natal Chamber of Industries, *Fifty Years of Progress*, p. 16.

50   Konczacki, *Public Finance and Economic Development*, pp. 11–12; Natal Chamber of Industries, *Fifty Years of Progress*, p. 7.

51   Konczacki, *Public Finance and Economic Development*, pp. 12–15, 175.

Chapter 13

The politics of dependence, 1893–9

RITCHIE OVENDALE

During the 1890s, British imperial interests in Southern Africa appeared to be threatened by the growing strength of the Transvaal Republic, especially after the development of the deep-level mines. It might have been expected that the two British colonies, the Cape and Natal, would have united to face this danger. Intercolonial jealousies and competition, however, prevented united action.

Intercolonial rivalry between the Cape Colony and Natal had a long history[1], and it had intensified after 1886 with the opening of the gold-fields in the Transvaal.[2] In 1889 a customs convention between the Cape and the Free State had precluded Natal from competing with its rival colony for Free State trade, and there seemed little hope of it being able to obtain a significant share in the trade to the interior.[3] Indeed, the 1890 negotiations over the Swaziland question between the Imperial Government and the Transvaal led to complaints from the Natal Governor, Sir Charles Mitchell, about a 'great concession to the Cape interests as opposed to those of Natal'.[4] Efforts by Sir Henry Loch, the High Commissioner, to dampen the colonial rivalry by offering Natal the bribe of a railway extension to the Transvaal through the Cape, were snubbed.[5] In the circumstances, there was nothing that Natal could do, Mitchell argued, but wait for the introduction of responsible government, whereafter the extension of the Natal line into the Republic[6] would provide a shorter route than that offered by the Cape (see Chapter 12). Bitter commercial rivalry with the Cape thus led Natal to court the Transvaal: Kruger was 'feted and flattered, as though he had been the Colony's best benefactor' during his visit in April 1891 on the occasion of the opening of the Natal railway extension to Charlestown, near the border with the Transvaal.

There were no immediate benefits, however, and it was not until the end

President Kruger was 'feted and flattered' on his visit to Natal in April 1891 when the Natal railway line reached Charlestown. He is photographed here with the Natal Governor, Sir Charles Mitchell. Sir David Hunter, the General Manager of the Natal Government Railways, is the tall man standing at the back.

of 1891, when Kruger realized that he was unlikely to acquire Kosi Bay as an independent outlet to the sea, that negotiations over railway extension were opened with Natal.[7] These were only tentative: the Republic was aware of Natal's desperate financial predicament, and that it could demand what it wanted,[8] Kruger's intention being to make it impossible for Natal to join the customs union the Cape and Free State had formed. The provisional agreement of December 1892 thus strongly favoured Transvaal interests, to the extent that Mitchell feared that it would allow the Transvaal to run the Natal railway as a commercial undertaking. He commented that this would place 'a most undesirable political lever in the hands of the government of the Republic, which might be used to force the hands of the Natal government in order to obtain some political advantage that might be considered of doubtful advantage to the Colony, to South Africa generally, or to Imperial interest in particular'. He had little faith in the Colony's loyalist sentiments, recognizing that imperial interests rested very insecurely upon 'a people so prone to sacrifice the future to any immediate present advantage as are the Colonists of Natal – or, rather, I should say, the mercantile element amongst the Colonists, which possesses, through its concentration and organization, so much power in the colony'. A Colonial Office minute similarly pointed out that Kruger's terms would make any union between the Cape and Natal impossible, while it would throw Natal into the arms of the Transvaal: 'The SA Republic wishes to get Natal into its power,' it commented.[9]

The behaviour of the Natal government during the ensuing months did everything to confirm these fears. The Executive Council rejected overtures from the Prime Minister of the Cape aimed at ending colonial rivalry, urging instead the cession of Swaziland to the Transvaal,[10] the hope being that there would then be nothing in the way of Natal's railway extension into the Republic,[11] which remained a matter of 'life or death' to the Colony.[12] With the coming of responsible government in Natal, the Transvaal Volksraad consented to investigate the railway extension. The resolution of late August 1893, however, promised nothing definite,[13] and it was only after the Natal government had threatened an alliance with the Cape, that the Volksraad was induced, early in January 1894, to give its approval.[14]

Natal had not seriously considered a customs union with the Cape. Indeed, the two colonies were at the time competing for the annexation of Mpondoland. The Natal Prime Minister, Sir John Robinson, commented that he wanted to let that matter ride until the Cape felt 'the pinch of railway competition' which would follow the extension of Natal's line into the Transvaal.[15] The Colony thus went ahead with the signing of the Charlestown Convention in April 1894 with the Transvaal government, an agreement which again illustrates Natal's obsession with obtaining entry into the Transvaal trade at almost any cost. The Natal government agreed not to undercut the Delagoa Bay railway line, and accepted conditions which made it difficult for it to join any customs union with the Cape and the Free State. Natal's gains were, however, slight: its share of the carrying trade was to be the heaviest and the least profitable. Natal also found at the conference that discussion of clause 16 of the agreement, which had been envisaged as a quid pro quo in that it would allow Natal produce to be admitted into the Republic duty-free, was conveniently sidestepped by the Transvaal delegates.[16] The Johannesburg Uitlander newspaper, the *Star*, commented:

> The alliance implied by the Convention between a Colony which is British to the backbone and a Republic which is the embodiment of all that is conservative and militant in Boerdom is on the face of it

unnatural, and must sooner or later be affected by broad political considerations which have up to now been kept conveniently in the background.[17]

The *rapprochement* between Natal and the Transvaal was initially tested in June 1894 by Kruger's commandeering of Uitlanders to participate in the campaign against Malaboch, the ill-fated northern Transvaal chief, for on this occasion the Natal government supported the affronted British subjects.[18] The honeymoon was further tried by arguments over the contentious clause 16, so that three of Natal's four leading newspapers soon became critical of the Ministry's 'truckling' to the Transvaal.[19] Robinson himself, however, remained firmly committed to his pro-Transvaal policy and, when the last rail of the railway was laid at Heidelberg on 10 October 1895, he spoke of his hope for a closer union between the two countries.[20]

Such an idea did not please the Secretary of State for the Colonies, Joseph Chamberlain, who had assumed office earlier in the year, committed to a vision of a federated South Africa and imperial consolidation. 'I do not like to see the English element in South Africa divided,' he commented. 'The condition of things in the Transvaal can hardly be permanent, and, if trouble arises there, matters will be complicated if the sentiment of the English population both in Natal and at the Cape is evoked on different sides.'[21]

After the resolution of the Malaboch crisis, a more serious challenge to the division of South Africa along economic lines came with the Jameson Raid. This attempt by Chamberlain and Cecil Rhodes, the Prime Minister of the Cape, to assert British supremacy in South Africa, led in Natal as elsewhere in southern Africa to outbursts of imperialistic fervour, so that 'truckling' to Kruger seemed more cowardly than ever.[22] The Natal Ministry, however, continued its traditional Transvaal policy in the face of mounting criticism. When it was reported that Sir Walter Hely-Hutchinson, who had succeeded Mitchell as Governor in August 1893, while arranging in Pretoria for the transportation of Jameson and his fellow prisoners, had expressed the sympathy of Natal to Kruger, there was an uproar.[23] Jameson and his followers were greeted with cheers on their journey through the Colony,[24] while Hely-Hutchinson was 'hooted' and received with 'three groans' in Pietermaritzburg.[25] Matters reached a crisis after it had become known that the German Kaiser had sent a telegram of congratulations to Kruger, whereupon a public meeting in Pietermaritzburg enthusiastically endorsed Chamberlain's assertion that British supremacy must be maintained.[26] Henry Bale, the Pietermaritzburg advocate, told the meeting that Natal had gained nothing from its 'subserviency and sycophancy' to Pretoria. The Colony's interests now demanded, he said, that it co-operate with the endeavour to safeguard British interests in South Africa, instead of allowing the two colonies to be kept apart by 'the Kruger wedge'.[27]

Despite this outburst of public indignation, the Natal government tried to maintain its conciliatory policy. In Hely-Hutchinson's opinion, it was only the 'noisy people' who had engaged in these 'Jingo' demonstrations. All the 'level-headed Englishmen' in the Colony were 'the other way of thinking'.[28]

Reaction to the Jameson Raid revealed the divisions that existed between interest groups in Natal. Commercial elements in Durban, dependent on the Transvaal trade, while maintaining that the expedition was inexcusable, had strongly supported Robinson and his policies.[29] Patriotic elements in Pietermaritzburg, less dependent on the railway connection to the Transvaal and suspicious of any Durban-based plan, protested that the time had come for the exertion of British influence.[30] The *Natal Afrikaner*, the mouthpiece of the Natal Afrikaner community, feared the possibility of racial conflict and praised the neutral policy of the Natal government.[31] Perhaps Afrikaner feelings in Natal were modified by the government's stance, with the result that the racial division was not as marked as it was elsewhere in South Africa, where the prodigious growth of the South African League testified to the depth of political excitement. When in July 1896 a province of the League was established in Natal, with the aim of supporting British supremacy in South Africa, it did not grow as rapidly as it had done in the Cape Colony.[32] Overriding all considerations of imperial, commercial or local interest was the observable fact that it was at the time impossible for Natal to move out of the Transvaal's orbit. By August 1896, the Colony was carrying the major share of the sea-borne traffic to the Transvaal.[33] The economy had boomed after the opening of the Charlestown railway extension, while gross railway revenue amounted to about one half of the Colony's total revenue.[34]

The immediate boom lasted until July 1897. In August of that year, railway revenue began to fall below the estimate, so that the Cape and Free State markets began to seem more enticing.[35] In February 1897, furthermore, Harry Escombe became Prime Minister in place of Robinson, who had been such a determined advocate of close relations with the

Sir David Hunter (1841–1914) was General Manager of the Natal Government Railways, 1879–1906. During the 1909 referendum he opposed Union because he believed that Natal's interests had not been properly secured.

Natal Archives, C60

Transvaal and, while in London for the jubilee celebrations in July, he wrote to Chamberlain asking for help in moving Natal towards a closer union with the Cape.[36] By then, there was growing dissatisfaction in Natal with Kruger's new aggressive policies, such as the Aliens Expulsion Act, the Press Law, and the Immigration Law, while the notorious judicial crisis which followed Kruger's refusal to accept the testing right of the Courts over Volksraad enactments, created a sensation in Natal.[37]

The election of September 1897, which followed the change in the Natal Ministry, did not centre around the Transvaal question. In Hely-Hutchinson's words, there was no 'political question' involved, so that the contest was between the leading politicians rather than between the policies they advocated.[38] The result, nevertheless, reflected dissatisfaction with 'truckling' to Kruger's Republic, for a large number of supporters of the South African League were returned, including Bale, F. S. Tatham, another Pietermaritzburg advocate, who had represented Pietermaritzburg City since 1893, and A. H. Hime, the former Colonial Engineer who had been a member of the Colony's Executive and Legislative Councils from 1876 until 1893. The Escombe Ministry was routed and Henry Binns, founder of the Umhlanga Valley Sugar Estate Company, formed a new government, after Bale had failed in his attempt to do so.[39]

In February 1897 Sir Alfred Milner was appointed as South African High Commissioner and Governor of the Cape. He intended to maintain

Sir Henry Binns (1837–1899). As Prime Minister of Natal during the diplomatic build-up to the Anglo-Boer War, he was faced with the difficult task of balancing Natal's imperial loyalties against her economic ties with the Transvaal.

Natal Archives, C52/1

'religiously' the ties of empire which existed and 'to seize every opportunity which naturally offers itself of developing new ones'.[40] While sailing to South Africa, he recorded:

> It is bad enough that there should be a danger of a Boer incursion into the Cape Colony and a rising to meet it. *But that might be chanced.* What ought never to be chanced, is our being turned out of Natal. And as things stand, we might be turned out of Natal tomorrow.[41]

He immediately made his position clear to those in authority in Natal, reacting sharply when he learnt that an extradition treaty between the Colony and the Transvaal was being negotiated. 'The British Colonies must not allow themselves to be used by the Republics for the purpose of a policy unfriendly to Great Britain', he wrote. 'Differentiation of Colonial and Imperial deserters can only be insisted upon by the Transvaal Government as a slight upon the Imperial Government and no British colony ought to lend itself to facilitate such a slight.'[42] Milner secured Hely-Hutchinson's co-operation in handling the 'disloyal' Binns, who had after assuming office as Prime Minister used unofficial channels to assure Kruger of his good intentions towards the Transvaal. Hely-Hutchinson explained that this was 'the old game of "sucking up" to Kruger in order to obtain commercial advantages'.[43] The issue became public when, after Kruger's re-election as President in February 1898, Binns sent a telegram of congratulations. This convinced Milner that there 'has got to be a separation of the sheep from the goats in this subcontinent, by which I don't mean the English and the Dutch, but those who disapprove and are not afraid to show this disapproval of the present dishonest despotism at Pretoria, and those who either admire or truckle to it'.[44]

Encouraged by Milner, a South African customs union conference led to a convention being drawn up to enable Natal to join the Cape-Free State organization, the terms being laid before the three Parliaments on 20 May 1898.[45] Opposition in Natal was immediate and vociferous: despite the insistence on how this move would consolidate the British interest, Natalians showed themselves more concerned with the price they paid for their food. But the Natal Parliament showed the same characteristic lack of concern for public protest as it had done at the time of the Jameson Raid and the convention came into effect at the beginning of 1899.[46]

For the Natal Ministry, this seems to have been a move of reinsurance, prompted not only by the High Commissioner's urgings but also by a fall-off in railway profits during the latter half of 1897.[47] Indeed, while the customs convention was being debated and the Press and Parliament were emphasizing the need for colonial solidarity and British supremacy, the Ministry supported Kruger over the 'Bunu [Bhunu] affair', during which the jurisdiction of the Transvaal over the courts in Swaziland was brought into question.[48] The Transvaal government thought that Bhunu, the Swazi king, was implicated in a murder and wanted to try him before a Swaziland court. Bhunu fled, whereupon the Natal Ministry, despite warnings from Milner, informed the republican government of Bhunu's arrival in Zululand. In July 1898 Hely-Hutchinson gave what was virtually a final warning that Natal should do nothing 'which might in any way tend to embarrass the High Commissioner in his delicate and responsible task of negotiating with the republics in matters of general and Imperial concern'. Bale, the Acting Prime Minister, gave the necessary assurances, and Hely-Hutchinson assured Milner by telegraph that Natal should not give any further cause for complaint.[49] When, however, there were rumours that Britain might be negotiating to acquire Delagoa Bay from Portugal, Natal tried to steal a lead over the Cape. Natal's ministers offered to ask

Parliament to sanction the annexation of Delagoa Bay to Natal and to refund the purchase money to Britain. Milner, however, doubted that Natal could be relied upon to co-operate fully with the British government in using Delagoa Bay as 'their trump card in the game for uniting South Africa as a British State' and Natal was snubbed.[50]

After the end of 1898, a marked change becomes perceptible in the Natal government's attitude towards the Transvaal. To some extent, this may be explained by the fact that Natal's finances had shown a marked improvement following its decision to join the customs union: for the first half of 1898, despite the depressed state of business with the Transvaal, the trade figures showed an increase of 11 per cent over the previous year.[51] As important, during this same period, patriotic opinion in the Colony was vociferous over the Uitlander question. When, on 18 December 1898, an Englishman, Edgar, was shot by a Johannesburg policeman, another outburst of public indignation swept through Natal. Newspapers editorials were resolute, with one editor calling for the 'waving of the Union Jack'.[52] A public meeting in Pietermaritzburg requested British intervention.[53] Responding to this, the Natal Ministry for the first time refrained from spoiling the image of a patriotic colony and when Chamberlain, speaking in the House of Commons in March 1899, referred to Kruger's 'illusory franchise promises', the Natal Ministry, despite the private opinion of Binns that Chamberlain's 'mischievous speech' could not have been 'more inopportune', kept quiet.[54] In March 1899 the Uitlanders forwarded another petition to the British government and, by the beginning of May, the patriotic forces in Natal saw the matter as being so serious that war was considered not too high a price to bring about reform in the Transvaal.[55]

It was gradually becoming clear to observers in Natal, as in the rest of South Africa, that the British government, urged on by Milner, was determined to force political reform upon the Transvaal in pursuit of its objective of a united British South Africa. That it was even prepared to contemplate the use of force was suggested by the steps that were taken from the middle of 1898 to strengthen Natal's defences and, thereafter, to reinforce the British garrison.[56]

While Milner might have felt more reassured about the position in Natal, by April 1899 he was faced with an Afrikaner Bond Ministry in the Cape. Chamberlain, in a memorandum to the British Cabinet dated 28 April, expressed the fear that Britain would not be able to expect any support from the Cape Bond government, with its strong leanings towards the Transvaal. 'The present state of things', he wrote, 'is a source of constant danger, and cannot continue indefinitely'.[57] On 4 May Milner sent a telegram (his so-called 'Helot despatch') to the Home Government. It prompted Chamberlain to comment that it was 'tremendously stiff, and if published, it will make either an ultimatum or Sir A. Milner's recall necessary'.[58] In this document, the High Commissioner observed:

> South Africa can prosper under two, three, or six governments, though the fewer the better, but not under two absolutely conflicting social and political systems, perfect equality for the Dutch and British in the British colonies side by side with permanent subjection of British to Dutch in one of the Republics.[59]

On 8 May, Milner thereupon instructed Hely-Hutchinson to 'stiffen the wobblers' in Natal, giving the impression that the Imperial Government was prepared to resort to war if necessary.[60]

In June, Milner and Kruger met in Bloemfontein at a conference that had been brought about by concerned parties in southern Africa and in Britain, in the hope that it would produce a peaceful solution to the Uitlander dispute. After the breakdown of the conference, the Press in Natal gave Milner unswerving support, and this seems to have reflected the opinion of the colonists.[61] The *Natal Afrikaner* alone continued to advocate 'conciliation', but even it envisaged the probability of war.[62] At this late stage, the Natal government continued to prevaricate as there were fears that, with the Cape making efforts to secure peace, the resolve of the British government might falter, in which case the Transvaal might avenge itself by curtailing Natal's trade.

At this crucial moment, early in June, Binns died. Bale again declined to form a Ministry, and the task fell to Hime. Both Bale and Hime had been foundation members of the South African League and were known imperial sympathizers.[63] On the surface, all seemed well. The Ministry was formed on the basis of the assurance of moral support given to the Governor for reasonable demands made by the Imperial Government on behalf of the Uitlanders: in the event of hostilities, the Natal government pledged 'its active and sympathetic co-operation'. But this front had been achieved only after the personal intervention of Hely-Hutchinson and concealed the misgivings of a group that included Escombe and was led by the former Minister of Native Affairs in the Robinson and Escombe Ministries, F. R. Moor, which favoured a resolution in Parliament claiming the right of the colonial governments in South Africa to be consulted by Her

Majesty's Government before any final step was taken.[64] A Colonial Office minute expressed surprise at Escombe's attitude, commenting that 'the Natal Ministers are in a blue funk'.[65]

Despite Hely-Hutchinson's opposition, on 17 June the Natal Ministry was however forced by Moor and C. J. Smythe, the Nottingham Road farmer, to subscribe to a minute containing their demands. On 22 June, Milner was then asked by the Natal Ministry to communicate its minute to the Cape government.[66] On the advice of Hely-Hutchinson, Milner agreed but he side-stepped the issue of Natal 'having its say' and would give no positive assurance regarding consultation.[67]

At the beginning of July, Hime assured Hely-Hutchinson that there was no longer any danger of a resolution in the Natal Parliament likely to hamper the High Commissioner.[68] Chamberlain's speech of 26 June at Birmingham probably reassured the Natal Ministry, for on that occasion the Colonial Secretary announced that 'having undertaken the business, we will see it through. We have tried waiting, patience and trusting to promises which were never kept. We can wait no more'.[69] By then, the Natal government was confronted by mounting public presure to support the High Commissioner. When, for example, Milner appealed at the end of June for equal rights in the Transvaal, about 3 000 residents of Durban gathered around Queen Victoria's statue and unanimously proclaimed their support for the stand taken by the High Commissioner, gave three cheers for the Queen, Milner and Chamberlain, and concluded by singing 'Rule Britannia' and 'God Save the Queen'.[70] The same evening, 2 000 Pietermaritzburg citizens passed a resolution which proclaimed their pro-imperial sentiments even more emphatically.[71] There were similar meetings at Escourt, Nottingham Road and Ladysmith[72] and by 10 July, 6 337 adult males had signed a petition to the Queen urging that the situation in the Transvaal be 'radically reformed'.[73] The Johannesburg *Star* commented that Natal had fallen 'into line with the loyal and fair-minded opinion of South Africa'.[74] Following these demonstrations of loyalty, Hely-Hutchinson explained to Chamberlain that 'in Durban and Pietermaritzburg, opinion seems to be practically unanimous in favour of the policy of Her Majesty's Government, and of the High Commissioner's attitude; and, I am of the opinion that, so long as there is no hint of yielding on the part of Her Majesty's Government, it will remain so'.[75]

As Natal public opinion began to make itself felt, the last remnants of opposition in the Natal Parliament disappeared. When on 14 July a motion had been introduced supporting the British government in its endeavour to secure equal rights for all Europeans in South Africa, Hime could obtain the support of Moor and five others only by means of dropping a request for additional troops. Only five days later, however, Escombe seconded Baynes's motion supporting the British government 'in its endeavour to secure equal rights and privileges for all Europeans in South Africa'. On 22 July it was carried unanimously amid cheers, with the two Afrikaner members also supporting it.[76] On 27 July a similar resolution, seconded by the Afrikaner member for Zululand, was passed unanimously by the Legislative Council.[77] Milner sent his congratulations to Hely-Hutchinson[78] and promptly used this stand by Natal to stiffen the Imperial Government against any acceptance of the franchise proposals that were being offered by Kruger at this time.[79] Reassured by the High Commissioner, the Natal Ministers on 25 July asked the British government for additional reinforcements and, by 29 July, Hely-Hutchinson was able to inform Chamberlain that the 'unmistakable trend of opinion in Natal' had 'sensibly diminished' friction in the Ministry.[80]

On 26 July Hely-Hutchinson telegraphed London to inform the Colonial Secretary that 'Her Majesty's Government can rely on practically unanimous support of an overwhelming majority of the whole population if war becomes necessary'. But, he warned, although opinion in Natal had 'consolidated and strengthened during the last six weeks in a remarkable manner', this support was given in the 'firm reliance' that Her Majesty's Government would accept 'nothing but a real and permanent settlement'. He amplified this in a dispatch a few days later:

> The present Transvaal oligarchy, if it be left, after this crisis, with power to injure, will undoubtedly revenge itself on Natal in one form or another for the attitude of uncompromising support of Her Majesty's Government which it has publicly adopted. Loyal and patriotic feeling has, at length, overcome the considerations of commercial prudence which have for so many years enabled the Transvaal to play Natal off against the Cape. Up to within the last six weeks, these considerations turned the balance in the minds of many. The definite declarations as to the permanence of the British flag in the Transvaal, which were nevertheless followed by the retrocession, have not been forgotten. Even now there is anxiety lest Her Majesty's Government should hesitate to effect a thorough and complete settlement, and to assert British supremacy in South Africa in an unmistakable manner.[81]

In this way, the suspect loyalty of Natal came to be employed by Milner in the last months before the outbreak of the Anglo-Boer War to induce the British government not to waver in its demands upon the Transvaal government. He was at the time presenting similar arguments regarding the need not to disappoint Uitlander expectations.[82] Milner was also able to use the predicament of the Natal Colony to persuade the Colonial Secretary and the British Cabinet of the need to send the further contingent to Natal, as had been requested on 25 July,[83] for at the end of August he informed Chamberlain: 'now the Colonial and Natal British, whose trade is greatly affected, are beginning to cry out, and with reason'.[84] Chamberlain thereupon urged his Prime Minister, Lord Salisbury, to increase the demands on the Transvaal, arguing that the colonists of Natal, whose interests could be seriously threatened, wanted the British government to raise its terms.[85]

The diplomatic tussle between the British and Transvaal governments was brought to a head by the resolve of the Transvaal to assert its independence. J. C. Smuts, the State Attorney, drew up a memorandum, dated 4 September, for submission to the Volksraad. The document held out the hope of South Africa becoming a great state with an Afrikaner republic stretching from Table Bay to the Zambesi, and went on to consider the possibility of European intervention in the event of war with Britain, revealing that overtures had already been made to Germany, the Netherlands and France. It also envisaged that, strategically and logistically, successful foreign intervention would be dependent upon the seizure of the port of Durban.[86]

In accepting this memorandum, the Transvaal and Free State Volksraads implicitly accepted the need for war, and in London Chamberlain immediately shifted the issue from the Uitlander franchise to British paramountcy in South Africa:

> What is now at stake is the position of Great Britain in South Africa – and with it the estimate formed of our power and influence in Colonies throughout the world . . . The Dutch in South Africa desire, if it be possible, to get rid altogether of the connection with Great Britain, which to them is not a motherland, and to substitute a United States of South Africa which, they hope, would be mainly under Dutch influences.[87]

Chamberlain urged that the British government formulate its demands in a categorical way, reinforcing its troops in South Africa. On 8 September the British Cabinet considered messages from Natal, urging that troops be sent to protect the Colony against attack from the Transvaal. It was decided to send 6 000 men from India, and four battalions with some artillery and cavalry from England. The Cabinet also at last set about making clear its demands on the Transvaal in the form of an ultimatum, for which the Natal Ministry minuted its thanks.[88]

In Natal, the emphasis also shifted to British paramountcy, it now being widely asserted that only British suzerainty over the whole of South Africa could guarantee the Colony's safety. The Ministry thus gave immediate effect to Chamberlain's request not to allow arms and ammunition to pass to the republics through the Colony.[89] On 6 September, 1 500 citizens in Pietermaritzburg unanimously approved a resolution that it was 'imperatively necessary' that the British government take action to 'enforce its demands and Suzerain Power'.[90] In Hely-Hutchinson's opinion, F. S. Tatham was expressing views that were widely-held when he wrote:

> Spurred on by the strong declaration made by Mr Chamberlain and other members of Her Majesty's Government, and by their strong sentiment of loyalty to the Crown, the people of Natal have unhesitatingly ranged themselves on the side of the Imperial Government . . . Natal is so deeply committed that she will be at the mercy of the Transvaal oligarchy if that Government be allowed to continue . . . The issue now is British supremacy or Boer supremacy, and upon a definite settlement of that issue hang the lives and fortunes of those who have stood by Great Britain in this controversy.[91]

Towards the middle of September, Hely-Hutchinson voiced his anxiety at the continued delay. He reiterated that Natal had made its stand in the firm conviction that British supremacy would be asserted in South Africa. Because of its relations with the Transvaal, the Colony had a great deal to lose. It had invested seven-ninths of its loan of £9 000 000 in a railway, the bulk of the revenue from which depended upon republican traffic, as well as over £1 000 000 on harbour works to facilitate the handling of these goods. It would, he pointed out, be easy for the Transvaal government to cripple the source of revenue from which the interest on Natal's debt of approximately £180 per head of the population was derived. The population of Natal, he went on to assert, was practically unanimous in its desire for a permanent settlement, if necessary at the cost of war: the Colony had in fact sacrificed much to support the cause of empire and discontent was growing over the delay and hesitation.[92]

The British government did not compromise. On 22 September the Cabinet authorized Chamberlain to inform the Transvaal that the British government was 'compelled to consider the situation afresh and to formulate their own proposals for a final settlement'.[93] When the Transvaal and the Free State presented an ultimatum on 9 October demanding the withdrawal of British troops, it only preceded the proposed British ultimatum by a few days.[94]

At the outbreak of the Anglo-Boer War, at which time South Africa seemed to be split along racial lines, Natal projected the image of a loyal colony sacrificing itself in the imperial interest. It was, however, only after the Natal government had become absolutely convinced of the inevitability of war and therefore only after the danger of Transvaal vengeance had been removed that the Colony had been able to afford the luxury of imperial sentiment.

Notes

1   B. A. le Cordeur, 'Relations between Natal and the Cape, 1856–1879' (unpublished Ph.D. thesis, University of Natal, 1963).

2   See S. E. Katzenellenbogen, *South Africa and Southern Mozambique: Labour, Railways and Trade in the Making of a Relationship* (Manchester, Manchester University Press, 1981), pp. 16–23.

3   Van der Poel, *Railway and Customs Policies*, pp. 12–43.

4   GH 1300, Folios 298–300, Unnumbered: Mitchell to Knutsford, Confidential, 13 May 1890 (copy).

5   GH 684, G187a/1891, Folios 11–24: Loch to Mitchell, Secret and Confidential, 21 May 1891; Enclosure, Unnumbered, Loch to Knutsford, Secret and Confidential, 20 April 1891 (copy).

6   GH 1352, Folio 55a, Unnumbered: Mitchell to Loch, Secret and Confidential, 2 June 1891 (copy).

7   R. Ovendale, 'Natal and the Jameson Raid', *Journal of Natal and Zulu History*, 4 (1981), pp. 1–3; *Natal Witness*, 8–13 April 1891.

8   Leyds Archives (TA), 80(3), Unnumbered: Leyds to Beelaerts van Blokland, 14 August 1892 (copy, extract).

9   GH 1300, Folios 333–8, Unnumbered: Mitchell to Ripon, Confidential, 19 December 1892 (copy).

10   *Natal Witness*, 23 May 1893, editorial.

11   NA Sir John Robinson Collection 3/2: Robinson to Mitchell, Telegram, 20 May 1893.

12   GH 1300, Folio 345, Unnumbered: Mitchell to Ripon, Confidential, 11 July 1893 (copy).

13   *Notulen der Verrichtinger van den Hoog Edel Achtbaren Eersten en Tweeden Volksraad der Zuid-Afrikaansche Republiek* (TA, 1893), pp. 402–6, Articles 1193–5.

14   Leyds Archives (80)1, Unnumbered: Van Boeschoten to Leyds, Secret, 5 January 1894 (copy).

15   See R. Ovendale, 'Profit or Patriotism: Natal, the Transvaal, and the Coming of the Second Anglo-Boer War', *Journal of Imperial and Commonwealth History*, 8 (1980), p. 211.

16   TA Transvaal State Secretary 4069, folios 185ff; Minutes of the Meetings of the Railway Delegates in Pretoria, 30 January 1894, 31 January 1894, 1–5 February 1894, dated 12 February 1894; The Railway Extension from Charlestown to Johannesburg, Copy of Agreements dated 3 and 12 February and 25 April 1894, pp. 9–10.

17   The *Star*, 26 April 1894, editorial.

18   The *Star*, 30 June 1894, editorial; *Natal Advertiser*, 18 June 1894; 29 June 1894, editorial; *Times of Natal*, 20 June 1894, editorial; *Natal Witness*, 23 June 1894, editorial, *Natal Mercury*, 22 June 1894.

19   Leyds Archives (80)2, GZ 82: Notes of Meeting between the Hon. T. K. Murray, Minister of Lands and Works, Natal and Government of the South African Republic held at Government Buildings, Pretoria, on 12 March 1895, Undated; GH 1301, Folios 56–9, Unnumbered: Hely-Hutchinson to Ripon, Confidential, 22 March 1894 (copy). Hely-Hutchinson attributed this to the personal biases and resentments of the editors. The *Natal Mercury*, which supported the alliance, was owned by the family of Sir J. Robinson, the Prime Minister: GH 1303, Folios 60–2, Unnumbered: Hely-Hutchinson to Ripon, Confidential, 29 March 1895 (copy); Sir John Robinson Collection, Pretoria, Minute Paper 1459/1895.

20   *Natal Witness*, 12 October 1895.

21   TA J. C. Chamberlain Papers 10/7/3: Chamberlain to Hely-Hutchinson, Secret, 3 September 1895; 10/7/7: Chamberlain to Hely-Hutchinson, Private, 30 November 1895, quoted by F. R. Carroll, 'The Growth and Co-ordination of Pro-War Sentiment in Natal before the Second Anglo-Boer War' (unpublished MA thesis, University of Natal, 1981), pp. 18–28.

22   *Natal Witness*, 4 January 1896; *Natal Mercury*, 7 January 1896; *Natal Afrikaner*, 14 January 1896, editorial.

23   GH 1429, Folios 37–9, No. 2: Hely-Hutchinson to Robinson, Telegram, 8 January 1896 (copy); Folio 41, No. 2: Robinson to Hely-Hutchinson, Telegram, 9 January 1896. What the Governor had done was to tell Kruger of the 'great grief' with which he had heard of Jameson's attack. It had been 'particularly painful' to him as an 'Englishman': NA Sir John Robinson Collection 3/46: Hely-Hutchinson to Robinson, Confidential for Ministers only, 12 January 1896; GH 1425, Folios 8–9, Transvaal Government to Hely-Hutchinson, 13 January 1896; folios 10–13: Enclosure, Account of Meeting between Hely-Hutchinson and Kruger.

24   GH 1423, Folio 45, Hely-Hutchinson to General Manager of Railways, 21 January 1896 (copy); Folio 46, General Manager of Railways, Durban, to Hely-Hutchinson, 21 January 1896.

25   GH 1423, Folio 146: Buddock, Newcastle, to Hely-Hutchinson, 23 January 1896; GH 1433, Folio 32, No. 1: Hely-Hutchinson to Robinson, 24 January 1896 (copy); Folios 58–61: General Manager of Railways to Hely-Hutchinson, 25 January 1896; *Natal Mercury*, 23 January 1896; *Natal Witness*, 24 January 1896.

26   GH 1228, Folio 40, No. 16: Hely-Hutchinson to Chamberlain, 25 January 1896.

27   *Natal Witness*, 25 January 1896; *Natal Advertiser*, 27 February 1896, editorial; *Times of Natal*, 31 January 1896 (supplement).

28   Ibid; NA Sir John Robinson Collection, 3/58, Hely-Hutchinson to Robinson, 17 March 1896.

29   *Natal Witness*, 9 January 1896.

30   Ibid., 17 January 1896.

31   *Natal Afrikaner*, 7 January 1896.

32   *Natal Advertiser*, 4 February 1897; *Natal Witness*, 4 February 1897; *The Star* 4 February 1897.

33   NA Sir John Robinson Collection 5/10: Minister of Lands and Works to Robinson, 3 October, 1896.

34   *Natal Advertiser*, 30 March 1897.

35   Ibid., 1 September 1896, editorial.

36   NA Escombe Papers 12/3/1: Escombe to Chamberlain, 24 July 1897 (copy).

37   *Natal Mercury*, 16 October 1896, editorial; *Natal Afrikaner*, 26 February 1897, editorial.

38   GH 1301, Folios 299–301, unnumbered: Hely-Hutchinson to Chamberlain, 8 October 1897 (copy).

39   *Natal Advertiser*, 22 September 1897, editorial; *Natal Afrikaner*, 1 October 1897, editorial; 25 January 1898; GH 1228, folio 424, No. 161: Hely-Hutchinson to Chamberlain, 8 October 1897 (copy).

40   A. Milner, *The Nation and Empire*, (London, Constable, 1913), pp. 1–6, Speech at London before Leaving for South Africa, 29 March 1897.

41   *The Milner Papers*, ed. C. Headlam (London, Cassell, 1931), 1, pp. 40–1: Milner to Selborne, 20 April 1897 (extract).

42   TA Milner Papers 1099, Folios 753–7: Milner to Hely-Hutchinson, Confidential, 17 August 1897, quoted by Carroll, 'Pro-War Sentiment in Natal', p. 103.

43   Chamberlain Papers (Birmingham University Library) JC10/7, No. 55: Hely-Hutchinson to Chamberlain, 16 December 1897, quoted by Brookes and Webb, *History of Natal*, pp. 198–9.

44   *Milner Papers*, ed. Headlam, 1, p. 216: Milner to Hely-Hutchinson, Private and Confidential, 18 February 1898 (extract).

45   Natal Parl. Papers 128/189, Sprigg to Binns, 18 March 1893; 579, 5/98: Minutes of the Conference and the proposed Convention.

46   *Natal Mercury*, 24 May 1898, editorial; *Times of Natal*, 31 May 1898, editorial; Natal Legislative Assembly Debates, 2 June 1898; *Natal Advertiser*, 17 June 1898, editorial, and 20 June 1898.

47   For the economic statistics see Ovendale 'Natal, the Transvaal and the Boer War', pp. 231–2.

48   Leyds Archives 31(1), GZR 374/98: Fraser to Reitz, 11 July 1898 (copy).

49   GH 1349, Folios 15–8, No. 2: Hely-Hutchinson to Milner, Secret, 30 July 1898 (copy).

50   GH 276, Folios 71–4, G436a/1898: Edward Wingfield to Hely-Hutchinson, 8 October 1898; Minute to Ministers, 29 Oct. 1898; *Milner Papers*, ed. Headlam, 1, p. 268: Milner to Hely-Hutchinson, 18 September 1898 (extract).

51   *Natal Advertiser*, 27 July 1899.

52   *Times of Natal*, 27 December 1898, editorial; *Natal Advertiser*, 27 December 1898, editorial.

53   GH 1229, Folio 112, 7/99: Hely-Hutchinson to Chamberlain, 18 January 1899.

54   South African Public Library, Cape Town, Merriman Papers 1899/204: Binns to Merriman, Private, 3 April 1899.

55   *Times of Natal*, 6 May 1899, editorial; *Natal Mercury*, 30 May 1899, editorial.

56   GH 1349, Folios 20–1, Hely-Hutchinson to Milner, Secret, 4 August 1898 (copy); GH 276, Folios 129–33, G218a/1899: Chamberlain to Hely-Hutchinson, Secret, 9 May 1899.

57   Public Record Office, London, CAB 37/49, No.28: Memorandum by Chamberlain, 29 April 1899.

58   R. H. Wilde, 'Joseph Chamberlain and the South African Republic, 1895–1899', *AYB*, 1956, 1, p. 102.

59   *Milner Papers*, ed. Headlam, 2, pp. 349–53: Milner to Chamberlain, Telegram, 4 May 1899.

60   Ibid., 1, pp. 358–9: Milner to Hely-Hutchinson, Very Confidential, 8 May 1899.

61   *Natal Mercury*, 6 June 1899, editorial; 8 June 1899, editorial; 10 June 1899, editorial, 16 June 1899, editorial; *Times of Natal*, 9 June 1899, editorial; *Natal Witness*, 12 June 1899, editorial.

62   *Natal Afrikaner*, 9 June 1899, editorial.

63   *Natal Advertiser*, 6 June 1899, editorial; *Natal Afrikaner*, 9 June 1899.

64   GH 1282, Folios 149–50, Unnumbered: Hely-Hutchinson to Chamberlain, Secret, 10 June 1899 (copy).

65   CO 179/205, Hely-Hutchinson to Chamberlain, Secret, 17 June 1899; Minute dated 11 July 1899.

66   GH 1282, folios 153–4, Unnumbered: Hely-Hutchinson to Chamberlain, Secret, 5 July 1899 (copy).

67   Ibid., 690, G268a/1899: Milner to Hely-Hutchinson, Confidential, 26 June 1899.

68   Ibid., 1282, Folios 153–4, Unnumbered: Hely-Hutchinson to Chamberlain, Secret, 5 July 1899 (copy).

69   *Milner Papers*, ed. Headlam, 1, p. 448.

70   *Natal Advertiser*, 3 July 1899, editorial.

71   *Natal Witness*, 3 July 1899, editorial.

72   GH 1229, Folio 212, 93/99: Hely-Hutchinson to Chamberlain, 11 July 1899

(copy); Folio 213, 95/99: Hely-Hutchinson to Chamberlain, 13 July 1899 (copy); Folio 213, 97/99: Hely-Hutchinson to Chamberlain, 13 July 1899 (copy).

73   *Natal Witness*, 12 July 1899, editorial.

74   The *Star*, 3 July 1899, editorial.

75   GH 1282, Folio 154, Unnumbered: Hely-Hutchinson to Chamberlain, Secret, 5 July 1899 (copy).

76   GH 1229, Folio 222, 103/99: Hely-Hutchinson to Chamberlain, 22 July 1899 (copy); Debates of the Natal Legislative Assembly, 19 July 1899.

77   *Natal Advertiser*, 26 July 1899, editorial.

78   *Milner Papers*, ed. Headlam, 1, p. 462, Milner to Hely-Hutchinson, Telegram, 21 July 1899 (extract).

79   Ibid., p. 468: Milner to Chamberlain, Telegram, 20 July 1899.

80   Ibid., 1282, Folio 159, Unnumbered: Hely-Hutchinson to Chamberlain, Secret, 29 July 1899 (copy).

81   *BPP* LXIV of 1899 (C. 9521), pp. 42–3, No. 32: Hely-Hutchinson to Chamberlain, Telegram, 26 July 1899, received 26 July 1899; GH 1282, Folios 159–62, Unnumbered: Hely-Hutchinson to Chamberlain, Secret, 29 July 1899 (copy).

82   See A. H. Duminy and B. Guest, *Interfering in Politics: a Biography of Sir Percy FitzPatrick* (Johannesburg, 1987), p. 73.

83   GH 1301, Folio 417, Unnumbered: Hely-Hutchinson to Chamberlain, Confidential, 29 July 1899 (copy); *Milner Papers*, ed. Headlam, 1, pp. 511–12: Milner to Chamberlain, Secret, Telegram, 30 July 1899 (extract); CAB 4111/25, No. 17, Salisbury to Victoria, 1 August 1899.

84   *Milner Papers*, ed. Headlam, 1, p. 499: Milner to Chamberlain, 30 August 1899 (extract).

85   E. Drus, 'The Chamberlain Papers concerning Anglo-Transvaal Relations, 1896–1899', *Bulletin of the Institute of Historical Research*, 27 (1954), p. 179: Chamberlain to Salisbury, 2 September 1899 (copy).

86   Leyds Archives, 192 (1), GR 1293/99: Memorandum on Military Situation, 4 September 1899; Minutes.

87   CAB 37/50, No. 70, Memorandum by Chamberlain, Confidential, 7 September 1899.

88   Ibid., 41/25, No. 18: Salisbury to Victoria, 9 Sept. 1899; GH 1282, Folio 168: Hely-Hutchinson to Chamberlain, Secret, 14 September 1899.

89   GH 1382, Folio 58: 29 August 1899; 1282, Folio 61, Unnumbered: Hely-Hutchinson to Chamberlain, Secret, 13 September 1899 (copy).

90   *Times of Natal*, 7 September 1899; *Natal Advertiser*, 7 September 1899; *BPP* LXIV of 1899 (C. 9521), p. 43, No. 33: Hely-Hutchinson to Chamberlain, Telegram, 7 September 1899.

91   *BPP* LVI of 1900 (Cd. 43), pp. 37–8: Hely-Hutchinson to Chamberlain, 13 September 1899, enclosure; GH 1229, Folio 269, 132/99: Hely-Hutchinson to Chamberlain, 13 September 1899 (copy); Folio 272, 134/99: Hely-Hutchinson to Chamberlain, 15 September 1899 (copy).

92   GH 1229, Folio 290, 134/99: Hely-Hutchinson to Chamberlain, 15 September 1899; 1301, Folio 432, Unnumbered: Hely-Hutchinson to Chamberlain, Confidential, 29 September 1899 (copy).

93   *BPP* LXIV of 1899 (Cd.9530), pp. 16–17: Chamberlain to Milner, Telegram, 22 September 1899.

94   Drus, 'Select Documents', pp. 182–8: Proposed Ultimatum Provided for Use of Cabinet, 9 October 1899.

Chapter 14

The Anglo-Boer War and its economic aftermath, 1899–1910

ANDREW DUMINY and
BILL GUEST

It soon became clear, following the outbreak of hostilities between the two inland Boer republics and Great Britain in October 1899, that the Colony of Natal could be no mere bystander. Even before the Transvaal government's ultimatum of 9 October had expired, the Volunteer Militia had been mobilized to meet the threatened invasion of the Colony. The bulk, including the A battery of the Natal Field Artillery, the Border Mounted Rifles, the Natal Carbineers and the Natal Mounted Rifles, were deployed at Ladysmith, while the Durban Light Infantry was ordered to assist in the defence of Colenso and Escourt, with Charlestown and Newcastle being abandoned to the Boers.[1]

In view of the danger of a Boer drive directed at the capture of Durban, the defence of Natal became an immediate preoccupation and by mid-September the order had already been given for the dispatch of 10 000 troops from India and Britain's Mediterranean bases. Disagreement then arose as to how these forces could best be deployed. Lieutenant-General Sir George White, who arrived on 7 October to assume command, rejected a plan to withdraw to the south of the Thukela in favour of concentrating his troops in Ladysmith, where sixty days' supply of stores had been accumulated. Major-General Sir William Penn-Symons, the commander of the Natal garrison before White's arrival, favoured holding the Boers closer to the Transvaal border, and had already taken 4 000 troops to Dundee.[2]

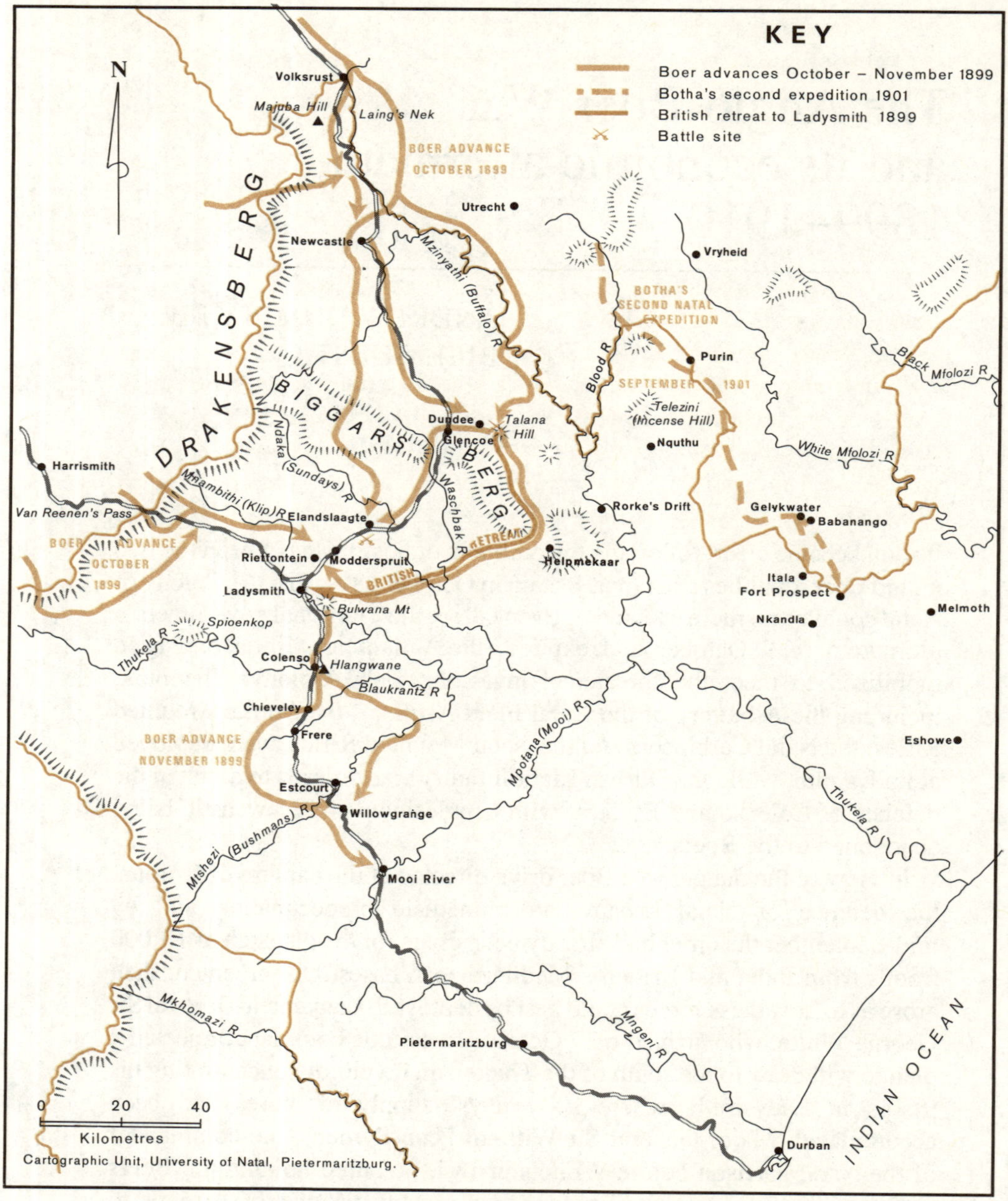

KEY

━━━ Boer advances October – November 1899
━ ━ ━ Botha's second expedition 1901
╫╫╫ British retreat to Ladysmith 1899
✕ Battle site

N

Volksrust

Majuba Hill ▲

Laing's Nek

**BOER ADVANCE
OCTOBER 1899**

Utrecht ●

Vryheid ●

Newcastle ●

Mzinyathi (Buffalo) R

**BOTHA'S
SECOND NATAL
EXPEDITION**

Purin ●

Blood R

SEPTEMBER 1901

Black Mfolozi R

Telezini
(Incense Hill)

D R A K E N S B E R G

B I G G A R S

Dundee

Glencoe

Talana
Hill

Nquthu ●

White Mfolozi R

Harrismith ●

Ndaka

(Sundays) R

B E R G

Rorke's Drift ●

Gelykwater ●

Babanango ●

Van Reenen's Pass

Mhambithi (Klip) R

Elandslaagte

Naschbek R

**BOER ADVANCE
OCTOBER
1899**

Rietfontein

Modderspruit

BRITISH

Helpmekaar ●

Itala
Fort Prospect ●

Melmoth ●

Ladysmith ●

Bulwana Mt

RETREAT

Nkandla ●

Spioenkop

Thukela R

Colenso ●

Hlangwane

Blaukrantz R

Chieveley ●

**BOER ADVANCE
NOVEMBER 1899**

Frere ●

Mpofana (Mool) R

Eshowe ●

Estcourt ●

Willowgrange ●

Mtshezi (Bushmans) R

Thukela R

Mooi River ●

Mkhomazi R

Pietermaritzburg ●

Mngeni R

I N D I A N   O C E A N

0   20   40
Kilometres

Cartographic Unit, University of Natal, Pietermaritzburg.

Durban ●

Map 21   Military operations during the Anglo-Boer War, 1899–1901

It was there that the first engagements of the war took place, apart from a few skirmishes involving the Natal Carbineers, who had been detailed to patrol along the railway line from Ladysmith to the Orange Free State border at Van Reenens.[3] On 20 October an attack was launched upon Talana Hill, overlooking Dundee, a position that had been occupied by the Boers (see Map 21). Although the assault was successful, Penn-Symons was killed and the pursuing cavalry were forced to surrender, having suffered over 200 casualties, after encountering another Boer force nearby. On the following day, after the Boers had occupied Elandslaagte railway station, cutting Dundee off from Ladysmith, an assault was launched on this position from Ladysmith (see Map 21). Aided by their newly-introduced khaki uniforms, which were less conspicuous than their traditional red jackets, the British took the Boer position along the edge of the plateau overlooking the railway station with a bayonet charge. A white flag appeared and, thinking that the Boers had surrendered, the British were surprised by a desperate counter-attack. The engagement left a bitter memory on both sides, for in the ensuing cavalry charge, many Boers were cut down by swords and lances.[4]

Instead of pushing home his advantage, White then ordered the abandonment of Dundee and prepared for a siege at Ladysmith. Most commentators agree that at this point the Boers should have launched their thrust to the coast,[5] disregarding the threat to their rear posed by the large British force that had been concentrated in Ladysmith. Whereas Pietermaritzburg was almost defenceless, twenty-eight guns had been removed from warships and positioned on the hills for the defence of Durban.[6] However, the Boer commander, General Piet Joubert, the hero of Majuba, favoured caution and would allow no more than the advance of a small force of 4 000 under General Louis Botha. This expedition proceeded in extremely wet conditions and the town of Estcourt was invested. Boer forces then advanced as far as Mooi River, (see Map 21) where an exchange of artillery fire took place on 22/3 November. At Estcourt the defenders successfully launched a surprise attack upon the Boer position on Beacon Hill, near Willow Grange, on 21 November. Joubert thereupon ordered the withdrawal of the Boer forces in order to concentrate on the siege of Ladysmith.[7]

While these events were taking place in what had become the main theatre of the war, a Boer commando entered Zululand, looting whatever cattle it could capture. During February 1900 another invaded from the east and captured the magistracies at Nquthu and Nkandla, necessitating the

Natal Archives, C1693

British troops en route *to the Natal front. They had abandoned the familiar red coats worn during previous South African campaigns.*

dispatch of naval guns and a contingent of 'Colonial Scouts' for the defence of Eshowe (see Map 21). The Boer forces, however, soon withdrew.[8]

British reinforcements were streaming in through Durban and the new commander-in-chief, Sir Redvers Buller, had already settled on the controversial strategy whereby the British expeditionary force was to be split and the republics invaded on three fronts, with two advancing along the Cape's rail routes, while the third, under Buller himself, advanced upon Ladysmith. After what seemed unnecessary delays, the invasions took place and between 10 and 17 December, during what became known in Britain as 'Black Week', all three of these detachments suffered major defeats. In Natal, the attempted assault upon the heights commanding the Thukela valley failed ignominiously, the best-known engagement being that at Spioen Kop which the British abandoned after it had been captured with 243 casualties. In all, it required over 50 000 troops and cost about 7 000 casualties before Ladysmith was eventually relieved on 28 February 1900. It had withstood a siege lasting 118 days. Although the town had been subjected to constant artillery fire, including that of two formidable 94-pounder 'Long Toms', there were relatively few casualties in the town itself resulting from the bombardment, while the sufferings of those under siege was lessened by Joubert's humane decision to allow the sick to be removed to a hospital between the Boer and British lines.[9] As had been the case at the sieges of Kimberley and Mafeking, the two Cape centres which had simultaneously been invested by the Boer forces, the major sufferers were probably the black population, whose food resources were already extremely meagre and who were therefore least well equipped to suffer the privations inflicted by war.

At the end of September 1900, after the theatre of military action had moved into the Orange Free State and Transvaal, the Natal Volunteer Militia was demobilized. Most of its members had been at Ladysmith

Natal Archives, C2970

A party of Boer volunteers pose in front of their supply wagons with their wagon drivers.

during the siege. It was replaced by a Volunteer Regiment, in which 500 militiamen promptly enlisted.[10] At this stage, it appeared that military activity had finally moved away from the Colony. Early in 1901, however, the British military authorities recruited Zulus to raid into the Transvaal, believing that this would assist in diminishing the sources of supply of the Boer commandos then operating in the south-eastern Transvaal. The move provoked an indignant response from the Natal government, which viewed with alarm the involvement of blacks in military operations, especially after fifty-six Boers had been massacred by the Zulus in the Vryheid district.[11]

During the closing months of 1901, parts of the Colony were again directly involved in hostilities as the result of a second invasion of Natal by Botha, who had become the Commandant-General of the Boer forces in place of the ageing and over-cautious Joubert. Like the invasions of the Cape Colony led by J. C. Smuts and C. de Wet, it was hoped to carry the war into a region in which there were many known Boer sympathizers and which had not been laid waste. To meet this threat, the Volunteer Militia was again called out and ordered to assemble at Pietermaritzburg and Greytown. Botha's threat was, however, soon dispelled when he unsuccessfully attacked the Itala and Fort Prospect positions[12] (see Map 21).

The war was formally ended by the Peace of Vereeniging signed in Pretoria on 31 May 1902. By then an estimated 2 710 Natalians had volunteered for military service, while another 474 served in non-combat units, including a corps of Indian stretcher-bearers. These figures represent nearly 20 per cent of the white male population.[13] Seventy-one VCs were awarded during the war but none were bestowed upon the Natal volunteers.[14]

Contemporary accounts of the war in Natal emphasized the sacrifices that were made by the Colony, one estimate being that nearly £500 000 was expended by the colonial treasury, including a rebate of customs duties on imported military stores. There was a sudden loss of customs and railway revenues following the cessation of trade with the Transvaal, and from the initial invasion of Boer forces which prevented the colonial government from collecting the hut tax, license fees, fines, stamp and transfer duties in the northern districts. Emphasis was also placed upon the effect of the war upon the white inhabitants as, during the early months, men volunteered for active service and women organized relief work.[15] The northern districts were directly affected by the Boer invasion, especially as on 10 November

1899 the region was annexed by Joubert in the name of the South African Republic. In Klip River County, the majority of 'Dutch' farmers co-operated with the invaders in a show of force against the black population before abandoning their farms for the interior Republics. After the war, they were to pay a price for their disloyalty, for they received no compensation for their losses.[16]

Despite these setbacks, and despite the two years of crippling drought that coincided with the war, it brought unprecedented prosperity to the Colony. The upkeep of the imperial army boosted its internal buying power, while military traffic inland more than compensated for the loss in railway earnings arising out of the war-time termination of the Overberg trade, even though few trucks used by the military returned to the coast with a payload. Moreover, the large number of imperial troops and the influx of refugees from the Transvaal increased the demand in Natal for imported goods, the duty on which offset the loss of revenue normally derived from transit dues on goods bound for the interior. The imposition of higher customs duties increased the cost of living, but this was compensated for by rising levels of income and employment as the private sector took advantage of the prevailing commercial climate.[17]

The prices of agricultural commodities soared and farmers found that they could also turn, as they had done during the Anglo-Zulu War, to highly profitable transport-riding. The major urban centres benefited as traders acted as middlemen for military provisions, while canteens and brothels flourished.[18] In Durban, with the harbour handling unprecedented traffic, warehouses bulged and heavy-engineering and other manufacturing enterprises responded to wartime demands.[19] Furthermore, no sooner had the occupation of Pretoria taken place in June 1900 than large numbers of immigrants began to arrive, fired by the belief that southern Africa offered limitless possibilities.

Always dependent upon customs duties as a major source of revenue, the Colony eagerly gathered the windfall which resulted from the surge in imports, so that for the first time its coffers began to bulge. In 1900–1 Natal's revenue increased by 57 per cent over the previous year to nearly £3 million and the trend continued into the immediate post-war period, with public revenue rising in 1902–3 to £4 334 000.[20] The Colony was sufficiently encouraged to embark upon extensive improvements to Durban harbour and expensive railway extensions.

On 26 June 1904 the 12 975 ton *Armadale Castle*, with a draught of 6,7 metres, became the first mail-steamer to negotiate the Bar and drop anchor

Before it became possible for larger vessels to cross the sandbar into Durban Bay, passengers were offloaded in a basket on to smaller vessels in the outer anchorage. This photograph was taken in 1900.

The Armadale Castle *was the first mail steamer to cross the bar into Durban Harbour in 1904.*

at the quayside in Durban harbour. No more would passengers and goods be landed through the surf in the outer anchorage, or in tugs across the Bar. In the same year, Durban's first floating dock, capable of lifting 8 500 tons of shipping dead weight, arrived off shore and was successfully moored in the harbour. It passed its first test just three days after the arrival of the *Armadale Castle* when it safely raised and lowered the 7 700 ton SS *Kent*. By that stage, the port was also endowed with a dry dock, a 213 metre timber wharf, numerous cranes and a coal shed.[21] The dream of Harry Escombe, who had died five years earlier, was fast becoming a reality. In 1903 Joseph Baynes, Natal's Minister of Lands and Works (1903–5) inaugurated a massive programme of land-reclamation and wharf extension which, although subjected to considerable criticism on the grounds of the expense involved, was continued by J. G. Maydon, Minister of Railways and Harbours,This substantially enlarged the harbour by creating the huge Maydon Wharf complex at Congella.[22]

Yet another significant harbour development was the opening in 1907 of a coal-loading plant at the Bluff. Constructed in London, it was equipped with an electric hoist or 'dumper' which was capable of lifting and sidetipping railway trucks with an average capacity of 45 long tons each. The coal was tipped onto an apron from whence it was conveyed in drop-bottom buckets of 6-ton capacity over the waiting holds of vessels tied up at the three-berth quay adjacent to the plant. By these means, three ships could be loaded simultaneously, a great improvement on the loading by means of baskets that was conducted at the Point.[23] This additional facility gave a boost to the local coal industry (see below) and to Durban's quest for recognition as a modern harbour. By 1910 it was already established as southern Africa's premier port, importing goods to the average annual value (1910–14) of £11 354 719, compared with £2 211 920 in 1887 and £102 512 in 1856.[24]

Railway construction in Natal had always been focused primarily on providing the shortest possible route into the republican interior, except for the north and south coast branch lines radiating from Durban. During the early years of the twentieth century, an additional 640 km of expensive branch line was constructed in a conscious effort to promote agricultural development in remote and hitherto neglected rural areas. By 1904 there were 1 198 kilometres of railway in Natal, compared with 173 in 1884, and there were 2 717 595 passenger journeys undertaken, compared with 464 496. Electric lighting and power was widely extended after its introduction in 1895, and in July 1904 a new Railway Power House was brought into operation at Durban. By 1909 the Colony had 1 588 kilometres of railway (see Map 20), over which more than three million tons of goods were carried in that year, compared with 192 500 tons in 1885, the bulk of the traffic being concentrated on the mainline into the interior.[25]

These extensive public works were accompanied by expensive undertakings in the towns, where the provision of telephones, electric lighting, macadamized streets and the construction of new railway stations, town halls, municipal and government offices, drill halls and schools testified to the rising expectations of the colonial community.[26]

This prosperity affected not only the white community. Like the white farmers, the homestead economy and the independent black producers benefited from the sharp rise in foodstuffs, while the surge in activity in Durban harbour created a new demand for unskilled labour. In the major towns, the military presence and the growing white immigrant population provided opportunities for, among others, rickshaw-pullers, stevedores and washerwomen. The result was the growth of black communities around the garrison centres, and particularly around Durban.[27]

As the war drew to a close, there seemed to be every prospect of Natal being able to reap the riches of the peace. Not only had its merchants gained important footholds in the Transvaal, its railway system seemed to have captured the bulk of the Transvaal trade. The Colony could also look with satisfaction upon the acquisition of considerable territorial gains. Although the request for the incorporation of Swaziland was brushed aside, the fertile Vryheid-Utrecht region, formerly the New Republic, was added to Natal.[28] The prospect of developing this region, as well as those parts of Zululand that were opened up for white settlement in 1905, added to the general euphoria.

The termination of hostilities in 1902 indeed fuelled a post-war boom. Property sales increased, there was an influx of capital and immigrants, and local merchants stockpiled imported goods in anticipation of an increased demand both in Natal and in the Transvaal, and in expectation of higher customs duties under the new customs convention that was about to be negotiated. In 1903 imports rose in value to an unprecedented £15,3 million, largely due to the post-war reconstruction programmes under way in the former Boer republics.[29]

It soon became clear, however, that post-war southern Africa would realize few of the expectations of those who, in the late 1890s, had envisaged the emergence of a prosperous new British dominion. When this happened, Natal found herself grappling not only with the difficulty of financing its ambitious operations, but of coping with new social problems. In the rural districts, recurrent drought, locusts and the spread of tick-borne disease created havoc.[30] In the towns, and especially the port of Durban, there was social distress, evidenced in an increase in drunkenness and a rising crime rate.[31]

The recession experienced in Natal from 1903 until 1909 was due partly to the decline of war-time expenditure in the Colony and to the termination of the inflow of funds which had previously been directed towards the repatriation and resettlement of refugees. At the same time, heavy demands were being made upon the colonial exchequer for the provision of improved agricultural services, the prevention of cattle diseases, the replenishment of railway stores and the completion of refugee repatriation. Imports declined as disappointed merchants found themselves saddled with stockpiles of foreign goods for which there was not the anticipated demand, and the situation was aggravated by the dumping on the local market of surplus military stores.[32]

In addition to these depressed trade conditions, public revenues were further reduced and administrative costs increased by another outbreak in 1904 of east coast fever, followed by the Bambatha 'Rebellion' in 1906 (see Chapter 15). The efforts of the Veterinary Department to keep east coast fever under control were undone within a few weeks when refugees from the 'Rebellion' spread the disease by moving livestock into non-infected areas, while the military contributed further to the process through the use of ox-drawn transport in and around the affected regions. The problem was compounded by the sale by public auction in Natal of cattle looted in Zululand during the uprising. By 1910 the disease had spread to the most westerly and southerly reaches of the Colony, with devastating effects on many farms, while the practice of dipping livestock that arose out of the investigations of Dr Watkins-Pitchford and was so staunchly advocated by Joseph Baynes had only begun to have beneficial effects.[33]

The economic depression was also to a large extent tied to events in the Transvaal. There, the recovery and expansion of the gold-mining industry, upon which the economic and political future of the subcontinent depended, was hampered by a shortage of unskilled labour. A substitute was found in imported Chinese indentured labour, but the Transvaal economy continued to lag behind expectations. As serious from Natal's point of view was a movement, supported both by a significant section of the mining industry as well as by the predominantly Boer farming community, to implement a 'ring-wall' policy such as would end the free importation of goods to the Transvaal from the other southern African colonies as laid down in a 1903 Customs Agreement, the details of which had been hammered out at a Customs Conference in Bloemfontein.[34] The mine owners, furthermore, had soon realized that their best interest lay in close co-operation with Portuguese Mozambique, from whence mine labourers could more easily be obtained. For this reason, in 1901 the military government of the Transvaal had negotiated an agreement (the so-called 'modus vivendi' agreement) whereby, in return for the supply of unskilled labour, the Portuguese were assured that, pending the signing of a formal convention, goods in transit to the Transvaal would have equal treatment with, and pay no higher duties than, goods in transit from the Cape or Natal. The local manufactures of Mozambique would also be exempted from import duty.[35]

Because railway rates were already lower on the Lourenço Marques line, and as Mozambique produced sub-tropical products in competition with those of Natal, Natal's interests were obviously at stake. At the 1903 Customs Conference it had been agreed that the division of the Transvaal trade between the coastal colonies and the Portuguese would be settled at a railway conference to be held in Johannesburg in the following year. However, although agreement in principle was then reached among the four colonial governments, negotiations with the Portuguese remained in the hands of the British government and, while these were continuing, Lourenço Marques's share of the Transvaal traffic grew from 30 per cent to 60 per cent.[36] Confronted by a dramatic fall-off in customs and railway revenue, the Natal government was faced with the problem of financing the extravagant plans it had laid during the boom years. Some of it could be met by means of taking out further loans but it soon became obvious that a source of revenue other than customs and railway receipts would have to be found.

A further cause of the mounting public debt was military expenditure. The cost of conquering the two Boer republics induced the British government to attempt to extract war contributions from Natal and the Cape Colony, as well as from the Transvaal and Orange River Colonies. It was, furthermore, made clear to the Natal administration that the Colony would in future have to bear the burden of its own defence, as had been stipulated in the granting of responsible government in 1893. The colonial government was now bluntly informed that the imperial garrison would be withdrawn by the end of the following year unless its cost was met from colonial funds. A government commission was hastily appointed to enquire into the Colony's defences, while urgent representations were made to London, pointing out the likely effects that the disappearance of British soldiers would have on black as well as Boer attitudes.[37]

After a plan to introduce compulsory military service was rejected on the grounds that it was unprecedented in the Empire, the 1903 Militia Act was passed. It provided for an active militia of 3 500, composed of white volunteers and ballotees, and three reserve militias, the first consisting of men between seventeen and thirty, the second of men between thirty and forty and the third of men between forty and fifty. This force was equipped with modern rifles, while a number of field guns were purchased, ostensibly for naval defence but in the knowledge that they could be used in the event of a 'native' uprising. These arrangements, which involved considerable expenditure at a time when it could be ill-afforded by the Natal government, fell far short of what local military experts regarded as necessary for quelling internal unrest.[38]

There was a slight improvement in the economic condition of the Colony in 1906/7, but this tendency was abruptly reversed by the world-wide recession in 1907, after which the local depression deepened. Attempts to reduce public expenditure by means of various economies were undermined by the additional costs involved in counteracting the spread of east coast fever. An effort to increase revenues by means of new taxation met with only limited success, for while the £1 poll tax on all adult males other than indentured Indians and certain categories of Africans helped to balance the Colony's 1905–6 budget, it was also a cause of the Bambatha 'Rebellion' which involved the government in further expense (see Chapter 15). After four consecutive years of budgetary deficits, Natal's legislature was obliged to accept the implementation of additional direct taxation simply in order to maintain public revenues at the same level.[39] During 1909 there were at last some indications of an economic upswing, in the wake of a similar recovery in Britain. In his budget speech of that year, the Colonial Treasurer felt sufficiently optimistic to declare that Natal had 'successfully pulled through a most difficult time', to the extent that some of the recently imposed taxes might eventually be reconsidered.[40]

In 1908 the Colonial Treasurer attributed a decrease in revenues raised from customs duties to the growth of local industry. This had occurred despite widespread criticism that the customs union tariff of 1903 provided insufficient protection against foreign competition.[41] In October 1905 local

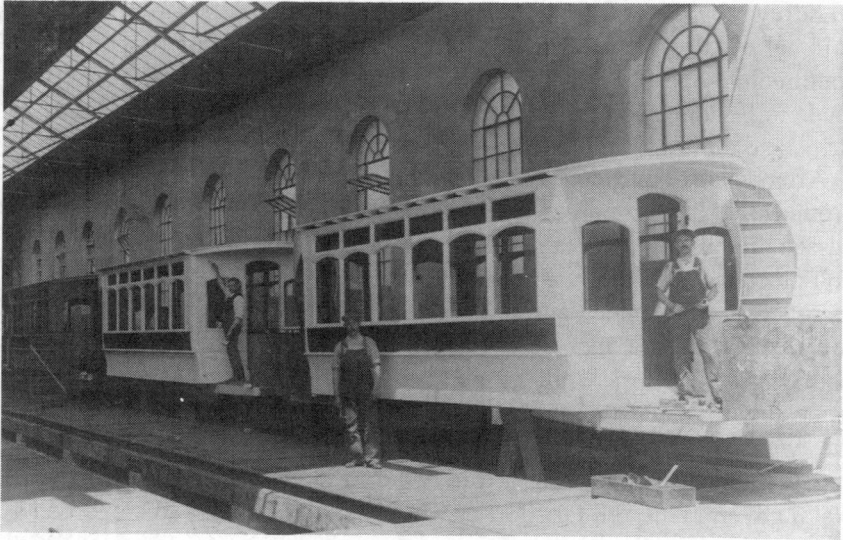

The construction of railway carriages and tramcars in Durban workshops brought many skilled artisans as immigrants to Natal after the Anglo-Boer War.

manufacturers, based largely in and around Durban, had already taken an important step towards promoting their collective interests by forming the Natal Manufacturers' Association, which was later to become the Natal Chamber of Industries. The variety of industries which the Association represented by 1910 provides some indication of the range of manufacturing activities which had been established by that time: engineering, baking, printing, coffee roasting, paints, mineral water, trunks and boxes, bricks and tiles, tent and sailmaking, tea merchants, stoves, castings and pots, preserves and canned fruit, soap and candles, matches, furniture, sugar refining, explosives, and chemicals, gates and wire, boots and leggings, biscuits, wagon and carriage builders, organ builders, saddles and harnesses, vinegar, druggists and joinery. Even so, by 1914 there were still no more than 500 manufacturing enterprises in Natal which ranked as 'factories' and the gross value of their output was less than £10 million a year.[42]

Towards the end of the colonial period, a new industry was launched when two Norwegians, Jacob J. Egeland (the consul in Durban) and Johan Bryde, formed the South African Whaling Company. In 1908 they began hunting off Durban with two whalers brought from Sandefjord. Their first whaling station was established on the Durban side of the Bluff, near the harbour entrance, but the nauseating odour produced and the large number of sharks attracted to what had previously been a popular picnic and bathing site led to public protests. This obliged them to re-locate their factory the following year on the ocean side of the Bluff, around which the whale carcasses were subsequently transported by train from the original slipway in the harbour. In 1909 Egeland withdrew from the partnership and, with his cousin Abraham Larsen, established the first British-financed whaling company in southern Africa, the Union Whaling and Fishing Company, which also operated from the Bluff. The new industry expanded rapidly, with 106 whales (mostly humpbacks) in 1908 producing 3 240 barrels of oil, 170 caught in 1909 and 532 in 1910. By 1912 there were thirteen whaling companies in Natal, although only six went into operation, and in that year over a thousand whales were brought in and 38 712 barrels of oil were produced.[43]

At the time of Union, the Natal whaling industry was obviously still in its infancy. By contrast, the local coal industry had already been in existence for two decades as a fairly large-scale commercial enterprise. Production was seriously disrupted in 1899 and 1900 by the Boer invasion of northern Natal. This not only forced the industry to close for six months but severely hampered its subsequent revival as a result of the damage inflicted on machinery and railway lines, and the looting of mine-stores and tools.[44]

Local History Museum, Durban

Durban's whaling industry was initiated by Norwegians – Jacob Egeland (left) is seen here with Captain Andersen of the whaler Omen, *the unidentified foreman of works and Abraham Larsen, Egeland's cousin.*

Electric coal-cutters greatly increased the output of Natal's coalmines after their introduction in the early 1900s. This photograph was taken at Elandslaagte Colliery, near Ladysmith, in 1903. (From the Commissioner of Mines Report, 1903.)

The most common method of working the coal deposits continued to be the pillar and stall (bord and pillar) system, based upon mining practice in the north of England and Scotland, whereby the coal is extracted leaving pillars, which are finally removed, allowing the roof to collapse. However, in the years immediately following the Anglo-Boer War, output was substantially increased by the introduction of American-made power-driven coal-cutters. The first of these was put into operation as early as 1899 at Elandslaagte and by 1909 there were 122 machines operating in fourteen Natal collieries, undercutting nearly 62 per cent of the industry's total annual output. Output was further improved by the introduction of mechanical haulages, which by 1909 were being used on the main roadways of virtually all producing collieries. Apart from power drills and pumps, very little machinery was used underground.[45]

During the first decade of the twentieth century there was also a noticeable improvement in the quality and variety of output following the installation of surface equipment for the sorting and cleaning of coal. By 1909 every producing colliery had a picking belt and ten of them were operating power-driven washing plants. Smaller sizes of coal, which constituted a significant percentage of gross output, could now be marketed. Gradually, as the consistency of the product improved, Natal coal lost its reputation for unreliability for steam-raising purposes.[46]

The speculative nature of the infant industry is reflected in the fact that more than sixty mines were opened between 1889 and 1909, yet over half had closed before Union due to inexperience, mismanagement and under-capitalization.[47] The financial performance of the surviving colliery companies varied considerably, with Natal Navigation and Elandslaagte yielding dividends as high as 20 per cent in 1902, when the collective dividend of the nineteen producing collieries was 6,56 per cent, on a combined total of £2 139 347 in paid-up capital, and 4,9 per cent and nil respectively in 1906, when eleven producing collieries paid a collective dividend of 2,71 per cent on £1 845 567.[48] Others, like the Dundee Coal Company, had a conservative long-term attitude towards profit-taking, arguing, as the chairman Benjamin Greenacre put it, that investors 'should be prepared to look to development as well as dividends'. In the pre-Union period most of the working collieries were locally owned, with the owners and directors usually resident in Durban, though several attracted British investment capital and the Dundee Coal Company even established a London as well as a Durban Board of Directors to facilitate the transfer of shares to English investors.[49]

Even though some collieries failed to produce, or closed within a few months, the new industry achieved an almost seventy-fold increase in output between 1889 (25 609 tons) and 1909 (1 786 583 tons), as well as an almost fourfold improvement in the output per man employed on 'productive' (i.e. non-developmental) work, from fifty-six tons per annum in 1889 to 222 tons in 1909.[50] The output of coal was obviously strongly influenced by market demand. The railways were initially a major consumer, amounting to 68 per cent of total output in 1889 but declining to 14,9 per cent in 1909, although the actual amount consumed increased steadily during that period.[51] There was fierce and often acrimonious competition among the collieries to supply the NGR, and also to secure trucks as and when needed to fulfill delivery contracts at both ends of the line. The shortage of trucks was a recurring problem, at its worst during and immediately after the Anglo-Boer War, as was traffic congestion on the single-track main line and the seasonal preferences accorded to the conveyance of perishable agricultural produce. The Colony's collieries successfully fulfilled the requirements of the Natal region but in 1909 domestic consumption (as distinct from that of the NGR) accounted for only 7,2 per cent of sales, less than half the NGR's 14,9 per cent. By that stage, the Overberg exportation of coal amounted to only 8,5 per cent of total consumption, for although the expanding Witwatersrand market initially promised to be very lucrative, Natal producers soon found themselves in unfavourable competition with the Transvaal collieries, which enjoyed the advantages of geographical proximity, a more plentiful labour supply and geologically more favourable mining conditions.[52]

Consequently, by the time of Union, the Natal coal industry had largely abandoned the inland trade to its Transvaal rival and was concentrating its marketing energies primarily on the export and bunker trade through Durban, which in 1909 accounted for 22,6 per cent and 46,8 per cent of sales respectively.[53] These markets were not easily developed, for although Natal's coal was of a quality superior to that of the Transvaal, it was already recognized that coal from the northern hemisphere was more effective for steam-raising purposes than any mined south of the equator because of the higher non-combustible ash content of southern coals and the differing nature of the vegetation in its original composition. Moreover, the resistance of vested British coal and steamship interests to the use of Natal coal had also to be overcome, after early samples used for bunkers off the Natal coast were found to contain a high percentage of clinker and ash, and had demonstrated a tendency to spontaneous combustion.[54]

The Union and Castle Companies, which merged in 1900 to form Union-Castle, conducted experiments with Natal coal over several years and initially concluded that it was suitable for coasters but could not be relied upon for their ocean-going steamers, which used Natal coal off the South African coast but bunkered coal from South Wales at Cape Town, where it was delivered by sailing vessels. It was only after the Union-Castle Company's largest liner, the *Kenilworth Castle*, completed the return journey to England entirely on Natal coal in 1907 that bunkering at Durban at last became a standard procedure for the mailships.[55]

Competition among the Natal collieries for export and bunker contracts (of which Union-Castle was only one) was understandably fierce, considering that collectively this trade already absorbed 32,4 per cent of the industry's output in 1898 and thereafter experienced a combined tenfold increase by 1909.[56] By 1901 coal had already become Natal's second largest export and from 1906 it was the largest. The industry owed a great deal to the efficiency and influence of the various shipping agents with which different collieries were associated: Bullard King and Co, J. T. Rennie and Sons, Lambert Bros., Mitchell Cotts and Co, and Mann George (SA) Ltd (a subsidiary of William Cory and Son Ltd of London).

The last named had assumed control of most of the coal trade through Durban by the end of 1909, in its capacity as agent for the Natal Coal Owners' Society formed in January of that year.[57] By then local coal was being marketed as far afield as the Cape Colony, India, Madagascar, Mauritius, Argentina and Singapore,[58] although the industry continued to struggle due to the variability of world prices and market demand, the fluctuating volume of shipping passing through Durban harbour, the cut-throat rivalry among colliery companies, the costs involved in transporting coal to the port, and the financial and physical hazards of mining.

While market demand was crucial to the survival of the Natal coal industry, so too was the provision of an adequate supply of labour. Prior to 1910 (and until the 1930s) the necessary skilled mine-labour and managerial expertise was drawn almost entirely from various parts of Britain. Skilled whites as a whole constituted only 11,1 per cent of the labour force employed on productive work in 1889 and as little as 4,53 per cent in 1909.[59] A high proportion of canny Scots were being appointed to manage collieries in an era when penny-pinching sometimes made the difference between closure and survival. In 1903 the colliery managers organized themselves into the Natal Mine Managers' Association, which soon proved to be an influential pressure-group within the industry.

In the recruitment of unskilled labour, upon which the coal industry relied heavily in view of its hand-got mining methods, it had to compete not only with the NGR and other local employers but, more seriously, with the Transvaal gold-mines which proved increasingly more successful in attracting unskilled black labour through higher wages (roughly 10 per cent more) and distinctly superior living and working conditions. Attempts to legislate against the recruitment of local labour for service outside Natal failed to stem the flow, while the Colony itself continued to cast an ever wider labour net into Mpondoland, Zululand, Swaziland and the Piet Retief district of the Transvaal.[60]

Several Natal collieries turned increasingly to indentured Indian labourers as a solution to the problem, on the grounds that, although considered physically weaker than Africans, they were more easily controlled, less prone to desertion and, after some training, more efficient.[61] After serving their indentures, Indians were usually encouraged to re-indenture or else to remain as 'free' employees of the collieries. Their numbers rose to as much as 44,5 per cent of the labour force employed on productive work in 1902, but declined to 40,83 per cent in 1909 as the drift into other more congenial avenues of employment gathered momentum and as the importation of indentured labourers approached its termination in 1911 (see Chapter 10). The employment of Indian women, primarily on the picking belts, followed a similar trend, amounting to 3,16 per cent of the industry's total work force in 1902 but only 1,14 per cent in 1909.[62]

The accommodation provided for white miners on Natal's collieries was spartan, while even less was spent on the housing and rations of Africans and Indians. In 1903 regulations were laid down regarding housing and sanitation, but unhygienic living conditions persisted well into the twentieth century, resulting in frequent outbreaks of disease and sometimes in death.[63] All mine employees shared the common hazard of death or injury by mining accident. Natal's early safety regulations were rudimentary and quite inadequate in view of the ever-present danger of firedamp (methane gas), coal dust and 'gob' fires.[64] Major explosions arising from these were not the most frequent type of serious accident experienced. The incidence of falls of mine roofs and worked coal, falls in shafts, accidents with coal-cutters and mechanical haulages, and surface mishaps were much higher. However, explosions such as those at St. George's Colliery in 1898, at New Campbell Colliery in 1901 and at the Glencoe and Cambrian Collieries in 1908 were invariably more dramatic, often involved many fatalities and usually prompted some improvements in the prevailing safety regulations.

Between 1897 and 1909 there were thirty-three such explosions and these were responsible for 146 of the 343 deaths which resulted from colliery accidents in Natal.[65] There was an overall decrease in the rate of death and injury from 17,94 to 12,19 per thousand,[66] though there was little room for complacency in view of the relative inexperience of the work-force, the deficiencies of mine overseers, many of whom had held menial posts in Britain, the willingness of some colliery owners to ignore safety measures in order to minimize costs and maximize output, and the inability of the under-staffed Mines Department to enforce what regulations existed as widely as it would have wished. The subsequent development of the still largely untouched Utrecht and Vryheid-Paulpietersburg coalfields following the extension of the railway line through Dundee to Vryheid, was to enlarge that task still further, though their deposits proved to be much more accessible and less fiery than those of Klip River.[67]

In 1904 a significant boost was given to the sugar industry by the report of the Zululand Delimitation Commission (see Chapter 8) which released

2 613 000 acres (more than a third of the territory) for white settlement.[68] This more than compensated for Natal's unsuccessful attempt to expand in a south-westerly direction when a bid to exploit the unrest in Mpondoland between the followers of chiefs Sigcau and Mhlangaza was abruptly terminated in 1894 by the British government's recognition of the Cape's right to annex and govern the region.[69]

The long-awaited opening of Zululand for white settlement enabled the local sugar industry to enter a new phase of sustained growth. In 1904 the Natal government established a Land Board, consisting of four representatives of the farming community and one government representative, to control the allocation of Crown land in the Natal-Zululand region. Prospective settlers were required to meet the cost of survey, to provide evidence that they possessed sufficient capital to launch themselves into farming, and to attend a formal interview in order to satisfy the Land Board that they were of the 'right type'. It was then the normal practice to require the purchase price to be repaid over twenty years, with the first payment being made at the end of the third year. In the case of Zululand, white farmers were allowed to acquire properties on 99-year lease at a rental of two shillings per acre for 'first-class' land in farm allotments of 300 to 400 acres, or of one shilling per acre in farms of between 400–500 acres that were designated as 'second class'. No rent was payable for the first two years of occupation but settlers were required to have at least £500 in capital and to bring at least 5 per cent of the land under cultivation during each of the first three years, thereafter maintaining at least 15 per cent of their respective properties under cultivation.[70]

The Zululand settlers were also required to sell their sugar cane to the concession mill which was erected in 1908 by J. L. Hulett at Amatikulu, where they were paid for their cane by weight delivered. This mill, built under government contract for the exclusive purpose of crushing for concession holders, proved so successful that Hulett was officially requested to erect another one on the Mhlathuze River. Known as the Felixton Mill, it came into operation in 1911 and had a milling capacity of thirty-five tons per hour compared to the Amatikulu's mill's thirty tons per hour.

Sugar farming in Zululand was initially impeded, first by the 1906 Bambatha 'Rebellion' and then by the outbreak of east coast fever, which necessitated the use of steam ploughs, mules and donkeys in place of oxen, but by 1908 between 6 000 and 7 000 acres had been brought under cultivation, producing an average yield of thirty tons per acre. There were

One of colonial Natal's most successful farmers was Sir James Liege Hulett (1838–1928). After experimenting with various crops, including arrowroot, maize, cotton and coffee, he developed his property Kearsney near Stanger into a productive tea estate (above), before rising to prominence in the local sugar industry. The Hulett family home (background) became the first Kearsney College between 1921 and 1939.

by then forty-seven 'first-class' and twenty-nine 'second-class' farms producing sugar, while the land in the low-lying malaria-ridden Umfolozi Block had been apportioned and farms in that region were already benefiting from the expertise provided by the government experiment station at Empangeni.[71] Immediately prior to Union, the Colony of Natal's annual output of cane was still only 86 790 tons but, with its expansion into Zululand, the local industry had entered a new and more complex era, and was poised for the dramatic changes which were to follow the First World War.[72]

In 1910, at the end of the colonial era, the Natal settlers looked with pride at the world they had made. Despite the economic depression of 1903–9, the mobilization of the Colony's manpower during the Bambatha 'Rebellion' and the rising level of Indian popular agitation, their self-confidence had scarcely faltered. What had once been an inhospitable corner of the African continent was now recognizably an extension of Europe.

What this view overlooked was that the smug well-to-do farmers and businessmen who dominated the small society were only a small part of the total population. Outside this successful clique income levels were low. The per capita income of whites in 1904 was £124 9s 10d, that of Indians £20 1s 0d and that of Africans £3 18s 6d.[73] The manufacturing sector was still mainly concerned with processing agricultural products and, although there was an increasing demand for sugar, maize and wattle bark, the agricultural sector was no more capable than before of giving any kind of impetus to the colonial economy as a whole.[74]

The apparent prosperity of the Colony therefore concealed the fact that there had been heavy overspending on capital works, that the transit trade and the hut tax remained the principal sources of revenue and that Natal's major industries, together with the lifestyle of its élite, depended upon cheap Indian and African labour.

Notes

1   The most comprehensive recent study of the Anglo-Boer War is T. Pakenham, *The Boer War* (Johannesburg, Jonathan Ball, 1979).

2   Pakenham, *Boer War*, p. 98.

3   C. H. Stott, *The Boer Invasion of Natal: Being an Account of Natal's Share in the Boer War of 1899–1900, as Viewed by a Colonist* (London, Partridge, 1900), pp. 35–44.

4   Pakenham, *Boer War*, pp. 133–41.

5   Ibid., pp. 168–9; Brookes and Webb, *History of Natal*, pp. 206–7.

6   E. M. G. Belfield, *The Boer War* (London, Leo Cooper, 1975), p. 46.

7   Stott, *Boer Invasion of Natal*, pp. 112–18; Pakenham, *Boer War*, p. 168–75.

8   Stott, *Boer Invasion of Natal*, pp. 219–20; P. Warwick, *Black People and the South African War*, 1899–1902 (Cambridge, Cambridge University Press, 1983), pp. 80–3.

9   Pakenham, *Boer War*, p. 267.

368   *White supremacy and black impoverishment*

10   H. R. Paterson, 'The Military Organisation of the Colony of Natal' (unpublished MA thesis, University of Natal, Durban, 1985), pp. 1–5.

11   P. Warwick, *Black People and the South African War,* pp. 87–9.

12   Pakenham, *Boer War*, p. 528–32; D. M. Moore, *General Louis Botha's Second Expedition to Natal* (Cape Town, Historical Publication Society, 1979).

13   Brookes and Webb, *History of Natal,* pp. 202–3.

14   See list of recipients of the Victoria Cross in L. Creswicke, *South Africa and the Transvaal War* (London, Blackwood,1900–2), 2, pp. 191–6.

15   Stott, *Boer Invasion of Natal*, pp. 214–24.

16   V. S. Harris, 'The Reluctant Rebels: the Impact of the Second Anglo-Boer War upon the Klip River Dutch Community, with Special Reference to the Dutch Community of Dundee' (BA Honours research essay, University of Natal, Pietermaritzburg, 1982), pp. 51–4.

17   Konczacki, *Public Finance and Economic Development*, pp. 54, 70–1; for a contemporary assessment of the effects of the war on Natal, see Stott, *Boer Invasion of Natal*, pp. 223–4.

18   R. Posel, '"A Modern Babylon": White Prostitution in Durban at the Turn of the Century' (Paper presented at ASSA Conference, Durban, 1986).

19   *Twentieth Century Impressions of Natal: its People, Commerce, Industries and Resources* (London, Lloyd's, 1906) pp. 67–83.

20   Konczacki, *Public Finance and Economic Development*, pp. 54–5, 72–3.

21   L. E. Neame, *Fifty Years of Progress: the Development of Industry in Natal, 1905–1955* (Durban, 1956), p. 16; Brookes and Webb, *History of Natal*, p. 214; Heydenrych, 'Port Natal Harbour', pp. 39–40.

22   Neame, *Fifty Years of Progress*, p. 16; Brookes and Webb, *History of Natal*, p. 214.

23   Steart, 'Coal in Natal', pp. 77–8.

24   *Official Year Book of the Union of South Africa, 1910–22*, p. 733; Brookes and Webb, *History of Natal*, pp. 162, 252.

25   *Blue Books for the Colony of Natal (Departmental Reports)*, Annual Report of the General Manager of Railways, 1904, pp. 9, 15–17; Konczacki, *Public Finance and Economic Development*, p. 23.

26   *Twentieth Century Impressions of Natal, passim*; A. H. Tatlow, *Natal Province: Descriptive Guide and Official Hand-Book* (Durban, South African Railways Printing Works, 1911).

27   M. W. Swanson,'"The Durban System": Roots of Urban Apartheid in Colonial Natal', *African Studies*, 35 (1976), pp. 159–176.

28   *BPP* LXIX of 1902 (Cd. 1163): *Further Correspondence re Affairs in South Africa*, pp. 5ff.

29   Konczacki, *Public Finance and Economic Development*, pp. 54–5, 72–3.

30   Ballard, 'The Repercussions of Rinderpest'.

31   *Report of an Official Inquiry into the Prison System of the Colony* (Pietermaritzburg, 1907) p. 21.

32   Konczacki, *Public Finance and Economic Development*, pp. 55–56, 75.

33   Union Government Report, No. 17 of 1944: East Coast Fever Commission, pp. 7–8; Pearse, *Joseph Baynes*, pp. 86–9; Brookes and Webb *History of Natal*, p. 215.

34   P. Richardson, *Chinese Mine Labour in the Transvaal* (London, Macmillan, 1982); A. H. Jeeves, *Migrant Labour in South Africa's Mining Economy: the Struggle for the Gold Mines' Labour Supply, 1890–1920* (Johannesburg, Witwatersrand University Press, 1985).

35   Katzenellenbogen, *South Africa and Southern Mozambique*, pp. 50–1.

36   Ibid., pp. 90–1.

37   Paterson, 'Military Organisation', p. 64.

38   Ibid., pp. 101–2.

39   Konczacki, *Public Finance and Economic Development*, pp. 57, 78, 82, 84.

40   Ibid., *Public Finance and Economic Development*, p. 57.

41   Ibid., pp. 57, 78.

42   Neame, *Fifty Years of Progress*, pp. 7, 17–18, 23–9; Brookes and Webb, *History of Natal*, p. 252.

43   For an account of the local whaling industry, see R. Gambell, 'A Short History of Modern Whaling off Natal', *Mercurius*, 14 (1971), pp. 37–44.

44   *Annual Reports of the Commissioner of Mines*, 1889–1909; Commissioner of Mines Records (Dundee), Files 126 and 149/1900: Correspondence re War Damage.

45   *Annual Reports of the Commissioner of Mines*, 1899–1909.

46   *Annual Reports of the Commissioner of Mines*, 1899, 1903, 1905, 1908, 1909; Commissioner of Mines Records (Dundee), File 550/910: Commissioner of Mines, 'Natal Mining', n.d., p. 3; GN No. 1, 1899: Natal Government Coal Commission Report of 1898, p. 6.

47   *Annual Reports of the Commissioner of Mines*, 1888–1909.

48   *Annual Reports of the Commissioner of Mines*: 1902, p. 49; 1903, p. 62; 1906, p. 75; 1909, p. 66.

49   GN No. 1, 1899: *Natal Government Coal Commission Report of 1898*, p. 4; Commissioner of Mines Records (Dundee), File 142/1905: Deputy Commissioner of Mines to Commissioner of Mines, 23 February 1905, enclosing list of secretaries and owners of Natal coal companies; Union Mines Department *Annual Report* for 1911, Section VII General, pp. 26–7; NA Dundee Coal Co Ltd. Minutes, Board of Directors, Add. 1/2: 9 November 1894 and 11 January 1895; 1/1/2, Annual Report, 30 September 1903.

50   *Annual Reports of the Commissioner of Mines*, 1889–1909.

51   *Annual Reports of the Commissioner of Mines*, 1889–1909; Commissioner of Mines Records (Dundee), file 400/1899: Report on official coal statistics, *Natal Mercury*, 22 July 1899.

52   *Debates of the Legislative Assembly*, 1902, pp. 338/9, 348/9, 371–8, 401, 557–560; *Annual Reports of the Commissioner of Mines*, 1900, 1901, 1902, 1909; J. McPhee, 'Coal in the Transvaal' (Paper presented to the third (Triennial) Empire Mining and Metallurgical Congress, South Africa, 1930).

53   *Annual Report of the Commissioner of Mines*, 1909; Ballard, 'Vital and Economic Statistics', *passim*.

54   R. Tavener-Smith, *Coal in Natal* (Inaugural Lecture) (Pietermaritzburg, University of Natal Press, 1973), pp. 8–9; PA K154: *1946/47 Coal Commission on the Past and Present Coal Position in South Africa and Future Prospects of the Industry*, p. 9; *Inter-Departmental Base Mineral Committee Report on 'The Export Coal and the Natal Coal Industry'*, 31 October 1935.

55   M. Murray, *Union Castle Chronicle, 1853–1953* (London, Longmans, Green, 1953), pp. 277–9.

56   *Annual Reports of the Commissioner of Mines*, 1898–1909.

57   *Annual Reports of the Commissioner of Mines*, 1901 and 1906; Ballard, 'Vital and Economic Statistics', *passim*; KCAL: Otto Siedle Papers: 'A Brief History of the Formation of the Natal Coal Owners' Society' (typescript); Talana Museum, Dundee: Natal Coal Owners' Society Minutes, 20 January 1909, pp. 1–5; PA K154: *Union Government Coal Commission of 1946–1947*, Minutes, Evidence and Correspondence, 4; 'Memorandum on the Past and Present Coal Position in South Africa and the Future Prospects of the Industry', submitted by African Coaling and Exporting Co Ltd, pp. 20, 24–6.

58   Commissioner of Mines Records (Dundee), File 550/1910: Commissioner of Mines, 'Natal Mining', n.d., pp. 3–4; Steart, 'Coal in Natal', p. 77.

59   *Annual Reports of the Commissioner of Mines, 1889–1909.*

60   *Supplement to the Blue Book for the Colony of Natal*: Annual Report of the Commissioner of Mines, 1889, p. H65; *Debates of the Legislative Asembly*, 1896, pp. 107–8, 485–6, 516, 545–6; 1901, pp. 106–18, 622–3; 1903, pp. 46–9, 97–9, 102, 221–4, 392–6; 1904, pp. 489–99; 1904, pp. 186–7, 601; 1907, pp. 503–20, 585–601, 622–34, 641; GN No. 1, 1899: *Natal Government Coal Commission Report of 1898*, pp. 4, 10.

61   *Annual Reports of the Commissioner of Mines*, 1889, p. H65, 1898, p. 5; 1901, p. 4.

62   *Annual Reports of the Commissioner of Mines*, 1889–1909; NA SNA 3686/1909: Report by Secretary for Native Affairs on visit to Natal Collieries to ascertain causes of labour shortage.

63   *Natal Mines Act, 1899*: pp. 15–16, Labour, Sanitation etc; *Annual Report of the Protector of Indian Immigrants* and *Annual Reports of the Health Officer*, 1903–1909; *Annual Reports of the Commissioner of Mines*, 1903–1909; Commissioner of Mines Records (Dundee), File 190/1903: 'Employment of Indian Immigrants at the Local Mines of the Colony'.

64   *Annual Reports of the Commissioner of Mines*: 1889, p. H65 and 1909, p. 26; *Natal Mines Act, 1899*, pp. 27–67. 'Firedamp' is a gas composed of carbon and hydrogen which, when mixed with air in sufficient quantities, is explosive. Its presence in a mine is not readily detectable as it is colourless, tasteless and odourless. When pillars are extracted in pillar and stall mines, the roof falls in and closes behind the excavation, creating what is called a 'gob'. If coal is left behind in the gob it is crushed by the weight of the strata above, heat is generated and, if oxygen is present, a fire can result. This creates the danger of carbon monoxide spreading through the mine. See A. Lupton, *Mining: an Elementary Treatise on the Getting of Minerals* (London, Longmans, Green, 1889), p. 255; Steart, 'Coal in Natal', pp. 24–9.

65   *Annual Reports of the Commissioner of Mines*: 1898, p. H110; 1901, pp. 15, 23–7; 1907/8, pp. 13–14; NGG Supplement, 22 December 1908, GN No. 732, 1908: *Report of the Glencoe Colliery Enquiry Commission*, pp. 1140/1.

66   *Annual Reports of the Commissioner of Mines, 1897–1909.*

67   *Annual Reports of the Commissioner of Mines*: 1906, pp. 6–7; 1907/8, p. 7; 1909, pp. 7, 51; Steart, 'Coal in Natal', pp. 24–9.

68   Eybers, *Select Constitutional Documents*, pp. 216–17; *Blue Book for the Colony of Natal (Departmental Reports)*, 1905: Report by the Joint Imperial and Colonial Commissioners of the Zululand Lands Delimitation Commission, 1902–1904, Final Reports, 18 October 1904, p. 46; Marks, *Reluctant Rebellion*, pp. 120–43; Richardson, 'The Natal Sugar Industry', p. 194.

69   A. M. Hutton, 'Pondoland: her Cape and Natal Neighbours, 1878–1894'
      (unpublished MA thesis, University of the Witwatersrand, 1935) *passim*;
      Davenport, *South Africa: a Modern History*, p. 99.

70   Tatlow, *Natal Province*, pp. 426–7, 431.

71   Osborn, *Valiant Harvest*, p. 195; Osborn, *This Man of Purpose*, pp. 73–81;
      Tatlow, *Natal Province*, pp. 431–4.

72   Richardson, 'The Natal Sugar Industry', p. 194; Osborn, *Valiant Harvest*,
      p. 93.

73   Konczacki, *Public Finance and Economic Development*, pp. 3–6, 27–8,
      175.

74   Konczacki, *Public Finance and Economic Development*, pp. 5–6, 175,
      183–99.

Chapter 15

From independence to rebellion
African society in crisis, *c.* 1880–1910

JOHN LAMBERT

Prior to white settlement, the African economy was centred around the homestead. Although there were exchanges of grain and livestock between homesteads, Africans cultivated crops and herded cattle primarily to provide for the needs of their own homesteads. A part of their surpluses could, however, be exchanged for specialist commodities such as ironware, baskets and pottery. As each homestead was required to pay tribute to its chief, there was a diversion of both produce and labour from the homestead to the chief. The chief controlled access to land and therefore was able to control the productive and reproductive resources of each homestead to a certain extent (see Chapter 3). African society had been profoundly affected by the rise of the Zulu kingdom and the devastation this caused. Chiefs were killed, homesteads destroyed, and most chiefdoms were dispersed. Even south of the Thukela, where a number of chiefdoms survived, their economic viability was undermined by excessive Zulu demands for labour and produce. By 1824, there were few cattle left in this region and very little grain was being produced. The surviving Africans were driven to seek refuge in broken and inaccessible tracts of land.[1]

When the British hunter-traders established themselves at Port Natal in 1824, Africans began congregating around the port. In return for protection, they had to provide the hunter-traders with produce and hides (see Chapter 5). By 1834 there were an estimated 6 000 refugees at Port Natal and in 1843 Henry Cloete commented that they were able to meet Durban's food requirements.[2]

After Shaka's assassination in 1828, Dingane abandoned much of Natal and the remnants of the original chiefdoms slowly began to return. This was hastened by the arrival of the Trekkers and the defeat of Dingane in

1838 (see Chapters 4 and 5). By 1843, Major T. C. Smith, the officer commanding the British force which took over Durban from the Trekkers in 1842, was able to refer to a 'superabundant population of the native tribes . . . and that from a very natural cause, viz., the protection they obtain and the profit they derive by finding a ready market for the grain and vegetables they cultivate'.[3] In return for supplying the Trekkers and settlers with produce, the Africans received livestock, particularly sheep and goats, and also a number of cattle.

By 1848 Shepstone (see Chapter 7) estimated that there were sixty-five chiefdoms in Natal. These consisted of the survivors of original chiefdoms which had retained their organization, of fragments of chiefdoms which had merged, or of refugees.[4] The surviving chiefs, or men who had taken advantage of the destruction of the dominant lineage to gain the chieftainship, had been able to reconstruct the tribal basis of society. They exacted labour services, particularly in their gardens, and extracted tribute. The more powerful among them recreated the *amabutho* or age-group regiments in an attempt to control the military services of their men.[5] A number of chiefs, such as Phakade, built up power by offering protection to refugees. As many refugees brought cattle with them, they strengthened the economic position of the chiefdoms they joined.[6]

Chiefs with *amabutho* were allowed to bring them together for the celebration of the First Fruits ceremony. The holding of this ceremony emphasized the authority of the chief within the chiefdom but, as it could only be held with official permission, it also symbolized the chief's position *vis-à-vis* the government. This could work to the chief's advantage. Teteleku of the Phumuza chiefdom, for example, used the First Fruits ceremony to maintain his authority over his widely-scattered followers.[7] Government support also enabled the appointed chief, Ngoza, to aquire considerable power. As a result, he attracted followers, so that by 1864 his chiefdom was larger than that of any hereditary chief.[8]

In general, however, the authority of most of the chiefs was weakened by the fragmented nature of the chiefdoms. The poor quality of the soil in most of the locations meant that they were unable to support the whole African population. A chief's people were, therefore, often scattered on location, crown and private land. In 1851 Shepstone estimated that two-thirds continued to live on private and crown lands. By 1881, there were 169 800 Africans on location and mission lands, compared to 162 606 on private lands and 42 600 on crown lands.[9]

The failure of the location system to segregate all Africans from the settler community had considerable economic advantages for the Colony. British rule had established an organized government in Natal and had been accompanied by the growth of urban and village centres. With these came the need to provide food for the towns and villages, to provide revenue for the administration, and to provide labour for the settlers and the government.

Had Natal become a colony of large-scale white settlement and intensive agriculture, these needs could have been met by the whites themselves. But the exodus of large numbers of Trekkers and the failure of immigration schemes to generate a prosperous British agricultural community, resulted in vast tracts of land being owned by absentee landlords and land speculation companies, such as the Natal Land and Colonization Company. Until the 1880s, most of the capital attracted to the Colony was invested in land speculation and in activities such as the transit trade to the interior, rather than in the development of new patterns of agriculture.[10] Furthermore, between the 1840s and the 1880s, almost half of the Colony's white population lived in Pietermaritzburg and Durban (13 859 of 30 198 in 1882).[11] Of those whites who were farmers, the majority, particularly in the Midlands and the interior, were involved in stock farming. In order to feed the white population, the development of the African peasantry was therefore encouraged.

African crop production was not only stimulated by market opportunities and by the attraction of augmenting herds. It was also necessitated by the financial demands made on Africans by both the colonial authorities and the white landowners. With the agricultural and industrial resources of the Colony undeveloped, it was tempting for the government to use African revenue to bolster its finances by means of the hut tax and indirect taxation on items which were used mostly by Africans (see Chapter 7).

In districts close to white settlement, there was thus a remarkable flowering of the homestead economy. As early as 1850, J. E. Methley, who had visited Natal and Zululand two years previously, referred to 'potatoes of several kinds, Indian and Kaffir corn, beans, fruits and a variety of other vegetables' being sold by Africans who, 'having no European competition to contend with, are beginning to find that the trade of a market gardener is one of the most lucrative'.[12] Two years later, the magistrate of Mpafana location referred to Africans as 'the only real peasantry of South Africa'.[13] African hawkers also provided the inhabitants of the towns with most of their supplies of fowls, eggs, milk and firewood.[14]

In the rural districts, too, and particularly in northern Natal, the specialization in stock farming and in wool production resulted in an inadequate grain crop on most white-owned farms and African cultivators provided the maize requirements of the farmers.

Between 1850 and 1880, there was a considerable increase in the amount of land cultivated by Africans and in the crops reaped. Although official statistics dealing with Africans in the nineteenth century must be approached with the greatest caution, the figures for 1867 (the first year in which statistics of African production were published) and 1882 attest to the increase. In the former year, the total area reaped by Africans was approximately 36 445 hectares and in the latter approximately 113 028. To a large extent, this was made possible by the eagerness with which cultivators adopted new agricultural implements such as ploughs. By 1872, Africans owned 1 122 ploughs and by 1882 this number had risen to 8 296.[15]

During the early years of British rule, the Africans also used the opportunities afforded by the market to increase their cattle holdings, so that by 1867 they possessed 301 934 head.[16] These purchases increasingly involved them in extra-colonial trade. Zululand was an obvious area from which to purchase cattle and in 1850 cattle were being bought there for as little as 25 shillings a head.[17] Livestock could also be obtained from Mpondoland. By the 1860s, Africans were involved in a trade network involving grain and livestock as far afield as the Orange Free State and the Cape.[18]

The growing prosperity of African agriculturalists was also encouraged by the fact that absentee landowners, who by 1880 owned just under 400 000 of the over two million hectares which had been acquired by whites, began to encourage squatting. With the price of land remaining low, there was little incentive for the land companies and other speculators to dispose of their lands. Instead, they looked to rent from African squatters as a way of making a profit. Despite the existence of Law 2 of 1865 which restricted the number of Africans squatting on a private farm to three families, by the 1880s landowners were encouraging squatting and were charging annual rentals ranging from £2 to £10 per hut.[19]

Although the exactions of government and landowners were considerable, the price of grain was high in the 1860s and 1870s, so that many Africans could meet the demands upon them with relative ease. This statement is more generally true of the areas that were close to the urban centres than it is of the outlying districts, particularly the more remote locations and crown lands, which were frequently arid and where there was no access to markets and where few traders operated. In these areas, the Africans were commonly drawn into the labour market, because they needed cash to buy food in times of shortage, because they had to pay the annual hut tax, or because they could convert their wages into traditional forms of wealth.

There was a constant demand from white Natal for labour. An *isibalo* or forced labour system existed whereby each chief was required to supply a certain number of men to work on the Colony's roads each year. Although this system was justified by Shepstone on the grounds that Africans traditionally supplied their chiefs with labour, it was a constant source of grievance because the rate of pay, between ten and twenty shillings in 1881, was lower than that obtainable on the open labour market.[20]

By far the greatest amount of labour was supplied by labour tenants on white farms, the custom being for farmers to allow homesteads on their farms on condition that its inhabitants provided labour. This occurred particularly in northern Natal, where there were few locations from which wage-labour could be drawn. The homestead head usually agreed that his sons would supply six months' labour each year at a nominal wage. During key periods, such as weeding and harvesting, all inhabitants had to provide labour without payment.[21]

Labour contracts were seldom in written form and this worked to the farmers' advantage. Many of them were able to insist upon periods of labour exceeding the normal six months, thus making it difficult for the tenants to seek work elsewhere. Friction frequently developed within homesteads as well as between homestead heads and farmers as a result of the inability of homestead heads to compel their men to work.

Labour tenants were generally unable to share in the prosperity enjoyed by the independent homestead producers. One reason for this was that the tenants were required to work for the farmers at precisely those times of the year when they should have been working their own gardens. This often meant that they were unable to plant more than the minimum needed for subsistence. Where surpluses could be planted, many farmers insisted on the right of refusal of the crop at a nominal price. Many tenants were also discouraged from investing in new agricultural implements for their own use because farmers frequently charged a rental for every plough used on their land. Insecurity of tenure also meant that they were reluctant to improve their position because of possible eviction.[22]

Despite these drawbacks, labour tenancy worked adequately until the

1880s. This was due not only to the fact that the price of agricultural commodities remained high, for it was often the case that tenants enjoyed a considerable degree of independence. On the stock farms of the interior, for example, very little land was required by the owners for cultivation. Many farmers had both winter and summer grazing farms and allowed their tenants virtually unrestricted use of their winter grazing farms.[23] The attraction of such tenancies must have been very considerable, particularly as it would have afforded men the opportunity to break free from the authority of their chiefs at a time when the chiefs were struggling to maintain their control over land allocation.

Until the 1880s, the majority of Africans were able to adapt to the colonial economy without abandoning their traditional methods of agriculture and without serious dislocation of the homestead economy. This is suggested by the fact that maize and sorghum continued to be the main crops, in 1882 accounting for 108 347 of a total of 113 028 hectares reaped by African producers.[24]

Changes were, however, occurring within the homestead economy. The introduction of the plough meant that men were becoming more involved in agriculture than they had been in the past. By enabling certain homesteads to cultivate far greater tracts of land, the plough also encouraged a growing differentiation between rich and poor. This happened particularly near the towns and villages, where it was easy to dispose of surplus produce. In these areas, large herds were built up through the proceeds of grain sales and, as cattle could be invested as lobola, polygyny flourished among wealthy homestead heads.[25]

One group of peasants in particular brought about changes in the homestead economy. They were the relatively few mission-educated *kholwa*, who by 1881 numbered approximately 7 500 individuals (see Chapter 11).[26] The growing prosperity of this community of wealthy African agriculturalists is shown by the increasing amount of freehold land they owned.[27] After 1880 it became possible for the public to purchase crown lands of the Colony on extended credit of ten years at an upset price of ten shillings an acre. The government was prepared to allow, and in fact encouraged, Africans to tender and syndicates of Africans, normally but not always *kholwa*, found it relatively easy to raise the amount for the initial instalment.[28] Although not all the purchasers were able to meet their annual payments and their lands therefore reverted to the Crown, the amount of land owned by Africans increased steadily. In 1877 they owned 33 631 hectares and by 1890 this had risen to 83 656 hectares.

It is true that, in some cases, the purchasers had no intention of farming the land other than by traditional means. Yet, in many cases these sales provided additional opportunities for the growth of a progressive peasantry and contributed to the development of colonial agriculture. This is particularly true as far as the *kholwa* were concerned. They used their access to European education and the market economy to restructure a life-style in which traditional values were replaced by those of the colonists. Their abandonment of tribal customs and obligations was particularly evident in their attitude to cattle, which they were prepared to hire or sell in order to buy land. Their abandonment of polygyny also reduced the need for lobola cattle and encouraged them to view livestock as having a market rather than a social value.[29]

There was constant friction between the independent 'westernized' African farmers, especially the *kholwa*, and the traditional Africans. This is particularly true of the chiefs, who were finding by the early 1880s that their position was steadily weakening. Despite the support Shepstone had given to chieftainship, the deposition of chiefs such as Sidoyi and Langalibalele (see Chapter 6) had shown that there were limits to their power. Furthermore, over 40 per cent of the chiefs were appointed and were without hereditary authority, while even the hereditary chiefs found that their authority was diminished by the fact that succession was dependent upon appointment by the Supreme Chief, the Governor.

By the 1870s, the chiefs had in fact become salaried officials. Their salaries were minimal (from £6 to £30 per annum in 1896) and this stressed their subordinate position. The government had also encouraged the fragmentation of the chiefdoms. Thus, by 1882, there were 173 chiefs in Natal compared to the sixty-five of 1852 and, of these, only thirty-eight had more than 700 huts under their control.[30] Chiefly authority was further undermined by the appointment of headmen or indunas over the scattered portions of various chiefdoms. Although these individuals were appointed by and remained responsible to the chiefs, they were often encouraged by the magistrates to defy the authority of their chiefs.

The presence of a magistrate in each division had also served to undermine a chief's authority, for the decisions of his court overrode those of the chief. The Native Administration Act of 1875, furthermore, deprived chiefs of jurisdiction in all criminal cases and required them to report all civil judgements to their magistrate.[31] Africans were quick to realize where real power lay and, by 1881, despite dissatisfaction with conditions in the magistrates' courts, they were taking cases to them rather than to the chiefs.[32] As Msutu told the 1881 Native Affairs Commission, 'The magistrate is really our chief'.[33]

The chiefs were not only faced by the gradual whittling away of their power by the administrative structure to which they belonged; the shortage of land meant that they were losing their ability to distribute it and so control the productive and reproductive resources of their chiefdoms. This, in turn, further undermined their authority as whole homesteads began to question the need to provide tribute or services if they received nothing in return. In many cases, even men in the locations were refusing to render tribute or service, while those on private lands were virtually free of chiefly jurisdiction. The drastic decline in the authority of the chiefs was to be seen in the fact that only a handful of chiefs actively retained the *amabutho* system. By 1881, chiefs like Mnini, Kukulela and Mganu were disbanding regiments because of their inability to feed the men at the First Fruits ceremony.[34]

The decline in the power of the chiefs was paralleled by that of the homestead head. Prior to white rule, a homestead normally broke up only on the death of its head, but now there was growing fragmentation as young men married and established their own homesteads by means of the opportunities offered by migrant labour or by moving on to white farms. This process was accelerated by regulations in 1869 which stipulated that no more than ten head of cattle could be given for a commoner's daughter. Paradoxically, while this strengthened the young men's chances of marrying and so encouraged the fragmentation of the homestead, it led to a decrease in the number of wives belonging to each homestead. This was because the fragmentation of the homestead led to a reduction in the size of cattle herds in each of them, thus reducing the potential for a man to have a large number of wives. After 1870, the number of polygamous marriages steadily declined: in 1871 4,9 per cent of marriages were of fifth wives or upwards; by 1880 this had dropped to 3,3 per cent and by the early twentieth century it averaged 0,9 per cent per annum. Between 1870 and 1909 the number of first marriages increased from 55,8 per cent to 70 per cent of the total marriages.[35]

The decline in the authority of chiefs and homestead heads was symptomatic of a growing crisis in African society. In the second half of the 1870s, a series of droughts caused crop failures while many herds were devastated by lungsickness and redwater fever. At the same time, a growing dependence by Africans on European-made products, and the need to find money for taxes and rents, meant that an increasing number of

Africans were raising their money by selling, not their surplus grain, but food they themselves needed to keep for times of dearth. This resulted in hunger and in the need to buy grain later in the season, when prices were inflated. The need to find money to replenish grain supplies led, in the more arid areas, to a steady increase in the number of men becoming migrant labourers.[36]

The extent of this growing crisis was masked by the Anglo-Zulu War of 1879, during which the presence of the military led to a general increase in wages, while it also inflated the price of oxen and created opportunities for wagon-hire. Magisterial reports between 1879 and 1882 thus refer to general prosperity, and contain references to the purchase of cattle from Zululand to restock herds depleted by disease in the 1870s.[37]

Despite this, a rise in land values and the opening of the crown lands for sale meant that Africans were beginning to find it more difficult to obtain access to private and crown lands as squatters. At the same time, there was a marked increase in the African population in the locations, from 113 000 in the 1850s to 169 800 in 1881.[38] As the increased demand for food was seldom met by the adoption of new agricultural techniques, the rapid exhaustion of existing agricultural lands forced encroachment onto grazing lands, the resultant over-grazing on the remaining pastures leading, in turn, to a deterioration in the quality of the livestock. To feed the growing population, the Colony's game and wild vegetational resources became rapidly depleted, making the African's diet less balanced than it had been.

Although migrant labour had to some extent bolstered the peasant economy, enabling it to survive these early crises, in the longer term it served to undermine traditional society. This was immediately seen in an increase in crime. Removed from tribal restraints in the towns and other labour centres, Africans were often susceptible to detrimental influences, so that criminal offences were becoming more common, while prostitution was becoming widespread in the towns.[39] In the rural areas, there was a marked increase in stock thefts and faction fights.

The growing crisis in African society was accelerated by the development of the Witwatersrand gold-fields after 1886. Apart from drawing off labour to the mines, it stimulated demands for labour in the Colony itself, for it led to the opening up of the Natal coalfields and the accelerated growth of the towns (see Chapter 12). The granting of responsible government (see Chapter 9) meant that the Natal administration was no longer subject to imperial control and was more

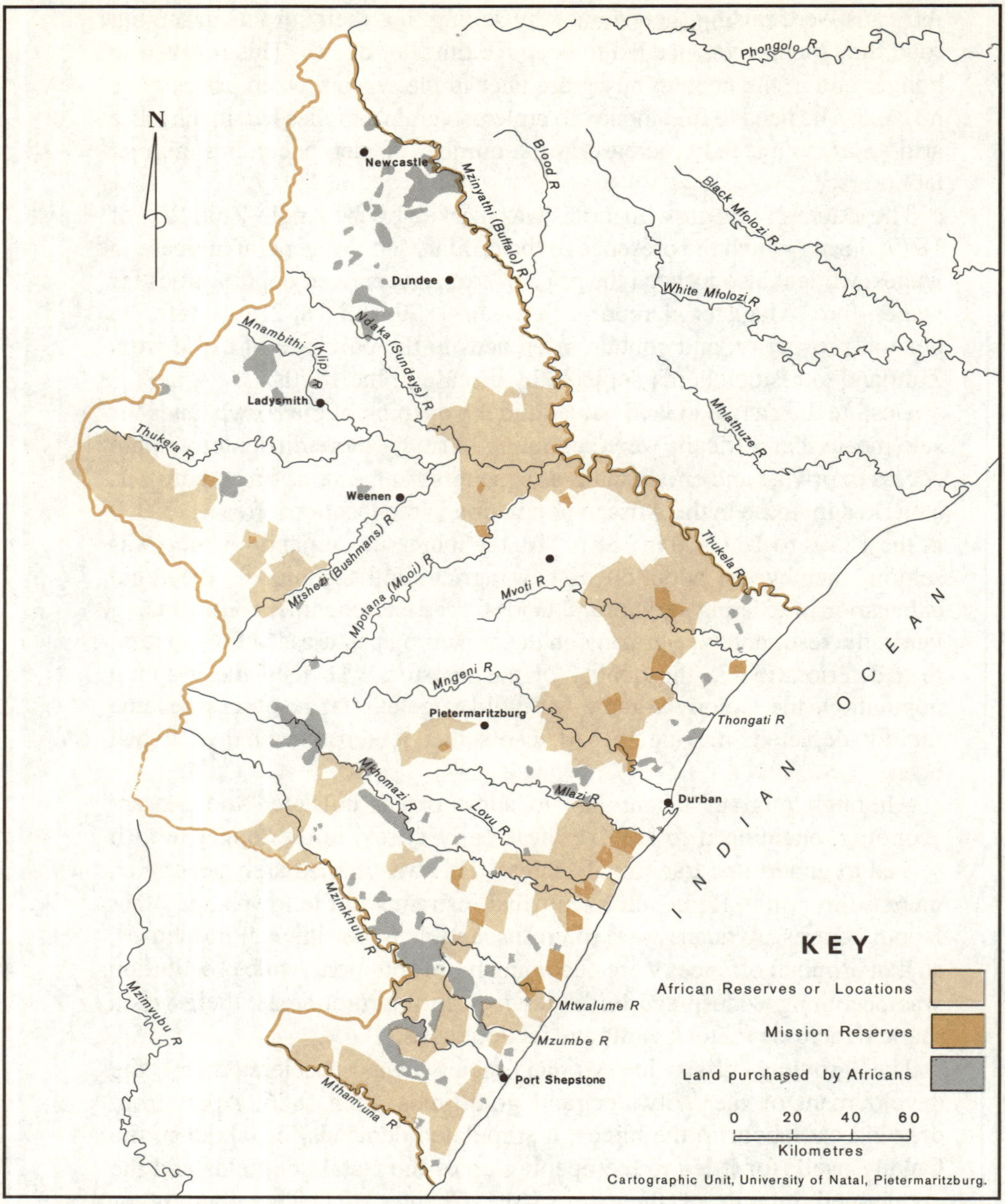

KEY

African Reserves or Locations

Mission Reserves

Land purchased by Africans

0   20   40   60
Kilometres

Cartographic Unit, University of Natal, Pietermaritzburg.

Map 22   Land occupied by Africans in Natal, 1905

susceptible to the demands of local pressure groups. With representation in the colonial Parliament heavily weighted in favour of the agricultural interests, it was difficult for any government between 1893 and 1910 to ignore the farmers. This was important because these years saw a significant new phase in farming as an increasing number of white farmers, responding to the increased demand for agricultural commodities, turned to the cultivation of foodstuffs (see Chapter 12). The result is seen in a dramatic increase in the amount of land on white farms on which crops were reaped, from 23 387 hectares in 1882 to 46 787 in 1895 to 166 642 in 1909.[40]

As white farming developed in this way, hostility towards the independent black producers showed a marked increase. One reason for this was that they were now seen as competitors for the colonial market; another was that squatting was no longer viewed as a profitable utilization of the land; a third was that the existence of a class of independent black producers seemed to stand in the way of the flow of labour from the black areas to white farms. The result was first seen in a rising demand for legislation to prevent Africans from purchasing land or squatting on white-owned land, while white farmers increasingly demanded labour from their tenants in lieu of rent and evicted those who were not prepared to comply with their demands.[41]

The first two responsible government ministries, headed by Robinson and Escombe, tended to pay more attention to urban, mercantile and mining interests than to farming. After 1897, however, farmers formed a majority in all Cabinets, where they could exert considerable influence. This was seen in the introduction of legislation to deprive Africans of access to land, to destroy their independence and to make it difficult for them to work outside the Colony. Among these enactments was the 1901 Labour Touts Act, which prohibited any person from touting for labour for use outside the Colony.[42] In the same year, the Act 'to Facilitate the Identification of Native Servants' provided that all Africans other than labour tenants had to possess an identification pass.[43] Many farmers were able to use this to tie their tenants to the land by refusing to allow them to obtain passes to work away from their farms.[44] In 1903, the Natal Native Trust, which since 1895 had been responsible for the mission reserves, levied a tax of £3 on every hut, while the government raised the annual hut tax paid by squatters on crown lands from £1 to £2.[45] These measures had the effect of forcing many Africans on to the labour market.

In 1903–4 individual purchases in the mission reserves were prohibited and the sale of crown lands to Africans was discontinued.[46] For the *kholwa*, against whom this legislation was specifically aimed, this was only part of a series of disasters that had followed the introduction of responsible government. Although 1 334 *kholwa* had been exempted from the observation of customary law by 1894,[47] in that year the Appeal Court ruled that exemption only released an African from the observance of tribal customs and did not give him a position of equality with Europeans. In 1905 the Native High Court ruled that children born to exempted parents would in future not themselves be exempted.[48]

Following the introduction of responsible government in 1893, a series of measures rapidly whittled away most of the remaining powers of the chiefs. In 1894 the appointment of headmen by chiefs was made subject to the approval of the magistrates, and in 1896 the government was given the power to remove them from office.[49] At the same time, the authority of chiefs in cases dealing with faction fights was replaced by that of the magistrates, while their right to manage their people in the locations was curtailed in 1896 when the Governor-in-Council was given the power to make and amend rules for the locations.[50] The authority of chiefs over their people on private lands was already tenuous and it was further reduced when, in 1895, the trial of civil cases involving Africans on private lands was removed to magisterial courts.[51] The effect of this measure was to leave the chiefs without any criminal or civil jurisdiction over their people living on private lands.

The impact of these government measures was heightened by a series of natural disasters which ravaged the Colony during this period. Between October 1894 and 1896 a devastating plague of locusts occurred and this caused widespread hardship, including famine and starvation in some areas.[52] The figures for African grain production in 1895 and 1896 give an indication of the losses suffered: production of maize dropped from 667 104 muids to 243 969 and of sorghum from 423 542 to 206 685.[53] This was followed in 1897–8 by a severe drought and by the great rinderpest plague which, due to inadequate fencing and the African practice of communal grazing, spread rapidly to all parts of the Colony. In general, white farmers were more successful than were Africans in isolating their herds, while they were also more prepared to inoculate them. Even amongst the white farming community, however, losses were very considerable. By 1898 they had lost nearly 90 000 head of cattle (about 34 per cent of their herds). By comparison, the Africans lost about 85 per cent, numbering nearly 420 000.[54]

The immediate problem facing the Africans was that of hunger. The ravages of locusts and drought meant that they had very little grain, so that they were forced to sell the few head of livestock they had left, or turn to traders or farmers for credit. In order to plant new crops, they borrowed or hired oxen from farmers for ploughing, while many, particularly in the locations, abandoned their ploughs and returned to hoes and picks.

By 1898, the drought had receded, so that despite the ravages of the rinderpest, in that year maize production rose to 497 497 muids and sorghum to 337 591.[55] African agriculturalists were, however, to find it very difficult to rebuild their cattle herds. They were once again at a distinct disadvantage when compared with white farmers who had lost fewer cattle and were able to profit from the rapid rise in the price of cattle, which soared from £5 a head in 1896 to £14 in 1898 and to almost £20 in 1900.[56] Most white farmers, furthermore, owned their land, so that it could be sold or mortgaged. They also customarily invested their capital in the share-market or deposited it in banks where it could earn interest, so that for them their cattle losses did not represent the same proportionate loss of capital as it did for the Africans, who were sometimes charged interest at a rate of between 600 and 800 per cent.[57]

Because cattle ownership was so important in African society, especially with regard to marriage contracts and status, the consequences of

In order to prevent the spreading of rinderpest, government inspectors destroyed many head of cattle. (From J. A. and A. Verbeek, Victorian and Edwardian Natal, *Shuter & Shooter, Pietermaritzburg, 1982.)*

rinderpest cannot be overestimated. One of the most important of these concerned the payment of lobola. Although the 1891 Code stipulated ten head of cattle as lobola for the wife of a commoner, it did not make this number enforceable in a court of law. If a father allowed his daughter to marry on the understanding that the cattle would be provided after the marriage, he therefore had no legal redress should the husband refuse to honour his commitment. The government, to deal with the situation caused by rinderpest, decreed that cattle could be replaced by money for bride-wealth but that the money equivalent of one head should be £3. As the price of cattle soared, few fathers were prepared to agree to such a sum, so that the number of marriages dropped considerably: from 5 087 in 1896 to 2 678 in 1899.[58] Not surprisingly, this was accompanied by a rise in sexual permissiveness.

To the Africans of northern Natal, the Boer invasion of Zululand and of the Colony in 1899 came as yet another blow as it led to the loss of wagons, cattle and crops. But to Africans in the rest of the Colony, the Anglo-Boer War provided an opportunity to recoup their rinderpest losses by providing the military with produce and with labour at wages higher than those paid by the colonists.[59] The prosperity experienced by some Africans was however short-lived, for by 1903 most of the imperial troops had been withdrawn, while the post-war years were to contain a new series of calamities. The first of these was the recurrence of the drought and locust plagues. This meant that much of the money earned during the war had to be spent on buying imported grain rather than on restocking herds. By 1905, in fact, the number of cattle owned by Africans had risen to only 271 798, far short of the 494 402 of 1896.[60]

The crisis for African society caused by these disasters was the greater because there had been a rapid rise in population, which between 1891 and 1904 increased from 456 000 to 608 527.[61] This increase was particularly serious in the locations which now had to support approximately 270 000 people. There the vulnerability of the homestead mode of production was particularly evident. Heavy over-grazing during the pre-rinderpest years and the constant ploughing of the shallow topsoils had caused widespread soil erosion. Encroachment into the land used for gardens worsened the resulting food shortages. In 1905 only 164 420 muids of maize and 86 218 of sorghum were grown by Africans in Natal,[62] these figures representing a drop of 75,35 per cent and 79,65 per cent respectively on the 1895 figure, at a time when the population had increased by 33,4 per cent. With their traditional foodstuffs, grain, meat and milk, now in short supply, Africans were unable to turn to natural vegetation and fauna, their traditional standby, for much of the natural vegetation had been destroyed, while whole game herds had been killed off by hunters or the rinderpest. In order to avoid starvation and to find money to pay their increased taxes and rents, Africans turned increasingly to migrant labour. This is revealed by the fact that by 1904 some 30 000 Africans (excluding labour tenants) were employed on white-owned farms, 71 299 were employed as migrant labourers within the Colony, and 32 878 were given passes to work outside the Colony.[63]

The plight of labour tenants on white-owned farms was scarcely different. By 1904 there were few cases of pure rent tenancy left,[64] so the majority of Africans on white-owned farms were labour tenants. They were paid a nominal wage of ten shillings a month and this became increasingly their sole source of livelihood as drought, cattle disease and locusts destroyed their independent means of subsistence. Inability to raise the money required for taxes and food led to widespread indebtedness which farmers were well able to exploit, particularly as they could refuse to grant permission to their tenants to seek work elsewhere. Where farmers themselves lent money to their tenants, repayment was normally in the form of labour, thus tightening the bonds that bound the tenant to the farm.

The increase in migrant labour had the effect of contributing to the further impoverishment of the black rural areas for, with men absent for a portion of each year, the normal distribution of work was upset and tasks such as ploughing were neglected.[65] As important, the disruption of family life helped to undermine African society, as is evidenced by an increase in the number of illegitimate births, both in the labour centres and in the homesteads. It is evidenced too in the rapid growth of the Ethiopian movement, with its politico-religious gospel (see Chapter 11), while Messianic prophecies of black revenge swept through the population.

These developments had been paralleled in Zululand (see Chapter 8), so that by 1905 a potentially explosive situation had developed. In many ways, the position of Dinuzulu in Zululand contributed to this situation. He had returned from exile in 1898, not as king but as the petty chief of the Usuthu people, living within the Nongoma district of the province of Zululand. By the end of the century, the Usuthu had lost the power and status that had been associated with their royal leadership, while a large part of the chiefdom now lay outside the borders of Zululand in the Vryheid district of the Transvaal, the land ceded by Dinuzulu as the New Republic.

After a controversial trial, King Dinuzulu was found guilty of harbouring 'rebels' during the Bambatha 'Rebellion' and in 1909 was sentenced to four years' imprisonment. After Union in 1910 his longstanding friend Prime Minister Louis Botha released him and he died in the Transvaal in 1913.

Killie Campbell Africana Library

Despite the determination of the Natal government and its officials in Zululand to play down Dinuzulu's role in the province, his prestige was enhanced by the fact that he received a salary of £500 a year, far higher than that of any other chief.[66] In addition, no attempt was made to stop men of the other chiefdoms from travelling to his homestead at Usuthu to pay their respects to him.

During the Anglo-Boer War, the military attempted to utilize the traditional loyalty to the royal house of the Usuthu in the Vryheid district and Dinuzulu was employed in the recruitment of scouts and cattle raiders for service against the Boers in the Transvaal. He was encouraged to raise an *ibutho* – the *Nkomindala* – and was also given authority over the Buthelezi and the Quluzi in Zululand.[67]

Despite his services during the war, there was considerable hostility towards him from officials and the colonists, especially after 1902, when he lost the extra authority that had been given to him during the war. There were widespread accusations of drunkenness and debauchery and, more seriously, of attempting to restore the power of the Zulu monarchy and conspiring to overthrow white rule in southern Africa.[68]

Dinuzulu was in fact in an extremely difficult position – far more difficult than that in which his predecessors had found themselves. On the one hand, he was the popularly-recognized head of the Zulu people and his presence in Zululand was regarded by many as evidence of the restoration of the royal house. On the other hand, his official status was merely that of chief and, like the other chiefs, he was subject to the authority of the Supreme Chief, sharing the restrictions placed on the other chiefs. As many chiefs in both Zululand and Natal were becoming frustrated with the attitude of government officials and with the laws they were enforcing in the name of the Supreme Chief, they turned to Dinuzulu as a potential leader.[69] As the position of Africans deteriorated, he thus came to be seen, not only in Zululand but also among traditionalists throughout Natal, as well as by many *kholwa*, as the embodiment of Zulu national pride and sentiment.[70]

This dual position must have imposed very considerable strains upon Dinuzulu. It is no wonder that, in the explosive situation that was developing in the region, he was to be trapped by the contradictions inherent in his position.

The developing crisis within Natal and Zululand needed far-sighted statesmanship on the part of the authorities. Instead, the colonial Parliament, intent on balancing the Colony's books, introduced a poll tax of £1 on every adult male, excepting those liable for hut tax.[71] As this new tax affected the young unmarried men in the homesteads, their hostility to it was particularly widespread and, by the beginning of 1906, rumours of rebellion were rife. Fired by the belief that European rule was drawing to an end, many Africans began killing white animals and destroying tools of European manufacture.

On 8 February, after an armed impi had adopted a threatening attitude near Richmond on the day on which the tax was to be collected, a small police detachment was sent to arrest the offenders. On reaching the homestead at Trewirgie Farm in fading light, a 'jeering, taunting and insolent' mob rescued two prisoners and, when the commander of the patrol, Sub-Inspector S. K. Hunt, attempted recapture and opened fire with his revolver, he and one of his troopers (Armstrong) were stabbed to death. In January, a farmer (Smith) was murdered at Camperdown, and in May the magistrate at Mahlabatini, H. M. Steinbank was killed.[72]

It seemed quite clear to those in authority that retribution should be swift,

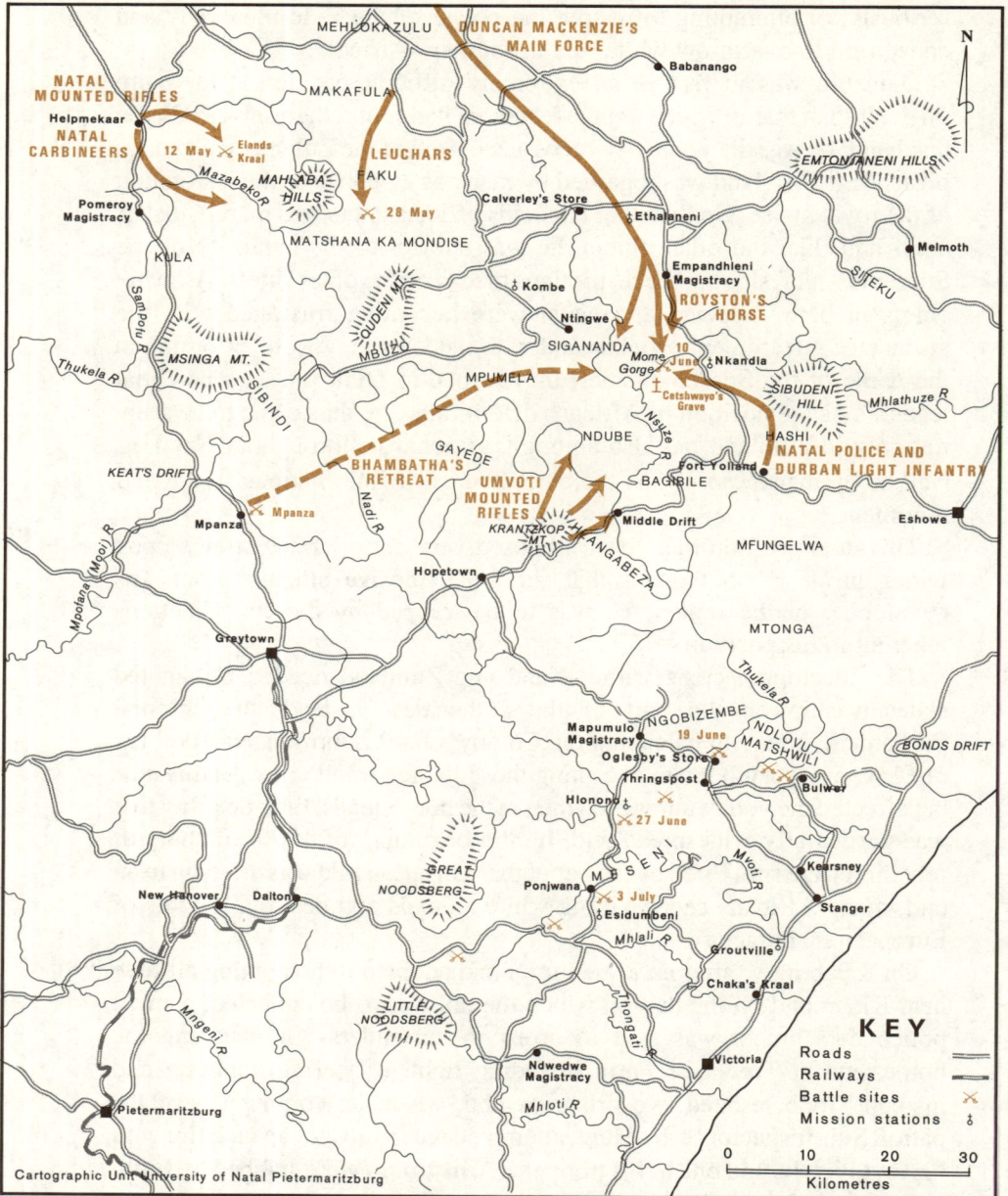

Map 23   The 'Rebellion' of 1906

Despite the protestations of the British government, twelve of those convicted by court martial of complicity in the killing of the two policemen Hunt and Armstrong were executed by firing squad at Richmond on 2 April 1906.

necessary as it was to maintain the illusion of power upon which white rule depended. HMS *Terpsichore* was due to arrive in Durban harbour in connection with a royal visit by the Duke and Duchess of Connaught and, with the promise of help from this quarter, the Natal government was encouraged to proclaim martial law and call out the militia. This body, together with tribal levies, assisted the police in their operations at Richmond. The leading participants in the killing of Hunt and Armstrong were publicly executed after being tried by court martial, some delay being caused by the attempted intercession of the Imperial Government (see Chapter 16); others received sentences of twenty years' imprisonment with hard labour, confiscation of property and lashes. While these proceedings were afoot, the military under the command of Colonel Duncan McKenzie, whose vigorous and crude measures had caused him to become known to the Africans as 'Shaka', made a show of force in the southern districts of Natal, where extensive crop and hut burning took place. The operation had not, however, achieved the desired effect of discouraging further resistance to the collection of the poll tax, and in March 1906 the focus of interest shifted to Bambatha, chief of the Zondi in the Umvoti district.[73]

Bambatha, although a very minor chief, had nursed a grievance against the government since 1890. He had been constantly involved in trouble

The Natal government forces against the Bambatha 'rebels' were commanded by Colonel Duncan McKenzie (standing, centre), seen here with his staff.

This photograph of Bambatha with his warriors was sold as a postcard at the time of the Bambatha 'Rebellion'.

with his white neighbours and in 1905 threatened to kill the magistrate if he attempted to collect the poll tax. He and the men of his chiefdom were accordingly ordered to pay the tax at Greytown. When they did not appear, a force was dispatched to arrest him, whereupon he fled into Zululand. After meeting Dinuzulu, whose part in the proceedings remains obscure, he returned to Umvoti, seized the chieftain who had been appointed in his stead and attacked a police contingent sent to investigate. A section of the relief force dispatched from Greytown was then ambushed at Mpanza, after which Bambatha sought shelter in the nearby Nklandhla forests. Anxious to avoid requesting imperial assistance because it was feared that this would lead to outside interference, the Natal government raised a special service force, Royston's Horse, to supplement the militia and, assisted by a small volunteer unit 500 strong from the Transvaal, this commenced operations against Bambatha late in April.[74] However, it required the full mobilization of the militia, the raising of another irregular unit, the Natal Rangers, half of which was recruited in Johannesburg and the other half in Durban, and the service of a battery of six maxims from the Cape Colony

A medical officer attends to the wounds of prisoners after the battle of Mome Gorge. The aged Chief Sigananda (seated, centre) was subsequently condemned to death, but died before sentence could be carried out.

Natal Archives, C568/2

During 1907, Natal government troops systematically destroyed the homesteads of suspected 'rebels' and others who refused to pay the new poll tax.

before the 'rebellion' was broken in an engagement lasting less than thirty minutes, during which nearly 600 of Bambatha's followers were massacred after they had been surprised at Mome Gorge (see Map 23), no opportunity being provided for surrender. Bambatha himself was one of the casualties. Thereafter, the colonial forces concentrated in the Mapumulo district (see Map 23), where the last resistance was quelled, the homesteads and crops of those suspected of disloyalty being put to the torch as an example to others. At the end of 1907 the militia was again mobilized in anticipation of trouble during the arrest of Dinuzulu, an action which was deemed necessary in the interests of white security.[75]

In the ensuing months, over 5 000 'rebels' were tried by court martial. Although a large number of death sentences were imposed, these were all commuted by the Governor to terms of life imprisonment, with hard labour. In March 1909 Dinuzulu was tried before a Special Court headed by the Chief Justice of the Transvaal, the other two members being the Natal judges H. C. Shepstone (brother of Theophilus Shepstone) and H. G. Boshoff. He was ably defended in court by W. P. Schreiner, the former Cape Prime Minister, and in the Press by Harriette Colenso, the daughter of Bishop J. W. Colenso, who saw in the trial the culmination of a long persecution of the Zulu king by the 'official clique' in Natal and Zululand, who feared the Zulu royal family as a focus of national resistance

M E S S A G E

From :--- COLONEL SIR DUNCAN McKENZIE, Commanding Troops.

To :-- DINUZULU KA CETSHWAYO, Usutu Kraal.

      I have received your Message. My reply thereto is as follows:---
      The Government has given you an order to surrender yourself at Nongoma and that order, you know as well as I do, must be obeyed.
      I am glad to hear, you say, you have done no wrong; if that is so, you can have no fear in obeying the order of the - Government.
      I have to inform you that Martial Law has been - proclaimed throughout Zululand. I now represent the Government here and your father and guardian Sir Charles Saunders is also here, therefore there is no reason for your messenger proceeding to Eshowe and on to His Excellency the Governor as proposed by you.

      Your compliance with this order will not only - give you the opportunity you desire of coming into the laager but also afford you, in due course, the opportunity you seek of being brought face to face with your accusers.

      I shall be pleased to afford you every assistance in my power; and, if you so wish, shall put a conveyance at - your disposal to bring you in.

Duncan McKenzie Col
        Commanding Troops.

Nongoma.
7th December, 1907.

The Natal government was convinced of the complicity of king Dinuzulu in the Bambatha 'Rebellion' and believed that the future security of the region depended on his being punished. Three days after this order had been issued he gave himself up, due largely to the intervention of Harriette Colenso and the barrister Eugene Renaud, who persuaded him that he would receive a fair trial.

to the ambitions of white settlers to obtain Zulu land and labour. Dinuzulu was nevertheless found guilty of complicity and sentenced to four years' imprisonment. He died in the Transvaal in 1913, after being released from imprisonment at the personal intervention of Louis Botha, the first Prime Minister of the Union of South Africa, who had known him as a companion during his childhood in Natal.[76]

Dinuzulu's attitude during the 'rebellion' and his long-term ambitions remain controversial. Whether he hoped to restore the kingship is debatable. What is beyond dispute is that he had an awareness of his responsibilities to the Africans of Natal as well as Zululand. He had also established a strong position for himself through a number of astute marriages which linked him to every important chief in Zululand and to others in Natal, Swaziland and the Transvaal. Yet, during the 'rebellion' he made no attempt to offer himself as a rallying point and at its conclusion he tried to act as an intermediary between the government and the 'rebels'. In the final analysis, it is probably true to say that his position was less important than that imagined by either the colonists or many of the Africans themselves, who had attempted to harness his prestige during the 'rebellion'.

The Bambatha 'Rebellion' is the last chapter in the saga which had seen, in the space of a mere quarter of a century, the undermining of the homestead economy. This was accompanied by the displacement of the traditional system of authority by one in which the chiefs became puppets of the colonial government, shorn of their traditional status, wealth and power. It was accompanied too by the dislocation of African society itself, under the impact of the dominant settler culture and as more and more of its members were sucked into the white economy as wage-labourers. Significantly, the 'rebellion' was followed by the deposition of Dinuzulu, the last remaining symbol of African independence, while the Natal government took the opportunity to confiscate firearms in the possession of Africans.

During 1906 the Natal government appointed a Native Affairs Commission to investigate the circumstances leading to the 'rebellion'. In its report, the commissioners attacked the system of African administration and urged the government to face the problems of over-crowding and indebtedness.[77] In response, certain minor reforms were introduced, but fundamental changes were ignored. Thus, for example, although interest rates were limited to 15 per cent per annum, contracts with employers for labour were specifically excluded.[78] The Commission thus failed to improve the lot of the Africans. As a final blow, the year of the 'rebellion' also saw the outbreak of east coast fever, the tick-transmitted disease which by 1909 decimated the cattle herds that had been built up by Africans since the rinderpest epidemic. Few Africans now had the resources to maintain an independent existence.

Significantly, Africans in Klip River County, where white agriculture remained backward and where there was a high proportion of *kholwa*-owned land, remained in general more prosperous than elsewhere in Natal. They were able to retain a certain measure of independence and, despite official discouragement, continued buying land. By 1905, Africans owned about 156 310 hectares in various parts of the Colony[79] (see Map 22). But less wealthy members of syndicates were finding it difficult to pay their instalments and were either losing their land or, in an attempt to raise money, were encouraging squatting. This was leading to a rapid increase in population on many African-owned farms, which would make it more and more difficult for them to produce sufficient for their own needs, let alone a surplus for the market. Even in the once-prosperous African community at Edendale, many inhabitants were by then no longer able to grow enough for themselves.[80]

After 1910, control of Natal's African population was placed in the hands of the Union government, which merely set the seal on a process that was already virtually complete when, in terms of the 1913 Land Act, it prevented Africans from purchasing land or remaining as squatters on the property of white land-owners.

Notes

1   For information on this period see Bryant, *Olden Times*, Chapter 39.

2   Welsh, *The Roots of Segregation*, p. 4; Bird, *The Annals of Natal*, 2, p. 311.

3   Ibid., pp. 212–13.

4   *BPP* Despatch with Enclosures from Lt. Governor Scott to His Grace the Duke of Newcastle, No. 34, 1864, Native Affairs (published separately, 26 February 1864), pp. 60–2.

5   *Proceedings of the Commission Appointed to Inquire into the Past and Present State of the Kafirs in the District of Natal* (Pietermaritzburg, Archbell, 1852), 2, pp. 29–30; L. Grout, *Zulu-Land; or, Life among the Zulu-Kafirs of Natal and Zulu-Land* (London, Presbyterian Publ. Comm., 1863), p. 164.

6   *Proceedings of the Commission*, 2, p. 34; Bird, *Annals of Natal*, 2, p. 313.

7   *Natal Witness*, 3 March 1890.

8   Welsh, *Roots of Segregation*, p. 114.

9   *Report of the Natal Native Commission, 1881–2* (Pietermaritzburg, Vause, Slatter, 1882), p. 35.

10   See Slater, 'Natal Land and Colonisation Company', pp. 257–83.

11   Natal Blue Book, 1882, pp. T4–5.

12   J. E. Methley, *The New Colony of Port Natal, with Information for Emigrants* (London, Houlston and Stoneman, 1850), p. 24.

13   *Proceedings of the Commission Appointed to Inquire into the Past and Present State of the Kafirs in the District of Natal* (Pietermaritzburg), 4, p. 7.

14   G. Russell, *The History of Old Durban and Reminiscences of an Emigrant of 1850* (Durban, P. Davis, 1899), p. 94; Lady Barker, *Life in South Africa* (New York, Negro Universities Press, 1969), p. 71; *Natal Mercury*, 20 August 1857.

15   Natal Blue Book: 1867, p. X7; 1882, p. X6; 1872, p. X18; 1882, p. X21.

16   Ibid., 1867, p. xii.

17   Methley, *The New Colony*, p. 23.

18   A. H. Manson, 'The Hlubi and Ngwe in a Colonial Society, 1848–1877' (unpublished MA thesis, University of Natal, Pietermaritzburg, 1979), p. 100; W. Beinart, *The Political Economy of Pondoland, 1860–1930* (Cambridge, Cambridge University Press, 1982), pp. 22–3.

19   *Evidence Taken Before the Natal Commission, 1881* (Pietermaritzburg, Vause, Slatter, 1882), pp. 30, 242, 351.

20   Ibid., p. 181, 234.

21   Ibid., p. 326.

22   *Report on the Condition of the Native Population, 1894*, p. 39.

23   Hurwitz, *Agriculture in Natal*, p. 28.

24   Natal Blue Book, 1882, p. X6.

25   *Proceedings of the Commission*, 3, p. 32.

26　*Report of the Natal Native Commission, 1881–2*, p. 33.

27　See *Crown Lands Commission, 1886* (Pietermaritzburg, P. Davis, 1886).

28　Natal Government Gazette, Supplement, March 1881, pp. 1–132; Association for Rural Advancement, Pietermaritzburg, Report 14, p. 1.

29　Etherington, *Preachers, Peasants and Politics*, p. 118.

30　*Report of the Natal Native Commission, 1881–1*, pp. 34, 40.

31　Act 26, 1875, 'Native Administration Act'.

32　*Evidence Taken Before the Natal Native Commission, 1881*, pp. 200, 354, 362.

33　Ibid., p. 367.

34　Ibid., pp. 196, 235, 337, 350, 362, 365, 380.

35　Welsh, *Roots of Segregation*, p. 83, 95.

36　*Crown Lands Commission, 1886* (Pietermaritzburg, Davis, 1886), p. 4; Natal Blue Book: 1876, pp. J8–9; 1882, p. GG63.

37　*Report on the Condition of the Native Population*, 1879–1882; Natal Blue Books, 1879–1882.

38　*Report of the Natal Native Commission*, 1881–2, p. 35.

39　Natal Legislative Council. Sessional papers, unnumbered, 1890, *Report of the Select Committee Appointed to Consider and Report on the Contagious Disease Prevention Bill*, pp. 7–8.

40　Natal Blue Book, 1882, p. X3; Natal Statistical Yearbook, 1895, p. N3, 1909, p. 95. The last figure excludes the territories annexed in 1903.

41　*South African Native Affairs Commission*, 3, p. 948.

42　Act 46, 1901, 'The Touts Act'.

43　Act 49, 1901, 'To Facilitate the Identification of Native Servants'.

44　*South African Native Affairs Commission*, 3, pp. 462, 532–7.

45　Act 48, 1903, 'To Amend the Squatters' Rent Law of 1884'.

46　Bundy, *South African Peasantry*, p. 190.

47　*Report on the Condition of the Native Population*, 1896, p. 4a.

48　U. S. Dhupelia, 'Frederick Robert Moor and Native Affairs in the Colony of Natal, 1893–1903' (unpublished MA thesis, University of Durban-Westville, 1980), pp. 49, 64.

49　Act 13, 1894, 'To Amend the Code of Native Law'; Act 40, 1896, 'To Amend the Code of Native Law'.

50   Act 11, 1896, 'To Provide for the Trial of Faction Fighting'; Act 40, 1896, 'To Amend the Code of Native Law'.

51   See SNA 1/1/274, Minute 3013/97, 6 February 1896.

52   SNA 1/1/229, Minute 1539/96, 11 September 1896.

53   *Natal Statistical Yearbook*, 1895, p. N7; 1896, p. P6.

54   Ibid., 1896, pp. P10, 15; 1897, pp. P10, P15.

55   Ibid., 1898, p. P7.

56   *Natal Agricultural Journal*, 9, 11 (23 November 1906), p. 1059.

57   *Natal Witness*, 28 May 1908.

58   *Report on the Condition of the Native Population*, 1898, p. A36.

59   For the impact of the war on Africans in Natal and Zululand see Warwick, *Black People and the South African War*.

60   *Natal Statistical Yearbook*, 1905, p. 92. This figure excludes the territories annexed in 1903.

61   *Report on the Condition of the Native Population*, 1902, p. B55; 1904, pp. 117–18. This figure excludes the territories annexed in 1903.

62   *Natal Statistical Yearbook*, 1905, p. 92. This figure excludes the territories annexed in 1903.

63   *Report on the Condition of the Native Population*, 1904, p. 174. These figures exclude the territories annexed in 1903.

64   By 1913 only 7,9 per cent of farms had absentee landowners. See L. M. Thompson, *The Unification of South Africa, 1902–1910* (Oxford, Clarendon Press, 1960), p. 490.

65   Brookes and Hurwitz, *The Native Reserves of Natal*, p. 86.

66   Zibhebhu received £200 while no other chief received more than £60.

67   Marks, *Reluctant Rebellion*, pp. 112–14.

68   Ibid., p. 111.

69   GH 1303, Confidential: Secretary of State to Administrator, 3 September 1904, enclosure.

70   Marks, *Reluctant Rebellion*, p. 114.

71   Act 38, 1905, 'To Impose a Poll Tax'.

72   Marks, *Reluctant Rebellion*, p. 216; R. J. H. King, 'The Premiership of C. J. Smythe, 1905–6, and the Bambatha Rebellion', MA thesis, University of Natal, Durban, 1979, pp. 181–9.

73 Marks, *Reluctant Rebellion*, pp. 202ff; Brookes and Webb, *History of Natal*, pp. 220–2.

74 Marks, *Reluctant Rebellion*, pp. 209 *passim*; Paterson, 'Military Organisation', pp. 116–9.

75 Marks, *Reluctant Rebellion*, pp. 260–3.

76 Ibid., pp. xxii, 190–5, 301.

77 *Report of the Natal Native Affairs Commission*, 1906–7 (Pietermaritzburg, P. Davis, 1907).

78 Act 41, 1908, 'To Regulate Claims against Natives for Interest'.

79 Association for Rural Advancement, Report 15, p. 2.

80 *Natal Native Affairs Commission*: Evidence, p. 910.

Chapter 16

Towards Union, 1900–10

ANDREW DUMINY

At about the turn of the century there was a marked increase in the racial prejudices of Natal's white colonial population. There are a number of possible explanations for this. One is that, as part of the world-wide English-speaking community, it was affected by ideas about the inferiority of other races that were then gaining popular acceptance.[1]

In the colonies, racial stereotypes seemed to be confirmed by the 'savagery' of Africans, as revealed by their nakedness, their heathenness and their apparent inability to perform anything beyond the simplest of manual tasks.[2] The Indian 'coolie' was viewed as being only slightly higher on the scale of civilization, their denigration being shared by the caste-conscious Indian élite. Relationships between colonists and Africans, and between colonists and 'coolie' Indians, were almost exclusively those between master and servant. As white employers attempted to direct and control their labourers or their domestic servants, making themselves understood with difficulty in pidgin English or in 'kitchen-kaffir', they readily accepted the prevailing assumptions that labourers had to be controlled with 'firmness', that accommodation in overcrowded communal rooms was adequate and that a diet of mealie-meal or rice with low-grade meat and sugar, was what Africans and 'coolies' were 'accustomed to'.[3]

One of the notions that swept through the English-speaking world at this time was that of 'The Yellow Peril'.[4] In Natal, the Asiatic menace was commonly seen as being that of the Indians, as evidenced in their increasing competition with white traders. Faced with this challenge, white society closed its ranks, so that by the end of the century, Indians had been disenfranchised, and a number of enactments had been passed that had the effect of minimizing the danger of Indian business competition (see Chapter 10).

The Anglo-Boer War appears to have sharpened these racial prejudices. This may have been due to the war hysteria, which produced throughout the Empire an added concern with imperial solidarity and hence with British racial exclusiveness.[5] During the immediate post-war years, a number of other factors came into play as far as the Colony of Natal was concerned. Shortly after the war, a census was held and this revealed that a very considerable increase in the African population had taken place, so that it then outnumbered the colonial white population by about 8 to 1, while the colonists were also by then outnumbered by the Indians.[6] Another observable fact was the growing urban black community, living in unsightly compounds, shacks or overcrowded and unsanitary buildings. While this spectacle began to stir the social conscience, the emergence of an urban black community undoubtedly added a new dimension to race relations. Not only was there inceased competition for unskilled and semi-skilled jobs between black and white workers, and especially between whites and Indians (see Chapter 10), the presence of the permanent and growing black community gave rise to new fears about crime and disease (see Chapter 14).

In Australia and New Zealand, the intrusion of race into politics had been spurred by the organization of trade unions, championing the interests of white skilled and semi-skilled workers, especially against the 'Asiatic Menace', the reality of which seemed to have been confirmed in the victory of the Japanese over the Russians in 1906.[7] This was also the case in Natal. In June 1906 the General Workers Political Association was formed to secure white labour representation in the Legislative Assembly and in the ensuing general election four of its members were elected to the Legislative Assembly. In the following year, the Natal Labour Party was formed. Although several of the labour representatives, especially N. H. Palmer, R. H. Tatham and M. S. Evans, the last a 'quasi-Labour' Member of the Legislative Assembly elected with Labour support, were sympathetic towards African interests, they stood united in their opposition to the Indians.[8]

It was during this post-war period that educated Africans also began to make their presence felt in politics. Largely the product of the mission schools, many of those trained for pastoral work had joined the Ethiopian movement, breaking away from the established Churches. Many of the *kholwa*, furthermore, were well-to-do farmers, were fluent in English, and had adopted western-style clothing (see Chapter 11). In 1900 the Natal Native Congress was formed. Its founders were Martin Luthuli, a leading

member of the American Zulu Mission at Groutville who had been
Dinuzulu's secretary during the 1880s, Saul Msane and Josiah Gumede,
both of whom had also been educated at mission institutions. They had
received the advice and encouragement of Sir James Liege Hulett, who had
been an active supporter of the African farming community at Groutville,
where the mission reserve had been cut up into individual allotments, and
Harriette Colenso, who had taken up the cause of the Zulu people after her
father's death. The new organization, modelled upon the Natal Indian
Congress, was thus representative of the small group of *Funemalungelo*, or
'exempted' Africans.[9]

The new mission-educated politicized African soon came to be
epitomized in the person of John L. Dube. Born in 1871, he was the son of
an American Zulu Mission pastor, his grandmother having been one of the
American missionary Lindley's (see Chapter 11) first converts. After
attending Adams College, he went to America to be trained for work in the

*John Langalibalele Dube (1871–1946), one of the founders of the African National
Congress in 1912, was regarded as a dangerous political figure after his return from the
USA in 1899. He is photographed here with his second wife, Angelina Khumalo, and
four of their six children.*

Killie Campbell Africana Library

American Board Mission. While attending Oberlin University, he met the American Negro leader Booker T. Washington, famous for his Normal and Industrial Institute for Negroes at Tuskegee, Alabama. Washington was the foremost advocate of the idea that Negro advancement lay in industrial education and gradual advancement rather than in political and civil rights. After collecting money for the project in America, Dube returned to Natal in 1899 and founded the Ohlange Institute at Inanda, about 25 kilometres from Durban, the intention being to provide African youths with training in practical skills so that they could be of service to their own community. In 1903 he founded the newspaper *Ilanga Lase Natal*, published in Zulu and English, which soon became the mouthpiece of the Natal Native Congress.[10]

The centre of controversy from the moment he returned from America, Dube has remained a controversial figure. Although he retained his formal links with the American Board Mission, he resigned as a pastor and was popularly viewed, in the white community at least, as a committed 'Ethiopian' (see Chapter 11). Although he took care to moderate his statements in public as well as in his newspaper to a degree that makes him appear timid and obsequious to the modern reader, constantly emphasizing the need for Africans to 'learn' from their white masters, he nevertheless persistently enunciated a courageous vision of equality, requiring that educated blacks be accorded the right to 'improve' themselves and, once they had done so, be accepted as equals in the colonial society.[11]

Almost without exception, the white community responded with near hysteria to this suggestion. As Dube complained, 'The reason that the Christian Native has a bad name, among the lower classes of European especially, is that he does not submit to being treated as a dog'.[12] He was watched after his return from America by special detectives and was detained during the Anglo-Boer War on the grounds that he had made seditious statements. Thinly-disguised, he features in George Heaton Nicholls's contemporary novel *Bayete* as the mastermind of a movement using the Church's following for political ends.[13]

It was not only in Natal that 'the Native Question' was beginning to engage attention. In 1903 an inter-colonial conference was convened in Bloemfontein to formulate a customs agreement whereby the South African colonies agreed at last to create a customs pool and to end the railway-tariff war that was being waged between the coastal colonies as the result of their rivalry for the trade of the interior (see Chapter 14). At this conference it was also agreed to appoint an inter-colonial commission

There were two Natal representatives on the 'Lagden' Commission of 1903–5 which provided guidelines for South Africa's future 'Native Policy'. They are (seated): Sir Marshall Campbell and H. O. Samuelson. The third person is the Secretary of the Commission, H. M. Taberer.

to formulate a common native policy.[14] The Natal representatives on this commission, the so-called Lagden Commission, were Marshall Campbell and H. O. Samuelson, the Under-Secretary for Native Affairs. Most Natalians who gave evidence before it argued in favour of tribal authority or 'Shepstonism', and against extending the franchise.[15] In any event, the Natal government ignored its recommendations regarding the granting of parliamentary representation to 'natives' albeit in special constituencies.[16]

The Lagden Commission undoubtedly stimulated discussion of the political dilemma which faced the colonial community in regard to admitting blacks to their society and to their political system. In one of several publications which followed the publication of the Commission's report, R. Plant, the Inspector of Native Schools, pleaded for policies that took into account 'the peculiarities of the Native mind'. 'The sympathetic relationship of father to child', he wrote, had been absent, with the result that the impression had been gained that everything the white colonists did in relation to the Africans was based purely upon self-interest.[17] In another publication, Maurice S. Evans, the Durban member of the Legislative Assembly who with Marshall Campbell, R. H. Tatham, F. O. Churchill, Nelson Palmer and Harriette Colenso, was a member of a small group of African sympathizers,[18] argued that the answer did not lie in making them 'white men'. 'Only foolish would-be friends or those who are enemies would wish them to ape the white man in all his ways', he wrote. Nor did it lie in African representation in Parliament: 'We have the responsibility of the governing race; we cannot transfer it by throwing part of it on to those who are as yet children; we must take up the white man's burden, and do the thinking for yet a long time'. He pleaded that a distinction be drawn between the 'kraal native' and those who had 'come out of the old life' and were 'trying to live on civilized lines'. For the 'kraal native', he advocated a system of paternal government, a programme of instruction in farming methods, the enforcement of a ban on liquor sales, and an improvement in working conditions to encourage migrant workers to remain for longer periods in employment. At the same time, it was necessary to curb the activities of white profiteers who charged exorbitant rates of interest on loans and high rentals to squatters. For the 'Amakolwa' he pleaded for the retention of the system of exemption and enfranchisement, suggesting that many of them could be drawn into a small military contingent. White colonists, he warned, must not fall into the mistake of reacting with hostility when 'they see an unpleasantly self-conscious, over-clothed dandy, who has lost the simple, natural, polite manners of his people'; nor must they assume that the criminals among them owed 'their unpleasant or criminal habits to association with mission work'.[19]

Statements such as these were by no means characteristic of Natal society as whole, if this can be gauged from the columns of the daily Press, the urgings of the Natal Native Reform League established in 1904 and the debates in the Natal Parliament. The period thus saw the enactment of a series of measures which were blantantly racialistic. Among these was a halt to the immigration of non-literate 'coolies' and 'Peruvian' Jews, amidst growing demands that the Indians should now be repatriated.[20] Other measures were aimed at imposing tighter controls on African education (see Chapter 11) and at controlling the urban black population (see Chapter 14). In 1903 it became a criminal offence for sexual intercourse to take place between white women and black men.[21]

The white Natal Parliament awaits detailed examination, for this period as well as before the Anglo-Boer War.[22] Largely the preserve of successful farmers and businessmen, anxious to retain their privileges and to increase their profits, its members were committed to nineteenth-century notions of *laissez-faire*, while they also prided themselves on their independence. The major issues of the day, apart from those relating to the treatment of Indians and Africans, tended to create further division because they were commonly seen as creating a conflict of interest between one district and another, and between farmer and merchant. This was particularly so in regard to government expenditure on roads and railways, while the division between town and country was laid bare after the 1906 session, when the Labour representatives called for the abolition of the system of multiple votes and the redelimitation of seats to provide urban constituencies, and Durban in particular, with a greater share of representation.[23] Because Natal governments continued to be formed as coalitions, with successive Prime Ministers attempting to obtain a cross-section of interest in their governments, the task of maintaining government unity was often very considerable.

The first post-war Prime Minister was Sir Albert Hime. Included in his Ministry was Moor who, as Minister of Native Affairs, piloted through parliament a series of measures aimed at controlling the mission schools.[24] By mid-1903, however, as the recession began to bite, he was forced to

A feature of Natal politics after 1900 was the growth of white labour organizations. This photograph shows a march down West Street of Natal railwaymen during their strike in 1909. The bearded figure, centre, is Dr Charles Haggar (1854–1934), who arrived in Natal from Australia in 1903 and remained to play a leading part in South African white labour politics.

Don Africana Library, Durban

Natal Government Archives, C506

During the years of responsible government, 1893–1910, a series of unstable coalitions attempted to draw together representatives of diverse interests. After only two years in office Sir George Sutton's Ministry was forced to resign when it failed to win support for its taxation proposals. Standing, left to right: *W. L'Estrange (who joined the Cabinet in 1904 after Joseph Baynes resigned) and W. F. Clayton.* Seated, left to right: *J. G. Maydon, G. M. Sutton, T. Watt and G. Leuchars.*

resign when the Supply Bill was thrown out. He was replaced briefly by Sir George Sutton, the Midlands farmer, who proposed to introduce a system of direct taxation. After the failure of his persistent efforts to obtain support for this very necessary measure, Sutton and his colleagues resigned in May 1905, offering to serve in a government headed by Charles Smythe, a man of unquestioned honesty who enjoyed great respect despite his limitations as a speaker. He was seen as the only person with a sufficient following to ensure the passing of taxation proposals which avoided a drastic increase in customs duties. After insisting upon being given a free hand, Smythe assumed the premiership and chose as his Ministers three who had served under his predecessor (Maydon, Watt and Clayton), adding the Midlands farmers T. Hyslop and H. D. Winter. A significant omission from his Cabinet was Moor, who refused to serve, possibly because he would not compromise himself on the taxation question, having emerged in the recent debates as the champion of an increase in customs duties. He now became the Leader of the Opposition.[25]

Smythe stalled on the taxation question, hoping to persuade the annual
Customs Conference, due to meet only in February 1906 when the 1903
Bloemfontein agreement was due for renewal, to accept an increase in
customs tariffs and railway rates, and to persuade the Transvaal to modify
the *modus vivendi* agreement (see Chapter 14). In the meantime, he
effected a cutback in expenditure by means of lowering the salaries of civil
servants by nearly 10 per cent and reducing the strength of the militia by
1 000.[26] However, after Lord Selborne, the High Commissioner, had
advised that the date of the next meeting of the Customs Conference could
not be brought forward, a £1 million loan was raised in London, providing
temporary relief. Smythe was thus brought face to face with the unpleasant
reality that an additional source of revenue had to be found, knowing that if
he attempted to proceed with the highly unpopular proposal to impose a
direct tax on the white community, which was already complaining loudly
about the effects of the recession, the ravages of east coast fever (see
Chapter 12) and not least about the reduction in civil service salaries, this
would be exploited by Moor and the Opposition, and would almost
certainly lead to the fall of his government.

It was in these circumstances that he proposed to replace the hut tax[27]
with a poll tax of £1 on every male 'Native', with an additional £1 for every
wife after the first. Fearing that this would be disallowed by the British
government, the proposal was linked at first with a small death duty, a tax
of 10s. per hut on landlords when the occupants were not employees, a tax
on unoccupied rural land, and tax on uninhabited urban houses. Although
the first of these was approved, the tax on urban housing was withdrawn in
the face of the opposition of local property-owners, that on uninhabited
land was thrown out in the Legislative Council and the substitution of the
poll tax for the hut tax ran into criticism on the grounds that it would be
more difficult to collect. The tax on polygynous marriages was abandoned
because it was thought that it could have a most unfortunate effect on 'the
Native mind'.[28] In the end, therefore, the government fell back upon a poll
tax of £1 on all males over 18, irrespective of race, with the exception of
Africans who already paid the hut tax.[29] This arrangement, while
theoretically treating all male inhabitants of the Colony as equals, threw the
major burden of the increase in taxation onto the African population.

The new taxation measures could do no more than provide temporary
relief, for the basic cause of Natal's financial difficulty was the fall-off in
customs and transit revenue, due largely to the continuing depression in the
Transvaal (see Chapter 14). Until the Customs Conference met, the only

hope of alleviation lay in adjusting railway and shipping rates, both of which affected the flow of traffic through the competing ports to the Transvaal. For a while hopes ran high after Selborne had convened a conference in Johannesburg to discuss the railway rates dispute, at which proposals for the unification of the South African railway systems were considered.[30] At the same time, it was agreed that an approach be made to the Imperial Government with regard to the secret negotiations that were then afoot with the Portuguese, after which, in a public speech in Durban, the High Commissioner condemned the preferential treatment that Mozambique was receiving.[31] Thereafter, a conference met in Durban later in the year to discuss shipping freight rates, followed by a shipping freights conference in London, with representatives of the shipping companies attending.[32]

These hopes were, however, soon dashed. At the Shipping Freights Conference, the shipowners refused to abandon the rebate system, while the Natal delegate, J. G. Maydon, insisted upon raising the thorny question of the rate structure which operated between the ports to Durban's disadvantage.[33] Even more disappointing was Maydon's inability while in London to influence the British government's negotiations on the *modus vivendi*, for the Colonial Secretary made it clear that the British government would respond only to the unanimous representations of the four South African colonies. From Natal's point of view, the trustworthiness of the British government was highly suspect, in view of its known anxiety not to antagonize the Portuguese, in view of the delicate European diplomatic climate, and in view of the Liberal government's declared opposition to the continued use of Chinese labour in the Transvaal gold-mines, for which no adequate substitute was likely to be found elsewhere than in Mozambique.[34]

After the failure of these two moves, hopes turned on the Customs Conference which assembled in Pietermaritzburg in March 1906. As the subject was closely related to railway and shipping freights, delegates were empowered to consider these at separate meetings, held concurrently. The results were, however, only moderately successful. Although a slight increase in customs duties was allowed, with preference of 3 per cent being given to imports from Britain and reciprocating colonies, and although it was hoped that this would yield an increase in revenue of about £120 000, the Transvaal representatives made it clear that their approval would have to be ratified after the new Transvaal constitution had been introduced and a new government elected.[35] It did not augur at all well for Natal that on their return from Pietermaritzburg, the Transvaal delegates were lambasted for their neglect of the Transvaal's interests.[36] While there was thus no hope of obtaining immediate relief from this quarter, a question mark hung over the final outcome. The decision of the conference regarding shipping freights was no more satisfactory, for there seemed no alternative to leaving negotiations with the shipping companies in the hands of the Imperial Government.[37] As for the railway dispute, although an agreement was reached which held promise of ending the competition for the Transvaal traffic by means of reducing rates, it was not long before Natal-Cape rivalry reasserted itself once more: this time in relation to the traffic to the Orange River Colony, following the completion of the Bethlehem-Kroonstad line.[38]

It was at this stage that the Colony found itself involved in the Bambatha 'Rebellion' of 1906, the reaction of a section of the Colony's African population to the series of blows which had been struck at their society and its economy during the previous quarter of a century (see Chapter 15). The 'rebellion' stretched the military resources of the Colony to their limit. Already in financial straights, it added about £700 000 to its debt.[39] As important, it left a trail of bitterness as criticism began to be voiced in Britain, particularly over the trial of over 5 000 of the 'rebels'. When twelve were sentenced to death by court martial for their complicity in the Richmond affair, the Secretary of State for the Colonies urged that the executions should not be carried out and when the Governor, Sir Henry McCallum, attempted to exercise the royal prerogative to cancel the warrants, Smythe and his Cabinet resigned. The issue was widely portrayed as interference in the affairs of a self-governing colony, a principle which the Liberals, who had assumed power at the end of 1905, were themselves wont to extol and, after protests had been received from other parts of the Empire, including Australia and New Zealand, the British government acknowledged the right of the Colony of Natal to manage its own affairs.[40]

Matters did not end there, for the Natal government went on to offer a reward of £500 for Bambatha's capture, dead or alive, and £20 for each of his followers. Thereafter, public opinion in Britain was outraged at the trial by court martial of the 'rebels', a private action being brought before the Privy Council against the Governor of Natal, while an application was made at Bow Street, charging him with homicide. Reports of atrocities in the field and of savage sentences in the courts continued to appear in the Press, wide publicity being given to the fact that Bambatha's head had been

Natal Archives, C548

During the trial of king Dinuzulu, Agnes and Harriette Colenso, the daughters of Bishop J. W. Colenso, vigorously supported Dinuzulu's cause. They are photographed here with Chief Mankulumana, another unidentified chief and Eugene Renaud, one of the defence lawyers.

severed and photographed in order to allay the rumour that he had escaped from Mome Gorge. Two cases attracted particular attention. The one was the trial of Sigananda, who despite his advanced age (estimated at 95) was brought before a military court after surviving the engagement at Mome Gorge. (He died before sentence could be carried out.) The other was the trial in the Supreme Court, and subsequent execution, of Mjongo and two others who had been involved in the Richmond affair, after they had recovered from serious wounds.[41]

The Natal government reacted sharply to these criticisms. While indignantly denying the sensational reports, it continued to support the contention of the military that severe action was necessary and remained resentful at what was regarded as uninformed outside interference. Political excitement ran high as the feelings of the local community, clamouring for vengeance, were fanned by the reaction of the British Liberal government and a section of the British Press, as reported in the local newspapers. One commentator, P. A. Silburn, who was prominent in military and political circles, went so far as to suggest that there were many in Natal who, 'embittered by the action of the Empire's traitors in power today' were now prepared to 'fight in support of a republican flag'.[42] The

Sir Charles Smythe (1852–1918) became Prime Minister in May 1905. He resigned 18 months later after the Colony's unsolved taxation problems had been aggravated by military expenditure brought about by action against the Bambatha 'rebels'. In opposition he played a leading part in the negotiations that preceded Union, after which he became the first Administrator of Natal.

Natal Archives, C145

lesson was not lost upon Smythe, who informed the Natal Parliament of the need for consolidating the military forces of the South African colonies. Privately, he had made up his mind that the military question, like the financial crisis, linked as this was to railway rates, customs and freight, pointed in one direction only and this was towards South African unification.[43] In the meantime, he returned to the seemingly impossible task of balancing the Colony's books, only to see his Income Tax Bill thrown out by the Legislative Council after a long struggle in the Assembly,[44] leaving him with no alternative other than to request the dissolution of Parliament.

The ensuing election of September 1906 was the most keenly contested since the introduction of responsible government in 1893. Smythe and his supporters were relentlessly opposed on the grounds that retrenchment, not an increase in taxation, was the only way out of the Colony's financial difficulties, Moor based his campaign upon the need for unification with the Transvaal, thereby provoking disagreement between members of Smythe's Cabinet on the course Natal should follow towards unification with the other colonies.[45] Despite these difficulties, Smythe won his own seat convincingly, as also did his leading supporters. When, however, a special session of Parliament assembled to consider the tax proposals, he won the no-confidence debate only with the support of the newly-elected Labour representatives, who made it clear that the price of their continued support included the allocation of a greater number of seats to the urban constituencies.[46] Anticipating that he would not command a majority on his tax proposals, Smythe resigned. Negotiations ensued to form a new government in which he would remain as Prime Minister, taking Moor and other leading members of the Opposition into his Cabinet. In the end, however, Smythe refused to abandon his colleagues and consequently it was the less effectual Moor who became Prime Minister in November 1906. His Cabinet was the least experienced to assume office, for none of its members had served in previous ministries. It included T. F. Carter, a former editor of the *Times of Natal*, E. A. Brunner, a Zululand trader, C. Hitchins, a Durban shipping businessman, W. A. Deane and C. O'G. Gubbins, a medical doctor trained in Dublin, who had after settling in Natal become a successful farmer in the Newcastle district and

Frederick Moor photographed with his Cabinet after assuming office in November 1906. Standing, left to right: *C. Hitchins, E. A. Brunner and T. F. Carter.* Seated, left to right: *C. O'G. Gubbins, F. R. Moor and W. A. Deane.*

Sir Matthew Nathan, Governor of Natal, 1907–9. The British Liberal government hoped that, with his wide experience of colonial administration, he would defend 'Native' interests more effectively than had previous governors of the Colony.

Natal Archives, C147

had served with the Natal Volunteers in the Anglo-Zulu War as well as during the Anglo-Boer War.[47]

The new administration was perhaps even more concerned than its predecessor about security and was as determined to brook no outside interference. Although Moor was known for his sympathy for the Africans,[48] Gubbins, Deane and Carter (Minister of Justice) formed a powerful group within the Cabinet urging a strong line on security and towards the Imperial Government. Although Governor McCallum insisted upon the appointment at the end of 1906 of a Commission to make recommendations on possible changes in 'native administration', its report was not ready until about a year later, with the result that action was delayed until the 1908 session of Parliament.[49] In mid-1907 McCallum was succeeded as Governor by Sir Matthew Nathan. The appointee of the British Liberal government which had been particularly critical of McCallum's failure to stand up to the Natal Ministry during the Bambatha 'Rebellion', it was hoped that Nathan, with his considerable experience in colonial administration and genuine concern for the welfare of the Africans, would be better able to control the local politicians. Shortly after his arrival, however, Moor and his ministers resolved to proceed with the arrest and trial of Dinuzulu (see Chapter 15) and Nathan was persuaded to agree to the declaration of martial law in Zululand. During the following months he was to experience continuing frustration in his dealings with the Cabinet. As he confided to his mother: 'The position of a Governor in a responsible government Colony is not a position for a gentleman'.[50]

In its report, the Native Affairs Commission at last addressed some of the causes of the 'rebellion', recommending a shake-up of native administration, with responsibility being placed in the hands of a permanent Secretary for Native Affairs, assisted by four new district commissioners, who would establish 'personal contact' with the African population and so assist in phasing out tribal authority. It also recommended the appointment of a Council of Native Affairs, consisting of four official and four non-official members with the Secretary for Native Affairs as Chairman, to advise the government on legislation affecting Africans. Some attention was also given to the question of direct African representation in Parliament and in the end it was recommended that 'exempted' Africans be represented in the Legislative Assembly by no more than three members elected from a list of nominees prepared by the Governor-in-Council. 'Tribal' Africans would be represented by four members of the Legislative Council, chosen by the Governor. These measures were recommended in association with others that provided separate schooling for Africans, with greater emphasis being placed upon technical and other skills, and the introduction of a form of leasehold individual tenure, similar to that operative in the Glen Grey district of the Cape Colony.[51]

Despite the active concern of the Governor, Sir Matthew Nathan, and despite the exertions of the Natal Native Congress, assisted by a small band of white sympathizers who formed the Native Affairs Reform Committee, these recommendations were considerably altered in terms of the legislation, commonly referred to at the time as 'the Moor Bills', that was subsequently enacted by the Natal Parliament. Act No. 1 of 1909 'to provide for the Better Administration of Native Affairs', in separating African administration from the purview of Parliament, gave additional powers, not envisaged by the Commission, to the Supreme Chief and his deputies, while the proposals to allow native representatives in the Legislative Council and to give 'exempted' Africans direct representation in the lower house were dropped. Even the proposal to introduce the new leasehold system was abandoned, after it had been opposed by Africans, who argued that the suggested 10-acre allotments were too small, and vociferous white opponents who maintained that they would be too large. Significantly, also, the Natal legislature refused to act on the recommendation of the Commission that it modify the measures it had enacted during the Bambatha 'Rebellion' which curbed the activities of the Ethiopian churches, although Nathan did succeed in persuading his ministers to make an exception of the American Zulu Mission.[52] Nathan also succeeded in persuading Moor to appoint A. J. Shepstone as the first Secretary for Native Affairs, passing over Samuelson, whom he disliked and distrusted, and to appoint James Stuart as Assistant Secretary. The four Commissioners for Native Affairs who were appointed in terms of the new legislation did not, however, meet with his approval.[53]

During the ensuing months, events moved rapidly in southern Africa towards unification, following a course very different from that which had been envisaged before Het Volk's victory in the Transvaal 1907 election shattered the dream of a British South Africa. It was immediately obvious that Smuts's vision of union was very different from that of Selborne and the closer-union enthusiasts who, during the first half of 1906, had been championing federation. Whereas they had been concerned with British imperial interests, Botha and Smuts had dedicated themselves to reducing imperial influence through the creation of a southern African state that would give expression to a broad South Africanism.[54]

A key figure in the ensuing events was to be Moor. A convinced federalist, he had attended the celebrations inaugurating Australian federation as Natal's representative and had on numerous occasions declared his commitment to a South African federation, which he believed to be necessary not only to rescue Natal from her financial difficulties but also to ensure future white domination in southern Africa. Furthermore, he knew Botha personally, having attended the same school before the Botha family moved from Greytown to the Transvaal.[55]

Moor was involved in the negotiations from the start, for he led the Natal delegation to the Pretoria customs conference in May 1908. The High Commissioner had made it clear that the railway and customs agreements, negotiated with such difficulty during 1905 and 1906, would have to be ratified by the new Transvaal government and the Natal delegates hoped that finality would at last be reached. However, to their consternation, Smuts made it clear that the Transvaal would scrap all its agreements with the coastal colonies and proceed with a ring-wall policy if the other colonies did not agree to unification. He thereupon proposed that the conference be re-formed to consider plans for a National Convention. In what may have been a calculated move on Smuts's part, Moor was then elected chairman, thus excluding the High Commissioner at the outset of the proceedings. Brushing aside the plea of the Natal representatives that the railway and customs questions should be discussed first, the conference then went on to agree that the Cape would be allowed twelve delegates at the convention, the Transvaal eight and Natal and the ORC five each.[56] Like Moor's election, this was a crucial development, for it meant that the federal principle was abandoned before the National Convention had even met.

On returning to Natal, Moor hotly defended his actions, which had been widely criticized in the Press and, after agreeing to allow the Natal delegates to be elected by a free vote and undertaking, at Smythe's insistence, to hold a referendum once the details of the new constitution were known, he obtained a large majority in the Legislative Assembly. He was thereupon elected one of the Natal delegates. Greene, the Minister of Railways and Harbours, was also elected. The others were opposition members (Smythe, Morcom and Watt),[57] who in this way became directly involved in the proceedings.

Before the National Convention was convened in Durban in October 1908, a stream of visitors came to Natal, intent upon persuading its leaders to join Union. Among them were Transvaal Progressives, anxious to disclaim any vested interest through their mining connections in the *modus vivendi* and eager to ensure that the English-speakers of Natal would help boost the number of 'British' in the future union. While Selborne paid a personal visit, Botha maintained contact with Moor, assuring him of his good intentions.[58]

Moor did not favour a rigid federal constitution but believed that there should be a large measure of local government to cater for Natal's interests.[59] However, the Natal delegation soon found that this proposal would obtain little or no support from the delegates representing the other colonies. The Transvaal delegation, which was able to speak from the position of strength which the Transvaal's dominance of the economy of the subcontinent accorded it, went to the National Convention united on this as on other important questions, while the plea that special provision be made for Natal's 'Britishness' fell on the deaf ears of Afrikaners, with their suspicion of the imperial factor and aspiration for national unity. As

Local History Museum, Durban

The members of the National Convention photographed outside the old Durban City Hall (now the Post Office), in October 1908.

important, Merriman, who had replaced Jameson as Prime Minister of the Cape Colony, was in close consultation with Smuts and an implacable opponent of federalism, besides having a very low opinion of Natal.[60]

The Natal delegates were therefore confronted at the outset with the choice of withdrawal or of attempting to negotiate the best possible deal compatible with Union. After their initial motion to the effect that the colonies should become known as 'states of the Union' and not 'provinces' had been defeated, they presented a list of twenty demands which included the right of a future province to raise taxes, to amend its constitution, and to control its own police, judicial system, and native administration. Only four of these were adopted, while eleven were rejected outright.[61] An important concession (not included in the list of demands) appeared to be that the provinces were given control of education, other than higher education.[62] However, as the financing of the Provincial Councils was to be in the hands of the central government and the Administrators appointed by, and responsible to, the central government, and as all enactments of the Provincial Councils could be overridden by the decisions of the central Parliament, it was clear that this concession was largely illusory. So also was the provision that a 'federal principle' was to be admitted in the future Senate for, although each province was to have eight senators, it was specifically stated that this would be guaranteed for only ten years.[63]

None of the Natal delegates represented Durban and for this reason Nathan took it upon himself to concentrate upon securing terms that would safeguard Natal's commercial interests. Through Selborne he obtained an assurance from Botha that Durban would receive no less than 30 per cent of the Transvaal trade, an agreement which Botha subsequently adhered to although he refused to write the railway agreement into the new constitution.[64] The Natal Governor was also responsible for an attempt, at Moor's request, to effect a compromise on the question of the African franchise. He produced a scheme whereby 'civilization' was to be assessed according to an ability to speak a European language, regular employment or occupation of property of a certain value, monogamy, and 'the habitual wearing of European clothes or living in a house as distinct from a hut'. He added a proposed sliding scale, whereby African votes would receive greater weighting with each new generation, with parity being achieved by the tenth generation.[65] Like the other compromises that were proposed, this too was rejected, it finally being agreed that each of the colonies would retain their existing franchise systems after unification had been effected. Fresh from their debate in the Natal legislature on the report of the Natal Native Commission, the other members of the Natal delegation emphatically rejected the proposal to give voting rights to blacks, while it was Greene who moved the amendment to exclude 'non-Europeans' from membership of both houses of the future Union Parliament.[66] Of more concern to them than votes for blacks was the decisive defeat of their plea for a federal constitution. The constitution they had assisted in drawing up was in fact to remain the cause of resentment in Natal for many years to come.

While the delegates to the National Convention were settling these details, of such importance to the black population of the subcontinent, various attempts were made by the blacks themselves to influence its proceedings and to bring pressure to bear on the British Parliament, in the hope that it would intervene in their interests. The Natal Native Congress, having been preoccupied with its contest with the Natal Parliament, was scarcely able to expand its activities. Dube urged the appointment of a 'Vigilance Committee' which would meet in Durban at the same time as the meeting of the National Convention and attempt to canvass support for the franchise. The Natal Native Congress presented its case in a letter to the National Convention. It was, however, only after the details of the new constitution had become known that a meeting of African leaders was convened in Bloemfontein to organize concerted action. After a six-man multiracial delegation led by W. P. Schreiner was unsuccessful in persuading the British government to modify the franchise provisions of the South Africa Act, the South African Native National Congress was formed. Dube was elected its first president.[67]

For Moor, the immediate problem was that of defending the new constitution before an irate Natal Parliament and a hostile Press. He placated Parliament by means of undertaking to insist upon eleven amendments at the ensuing Bloemfontein session of the Convention, such as would safeguard the new Provincial Councils as well as Natal's economic interests. However, none of these were accepted, the only concession offered being a provision that any bill which altered or reduced the powers of the Provincial Councils would be reserved for the King's assent.[68] Thereafter, as the head of a government which had never received popular endorsement and which was generally held to be 'unpopular', he had to face a referendum. To make matters worse, shortly before the referendum took place on 10 June, details of the Transvaal-Mozambique Convention, which had at last been finalized, were published. It preserved the main features of the *modus vivendi* agreement and allotted only 30 per cent of the Transvaal trade to Natal, leaving the Portuguese 50 per cent of the Transvaal traffic for a minimum of ten years.[69]

Despite underlying hostility to what the *Natal Advertiser* described as 'a sentence of death', approximately 85 per cent of the electorate voted in favour of Union, with 11 121 votes in favour and 3 701 against.[70] This result may be ascribed to a number of things. The most important of these was probably that all the leading Natal politicians, including the influential members of the opposition, Smythe, Hyslop and Morcom, who had been delegates to the Convention, supported Union and defended the constitution as the best that Natal could obtain in the circumstances. This meant that the opposition Natal League was led by a small group of lesser figures. Included in this group was Maydon, who was disgusted at the Transvaal government's renewal of the *modus vivendi* agreement. Another was Silburn, who viewed unification as a sell-out of imperial interests to Afrikaner nationalism. A third was Sir David Hunter, the former General Manager of the Natal Government Railways, who up till this point had played no part in politics.[71]

Prior to the referendum, Natal was bombarded by a stream of visitors, most of them forecasting a new political dispensation after Union such as would give expression to the 'spirit of Union' which had emerged during the Convention.[72] The *Mercury* urged its readers to vote for union as a

Natal was the only one of the four future provinces of the Union of South Africa in which the decisions of the National Convention were ratified by the white electorate (10 June 1909).

means of 'getting rid of Mr Moor and his incapable government',[73] and this might well have reflected the mood of a significant section of the electorate. In the final resort, however, the option could be starkly imagined by any voter: isolation would mean a continuation of the economic depression, with its spectre of increased taxation, as Natal would be forced to continue to compete for the Transvaal traffic, but with the disadvantage that the Cape's interests would receive priority. It would also mean that Natal would have to cope with future internal unrest and deal with its 'Indian problem' singlehanded. Union, on the other hand, would mean the wiping out of the Colony's debts, £24 000 for Pietermaritzburg annually for twenty-five years as compensation for not having been included in the Pretoria-Cape Town-Bloemfontein capital compromise, and the guarantee of sharing in the prosperity which was confidently predicted for the new South Africa.

Notes

1 Bolt, *Victorian Attitudes towards Race*. An interesting example of this racism was the growth of anti-Jewish feeling at the Cape. See M. Shain, *Jewry and Cape Society: the Origins and Activities of the Jewish Board of Deputies for the Cape Colony* (Cape Town, Historical Publications Society, 1983), pp. 45–56.

2 See, for example, W. A. Squire, 'The Races of Natal', *Twentieth Century Impressions of Natal*, pp. 212–19.

3 See, for example, P. R. Warhurst, 'Obstructing the Protector', *Journal of Natal and Zulu History*, 7 (1984).

4 R. Huttenback, *Racism and Empire: White Settlers and Colored Immigrants in the British Self Governing Colonies, 1830–1910* (Ithaca and London, Cornell University Press, 1976).

5 Ibid., pp. 69ff.

6 Konczacki, *Public Finance and Economic Development*, pp. 3–6.

7 Huttenback, *Racism and Empire*, pp. 73–82.

8 E. Gitsham and J. F. Trembath, *A First Account of Labour Organisation in South Africa* (Durban, E. P. and Commercial Printing Co., 1926); M. Bennett, 'The 1909 Natal Government Railways Strike' (unpublished Honours essay, University of Natal, 1982), pp. 1–6.

9 Marks, *Reluctant Rebellion*, pp. 68–71; S. Marks, 'Harriette Colenso and the Zulus, 1874–1913', *Journal of African History*, 4, 3 (1963), pp. 403–11.

10 Ibid., pp. 73–5; W. C. Wilcox, 'The Booker Washington of South Africa: the Story of John Dube', *The Congregational*, 10 March 1927.

11 For a recent assessment of Dube see S. Marks, *The Ambiguities of Dependence in South Africa* (Johannesburg, Ravan Press, 1986), pp. 42–73.

12 Quoted in Marks, *Reluctant Rebellion*, p. 76.

13 G. Heaton Nicholls, *Bayete. 'Hail to the King!'* (London, Allen and Unwin, 1923).

14 Marks, *Reluctant Rebellion*, pp. 11–12, 14; Davenport, *South Africa: a Modern History*.

15 *BPP* LV of 1905 (Cd. 2399) *Report of the South African Natives Affairs Commission*.

16 Marks, *Reluctant Rebellion*, pp. 11–12, 340–57.

17 Plant, *The Zulu in Three Tenses*.

18   Marks, *Reluctant Rebellion*, pp. 12, 359–62.

19   M. S. Evans, *The Native Problem in Natal* (Durban, P. Davis, 1906). See also M. S. Evans, *Black and White in South-East Africa: a Study in Sociology* (London, Longmans, Green, 1911), in which these ideas are developed further, the author arguing that Africans should be accorded 'local self-government' so that they could 'develop along their own lines'.

20   Posel, 'A Modern Babylon'; Pachai, *International Aspects*, p. 50 *passim*.

21   Posel, 'A Modern Babylon'.

22   Marks, *Reluctant Rebellion*, pp. 17ff; Thompson, *The Unification of South Africa*, p. 127.

23   King, 'Smythe', p. 200.

24   U. S. Dhupelia, 'Frederick Robert Moor and Native Affairs in the Colony of Natal'; Switzer, 'American Zulu Mission in South Africa'.

25   King, 'Smythe', pp. 8–13.

26   Ibid, p. 42.

27   Ibid., pp. 15–21.

28   *Natal Mercury*, 9 August 1905.

29   King, 'Smythe', pp. 26–39.

30   Ibid., pp. 43–5.

31   *Natal Mercury*, 17 October 1905.

32   King, 'Smythe', p. 50; V. E. Solomon, *The South African Shipping Question, 1886–1914* (Cape Town, Historical Publications Society, 1981), pp. 144ff.

33   King, 'Smythe', p. 56; Solomon, *Shipping Question*, p. 152.

34   King, 'Smythe', p. 60.

35   Thompson, *Unification of South Africa*; King, 'Smythe', pp. 61–4.

36   *The Star*, 14 July 1906.

37   King, 'Smythe', p. 67.

38   Ibid., p.62.

39   Paterson, 'Military Organisation', p. 124.

40   King, 'Smythe', pp. 99–102.

41   Marks, *Reluctant Rebellion*, p. 190 *passim*. For the charges against McCallum see Ibid, p. 364 and King, 'Smythe', pp. 147–9.

42   P. A. B. Silburn, *The Constitutional Crisis in South Africa* (Durban, Robinson, 1909).

43.   King, 'Smythe', pp. 143–4.

44   Ibid., pp. 168–78.

45   Ibid., pp. 194–7.

46   Ibid., p. 200.

47   Entries in *Dictionary of South African Biography*.

48   Marks, *Reluctant Rebellion*, p. 22.

49   A. P. Haydon, *Sir Matthew Nathan: British Colonial Governor and Civil Servant* (St. Lucia, University of Queensland Press, 1976), p. 135.

50   Ibid., pp. 127–31, 134.

51   Marks, *Reluctant Rebellion*, p. 340–3.

52   Marks, *Reluctant Rebellion*, pp. 343–50, 362–3.

53   Haydon, *Sir Matthew Nathan*, p. 144.

54   W. K. Hancock, *Smuts, The Sanguine Years, 1870–1919* (Cambridge, Cambridge University Press, 1962), p. 246.

55   J. M. Mendel, 'Frederick Robert Moor and the Unification of South Africa' (Unpublished BA Honours Research Essay, University of Natal, Durban, 1981), p. 54.

56   Marks, *Reluctant Rebellion*, pp. 339, *passim*.

57   Ibid., pp. 360–3.

58   Thompson, *Unification of South Africa*, p. 165.

59   Mendel, 'Moor', p. 33.

60   Hancock, *Smuts*, pp. 246ff.

61   *Minutes of Proceedings with Annexures of the South African National Convention* (Cape Town, Government Printer, 1911), p. 11.

62   Thompson, *Unification of South Africa*, p. 260.

63   Mendel, 'Moor', p. 50.

64   Haydon, *Sir Matthew Nathan*, pp. 155–7.

65   Ibid., p. 159.

66   Marks, *Reluctant Rebellion*, p. 348.

67   Ibid., pp. 362–3; *Ilanga Lase Natal*, 20 November 1908; A. Odendaal, *Vukani Bantu!: the Beginnings of Black Protest Politics in South Africa to 1912* (Cape Town, David Philip, 1984), p. 40 *passim*; P. Walshe, *The Rise of African Nationalism in South Africa* (Los Angeles, 1970), pp. 7–17.

68   Section 64 of the South Africa Act; Mendel, 'Moor', p. 50.

69   Katzenellenbogen, *Mozambique*, p. 98.

70   Brookes and Webb, pp. 243–5; Haydon, *Sir Matthew Nathan*, p. 161.

71   Ibid., pp. 161–2.

72   See A. H. Duminy, 'The "Natal Party"', in Natal, 1909–61: a Collection of Papers Presented at a Workshop at the University of Natal, 1982 (Pietermaritzburg, Department of Historical Studies, University of Natal, 1983).

73   Brookes and Webb, *History of Natal*, p. 244.

Conclusion

ANDREW DUMINY and
BILL GUEST

When, during 1908 and 1909, the decision was reached to terminate the separate existence of the Colony of Natal, few observers entertained the possibility that Afrikaner nationalism would gather momentum and could in time dominate the Union of South Africa. Indeed, on the eve of Union, two of Natal's leading politicians – Moor and Gubbins – accepted positions in Botha's Cabinet, while Greene became one of the Union's Railway Commissioners. Afrikaners had in fact featured only briefly in Natal's history before 1910. Although the establishment of the Republic of Natalia had predated the British annexation, the majority of Trekkers had moved back into the interior rather than accept British rule. Those that remained were soon outnumbered by the British settler population, which was especially predominant in the growing urban centres. Even Pietermaritzburg, the capital of the old Republic of Natalia, after becoming the seat of an English-speaking administration, grew into a city which still prides itself on its Victorian character.

It may therefore be doubted whether the average British settler had any personal contact with the Afrikaners, whose destiny in the subcontinent they shared, until the Afrikaner rural population began to drift to the towns in the twentieth century. Even though most of them felt the same superiority towards the Afrikaner as they did towards Indians and Africans, they had thus, during the disputes that arose at the end of the nineteenth century from competition for the trade of the republican Transvaal, easily been able to develop and enunciate sympathies with the inhabitants of the Transvaal or the Orange Free State without having to relate them to a racial stereotype (see Chapter 13). In 1902, when the coal-rich Utrecht-Vryheid farmlands, with their large and almost exclusively Dutch-speaking population, were added to Natal, this was regarded as a substantial gain and not viewed as likely to give rise to political difficulties. During the 1909 referendum, Natal's politicians were able to pride themselves on the absence of tension between the two white 'racial' groups, discounting the significance of the establishment at this time of a *Boerekongres* movement, modelled upon that which had led in 1906 to the establishment of Het Volk in the Transvaal.[1]

In 1910 it also seemed that white supremacy was assured. The once-feared Zulu military machine had been smashed and the Bambatha 'Rebellion' had provided the pretext for the imprisonment of Dinuzulu, the heir of Shaka and one of the last remaining symbols of Zulu political and economic independence. As settlers moved into Zululand and as more and more Africans moved into the employment of whites, it seemed that unification was the prelude to further rapid economic growth.

The visible evidence of the growth of Natal's economy was the alteration of the physical environment.[2] It is generally argued that in pre-colonial times, although Africans needed vast numbers of animal skins for clothing, feathers for ornamentation and saplings for stockades and huts, there was no wholesale plundering of these natural resources. When, furthermore, the fertility and carrying-capacity of the land had been affected by overcultivation and overgrazing, they could move to other parts, allowing the veld to recover. White penetration into the region had, however, led to African hunters joining whites in the systematic slaughter of game to provide items such as horn and tortoise-shell to satisfy the demands of Victorian fashion, and especially the ivory that was used in making billiard balls, ornaments and the keys of the pianos that graced every Victorian drawing-room. Whole herds of animals were often trapped and butchered so that their skins could be sold for a shilling each. In the mid-1870s a traveller through the north-eastern districts of Natal commented that throughout his journey he had not lost sight of herds of game. Twenty years later, most of it had disappeared, in spite of the introduction of the Colony's first game law in 1866.[3]

The destruction of the game was followed by the rape of the natural forests and by the clearing of land to make way for cultivated fields, a process that was accompanied by the fencing of land. Again, the destruction was extensive, the effect being most noticeable in the river estuaries, which by the 1870s had already silted up and become polluted.[4] For the African population, the effect was disastrous, because migration was no longer possible in times of drought or once the soil had become exhausted. Confined by the Shepstone system to locations which were becoming overcrowded, or living as squatters or labour-tenants on privately-owned farmland, they were trapped in a system from which the only eventual outlet for many would be to enter the labour market.

To these onslaughts on the environment must be added those of diseases. This is a topic that has until recently received little attention, especially as far as pre-colonial Natal is concerned,[5] it being commonly assumed that Nguni-speaking society had been relatively free of disease. In other parts of the British Empire, contact between colonists and aborigines during the nineteenth century had led to a decline in the aboriginal populations, as they were ravaged by disease and addiction to strong European liquor. In the Natal-Zululand region this happened in the case of the San but it did not occur with the Africans. To some extent, this may be explained in terms of the unexpectedly high fertility rate of the African peoples. It was popularly believed in the colonial community that there was also a decline in the death rate due to medical advances and the imposition of stability upon the region by colonial rule. The latter assertion would to some extent rest upon the assumption that the Nguni-speaking population had been kept down by a large number of battle casualties during the Shakan period and during the many internecine disputes that ensued until the final annexation of Zululand took place in 1887. It is however possible that the casualty figures of Zulu battles have been exaggerated by the participants as well as by second-hand recorders, so that a better explanation for the limitation of the population prior to the period of colonial conquest may lie in the social taboos that discouraged early marriages until the fabric of African society began to crumble towards the end of the century (see Chapter 15).

The increase in Natal's white population was circumscribed primarily by the failure of the Colony to attract immigrants in sufficiently large numbers, but also by a high rate of infant mortality at a time when little could be done to overcome the handicap of premature birth and when artificial methods of feeding were limited and inefficient. The medical care available to whites living in Pietermaritzburg and Durban was decidedly better than that accessible to settlers in the remote country districts, especially after the establishment of Grey's hospital in 1857 and of Addington in 1879, where abdominal surgery became a routine matter from the 1880s after the introduction of anaesthetics. These institutions also proved to be invaluable for dealing with outbreaks of infectious diseases, while in 1880 a mental asylum was established at Town Hill in Pietermaritzburg. The hospitals tended to attract better qualified doctors and nurses to the Colony. In the country districts, where there were few medical men other than missionary doctors, families still had to rely largely upon their own ingenuity and home cures, some of them 'Dutch remedies' which had been introduced into the region by the Trekkers.[6]

A marked feature of the first years of the twentieth century was the accelerated growth of Pietermaritzburg and Durban. This was due not only to the influx of immigrants during the boom years but also to the many hardships that were experienced by the farming community during the depression. Whereas in 1887 the white population of Durban had been 8 762, by 1910 it had risen to 29 836. As there were then over 12 000 whites living in Pietermaritzburg, this meant that almost half of the white population of Natal was resident in the two major urban centres. The growth of the African and Indian urban population was no less spectacular. The Indian population of Durban grew from 9 562 in 1899 to 16 131 in 1910, while that of Africans grew from 11 935 to 16 489, reaching a peak of 19 600 in 1905–6. By then only 4 per cent of the Colony's estimated 904 000 Africans were employed at any given time in the towns, but an increasing number were experiencing urban life for varying periods of employment, primarily as domestic servants and 'togt' daily labourers.[7]

Africans and Indians had always been subject to controls in the towns.

Many of those Africans who found employment in the towns, especially Pietermaritzburg and Durban, were rickshaw-pullers. Rickshaws were first introduced to Natal by the sugar magnate Marshall Campbell. They had been invented in Japan in the 1880s.

After the Anglo-Boer War the Durban Borough Police was expanded by utilizing revenues obtained from fines, togt licence-fees and, after 1908, the sale of 'kaffir beer' in municipal canteens.

Togt labourers, for example, had since the 1870s been required to obtain licences to seek work (see Chapter 7) and this enabled the authorities to limit influx and exclude 'undesirables'. Municipal by-laws also required Africans to be 'decently clothed', while Indians as well as Africans were barred from the streets after a curfew had been sounded at 9 p.m. and were not permitted to walk on pavements. In 1901 the Identification of Native Servants Act made it impossible, in the words of Durban's Superintendent of Police, to 'move an inch without a pass'. In 1902 the Togt Labour Amendment Act tightened up the regulations controlling togt labourers, requiring them to live in licensed premises or in barracks and specifying the wages they would receive, while giving municipal officials the authority to refuse to issue togt badges to Africans who were 'diseased' or 'of dissolute habits'.[8] The control of Africans in Durban was then streamlined by means of utilizing the revenue obtained from registration fees and fines to pay a local police force consisting of seventy white officers and 400 African policemen. Between 8 000 and 20 000 African workers were arrested each year for misdemeanours which included disorderliness, using 'provocative language' and 'indecent conduct'.[9] Between 1902 and 1906 an outbreak of plague, arising from the importation of infected rats on a passing ship, caused panic amongst the inhabitants of Durban as the disease claimed 124 victims. The response of the local authorities was a series of sanitary regulations and a number of emergency measures, carried out with great resolution, including the burning of the contents of warehouses, the demolition of overcrowded 'insanitary' shacks and buildings and the forced removal of Africans and Indians to locations on the outskirts of the town.[10] In 1908 the so-called 'Durban System' was devised, whereby the sale of liquor was controlled by means of a municipal monopoly of the sale of 'Kaffir Beer', which then provided the local authority with additional funds to control Africans in the municipal area.[11]

It may thus be seen that the black population of the Colony was increasingly subjected, not only to the effects of drought, disease and economic depression, but also to legislation enacted in the interests of the white colonial electorate and carried out by a state whose instruments of coercion were becoming more effective.

A similar pattern may be distinguished in the field of education. During the nineteenth century, education had been provided by three types of school. In the first category were state schools, directly financed by the government. The second category comprised the so-called state-aided

In 1903 squatter shacks on Durban's Point known as 'Bamboo Square' were demolished after an outbreak of plague had alarmed the urban white population. (From J. A. and A. Verbeek, Victorian and Edwardian Natal, *Shuter & Shooter, Pietermaritzburg, 1982.)*

Natal Archives, C3295

As the urban centres expanded, civic authorities began to provide 'barrack' accommodation for African and Indian labourers, in the interests of sanitation and control. This photograph is of the Durban Indian barracks.

schools, organized by local interested bodies such as churches, while there were also a number of private schools, some of them supported by missions and others by wealthy associations of parents. During the major part of the nineteenth century, all schools admitted children of all races, provided that they were able to pay the fees and provided that they 'conformed in all respects to European habits and customs'. During the early years of the twentieth century, however, mission schools were brought under closer control (see Chapter 11), while the state schools began to be organized more and more on racial lines. To some extent, the growing racial exclusiveness of the schools reflected the inability of a more impoverished black population to meet the costs of education. Also, many of the new schools were established in white neighbourhoods, where there were few if any black children. It was, however, also the result of the conscious direction of the Natal Education Department, created in 1894, whose policies were a response to the demands of the white colonial public and reflected the belief that the educational needs of African and Indian children differed from those of whites.[12]

At the same time as the Colony's black population began to feel the effects of these measures, the taxation system effectively ensured that it continued to provide the necessary supply of cheap labour to meet the demands of white employers, being rewarded with only a fraction of what it was contributing to the colonial Treasury. The Colony's legal system not only upheld the legislation of the colonial Parliament but also applied the Roman-Dutch legal code. For the African population, this meant the whittling away of Native Customary Law as well as the continuing usurpation of the role of the chiefs by that of white magistrates. In the colonial courts, Africans as well as Indians who had to rely upon interpreters and those who could not afford lawyers' fees were at an immediate disadvantage, while white juries and the officials who dispensed justice were frequently unsympathetic, especially in cases in which it seemed necessary to uphold the authority of the government or of white employers.[13]

White colonial society, which has attracted less attention from historians than black society, was no less affected by the changes that had taken place in the colonial economy during the two or three decades before 1910. During the early colonial period, white immigrants, even those with only a small amount of capital, had been able to enrich themselves in a number of ways. Land was cheap, trading opportunities were many and the frontier offered a good living to the hunter. As land values rose, as frontier commodities became exhausted and as the network of trading stores spread, these opportunities diminished. Undercapitalized white farmers, furthermore, were as vulnerable as were independent black producers to the effects of falling agricultural prices, droughts, locust plagues and animal diseases. Like the independent black producers who found that they could no longer compete, the white drop-outs received little or no sympathy from the strata of successful businessmen and farmers which dominated the small colony. Many of those who left the land were presumably attracted to the Witwatersrand, where between 1890 and 1910 Johannesburg grew from a mining camp to a city with a white population of over 200 000.[14] Those who remained in Natal helped to swell the growing urban populations. Ill-equipped to compete for jobs with immigrant artisans, they found employment as labour-overseers, policemen, stock inspectors or in the expanding government service. They became yet another element in the complex capitalist state that was rapidly being forged in Natal, as in other parts of southern Africa.

Notes

1   E. G. Jansen, *Die Natalse Boerekongres, 1906–11* (Pietermaritzburg, Natalse Pers, n.d.); Harris, 'Reluctant Rebels', p. 55; A. J. van Wyk, 'Politieke Woelinge in Natal, 1910–15' (unpublished D.Phil. thesis, University of the Orange Free State, 1977), p. 16.

2   B. Ellis, 'The Impact of White Settlers on the Natural Environment of Natal, 1845–70', in *Enterprise and Exploitation in a Victorian Colony*, eds. Guest and Sellers.

3   J. P. FitzPatrick, 'Jock of the Bushveld and Those who Knew Him', *The State*, 1 (1909); J. B. Taylor, *A Pioneer Looks Back* (London, Hutchinson, 1939).

4   GN No. 388, 1881: Report of the Commission . . . on the Pollution of Streams, 1881.

5   C. Dyer, 'A Case of Money and Life: an Examination of the Relationship between Health and the Political Economy in Durban at the Turn of the Century' (unpublished BA Honours essay, University of Natal, Durban, 1986); K. Gascoigne, 'Health and Disease in the 19th century, with Reference to Colonial Natal' (unpublished BA Honours essay, University of Natal, Durban, 1986).

6   J. B. Brain, 'Health and Disease in White Settlers in Colonial Natal', *Natalia*, 15 (November 1985), pp. 64–77.

7   Konczacki, *Public Finance and Economic Development*, pp. 3–6, 27–8, 175.

8   P.A.M.S. la Hausse, 'Beer, Social Control and Segregation: the Durban System and the 1929 Beerhall Riots' (unpublished BA Honours essay, University of Natal, Durban, 1980); Dyer, 'Health and Political Economy in Durban', p. 50; Posel, 'A Modern Babylon'.

9   La Hausse, 'Beer, Social Control and Segregation', p. 18.

10   Ibid; Dyer, 'Health and Political Economy in Durban', *passim*.

11   M. W. Swanson, '"The Fate of the Natives": Black Durban and African Ideology', *Natalia*, 14 (December 1984), pp. 60–1; 'The Urban Factor in Native Policy, 1843–73', *Journal of Natal and Zulu History*, 3 (1980), pp. 7–12.

12   A. L. Behr and R. G. Macmillan, *Education in South Africa* (Pretoria, Van Schaik, 1966), pp. 112–18, 333–6; A. M. Barrett, *Michaelhouse, 1896–1968* (Pietermaritzburg, Michaelhouse Old Boys' Club, 1969); S. Vietzen, *A History of Education for European Girls in Natal 1837–1902* (Pietermaritzburg, University of Natal Press, 1980).

13   Welsh, *The Roots of Segregation*, pp. 217ff, P. Spiller. 'The Jury System in Colonial Natal, 1846–1910', *Journal of Natal and Zulu History*, 9 (1986), pp. 1–11.

14   C. van Onselen, *Studies in the Social and Economic History of the Witwatersrand, 1886–1914*; Vol. 1: New Babylon (Johannesburg, Ravan Press, 1982), pp. 1–2.

Bibliography of works cited

A bibliography of published work on Natal and Zululand prior to 1910 was originally planned as the final contribution to this new history. This bibliography would further update the listing in Edgar H. Brookes and Colin de B. Webb's *A history of Natal* (Pietermaritzburg: University of Natal Press, 1965; and second edition with bibliography updated to 1985), and would include journal articles and chapters in edited collections of papers, conference and seminar papers, and theses. In addition, entries would be listed in subject categories. However, the extent of the bibliography which resulted made inclusion in this book impractical, and publication thereof has been postponed.

What follows, then, is a bibliography of the non-archival works upon which this new history of Natal is based; presenting to the reader the full bibliographic citation for any book, serial, article, thesis, unpublished paper, newspaper or government publication mentioned in the footnotes of the preceding chapters. Both the South African and overseas editions of works are included, and revised, expanded and new editions noted. If a thesis or unpublished paper cited in the text has been published, bibliographic details are given for both versions.

The entry format for each item has been standardized according to the *Anglo-American cataloguing rules* (2nd edition; edited by M. Gorman and P. W. Winkler; London: The Library Association, 1982), K. L. Turabian's *A manual for writers of research papers, theses, and dissertations* (1st British edition; London: Heinemann, 1982), and *The Chicago manual of style: for authors, editors, and copywriters* (13th edition, revised and expanded; Chicago: University of Chicago Press, 1982). Each entry contains sufficient bibliographic information to trace the item in a library catalogue. Series statements, for example, are given only when they may be necessary for identifying the item. Copyright dates (e.g. c1969) are given if dates of publication are unavailable. Information given in square brackets indicates that such information has been established from some other source than the prescribed source(s) of information in the item itself. Theses reproduced and distributed by University Microfilms International have been taken as published, and are listed with books in the secondary sources section.

For further information about manuscript and archival material cited in this book, readers are referred to the *List of archivalia in South African Archives Depots: Natal Archives Depot* (3rd edition, Pretoria: State Archives Service, 1987) and *A guide to unofficial sources relating to the history of Natal* by A. H. Duminy, M. L. Honnet and R. J. H. King (University of Natal, Department of History and Political Science research monograph no. 4. Durban: The Department, 1977). Enquiries may also be directed to the Natal Archives Depot (Private Bag X9012, Pietermaritzburg, 3200, or 231 Pietermaritz Street, Pietermaritzburg, 3201) and the Killie Campbell Africana Library (220 Marriott Road, Durban, 4001).

The bibliography is arranged as follows:

Bibliographies, dictionaries, guides

Primary sources
  Books
  Articles
  Newspapers and other periodical publications
  Official publications

Secondary sources
  Books
  Articles
  Theses
  Unpublished seminar and conference papers, reports, etc.

BIBLIOGRAPHIES, DICTIONARIES, GUIDES

Bryant, A. T.   *A Zulu-English dictionary.* Mariannhill: Mariannhill Mission Press, 1905.

Cherry, M. A.   'Bibliography of rock art in Natal and Lesotho, 1874–1981.' *Annals of the Natal Museum* 25 (1982), pp. 173-220.

Dictionary of South African biography. Vol. 1 (1968)– . Edited by W. J. de Kock. Cape Town: Nasionale Boekhandel [for the Human Sciences Research Council], 1968– . 5 v. [proceeding].

Palmer, A. W.   *A dictionary of modern history, 1789–1945.* London: Cresser Press, 1962.
– – Harmondsworth: Penguin, 1974.
– – 2nd edition. 1983.

Rosenthal, E., comp.   *Southern African dictionary of national biography.* London: Frederick Warne, 1966.

Samuelson, R. C. A.   *The king Cetywayo Zulu dictionary.* Durban: Commercial Printing Co., 1923.

Webb, C. de B.   *A guide to the official records of the Colony of Natal.* Pietermaritzburg: University of Natal Press, 1965.
– – 2nd, revised edition. 1968.

Webb's guide to the official records of the Colony of Natal. Expanded and revised edition. Compiled by J. Verbeek, M. Nathanson and E. Peel. Pietermaritzburg: University of Natal Press, 1984.

PRIMARY SOURCES

BOOKS

Barker, Lady   *see* **Broome, M. A.**

Barter, C.   *Adventures of an Oxford collegian in Africa, The dorp and veld, or, Six months in Natal.* London: Ward and Lock, n.d.

————. *The dorp and veld, or, Six months in Natal.* London: William S. Orr and Co., 1852.

Bell, K. N. and Morrell, W. P., eds. *Select documents on British colonial policy, 1830–1860.* Oxford: Oxford University Press at the Clarendon Press, 1928.

Bird, J., [comp.]   *The annals of Natal: 1495 to 1845.* Pietermaritzburg: P. Davis and Sons, 1888. 2v.
– – Cape Town: Maskew Miller, [192-?].
– – Pietermaritzburg: L. Bayly, [192-?].
– – Facsimile of Maskew Miller edition. Cape Town: Struik, 1965.

Boxer, C. R.   *The tragic history of the sea.* See **Gomes de Brito, B.**, *The tragic history of the sea.*

Brackenbury, H.   *Some memories of my spare time.* Edinburgh; London: William Blackwood and Sons, 1909.

Broome, M. A. (Lady Barker)   *Life in South Africa.* By Lady Barker. Philadelphia: J. P. Lippincott and Co., 1877.
– – Reprint edition. New York: Negro Universities Press, 1969.
[American edition of *A year's housekeeping in South Africa.*]

————. *A year's housekeeping in South Africa.* London: Macmillan, 1877.
– – Leipzig: Bernhard Tauchnitz, 1877.
– – New edition. London: Macmillan, 1879.
– – 1883.
– – 1886.

Bryant, A. T. *A history of the Zulu and neighbouring tribes.* Cape Town: Struik, 1964.

————. *Olden times in Zululand and Natal: containing earlier political history of the Eastern-Nguni clans.* London: Longmans, Green, 1929.
– – Facsimile reprint edition. Cape Town: Struik, 1965.

————. *The Zulu people as they were before the white man came.* Pietermaritzburg: Shuter & Shooter, 1949.

Callaway, H. *Izinganekwane, Nensumansumane nezindaba Zabantu = Nursery tales, traditions and histories of the Zulus.* Vol. 1, part I [–VI]. Springvale, Natal: John A. Blair; Pietermaritzburg: Davis and Sons; London: Trübner and Co., 1866-1868.
– – Reprint edition. Westport: Negro Universities Press, 1970.

————. *Missionary sermons: selected from those preached during a visit to Great Britain in 1873–4.* London: George Bell and Sons, 1875.

————. *Nursery tales, traditions, and histories of the Zulus, in their own words, with a translation into English, and notes.* (Students' edition). Vol. 1. Springvale, Natal: John A. Blair; Pietermaritzburg: Davis and Sons; London: Trübner and Co., 1868.

————. *The religious system of the Amazulu.* Springvale, Natal: John A. Blair; Pietermaritzburg: Davis and Sons; Cape Town: J. C. Juta; London: Trübner and Co., 1868–1870.
– – Springvale: J. A. Blair; London: Trübner and Co., 1870.
– – [London: Folk-lore Society, 1885?].
– – Re-edited by Rev. W. Wanger. [Mariannhill]: Mariannhill Mission Press, 1913.

Carnarvon, Lord *see* **Herbert, H. H. M., 4th Earl of Carnarvon**

Cetshwayo kaMpande *A Zulu king speaks: statements made by Cetshwayo kaMpande on the history and customs of his people.* Edited by C. de B. Webb and J. B. Wright. Pietermaritzburg: University of Natal Press; Durban: Killie Campbell Africana Library, 1978.
– – Paperback edition. 1983.

Colenso, F. *Colenso letters from Natal.* Arranged with comments by Wyn Rees. Pietermaritzburg: Shuter & Shooter, 1958.

Colenso, F. E. *The ruin of Zululand: an account of British doings in Zululand since the invasion of 1879.* London: William Ridgway, 1884-5.

Colenso, F. E. and Durnford, E. *History of the Zulu War and its origin.* London: Chapman and Hall, 1880.
– – 2nd edition. 1881.
– – Reprint edition. Westport: Negro Universities Press, 1970.

Colenso, H. E. *Mr Commissioner Osborn as one cause of confusion in Zulu affairs.* [London]: Burt and Sons, (1892).

————. *The present position among the Zulus, 1893, with some suggestions for the future.* London: Burt, [1893].

————. *The Zulu impeachment of British officials in 1887–8, confirmed by official records in 1892.* London: Burt and Sons, (1892).

Colenso, J. W. *Church missions among the heathen in the Diocese of Natal.* [London]: R. Clay, [1853?].
– – In *Bringing forth light: five tracts on Bishop Colenso's Zulu mission,* pp. 1–28. Edited by R. Edgecombe. Pietermaritzburg: University of Natal Press; Durban: Killie Campbell Africana Library, 1982.

————. *Langalibalele and the Amahlubi tribe: being remarks upon the official record of the trials of the chief, his sons and induna, and other members of the Amahlubi tribe.* London: Spottiswoode and Co., 1874.
– – [With] Appendix VII 'Sequel to the story of Matyana'.

‒ ‒ [Published as a British Parliamentary command paper] C. 1141. Vol. LIII. January 1875. London: HMSO, 1875.
‒ ‒ [As a command paper] In *Papers relating to Natal and Zululand, 1875–82*, pp. 267–382. Irish University Press series of British Parliamentary papers. Colonies Africa; 30. Shannon: IUP, 1971.

Creswicke, L. *South Africa and the Transvaal War*. Edinburgh: T. C. and E. C. Jack, 1900–[1902]. 7 v.
‒ ‒ London: Caxton Publishing Co., [1903?]. 8 v.
‒ ‒ London: Blackwood, Le Bas and Co., [1903]. 8 v.

Dlamini, P. *Paulina Dlamini: servant of two kings*. Compiled by H. Filter; edited and translated by S. Bourquin. Durban: Killie Campbell Africana Library; Pietermaritzburg: University of Natal Press, 1986.

Emery, F. *The red soldier: letters from the Zulu War, 1879*. London: Hodder and Stoughton, 1977.

Empire Mining and Metallurgical Congress (3rd (Triennial): 1930: South Africa) *Proceedings*. Edited by J. A. Vaughan. Johannesburg: The Congress, 1930. 4 v.

Escombe, H. *Speeches of the late Right Honourable Harry Escombe*. Edited by J. T. Henderson; with an introduction by the late Honourable Sir J. Robinson. Pietermaritzburg: P. Davis and Sons, (1903).

Evans, M. S. *Black and white in southeast Africa: a study in sociology*. Preface by Lt.-Col. Sir Matthew Nathan. London: Longmans, Green, 1911.
‒ ‒ 2nd edition. 1916.

──────. *The native problem in Natal*. Durban: P. Davis and Sons, 1906.

Eybers, G. von W., [ed.] *Select constitutional documents illustrating South African history, 1795–1910*. London: George Routledge and Sons; New York: E. P. Dutton, 1918.

‒ ‒ Reprint edition. New York: Negro Universities Press, 1969.

Fannin, N., comp. *Pioneer days in South Africa: an absorbing record of the Zulu War and the diamond fields, and of expeditions and incidents now written in the history of the 19th century*. Durban: Robinson, 1932. [Cover title: *The Fannin papers: a pioneer's story of the diamond fields and the Zulu War*].

Fuze, M. M. *The Black people and whence they came: a Zulu view*. Translated by H. C. Lugg; edited by A. T. Cope. Pietermaritzburg: University of Natal Press; Durban: Killie Campbell Africana Library, 1979.

Fynn, H. F. *The diary of Henry Francis Fynn*. Compiled from original sources and edited by James Stuart and D. McK. Malcolm. Pietermaritzburg: Shuter & Shooter, 1950.
‒ ‒ [2nd edition]. 1969.

Gardiner, A. F. *Narrative of a journey to the Zoolu country in South Africa, undertaken in 1835*. London: William Crofts, 1836.
‒ ‒ New York: Thomas George, 1836.
‒ ‒ Facsimile of William Crofts edition. Cape Town: Struik, 1966.

Gibson, J. Y. *The story of the Zulus*. Pietermaritzburg: P. Davis and Sons, 1903.
‒ ‒ New edition. London: Longmans, Green and Co., 1911.

Gomes de Brito, B. *The tragic history of the sea, 1589–1622: narratives of the shipwrecks of the Portugese East Indiamen* São Thomé *(1589)*, Santo Alberto *(1593)*, São João Baptista *(1622)*, *and the journeys of the survivors in south east Africa*. Edited from the original Portugese by C. R. Boxer. Cambridge: Hakluyt Society at the University Press, 1959.

Grout, L. *Zulu-land, or, Life among the Zulu-Kafirs of Natal and Zulu-land, South Africa*. London: Trübner and Co., [186–].

– – Philadelphia: Presbyterian Publication Committee, [1864].
– – Facsimile of Trübner and Co. edition. London: African Publication Society, 1970.

Herbert, H. H. M., 4th earl of Carnarvon *Speeches on the affairs of West Africa and South Africa*. London: John Murray, 1903.

Karis, T. and Carter, G. M. *From protest to challenge: a documentary history of African politics in South Africa, 1882–1964*. Stanford: Hoover Institution Press, 1972–1977. 4 v.
– – Paperback edition. 1987.

Lupton, A. *Mining: an elementary treatise on the getting of minerals*. London: Longmans, Green and Co., 1889.

MacKinnon, J. P. and Shadbolt, S., comps. *The South African campaign, 1879*. London: Sampson Low, Marston, Searle and Rivington, 1880.
– – London: J. B. Hayward, 1882.
– – Facsimile of 1882 edition. Portsmouth: Eyre and Spottiswoode, 1973.

Methley, J. E. *The new colony of Port Natal, with information for emigrants*. London: Houlston and Stoneman; Leeds: H. W. Walker, 1849.

————. *The new colony of Port Natal, with information for emigrants, accompanied by an explanatory map*. By the Government Official Surveyor. 2nd edition. London: Houlston and Stoneman, 1850.
– – 3rd edition. 1850.
– – Facsimile of 3rd edition. [Pietermaritzburg: University of Natal, 1968].

Milner, A., 1st viscount Milner *The Milner papers: South Africa, 1897–1907*. Edited by C. Headlam. London: Cassell, 1931–1933. 2 v.

————. *The nation and empire: being a collection of speeches and addresses, with an introduction*. London: Constable and Co., 1913.

Mitford, B. *Through the Zulu country: its battlefields and its people*. London: Kegan Paul, Trench and Co.. 1883.
– – Reprint edition. Durban: T. W. Griggs, 1975.

Molteno, P. A. *The life and times of Sir J. C. Molteno, KCMG, first premier of Cape Colony: comprising a history of representative institutions and responsible government at the Cape, and of Lord Carnarvon's confederation policy, and of Sir Bartle Frere's High Commissionership of South Africa*. London: Smith, Elder and Co., 1900.

Moodie, D., comp., transl. and ed. *The record, or, A series of official papers relative to the condition and treatment of the native tribes of South Africa*. Cape Town: A. S. Robertson, 1838–[1841]. 3 vols in 1.
– – Facsimile reprint. Amsterdam: A. A. Balkema, 1960.

Norris-Newman, C. L. *In Zululand with the British throughout the war of 1879*. London: W. H. Allen and Co., 1880.

Owen, F. *The diary of the Rev. Francis Owen, missionary with Dingaan in 1837–38, together with extracts from the writngs of the interpreters in Zulu, Messrs Hulley and Kirkman*. Edited by G. E. Cory. Cape Town: Van Riebeeck Society, 1926.

Plant, R. *The Zulu in three tenses: being a forecast of the Zulu's future in the light of his past and present*. Pietermaritzburg: P. Davis and Sons, 1905.

Robinson, J. *A life-time in South Africa: being the recollections of the first premier of Natal*. London: Smith, Elder and Co., 1900.
– – Reprint edition. Pretoria: State Library, 1968.

Russell, G. *The history of old Durban and reminiscences of an emigrant of 1850*. Durban: P. Davis and Sons, 1899.
– – London: Simpkin Marshall and Co., 1899.
– – Facsimile of P. Davis and Sons edition. Durban: T. W. Griggs, 1971.

Sanderson, J. *Memoranda of a trading trip into the Orange River (Sovereignity) Free State and the country of the Transvaal Boers, 1851–1852.* London: W. Clowes and Sons, [1860].

Silburn, P. A. B. *The constitutional crisis in South Africa.* Durban: Robinson and Co., [1908?].

Stott, C. H. *The Boer invasion of Natal: being an account of Natal's share of the Boer War of 1899–1900, as viewed by a Natal colonist.* London: S. W. Partridge and Co., 1900.

Stow, G. W. *The native races of South Africa: a history of the intrusion of the Hottentots and Bantu into the hunting grounds of the Bushman, the aborigenes of the country.* Edited by G. M. Theal. London: Swan Sonneschein, 1905.
– – Facsimile edition. Cape Town: Struik, 1964.

Tatlow, A. H., ed. *Natal province: descriptive guide and official hand-book.* Durban: South African Railways Printing Works, 1911.

Taylor, J. B. *A pioneer looks back.* London: Hutchinson, 1939.

Theal, G. M., [comp.] *Records of southeastern Africa, collected in various libraries and archive departments in Europe.* London: Clowes, printers, for the Government of the Cape Colony, 1898–1903. 9 v.
– – Facsimile reprint. Cape Town: Struik, 1964.

Twentieth century impressions of Natal: its people, commerce, industries, and resources. [Durban]: Lloyd's Greater Britain Publishing Co., 1906.

Vijn, C. *Cetshwayo's Dutchman: being the private journal of a white trader in Zululand during the British invasion.* Translated from the Dutch and edited with preface and notes by the Right Reverend J. W. Colenso. London: Longmans, Green and Co., 1880.
– – Reprint edition. New York: Negro Universities Press, 1969.

Webb, C. de B. and Wright, J. B., eds. and transl. *The James Stuart archive of recorded oral evidence relating to the history of the Zulu and neighbouring peoples.* Pietermaritzburg: University of Natal Press; Durban: Killie Campbell Africana Library, 1976– . 4 v. [proceeding].

Wolseley, G. *The South African diaries of Sir Garnet Wolseley, 1875.* Edited by A. Preston. Cape Town: A. A. Balkema, 1971.

————. *The South African journals of Sir Garnet Wolseley, 1879–1880.* Edited by A. Preston. Cape Town: A. A. Balkema, 1973.

ARTICLES

Alexander, R. C. 'Our Indians.' In Durban Corporation, *Mayor's minute, with departmental reports, appendices and balance sheets for the municipal year ended 31st July 1889*, p. 34. [Durban: The Corporation], 1889.

Andree, R. 'Die Steinzeit Afrika.' *Globus* 41 (1882), pp. 185–190.

Bryant, A. T. 'A sketch of the origin and early history of the Zulu people.' Preface to *A Zulu-English dictionary*, pp. 12–66. Mariannhill: Mariannhill Mission Press, 1905.

Delegorgue, A. 'Travels in southern Africa.' In *The annals of Natal, 1495–1845*, vol. 1, pp. 553–76. [Compiled] by J. Bird. Pietermaritzburg: P. Davis and Sons, 1888.

Fitzpatrick, P. 'Jock of the Bushveld and those who knew him.' *The State* 1 (1909), pp. 30–5; 2 (1909), pp. 148–58; 3 (1909), pp. 256–66.

Griesbach, C. L. 'On the geology of Natal in South Africa.' *Quarterly journal of the Geological Society of London* 27 (1871), pp. 52–72.

Mason, F. 'Colonial views adverse to missionary work and how to meet them.' In *Proceedings of the Natal Missionary Conference, held in the Wesleyan Chapel, Durban, May 1878*, pp. 48–54. Durban: Printed at the *Natal mercury* Office, 1878.

McPhee, J. 'Coal in the Transvaal.' In *Proceedings of the Third (Triennial) Empire Mining and Metallurgical Congress, held in South Africa, March 24th to May 9th, 1930. Part 111: Papers and discussions, South African mining, ex Witwatersrand*, pp. 680–703. Edited by J. A. Vaughan. Johannesburg: The Congress, 1930.

Sanderson, J. 'Memoranda of a trading trip into the Orange River (Sovereignty) Free State and the country of the Transvaal Boers, 1851–1852.' *Journal of the Royal Geographic Society* 30 (1860), pp. 233–55.
– – Separately published. London: W. Clowes and Sons, [1860].

Steart, F. A. 'Coal in Natal.' In *Proceedings of the Third (Triennial) Empire Mining and Metallurgical Congress, held in South Africa, March 24th to May 9th, 1930. Part 111: Papers and discussions, South African mining, ex Witwatersrand*, pp. 595–679. Edited by J. A. Vaughan. Johannesburg: The Congress, 1930.

Webb, C. de B., ed. 'A Zulu boy's recollections of the Zulu War.' *Natalia* 8 (1978), pp. 6–21.

NEWSPAPERS AND OTHER PERIODICAL PUBLICATIONS

For holdings of newspapers listed here, see *A list of South African newspapers, 1800–1982, with library holdings* (2nd edition; Pretoria: State Library, 1986).

The Cape argus. 3 Jan. 1857–29 Nov. 1969. Cape Town: The Argus Group, 1857–1969. Issued twice a week (Jan. 1857–Mar.1858), three times a week (30 Mar. 1858–Mar. 1880), daily (1880–1969). Continued by *The Argus*.

Ilanga lase Natal. Vol. 1, no. 1 (April 1903)–6 Mar. 1965. Durban: World Printing and Publishing Co., 1903–1965. Weekly. Continued by *Ilanga*.

Izindaba zabantu. Oct. 1910–Dec. 1928. Mariannhill: Society of the Missionaries of Mariannhill, 1910–1928. Fortnightly (1910–11), weekly (1911–28). Continued by *Umafrika*.

Madras mail. [Articles from the *Madras mail* referred to in Chapter 10 are to be found attached to documents II (Indentured Indians) A/2/11:340/06 in the Natal Archives Depot, Pietermaritzburg].

De Natal Afrikaner. 1886–[Jan. 1921?]. Pietermaritzburg: [n.p.], 1886–[1921?]. Issued twice a week. Continued by *Die Afrikaner* (Pietermaritzburg).

The Natal almanac and yearly register. 1863–1870.
The Natal almanac, directory, and yearly register. 1871–1906.
Natal directory (almanac and directory). 1907.
Natal directory. 1908–1910. Pietermaritzburg: P. Davis and Sons, 1862–1909. Annual. Title varies.

The Natal colonist and herald. No. 1 (3 May 1866)–December 1870; vol. 1, no. 1 (3 Jan. 1871)–no. 1113 (24 April 1880). Durban: [n.p.], 1866–1880. Issued three times a week. From 1866–1870 as *Natal herald*. Suspended 28 Dec. 1877–17 Aug. 1878.

Natal mercantile advertiser. [1863?–1864?]. Durban: [n.p.], 1863–1864. Weekly?

Natal mercantile advertiser. 1878–9 July 1886. Durban: Allied Publishing, 1878–

1886. Daily. Continued by *Natal advertiser, Natal daily news, The Daily news* [Durban].

Natal mercury. No. 1 (25 Nov. 1852)– . Durban: Allied Publishing, 1852– . Weekly (1852–1863), thrice weekly (1864–1877), daily (1878–). First published as *Natal mercury and commercial and shipping gazette.*

Natal Missionary Conference *Proceedings of the Natal Missionary Conference . . .* [1st to 44th, 1877–1925]. [Various publishers], 1877–1925. [44?] v.

Natal witness. No. 1 (27 Feb. 1846)– . Pietermaritzburg: *Natal witness,* 1846– . Weekly (1846–1863), twice weekly (1864–1877), thrice weekly (1878–1880), daily (4 Jan. 1881–). From [1863?]–1873 as *Natal witness, and agricultural and commercial advertiser.*

South African Indian who's who and commercial   directory . . . *1938–1940*. Second issue. Compiled and edited by D. Bramdow. Pietermaritzburg: *Natal witness,* 1939.

South African Indian who's who. Third edition. Compiled and edited by S. Bramdow. Pietermaritzburg: *Natal witness,* 1960.

The Star. 5 April 1889– . Johannesburg: *The Star,* 1889– . Daily. From 25 Mar. 1897–13 April 1897 as *Comet.* Continues *Eastern star.* Suspended 1900–1901.

Times of Natal. No. 1 (19 Aug. 1865)–no. 15348 (31 Aug. 1927); 15 Sept. 1927–29 Dec. 1927. Pietermaritzburg: *Times* Printing and Publishing Co., 1865–1927. Frequency varies, daily (1882–1927). From 1865–11 March 1876 as *Times of Natal and agricultural chronicle.* Continues *Natal mercury* [Pietermaritzburg]. Absorbed by *Natal witness?*

OFFICIAL PUBLICATIONS

NATAL

Webb's guide to the official records of the Colony of Natal (compiled by Jennifer Verbeek, Mary Nathanson and Elaine Peel; Pietermaritzburg: University of Natal Press, 1984) lists official Natal colonial publications housed in South African archives depots and in major South African libraries. The publication format of each document, indicating publication in the *Natal government gazette* (G.G.), the *Blue books* (B.B.), or separate publication (Sep. pub.) is given, together with available holdings information for each item. All published Natal government publications referred to in this book are listed with the *Webb's guide* reference or indexing code.

Unpublished or archival official material is not listed here. This includes items referred to as *NPP* (*Natal Parliamentary Papers*), the 'Reports on the condition of the native population', and the minutes of the Natal Executive Council for 1846. For this material, the reader is referred to the *List of archivalia in South African Archives Depots: Natal Archives Depot* (3rd edition. Pretoria: State Archives Service, 1987) for holdings of the Natal Archives Depot (Private Bag X9012, or 231 Pietermaritz Street, Pietermaritzburg 3200), and the listing of unpublished government records in Part 1 of *Webb's guide.*

Publishers and printers of Natal government publications are specified where possible. If a serial publication was issued by more than one publisher, the indication 'Various publishers' is given. Printers and publishers used by the Natal government in this instance include William Watson, May and Davis, P. Davis and Sons, Robert Richards, and Vause, Slatter and Co. of Pietermaritzburg.

Natal (Colony). *Natal government gazette*. 1849–1910. [Pietermaritzburg]: 'Published by authority', 1849–1910. Weekly, with extraordinary issues and supplements. [*Webb's guide* B39]

Natal (Colony). [Blue books (Statistical year books and departmental reports)]. *Blue book for the Colony of Natal*. 1850–1883. Pietermaritzburg: [Various publishers], 1850–1883. Annual. [*Webb's guide* B41]

———. *Blue book for the Colony of Natal and its supplement* . . . 1884–1892/3. Pietermaritzburg: [Various publishers],

1884–1893. Two v. annually. Vol. 1: Blue book (Statistical returns); vol. 2: Supplement (Departmental reports). [*Webb's guide* B42–3]

———. *Statistical yearbook*. 1893/4–1909. Pietermaritzburg: [Various publishers], 1894–1909. Annual. Continues Blue book v. 1 (Statistical returns). [*Webb's guide* B44]

———. *Departmental reports*. 1893/4–1909. Pietermaritzburg: [Various publishers], 1894–1909. Annual. Continues Blue book v. 2 Supplement (Departmental reports). [*Webb's guide* B45]

Note: The '*Blue books*' for the Colony of Natal contain annual departmental reports and statistical information, published for public information and submission to the colonial authorities in Britain. Information mentioned in this book which is to be found in the *Blue books* includes:
  – Reports of the Resident Magistrates in the various magisterial districts (1878, 1879, 1881, 1885) [see *Webb's guide* D706–36] [Note that parts of the 'Reports on the condition of the native population' appear to be included in these annual reports of the Resident Magistrates];
  – Returns for agriculture (1879, 1881);
  – Statistical summaries of public finance (1900) [see *Webb's guide* D68];
  – Reports of the Protector of Indian Immigrants (1886) [see *Webb's guide* D568–605];
  – Reports on the mining industry of Natal by the Mining Commissioner (1889–1893/4, 1897–1900) [see *Webb's guide* D257–78];
  – Reports of the General Manager of the Natal Government Railways (1887, 1889, 1890, 1891, 1896) [see *Webb's guide* D971–1003].
Many of the annual reports of government officials and departments were published in the *Natal government gazette*, and/or issued separately by the official printers and publishers. Details of the manner in which each item was published are indicated in *Webb's guide*, together with holdings information.
Those reports cited in the preceeding text which do not appear in the *Blue books* are:
  – Reports on the mining industry of Natal by the Mining Commissioner (1894/5–1896, 1901–9) [*Webb's guide* D264–265, D271–8];
  – Report of the General Manager of the Natal Government Railways (1904) [*Webb's guide* D998];
  – Reports of the Health Officer (1903–1909) [*Webb's guide* D829–38].

Natal (Colony). Commission appointed to inquire into the past and present state of the Kafirs in . . . Natal. *Proceedings of the Commission appointed to inquire into the past and present state of the Kafirs in the district of Natal, and to report upon their future government, and to suggest such arrangements as will tend to secure the*

peace and welfare of the district, for the information of His Honor the Lieutenant Governor. Pietermaritzburg: J. Archbell and Son at the office of the *Natal independent*, and *Natal government gazette*, 1852–1853. [Separately published report, and proceedings in the *Natal government gazette*, are listed in *Webb's guide* E8.]

Natal (Colony). Commission on Crown Lands *Report of the Commission on Crown Lands.* [N.p., 1886]. [*Webb's guide* E102]

Natal (Colony). Commission . . . on the Pollution of Streams *[Report of the] Commission appointed to enquire into and report upon the pollution of streams in the coast districts.* Pietermaritzburg: Vause, Slatter and Co., 1881. [*Webb's guide* E77]

Natal (Colony). Commission upon the Coal Industry of Natal *Report of the Commission upon the Coal Industry of Natal.* [N.p., 1898]. [Also known as *Report of the Commission upon the Coal Industry of the Colony.*] [*Webb's guide* E139]

Natal (Colony). Glencoe Colliery Enquiry Commission *Report of the Glencoe Colliery Enquiry Commission.* [N.p., 1908]. [*Webb's guide* E181]

Natal (Colony). Indian Immigrants' Commission *Report of the Indian Immigrants' Commission, 1885-7.* Pietermaritzburg: P. Davis and Sons, 1887. [*Webb's guide* E108] [Also known as the *Wragg Commission* after its chairman Walter Wragg.]

Natal (Colony). Indian Immigration Commission *Report of the Indian Immigration Commission. Pietermaritzburg: P. Davis and Sons, 1909.* [Also known as *Report of the Commission . . . [on] Indian immigration to Natal.*] [*Webb's guide* E184]

Natal (Colony). [Laws, etc.] *Ordinances, laws and proclamations of Natal.* Compiled and edited by C. F. Cadiz; assisted by R. Lyon. Pietermaritzburg: Vause, Slatter, 1879-1880. 2 v. Vol. 1: 1843-70; vol. 2: 1870-79. [*Webb's guide* B30]

Natal (Colony). Legislative Council. *Debates of the Legislative Council . . . 1879(?)-1893.* Pietermaritzburg: [Various publishers], [1879?]-1893. Annual. [*Webb's guide* B4]

————. *Votes and proceedings of the Legislative Council . . . 1857-1893.* Pietermaritzburg: [Various publishers], 1857-1893. Annual. [*Webb's guide* B3]

Natal (Colony). [Natal Mines Act no. 43 of 1899] In *Statutes of Natal: being a compilation of the statutes of the Colony of Natal from the years 1845-1899 inclusive, with footnotes, and with appendix containing the acts of 1900.* Vol. 2. Compiled and edited by R. L. Hitchins; revised by G. W. Sweeney. Pietermaritzburg: P. Davis and Sons, 1901. [*Webb's guide* B28]

Also in *Acts of the Parliament of the Colony of Natal, passed in the third session of the Second Colonial Parliament, 1899.* Natal: William Watson, 1899. [*Webb's guide* B25]

Natal (Colony). Native Affairs Commission *Report of Native Affairs Commission, 1906-7.* Pietermaritzburg: P. Davis and Sons, 1907. [*Webb's guide* E175]

Natal Native Commission. *Evidence taken before the Natal Native Commission, 1881.* Pietermaritzburg: Vause, Slatter and Co., 1882. [*Webb's guide* E86]

————. *Report of the Natal Native Commission, 1881-2.* Pietermaritzburg: Vause, Slatter and Co., 1882. [*Webb's guide* E85]

Natal (Colony). Parliament. Legislative Assembly *Debates of the Legislative Assembly. . . . 1893-1910.* Pietermaritzburg: [Various publishers], 1893-1910. Annual. [*Webb's guide* B8]

Natal (Colony). Prison Reform Commission *Report of the Prison Reform Commission.* Pietermaritzburg: P. Davis and Sons, 1907. [Cover title of separately published edition: *Report of an official enquiry into the prison system of the Colony, with recommendations touching the sentencing, punishment and treatment of prisoners.*] [*Webb's guide* E171]

Natal (Colony). Select Committee . . . on the Contagious Diseases Prevention Bill *Report of the Select Committee . . . on the Contagious Diseases Prevention Bill (no. 19, 1890) and the evidence . . . .* In *Sessional papers of the Legislative Council of Natal* (Sixth Session, Twelfth Council), 1890 [unnumbered]. [*Webb's guide* C1197]

Natal (Colony). Zululand Lands Delimitation Commission *Zululand Lands Delimitation Commission, 1902–1904: re-*

ports by the joint imperial and colonial commissioners, with annexures and maps. Pietermaritzburg: P. Davis and Sons, 1905. [*Webb's guide* E166]

North, F. W. *Report upon the coalfields of Klip River, Weenan, Umvoti and Victoria counties, together with tabulated statement of results obtained from a series of trials of colonial coal upon the Natal Government Railways, September 1881.* London: Harrison and Sons, printers to Her Majesty, 1881. [*Webb's guide* C815]

SOUTH AFRICA

Most Commission reports issued by the government of the Union of South Africa appeared as part of the UG (Union government) series. This used a simple annual sequential numbering system, which is followed by most libraries and archives depots in filing and retrieving these publications. The UG numbers for commission reports referred to in this book, are given here.

South Africa (Union) *Official year book of the Union . . .* Vol. 1–30, 1918–1960. Pretoria: Government Printer, 1918–1961. 30 v.

South Africa (Union). Coal Commission *Report of the Coal Commission, 1946–7.* UG 29–1948. Pretoria: Government Printer, 1948.

South Africa (Union). East Coast Fever Commission *Report of the East Coast Fever Commission. Pretoria, 25 November 1943.* UG 17–1944. Pretoria: Government Printer, 1944.

South Africa (Union). Mines Dept *Annual report . . . for the calendar year ended 31st December, 1911.* UG 49–'12. Pretoria: Government Printing and Stationery Office, 1912.

UNITED KINGDOM

British Parliamentary papers are in date and command number (C/Cd/Cmd) order. Those which have been republished in facsimile as part of the Irish University Press series of British Parliamentary papers have been given their IUP reference as well.

United Kingdom official publications cited here, which appear in the 'non-Natal publications' section of *Webb's guide to the official records of the Colony of Natal* (compiled by Jennifer Verbeek, Mary Nathanson and Elaine Peel; Pietermaritzburg: University of Natal Press, 1984), are listed below with the *Webb's guide* indexing code in parentheses.

United Kingdom. Court of the Special Commissioners for Zululand *The Court of the Special Commissioners for Zululand,* *Nov. 15th, 1888 to April 27th, 1889.* London: Waterlow and Sons, 1889. [*Webb's guide* G283]

450   *Bibliography*

United Kingdom. Parliament. *Correspondence relative to the establishment of the settlement of Natal*. [980]. Vol. XLII. July, 1848. London: William Clowes & Sons for HMSO, 1848.
– – In *Correspondence regarding the establishment of the settlement of Natal, 1847–51*, pp. 9–242. Irish University Press series of British Parliamentary papers. Colonies Africa; 28. Shannon: IUP, 1971. [*Webb's guide* G8]

––––––. *Settlement of Natal: correspondence relating to the settlement of Natal*. [1292]. Vol. XXXVIII. 14 August 1850. London: William Clowes & Sons for HMSO, 1850.
– – In *ibid*., pp. 353–590. [*Webb's guide* G15]

––––––. *Papers relating to the late Kafir outbreak in Natal*. C. 1025. Vol. XLV. 1874. London: William Clowes & Sons for HMSO, 1874.
– – In *Correspondence and other papers regarding affairs of Natal Colony and the Kaffir rebellion, 1852–75*, pp. 451–540. Irish University Press series of British Parliamentary papers. Colonies Africa; 29. Shannon: IUP, 1971. [*Webb's guide* G70]

––––––. *Further papers relating to the late Kafir outbreak in Natal*. C. 1119. Vol. LIII. February, 1875. London: William Clowes & Sons for HMSO, 1875.
– – In *ibid*., pp. 541–606. [*Webb's guide* G71]

––––––. *Further papers relating to the Kafir outbreak in Natal*. C. 1121. Vol. LIII. February, 1875. London: Harrison and Sons, [1875].
– – In *ibid*., pp. 607–712. [*Webb's guide* G72]

––––––. *Langalibalele and the AmaHlubi tribe: being remarks upon the official record of the trials of the chief, his sons and induna, and other members of the AmaHlubi tribe*. By the Bishop of Natal. C. 1141. Vol. LIII. January, 1875. London: William Clowes & Sons for HMSO, 1875.
– – In *Papers relating to Natal and Zulu-land, 1875–82*, pp. 95–266. Irish University Press series of British Parliamentary papers. Colonies Africa; 30. Shannon: IUP, 1971. [*Webb's guide* G81]

––––––. *Further correspondence relating to affairs in Natal*. C. 1187. Vol. LIII. April 1875. London: Harrison and Sons, [1875].
– – In *Correspondence and other papers regarding affairs of Natal Colony and the Kaffir rebellion, 1852–75*, pp. 723–37. Irish University Press series of British Parliamentary papers. Colonies Africa; 29. Shannon: IUP, 1971. [*Webb's guide* G76]

––––––. *Correspondence relating to the colonies and states of South Africa: part II: Natal*. C. 1342–1. Vol. LII. August 6, 1875. London: Harrison and Sons, [1875].
– – In *Papers relating to Natal and Zulu-land, 1875–82*, pp. 9–66. Irish University Press series of British Parliamentary papers. Colonies Africa; 30. Shannon: IUP, 1971. [*Webb's guide* G78]

––––––. *Correspondence respecting the proposed conference of delegates on affairs of South Africa*. C.1399. Vol. LII. February 1876. London: Harrison and Sons for HMSO, 1876.
– – In *Correspondence regarding Carnarvon's proposed confederation, the annexation of Transvaal and other papers on South Africa, 1851–1877*, pp. 37–134. Irish University Press series of British Parliamentary papers. Colonies Africa; 9. Shannon: IUP, 1970. [*Webb's guide* G80]

––––––. *Further correspondence relating to the colonies and states of South Africa: Natal*. C. 1401–1. Vol. LII. Februrary, 1876. London: Harrison and Sons for HMSO, 1876.
– – In *Papers relating to Natal and Zulu-land, 1875–82*, pp. 267–382. Irish University Press series of British Parliamentary papers. Colonies Africa; 30. Shannon: IUP, 1971. [*Webb's guide* G81]

––––––. *Further correspondence respecting the affairs of South Africa*. C. 2308. Vol. LIII. 7 April 1879. London: George Edward Eyre and William Spottiswoode for HMSO, 1879.

– – In *Correspondence regarding the Anglo-Zulu War and Boer unrest, 1878–79*, pp. 581–658. Irish University Press series of British Parliamentary papers. Colonies Africa; 12. Shannon: IUP, 1970. [*Webb's guide* G100]

———. *Natal: instructions addressed to Sir H. Bulwer, KCMG, on his appointment to the government of Natal and papers relating thereto*. C. 3174. Vol. XLVII. March 1882. London: George Edward Eyre and William Spottiswoode for HMSO, 1882.
– – In *Correspondence regarding King Cetshwayo and other affairs, 1882–83*, pp. 9–44. Irish University Press series of British Parliamentary papers. Colonies Africa; 31. Shannon: IUP, 1971. [*Webb's guide* G131]

———. *Natal: correspondence relating to the proposal to establish responsible government in Natal*. C. 6487. Vol. LVII. July 1891. London: Eyre and Spottiswoode for HMSO, 1891.
– – In *Correspondence and other papers regarding Zululand, Tongaland and the establishment of responsible government on Natal, 1890–99*, pp. 117–98. Irish University Press series of British Parliamentary papers. Colonies Africa; 35. Shannon: IUP, 1971. [*Webb's guide* G184]

———. *Natal (responsible government): return to an address of the Honourable The House of Commons, dated 10 February 1893, for copies of correspondence in continuation of previous correspondence relating to the proposal to establish responsible government in Natal*. (216). Vol. LX. 15 May 1893. London: Eyre and Spottiswoode for HMSO, [1893].
– – In *ibid.*, pp. 277–338. [*Webb's guide* G190 and G191]

———. *South African Republic: further correspondence relating to political affairs in the South African Republic*. C. 9521. Vol. LXIV. September, 1899. London: Darling & Son for HMSO, 1899.
– – In *Papers regarding affairs of the South African Republic, 1899*, pp. 689–762. Irish University Press series of British Parlia-
mentary papers. Colonies Africa; 43. Shannon: IUP, 1971.

———. *South African Republic: further correspondence relating to the political affairs of the South African Republic*. C. 9530. Vol. LXIV. October, 1899. London: Darling & Son for HMSO, 1899.
– – In *ibid.*, pp. 763–840.

———. *South Africa: further correspondence relating to affairs in South Africa*. Cd. 43. January, 1900. London: Darling & Son for HMSO, 1900.

———. *South Africa: further correspondence relating to affairs in South Africa*. Cd. 1163. July, 1902. London: Darling & Son for HMSO, 1902. [*Webb's guide* G225]

———. *Report of the South African Native Affairs Commission, 1903–1905*. Cd. 2399. Vol. 82. April, 1905. London: HMSO, 1905.
– – [also published in South Africa and 'presented to His Excellency the High Commissioner and the Government of the colonies and territories in British South Africa'] Cape Town: Cape Times, Government Printers, 1905. [*Webb's guide* G236]

United Kingdom. War Office. Intelligence Division. *Narrative of the field operations connected with the Zulu War of 1879*. Prepared in the Intelligence Branch of the Quartermaster-General's Department, Horse Guards, War Office. London: HMSO, 1881.
– – Reprinted 1907.

———. *Précis of information concerning Zululand, with a map*. Prepared in the Intelligence Branch, War Office. Corrected to December, 1894. London: HMSO, 1895.

OTHER

Conacher, J.   *Report by Mr J. Conacher upon the distribution of overseas traffic between the South African Railways and upon certain other matters . . . .* Pretoria: Government Printing and Stationery Office, 1908. [*Webb's guide F631 and G359*]

Goswami, K. P., comp. *Mahatma Gandhi: a chronology.* New Delhi: Publications Division, Ministry of Information and Broadcasting,Government of India, [1971].

South African National Convention *Minutes of proceedings with annexures (selected) of the South African National Convention held at Durban, Cape Town and Bloemfontein, 12th October, 1908 to 11th May, 1909.* Cape Town: Government Printer, 1911. [*Webb's guide G375*]

South African Native Affairs Commission *South African Native Affairs Commission, 1903–5.* 5 v. Cape Town: Cape Times, Government Printers, 1905. Vol. 1: Report of the Commission; vols. 2–4: Evidence (Cape; Natal; Rhodesia, Bechuanaland, Orange River Colony, Basutoland, Transvaal, Cape); vol. 5: Index and annexures to evidence . . . . [*Webb's guide G318*]

SECONDARY SOURCES

BOOKS

Allen, G. and Allen, D.   *The guns of Sacramento.* London: Robin Garton, 1978.

Archives year book for South African history. Vol. 1 (1938)–   . Pretoria: Government Printer, 1938–   . [84?] v. [proceeding].

Argyle, W. J. and Preston-Whyte, E. M. *Social system and tradition in South Africa: essays in honour of Eileen Krige.* Cape Town: Oxford University Press, 1978.

Arkin, A. J.   *The contribution of Indians to the South African economy, 1860–1970.* Durban: Institute for Social and Economic Research, University of Durban-Westville, 1981.

Ballard, C. C.   *John Dunn: the white chief of Zululand.* Johannesburg: Ad Donker, 1985.

Barrett, A. M. *Michaelhouse, 1896–1968.* Pietermaritzburg: Michaelhouse Old Boys' Club, 1969.

Behr, A. L. and Macmillan, R. G. *Education in South Africa.* Pretoria: Van Schaik, 1966.
– – [2nd edition]. 1971.

Beinart, W.   *The political economy of Pondoland, 1860–1930.* Cambridge; New York: Cambridge University Press, 1982.

Belfield, E. M. G.   *The Boer War.* London: Leo Cooper; Hamden, Conn.: Archon Books, 1975.

Benyon, J. A. *Mr Hoggenheimer's weight problem.* Pietermaritzburg: University of Natal Press, 1977. [Inaugural lecture]

————. *Proconsul and paramountcy in South Africa: the High Commission, British supremacy and the sub-continent, 1806–1910.* Pietermaritzburg: University of Natal Press, 1980.

Bergh, J. S. with the assistance of Bergh, A. P. *Tribes and kingdoms.* Cape Town: D. Nelson, 1984.

Binns, C. T. *Dinuzulu: the death of the house of Shaka*. London: Longmans, 1968.

————. *The last Zulu king: the life and death of Cetshwayo*. London: Longmans, 1963.

Bodelsen, C. A. G. *Studies in mid-Victorian imperialism*. Copenhagen: Gyldendalske Boghandel; Nordisk Forlag, 1924.
– – Copenhagen: Gyldendal; London: Heinemann, 1960.
– – Reprint of 1924 edition. New York: H. Fertig, 1968.

Bolt, C. *Victorian attitudes to race*. London: Routledge and Kegan Paul, [1971].

Bond, J. *They were South Africans*. Cape Town; New York: Oxford University Press, 1956.

Bonner, P. *Kings, commoners and concessionaires: the evolution and dissolution of the nineteenth-century Swazi state*. Cambridge; New York: Cambridge University Press, 1983, c1982.
– – Johannesburg: Ravan Press, 1983.

Booth, A. R. *The United States experience in South Africa, 1784–1870*. Cape Town; Rotterdam: A. A. Balkema, 1976.

Brain, J. B. *Catholics in Natal 2, 1886–1925*. Durban: Archdiocese of Durban, 1982.

————. *Christian Indians in Natal, 1860–1911: an historical and statistical study*. Cape Town: Oxford University Press, 1983.

Brookes, E. H. *The history of Native policy in South Africa, 1830 to the present day*. Cape Town: Nasionale Pers, 1924.
– – 2nd, revised edition. Pretoria: Van Schaik, 1927.

Brookes, E. H. and Hurwitz, N. *The Native reserves of Natal*. Natal regional survey; v. 7. Cape Town: Oxford University Press for the University of Natal, 1957.

Brookes, E. H. and Webb, C. de B. *A history of Natal*. Pietermaritzburg: University of Natal Press, 1965.
– – 2nd (paperback) edition. 1987.

Bryant, A. T. *A history of the Zulu and neighbouring tribes*. Cape Town: Struik, 1964.

————. *Olden times in Zululand and Natal: containing earlier political history of the Eastern-Nguni clans*. London: Longmans, Green, 1929.
– – Facsimile reprint edition. Cape Town: Struik, 1965.

————. *The Zulu people as they were before the white man came*. Pietermaritzburg: Shuter & Shooter, 1949.

Bulpin, T. V. *To the shores of Natal*. Cape Town: Timmins, [1953?].

Bundy, C. *The rise and fall of the South African peasantry*. Berkeley: University of California Press, 1979.
– – London: Heinemann, 1979.
– – 2nd edition. London: James Currey; Cape Town: David Philip, 1988.

Burness, D. *Shaka, king of the Zulus in African literature: and two special essays, 'Shaka's social, political and military ideas' by Jordan K. Ngubane, and 'Shaka in the literature of southern Africa' by Daniel P. Kunene*. Washington: Three Continents Press, 1976.

Cable, [J. H.] C. *Economy and technology in the Late Stone Age of southern Natal*. Cambridge monographs in African archaeology, 9. BAR international series, 201. Oxford: British Archaeological Reports, 1984.

***Cambridge history of the British Empire*.** Cambridge: Cambridge University Press, 1929–1940. 8 v. in 9.
– – Vol. 8. 2nd edition. 1963.

Carter, G. M. *The politics of inequality: South Africa since 1948*. London: Thames and Hudson, 1958.

– – Revised edition. [1959]. [1962].
– – New York: Praeger, 1959.
– – New York: Octagon Books, 1977.

Clarke, S. H. *Zululand at war, 1879: the conduct of the Anglo-Zulu War.* Houghton, Johannesburg: Brenthurst Press, 1984.

Cohen, R. and Middleton J., eds. *From tribe to nation in Africa: studies in incorporation processes.* Scranton, Penn.: Chandler Publishing Co., [1970].

Coupland, R. F. *Zulu battle piece: Isandhlwana.* London: Collins, 1948.

Crummey, D. and Stewart, C. C., eds. *Modes of production in Africa: the precolonial era.* Beverley Hills, Ca.: Sage Publications, c1981.

Dalby, D., ed. *Language and history in Africa.* London: Frank Cass and Co., 1970.

Davenport, T. R. H. *South Africa: a modern history.* Toronto: University of Toronto Press; London: Macmillan, 1977.
– – 2nd edition. 1978.
– – 3rd edition, updated and extensively revised. Johannesburg; Basingstoke: Macmillan; Bergvlei: Southern Books, 1987.

Davenport, T. R. H. and Hunt, K. S., eds. *The right to the land. Cape Town: David Philip, 1974.*

De Kiewiet, C. W. *A history of South Africa: social and economic.* London: Clarendon Press; Oxford University Press, 1941.

————. *The imperial factor in South Africa: a study in politics and economics.* London: Cass; Cambridge: Cambridge University Press, 1937.

Delius, P. *The land belongs to us: the Pedi polity, the Boers and the British in the nineteenth century Transvaal.* Johannesburg: Ravan Press, 1983.
– – Berkeley: University of California Press, c1984.
– – London: Heinemann, c1984.

Denoon, D. with Nyeko, B. *Southern Africa since 1800.* London: Longman, 1972.
– – 2nd edition. 1984.

Dictionary of South African biography. Vol. 1 (1968)– . Edited by W. J. de Kock. Cape Town: Nasionale Boekhandel [for the Human Sciences Research Council], 1968– . 5 v. [proceeding].

Duignan, P. and Gann, L. H. *The United States and Africa: a history.* Cambridge: Cambridge University Press, 1984.

Duminy, A. H. *Truth and illusion in history.* Pietermaritzburg: University of Natal Press, 1984. [Inaugural lecture]

Duminy, A. H. and Guest, B. [W. R.] *Interfering in politics: a biography of Sir Percy Fitzpatrick.* Johannesburg: Lowry, 1987.

Duminy, A H. and Ballard, C. C., eds. *The Anglo-Zulu War: new perspectives.* Pietermaritzburg: University of Natal Press, 1981.

Ellenberger, D. F., comp. *History of the Basuto: ancient and modern.* Written in English by J. C. MacGregor. London: Caxton, 1912.
– – New York: Negro Universities Press, [1969].

Emery, F. *The red soldier: letters from the Zulu War, 1879.* London: Hodder and Stoughton, 1977.

Etherington, N. A. *Preachers, peasants and politics in south east Africa, 1835–1880: African Christian communities in Natal, Pondoland and Zululand.* London: Royal Historical Society, 1978.

————. *The rise of the Kholwa in southeast Africa: African Christian communities in Natal, Pondoland and Zululand, 1835–1880.* Ann Arbor, Mich.: University Microfilms International, 1971. (Ph.D. thesis).

Fortes, M. and Evans-Pritchard, E., eds. *African political systems.* London: Oxford University Press for the International African Institute, 1940.

Fox, F. W. and Young, M. E. Norwood *Food from the veld: edible wild plants of southern Africa botanically identified and described.* Johannesburg: Delta Books, 1982.

French, G. *Lord Chelmsford and the Zulu War.* London: John Lane, the Bodley Head, 1939.

Fried, M. H. *The notion of tribe.* Menlo Park, Ca.: Cummings Publishing Co., 1975.

Galbraith, J. S. *Reluctant empire: British policy on the South African frontier, 1834–1854.* Westport, Conn.: Greenwood Press, 1963.
– – Berkeley: University of California Press, 1963.

Gluckman, M. *Custom and conflict in Africa.* Oxford: Basil Blackwell, c1956.
– – New York: Barnes and Noble, 1964.

———. *Order and rebellion in tribal Africa.* London: Cohen and West, 1963.

Gitsham, E. and Trembath, J. F. *A first account of labour organisation in South Africa.* Durban: E. P. and Commercial Printing Co., 1926.

Godelier, M. *Perspectives in Marxist anthropology.* Translated by R. Brain. New York; Cambridge: Cambridge University Press, 1977.

Gon, P. *The road to Isandlwana: the years of an imperial battalion.* London; Johannesburg: Ad Donker, 1979.

Goodfellow, C. F. *Great Britain and South African confederation, 1870–1881.* Cape Town: Oxford University Press, 1966.

Gordon, R. E. *Shepstone: the role of the*

family in the history of South Africa, 1820–1900. Cape Town: A. A. Balkema, 1968.

Goswami, K. P., comp. *Mahatma Gandhi: a chronology.* New Delhi: Publications Division, Ministry of Information and Broadcasting, Government of India, [1971].

Gray, R. and Birmingham, D., eds. *Precolonial African trade: essays on trade in central and eastern Africa before 1900.* London; New York: Oxford University Press, 1970.

Greyling, J. J. C. and Davies, R. J. *Land-subdivision, land-ownership and land occupation.* Indian agricultural holdings on the Natal North Coast; report 1. Pietermaritzburg: Natal Town and Regional Planning Commission, 1970. 3 v.

Guest, B. [W. R.] *Langalibalele: the crisis in Natal, 1873–1875.* University of Natal, Department of History and Political Science research monograph no. 2. Durban: The Department, 1976.

Guest, B. [W. R.] and Sellers, J. M., eds. *Enterprise and exploitation in a Victorian colony: aspects of the economic and social history of colonial Natal.* Pietermaritzburg: University of Natal Press, 1985.

Gutkind, P. C. W., ed. *The passing of tribal man in Africa.* Leiden: Brill, 1970.

Gutkind, P. C. W. and Wallerstein, I., eds. *The political economy of contemporary Africa.* Beverly Hills, Ca.: Sage Publications, c1976.
– – 2nd edition. 1985.

Guy, J. J. *The destruction of the Zulu kingdom: the civil war in Zululand, 1879–1884.* London: Longman, 1979.
– – Johannesburg: Ravan Press, 1982.

———. *The heretic: a study of the life of John William Colenso, 1814–1883.* Johannesburg: Ravan Press; Pietermaritzburg: University of Natal Press, 1983.

Hall, M.   *Settlement patterns in the Iron Age of Zululand: an ecological interpretation.* Cambridge monographs in African archaeology, 5. BAR international series, 119. Oxford: British Archaeological Reports, 1981.

Hall, M. *et al.*, eds.   *Frontiers: southern African archaeology today.* Edited by M. Hall, G. Avery, D. M. Avery, M. L. Wilson and A. J. B. Humphreys. Cambridge monographs in African archaeology, 10. BAR international series, 207. Oxford: British Archaeological Reports, 1984.

Hancock, W. K. *Smuts* . . . . Cambridge: Cambridge University Press, 1962–1969. 2 v. Vol.1: *The sanguine years, 1870–1919*; vol. 2: *The fields of force, 1919–1950.*

Harington, A. L.   *Sir Harry Smith: bungling hero.* Cape Town: Tafelberg, 1980.

Hassan, F. A. *Demographic archaeology.* New York: Academic Press, 1981.

Hattersley, A. F.   *The British settlement of Natal: a study in imperial migration.* Cambridge: Cambridge University Press, 1950.

————. *Hilton portrait: South African public school, 1872–1945.* Pietermaritzburg: Shuter & Shooter, 1945.

————. *Pietermaritzburg panorama: a survey of one hundred years of an African city.* Pietermaritzburg: Shuter & Shooter, 1938.

————. *Portrait of a city.* Pietermaritzburg: Shuter & Shooter, 1951.

————. *Portrait of a colony: the story of Natal.* Cambridge: Cambridge University Press, 1940.

Haydon, A. P.   *Sir Matthew Nathan: British colonial governor and civil servant.* St. Lucia: University of Queensland Press, 1976.

Henige, D. P.   *The chronology of oral tradition: quest for a chimera.* Oxford: Clarendon Press, 1974.

– – Westport, Conn.: Green Press, (1987), c1974.

Hinchliff, P. *John William Colenso, Bishop of Natal.* London: Nelson, 1964.

Hodder, I. *Symbols in action: ethnoarchaeological studies of material culture.* Cambridge; New York: Cambridge University Press, 1982.

Holme, N. *The silver wreath: being the 24th Regiment at Isandhlwana and Rorke's Drift, 1879.* London: Samson Books, 1979.

Hunt, J. D. *Gandhi in London.* New Delhi: Promilla and Co., c1978.

Hurwitz, N. *Agriculture in Natal, 1860–1950.* Natal Regional Survey; v. 12. Cape Town: Oxford University Press for the University of Natal, 1957.

Huttenback, R. A. *Gandhi in South Africa: British imperialism and the Indian question, 1860–1914.* Ithaca: Cornell University Press, 1971.

————. *Racism and empire: white settlers and colored immigrants in the British self-governing colonies, 1830–1910.* Ithaca: Cornell University Press, 1976.

Iliffe, J. *A modern history of Tanganyika.* New York; Cambridge: Cambridge University Press, 1979.

Jansen E. G. *Die Natalse Boerekongres, 1906–1911.* Pietermaritzburg: Natalse Pers, n.d.

Jeeves, A. H.   *Migrant labour in South Africa's mining economy: the struggle for the gold mines' labour supply, 1890–1920.* Kingston: McGill-Queen's University Press; Johannesburg: Witwatersrand University Press, 1985.

Junod, H. A.   *The condition of the natives of south-east Africa in the sixteenth century, according to the early Portugese documents.* Cape Town: South African Association for the Advancement of Science, 1914.

Katzenellenbogen, S. E. *South Africa and southern Mozambique: labour, railways and trade in the making of a relationship.* Manchester: Manchester University Press, 1981.
– – Atlantic Highlands, NJ: Distributed in North America by Humanities Press, c1982.

Kennedy, P. A. *The fatal diplomacy: Sir Theophilus Shepstone and the Zulu kings, 1839–1879.* Ann Arbor, Mich.: University Microfilms International, 1976. (Ph.D. thesis).

Klein, M. and Johnson, G. W., eds. *Perspectives on the African past.* Boston: Little, Brown and Co., [1972].

Klein, R. G., ed. *Southern African prehistory and paleoenvironments.* Rotterdam: Balkema, 1984.

Knight, I., ed. *There will be an awful row at home about this.* Shoreham-by-sea: Zulu Study Group, Victorian Military Society, 1987.

Knowles, L. C. A. and Knowles, C. M. *The economic development of the British overseas empire.* Vol. 3: *The Union of South Africa.* London: George Routledge, 1936.

Konczacki, Z. A. *Public finance and economic development of Natal, 1893–1910.* Durham, N C: Duke University Press, 1967.

Krige, E. J. *The social system of the Zulus.* London: Longmans, Green, 1936.
– – Johannesburg: University of the Witwatersrand, 1936.
– – 2nd edition. Pietermaritzburg: Shuter & Shooter, 1950.
– – 3rd edition. 1957.

Laband, J. P. C. *Fight us in the open: the Anglo-Zulu War through Zulu eyes.* Pietermaritzburg: Shuter & Shooter; Ulundi: KwaZulu Monuments Council, 1985.

Laband, J. P. C. and Thompson, P. S. *A field guide to the war in Zululand, 1879.* With cartography by B. Martin. Pietermaritzburg: University of Natal Press, 1979.

––––––. *Field guide to the war in Zululand and the defence of Natal, 1879.* With cartography by B. Martin. 2nd, revised edition. Pietermaritzburg: University of Natal Press, 1983.

––––––. *War comes to Umvoti: the Natal-Zululand border, 1878–79.* University of Natal, Department of History research monograph no. 5. Durban: The Department, 1980.

Laband, J. P. C. and Thompson, P. S.; with Henderson, S. *The buffalo border, 1879: the Anglo-Zulu War in northern Natal.* University of Natal, Department of History research monograph no. 6. Durban: The Department, 1983.

Laband, J. P. C. and Wright, J. B. *King Cetshwayo kaMpande, c. 1832–1884.* Pietermaritzburg: Shuter & Shooter; Ulundi: KwaZulu Monuments Council, 1983.

Lewis-Williams, J. D. *Believing and seeing: an interpretation of symbolic meanings in southern San rock paintings.* London; New York: Academic Press, 1981.

Lodge, T., ed. *Resistance and ideology in settler societies.* Johannesburg: Ravan Press in association with the African Studies Institute of the University of the Witwatersrand, 1986.

Lugg, H. C. *Historic Natal and Zululand: containing a series of short sketches of the historical spots, game reserves, fishing resorts, and places of scenic beauty, etc. to be found in the province, together with some notes on a number of outstanding characters, both European and Native, associated with its past history & development.* Pietermaritzburg: Shuter & Shooter, 1948.

Mael, R. *The problem of political integration in the Zulu empire.* Ann Arbor, Mich.: University Microfilms International, 1974. (Ph.D. thesis).

McCracken, J. L. *The Cape parliament, 1854–1910.* Oxford: Oxford University Press; Clarendon Press, 1967.

MacKeurtan, [H.] G. *The cradle days of Natal, 1497–1845.* London; New York: Longmans, Green, 1930.
– – New edition. London: Longmans, 1931.
– – 2nd edition. Pietermaritzburg: Shuter & Shooter, 1948.
– – Facsimile of 1930 edition. Durban: T. W. Griggs, 1972.

Marks, S. *The ambiguities of dependence in South Africa.* Johannesburg: Ravan Press, 1986.

————. *Reluctant rebellion: the 1906–8 disturbances in Natal.* Oxford: Clarendon Press, 1970.

Marks, S. and Atmore, A., eds. *Economy and society in pre-industrial South Africa.* London: Longman, 1980.

Marks, S. and Rathbone, R., eds. *Industrialisation and social change in South Africa: African class formation, culture and consciousness, 1870–1930.* London: Longman, 1982.

Mason, R. *Prehistory of the Transvaal: a record of human activity.* Johannesburg: Witwatersrand University Press, 1962.

Maurice, F. B. and Arthur, G. C. A. *The life of Lord Wolseley.* London: William Heinemann, 1924.
– – Garden City, New York: Doubleday, Page and Co., 1924.

Maylam, P. R. *A history of the African people of southern Africa, from the Early Iron Age to the 1970s.* London: Croom Helm; Cape Town: David Philip, 1986.

Miller, J. C., ed. *The African past speaks: essays on oral tradition and history.* Folkestone, Eng.: Dawson; Hamden, Conn.: Archon Books, 1980.

Moore, D. M. *General Louis Botha's second expedition to Natal during the Anglo-Boer War, September-October, 1901.* Cape Town: Historical Publication Society, 1979.

Morris, D. R. *The washing of the spears: a history of the rise of the Zulu nation under Shaka, and its fall in the Zulu War of 1879.* New York: Simon and Shuster, [1965].
– – London: Jonathan Cape, 1966.
– – London: Sphere Books; Johannesburg: Jonathan Ball, 1968.

Murray, M. *Union Castle chronicle, 1853–1953.* London: Longmans, Green, 1953.

Myklebust, O. G. *H. P. S. Schreuder: kirke og misjon.* Oslo: Gyldendal Norsk Forlag, 1980.

Natal Chamber of Industries *Fifty years of progress.* See **Neame, L. E.** *Fifty years of progress.*

Neame, L. E. *Fifty years of progress: the development of industry in Natal, 1905–1955.* [Durban]: Natal Chamber of Industries, [1956].

Nicholls, G. Heaton *Bayete! 'Hail to the King!'* London: George Allen and Unwin, 1923.

Odendaal, A. *Black protest politics in South Africa to 1912.* Cape Town: David Philip; Totawa, NJ: Barnes and Noble, 1984.

————. *Vukani Bantu: the beginnings of Black protest politics in South Africa to 1912.* Cape Town: David Philip, 1984.

Oliver, R. and Fage, J. D. *A short history of Africa.* Harmondsworth: Penguin, 1962.
– – New York: New York University Press, 1963.
– – 2nd edition. Harmondsworth: Penguin, 1966.
– – 3rd edition. 1970.
– – [3rd edition]. London: Collings, 1974.
– – 4th edition. Harmondsworth: Penguin, 1972.

– – 5th edition. 1975.

Omer-Cooper, J. D. *The Zulu after-math: a nineteenth century revolution in Bantu Africa.* London: Longmans, Green and Co., 1966.
– – 2nd edition. 1969.

Osborn, R. F. *This man of purpose: Sir James Liege Hulett, pioneer of Natal and Zululand: a biography.* Umhlali: North Coast Sales Promotions, 1973.

–––––. *Valiant harvest: the founding of the South African sugar industry, 1848–1926.* Durban: South African Sugar Association, 1964.

Pachai, B. *The international aspects of the South African Indian question, 1860–1971.* Cape Town: Struik, 1971.

–––––. *South Africa's Indians: the evolution of a minority.* Washington: University Press of America, 1979.

Pager, H. *Ndedema: a documentation of the rock paintings of the Ndedema Gorge.* With a foreword by R. A. Dart and contributions by R. J. Mason and R. G. Welbourne. Graz: Akademische Druck- u. Verlagsanstalt, 1971.

Pakenham, T. *The Boer War.* Johannesburg: Jonathon Ball, 1979.
– – London: Weidenfeld and Nicolson, 1982.

Parkington, J. and Hall, M., eds. *Papers on the prehistory of the Western Cape, South Africa.* BAR international series, 332. Oxford: British Archaeological Reports, 1987.

Pearse, R. O. *Joseph Baynes: pioneer.* Pietermaritzburg: Shuter & Shooter; Baynesfield Board of Administration, 1983.

Peires, J. B., ed. *Before and after Shaka: papers in Nguni history.* Grahamstown: Institute of Social and Economic Research, Rhodes University, 1981.

Phillips, J. *The agricultural and related development of the Tugela Basin and its influent surrounds: a study in tropical Africa.* Natal town and regional planning report; 19. Pietermaritzburg: Natal Town and Regional Planning Commission, 1973.

Phillipson, D. W. *The later prehistory of eastern and southern Africa.* London: Heinemann, 1977.

Ranger, T. *Revolt in Southern Rhodesia, 1896–7: a study in African resistance.* London: Heinemann, 1967.
– – New edition. 1979.

Rasmussen, R. *Migrant kingdom: Mzilikazi's Ndebele in South Africa.* London: Rex Collings; Cape Town: David Philip, 1978.

Richardson, P. *Chinese mine labour in the Transvaal.* London: Macmillan, 1982.
– – Atlantic Highlands, NJ: Humanities Press, 1982.

Robinson, R. and Gallagher, J.; with Denny, A. *Africa and the Victorians: the climax of imperialism in the Dark Continent.* New York: St. Martin's Press, 1961.
– – New York: Anchor Books, 1968.

–––––. *Africa and the Victorians: the official mind of imperialism.* London: Macmillan; New York: St. Martin's Press, 1961.
– – 2nd edition. 1981.

Ross, R., ed. *Racism and colonialism.* The Hague: Martinus Nijhoff Publishers for Leiden University Press, 1982.

Saunders, C. *The making of the South African past: major historians on race and class.* Cape Town: David Philip; Totawa, NJ: Barnes and Noble, 1988.

–––––. , ed. *Black leaders in southern African history.* London: Heinemann, 1979.

Shain, M. *Jewry and Cape society: the origins and activities of the Jewish Board of Deputies for the Cape Colony.* Cape Town: Historical Publication Society, 1983.

Shepperson, G. and Price, T. *Independent African: John Chilembwe and the origins, setting and significance of the Nyasaland native rising of 1915.* Edinburgh: Edinburgh University Press, 1958.

Smith, K. *The changing past: trends in South African historical writing. Johannesburg; Southern Book Publishers, 1988.*

Solomon, V. E. *The South African shipping question, 1886–1914.* Cape Town: Historical Publication Society, 1981.

Spencer, S. O'Byrne *British settlers in Natal, 1824–1857: a biographical register.* Pietermaritzburg: University of Natal Press, 1981– . 4 v. [proceeding].

Sundkler, R. *Bantu prophets in South Africa.* London: Lutterworth Press, 1948.
– – 2nd edition. Oxford: Oxford University Press, 1961.

Swan, M. [Tayal, M.] *Gandhi: the South African experience.* Johannesburg: Ravan Press, 1985.

Tavener-Smith, R. *Coal in Natal.* Pietermaritzburg: University of Natal Press, 1973. [Inaugural lecture].

Theal, G. M. *History and ethnography of Africa south of the Zambesi from the settlement of the Portugese at Sofala in September 1505 to the conquest of the Cape Colony by the British in September 1795.* London: Swan Sonnenschein, 1907–1910. 3 v.
– – London: George Allen, [19–?]. 2 v.

––––––. *History of South Africa from 1873 to 1884: twelve eventful years; with continuation of the history of Galekaland, Tembuland, Pondoland and Betshuanaland until the annexation of those territories to the Cape Colony, and of Zululand until its annexation to Natal.* London: George Allen and Unwin, (1919). 2 v.
– – London: George Allen and Unwin; Cape Town: T. Maskew Miller, [1919].

Thompson, L. M. *The unification of South Africa, 1902–1910.* Oxford: Clarendon Press, 1960.

Thompson, L. M., ed. *African societies in southern Africa: historical studies.* London: Heinemann, 1969.
– – New York: Praegar, [1969].

Tinker, H. *A new system of slavery: the export of Indian labour overseas, 1830–1920.* Oxford: Oxford University Press, 1974.

Uys, C. J. *In the era of Shepstone: being a study of British expansion in South Africa, 1842–1877.* Lovedale: Lovedale Press, [1933].

Van der Poel, J. *Railway and customs policies in South Africa, 1885–1910.* London: Longmans Green, 1933.

Van Onselen, C. *Studies in the social and economic history of the Witwatersrand, 1886–1914.* Harlow, Essex: Longman, 1982. 2 v. Vol. 1: *New Babylon*; vol. 2: *New Nineveh.*
– – Johannesburg: Ravan Press, 1982. 2 v.

Vansina, J. *Oral tradition: a study in historical methodology.* Translated by H. M. Wright. London: Routledge and Kegan Paul, 1965.
– – Chicago: Aldine Publishing Co., 1965.
– – Harmondsworth: Penguin, 1973.

Vietzen, S. *A history of education for European girls in Natal, 1837–1902.* Pietermaritzburg: University of Natal Press, 1973.
– – 2nd edition, with illustrations. 1980.

Vinnicombe, P. *People of the eland: rock paintings of the Drakensberg Bushmen as a reflection of their life and thought.* Pietermaritzburg: University of Natal Press, 1976.

Walker, E. A. *A history of South Africa.* London; New York: Longmans, Green, 1928.

– – Reissue with extensive additions. 1935.
– – 2nd edition. 1940.
– – New impression. London; New York: Longmans, Green and Co., 1941.
– – With minor corrections. 1947.
– – [3rd edition]. *A history of southern Africa.* London; New York: Longmans Green, 1957.

–––––. *W. P. Schreiner: a South African.* London: Oxford University Press, 1937.
– – Abridged edition. Johannesburg: Central News Agency, [1960?].
– – 2nd edition. London: Oxford University Press, 1969.

Walshe, P. *The rise of African nationalism in South Africa: the African National Congress, 1912–1952.* London: C. Hurst, 1970.
– – Berkeley: University of California Press, 1971.
– – Johannesburg: Ad Donker, 1987.

Walter, E. V. *Terror and resistance: a study of political violence, with case studies of some primitive African communties.* London; New York: Oxford University Press, 1969.

Warwick, P. *Black people and the South African War, 1899–1902.* Cambridge; New York: Cambridge University Press, 1983.
– – Johannesburg: Ravan Press, 1983.

Welsh, D. *The roots of segregation: native policy in colonial Natal, 1845–1910.* Cape Town: Oxford University Press, 1971.

Wight, M. *The development of the legislative council, 1606–1945.* London: Faber and Faber under the auspices of Nuffield College, 1946.

Willcox, A. R. *Rock paintings of the Drakensberg, Natal and Griqualand East.* London: Parrish, 1956.
– – 2nd edition. Cape Town: Struik, 1973.

Wilson, M. and Thompson, L., eds. *The Oxford history of South Africa. Oxford: Clarendon Press, 1969–1971. 2 v. Vol. 1: South Africa to 1870*; vol. 2: *South Africa, 1870–1966.*

Wright, H. M. *The burden of the present: liberal-radical controversy over South African history.* Cape Town: David Philip; London: Rex Collings, 1977.

Wright, J. B. *Bushman raiders of the Drakensberg, 1840–1870: a study of their conflict with stock-keeping peoples in Natal.* Pietermaritzburg: University of Natal Press, 1971.

Wright, J. B. and Manson, A. *The Hlubi chiefdom in Zululand-Natal: a history.* Ladysmith: Ladysmith Historical Society, 1983.

ARTICLES

Alpers, E. A. 'State, merchant capital, and gender relations in southern Mozambique to the end of the 19th century: some tentative hypotheses.' *African economic history* 13 (1984), pp. 23–55.

Atmore, A. and Marks, S. 'The imperial factor in South Africa in the nineteenth century: towards a reassessment.' *Journal of imperial and Commonwealth history* 3 (1974), pp. 105–39.

Auret, C. and Maggs, T. M. O'C. 'The great ship *São Bento*: remains from a mid-sixteenth century Portugese wreck on the Pondoland coast.' *Annals of the Natal Museum* 25 (1982), pp. 1–39.

Ballard, C. C. 'Migrant labour in Natal, 1860–1879, with special reference to Zululand and the Delagoa Bay hinterland.' *Journal of Natal and Zulu history* 1 (1978), pp. 25–42.

———. 'Natal, 1824–44: the frontier inter-regnum.' *Journal of Natal and Zulu history* 5 (1982), pp. 49–64.

———. 'The repercussions of rinderpest: cattle plague and peasant decline in colonial Natal.' *The international journal of African historical studies* 3 (1986), pp. 421–50.

———. 'The role of trade and hunter-traders in the political economy of Natal and Zululand, 1824–1880.' *African economic history* 10 (1981), pp. 3–21.

———. 'Sir Garnet Wolseley and John Dunn: the architects of the Ulundi settlement.' In *The Anglo-Zulu War: new perspectives*, pp. 120–47. Edited by A. Duminy and C. C. Ballard. Pietermaritzburg: University of Natal Press, 1981.

Ballard, C. C. and Lenta, G. 'The complex nature of agriculture in colonial Natal, 1860–1909.' In *Enterprise and exploitation in a Victorian colony: aspects of the economic and social history of colonial Natal*, pp. 120–49. Edited by B. Guest and J. M. Sellers. Pietermaritzburg: University of Natal Press, 1985.

Beall, J. D. and North-Coombes, M. D. 'The 1913 disturbances in Natal: the social and economic background to "passive resistance".' *Journal of Natal and Zulu history* 6 (1983), pp. 48–81.

Bell-Cross, G. 'Problems associated with the location and identification of early shipwrecks.' *South African Museum bulletin* 14 (1981), pp. 326–40.

Benyon, J. A. 'Isandhlwana and the passing of a proconsul.' *Natalia* 8 (1978), pp. 38–45.

Bhana, S. 'Indian trade and trader in colonial Natal.' In *Enterprise and exploitation in a Victorian colony: aspects of the economic and social history of colonial Natal*, pp. 234–63. Edited by B. Guest and J. M. Sellers. Pietermaritzburg: University of Natal Press, 1985.

Bonner, P. L. 'Classes, the mode of production and the state in pre-colonial Swaziland.' In *Economy and society in pre-industrial South Africa*, pp. 80–101. Edited by S. Marks and A. Atmore. London: Longman, 1980.

———. 'The dynamics of late eighteenth century, early nineteenth century northern Nguni society: some hypotheses.' In *Before and after Shaka: papers in Nguni history*, pp. 74–81. Edited by J. B. Peires. Grahamstown: Institute of Social and Economic Research, Rhodes University, 1981.

Bradlow, E. 'Indentured Indians in Natal and the £3 tax.' *South African historical journal* 2 (1970), pp. 38–53.

Brain, J. B. 'Health and disease in white settlers in colonial Natal.' *Natalia* 15 (1985), pp. 64–77.

———. 'Indentured and free Indians in the economy of colonial Natal.' In *Enterprise and exploitation in a Victorian colony: aspects of the economic and social history of colonial Natal*, pp. 198–233. Edited by B. Guest and J. M. Sellers. Pietermaritzburg: University of Natal Press, 1985.

Brain, J. B. and Brain, P. 'Nostalgia and alligator bite: morbidity and mortality among Indian migrants to Natal, 1884–1911.' *South African medical journal* 65 (21 January 1984), pp. 98–102.

Bryant, A. T. 'A sketch of the origin and early history of the Zulu people.' Preface to *A Zulu-English dictionary*, pp. 12–66. Mariannhill: Mariannhill Mission Press, 1905.

Butler, J. R. M. 'Colonial self-government, 1838–1852.' In *The Cambridge history of the British empire*. Vol. 2: *The growth of the new empire, 1783–1870*, pp. 335–87. Edited by J. Holland Rose, A. P. Newton and E. A. Benians. Cambridge: Cambridge University Press, 1940.

———. 'Imperial questions in British politics, 1868–1880.' In *The Cambridge history of the British Empire*. Vol. 3: *The Empire-Commonwealth, 1870–1919*, pp. 17–64. Edited by E. A. Benians, J. Butler, C. E. Carrington. Cambridge: Cambridge University Press, 1959.

Cable, J. H. C.; Scott, K. and Carter, P. L. 'Excavations at Good Hope Shelter, Underberg District, Natal.' *Annals of the Natal Museum* 24 (1980), pp. 1–34.

Carter, P. L. 'The effects of climatic change on settlement in eastern Lesotho during the Middle and Later Stone Age.' *World archaeology* 8 (1976), pp. 197–206.

————. 'Late Stone Age exploitation patterns in southern Natal.' *South African archaeological bulletin* 25 (1970), pp. 55–8.

Chanaiwa, D. S. 'The Zulu revolution: state formation in a pastoralist society.' *African studies review* 23 (1980), pp. 1–20.

Cobbing J. 'The evolution of the Ndebele Amabutho.' *Journal of African history* 15 (1974), pp. 607–31.

Cohen, R. and Middleton, J. 'Introduction.' In *From tribe to nation in Africa: studies in incorporation processes*, pp. 1–2. Edited by R. Cohen and J. Middleton. Scranton, Penn.: Chandler Publishing Co., [1970].

Colenbrander, P. J. 'External exchange and the Zulu kingdom: towards a reassessment.' In *Enterprise and exploitation in a Victorian colony: aspects of the economic and social history of colonial Natal*, pp. 98–119. Edited by B. Guest and J. M. Sellers. Pietermaritzburg: University of Natal Press, 1985.

————. 'The Zulu political economy on the eve of the war.' In *The Anglo-Zulu War: new perspectives*, pp. 78–97. Edited by A. H. Duminy and C. C. Ballard. Pietermaritzburg: University of Natal Press, 1981.

Comaroff, J. L. 'Rules and rulers: political processes in a Tswana chiefdom.' *Man* 13 (1978), pp. 1–20.

Cope, R. L. 'Strategic and socio-economic explanations for Carnarvon's South African confederation policy: the historiography and the evidence.' *History in Africa* 13 (1986), pp. 13–34.

Coquery-Vidrovitch, C. 'The political economy of the African peasantry and modes of production.' In *The political economy of contemporary Africa*, pp. 90–111. Edited by P. C. W. Gutkind and I. Wallerstein. Beverly Hills, Ca.: Sage Publications, c1976.

'Research on an African mode of production.' In *Perspectives on the African past*, pp. 33–51. Edited by M. Klein and G. W. Johnson. Boston: Little, Brown and Co., [1972].

Cramb, J. G. 'A Middle Stone Age industry from a Natal rock shelter.' *South African journal of science* 48 (1952), pp. 181–6.

————. 'A second report on work at the Holley Shelter.' *South African journal of science* 57 (1961), pp. 45–8.

Davenport, T. R. H. 'The fragmentation of Zululand, 1879–1918.' *Reality: a journal of liberal and radical opinion* 11, 5 (1979), pp. 13–15.

————. 'The responsible government issue in Natal, 1880–1882.' *Butterworth's South African law review* 1957, pp. 84–133.

Davies, O. 'Excavations at Blackburn.' *South African archaeological bulletin* 26 (1971), pp. 165–78.

————. 'Excavations at Shongweni South Cave: the oldest evidence to date for cultigens in southern Africa.' *Annals of the Natal Museum* 22 (1975), pp. 627–62.

————. 'Excavations at the walled Early Iron Age site in Moor Park near Estcourt,

Natal.' *Annals of the Natal Museum* 22 (1974), pp. 289–324.

————. 'The older coastal dunes in Natal and Zululand and their relation to former shorelines.' *Annals of the South African Museum* 71 (1976), pp. 19–32.

————. 'The palaeolithic sequence of Umgababa ilmenite diggings.' *Annals of the Natal Museum* 25 (1982), pp. 41–59.

————. 'Pleistocene beaches of Natal.' *Annals of the Natal Museum* 20 (1970), pp. 403–42.

————. 'The 'Sangoan' Industries.' *Annals of the Natal Museum* 22 (1976), pp. 885–911.

Davies, O. and Gordon-Gray, K. 'Tropical African cultigens from Shongweni excavations, Natal.' *Journal of archaeological science* 4 (1977), pp. 153–62.

Dominy, G. 'The New Republicans: a centennial reappraisal of the 'Nieuwe Republiek', 1884–1888.' *Natalia* 14 (1984), pp. 87–97.

Drus, E. 'The Chamberlain papers concerning Anglo-Transvaal relations, 1896–1899.' *Bulletin of the Institute of Historical Research* 27, 76 (1954), pp. 156–89.

Edgecombe, [D.] R. 'Sir Marshall Clarke and the abortive attempt to 'Basutolandise' Zululand, 1893–7.' *Journal of Natal and Zulu history* 1 (1978), pp. 43–53.

Edgecombe, [D.] R. and Guest, B. [W. R.] 'An introduction to the pre-Union Natal coal industry.' In *Enterprise and exploitation in a Victorian colony: aspects of the economic and social history of colonial Natal*, pp. 308–51. Edited by B. Guest and J. M. Sellers. Pietermaritzburg: University of Natal Press, 1985.

Ellis, B. 'The impact of white settlers on the natural environment of Natal, 1845–1870.' In *Enterprise and exploitation in a Victorian colony: aspects of the economic and social history of colonial Natal*, pp. 70–97. Edited by B. Guest and J. M. Sellers. Pietermaritzburg: University of Natal Press, 1985.

Etherington, N. A. 'African economic experiments in colonial Natal, 1845–1880.' In *Enterprise and exploitation in a Victorian colony: aspects of the economic and social history of colonial Natal*, pp. 264–85. Edited By B. Guest and J. M. Sellers. Pietermaritzburg: University of Natal Press, 1985.

————. 'Anglo-Zulu relations, 1856–1878.' In *The Anglo-Zulu War: new perspectives*, pp. 13–52. Edited by A. H. Duminy and C. C. Ballard. Pietermaritzburg: University of Natal Press, 1981.

————. 'Frederic Elton and the South African factor in the making of Britain's East African empire.' *Journal of imperial and Commonwealth history* 9 (1981), pp. 255–74.

————. 'Labour supply and the genesis of South Africa confederation in the 1870s.' *Journal of African history* 20 (1979), pp. 235–53.

————. 'Why Langalibalele ran away.' *Journal of Natal and Zulu history* 1 (1978), pp. 1–24.

Gambell, R. 'A short history of modern whaling off Natal.' *Mercurius* 14 (1971), pp. 37–44.

Gluckman, M. 'Analysis of a social system in modern Zululand. A: the social organisation of modern Zululand.' *Bantu studies* 14 (1940), pp. 1–30.

————. 'Analysis of a social system in modern Zululand. B: Social change in Zululand.' *Bantu studies* 14 (1940), pp. 147–74.

————. 'The individual in a social framework: the rise of King Shaka of Zululand.'

Journal of African studies 1 (1974), pp. 113–44.

———. 'The kingdom of the Zulu of South Africa.' In *African political systems*, pp. 25–55. Edited by M. Fortes and E. E. Evans-Pritchard. London: Oxford University Press for the International African Institute, 1940.

———. 'The rise of a Zulu empire.' *Scientific American* 202 (April 1960), pp. 157–68.

Gooch, W. D. 'The Stone Age of South Africa.' *Journal of the Royal Anthropological Institute* 11 (1882), pp. 124–82.

Goodwin, A. J. H. 'A new variation of the Smithfield culture from Natal.' *Transactions of the Royal Society of South Africa* 19 (1930), pp. 7–14.

———. 'The Rhodesian origin of certain Smithfield "N" elements.' *Proceedings of the Rhodesian Scientific Association* 34 (1934), pp. 28–34.

Goodwin, A. J. H. and Van Riet Lowe, C. 'The Stone Age cultures of South Africa.' *Annals of the South African Museum* 27 (1929), pp. 1–279.

Guest, B. [W. R.] 'The meaning of Majuba for Natal.' *Natalia* 11 (1981), pp. 27–8.

———. 'The war, Natal and confederation.' In *The Anglo-Zulu War: new perspectives*, pp. 53–77. Edited by A. H. Duminy and C. C. Ballard. Pietermaritzburg: University of Natal Press, 1981.

Guy, J. J. 'Cetshwayo kaMpande, c. 1832–1884.' In *Black leaders in southern African history*, pp. 75–99. Edited by C. Saunders. London: Heinemann, 1979.

———. 'The destruction and reconstruction of Zulu society.' In *Industrialisation and social change in South Africa: African class formation, culture, and consciousness, 1870–1930*, pp. 167–94. Edited by S. Marks and R. Rathbone. London: Longman, 1982.

———. 'Ecological factors in the rise of Shaka and the Zulu kingdom.' In *Economy and society in pre-industrial South Africa*, pp. 102–19. Edited by S. Marks and A. Atmore. London: Longman, 1980.

———. 'A note on firearms in the Zulu kingdom, with special reference to the Anglo-Zulu War, 1879.' *Journal of African history* 12 (1971), pp. 557–70.

———. 'The role of colonial officials in the destruction of the Zulu kingdom.' In *The Anglo-Zulu War: new perspectives*, pp. 148–74. Edited by A. H. Duminy and C. C. Ballard. Pietermaritzburg: University of Natal Press, 1981.

Hall, M. 'Archaeology and modes of production in precolonial southern Africa.' *Journal of southern African studies* 14 (1987), pp. 1–17.

———. 'Enkwazini, an Iron Age site on the Zululand coast.' *Annals of the Natal Museum* 24 (1980), pp. 97–110.

———. 'The role of cattle in southern African agropastoral societies: more than bones alone can tell.' *South African Archaeological Society, Goodwin series* 5 (1986), pp. 83–7. [Journal issue entitled *Prehistoric pastoralism in southern Africa*, edited by M. Hall and A. B. Smith.]

Hall, M. and Mack, K. 'The outline of an eighteenth century economic system in south-east Africa.' *Annals of the South African Museum* 91 (1983), pp. 163–94.

Hall, M. and Maggs, T. M. O'C. 'Nqabeni: a Later Iron Age site in Zululand.' *South African Archaeological Society, Goodwin series* 3 (1979), pp. 159–76. [Journal issue entitled *Iron Age studies in southern Africa*, edited by N. J. van der Merwe and T. N. Huffman.]

Hall, M. and Vogel, J. C. 'Some recent

radiocarbon dates from southern Africa.' *Journal of African history* 21 (1980), pp. 431–55.

Hamilton, C. A. 'Shaka: one kind of folklore or the other.' *Weekly mail*, 31 Oct.–6 Nov. 1986, p. 22.

Hammond-Tooke, W. D. 'In search of the lineage: the Cape Nguni case.' *Man* 19 (1984), pp. 77–93.

Harlow, V. 'The new imperial system, 1783–1815.' In *The Cambridge history of the British empire*. Vol. 2: *The growth of the new empire, 1783–1870*, pp. 129–87. Edited by J. Holland Rose, A. P. Newton and E. A. Benians. Cambridge: Cambridge University Press, 1940.

Harries, P. 'History, ethnicity and the Ingwavuma land deal: the Zululand northern frontier in the nineteenth century.' *Journal of Natal and Zulu history* 6 (1983), pp. 1–27.

Henderson, S. 'Colonial coalopolis: the establishment and growth of Dundee.' *Natalia* 12 (1982), pp. 14–26.

Heydenrych, [D.] H. 'Indian railway labour in Natal, 1879–1895: the biggest Indian workforce in the Colony.' *Historia* 31, 3 (1986), pp. 11–20.

————. 'Railway development in Natal to 1895.' In *Enterprise and exploitation in a Victorian colony: aspects of the economic and social history of colonial Natal*, pp. 46–69. Edited by B. Guest and J. M. Sellers. Pietermaritzburg: University of Natal Press, 1985.

Heydenrych, L. 'Port Natal harbour, c.1850–1897.' In *Enterprise and exploitation in a Victorian colony: aspects of the economic and social history of colonial Natal*, pp. 17–46. Edited by B. Guest and J. M. Sellers. Pietermaritzburg: University of Natal Press, 1985.

Huffman, T. N. 'The origins of Leopard's Kopje: an 11th century *difaqane*.' *Arnoldia* 8, 23 (1978), pp. 1–23.

Jackson, F. W. D. [Correspondence between D. Morris and F. W. D. Jackson on Isandhlwana] *Soldiers of the Queen* 29/30 (1982), pp. 3–22; 33 (1983), pp. 9–20.

————. 'Isandhlwana, 1879: the sources re-examined.' *Journal of the Society of Army Historical Research* 43 (1965), pp. 30–43; 113–32.

Junod, H. A. 'The condition of the natives of south-east Africa in the sixteenth century, according to the early Portugese documents.' *South African journal of science* 10 (1914), pp. 137–61.
– – [separately published]. Cape Town: South African Association for the Advancement of Science, 1914.

Kennedy, P. A. 'Mpande and the Zulu kingship.' *Journal of Natal and Zulu history* 4 (1981), pp. 21–38.

King, P. 'Tribe: conflicts in meaning and usage.' *West African journal of sociology and political science* 1 (1976), pp. 186–94.

Kjonstad, S. 'The development of the Marburg settlement, Natal.' *JNGA: journal of the Natal Geographical Association* 5 (1987), pp. 22–34.

Klapwijk, M. 'An Early Iron Age site near Tzaneen, N E Transvaal.' In 'Early Iron age settlement of southern Africa', p. 324. *South African journal of science* 69 (1973), pp. 324–6.

Klein, R. G. 'The mammalian fauna from the Middle and Later Stone Age (Late Pleistocene) levels of Border Cave, Natal Province, South Africa.' *South African archaeological bulletin* 32 (1977), pp. 14–27.

————. 'The prehistory of Stone Age herders in the Cape Province of South Africa.' *South African Archaeological Society, Goodwin Series* 5 (1986), pp. 5–12. [Journal issue entitled *Prehistoric pastoralism in southern Africa*, edited by M. Hall and A. B. Smith.]

Kline, B. J. 'The establishment of responsible government in Natal, 1887–1893: the legacy of apartheid.' *Journal of Natal and Zulu history* 9 (1986), pp. 55–70.

Laband, J. P. C. 'The battle of Ivuna (or Ndunu Hill).' *Natalia* 10 (1980), pp. 16–22.

———. 'The battle of Khambula, 29 March 1879: a re-examination from the Zulu perspective.' In *There will be an awful row at home about this*, pp. 20–9. Edited by I. Knight. Shoreham-by-sea: Zulu Study Group, Victorian Military Society, 1987.[†]

———. 'British fieldworks of the Zulu campaign of 1879, with special reference to Fort Eshowe.' *Military history journal* 6, 1 (1983), pp. 1–5.[†]

———. 'Bulwer, Chelmsford and the border levies.' *Theoria* 57 (1981), pp. 1–15.[†]

———. 'The cohesion of the Zulu polity under the impact of the Anglo-Zulu War: a reassessment.' *Journal of Natal and Zulu history* 8 (1985), pp. 33–62.[†]

———. 'The establishment of the Zululand administration in 1887: a study of the criteria behind the selection of British colonial officials.' *Journal of Natal and Zulu history* 4 (1981), pp. 62–73.[†]

———. 'Humbugging the general?: King Cetshwayo's peace overtures during the Anglo-Zulu War.' *Theoria* 67 (1986), pp. 1–20.[†]

Lambert, J. 'Sir John Robinson, 1839–1903.' *Journal of Natal and Zulu history*, 3 (1980), pp. 45–56.

Le Cordeur, B. A. 'The relations between the Cape and Natal, 1846–1879: agency and island.' In *Archives year book for South African history*, 1965, part 1, pp. 1–264. Cape Town: Government Printer, 1965.

Leverton, B. J. T. 'Government finance and political development in Natal, 1843–1893.' In *Archives year book for South African history*, 1970, part 1, pp. 1–317. Cape Town: Government Printer, 1971.

Lewin, R. 'Ethiopian stone tools are the world's oldest.' *Science* 211 (1981), pp. 806–7.

Lewis-Williams, J. D. 'The San artistic achievement.' *African arts* 18 (1985), pp. 54–9.

———. 'The social and economic context of southern San rock art.' *Current anthropology* 23 (1982), pp. 429–49.

———. 'The thin red line: southern San notions and rock paintings of supernatural potency.' *South African archaeological bulletin* 36 (1981), pp. 5–13.

Liesegang, G. 'Dingane's attack on Lourenco Marques in 1833.' *Journal of African history* 10 (1969), pp. 56–79.

Maggs, T. M. O'C. 'The great galleon *São João*: remains from a mid-sixteenth century wreck on the Natal coast.' *Annals of the Natal Museum* 26 (1984), pp. 173–86.

———. 'The Iron Age sequence south of the Vaal and Pongola Rivers: some historical implications.' *Journal of African history* 21 (1980), pp. 1–15.

———. 'Iron Age settlement and subsistence patterns in the Tugela River Basin, Natal.' In *Frontiers: southern African archaeology today*, pp. 194–206. Edited by M. Hall et al. Cambridge monographs in African archaeology, 10. BAR international series, 207. Oxford: British Archaeological Reports, 1984.

———. 'The Iron Age south of the Zambezi'. In *Southern African prehistory and paleoenvironments*, pp. 329–60. Edited by R. G. Klein. Rotterdam: Balkema, 1984.

[†] J. P. C. Laband's articles on the Anglo-Zulu War will be published by the University of Natal Press in 1990 under the title *King and colony at war*, edited by J. P. C. Laband and P. S. Thompson.

————. 'Mabhija: pre-colonial industrial development in the Tugela Basin.' *Annals of the Natal Museum* 25 (1982), pp. 123–41.

————. 'Mgoduyanuka: terminal Iron Age settlement in the Natal grasslands.' *Annals of the Natal Museum* 25 (1982), pp. 83–114.

————. 'Mzonjani and the beginning of the Iron Age in Natal.' *Annals of the Natal Museum* 24 (1980), pp. 71–96.

————. 'Ndondondwane: a preliminary report on an early Iron Age site on the lower Tugela River.' *Annals of the Natal Museum* 26 (1984), pp. 71–93.

Maggs, T. M. O'C. and Davison, P. 'The Lydenburg heads.' *African arts* 14, 2 (1981), pp. 28–33.

Maggs, T. M. O'C. and Michael, M. A. 'Ntshekane: an early Iron Age site in the Tugela Basin, Natal.' *Annals of the Natal Museum* 22 (1976), pp. 705–40.

Maggs, T. M. O'C.; Oswald, D.; Hall, M. and Ruther, H. 'Spatial parameters of Late Iron Age settlements in the Upper Thukela Valley.' *Annals of the Natal Museum* 27 (1986), pp. 455–79.

Marks, S. 'Harriette Colenso and the Zulus, 1874–1913.' *Journal of African history* 4 (1963), pp. 403–11.

————. 'The Nguni, the Natalians, and their history.' *Journal of African history* 8 (1967), pp. 529–40.

————. 'The traditions of the Natal "Nguni": a second look at the work of A. T. Bryant.' In *African societies in southern Africa: historical studies*, pp. 126–44. Edited by L. M. Thompson. London: Heinemann, 1969.

Marks, S. and Atmore, A. 'The problem of the Nguni: an examination of the ethnic and linguistic situation in South Africa before the *mfecane*.' In *Language and*

history in Africa, pp. 120–32. Edited by D. Dalby. London: Frank Cass and Co., 1970.

Mason, M. 'Production, penetration and political formation: the Bida state, 1857–1901.' In *Modes of production in Africa: the precolonial era*, pp. 205–26. Edited by D. Crummey and C. C. Stewart. Beverly Hills, Ca.: Sage Publications, c1981.

Mazel, A. D. 'The archaeological past from the changing present: towards a critical assessment of South African Later Stone Age studies from the early 1960s to the early 1980s.' In *Papers in the prehistory of the Western Cape, South Africa*, pp. 504–29. Edited by J. Parkington and M. Hall. BAR international series, 332. Oxford: British Archaeological Reports, 1987.

————. 'Diamond 1 and Clarke's Shelter: report on excavations in the northern Drakensberg, Natal, South Africa.' *Annals of the Natal Museum* 26 (1984), pp. 25–70.

————. 'Evidence for pre-Later Stone Age occupation of the Natal Drakensberg.' *Annals of the Natal Museum* 25 (1982), pp. 61–5.

————. 'Mbabane Shelter and eSinhlonhlweni Shelter: the last two thousand years of hunter-gatherer settlement in the central Thukela Basin, Natal, South Africa.' *Annals of the Natal Museum* 27 (1986), pp. 389–453.

Mazel, A. D. and Parkington, J. E. 'Stone tools and resources: a case study from southern Africa.' *World archaeology* 13 (1981), pp. 16–30.

Miller, J. C. 'Introduction: listening for the African past.' In *The African past speaks: essays on oral tradition and history*, pp. 1–59. Edited by J. C. Miller. Folkestone, Eng.: Dawson; Hamden, Conn.: Archon Books, 1980.

Morris, D. [Correspondence between D. Morris and F. W. D. Jackson on

Isandhlwana] *Soldiers of the Queen* 29/30 (1982), pp. 3–22; 33 (1983), pp. 9–20.

Myklebust, O. G. 'Norsk misjon og British imperialisme in Syd Afrika.' *Norsk tidsskrift for misjon* 31 (1977), pp. 65–72.

Ngubane, J. K. 'Shaka's social, political and military ideas.' In Burness, D. *Shaka, King of the Zulus in African literature: and two special essays, 'Shaka's social, political and military ideas' by Jordan K. Ngubane, and 'Shaka in the literature of southern Africa' by Daniel P. Kunene*, pp. 127–64. Washington: Three Continents Press, 1976.

Okoye, F. N. C. [N. C. F.] 'Dingane: a reappraisal.' *Journal of African history* 10 (1969), pp. 221–35.

Ovendale, R. 'Natal and the Jameson Raid.' *Journal of Natal and Zulu history* 4 (1981), pp. 1–20.

―――. 'Profit or patriotism: Natal, the Transvaal, and the coming of the Second Anglo-Boer War.' *Journal of imperial and Commonwealth history* 8 (1980), pp. 209–34.

Pachai, B. 'Aliens in the political hierarchy.' In *South Africa's Indians: the evolution of a minority*, pp. 1–68. Edited by B. Pachai. Washington: University Press of America, 1979.

Park, M. G. 'The history of early Verulam, 1850–1860.' In *Archives yearbook for South African history*, 1953, part 2, pp. 241–306. Cape Town: Government Printer, 1953.

Parkington, J. E. 'Time and place: some observations on spatial and temporal patterning in the Later Stone Age sequence in southern Africa.' *South African archaeological bulletin* 35 (1980), pp. 73–83. [Commentary and reply pp. 84–112.]

Ranger, T. O. 'Race and tribe in southern Africa: European ideas and African acceptance.' In *Racism and colonialism*, pp. 121–42. Edited by R. Ross. The Hague: Martinus Nijhoff Publishers for Leiden University Press, 1982.

Richardson, P. 'The Natal sugar industry, 1849–1905: an interpretative essay.' *Journal of African history* 23 (1982), pp. 515–27.
― – In *Enterprise and exploitation in a Victorian colony: aspects of the economic and social history of colonial Natal*, pp. 180–197. Edited by B. Guest and J. M. Sellers. Pietermaritzburg: University of Natal Press, 1985.

Robey, T. 'Mpambanyoni: a Late Iron Age site on the Natal South Coast.' *Annals of the Natal Museum* 24 (1980), pp. 147–64.

Sackett, J. R. 'Style and ethnicity in the Kalahari: a reply to Wiessner.' *American antiquity* 50 (1985), pp. 154–59.

Sellers, J. M. 'The origin and development of the woolled sheep industry in the Natal Midlands in the 1850s and 1860s.' In *Enterprise and exploitation in a Victorian colony: aspects of the economic and social history of colonial Natal*, pp. 150–79. Pietermaritzburg: University of Natal Press, 1985.

Shenk, W. R. 'Rufus Anderson and Henry Venn: a special relationship.' *International bulletin of missionary research* 5 (1981), pp. 168–72.

Slater, H. 'The changing pattern of economic relationships in rural Natal, 1838–1914.' In *Economy and society in pre-industrial South Africa*, pp. 148–70. Edited by S. Marks and A. Atmore. London: Longman, 1980.

―――. 'Land, labour and capital in Natal: the Natal Land and Colonisation Company, 1860–1948.' *Journal of African history* 16 (1975), pp. 257–83.

Smith, A. 'Delagoa Bay and the trade of south-eastern Africa.' In *Pre-colonial African trade: essays on trade in central and* eastern Africa before 1900, pp. 265–89. Edited by R. Gray and D. Birmingham. London; New York: Oxford University Press, 1970.

———. 'The trade of Delagoa Bay as a factor in Nguni politics, 1750–1835.' In *African societies in southern Africa: historical studies*, pp. 171–89. Edited by L. M. Thompson. London: Heinemann, 1969.

Southall, A. W. 'The ethnic heart of anthropology.' *Cahiers d'etudes Africaines* 25, 100 (1985), pp. 567–72.

———. 'The illusion of tribe.' In *The passing of tribal man in Africa*, pp. 28–50. Edited by P. C. W. Gutkind. Leiden: Brill, 1970.

Spiller, P. 'The jury system in colonial Natal, 1846–1910.' *Journal of Natal and Zulu history* 9 (1986), pp. 1–11.

Stein, H. B. 'Stone implements from the Cathkin Peak area.' *Bantu studies* 7 (1933), pp. 159–82.

Swanson, M. W. '"The Durban system": roots of urban apartheid in colonial Natal.' *African studies* 35 (1976), pp. 159–76.

———. '"The fate of the Natives": Black Durban and African ideology.' *Natalia* 14 (1984), pp. 59–68.

———. 'The urban factor in Natal Native policy, 1843–1873.' *Journal of Natal and Zulu history* 3 (1980), pp. 1–14.

Tayal, M. [Swan, M.] 'Indian indentured labour in Natal, 1890–1911.' *Indian economic and social history review* 14 (1977), pp. 519–47.

Terray, E. 'Long-distance exchange and the formation of the state: the case of the Abron Kingdom of Gyaman.' *Economy and society* 3 (1974), pp. 315–45.

Thackeray, A. I. 'Dating the rock art of southern Africa.' *South African Archaeological Society, Goodwin series* 4 (1983), pp. 21–6. [Journal issue entitled *New approaches to southern African rock art*, edited by J. D. Lewis-Williams.]

Thackeray, A. I.; Thackeray, J. F.; Beaumont, P. B. and Vogel, J. C. 'Dated rock engravings from Wonderwerk Cave, South Africa.' *Science* 214 (1981), pp. 64–7.

Thompson, L. M. 'Co-operation and conflict: the High Veld.' In *The Oxford history of South Africa*. Vol. 1: *South Africa to 1870*, pp. 391–446. Edited by M. Wilson and L. M. Thompson. Oxford: The Clarendon Press, 1969.

———. 'Indian immigration into Natal, 1860–1872.' In *Archives year book for South African history*, 1952, part 2, pp. 1–76. Cape Town: Government Printer, [1953?].

———. 'The subjection of the African chiefdoms, 1870–1898.' In *The Oxford history of South Africa*. Vol. 2, *South Africa, 1870–1966*, pp. 244–86. Edited by M. Wilson and L. Thompson. Oxford: Clarendon Press, 1971.

Thompson, P. S. 'Captain Lucas and the border guard: the war on the lower Tugela, 1879.' *Journal of Natal and Zulu history* 3 (1980), pp. 30–44.[†]

———. '"The Zulus are coming!": the defence of Pietermaritzburg, 1879.' *Journal of Natal and Zulu history* 6 (1983), pp. 28–47.[†]

Thornton, R. 'Evolution, salvation and history in the rise of the ethnographic monograph in southern Africa, 1860–

[†] P. S. Thompson's articles on the Anglo-Zulu war will be published by the University of Natal Press in 1990 under the title *King and colony at war*, edited by J. P. C. Laband and P. S. Thompson.

1920.' *Social dynamics* 6, 2 (1980), pp. 14–23.

Trapido, S. 'Natal's non-racial franchise, 1856.' *African studies* 22 (1963), pp. 22–32.

Unterhalter, E. 'Confronting imperialism: the people of Nquthu and the invasion of Zululand.' In *The Anglo-Zulu War: new perspectives*, pp. 98–119. Edited by A. H. Duminy and C. C. Ballard. Pietermaritzburg: University of Natal Press, 1981.

Van der Merwe, N. J.; Sealy, J. and Yates, R. 'First accelerator carbon–14 date for pigment from a rock painting.' *South African journal of science* 83 (1987), pp. 56–7.

Van Riet Lowe, C. 'The Smithfield "N" culture.' *Transactions of the Royal Society of South Africa* 23 (1936), pp. 367–72.

Van Wyk, A. J. 'Dinuzulu en die Usutu-opstand van 1888.' In *Archives year book for South African history*, 1979, part 1, pp. 1–174. Pretoria: Government Printer, 1983.

Van Zyl, D. A. 'Boom or bust: the economic consequences of the Anglo-Zulu War.' *Journal of Natal and Zulu history* 9 (1986), pp. 26–55.

Voigt, E. A. 'The faunal remains from Magogo and Mhlopeni: small stock herding in the Early Iron Age in Natal.' *Annals of the Natal Museum* 26 (1984), pp. 141–63.

Voigt, E. A. and Von den Driesch, A. 'Preliminary report on the faunal assemblage from Ndondondwane, Natal.' *Annals of the Natal Museum* 26 (1984), pp. 95–104.

Volman, T. P. 'Early prehistory of southern Africa.' In *Southern African prehistory and palaeoenvironments*, pp. 169–220. Edited by R. G. Klein. Rotterdam: Balkema, 1984.

Walter, R. C. and Aronson, J. L. 'Revisions of K/Ar ages for the Hadar hominid site, Ethiopia.' *Nature* (London) 296 (1982), pp. 122–27.

Warhurst, P. R. 'Obstructing the Protector.' *Journal of Natal and Zulu history* 7 (1984), pp. 31–40.

Webb, C. de B. 'Great Britain and the Zulu people, 1879–1887.' In *African societies in southern Africa: historical studies*, pp. 302–324. Edited by L. M. Thompson. London: Heinemann, 1969.

————. 'Lines of power: the High Commissioner, the telegraph and the war of 1879.' *Natalia* 8 (1978), pp. 31–7.

————. 'The origins of the war: problems of interpretation.' In *The Anglo-Zulu War: new perspectives*, pp. 1–12. Edited by A. Duminy and C. C. Ballard. Pietermaritzburg: University of Natal Press, 1981.

Wendt, W. E. 'Art mobilier from the Apollo Cave, South West Africa: Africa's oldest dated works of art.' *South African archaeological bulletin* 31 (1976), pp. 5–11.

Wiessner, P. 'Style or isochrestic variation?: a reply to Sackett.' *American antiquity* 50 (1985), pp. 160–6.

Wilcox, W. C. 'The Booker Washington of South Africa: the story of John Dube.' *The Congregational*, [10 March 1927?]. (To be found in Killie Campbell Africana Library's Mrs Tyler Gray Newscutting Book 4, p. 131.)

Wilde, R. H. 'Joseph Chamberlain and the South African Republic, 1895–1899: a study in the formulation of imperial policy.' In *Archives year book for South African history*, 1956, part 1, pp. vii–xiv, 1–158D. Cape Town: Government Printer, 1956.

Willcox, A. R. 'Reasons for the non-occurrence of Middle Stone Age material in the Natal Drakensberg.' *South African journal of science* 70 (1974), pp. 273–5.

Wilson, M. 'The early history of the Transkei and Ciskei.' *African studies* 18 (1959), pp. 167–79.

Wobst, M. W. 'Boundary conditions for paleolithic social systems: a simulation approach.' *American antiquity* 39 (1974), pp. 147–78.

Wright, J. B. 'Clash of paradigms: a review of Harrison M. Wright's *The burden of the present: liberal and radical controversy over southern African history* (Cape Town and London).' *Reality: a journal of liberal and radical opinion* 9 (1977), pp. 14–17.

———. 'Politics, ideology and the invention of "Nguni".' In *Resistance and ideology in settler societies*, pp. 96–118. Edited by T. Lodge. Johannesburg: Ravan Press in association with the African Studies Institute of the University of the Witwatersrand, 1986.

———. 'Pre-Shakan age-group formation among the Northern Nguni.' *Natalia* 8 (1978), pp. 22–30.

Wright, J. B. and Edgecombe, [D.] R. 'Mpande kaSenzangakhona, *c.*1798–1872.' In *Black leaders in southern African history*, pp. 45–60. Edited by C. Saunders. London: Heinemann, 1979.

Yates, R.; Golson, J. and Hall, M. 'Trance performance: the rock art of Boontjieskloof and Sevilla.' *South African archaeological bulletin* 40 (1985), pp. 70–80.

Young, L. M. 'The Native policy of Benjamin Pine in Natal, 1850–1855.' In *Archives year book for South African history*, 1951, part 2, pp. 209–346B. Cape Town: Government Printer, [1952?].

THESES

Theses marked with an asterisk have subsequently been published with the same, or a similar, title. The published version is listed under ARTICLES or BOOKS as applicable.

Arkin, A. J. 'The contributions of Indians in the economic development of South Africa, 1860–1970: an historical-income approach.' Ph.D., University of Durban-Westville, 1981.*

Barbour, M. R. 'Natal, 1824–1856: a review of some economic aspects of the colony from its foundation to the granting of representative government.' BA Honours, University of Natal, Pietermaritzburg, 1972.

Barrett, A. M. 'A history of Michaelhouse, 1896–1952.' M.Ed., University of Natal, Pietermaritzburg, 1968.*

Beaumont, P. B. 'Border Cave.' MA, University of Cape Town, 1978.

Behn, M. M. 'The Klip River insurrection, 1847.' MA, University of South Africa/Natal University College, 1932.

Bennet, M. 'The 1909 Natal Government Railways strike.' BA Honours, University of Natal, Durban, 1982.

Bitensky, M. F. 'The economic development of Natal, 1843–1885.' MA, London School of Economics, 1954/5.

Bruss, G. G. 'The impact of the First World War on the German community in Natal.' MA, University of Natal, Durban, 1981.

Carroll, F. R. 'The growth and coordination of pro-war sentiment in Natal before the Second Anglo-Boer War.' MA, University of Natal, Pietermaritzburg, 1981.

Carter, P. L. 'The prehistory of eastern Lesotho.' Ph.D., Cambridge University, 1978.

Cope, R. L. 'The British annexation of Zululand, 1887.' BA Honours, University of Natal, Pietermaritzburg, 1959.

Cubbin, A. E. 'Origins of the British settlement at Port Natal, May 1824–July 1842.' D.Phil., University of the Orange Free State, 1983.

Davenport, T. R. H. 'The responsible government issue in Natal, 1880–1882.' MA, University of South Africa/Rhodes University College, 1948/9.*

Denoon, D. J. N. 'Sir John Robinson: his career from 1884 until the achievement of responsible government by Natal in 1893.' BA Honours, University of Natal, Pietermaritzburg, 1962.

Dhupelia, U. S. 'Frederick Robert Moor and Native affairs in the Colony of Natal, 1893–1903.' MA, University of Durban-Westville, 1980.

Doolan, J. P. 'Country notes by Agricola: an analysis of the journalism of G. M. Sutton in *The Natal witness*, 1883–1903, as a commentary on the progress of Natal agriculture.' BA Honours, University of Natal, Pietermaritzburg, 1978.

Dyer, C. 'A case of money and life: an examination of the relationship between health and the political economy in Durban at the turn of the century.' BA Honours, University of Natal, Durban, 1986.

Etherington, N. A. 'The rise of the Kholwa in southeast Africa: African Christian communities in Natal, Pondoland and Zululand, 1835–1880.' Ph.D., Yale University, 1971.*

Feather, S. A. 'A culutural-social study of the Norwegian settlement at Marburg.' MA, University of Natal, Pietermaritzburg, 1980.

Gascoigne, K. 'Health and disease in the 19th century with reference to colonial Natal.' BA Honours, University of Natal, Durban, 1986.

Ginwala, F. 'Class consciousness and control: Indian South Africans, 1860–1946.' Ph.D., Oxford University, 1974.

Guest, B. [W. R.] 'Natal and the confederation issue in the 1870s.' MA, University of Natal, Durban, 1967.

Hamilton, C. A. 'Ideology, oral traditions and the struggle for power in the early Zulu kingdom.' MA, University of the Witwatersrand, 1985.

Harris, V. S. 'Reluctant rebels: the impact of the Second Anglo-Boer War upon the Klip River Dutch community, with special reference to the Dutch community of Dundee.' BA Honours, University of Natal, Pietermaritzburg, 1982.

Hedges, D. W. 'Trade and politics in southern Mozambique and Zululand in the eighteenth and early nineteenth centuries.' Ph.D., London School of Oriental and African Studies, 1978.

Hutton, A. M. 'Pondoland: her Cape and Natal neighbours, 1878–1894.' MA, University of the Witwatersrand, 1935.

Kaissier, W. E. 'An economic analysis of wattle farming in South Africa.' M.Sc., University of Natal, Pietermaritzburg, 1960.

Kennedy, P. A. 'The fatal diplomacy: Sir Theophilus Shepstone and the Zulu kings, 1839–1879.' Ph.D., University of California, Los Angeles, 1976.*

Kiernan, M. P. 'The work for education in Natal of Robert James Mann, 1857–65.' M.Ed., University of Manchester, 1982.

King, R. J. H. 'The premiership of C J Smythe, 1905–1906, and the Bambatha Rebellion.' MA, University of Natal, Durban, 1979.

Laband, J. P. C. 'Dick Addison: the role of a British official during the disturbances in the Ndwandwe district of Zululand, 1887–1889.' MA, University of Natal, Pietermaritzburg, 1980.

La Hausse, P. A. M. S. 'Beer, social control and segregation: the Durban system and the 1929 Beerhall Riots.' BA Honours, University of Natal, Durban, 1980.

Lambert, J. 'Sir John Robinson and responsible government, 1863–1897: the making of the first Prime Minister of Natal.' MA, University of Natal, Pietermaritzburg, 1975.

Le Cordeur, B. A. 'Relations between the Cape and Natal, 1846–1879.' Ph.D., University of Natal, Durban, 1962.*

Leverton, B. J. T. 'Government finance and political development in Natal, 1806–1834.' MA, University of Natal, Durban, 1959.

———. 'Government finance and political development in Natal, 1843 to 1893.' D.Litt. et Phil., University of South Africa, 1968.*

Lewis-Williams, J. D. 'Believing and seeing: an interpretation of symbolic meanings in southern San rock paintings.' Ph.D., University of Natal, Durban, 1977.*

Loudon, J. G. 'The responsible government issue in Natal, 1880–1882: parliamentary elections in coastal constituencies.' MA, University of South Africa/Natal University College, 1940.

Mael, R. 'The problem of political integration in the Zulu empire.' Ph.D., University of California, Los Angeles, 1974.*

Manson, A. H. 'The Hlubi and Ngwe in a colonial society, 1848–1877.' MA, University of Natal, Pietermaritzburg, 1979.

Mathews, J. 'Lord Chelmsford and the problems of transport and supply during the Anglo-Zulu War of 1879.' MA, University of Natal, Pietermaritzburg, 1979.

———. 'Lord Chelmsford, British general in southern Africa, 1878–1879.' D Litt. et Phil., University of South Africa, 1987.

Mazel, A. D. 'Up and down the Little Berg: archaeological resource management in the Natal Drakensberg.' MA, University of Cape Town, 1981.

Mendel, J. M. 'Frederick Robert Moor and the unification of South Africa, 1907–1910.' BA Honours, University of Natal, Durban, 1981.

Moore, D. M. 'General Louis Botha's second expedition to Natal during the Anglo-Boer War, September-October 1901.' MA, University of South Africa, 1978.*

O'Byrne, S. P. M. 'Natal during the administration of Sir Arthur Havelock.' BA Honours, University of Natal, Pietermaritzburg, 1961.

Pachai, B. 'The emergence of the question of the South African Indians as an international issue, 1860–1961.' Ph.D., University of Natal, 1963.

Paterson, H. R. 'The military organisation of the Colony of Natal.' MA, University of Natal, Durban, 1985.

Pridmore, J. 'The reaction of colonial Natal to Sir Garnet Wolseley's settlement of Zululand, June-December, 1879.' BA Honours, University of Natal, Pietermaritzburg, 1983.

Rolando, S. C. 'The establishment of veterinary services in Natal: the career of Samuel Wiltshire, 1874–1896.' BA Honours, University of Natal, Durban, 1987.

Slater, H. 'Transitions in the political economy of south-east Africa before 1840.' Ph.D., University of Sussex, Brighton, 1976.

Smith, A. 'The struggle for control of southern Mocambique, 1720–1835.' Ph.D., University of California, Los Angeles, 1970.

Swanson, M. W. 'The rise of multi-racial Durban: urban history and race policy in South Africa, 1830–1930.' Ph.D., Harvard University, 1964.

Switzer, L. E. 'The problems of an African mission in a white-dominated multi-racial society: the American Zulu Mission in South Africa, 1885–1910.' Ph.D., University of Natal, Pietermaritzburg, 1971.

Talbot, C. J. 'Harry Escombe and the politics of responsible government in Natal, 1879–1885: a search for power.' MA, University of Natal, Pietermaritzburg, 1974.

Theunissen, A. B. 'Natal under Lieutenant-Governor Scott, 1856–1864.' MA, University of South Africa/Natal Univeristy College, Durban, 1936.

Van Wyk, A. J. 'Dinizulu en die Usutu-opstand van 1888.' MA, University of the Orange Free State, 1972.*

———. 'Politieke woelinge in Natal, 1910–1915.' D.Phil., University of the Orange Free State, 1977.

Walker, M. J. 'The Provincial Council and Natal, 1924–1932.' MA, University of Natal, Durban, 1976.

Wells, R. W. 'The operation of the Jamaica reforms in the Natal constitution, 1875–1880.' MA, University of South Africa/Natal University College, Durban, 1935.

Williams, B. O. 'The dispute between Lieutenant-Governor Keate and the Legislative Council, Natal, 1867–1872.' MA, University of South Africa/Natal University College, Durban, 1935.

UNPUBLISHED CONFERENCE AND SEMINAR PAPERS, REPORTS, ETC.

Papers which have subsequently been published are marked with an asterisk. The published version is also listed in the ARTICLES listing.

Ballard, C. C. 'A survey of selected vital and economic statistics for the Colony of Natal, 1844–1909.' Report submitted to the University of Natal Research Committee, 1981.

Beaumont, P. B. 'The Stone Age culture stratigraphy of Border Cave.' Paper presented at a workshop on 'Towards a better understanding of the Upper Pleistocene in sub-Saharan Africa', organized by the Southern African Association of Archaeologists, Stellenbosch, June 1979.

Bhana, S. and Brain, J. B. 'Movements of Indians in southern Africa, 1860–1911.'

Preliminary report presented to the Human Sciences Research Council, 1984.

Brain, J. B. 'Natal's Indians: religion, missionaries and indentured Indians.' Paper presented at the conference held to mark the 125th anniversary of the arrival of indentured Indians, University of Durban-Westville, October 1985.

Camp, B. E. 'A history of the district of Alfred.' Report for the Magistrate's Office, Harding, [1960?].

Cobbing, J. 'The case against the *mfecane.*' Seminar paper given at the Centre for

African Studies, University of Cape Town, 1983. Revised version with the same title given at the African Studies Institute, University of the Witwatersrand, 1984.

Duminy, A. H. 'The "Natal Party", 1910.' Paper presented at a workshop on Natal in the Union period, University of Natal, Pietermaritzburg, 27–28 October 1982.

Guy, J. J. 'Segmentation and Nguni history.' Paper presented at Rhodes University, Grahamstown, 1973.

Hamilton, C. A. 'The AmaLala in Natal, 1750–1826.' Seminar paper presented in the Department of History, University of the Witwatersrand, 10 November 1982.

Hamilton, C. A. and Wright, J. B. 'The making of the Lala: ethnicity, ideology and class formation in a precolonial context.' Paper presented at the Third History Workshop conference, University of the Witwatersrand, 1984.

Heydenrych, D. H. 'The construction of public works and the constitutional status of Natal, 1875–1893: the railway case.' Paper presented at the Conference on the History of Natal and Zululand, University of Natal, Durban, 2–4 July 1985.

————. 'Indian railway labour in Natal, 1879–1895: the biggest Indian work force in the Colony.' Paper presented at a workshop on the development of Natal before Union, Department of Historical Studies, University of Natal, Pietermaritzburg, 24–25 October 1984.*

Loubser, J. H. N. 'Excavations at Ndondondwane on the Tugela River.' Report for the KwaZulu Monuments Council, 1984.

Mazel, A. D. 'The ecology of the Holocene Later Stone Age communities of the northern Natal Drakensberg and Tugela River catchment.' 1983/84 HSRC progress report, 1984.

————. 'The Holocene Later Stone Age prehistory of the Tugela Basin.' 1984/85 HSRC Progress Report, 1985.

Ovendale, R. 'Natal, the Transvaal, and the origins of the Second Anglo-Boer War.' Paper presented at the Conference on the History of Natal and Zululand, University of Natal, Durban, 2–4 July 1985.

Posel, R. '"A modern Babylon": white prostitution in Durban at the turn of the century.' Paper presented at the ASSA (Association for Sociology in Southern Africa) Conference, Durban, 1986.

Slater, H. 'The changing pattern of economic relationships in rural Natal, 1838–1914.' Seminar paper given at the Institute of Commonwealth Studies, London University. Reproduced in the Institute's 'Collected seminar papers on the societies of southern Africa in the 19th and 20th centuries' vol. 3, pp. 38–52, [1972?].*

INDEX

Birth and death dates of people are provided except where this information has not been available, as in the case of many Africans, Indians and early white settlers. Page numbers in italics refer to illustrations.